Everyday PC Maintenance You Should Perform

The best way to be sure that nothing goes wrong with your computer is to perform computer maintenance on your hard disk regularly. Take the following steps to avoid problems with your computer *before* they arise.

Scan Your Hard Drive for Errors

Click the **Start** menu, choose **Programs**, and then click **Accessories**. From the **Accessories** menu, choose **System Tools**, and then choose **Scandisk**. Select **Standard, Automatically fix errors**, then click **Start**.

Defragment Your Hard Drive

Click the **Start** menu, choose **Programs**, and then click **Accessories**. From the **Accessories** menu, choose **System Tools**, and then choose **Disk Defragmenter**. Select a drive to defrag, and click **OK**.

Create an Emergency Diskette

Click the **Start** menu, and then choose **Control Panel**. After Control Panel opens, double-click **Add/Remove Programs**. From the window that appears, click either the **Start Disk** or the **Startup Disk** tab and click **Create Disk**. If you use Windows 95, copy the additional files listed in Chapter 4, "What You Need to Know *Before* You Open Your PC," to the diskette.

Back Up Your Hard Disk

Microsoft Backup is no longer a regular part of Windows. To ensure reliable backups, you need the most reliable backup media available. See Chapter 18, "Adding an Optical Drive," for details on recordable CD- and DVD-based media.

ALPHA

tear here

Scan for Viruses

A malicious file can enter your computer as an attachment to your e-mail, unwanted macro in a document, as a component of a Web page, or through the boot sector of a removable disk such as a diskette. Viruses are a serious threat to the efficiency of your system and the integrity of your data.

Scan for Unwanted Code

Advertisements and other pesky and irritating code fragments can make their way into your PC through the Internet and send data back to their sources. You have the right to privacy on your PC. See the Halftime Report for ways to protect yourself from *non*viral unwanted code.

Back Up Your System Registry

The Registry is the working set of parameters for most every Windows application, as well as the Windows operating system. It is stored on your system as two or three gargantuan files. Click the **Start** menu, choose **Run**, and type `SCANREGW.EXE`.

Clean Your Internet Cache

Unwanted and malicious code can lurk inside your Internet cache. Click **Start**, and choose **Control Panel**. Double-click **Internet** (or **Internet Options** or **Internet Settings**, depending on your version of Windows). Under **Temporary Internet Files**, click **Delete Files**.

Expunge Your TEMP Directory

Unwanted and malicious code, plus just plain ol' *junk,* can lurk in your TEMP directory. Reboot your computer; then immediately after startup, use Windows Explorer to navigate to your TEMP directory (generally `C:\Windows\Temp`). From the **Edit** menu, select **Select All**. Then from the **File** menu, select **Delete**.

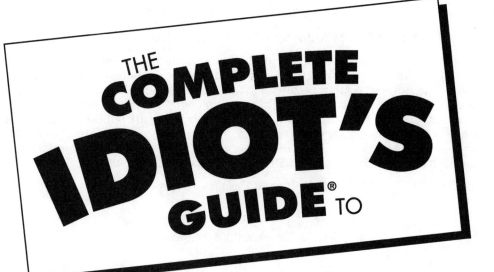

THE COMPLETE IDIOT'S GUIDE® TO

Upgrading and Repairing PCs

Fifth Edition

by Jennifer Fulton

ALPHA

A Pearson Education Company

To my husband Scott—my friend, my love, my rock.

Copyright © 2002 by Pearson Education, Inc.

International Standard Book Number: 0-02-864239-2
Library of Congress Catalog Card Number: 2001095865

04   03   02   8   7   6   5   4

Interpretation of the printing code: The rightmost number of the first series of numbers is the year of the book's printing; the rightmost number of the second series of numbers is the number of the book's printing. For example, a printing code of 02-1 shows that the first printing occurred in 2002.

Printed in the United States of America

Publisher
Marie Butler-Knight

Product Manager
Phil Kitchel

Managing Editor
Jennifer Chisholm

Acquisitions Editor
Eric Heagy

Development Editor
Nancy D. Warner

Production Editor
Billy Fields

Copy Editor
Daryl Kessler
Rachel Lopez

Illustrator
Jody Schaeffer

Cover Designers
Mike Freeland
Kevin Spear

Book Designers
Scott Cook and Amy Adams of DesignLab

Indexer
Ginny Bess

Layout/Proofreading
Svetlana Dominguez
Timothy Osborn

Contents at a Glance

Contents

xi

Introduction

This is a book about maintaining the single most complex, unfathomable, and over-hyped appliance you will ever own. Upgrading and maintaining your computer is a difficult and bewildering task, and yet you are the most qualified person to handle it. The main reason is because you are perhaps the only person you can trust entirely to do the job right.

You are an intelligent, mature adult. You can balance a budget, which is more than I can say for most organized governments. You can plan the annual week-long sales convention. You can get the copier to collate and even to staple, on one side, so that the other side opens up. Yet there's something about a computer that just makes you feel foolish.

You feel foolish when the darned thing freezes up and you can't get all your files saved. You feel foolish when the program you're trying to install tells you there are not enough megabytes here or gigabytes there. You feel foolish when you pop the cover, see more green and gold staring up at you than at a Notre Dame football rally, you can't spot the CPU, the SEC, or the PDQ, and you end up snapping the cover back on.

It's a normal feeling. To paraphrase *Mystery Science Theater 3000,* you should breathe and just relax. Upgrading your computer has become a part of its everyday maintenance. It's no longer merely a way to make your machine keep up with the capabilities of your neighbor's. In some cases, you really do have to upgrade your computer simply so it can keep on doing what it has done before. Yes, it is not an easy job. Yes, it can be time consuming, and even boring. And yes, it can be expensive.

But it is not insurmountable. Even though the Sci-Fi Channel frequently depicts computers as having diabolical wishes to conquer the world—or, at least, northern Iowa—your computer is merely a machine. The way that machine works is far, far simpler than the way you might think it works.

The Complete Idiot's Guide to Skipping Chapters

With so many computer books on the market with titles like "Upgrade and Repair Everything Yourself In Twenty-Two Seconds," why do you need *this* one? First of all, this book doesn't assume you want to become a computer technician in your spare time. Instead of overloading you with technical mumbo jumbo, it shows you how to do just about any repair or upgrade task you would want or need to attempt, while guiding you along with simple-to-follow steps and illustrations.

Although comprehending how computers work and how to fix or upgrade them are mysteries of the ages, this book is not a mystery novel. Feel free to skip around, even to the end. There's no surprise ending to spoil the rest of the book for you; in fact, if this book does its job, there shouldn't be too many surprises at all, except the one that comes from making some sense of it all.

You'll find the best part about this book is that you don't have to read any one specific topic unless you need to. Just find the chapter that mentions your problem and go to it. If you do choose to read this book all the way through, you don't necessarily need to read every chapter in sequence. When you come to a part of the book that refers to something printed earlier, I'll tell you where that something is so you can jump right to it.

If you are the sort who appreciates reading this type of book front to back, then have someone loosen the restraints on your strait jacket so you can lean up against the bed rails and get comfy, and you'll find that I did indeed give some thought to the arrangement of this book.

To enhance your enjoyment of this volume in any way I possibly can, I've chosen to employ a Gratuitous Sports Motif (GSM), whereby the book is divided into four "quarters," each of which contain several chapters. Each quarter gathers together those topics relative to a particular aspect of caring for your system. There's a halftime break where I talk about an important topic (for this edition, it's system security), and there's post-game analysis at the end. You'll be surprised; upgrading PCs and football actually share some similarities: You go back and forth all the time, you find yourself moping around, trying to wind down the clock, and when you're only a few inches from your goal and things get tight, you sometimes still feel like punting the thing away. If only I had John Madden to draw meaningless circles and arrows all over the pages, the illusion would be complete.

> ➤ **First Quarter: Assessing Whether Upgrading Is Really Necessary**—I kick things off by helping you ask yourself whether you really need to do anything to your system at all. Granted, if you flick the switch, and you see smoke, that question's answered. But even if you're happy with the way things are, won't you still have to upgrade, or else miss out on the next great graphics or performance or Internet innovation? Maybe not. If your five-year-old computer works for you, all the equipment you've installed is in working order, and watching the Death Star implode in breathtaking 12-D isn't your idea of progress, you might be just fine where you are now.

> ➤ **Second Quarter: Preventative Maintenance and Other Ways to Avoid Upgrading**—There are procedures you should know that will help you extend the life of your system and that can improve its performance without draining your bank account. If you can keep your hard disk drive optimized, your printer free of toner dust and chewing gum, and your operating system on good speaking terms with your peripherals, you can effectively push *forward* the time at which you'll need to seriously consider hardware upgrades or replacement.

➤ **Third Quarter: Taking Everything Apart**—You knew it had to come sooner or later. If you've ever put together an automobile from a mail-order kit, or constructed a scale-model battleship out of toothpicks inside a Seagram's bottle, or even if the most you've ever done is build your own five-story office complex with no more than a chisel and a sledgehammer, getting inside your computer and swapping components will be ... okay, not the easiest thing in the world, but it isn't brain surgery. Well, all right, it *is* brain surgery, but it's simple ... as brain surgeries go. Every major component you might need to replace is given its own exclusive chapter—memory, processors, hard disk, CD-ROM and/or DVD-ROM, power supply, motherboard, modem, network card, system case, video card, sound card, interface card.

➤ **Fourth Quarter: Putting Everything Back Together**—Don't you just love happy endings? In the tradition of Laura Ingalls Wilder (whose Little House burned to the ground more often than Charles Keating's real estate portfolio) I wrap things up with a new home for your equipment, hugs all around, and a Moral for Our Times. But if you're still interested in things burning to the ground, you'll want to read the chapter on making Microsoft Windows understand what you've done to your computer, even if you made it better. Oftentimes, you'll find your computer's so dumb that it won't know what you've added or subtracted until you go deep into its internal memory and tell it. Sometimes adding a new modem, sound card, or video card will cause a conflict with some other device in your computer or attached to it. When that happens, you might have to change some settings or edit some configuration files to get everything and everyone to live together peacefully. Sometimes it takes conflagration to be the spark that makes rebuilding happen in your life. Let it out. Let the flames flow through you. Then give everybody a big hug.

Special Reminders

As you read this book, watch out for these special features that will enhance your life and enrich your consciousness:

Note

These sidebars give you time-saving tips and hints for staying out of trouble.

Check This Out

In these boxes, you'll find a cornucopia of information, including easy-to-understand definitions and amusing anecdotes from yours truly.

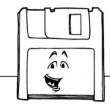

Techno Talk

In these boxes, you'll find some of the terms and terminology you might want to know more about, but you can still live without knowing—like "Flash BIOS," "Run Length Limited," and "IRQ."

Acknowledgments

As always, I thank the bright, capable, and hard-nosed people of Alpha Books. (I'll just have to get used to that new name.) Eric Heagy was a great help, and kept this project running steadily. And the original vision of Marie Butler-Knight, creator of *The Complete Idiot's Guide* series, continues with her guidance and her wisdom. Marie, you're the best.

In my work, I read quite a bit of material frequently posted to independent Web sites. A full and complete listing of the Web sites I read would spill out the back end of this book, but a listing of the sites I *trust* is short enough. My thanks to these sites for their persistence and their inspiration: Anandtech (www.anandtech.com), Tom's Hardware Guide (www.tomshardware.com), 3DnHardware (www.3dhardware.com—careful, there's no "n" in the URL), and PC Guide (www.pcguide.com). I mention other Web sites throughout the text of this book, where you can go to get splendid, up-to-the-minute information on PC hardware and devices.

About the Author

Jennifer Fulton is a consultant, trainer, and best-selling author of over 100 books covering many areas of computing, including MS-DOS, Windows, and Microsoft Office. Jennifer is a self-taught computer guru, and after working with computers all day, Jennifer brings what's left of her sense of humor to her many books, including *How to Use Office XP, Teach Yourself Windows Me in Ten Minutes,* and *How to Use Publisher 2000.*

Jennifer began her writing career as a staff writer for Macmillan Computer Publishing, before escaping to the life of a freelance author, trainer, and consultant. She lives in Indiana with her husband, Scott—himself an author and editor for over 17 years—and her daughter, Katerina, author-to-be. They live together in a small home filled with many books, some of which they have *not actually* written themselves.

Special Thanks to the Technical Reviewer

The Complete Idiot's Guide to Upgrading and Repairing PCs, Fifth Edition, was reviewed by Hethe Henrickson, an expert who double-checked the accuracy of what you'll learn here, to help us ensure that this book gets all its facts straight. (For instance, it's a CAT5 *cable* with RJ-45 *connectors*, not a RJ-45 cable with CAT5 connectors!) Thanks, Hethe, very much.

Hethe Henrickson is a networking expert based in Sioux Falls, SD. He is an MCSE in Windows NT4 and in Windows 2000. Additionally, he is a Novell CNA, a cisco CCNA, and is A+ certified. Hethe teaches MCSE classes at National American University and has a column on swynk.com.

Trademarks

All terms mentioned in this book that are known to be or are suspected of being trademarks or service marks have been appropriately capitalized. Alpha Books and Pearson Education, Inc., cannot attest to the accuracy of this information. Use of a term in this book should not be regarded as affecting the validity of any trademark or service mark.

Assessing Whether Upgrading Is Really Necessary

The most important decision you will have to make regarding your computer is this: Should you upgrade it or replace it? This is a more difficult decision now than it ever has been, primarily because pre-assembled PCs are so inexpensive nowadays. However, the nearly "free" PCs offered by a lot of companies come with their own share of headaches, including high-cost Internet connections, a lack of certain frills which may force you to upgrade anyway, and a potential loss of privacy. In this quarter, you'll get off to a great start with an in-depth look at all your options.

If you think owning a PC is frustrating, upgrading one can be even more so. So you'll also learn what it will take to upgrade your computer, and some steps you can take to prevent disaster during the process.

Chapter 1

Making the Call: When, Why, and Whether You Should Upgrade

In This Chapter

➤ Assessing the upgradability of your PC

➤ Deciding whether an upgrade is worth your time, money, and effort

➤ What upgrading means if you own a notebook PC

➤ Deciding whether you can get away with a simple repair job instead

---

The main reason people want to upgrade their computers is that they need them to run some piece of software—a bigger spreadsheet, the newest version of Windows, a better Web browser, or today's most awesome games. People consider upgrading their PCs because they want their machines to do or run something they cannot do or run today. They're also thinking maybe—just maybe—they'll save some money by doing it themselves instead of hiring a service technician to do the work or buying a new PC altogether.

Chances are you're in the same boat with these people. You might not know everything about computers, but you do know—or at least you have a deep suspicion—that the PC you have now isn't good enough. If you don't have to replace the whole thing, and you perform the upgrade yourself, you should save some money and the experience might be rewarding in itself ... right?

... Maybe. This chapter is about all those questions you're asking whose answers start with "maybe." The rest of this book will show you exactly what you need to do to make those crucial repairs and upgrades once you've decided to take the plunge and do those jobs yourself. However, before you go that far, this chapter will help you make some critical decisions.

Assessing What You Really Want from Your PC

Believe it or not, depending on what you need your current PC to do, you could save money simply by chucking it and buying a new one. Often the whole is significantly cheaper than the sum of its parts. If after all the reading you're about to do, you end up chucking your old system for a new one, and you've saved money in so doing, and you're happy, then this book will have done its job. (Of course, you'll want to keep this book handy, because who knows when you'll need to repair or upgrade something later?)

You Should Upgrade If You Can Make a Great System

On the other hand, you can build your current PC using relatively inexpensive parts to give it performance and features you cannot purchase in a pre-manufactured system. Computer parts are cheaper than they have ever been and their performance levels are astounding. Fact: Some parts that are available on the open market for upgrades or replacements are not available to brand-name PC manufacturers. So you really can build a hot rod PC—perhaps leveraging some of your old system's parts—without spending too much money or time.

PC manufacturers usually don't equip their systems with the best possible equipment. By "best," I don't necessarily mean "fastest"; I'm also taking into account reliability and quality of service. Fact: Manufacturers have access to new sound cards at less than $5 per unit, wholesale price. These cards might be adequate at best; however, you'll find them even in relatively expensive systems whose total retail price exceeds $1,000. Why? The manufacturer can reasonably mark up the value of the sound card more than it can almost any other part inside the system—for example, $40 more for the sound card while only $20 more for the motherboard. Yet for a retail price of around $30, you can replace that inadequate sound card for which you might have paid $45 with one whose quality exceeds that of some consumer stereo sets.

You Should Upgrade a PC to Keep It Alive

The second most common reason PCs need upgrades is that upgrades have become part of everyday maintenance. In some cases you really do have to upgrade your computer simply so it can keep on doing what it did before. When a part goes out you have to replace it with what's available to you. Older equipment is not always readily available and is not necessarily cheaper than newer equipment. This is not because old equipment has appreciated in value; the price of new equipment has plummeted faster than the value of the old equipment has depreciated.

This presents an entirely new problem: a compromise between availability, reliability, compatibility, and affordability. You may find yourself upgrading an old part because that's the cheaper route. New 1999 model 19" diagonal monitors sold for more than $1,000 then, but they sell for about $500 used today; meanwhile, new 2001 19" models sell for less than $300. Here's another example: A Pentium MMX 233 CPU (unused) with heat sink and fan sells for about $55; meanwhile, a newer Celeron 366 with the same heat sink and fan sells for $49.

You Shouldn't Upgrade If It Costs More Money

Today the average price of a fully configured, off-the-shelf, consumer-level desktop PC is about $750. That price might dip down during the holidays but for at least the next few years, $750 probably represents the permanent average PC system price. From now on, consumer-level PCs will simply adopt newer, higher-performance features, but sell them in $750 systems. So next year's everyday $750 system might be the equivalent of today's "power-user" $2,000 system. $750 is a price point that retailers can live with.

If you subtract the discounted values of all the peripheral equipment (monitor, speakers, printer, scanner, keyboard, mouse, Internet subscription) from that $750 average, the price of just the system unit (a computer without a monitor) likely is about $300. Keep this figure in mind as you consider whether to upgrade anything inside the box you have now; you probably can find a computer store near you (or on the Internet) where you can buy a new computer without a monitor for around $300. Even if you decide to go this route, you'll probably want to add things to this new computer or move things from your old computer to the new one; so don't think you can bypass the upgrading process completely. Still, this usually is a great way to go; especially if your computer is more than two years old.

You Shouldn't Upgrade If It Launches a Cascade

If your objective is to convert your existing PC into a high-performance computer and your machine was built in 1996 or earlier, you probably should abort now. The money you'd have to spend to make an adequate system live and thrive in your existing case easily exceeds what you'd spend for a more-than-adequate, complete PC.

If your old machine was built in 1997 or later and you plan to make it "state of the art," splash some cold water on your face and heed the following words: High performance is achieved through the cooperative effort of all your PC's components. This, of course, includes your *CPU* (the central processing unit, which is the main processor in your PC). But you must also take into account your *memory* (where all the data you're working on is stored); your *motherboard* (the platform upon which your computer is built, and which links all its parts together); and, without question, your *video* (graphics) *card* (which is responsible for everything you see on your monitor). Each of these components expects the other to operate more or less on its plateau; for instance, the fastest video card you can buy won't be the fastest it can be—and it might not even work—if your CPU doesn't meet its minimum requirements. Further, the fastest RAM you can buy won't be the fastest if it's installed in a system whose motherboard is designed for slower memory components. For more information on memory, motherboard, and bus, see Chapter 3, "What It Takes to Upgrade Each Part of Your Computer."

Even if your system is relatively new, upgrading one component could force you to upgrade one or more of the others. By the time you've done that, you've more than purchased your own PC all over again. I call this effect the *Upgrade Cascade;* unless you are a fan of Dominos, you should avoid this chain of events at all cost.

You Shouldn't Upgrade Just to Own the Best or Fastest

The relative performance of any single PC model, from the point of view of the overall market, goes from state of the art to obsolete in less than one year. This is not a joke. When the Fourth Edition of this book was published in late 1999, the first 566 MHz processors were just being shipped. By April of 2000, AMD was shipping its first 1.2GHz (1,200MHz) Athlon processors. At the time of this writing in May 2001, Intel's factories are gearing up to make 2.2GHz processors.

Is it really necessary for you to own the fastest system on the market? Why not instead own, or build, precisely the system you need to get the job done? Does the fact that the market claims your computer is old mean you're not allowed to balance your checkbook with it? Thankfully, the answer is no. If your computer continues to serve the purposes for which you originally purchased it—and you don't smell smoke—there's no clear reason—aside from maintaining your edge in certain social circles—that you can't still use it.

Keeping up with the public perception or market perception of your PC's relative performance capabilities is just not a good enough reason for you to continue investing in PC upgrades. First, if you keep spending on incremental upgrades just to stay on top, you'll be spending more than if you simply replace your entire system every six months. (Think I'm kidding? You can easily spend more than $1,500 on top-of-the-line upgrades every six months...and that's the entry price of a high-performance PC.) Second, speed is a very relative thing in PCs. If it helps, a 1.2GHz processor is less than twice as fast as a 566MHz processor. Additionally, there are 566MHz PCs that are faster—*way* faster—than 1.2GHz PCs. How this happens will become clear in Chapter 9, "Accelerating Your PC with a New CPU."

You Shouldn't Upgrade to Compensate for Depreciation

Your computer is the most liquid asset you own; it loses value more rapidly than Eddie Murphy's latest sequel. Depending on what business you're in, the IRS still might require you to depreciate its value over five years' time; in five years they'll be giving your PC away free with breakfast cereal. When you evaluate any computer, it's a waste of time to consider its resale value; instead evaluate it by how much work it can do for you and how well it can do that work.

What *Should* You Upgrade?

What parts of your old computer are practically jumping out at you and demanding an upgrade? It's time to make a serious assessment. Your judgment criteria should not be whether your next-door neighbor has more Hertz in his processor than you do. Instead, find out how much computer you really need, even if everything seems to work fine; then assess what doesn't work and what could work better than it does now.

The first consideration when deciding what you want your computer to do is how much power your software needs. Get more power than your computer needs because your needs probably are going to change and adapt over time. What you don't want is to get caught (again) with too little computer for the work (or play) you plan to do.

Here is one of the dirty little secrets of the software industry: Modern computers generally are far more capable than the nature of the jobs for which they're used. One example involves everyday accounting. Adding and subtracting numbers puts extremely little strain on today's processors. The truth of the matter is it takes far more computing power to support those fancy windows and that fast, responsive mouse pointer than it does to keep your books.

How Fast Is Fast Enough?

So how do you make a fair judgment? Take a good look at the requirements of the software you own or want to buy; generally they're printed on the side of the box or on their download page on the Web. You should find five requirements: CPU type, speed, memory space, hard drive space, and operating system revision number. However, some manufacturers list only one space requirement, as in "Requirements: 180MB." This might leave you wondering whether they mean RAM or hard drive space. Usually it means drive space; not memory. However, if you're evaluating software that's two years old or older, it probably means memory (RAM).

With these numbers in hand, realize the following: Minimum requirements generally are very conservative. A program may consume 180MB of hard drive space once installed; however, once you use it to generate new documents or databases or drawings, how much space will you have used then? Also keep in mind that the CPU speed listed usually is the slowest PC on which the manufacturer tested its software.

How Fast Is Fast?

The CPU in your computer probably is more than fast enough for your operating system to handle everyday jobs such as adding numbers together, forecasting expenditures, and tracking your portfolio. What really makes your blazingly fast computer seem slow is the introduction of graphics- and sound-intensive jobs. Blowing-up-the-planet Xenon jobs. Passing-Michael Andretti-on-the-back-stretch jobs. Those are the extreme cases. In the middle of this picture are the real-world jobs that take some graphics and sound to accomplish properly. These include planning the back garden, plotting the family tree, and downloading everything but the kitchen sink from the Internet. These jobs require speed from your computer because graphics and sound require far more processor power than mere accounting jobs.

To put this another way (I'm a qualified expert at putting things another way): The tasks for which you originally purchased your computer are not the tasks it spends most of its time performing. Thus, the more work your computer has to do to maintain itself, the less time it spends doing what you think it should be doing. Now add all the other background tasks you might have assigned to your computer: antivirus monitoring, instant e-mail and messaging, printer status monitoring, streaming media provision, automatic alarms reminding you to feed the cat. Users typically overtax their high-performance PCs with ever-increasing background tasks, resulting in a system that seems slower than even their old PCs were.

In the end your PC may be spending one-hundredth of its real time actually doing the real work you want it to do. That might be perfectly normal—and even acceptable—if your PC is designed and maintained in such a way that your operating system can keep up with the workload. Speed comes from a number of different sources; believe it, or not, the CPU is not on the top of that list. In short, PCs have to be really fast to not appear slow. For many users the faster their PCs become, the more they expect those PCs to do for them; therefore the slower their systems appear to them over time.

That said, how fast does your CPU really need to be? As a rule, add the minimum CPU speed requirements in megahertz (MHz) for all the programs you plan to run together (including your operating system); then divide the sum by the number of programs. Add the result to the fastest speed requirement in your list; your total should be your approximate CPU speed requirement. When a program (especially an application) doesn't present a minimum speed requirement, you should assume it is capable of running with the CPU speed of the entry-level PC produced when the software was introduced. For example, a Microsoft application introduced two years ago probably will run on a Pentium 266.

How Fast Is Slow?

Consider the extent to which the programs you (and your kids) have chosen will require graphics and sound. Realize that a computer with even the fastest CPU will seem slow to you if the video and sound processors in that same computer (yes, they're separate from the CPU) aren't up to speed. In fact, because of the way CPUs and video cards interact, a fast CPU with slow video could yield a slower overall computer than a *slow* CPU with slow video.

The video card you choose for your computer provides a far more perceivable speed increase than the CPU you choose. In other words, if you double the speed of your graphics processor, you'll notice and appreciate the overall speed increase in your computer far more than if you doubled the speed of your CPU. Why? You won't believe it, but I'll tell you anyway: The one job the CPU performs more often than any other job is waiting. If you speed up the CPU, from the CPU's perspective it waits nearly twice as long—because it really does wait nearly twice as much. More processor cycles are spent in the interim while other things are happening in your computer—your hard drive is fetching data, your video card is setting up the display, and your BIOS is waiting for you to touch the keyboard. Conversely, if you speed up the graphics it takes less time—fewer processor cycles—for your computer to display results or changes ... so the CPU doesn't wait as much as it did before.

Note

Before you open your wallet, be sure to check out the Second Quarter of this book, which contains several easy things you can do to speed up a slow PC. Best of all, most of these tricks don't cost you a thing!

What *Can* You Upgrade?

If you're lucky enough to own a computer that looks like a dumpy little putty-colored box that someone from an earlier era might have thought was used to store cold beer or fishing tackle, there's a good chance you can upgrade or repair it. Here are some of the things that make a system upgradeable:

➤ **An ordinary-looking system case**—Is it rectangular, with access to floppy and CD-ROM drives in the front? Is it a tower system that sits on the floor (really a desk-side unit rather than a desktop), as opposed to a box that sits beneath your monitor? Chances are the system case was built for relatively easy entry by human fingers and hands—a definite plus when upgrading.

➤ **One or two categories of bays**—Find your CD-ROM drive. (You don't have one? Uh-oh. Check out Chapter 18, "Adding an Optical Drive," to see whether we can solve that little problem.) Is it a rectangular unit that looks like with a few screws loosened it could be pulled out from the front like a drawer? Are there other rectangular plastic panels in its vicinity? Congratulations! Those are standard drive bays. You might find a smaller series of such bays in the vicinity of your floppy drive. Bays are built for easy access and replacement. Anything that's installed in a bay is something you can take out and replace. There could be a hard drive in one of those bays; Chapter 16, "Hands-On Hard Disk Replacement," will show you how to replace it.

➤ **The plugs and connectors in the back**—Hopefully they are in the back. Your printer, external modem, telephone line, and scanner might be connected here. Are the plugs arranged in silver aisles, or strips, with one or two plugs per strip? Are there between five and eight strips running perpendicular to how your PC is sitting (horizontal for a tower system; vertical for a desktop case)? If so, those plugs are provided by cards—some of the easiest things to replace in your PC. Chapter 12, "Face the Interface," shows you how to take out and replace a card, any card.

➤ **Ordinary peripheral thingies dangling off the side**—As a general rule, anything belonging to your computer that plugs into it from the outside is something you can easily replace. Chapter 8, "The Easiest Things to Upgrade," covers all of these items. That's right: All of them. They're so easy to replace, all that information is in one chapter.

Repairs That Enable You to Avoid Upgrades

There might be things you can do to your PC right now, today, that could improve its performance to such an extent that you might not need an upgrade. Consider these possibilities:

➤ **Reducing Windows clutter**—If your main complaint is how slow your programs run, there are some things you can do about it without upgrading your CPU or adding more RAM. First you want to get the most out of Windows by streamlining it. (This book presumes Windows is your operating system.) See Chapter 6, "Cleaning Windows," for help in that department.

➤ **Adjusting, moving, and cleaning your peripherals**—As you've probably surmised, when you're the victim of an odd problem with no known origin—strange buzzing noises, tiny blips onscreen, occasional computer lockups—these might be symptoms of a larger problem. Or (if you're lucky) it might be something simple such as a loose cable. Who knows? Instead of guessing, check out Chapter 5, "Fixing the Most Common Problems."

➤ **Making the most of the RAM you have**—Everything your PC does—every program it runs, every calculation it makes—is placed in memory first so the computer can manipulate the data. Each program in turn grabs its own share of memory, which it uses to keep track of its own stuff. Windows especially needs lots of memory. By making sure your PC uses its memory wisely, you provide as large a working area as possible for Windows. And, with a bigger working area, Windows is able to get more things done at the same time. Thanks to the advent of jargon, the memory inside your computer where all your running programs reside, and the memory required by those same programs to do their business, technically is not the same memory. As a result, there are ways to make more "memory" for your computer without adding memory. (Are you getting more curious?) For help maximizing memory, see Chapter 6.

➤ **Reorganizing your hard drive**—If you're running out of space for all those files you download from the Internet, but you're scared at the thought of having to open your PC to add a new hard drive, it's time to rearrange your hard disk. Chapter 7, "'Repairing' the Hard Disk Instead of Replacing It," is filled with lots of easy things you can do to grab that space you need, whether you use Windows 95, 98, or Me. Also, reorganizing the files on your hard disk can make it easier and quicker for the computer to retrieve them.

Is Your Old Computer Worth Fixing or Upgrading?

The sad fact for most computers built before 1997 is that it's simply easier to throw them away and start over (and cheaper, too). I know … this probably goes against the grain; after all, you hung onto that old toaster for three years, and now it makes a darn good doorstop. But really, new PCs are just too inexpensive today for you to not consider simply buying a new one instead of upgrading your old geezer. I can't really tell you what to junk, but I can give you some leading indicators of old age:

➤ If your PC is a 486, consider scrapping it if the upgrades you're considering will cost you more than $200. You might be able to install some used parts, such as a Pentium Overdrive processor; they're still available, even though they're no longer manufactured. However, Overdrive processors—even used ones—aren't cheap, whereas ordinary Pentium or Celeron processors are dirt cheap. Thus, your cost still might be prohibitive; especially considering an entirely new motherboard with a faster processor might cost less than $200 total.

➤ Does your RAM come in single *chips*, with the little tin legs sprawling out of the side like a dead spider? Yep. Haul out the chipper-shredder.

➤ Does your RAM come in the form of SIMMs—small modules with the memory chips soldered onto just one side, not both? Replacing SIMMs is cost prohibitive when compared to newer DIMMs (which have the chips soldered onto both sides), as DIMMs have become dirt cheap by comparison, SIMMs aren't made anymore, and are hard to get ahold of.

> **Note**
>
> If you're currently leasing your computer, there's a good chance you aren't allowed to upgrade it yourself—not without a substantial penalty involved. Contact the company with which you have the lease agreement.

➤ Can you plug a brand new internal modem into any of the open expansion slots in your computer? If you cannot, you may have a very old 8-bit expansion bus. If you have an IBM PS/2 (that's an indicator right there), you may be stuck with the old 32-bit MicroChannel (MCA) bus, which IBM dropped support for in 1991. If some of the cards in your slots have little notches in their plugs every half-inch or so, they may belong to the old Extended Industry Standard Architecture (EISA) 32-bit bus, which also never caught on.

If your PC is a Pentium I (predating the advent of Pentium II), there is a limit to how far you can upgrade your CPU. Some of Intel's Celeron processors are still compatible with so-called Socket 7 motherboards, but your current motherboard may not support the speed a new Celeron may require.

Meanwhile, Pentium II, III, and 4 models (the Roman numeral died out with model 4) are entirely different types of CPU than the old socketed models—so you can't really upgrade to this level from a Pentium I. These newer CPUs slide neatly between two posts for installation, which is about as simple as changing the batteries in your Walkman. Even though they share the same names, because the older Pentium is a chip and the later one is a two-chip cartridge they are physically incompatible with one another. Pentium, Pentium Pro, and Pentium II were designed in three different eras in the history of CPUs and are as incompatible with one another as Ford Model T, Ford Falcon, and Ford Mustang.

If your PC has a Pentium II, you probably can upgrade to a PIII or P4. However, you could see more performance improvement from a video card upgrade.

Nonobvious Factors That Render Your PC Nonupgradeable

Aside from the obvious factors—excessive age, sounding like a foghorn, being shaped like an eggplant—that would indicate your PC probably cannot be upgraded by anyone sane, there are some factors beneath the surface that you should consider:

➤ **Proprietary hardware**—Some major brand-name PCs are somewhat more expensive and difficult to upgrade than just the average built-in-someone's-garage model. Cases in point include Compaq Presario, HP Vectra, Sony VAIO, and IBM NetVista. These are all quality machines, but often they are so full of proprietary hardware that parts made by other manufacturers just don't jive well with them. In some cases the system case is so funky, so hip, so cool, you can't even get into the thing to replace your modem. These designs leave you beholden to your local repairperson ... which was the manufacturers' intention in the first place.

➤ **Accessibility inside your system case**—Of course, everything's relative but in my opinion, opening up the vast majority of PCs is no mean feat. From there, taking out whatever you need to take out without raking your hand off is a stunt worthy of newspaper coverage. After that, inserting whatever new thing that needs to be inserted without shorting anything out is a feat of endurance that beats sitting through an entire episode of *Emeril*. Finally, getting the new device to play well with all the other devices already in your PC is, to borrow a phrase from Sgt. Friday himself, Jack Webb, an endless, glamourless, thankless job that's gotta be done.

➤ **Total cost**—Money's always an issue. Memory and CPU upgrades can become cost prohibitive as the age of your system increases. In the case of a "generation jump," in which you're moving from a Pentium 150 MMX to a Pentium II 566, your CPU, memory, and motherboard will almost certainly need to be upgraded together, at the very least. Once you've done that, you'll probably also need a new graphics card; not just to satisfy your wants, but to get your new system booted up in the first place. Welcome once again to the Upgrade Cascade. So, you'll want to sum up all your expenses to see whether they overshoot that $500 entry level, or $750 average-price retail system.

The best way to find out whether an upgrade component might fail on your system is to contact the manufacturer of that component, as opposed to the manufacturer or builder of your computer. The best way to contact this manufacturer is through its Web site. You can also use an Internet search engine to look up the name of your upgrade and the brand name of your PC, to see if someone has posted a message on some cyber-something network saying they, too have had problems and need help. While you're on the net, check out the Usenet newsgroups that begin with comp.sys.IBM.pc.hardware.*something* (if you don't have a newsgroup reader, use Google on the Web at groups.google.com.) Also visit these Web sites: computershopper.com, computers.cnet.com, and computers.yahoo.com.

Why Upgrading a Notebook PC Might Not Be Doable

As a general rule there is not much about a notebook computer that you can upgrade yourself. (Whereas notebook PCs used to be smaller, by definition, than laptop PCs, once laptop systems became small enough, manufacturers decided to eschew the anatomical reference, merging the two form factors with the "notebook" moniker surviving.) If you can get inside the case—a feat generally prohibited by both common sense and your warranty—you can perhaps swap or add memory, but only if your computer was manufactured after 1996.

In rarer circumstances, you might be able to replace the CPU if you don't mind risking the entire computer to do it; however, if you don't know for sure, it's safe to bet that you cannot. You cannot upgrade the built-in LCD monitor, although most notebook PCs can attach to external monitors. You might have your choice of mouse devices, including some that attach to the unit itself or the ordinary desktop-style mouse, even if your notebook has a pointing device built in. However, as a rule you can replace your keyboard component only with another part of exactly the same type—and even then, you have to go inside the machine to do it.

Part of the problem is that there is not now, nor has there ever been, any standard design for notebook PC hardware. Only major manufacturers produce these kinds of computers; when they do, they implement their own designs at their own factories. (This is how the desktop computer industry might be now if smaller companies hadn't successfully forced standardization of components and interfaces.)

Throughout this book, especially in the Third Quarter—as we discuss how to upgrade, repair, and manage certain desktop PC components—we also will discuss whether their notebook counterparts can be upgraded. A few notebook PCs were designed with upgradability in mind; the problem is you might be locked into purchasing new components from the same manufacturer. Whenever you don't have a choice about from where you get a part, you generally pay a higher price.

The average price of a notebook PC these days is about $1,500. So whatever you decide to do to a notebook (if it can be done, that is), better cost you less than that, or you should simply chuck the idea of upgrading altogether and replace the notebook with a new one.

The Least You Need to Know

➤ With a few simple repairs and a bit of maintenance, you might be able to improve your PC enough that you can live with it a while longer without upgrading.

➤ If the programs you are using work adequately now and are likely to work adequately tomorrow, even a major CPU speed upgrade might not be noticeable to you; especially with programs that make quick calculations, such as checkbook balancers.

➤ The speed of any PC is determined by how well its main components work together: CPU, motherboard, RAM, and video.

➤ When deciding whether it's worth it to upgrade a particular part, be sure to consider the expense, the difficulty factor, and your risk tolerance level.

➤ Beware of the Upgrade Cascade, a phenomenon that causes you to buy additional parts just to get any one new part to work.

Chapter 2

Now, Let's Find Out What Kind of Computer You Have

In This Chapter

➤ Determining what you own and can still use right now

➤ Extracting vital system information from your PC

➤ Judging the net value of the PC you need just to get by

➤ How much (and how little) computer do you need to upgrade to the next step?

It seems like only yesterday, probably because it was. After months of sweating over the decision, you made that first investment of hard-earned money in a new computer (or at least money you hope to hardly earn), and you even witnessed your software running for a minute or two. So why not relax ... after all, the hard part's over, right? Wrong. I know, I know. You're thinking, why should I worry about what makes the thing work when the sales guy promised all I had to do was switch the computer on, "point and click" on some corny little picture, and everything would happen automatically?

The problem is now you have the urge to run some new software. To do that, you probably have to install the latest version of Windows. So you march down to the local computer store and, as you're standing in the checkout line, you glance at the back of the Windows box at the list marked "System Requirements," only to discover that your one-year-old computer is now an antique.

Suddenly you realize the guy at the computer store lied—and you really do need to know how the dumb PC works because now you have to upgrade it. No, as much as you might want to, you can't just take it in to some computer store and say, "Upgrade this thing" because at the very least you have to tell the guy what to upgrade. Plus, the more you know, the less likely you are to pay $500 for a $50 part. Luckily, learning more about your PC is what this chapter is all about.

What You Can Tell by Looking at the Outside

Chances are you probably already know one thing about your computer: the clock speed of its CPU. Amid the sea of adjectives, synonyms for "speed" and "productivity," and references to the word "solution," almost the only fact visible in most modern-day retail PC ads is the CPU clock speed. You'll find it hiding uncomfortably inside the model name, as in "eMachines 400id" or "Compaq Presario 650." Hewlett-Packard no longer incorporates clock speed in its model names (for instance, "Pavilion 7855"), although HP is better than most at revealing its machines' contents in all its advertising.

You can tell a lot about an automobile by looking at it from any one side; it doesn't have to be running. Computers rarely are so self expressive. The only distinctive visible elements of 90 percent of computer models manufactured today—specifically when they're turned off—are the locations of their built-in devices and plugs to outside peripherals. Hard drives now are very well hidden; one could be lurking behind one of those covered-up bays or tucked away in the corner somewhere. However, the hard drive activity indicator light generally is nowhere near the drive itself, so there's no point in searching for your hard drive without actually taking off the cover.

Techno Talk

This book has taken to the new convention of calling CD-ROMs, DVD-ROMs, and their read/write counterparts **optical discs** to collect them into one happy family. I leave the "c" in "discs" to pay homage to the Norwegian folks who invented the things.

Continuing our outside look, you won't be able to learn anything about the floppy drive (assuming your computer has one; a lot of them nowadays do not) just by looking at it, other than the fact that it exists at all. There used to be two different size floppy drives; now most are of the 3½-inch disk variety (encased in hard plastic; not floppy at all).

Your optical disc drive (CD-ROM, DVD-ROM, or CD-RW) actually might divulge a bit more about itself. If your optical drive is a DVD-ROM, it should bear a distinctive, bold "DVD" logo on the front—the very same logo worn by DVD video players. A DVD-ROM drive will read CD-ROM discs; there are no exceptions to this rule. A CD-*RW* (ReWritable) drive can write data to an *optical disc*. The only indicator some models give you that indeed they are CD-RW drives is the presence of a "Write" activity light, meant to go on whenever the drive is writing data to a disc.

You'll learn the most about your computer by looking at the back, where all the spaghetti-looking cables generally are plugged in. Even if nothing's plugged in at the moment, usually you can find some critical clues to the way your computer is built:

➤ Well-built PCs or otherwise helpful system cases will label the meanings of plugs with either words or little pictograms.

➤ Suppose nothing's plugged in at the moment and you have no words or pictograms to guide you. If you can find a plug that's exactly 1½ inches wide with two rows of tiny little holes, you've found what's called a *parallel port*. That's where most printers can be plugged in.

➤ If you find a plug that's 1½ inches wide, with two rows of metal pins pointing out, you may have found the 25-pin serial port. External modems generally plug in here. You also might get a clue to this computer's relative age. Many brand-name systems built after 1998 don't have this style of serial port.

➤ If you're not sure where your monitor plugs in, look for a plug that's ⁹⁄₁₆ inches wide. If you find one that has three rows of holes rather than the usual two, you've found the *SVGA* (*Super VGA*) plug for your monitor. You now know for certain that you have a modern SVGA video port into which most of today's monitors made will plug. If you don't find one, chances are the video you have installed on your computer follows an older standard that's incompatible with newer monitors. SVGA plugs have three rows of five holes each. They're also ⁹⁄₁₆" wide.

➤ Look for the round plug where your keyboard connects; if that plug is ⅝ inches in diameter, you may have a system constructed before 1998. No problem; most replacement keyboards still use this older plug as an option. If the round plug is more like ⅜ inches in diameter, undoubtedly you have a newer system.

What Your BIOS Can Tell You Before You Look Inside

As you'll find out in detail in the next chapter, your computer's *BIOS* (*Basic Input/Output System*) is the primary program that your computer runs. In essence, the BIOS teaches your computer how to be a computer and it repeats that task every time you turn your computer on. You may have seen the term "BIOS" appear for a few seconds, right at the beginning of your computer's boot (startup) sequence.

Unless your computer qualifies as antiquated, there's a very good chance that, during its boot sequence, it displays a screen that tells you pretty much what's inside your PC. Not just memory or hard drive space, but how many storage devices you have, what type of interface they use (ATA, SCSI), and what type of transfer mode your devices use (Mode 1, Mode 3). This information is crucial when you decide to replace these devices or simply move them around to make room for new ones.

Why haven't you ever seen this information before, you ask? Because Microsoft's Windows logo actually covers it up; its pretty little "blue sky" conceals some of the most important information your computer will ever tell you about itself. Why would Microsoft intentionally cover up this information? (Sounds like a question attorney David Boies would have asked, eh?) Just trust me for now that the answer has to do with political issues between Microsoft and the BIOS manufacturers, and reading about them probably wouldn't be your favorite pastime.

However, there may be a brief moment, just between the initial single "beep" that signals your motherboard's okay and when the Microsoft logo appears, when the startup information is visible. It's too fast for anyone to actually read it, but unless your computer's manufacturer makes a little billboard of its own, then this information does show itself. Here is where you can take advantage of one of the least-remembered aspects of old-style computing: Take a good look at your keyboard. Generally along the right of the top row of keys, you'll see one marked "Pause." This key does nothing whatsoever in Windows (although some games do recognize it); but before Windows boots up, your computer thinks it's an old command line system—in other words, it's getting ready to load MS-DOS.

So until Windows starts booting up, the Pause key really works. To defeat Microsoft's cover-up ploy and read the information your computer is trying to tell you about itself, wait for the single beep; then immediately press the Pause key. This should hold the startup sequence just before Windows has an opportunity to take over. You can't hurt your computer at this point; it's perfectly safe.

You now have all the time in the world to read the screen. Take this opportunity to get out a piece of paper and write down exactly what you see, as your BIOS tells you about the following:

Check This Out

If you press Pause during the boot sequence and you see only some of these items listed, you pressed Pause before your PC could show the entire report. Solution: Very, very quickly press Enter; then press Pause again. Your report should become fuller. However, if you see the Windows logo, you waited too long. Press Ctrl+Alt+Delete and start over. (Sigh!)

➤ **CPU type**—The family to which your CPU belongs, as reported to your computer's BIOS by the CPU itself. Here you'll become certain whether you have a PENTIUM, a PENTIUM MMX, a PENTIUM II, a CELERON, or a non-Intel brand such as an AMD or Cyrix.

➤ **Co-processor**—Most likely this registers "Installed." Originally, a co-processor was a separate chip but beginning with the 486DX series, and carrying on with every Pentium ever made, Intel integrated the co-processor into the CPU package.

➤ **CPU clock**—The reported clock speed of your CPU. This is not necessarily how fast the CPU is actually operating; even if something about your computer makes the CPU run slower or faster, this entry will register the clock speed at which your CPU was designed to run.

➤ **Base memory**—Unless your PC qualifies as one of those old computers mentioned in Chapter 1, "Making the Call: When, Why, and Whether You Should Upgrade," this probably reads "640K." The K stands for kilobytes, or 1,024 bytes, as you'll see explained in dramatic detail in Chapter 3, "What It Takes to Upgrade Each Part of Your Computer."

➤ **Extended memory**—Add this number to the preceding 640K figure, to arrive at how many kilobytes of memory your computer actually has installed. Divide this number by 1,024 (for this job you might even need a computer) to arrive at the more familiar number of megabytes of RAM you have installed.

➤ **Cache memory**—This is not part of your computer's main memory bank of RAM. Instead, this is very fast memory that is exclusively available to your CPU. The more cache memory you have, the faster your system performs; you'll learn why in Chapter 9, "Accelerating Your PC with a New CPU."

➤ **Diskette drives**—Otherwise known as "floppy disk drives." If your drives are working and your BIOS detects them, it'll report that fact here.

➤ **Primary and secondary master and slave disks**—Most motherboards manufactured since 1996 can manage up to four main storage devices, which include your hard disks and optical disc drives. Hard disks show up in this list with three important parameters; usually in this order: *access mode, interface type,* and *capacity*. The third is the most obvious; for the meanings behind the other two, check out Chapter 16, "Hands-On Hard Disk Replacement."

➤ **Display type**—Generally SVGA or some variant of that phrase, but basically that same standard.

➤ **Serial and parallel ports**—Even if you use an internal modem, your PC will need to reserve one serial port for it. From your PC's vantage point, ports are logical things, not physical like plugs. All the ports that register on your PC will show up here.

➤ **RAM banks**—Your motherboard may be managing two different types of memory in separate banks, although perhaps not simultaneously. The amounts of memory your BIOS currently recognizes in your motherboard's one or two banks will be registered here.

➤ **PCI device listing**—Most motherboards produced after 1994 support the PCI expansion bus, which is the 32-bit bus that made Plug-and-Play (PNP) possible. PNP devices plugged into the PCI bus are capable of identifying themselves—saying hello, if you will, to the BIOS. Once they do say hello, you'll see the listings for each device at the bottom of the BIOS startup screen. You might not recognize everything listed here and you may be introduced to some things you never thought you had or needed. Chapter 12, "Face the Interface," will explain the meanings of these things in greater detail.

➤ **AGP device listing**—In 1998, Intel introduced a specification for integrating many of the video processing procedures into the CPU's main bus. Although this was supposed to reduce or eliminate the need for separate video RAM banks, AGP ended up giving the CPU access to the separate video RAM. Thus, if you have AGP, you still need a separate video card with its own memory; however, you'll still notice a speed increase. You'll also notice an AGP device listing in your BIOS's startup screen.

Now that you've made out a checklist of your PC's essential parts, what do you do with it? Keep it very handy—perhaps in the front of your desk drawer. Whenever you need to upgrade or repair a part or two, you'll need to investigate what you can afford and what your PC requires. You might need to ask questions of other people (egad!); inevitably, they'll ask exactly what you own today. If your PC won't boot, you won't have this list available to you at startup, so reach in your desk and pull it out.

If the Pause key method just isn't working out for you, there's an alternative method that might make Microsoft angry if they heard about it, but won't harm your computer. Just start up your computer with an unformatted floppy disk firmly in your drive. True, your computer will become irritated—you'll probably get an "Invalid System Disk" message. But once you do get that message … look at what's immediately above it! It's the BIOS report! What you've done is tick off Windows before it had a chance to overlay the BIOS report with its cheesy little startup screen. (Hey, it's your computer!)

Matching Your Computer to Your Operating System's Requirements

In Chapter 1 we discussed some methods for determining how much computer you actually need to run the software you intend to run. The operating system of your computer qualifies as software. Windows is not an integrated part of your PC; computers that are referred to today as "Windows PCs" are merely PCs with Windows installed on their hard drives.

To paraphrase an airline attendant, I realize that you have other choices when running your software and I appreciate that you've chosen Windows. (You have chosen Windows, right?) First of all, if you chose Linux, I'd have to at least double the size of this book. There have always been alternative operating systems to Windows—before Linux, there was IBM's OS/2. However, with each edition of this book I've done the requisite soul-searching and come to the following conclusion: If you truly were the sort of person who would jump head-first into the deep end of computing without a second thought—like Butch Cassidy leaping off the cliff into the river—this book would not serve you well as a flotation device once you had landed smack in the shallow river that is Linux Software. I reckon you're more the Sundance Kid type—in other words, both smart and sensible. You know as well as I do that, when you take up Linux as a hobby, "the fall will probably kill ya'." Your intention is to take the easiest, safest, most sensible route—three adjectives that do not describe Linux.

These are the reasons that in this book I don't cover other operating systems; just Windows. Does this mean I have some bias or fondness toward Microsoft, on the order of my bias or fondness toward—say, Robert Redford? Let's face facts: Despite its relative ease of use, Windows is the most problematic operating system there ever was. However, it's the most widely used operating system there is. If Windows truly were the easiest, most reliable, most agreeable piece of software that ever ran, I wouldn't be in business. Now that I think about it, I'd be hard at work helping the Linux folks off the river bank.

Moving On Up (or Down) to Windows 98 SE

Most of the time, this book will offer the judgment criteria you need to make reasonable decisions about your computer. However, here's one decision this book is going to make for you: Your upgraded computer should run Windows 98 Second Edition (SE).

Why not Windows 95? Because Win98 SE is faster and has fewer bugs, so it will aggravate you less frequently. Also, the newer equipment Win98 SE requires might be less expensive than the older equipment Win95 requires. Why not just run Win95 on newer equipment? Because Win95 requires drivers and other software tools to manage and manipulate your hardware—and if your hardware is too new, it won't work.

Why not Windows 95 OSR2, the nonpublic "corrected" version released to PC manufacturers? Because the best implementations of the "corrections" that appeared in OSR2, are to be found in Win98 SE.

Why not Windows 98, the first edition? Because Win98 was, as operating systems go, a tragic mistake. Win98 SE corrected most of those mistakes; perhaps something to do with Microsoft's losing streak in the federal courts—perhaps you read about it. If you're a multibillion dollar corporation whose success rests pretty much on the success of one product, suddenly coming one step away from being split in two has a unique and interesting way of making you improve the quality of that product really fast. Thus, the Second Edition.

Why not Windows Millennium Edition (Me), the version released after Win98 SE (other than for the sake of its stupid name)? Because despite the sound of an approaching federal axe, Microsoft tried some new features in WinMe that ended up not working very well. For instance, a new memory management technique resulted in the code of terminated programs hanging around memory for a while … sometimes forever. So there's actual running computer code hanging around inside your system, waiting for something to happen when nothing *can* happen. (Adobe Acrobat, for example, never actually shuts down on WinMe until you turn your computer off.) As a result, this code wastes both your computer's space and time, and your own.

Another WinMe feature was a method for self upgrading that involved being online all the time and letting Microsoft's servers check out your computer at random. (Scary thought, isn't it?) Finally, I can tell you through personal experience that Windows Me is darn slow, so paying money to upgrade your computer to run WinMe makes no sense. Any of the WinMe features you might really like—such as Internet Explorer 5.5 or Windows Media Player 7—can be downloaded free from Microsoft's Web site and installed on Win98 SE; they work just fine. So don't upgrade to Windows Me.

Why not Windows 2000, the operating system formerly known as Windows NT? Several reasons. First of all, you're not a system administrator. Even if you do decide to run a PC network in your home, you don't need Windows 2000 to do it. Also, you may want to run a game once in a while. Most PC games are tested for Windows 98 and WinMe, not for 2000. Maybe you run Windows 2000 on your office system, and maybe you don't notice a lot of differences. That's probably because you're not the administrator of your system at work. (If you are—hey, you're an admin? I've been having this problem, perhaps you could help me out …) Windows 2000 requires a lot of overhead on your computer. You don't need it to run everyday applications, and you don't want it if you're going to be running entertainment software of any kind.

If you're running Windows 95 now, you can run Windows 98 SE. Upgrading your hard drive should be no problem—your only concern should be having enough space for the upgrade (from 120 to 200MB of free hard disk space). If you run Windows Me now, you can attempt to uninstall it using the Uninstall Windows Me option in the Add/Remove Programs window (assuming you upgraded from a previous version of Windows and you didn't erase the uninstall files). However, based on what I've seen online and experienced myself, uninstalling Windows Me doesn't always work and the process may trash your system. As an option, consider (if you're buying a new hard disk anyway) purchasing Windows 98 SE and using it when you install the operating system instead of your Windows Me disc.

Building the Computer That Runs Windows 98 SE

Microsoft publishes a list of minimum system requirements for running Windows 98 Second Edition. The company could not be dreaming any more if it said you could run SE on a Proctor-Silex toaster oven. The following table of our recommendations versus theirs comes from years of experience installing and tinkering with Win98 SE (see Table 2.1).

Table 2.1   Recommendation Comparison

What Microsoft Says You Need	What You Actually Need
486DX/66 CPU	This is a joke. You actually cannot run many of Win98 SE's features without a Pentium 266 CPU minimum.
24MB of memory (RAM)	Try 64MB if you want to avoid pulling your hair out. However, depending on your motherboard, 128MB may be cheaper.
140–315MB hard disk space	To make installation quicker, you must re-serve twice the space you actually use. Shoot for 1GB.
VGA monitor	This also implies the presence of a VGA video card. The truth is you need an SVGA monitor; all new monitors sold today are SVGA, even if they don't bear that old moniker. However, many older VGA monitors are not SVGA.
CD-ROM drive	If Windows 98 SE were released on diskettes, you'd need several wooden crates to carry them. Consider a CD-RW instead for its potential as a backup device.
What else?	Uh, how about a printer? Think you might need one of those? Also, either a modem or network card with broadband gear and, of course, a sound card.

Let's run these numbers through the cash register. Suppose instead of upgrading you are building from scratch as minimal a system as you can find. Avoiding the fancy equipment, let's examine some reasonable, low-cost parts in Table 2.2 that combine to produce a Windows 98 SE system (keeping in mind that some of SE's minimum system requirements—such as a 266 MHz CPU—are no longer available as new parts).

Table 2.2 Parts to Combine

Item	What It'll Cost You
Celeron 366 CPU (PPGA)	$49
Socket 370 Motherboard	$98
64MB PC100 ECC RAM	$44
30GB hard disk	$150
12× CD-RW drive	$180
3½" diskette drive	$19
16MB 128-bit video card	$110
Wavetable sound card	$38
56K internal fax modem	$36
ATX form factor system case	$50
17" SVGA monitor	$180
1200 dpi color inkjet printer	$139
Grand total	**$1,093**

At the time of this writing, a comparable fully assembled system sold for $1,018. It would give you an 800MHz Celeron with 128MB RAM, 30GB hard drive, 24× CD-RW, 56K modem, and Windows Me. (I added in the price of the monitor and printer.) Obviously, when it comes time to upgrade everything, as I said in Chapter 1, your best bet is to purchase a new system.

Other Upgrading Concerns

Suppose you have an older edition of Windows than Win98 SE. You're pondering the move to Win98 SE. Here are some other matters you should be concerned about:

➤ **Upgrading your programs**—You can run DOS, Windows 3.1, Windows 95, and Windows 98 programs under Windows 98 SE. The only thing you need to be careful of here is utilities such as antivirus programs (updated with the latest virus signature files), disk optimizers, rescue utilities, uninstallers, and so forth. You definitely should use Windows 98 versions of these programs with Windows 98, unless you like playing Russian Roulette with your data.

➤ **Upgrading your drivers**—The Windows 98 SE CD-ROM contains a plethora of drivers, along with a categorized list of those drivers; yet there's still the possibility that a driver for your specific hardware might be missing. Check online with Microsoft at microsoft.com/windows98/support/critical/default.asp.

➤ **FAT32**—FAT32 is a file management system specially designed for the larger hard disks in use today. If you use Windows 98 SE to convert your hard disk to FAT32, your files consume less space and hard disk access is much faster. In addition, a FAT32 drive uses less of your precious Windows resources. However, FAT32 is not compatible with FAT16, the (retroactively named) file management system in use under DOS, Windows 3.1, and Windows 95. This doesn't present any real problem to your programs. If you have two hard disks—one formatted with FAT32, the other with FAT16—you'll have no problem.

➤ **Plug-and-Play**—Windows 98's "support" of Plug-and-Play devices has become something of an acknowledgement that the BIOS knows better how to set them up than does the operating system. Windows therefore has become relegated to the status of a "Plug-and-Play *Aware*" operating system—and believe me, this is an enhancement you want.

➤ **Using your old Windows 3.1 programs**—Most Windows 3.1 applications run just fine under Windows 98 SE. However, there are some 3.1 applications that, like some cats, just don't take well to new surroundings. If you need to make sure your program will run okay under 98 SE, contact that program's manufacturer. Keep in mind that you can't use your Windows 3.1 application to save documents with SE's longer filenames. If you use a 3.1 application to try to open a file with a long name, you will see that the 3.1 application has translated it into an abbreviated form that fits the old naming conventions. For example, files called `Really Big Dog.DOC` and `Really Big Cat.DOC` will appear as `REALLY~1.DOC` and `REALLY~2.DOC`. The files will still work but you might have to do some guessing to figure out which file is which.

The Least You Need to Know

➤ The more ordinary your PC is from the outside, the more upgradeable it is on the inside.

➤ When you look at the back of your computer to see what can be plugged into it, you can learn a few things about its capabilities and perhaps even its age.

➤ Your computer's BIOS really does try to tell you about itself and all the parts of your PC as it boots up. Start your computer, wait for the beep, and hit Pause; then read what your PC is trying to tell you.

➤ If you have an older operating system and want to install newer parts, you should consider upgrading to Win98 SE, as it is the most reliable operating system released thus far from Microsoft.

➤ Windows Me is newer, but not necessarily better, and many of its features are available as free downloads from Microsoft.

➤ Microsoft's published requirements for a minimum Win98 SE system fell out of a warp in the space/time continuum, in which beings in a parallel universe can run Win98 SE on a turnip. Consider a Pentium or Celeron 266 system to be your true minimum.

Chapter 3

What It Takes to Upgrade Each Part of Your Computer

In This Chapter

➤ That which lurks beneath the putty-colored skin of your computer

➤ The truth about your PC's guts: RAM, the hard disk, and so on

➤ What to expect when upgrading a particular component

Now that you've found out something about your own computer, you're probably anxious to get down to the question of which parts you should upgrade and which parts might be too much trouble. I'll start this chapter by opening a computer and giving you the lay of the land. Next we'll discuss each part of the computer and the reasons you should or should not upgrade that particular part. After reading the section that follows ("Parts Is Parts"), feel free to skip ahead to the parts in which you're most interested.

Parts Is Parts

A person has many parts: a heart that pumps blood, a stomach that changes food into energy, and a brain that ignores pointless information. A computer also has many parts; each serving its own function. The *system unit* (the big box into which everything plugs) contains most of these parts. Here's a look inside one of my very own system units (see Figure 3.1); the table that follows gives you a description.

Figure 3.1

The guts at a glance.

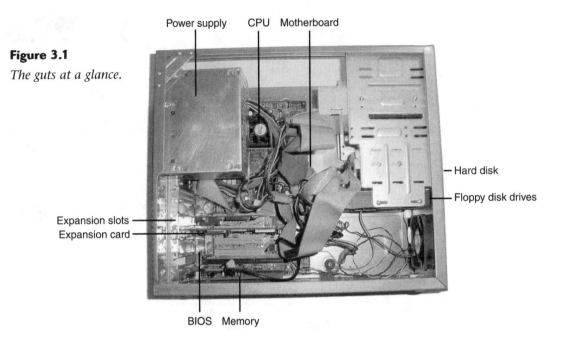

Table 3.1 Parts Description from Figure 3.1

Item	Description
Motherboard	Your house might be built on a slab; PCs are built on motherboards (also called "mainboards"). It electronically connects all the other parts of the computer. You could think of the motherboard as being the nervous system of the computer.
CPU	Nicknamed the "brain," the central processing unit has the job of executing all the instructions presented to it by your programs and your operating system.
BIOS	If the CPU is the brain, the Basic Input/Output System is the computer's instinct. It's your computer's main program; it tells your computer how to run a program or read input from the keyboard or a disk drive. BIOS also is known as *firmware*, because it's the interface between the computer's hardware and its software.
Memory	Nicknamed "RAM" for Random Access Memory, this is the work area of the computer. If you upgrade this, the computer has a bigger area in which to work. A small part of your RAM is reserved for internal use only; it's called *system memory*.
Hard disk	This is where the computer stores programs and permanent data (stuff you create and save). If you upgrade this, you can install more of those mega-do-it-all programs you love.

Item	Description
Diskette drive	This enables you to transfer stuff from one PC to another or store data you don't need on the hard disk all the time. PCs used to come with at least one of these but newer ones don't. Little chance you'll want to add one of these but you might need to replace one you've been using if yours breaks down.
Power supply	This is the thing that powers it all. After upgrading, you might find that you need more juice to run all your new toys. In that case, you can upgrade the power supply.
Expansion slots	These gizmos enable you to add new stuff to your PC such as an internal fax modem, a tape backup, or a much better video card. You can't add these to a computer—they are part of its motherboard. However, you can replace the motherboard and get different (and perhaps better) expansion slots.
Expansion card	Here's one of the little devils now—in Figure 3.1, an internal modem.

The Motherboard Makes the Right Connections

The motherboard serves two purposes, architecturally speaking. First, it provides the foundation for all your other components. It also serves as the chassis for those components, linking them together with buses and interfaces so that they cooperate (see Figure 3.2).

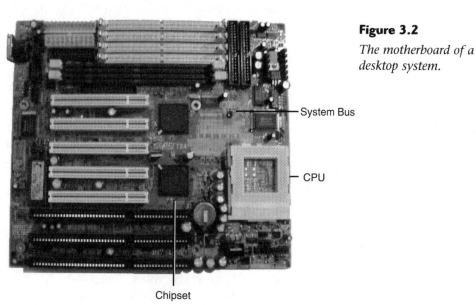

Figure 3.2

The motherboard of a desktop system.

System Bus

CPU

Chipset

What Does a Motherboard Do?

From the outside the motherboard looks like a small city. Etched onto its surface are *leads* (pronounced "leeds") running from the CPU (a computer chip that acts like the brain of your computer) to all the other parts. These leads form an electronic highway called the *system bus* (or *data bus*). Like commuters at rush hour, computer instructions ride the system bus from memory, the hard disk, or wherever to the CPU and back again. (For example, an instruction must go through the CPU—it can't go from memory directly to the hard disk.) The system bus (or highway) weaves in, out, and around every chip on the motherboard; at the end it forms a complete circuit by closing itself and ending where it started.

Your PC has another, equally important bus called the *peripheral bus* (or *expansion bus*), into which all your expansion cards plug. Expansion cards act like stops along the peripheral bus route. The peripheral bus connects to the system bus at the peripheral bus controller, which acts as a traffic signal for data going to one of the expansion boards.

The first motherboards for IBM's PCs utilized literally dozens of soldered-on chips from a variety of manufacturers. In the mid-1990s, motherboard manufacturers realized it could be advantageous to simply standardize and incorporate the functionality of all these different chips into two or three chips that would be much easier for factories to install. Thus the *chipset* was born. Today, the three defining factors of the capability of any motherboard are, in order: 1) which chipset it has; 2) which BIOS it has; 3) which manufacturer assembled them all together (you'll find this name on the motherboard itself—it may not be the name on the outside of the motherboard box). Professional PC technicians identify motherboards more by their chipset than by any other identifying mark or name.

Note

When researching the prices and availability of motherboards, you'll notice they're often organized by their clock speed. You'll find 66MHz, 100MHz, 133MHz, and today 200MHz. Don't confuse CPU clock speed (1.2GHz) with motherboard (system bus) clock speed (133MHz). CPUs often run faster than motherboards; generally in easy multiples for the CPU and the system bus to be synchronized.

So what happens on an average motherboard? Imagine the CPU living in its very own, narrowly confined world, in which all that it can ever see and know is mapped in its memory, its own castle, from which it never emerges. Everything that it can directly address—all of its "subjects," as it were, including all of the contents of RAM plus the chipset and BIOS—constitutes the sum total of the CPU's universe. All these items reside on the system bus.

On the peripheral bus is the rest of the world—your display adapter, modem, printer port, hard drive controller, CD-ROM controller, audio—which the CPU doesn't allow itself to see. Each card that sits on the peripheral bus really is a computer unto itself, each having a central processor of sorts, and even something that qualifies as memory (yes, even a modem maps its own memory). But inside your computer, all of these cards aren't given the royal, majestic status of the CPU.

The chipset manages all the processes taking place on the motherboard, including the transfer of data emerging from the CPU, from the system bus to the peripheral bus. So the chipset acts as the liaison between these two buses, fulfilling a role that used to be undertaken by a separate peripheral bus controller chip.

Data the CPU must utilize is summoned through this liaison. As data leaves the CPU unit proper, heading toward an expansion card, traveling over the leads that make up the system bus, it actually hops off that system bus at a crossover station and gets on the peripheral bus. Each expansion card has its own bus; however, you don't have to be concerned about it because the card can maintain its own affairs. On the return trip data hops off the card's own bus and onto the peripheral bus where it finds the same crossover station as before, and rides the system bus back to the CPU.

Why Upgrade the Motherboard?

First of all, some PCs come with CPUs you can't remove, so there's no other way to upgrade them. (What's a CPU? See the section named "The Brain of Your PC: The CPU" later in this chapter.) Also, if you have an old PC (first edition Pentium, 486, 386, and so forth) upgrading (as in *replacing*) the motherboard is the only option that makes sense. That's because the real speed of the CPU is determined by the speed of the system bus. If you purchase a blazingly fast CPU—even one that fits in the socket—and your system bus is slow, the motherboard can't support a high enough *multiplier* to produce the CPU speed you paid for, and you have wasted money. Plus, for the relatively low price of a motherboard (always less than $200, with the most common models selling for around $100), you can essentially make yourself a new PC.

You'll read about this a lot in this book, but I thought I'd introduce it to you here first: When you choose a new motherboard, you'll find it supports its own system bus speed. For that bus to support the CPU of your choice, the BIOS on that motherboard must support the discrete *multiplier* that factors in how much the system bus speed must be *sped up* in order to equal the designated CPU speed. Simply put, if you're considering a 100MHz system bus motherboard and a 600MHz processor, the motherboard's BIOS must support a 6x multiplier for the two to work together. You'll read a lot more about this in Chapter 9, "Accelerating Your PC with a New CPU."

Why Not Upgrade the Motherboard?

Replacing the motherboard might seem like a quick fix for an old PC—and usually it is, but keep in mind that replacing a motherboard creates its own set of problems. In the end everything connects to the motherboard; if you replace it, you also might have to replace a lot of other things. If your PC is pretty old, most of your existing components probably won't work with a new motherboard.

For example, the older memory modules on a first edition Pentium system won't work with modern motherboards that require different configurations—literally different *shapes* of modules. Also, the new motherboard might not be compatible with the type of expansion cards you use. For example, your existing video graphics card might not work with the new motherboard. (See the description of various expansion slot types later in this chapter for more information.)

In addition, your hard disk might not be compatible with the new motherboard's on-board disk controller. Also, your various drives (hard disk, floppy, CD-ROM, tape, and so forth) might use connectors that are incompatible with the new power supply. This isn't any really big deal because you can get converters for them, but keep it in mind.

Also, replacing the motherboard (a process described in excruciating detail in Chapter 10, "Replacing the Motherboard and Its Parts") means having to unplug everything and then decide where each piece fits into the new motherboard—a nasty business at best.

You'll also have to reformat your hard drive. Microsoft Windows maintains information about the CPU of its computer at the time it was installed on the boot sector of the hard drive. The reason is quite simple: Without this information on the boot sector, swapping a hard drive between systems would be way too easy. (From a legal standpoint, it would be in violation of one of those small-print clauses you don't read. And we don't want that, now, do we?)

So whenever you swap motherboards out from under a hard drive, the information on the drive doesn't jive with the information in the BIOS. (Why doesn't Windows simply trust the BIOS to tell it what system it's in? Because that's what Windows used to do … and that worked just too well.) Consider whether the motherboard will fit your system. For most PCs, finding one that fits your case's form factor is easy but you have to make sure the motherboard you get has holes that match up with the ones in your PC's case. If you can't find a compatible motherboard, you have to buy a new case—and that can add to the expense of upgrading. Keep in mind that a motherboard is easy to break. If you shove it too hard or if you're not careful of the sharp, silver solder points on the bottom, something could snap inside. You won't notice it until you've plugged everything in and nothing happens.

The Brain of Your PC: The CPU

Sometimes I say the CPU is the "brain" of your computer, which is all well and good; however, it's really more correct to say it's the "engine" of your computer. While your chipset is running your system bus, and your BIOS is busy coordinating all the data input from various devices (and from you, the user), the CPU runs your operating system and your software.

The Limits to Upgrading Your CPU, in Brief

Although originally the whole idea behind the standardization of CPU *sockets* (the plugs where your CPU fits into your motherboard) was to introduce the notion of interchangeability in PC construction, an "equal and opposite reaction" was born from that idea. Standardized sockets led to the creation of market competition—a force that Intel, at that time, thought it would never have to face. Other companies could build CPUs that fit into Intel sockets.

As these companies started building trademarks for themselves, Intel responded by changing its sockets. (And by suing, but you don't need to hear about that part.) The competitors—most notably, Advanced Micro Devices (AMD) and Cyrix (now part of VIA)—responded by changing their sockets, and introducing new CPU connection technology into the mix. This made Intel change its design yet again, the end result being more sockets and slots than there are CPUs currently manufactured. No joke. It also has become a very rare circumstance where any one CPU can be easily replaced on the same motherboard with a CPU that's two years younger. Today if you want or need to replace a CPU built in 1999 or earlier with a new model, you'll also probably need a new motherboard. Chapter 9 will spell out for you exactly what you can and cannot upgrade.

Judging When to Make a CPU Investment

At the incredible rate at which CPUs improve in performance and decline in cost, how can you determine the best time to invest in any particular model? Regardless of how the CPU market plays out in the future, it probably will always abide by a basic, unwritten law (unwritten until now, that is). There are always four classes of retail CPUs available:

➤ **Incoming** models reflect the top of the line in speed and performance. For a brief period, these will always be the most expensive models. How brief a period? No longer than eight months, at the current rate in which CPU foundries are improving their production lines. Before the advent of gigahertz clock speeds, newer models generally were 33MHz faster than the older ones; now they're 200MHz (.2GHz) faster. Upgrading to a CPU in this class is almost always more expensive than it needs to be, but it does put off the next upgrade the longest.

➤ **Standard** models represent those most often installed in the average consumer PC—the one with the $750 price tag. These models have been available for eight months or more; once they become standard they probably will continue to be available for another eight months. By the time an incoming model becomes a standard model, its street price probably has decreased by 66 percent. Upgrading to a CPU in this class usually is your best bet—reasonably priced and fast as heck.

➤ **Outgoing** models are no longer in production by their manufacturer, although remaining inventory still is being sold off. They've probably been publicly available for no more than 16 months. Their street price probably will never go lower than 25 percent of their original asking price. Upgrading to a CPU in this class will save you the most money, making it sometimes an even better bargain than upgrading to a standard model CPU, although you might find yourself upgrading again in a year or so.

➤ **Discontinued** models often are sold as used parts, or by retailers that purchased them in bulk when their manufacturers were clearing them out. As they get rarer in quantity, the street price of nonused models will rise again; often back to their former standard retail price. If you can find a CPU in this class that suits your needs without replacing the motherboard, buy it, unless the popularity (and scarcity of the CPU) has driven the price up beyond reason.

Many retailers—especially the online variety—bundle their top-of-the-line motherboards with top-of-the-line CPUs and top-of-the-line memory modules pre-installed. These bundles sell for between $200 and $450, saving you more than a hundred bucks versus purchasing these items individually. However, you rarely find bundles for less than top-of-the-line stuff.

Techno Talk

Everything happens in a computer within a **cycle.** For example, if you read a file from the hard disk so that you can make changes to it, the hard disk reads a small amount of the file per cycle until it reads the entire file. The speed of the computer's CPU determines the number of cycles per second (Hertz, or Hz) in the computer.

How Speed Plays a Factor in Your Computer's ... Uh, Speed

Every process in a CPU takes place to a beat, almost as if it were playing to music. The speed of this beat regulates how fast the CPU can think. If you've ever been to an amateur piano recital and seen a metronome sitting on top of the piano, bobbing back and forth like a presidential candidate, you understand the principal of performing to a fixed beat. If you adjust the dial on that metronome so the tick is sped up from 2 ticks per second to 500 million ticks per second, you can understand the beat that regulates a 500MHz CPU. (Computer engineers don't actually use the term "ticks;" they prefer *cycles*. Sounds sexier.)

So how much faster is a 750MHz processor than a 500MHz processor? Fifty percent? Believe it or not, no. The 750MHz processor is somewhat faster, but by how much depends on the work it's doing at the time. Some spreadsheet operations take more time than most word processing operations, given the same CPU. How noticeable is the difference? For a simple accounting program, perhaps the change is not very noticeable at all, whereas a graphics-intensive game might be significantly faster.

Remember, all computers do simple math faster than you can blink. As a result, balancing your checkbook might take two thousandths of a second rather than three. But Mighty-Battle-Mega-Tron XII might just be 50 percent faster, if not more, because of a cascade effect in which faster operations (such as high-resolution graphics rendering) reduce the workload on future operations, making them faster in turn.

So if you use your PC for math-intensive tasks such as creating spreadsheets, playing games, manipulating complex graphics, or spending time online with the most graphically replete Web sites, a CPU upgrade will improve your disposition more than if you're the type of user who only uses a word processor.

Why Upgrade the CPU?

A brand-new CPU, whose speed essentially was considered top of the line less than one year earlier than whenever you're reading this book, probably can be had for about $60. However, because of the many generation shifts CPUs have undergone in the past five years, you might have to replace your motherboard to upgrade that CPU at all.

Also, it's very unlikely that you'd find the $60 CPU bundled with a $100 motherboard. If you want to take advantage of savings from bundling, you have to set your sights a little higher and be prepared to spend $200 or more. This of course presumes that you don't fall into the Upgrade Cascade discussed in Chapter 1, "Making the Call: When, Why, and Whether You Should Upgrade," where you have to purchase even more hardware to justify your initial purchase. Thus, because you might be facing a substantial financial hurdle, here are some reasons that could be powerful enough to coerce you to make the jump:

➤ **The educational software, games, or other graphics-intensive programs you want to run require speed.**   Graphic-intensive programs often spell out their minimum CPU speed requirements right on the box. This is because the CPU is the component that manages all the math necessary to produce all those pretty pictures; especially the 3D, real-time variety. Although it's really the graphics processors on modern video cards that handle the display, the CPU has to be fast enough to keep pace with the video card.

➤ **You plan to install a high-capacity hard drive.**   What has this to do with anything? High-capacity drives are, by design, fast—and with Ultra DMA (a marketing term for a mode of data transfer that means, essentially, "pretty darn fast") on the motherboard these drives are extremely fast. With hard drives, "fast" is defined by how much data can be fetched in one cycle. If your CPU is too slow, the data that was fetched so quickly is kept waiting in the queue. When that happens, "fast" becomes slow.

➤ **You intend to use your computer to play music or video *while* you're using it to do other things.** Your computer store can set up any demo machine to play "Top Gun" on DVD and quad-channel Dolby, using a CPU as old and slow as a Pentium 75. However, I bet you they don't use that machine as a cash register at the same time. Real-time video and sound streams are processed mainly by your CPU and merely projected by your video and sound cards. Streaming media is the single most time-intensive job your CPU can undertake. If you want to run BBC News 24 in the corner of your screen while you manage your portfolio in Excel, you need a screaming CPU.

Why Not *Upgrade the CPU?*

Upgrading the CPU might sound like the answer to a prayer, but remember that you might not always want what you think you need. There are some realities to consider. And here they are:

➤ **Faster CPUs may lead you to make subsequent purchasing decisions (motherboard, video, RAM) that leave you with a slower computer overall.** No kidding. For this reason you should avoid purchasing your parts piecemeal. First, uncover some evidence that the equipment you're buying really does lead to performance improvements when it all works together. Look up the manufacturers of your components online, and run searches for their names (Google is a great search engine for that purpose). This way, you'll get listings for *independent* sources who have tried the combination you're considering already.

➤ **You might run up against a socket/slot compatibility wall.** At one time, Intel purposefully installed 486DX CPUs in sockets that were too big for them, for the express purpose of enabling owners to upgrade to the newer, bigger Pentium series after it was invented. This was the final time in history that Intel or anyone else planned a socket that would sustain a crossover in generations. A newer CPU simply might not fit into your old connector; especially if the new CPU uses a slot and you have a socket—or the new CPU uses a socket and you have a slot.

➤ **There are limits to what a CPU upgrade can accomplish.** Although a new CPU can think faster, it still may be talking to really slow, stupid PC parts. The bottlenecks between a fast CPU and its slow fellow components can be much greater than between a slow CPU and those same components. Yes, a faster CPU can lead to a performance downgrade.

➤ **You might experience problems with overheating.** Faster CPUs run hotter. All new CPUs sold today come complete with a snap-on gadget called a *heat sink*—either a cute little fan, or an array of jet-black spikes that look more like weapons than computer parts. (You'll learn more about these in Chapter 20,

"Cooling and Ventilating Your System.") However, in the tightest system cases, such as Slimlines and mini-towers, if the heat sink has no space in which to disperse the heat emanating from the CPU, they're about as much good to the CPU as a felt hat would be to a fellow walking through a desert. You can buy inexpensive, cute, snap-on miniature fans that do a better job of dispersing the heat from socketed CPUs. But again, without proper ventilation, you might find yourself needing a bigger system case. That might also mean a new motherboard, as well.

Basic Functions Are in the System BIOS

BIOS, short for Basic Input/Output System, is a set of instructions for how the CPU communicates with the other principal devices in your computer—mainly your hard disk; your floppy disk; and the input devices, including your keyboard and mouse. There are a few other, minor elements of your computer which, thanks to a shortage of available words in the world's collective vocabulary, also are called "BIOS." However, when this book uses the term "BIOS" by itself it means the more important system BIOS.

The system BIOS plays the role of the PC's butler—performing the lowly tasks that the CPU doesn't want to waste its time doing. This includes basic input and output chores such as paying attention to something the user is doing and shuttling data from the hard disk stream to memory. The BIOS also contains the primary routines—namely, Power-On Self-Test (POST)—that start up the computer, tell the computer that it is a computer, and shut the computer down. Meanwhile, the CPU is free to concentrate on upper-class tasks such as calculating the square root of 234,567,483,094 and spell checking a 200-page document.

When you start your PC, the BIOS checks everything out to make sure it's functioning properly. For example, the POST routine checks out the keyboard to make sure it's plugged in and it checks out memory to make sure a memory module hasn't committed suicide in the middle of the night.

For Plug-and-Play (PNP) systems (basically all PCs produced since 1996), the BIOS also might give certain connected peripherals (such as hard drives, CD-ROMs, devices connected to the USB interface, and devices on the PCI bus) a chance to identify themselves and reveal their resources to the computer. This was a job formerly handled by the operating system; however, with each revision of Windows, this job was handled increasingly poorly. Peripheral manufacturers actually compelled BIOS manufacturers to develop a PNP standard that sneaked behind the back of Windows and brought peripherals online before Windows noticed they were ever offline.

The BIOS also acts as an intermediary between your operating system and your video card. The operating system knows what it wants to display; the video card has the facilities for displaying it. The operating system has just one way to communicate with the BIOS; however, there are several types of video cards. Video drivers consist of software that informs the operating system what the video card is capable of or willing to display; however, technically the drivers don't do the job of generating the display data. Because of this, the moment you switch your PC on you see the insignia of your video BIOS seconds before you see that of your main BIOS.

Another important function of the BIOS is to kick start the operating system, whatever that might be. After the POST, the BIOS loads the operating system into memory and then tells it, "Okay, George, I brought 'er in. Now this baby's yours." From here, the operating system handles the big jobs, sending requests to the CPU. The lowly BIOS continues to run—fetching data, watching for key presses, and scanning for mouse movement.

Check This Out

Want to know what brand and version of BIOS you have? Just start your PC, and watch for a message onscreen, such as **Award Modular BIOS v4.51PG.**

The BIOS generally is stored on one ROM (Read-Only Memory) chip, located on the motherboard. On all PC motherboards produced since 1996, the chip in use here is called a *flash ROM*. The chip retains the BIOS program without any power being supplied to it at all; however, you can replace the program on that chip with a newer edition using a technique called *flashing*. (The word derives from the cooking technique in which meat is barely introduced to the barbeque; then served rare.) For this reason, modern PCs are said to have *flash BIOS*.

Why Upgrade the BIOS?

The first and perhaps most compelling reason you might want to *reflash* (*reprogram*) your BIOS is it's generally free; you can download new BIOS programs from the Web. The trick is locating the version you need for the motherboard and CPU you own. There are countless motherboard models in the world, each of which uses an edition of an Award, Phoenix, AMI, or other BIOS especially tailored to it. You can learn the trick to finding the BIOS you need by reading Chapter 10, "Replacing the Motherboard and Its Parts."

You normally don't have to upgrade your BIOS because it contains all the information it needs to run the major input and output devices in your system. What it doesn't know it learns through *device drivers*—special files that supplement its language skills, as it were. Device drivers are maintained by the operating system (Windows). For example, if you add a CD-ROM drive to your computer, you also must install its device driver so the BIOS can communicate with it.

With device drivers widely available and (relatively) easy to install, do you ever need to upgrade your BIOS? Well, if you have an older system, you might notice when you add a fancy new part that its technology can be so advanced that the old, pokey BIOS just can't keep up, even with the help of a driver. In such a case, you must upgrade the BIOS as well.

By the way, because the BIOS is a chip, how do you replace it? Replacement usually is a matter of pulling the old BIOS chip off the motherboard socket (it isn't welded in) and pushing in a newer one. You might have to replace your chip if it becomes defective. One problem you might experience is a BIOS chip whose program fails as your system warms up. A new BIOS chip costs between $30 and $100.

Why Not Upgrade the BIOS?

The best reason for you not to upgrade your BIOS is that everything you use with your computer now, and everything you plan to use with it in the near future, works just fine with it now. You should only try reflashing your BIOS to improve its speed if you notice a lag or lull in hard drive access or graphics speed. But if you're comfortable with the speed at which your PC makes contact with its peripherals, don't bother.

Also, there's one very real, very strange reason for not wanting to upgrade your BIOS: Even though doing so might make something new work, it might make something old fail. It's been known to happen. In Chapter 10, I'll discuss some of the strange consequences and real dangers involved in flashing your own BIOS ... besides, of course, being indicted for public indecency.

Don't let potential problems prevent you from upgrading a flash BIOS. You can always reflash your old BIOS back onto your computer if later on, even though you're able to boot it up again, you experience some problems. What sort of problems? Recently when I reflashed a BIOS with a newer version, Windows insisted I had some kind of infrared keyboard or pointer device attached to my computer, which it couldn't find. In other words, Windows was complaining that I had installed a device I hadn't installed, because I hadn't installed it. The reason: Some BIOS register was informing Windows that this device was present. Windows looked for its associated device driver, couldn't find it, then reported an error. The solution: I reflashed my old BIOS and the problem went away.

The PC's Think Tank: RAM

Random Access Memory basically is the computer's work area. The computer stores data and instructions temporarily in RAM, where they wait until the CPU summons them. For example, when you start a program your computer places the instructions that make up the program (literally a bunch of numbers) into RAM. The CPU then retrieves, or "fetches," these instructions in sequence as if they were written out on a long scroll or tape. Imagine this tape being fed through a series of virtual spools inside the CPU, with one or more virtual heads reading the instructions on this imaginary tape in one or more places. This is a pretty realistic idea of what goes on inside a CPU with the instructions from RAM.

Aside from program instructions, data also is placed in RAM. When you use an application to create something, such as a letter to my editors telling them what a great book you think this is, your computer stores that letter in RAM so that the CPU can make your changes to it.

However, RAM is not a permanent thing—that is to say all the data and instructions that make up the contents of RAM are not permanent. When you reboot the computer (turn it off and on again using the switch located on the machine itself), everything in RAM is erased. That means I'll never get to hear your wonderful words of praise unless you save your letter to the hard disk (or at least print it out) before you turn the computer off.

Because RAM is the computer's working area (or its desk, if you will), it places a limit on the amount of things you can ask your computer to do at one time—there's only so much room on that desk. When you try to run a lot of programs without a lot of memory, Windows will shuffle stuff out of memory to the hard disk, then back again when it's needed. By doing this, Windows reserves RAM for the stuff on which you're currently working. This back and forth business really slows things down, believe me, because the hard drive is slower than the RAM. That's why adding more RAM probably is the best thing you can do for a computer. (You'll find more on Windows in the Fourth Quarter of this book.)

Techno Talk

Memory today is measured in megabytes. A **byte** is the amount of memory it takes to store a single character, such as the letter J. A **kilobyte** is roughly one thousand bytes; a megabyte is roughly one million bytes. (Okay, if you've just gotta know, it's really 1,048,576 bytes.)

The Different Types of RAM

The type of RAM that constitutes the computer's working area is *dynamic RAM,* or *DRAM.* Information stored in DRAM is made up of electrical charges, which degrade and decay when left to themselves. Because of this, periodically DRAM has to be dynamically *refreshed* (hence, the name) so that all those bits don't literally blow away.

The other type of RAM (referred to scientifically as "The Other Type of RAM") is *static RAM,* or *SRAM.* Modern computers have a little bit of SRAM tucked away somewhere, in a location referred to as a *cache.* What makes SRAM different from DRAM is that SRAM uses fewer transistors for each bit of storage, so 1) it's more densely packed, so it takes up less space; and 2), it doesn't need to have its contents refreshed as long as it's getting power; thus the term *static.* SRAM is significantly faster than DRAM.

So, why not use all SRAM? For one thing, SRAM is too expensive right now to use as your PC's main memory. More important, SRAM can't be mapped the same way as DRAM—meaning, for chunks of memory 32MB or larger, the CPU can't call an address from SRAM the same way as from DRAM. It would not be hard to enable the

CPU to do that, except that today's CPU must access RAM the same way as *yesterday's* CPU does for software to remain compatible.

The system memory on most motherboards manufactured during the 1990s is provided by easy-to-install *memory modules.* When you upgrade your RAM, you can just snap in some modules and you're done. The original PC memory module, used in motherboards between 1990 and 1997, was the *Single Inline Memory Module (SIMM)*. What's "single" about it? It has a single row of pins along the bottom edge connector. And unless you have the attention span of toddler, you know by now that *inline* means "in line" or, more accurately, "in a line." There are three varieties of SIMMs: 30-pin with 9 chips, 30-pin with 3 chips (denser memory per chip), and 72-pin with 8 chips.

The most commonly used memory module today is the *Dual Inline Memory Module (DIMM)*. Contrary to what you might read, both SIMMs and DIMMs have surface-mounted DRAMs on one or both sides. So what's dual about a DIMM? It's the architecture of the pins that connect these modules to the motherboard.

In a SIMM, even though you might see two rows of metal pins on both sides of the module, each pin in those rows is connected—so technically, each pair really is the same pin. For a DIMM, both rows of pins are not connected. You can't see that they're not connected, but take my word for it. This means that a greater number of real pins can be attached to the same amount of real estate, resulting in a broader interface between memory and the data (system) bus.

There's one more difference that stands out and says, "I'm a DIMM": the presence of an extra notch in the connector that's *offset,* so you can't install a DIMM the wrong way; the plug on the motherboard won't let you (see Figure 3.3).

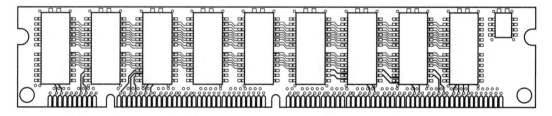

Figure 3.3

A common DIMM module.

Although the sizes of the first DIMM modules were all over the board—small being a 72-pin model that had 32 pins and 8 chips per side; medium having 144 pins and 16 chips (usually) split in two sides the same way—the most common DIMM form factor today is the large 168-pin 16-chip model that's a full 5¼ inches long.

The Differences in RAM on the Inside

In 1998 the leading PC manufacturers decided that the 50MHz speed limit of the PC's system bus simply was too slow to handle modern applications. The only way to improve a computer's performance as CPU speed becomes faster would be to remove all limitations to system bus speed imposed by any standards. So it was that the 100MHz system bus and 100MHz DRAM were developed simultaneously. In fact, the S in the name chosen for the new memory standard—SDRAM—stands for simultaneous. Engineers learned that the only way to ensure memory reliability as speeds increase is to synchronize its speed with that of the system bus. This way, the CPU would never have to wait to fetch memory contents. The era of so-called "wait states" is over.

Today's most common memory modules are 168-pin DIMMs equipped with SDRAM. A competing standard at the time of this writing, and a contender for SDRAM's replacement, is *Direct Rambus DRAM (DRDRAM, sometimes called RDRAM)*. This is a proprietary technology developed by Intel and Rambus, which replaces the front side of the system bus with an entirely separate memory bus currently clocked at 400MHz. I'll talk more about DRDRAM and its potential replacement memory module, the RIMM in Chapter 11, "Memorize This! Upgrading Memory."

Before the advent of SDRAM, the most common RAM standard utilized a DRAM architecture called *Extended Data Out*. In a strange sense, EDO is a purposefully de-evolved form of DRAM, with certain memory flushing safeguards removed, mainly because with modern CPUs these safeguards are simply not needed. The details of this feature would bore the common sea snail. Suffice it to say that if your computer uses a Pentium and uses EDO DRAM, it cannot use any other type.

Check This Out

Your CPU might have a small but powerful amount of SRAM in one or more *caches*. A cache is a special area where the PC keeps data that it has been using a lot. The idea is that if the PC requests the data several times, chances are it will do it again; thus, it's best to keep the data someplace where the CPU can get to it fast. The data in the cache is constantly evaluated so that it contains the data that was most recently accessed, under the presumption that the data that will be accessed next most likely will be in the same block. When it isn't, the cache gets loaded with a block of data from the region that is being accessed currently, which does consume some time but not as much as fetching data directly from DRAM each and every time.

If your PC doesn't have EDO memory, it might have Fast Paging Mode. Like EDO, FPM is faster memory because it makes intelligent guesses about which page of data is most likely to be needed next, and loads that into memory. FPM was replaced by the EDO standard.

So How Much Memory Do I Need?

To run big programs and not have to wait a long time to do it, you need to have lots of memory. How much is enough? Well, some nerds will tell you there's no such thing as enough when you're talking about a computer; however, for a Windows 95/98 computer, a good minimum is 64MB (that is, if you don't mind taking frequent siestas). Me, I run with 128MB.

If you prefer a more scientific method, check out the minimum requirement of the programs you want to run—you're not adding them together; you're just looking for the program that needs the greatest amount of memory. Now take that number and double it.

How Do I Tell How Much Memory I Have?

To figure out how much memory you already have, watch the screen the next time you start your PC. As your computer gets its stuff together so it can face another work-day, the Power-On Self-Test counts down the amount of memory you have. If you have an older system this amount might be shown in kilobytes (KB) rather than megabytes (MB). To get the amount of megabytes your PC has, divide the K number you see by 1,024, which is the number of kilobytes in one megabyte.

For example, when I start my PC I see the total add up to this number: 131,072. If I divide this by 1,024 I get 128MB. If your PC counts up memory too fast for you to read it, Windows can tell you. Right-click My Computer and select Properties. Your PC's total RAM appears on the General tab.

Why Upgrade Memory?

This is one of those topics that seems self-answering on the surface; I could just say, "More is better" and be done with that. However, I've put all my cards on the table with every other topic, so let's examine this one just as fairly. Adding memory offers the greatest performance upgrade you can make to your computer for the lowest price. Basically, when you add more memory, your Windows computer will be able to handle more tasks simultaneously without paging unused memory to your hard drive nearly as often. Remember, every time Windows has to pull its resource data off of your hard drive rather than RAM, it takes several hundred times longer to do so. No joke.

Oh, and did I mention price? RAM—specifically, DRAM—is cheap. Granted, its price is prone to fluctuation. At least once per year there's some political brouhaha among the

Asian nations where the world's major memory foundries are based that results in a threat of chip shortages that parallels the now Semiannual OPEC Threat of Oil Supply Shutoffs. During these periods RAM prices tend to rise as demand rises, although recently even their peak prices have been cheap from the vantage point of the last four years of history. However, once these threats subside—and they always do—RAM prices drop below the floor. How low is that? Today, using the 128MB SDRAM DIMM as a benchmark, RAM is available on the open market at about 22.6¢ per megabyte. If the price drops any lower, they're going to find where that loose plutonium from Chernobyl ended up.

Why Not Upgrade Memory?

As you might expect, all motherboards have a maximum amount of memory they can contain. The fact that SIMMs and DIMMs come in denser packages doesn't mean you can just add these dense packages to your old motherboard and suddenly you have all the memory of a herd of elephants. It's up to the motherboard's chipset and system bus to determine how much memory is its maximum. (The BIOS also plays a limited role in determining this maximum.)

If you're at the point where you really do need more memory than your motherboard is able to handle, you should consider replacing your motherboard. Of course the fact that you're considering this should raise a red flag in your mind that perhaps your computer is too old for what you want it to do.

There's another point to consider, which involves computer capacity versus human capacity: At some point simply adding memory might be pointless for you. For instance, if your computer is used only for running the average spreadsheets, a 256MB computer probably won't give you a lot of noticeable performance gains over a 128MB computer. Thus the question here really becomes …

Can I Upgrade Memory?

Funny question. You might be thinking, "If there's a will, there's a way." That's not always so. The theoretical address limit of your PC's CPU, and of both Windows and Linux for PCs, is 4GB (gigabytes). Today, this is still a pretty high number, although with 100GB hard drives becoming abundant, it doesn't seem as high as it used to. Even if you double the highest maximum requirement of the software you plan to run, your total won't even approach 4GB.

The true limit of addable memory likely is physical rather than theoretical: Your motherboard has only so many slots open (see Figure 3.4). There is no longer any such thing as a memory expansion card for modern PCs; your CPU can access only the memory that's directly linked to your computer's system bus. In Chapter 11, you'll see that the fact that there are so many empty module slots on your motherboard does not necessarily mean you can add that many modules to your system.

You might have to add more modules to increase your memory—meaning you have to remove the modules you have—or you might not be able to add as many modules of the same type as you have open slots. You probably will need a notepad with several unused sheets of paper to help you figure out how much you can upgrade your RAM, if at all.

Figure 3.4

Memory is arranged on your motherboard in banks.

Now suppose your PC has two banks of memory with four rows each, and that it uses SIMMs. If your PC is circa 1992, it probably accepts only the 1MB or 4MB 30-pin SIMMs, so let's assume that's the case here. To upgrade memory you have to fill a bank, and because your PC has four rows in each bank, you have to buy enough memory to fill those four rows. You can't mix and match the SIMMs you use in a single bank, so you have to fill your bank with either four 1MB or four 4MB SIMMs. This gives you either 4MB of memory (if you fill a bank with four 1MB SIMMs) or 16MB (if you use the 4MB SIMMs instead). It also means you can't add only 1 or 2MB of RAM to this PC—you have to add at least 4 or 16MB, because your PC accepts only 1 or 4MB SIMMs.

Socket 7-based Pentium PCs and some 486s use 72-pin SIMMs, which come in a lot more varieties, including 512K, 1MB, 2MB, 4MB, 8MB, and 16MB. This means you'll have more flexibility when adding memory to these systems. Although DIMMs are just as easy to install as SIMMs, they actually come in several more varieties (the reasons for which I plan to bore you with in Chapter 11). Suddenly there are *buffered* and *unbuffered* flavors, and both of those kinds come in two different voltage capacities. So finding the right DIMM for your socket might remind you of finding the right replacement bulb for your string of Christmas lights.

Another problem you might run into is a motherboard whose banks are full. At this point you can decide to replace your RAM chips with higher capacity ones. For example, in the sample system, you could replace the 8 rows of 1MB SIMMs with 8 rows of 4MB SIMMs, taking you from 8MB of memory to 32MB.

Check This Out

For years, computer mechanics (the ones getting paid money to do the things you want to do to your own PC) were wondering why some memory modules seemed to short out for no reason at all. Just recently, the culprit was discovered: Some memory manufacturers use gold for the pins on their memory modules; others use tin. Likewise, some memory socket manufacturers use tin or some other silver metal for their connectors; others use gold. Mixing the two metals by shooting electricity through them literally creates a chemical imbalance that could cause the module—and even the motherboard—to short out. So pay attention to whether the module sockets on your motherboards have a heart of gold, and if they do, don't break that heart by offering it mere tin.

Save It for the Hard Disk

The hard disk is where you store your permanent data, such as programs and the stuff you create with them, letters, and other things. When you look inside your PC at the hard disk, all you see is a boring metal case about the size of a sandwich. You can't see or touch the hard disk itself; it's protected against the smog, smoke, pollen, and other crud that you and I breathe every day without even thinking about it.

If you could open the hard disk you'd see it's actually a series of disks (platters) that look like CDs suspended on a central hub (see Figure 3.5). These platters are coated with magnetic particles to form a pattern that, when translated from the ancient Sanskrit (okay, the bits and bytes), forms your data. Read/Write heads are the magnetic devices inside a hard disk, that float over the platters (never touching them), sensing and depositing data, eagerly waiting to grab this data when you request it. Reading is the process of retrieving data from a disk. Writing is the process of saving data onto a disk.

Figure 3.5

The guts of a hard disk.

Partitioning and Formatting Your Hard Disk

How exactly does a computer save data onto a magnetic disk? I'm glad you asked. First you must understand that your computer usually treats the hard disk as one unit, although you can divide the hard disk into smaller units called *partitions*. Windows assigns each of these partitions a letter, starting with C and working toward Z.

For your computer to start using a new hard disk, you have to partition it—give it an area of space that the operating system, not just the BIOS, recognizes as a hard disk. Even with all active versions of Windows, you partition your hard disk using the FDISK command from the DOS command line. When your hard disk is within the maximum size limits of the BIOS, basically all you're doing with FDISK is telling the computer the size of each partition. However, when your hard disk's capacity exceeds that maximum size, you can use FDISK to create two or more partitions, thereby making the operating system think you have more than one hard disk.

After you partition a hard drive, you *format* it. Formatting is a process that divides the platters into cylinders, tracks, and sectors. A hard disk generally has more than one *platter* (very few do not), stacked atop one another without touching, not unlike an old Wurlitzer jukebox. A *track* is a circle on which the hard disk actually places the data. Think of a *cylinder* as a cross section of all the tracks on each platter that are in the same location. Each track is divided into parts called *sectors*. When you save a file to the hard disk, it becomes divided into *clusters,* which are scattered among these sectors.

The logical location of a file is stored within a special group of sectors called the *file allocation table* (*FAT*), whose location begins at the second sector of the first track of the hard disk, just after the master boot record, which makes the hard drive work in the first place.

Why Upgrade the Hard Disk?

This one's easy: If you need more room for your programs or data, you've gotta add a hard disk. A hard disk offers the least expensive storage per megabyte you can purchase today, with CD-R discs coming in a close second. But you can't rely on optical storage for everyday access (every minute access, actually) as well as you can with a hard disk drive.

Another reason: *speed*. High-capacity hard disks today are orders of magnitude faster than their predecessors, which date back merely to 1996. Windows makes use of any free hard disk space you have for use as extra Windows memory. (You can ask Windows not to but it will punish you, and you might receive a mysterious subpoena in the mail.) Installing a faster hard disk could significantly speed up all memory management operations in your computer, which could speed up your entire PC more noticeably than even a CPU upgrade.

Here's a hard disk option you should consider, and which I discuss in further detail in Chapter 7, "'Repairing' the Hard Disk Instead of Replacing It": For reasons purely of safety—not excess—consider adding a second hard disk drive. Keep your operating system on the first drive (C) and your important data files on the second drive (D). Why? Have you ever had a hard disk crash on you? Maybe it crashed on account of something the operating system did? Notice how when a hard disk crashes, *all* of it crashes? This means your vital data files are dragged down along with everything else, right?

If you keep your vital data files on a separate drive, they're safe. And because those files are on a drive that did not contain the operating system, the chances of it crashing are reduced. Why? Because the operating system—okay, Windows—consumes more data transfer time than the simple storage and recall of data files. Besides, most Windows applications currently store backup images of files under construction in the \TEMP directory on drive C, and update those files every few minutes or so. So the wear and tear is always on drive C. Thus, when you move your vital data to drive D, you reduce the chances of that data being part of the cause of your next hard disk crash.

Why Not Upgrade the Hard Disk?

Here again, the question becomes whether you *can* add a hard disk. There are several factors to ponder, depending on whether you're adding a drive or replacing your existing one. If you're adding a second drive, you have to find a drive that works well with your first drive. If you don't mind ditching your first drive, you open more options; however, you still have to find one that's compatible with your PC.

Another factor here is whether you feel up to the task of replacing or adding a hard disk to your PC. If you're replacing your old hard drive, you have to take the old drive out, of course. This usually means removing some other stuff so you have enough room to remove the drive.

After you slide the new drive into the empty drive bay and plug in its data and power cables, you have to set up the drive. This can get pretty nerdish, so you might want to bribe a guru to help you out here. If you have to brave the depths of CMOS, FDISK, and FORMAT yourself, don't despair—I provide the necessary help in Chapter 16, "Hands-On Hard Disk Replacement."

If your existing hard disk drive is connected to a SCSI host adapter card, you don't intend to replace that drive, and you want to add another drive, you pretty much have to go with SCSI. SCSI devices connect to each other in what's called a *daisy chain*— kind of like holding hands for a game of whip. Unfortunately, you can't assume that your existing SCSI host adapter works with both your old and your new SCSI drive. Some are just incompatible. That means you might have to buy an additional SCSI controller for the new drive. If you're replacing your old SCSI drive, you shouldn't run into a problem. See Chapter 12, "Face the Interface," for more details about these host adapter thingies.

Your PC's Video System

Increasing your system RAM is the least expensive performance improvement you can buy for the greatest performance gain (more so than a CPU upgrade). However, replacing your video (graphics) card—possibly the most expensive upgrade there is— easily is the most dramatic and most appreciable performance gain you can buy (much more so than a CPU upgrade).

Your computer's video system is composed of the following parts: a video controller (graphics card), a graphics accelerator (which may or may not be separate from the main card), perhaps a local bus or port linking the video controller to the CPU, graphics production capability inside the CPU itself, and, of course, a monitor.

A video card you purchase today can plug into any of four types of expansion ports, listed here in order of most advanced to least advanced:

➤ **The AGP port**—This is the most commonly used dedicated expansion port found on motherboards constructed from 1999 on. The port gives the video card direct access to the system bus (or, as AGP engineers are now calling it, the *frontside bus*). This links the video processor to both the CPU and memory—a direct route, unencumbered by any other devices that would reside on a more general expansion bus such as PCI. Theoretically, you can leave the AGP port open and install a PCI or ISA video card on a motherboard that supports AGP— but frankly, why would you want to? AGP cards offer high performance and are now inexpensive. The AGP slot is divided into three segments, but is identified by a distinguishing *hook*—so there's a trick to inserting the card that you'll learn in Chapter 12.

➤ **The PCI port**—This is the high-speed, 32-bit expansion bus designed for everyday devices including video, sound, modem, and networking cards. PCI video cards still are being manufactured at the time of this writing. They continue to provide more than adequate performance for everyday computing tasks, although as AGP cards become more mass produced, PCI video cards are no longer the least expensive. They also don't provide the highest performance available for intense graphics, especially for gaming.

➤ **The VESA (VL-Bus) port**—The original frontside bus connection for video cards, its design was the predecessor to AGP and was deployed in motherboards mainly between 1992 and 1994. These cards are no longer in production; if you have a VESA port in your computer, it may be too old to be upgraded.

➤ **The ISA port**—Especially for older computers, you still can find inexpensive, general-purpose SVGA cards for everyday Windows work; however, you probably won't be able to play the latest games with them. The problem with ISA video cards is that they're noticeably slower, even for everyday work. If your motherboard doesn't offer an AGP or PCI port, consider replacing it unless you need to artificially extend the time it takes for you to get any work done as a way to avoid stress.

When you decide to upgrade your video, you should utilize the most advanced expansion port available to you. If you find you have to replace your motherboard to upgrade your video, you might encounter a situation where you have to replace your CPU. Video upgrades are the central gateways to the Upgrade Cascade. The most sensible choice might be to either purchase the best performing video card your system can handle or replace the entire system.

So What's VGA?

When there were several standards for the CPU transmitting data to the graphics processor, the *Video Graphics Adapter* (*VGA*) standard became the most advanced of the mix way back in 1984. The SVGA standard was the latest revision to VGA— actually a specification for how VGA could be extended and amended in the future to account for improvements in video technology. Because it was a standard that could stretch itself, SVGA became so ubiquitous that, even though all PC video cards produced today use SVGA, they don't even say so. The abbreviation has fallen out of common use; however, the standard is very strong and unlikely to be replaced in the near future. (How many computer standards can you say that about?)

SVGA took the old VGA standard and blew it wide open. The result is that SVGA gives you the capability to display more colors at higher *resolutions*. The image you see onscreen is made up of tiny dots called *pixels*. A screen's resolution is determined by the number of pixels that appear on the screen. Common resolutions include 640h × 480v (that's 640 pixels across by 480 pixels down), 800h × 600v, 1024h × 768v, and 1280h × 1024v. At lower resolutions, there are fewer pixels to fill the screen, so they're bigger and fatter. At higher resolutions there are more pixels, which are smaller so they provide finer detail to an image.

All new monitors sold today—both tubes and LCD panels—use SVGA. Because the SVGA standard is so extensible, higher resolutions and greater color tables could conceivably be adopted over the next few years; all without dumping the existing video modes SVGA supports now.

What's This About "Acceleration"?

Many expensive video cards tout themselves as "graphics accelerators." At one time, graphics cards and graphics accelerators were separate entities unto themselves. Suffice it to say that most so-called "accelerator cards" today also are video cards in and of themselves, with acceleration technology built in.

What do I mean by "acceleration technology?" Basically, it consists of much of the programming and instructions necessary for graphics-intensive programs (read: games) to render exquisite images saved permanently in the hardware (namely, ROM chips). This makes rendering such images substantially faster, especially when the manufacturers of such graphics-intensive binary code (read again: games) agree to subscribe to this new hardware standard so their programs can benefit.

3D accelerators contain in hardware much of the programming necessary to render detailed, three-dimensional, moving images. Graphics rendering standards now are built in to the firmware of video cards; and games that aim to provide their players with otherworldly experiences (for instance, virtual worlds where computers make sense) know how to communicate specifically with the video hardware. The graphics accelerator then tells that hardware what scenes to render rather than doing it itself or relying on mere software to do it. The result is an experience that is not only very fast but shockingly fluid and surprisingly detailed. Chapter 14, "I Can See Clearly Now: Upgrading Your Video," will give you some valuable pointers for choosing the right video card for your jobs, your needs, and your wants.

To make use of accelerator technology, you really need a computer with a Pentium-class CPU no slower than 266MHz. In other words, your CPU has to be fast enough itself to be able to drive the accelerator—sort of like when your automobile has to be going at least 45MPH for your turbocharger to kick in.

Why Upgrade the Video?

The best reason in the world to consider upgrading your video is your own personal health. Any image produced on a projected monitor (that is, a CRT such as your television set, although not an LCD screen such as the one on your laptop or note-book) flickers by nature. It might flicker so fast that you don't notice it much, but deep inside your head, something does notice it. If it notices this too much, it sounds an alarm in the form of a headache. If you happen to like your eyes and you want to be able to continue to see out of them, consider a high-speed video card (remember, 3D isn't necessary for speed) with a sharp, big monitor (17" diagonal or greater).

With a good SVGA tube monitor (CRT), you can get rid of that annoying flicker, stop squinting, and actually see what it is you're working on. With a more expensive, flat-panel monitor (LCD), there's no flicker at all. However, you sacrifice the capability of changing resolutions, which often is helpful in advanced gaming.

Why Not *Upgrade the Video?*

To get the best image, you need to match a good video card with a good monitor. Monitors still are among the most expensive PC components currently available, aver-aging about $250 to $1,000. (Meanwhile, the average video card sells for about $125.) The best video cards available might not be able to show off their best performance modes—and might not be able to work at all—with an older SVGA monitor.

If you have an older PC (months and months old), you might already be using the best performing video card available to it. The optimum speed of PCI-based video cards probably has already been reached. If you have a top-of-the-line PCI video card now, but no AGP port on your motherboard, the only way up is down … jump on that inner tube and take a wild, watery ride down the Upgrade Cascade!

The Least You Need to Know

➤ The motherboard is the chassis of the system unit; everything connects to it. It uses an electronic transportation system called the system bus to transfer data back and forth between devices.

➤ The BIOS handles routine tasks such as reading and writing data, updating the monitor display, and monitoring keyboard and mouse activity.

➤ RAM is the working area of the computer. If you add more RAM (memory), the PC can handle larger workloads.

➤ You use the hard disk to store permanent data, which is connected to a con-troller that's on the drive (IDE, EIDE) or on a card (SCSI, ESDI) or on the motherboard (OLD).

➤ Your computer's video family contains up to four members: the monitor, the video graphics controller, local bus, and VRAM (except for AGP).

Chapter 4

What You Need to Know *Before* You Open Your PC

In This Chapter

➤ Preparing for the next big disaster of the day

➤ Backing up important stuff

➤ Getting ready for the big moment

➤ Uncovering your PC's innards

For me, opening a PC and playing around with its guts is about as much fun as playing around with real guts. But when I absolutely have to, I perform upgrades to my PC; even if you're not much of a mechanic either, you can, too.

If you've upgraded a few things on your PC already, you probably started the same way I did: with the easy stuff such as the keyboard, mouse, or printer. If you want to upgrade anything else, there's a good chance you'll need to actually open up your PC—and that can be scary. This entire chapter is about two things: preparing to open up your PC and actually doing it. This way, both you and your PC are completely prepared for the momentous event: the *internal upgrade*.

Creating an Emergency Diskette

Before you upgrade anything on your PC (or even install a new program, for that matter), you should update your emergency diskette. With an emergency diskette, you'll be able to restart your PC if something critical happens to the hard disk, or to the interface to the hard disk. If something happens to prevent your PC from starting normally, just slip the emergency diskette into drive A: and use it to restart your PC.

The ordinary contents of an emergency diskette include the core component of your operating system (Windows and/or DOS), namely two hidden files called IO.SYS and MSDOS.SYS. Also included are two configuration files: AUTOEXEC.BAT and CONFIG.SYS. When your PC starts, usually it checks drive A for a copy of the operating system and these two configuration files. (If your BIOS is set to check drive C: first, it should default to A: if it can't find anything on C:—for instance, if C: has crashed.) If there isn't a diskette in drive A, your PC boots with the copy of the operating system it finds on the hard disk. Since the advent of Windows 98, you no longer have to have these configuration files on the root directory of the disk you use to start your computer; however, if they are there, Windows does pay attention to them.

When you have a bootable diskette such as an emergency diskette, these two hidden files and two configuration files are installed there. These are what makes the diskette *bootable* (uh, it's what makes the PC start from the diskette instead of using the hard drive). If something you do during your upgrade (such as changing the configuration files) accidentally causes the hard disk to fail, you can insert your emergency diskette in drive A: and start your computer from there.

Keep your emergency diskette in some handy place where you can get to it quickly when you need it. No, not on top of your computer—it'll just get warped by the heat. And not next to the telephone, where there's a small chance the magnet inside might mess with the data. Put it in your top desk drawer or in your file cabinet.

Emergency Diskette for Windows 95

If you use Windows 95, here's what you do to create an emergency diskette:

1. Click the Start button, and then from the Settings menu that pops up, select Control Panel.

2. Double-click Add/Remove Programs. (A natural place for you to locate the emergency diskette setup button, isn't it?)

3. Depending on the version of Windows 95 you have installed, from here you select either the Start Disk tab and click Start, or select the Startup Disk tab and click Create Disk.

Windows 95 may or may not copy the files you need to your diskette, and I can neither confirm nor deny that this is one heck of a crazy way to run a computer. Regardless, be sure to copy WIN.INI and SYSTEM.INI onto the diskette. In addition, look for these hidden files in the Windows directory and copy them to drive A: SYSTEM.DAT and USER.DAT.

Make sure these files have been copied over (most of them from the Windows\Command directory, others from the Windows directory, and still others from Windows\System). If they haven't, copy them yourself: ATTRIB.EXE, CHKDSK.EXE, DRVSPACE.BIN, EBD.SYS, EDIT.COM, FDISK.EXE, FORMAT.COM, MEM.EXE, MSAV.EXE, MSCDEX.EXE, MSD.EXE, REGEDIT.EXE, RESTORE.EXE, SCANDISK.*, SYS.COM, UNDELETE.EXE. Microsoft Diagnostics (MSD.EXE) may or may not be on your computer; if it isn't, there isn't much you can do about it. The replacement for MSD, called MSINFO32.EXE, runs only in the Windows environment; the floppy disk can take you only as far as the DOS prompt.

At this point, your emergency diskette will start up your computer easily enough but won't necessarily start your CD-ROM. You'll need your CD-ROM very badly, so skip over the upcoming part about Windows 98; then I'll tell you what to do.

Emergency Diskette for Windows 98 and Windows Me

With the advent of Windows 98, Microsoft put some punch into the ol' emergency diskette. The old system merely booted up the computer, gave you a DOS prompt, and left you on your own. No longer do you have to copy a bunch of files manually over to the diskette; Windows now does this part of the job for you. Here's the process:

1. Click the Start button; then from the Settings menu, select Control Panel. Double-click Add/Remove Programs (although you'll be neither adding nor removing any programs).

2. Select the Startup Disk tab; then click Create Disk. The next few screens that come up walk you through formatting the floppy disk and then copying all the files you'll need to actually *do* something to your system if it's all fouled up.

As I mentioned earlier, you don't have to copy any DOS mode drivers onto the diskette for your optical disc. Windows 98 copies some generic drivers for you when it creates the diskette; it prefers to use them. When you insert this diskette and start your computer, it engages these generic DOS-mode drivers for your hard drives and CD-ROMs, and gets them up and running—something the previous Windows emergency diskettes did not do automatically. It then creates a specialized region of memory called a *RAMdisk*—in essence, a portion of memory that DOS will think is a disk drive.

When your computer boots up, you'll be able to access the files in this RAMdisk through a separate drive letter, such as E: or F:. The diskette contains a compressed file that gets copied into this RAMdisk during the boot process. The file then is auto-matically uncompressed to reveal SCANDISK, FDISK, FORMAT, and some of the other tools you'll need to find out what's wrong; and perhaps get your hard disk back in working order.

Check This Out

When you installed your antivirus program, it might have given you the option to make a special emergency diskette at that time. Can you use that in place of the startup disk made by Windows? Not for all purposes. The antivirus versions of emergency diskettes are designed to be used if either you or your antivirus program believes your system is in-fected. However, as antivirus program manufacturers don't always want to believe, other things can go wrong with your system besides viruses. So you should go ahead and make the specialized diskette, but reserve it for virus disinfecting purposes only. If you have a more general problem, like Windows getting ready to blow up on you, use your Windows emergency diskette instead.

Be Certain You Can Boot with Your Optical Disc Drive

You should test your emergency diskette's capability to start up not only your com-puter, but all its components as well. Here's why: Different operating systems have different procedures for making an emergency diskette; the resulting diskettes them-selves are a bit different.

The Windows 98 emergency diskette—and those for Win98 SE and WinMe—feature a startup routine that searches for your optical disc and, if it finds a respectable IDE ver-sion of one (unfortunately, no SCSI allowed), it will boot up that drive. This is impor-tant because without this feature in the startup routine, Windows won't boot your optical disc. If your emergency diskette hasn't booted your optical disc, you can't get to your Windows installation disc. You'll need that to reinstall Windows if you ever have to reformat your hard drive or relocate your hard drive in a new system.

Here's how silly Windows 95 is: To boot a CD-ROM, you need two driver files: one that makes the drive recognizable by the system (turns it on, in other words); a sec-ond that plugs its file system into Windows. Win95 copies this second driver onto the emergency diskette, but not the first one. Because the first one (the DOS-mode device driver) is supplied by the drive's manufacturer rather than Microsoft, there is no way for the emergency diskette creation process to know what that driver would be called. Being unable to complete the process successfully, Win95 simply stops trying.

If your Windows 98/SE/Me emergency diskette is capable of locating and booting your CD-ROM or DVD-ROM, it will contain as many as nine drivers whose filenames have the *.SYS extension; especially including ASPICD.SYS. The startup routine will try all of these drivers in sequence until it finds one that boots your optical disc.

If your emergency diskette won't boot your optical disc—or worse, if you're stuck with Windows 95 or even an older version—you should locate the drivers that allow your optical drive to boot up in DOS mode (from the C:\> prompt). They may have come on a disc or diskette with your optical drive or with your system, or they may even be installed on your hard disk at this moment—although that's unlikely. (Because the DOS mode drivers are not needed by Windows to run your optical drive, they probably were not installed on your computer.) If you can't find a diskette that contains your DOS mode drivers—especially if you don't know in which files they would be in the first place—there's a good chance you can download the drivers you're looking for from the Internet at www.drivershq.com. Just search for the drive's manufacturer and model number.

Don't know who your optical drive's manufacturer is? Not everyone is kind enough to print their own logo on the front. You can find out easily using Windows by right-clicking My Computer on the Windows Desktop and selecting Properties. Select the Device Manager tab. Click the + sign in front of CDROM or DVDROM. The listing that appears should state the manufacturer and model number of the drive you have installed.

If you own a DVD-ROM drive, there may not be such a thing as a DOS-mode driver for your device. On the other hand, you're probably not using Windows 95, because most DVD-ROM drivers are too new for Win95. In any case, be certain your emergency diskette boots your DVD-ROM drive before you start your upgrade or repair. If it doesn't work, check your manufacturer's Web site for any special procedures you might have to perform for its specific brand of drive.

To explain why you're doing all this and to clear up any possible confusion (there's nothing here that could possibly confuse you, is there?): Windows can run your CD-ROM because it has its own drivers for the thing but they're separate from the drivers that MS-DOS would need to run the same device. Your emergency diskette will boot your computer in MS-DOS mode so the drivers and other programs you use on this diskette are those intended for use with MS-DOS.

Backing Up the Backup of Your System Registry

Windows 98, SE, and Me contain two programs—one for Windows; the other for MS-DOS mode—both of which are called *Registry Scanner*. The Scanner's purpose is to enable you to periodically back up the key configuration files of Windows: WIN.INI, SYSTEM.INI, SYSTEM.DAT, USER.DAT, and with Windows Me, CLASSES.DAT. These are four (or five) files without which Windows cannot run. If they go down, your entire computer is in trouble.

Rather than simply copying these files to the same directory under a different filename (which is what Windows 95 did by copying SYSTEM.DAT to SYSTEM.DA0, and USER.DAT to USER.DA0), Registry Scanner produces a single compressed file called a *cabinet file* (basically a file whose contents were mathematically compressed to consume less space), which contains copies of these key files. The resulting compressed file is stored in the Windows\SYSBCKUP directory, along with backups made earlier.

Windows is smart enough to run the Registry Scanner automatically at startup and maintains a handful of older Registry backups (not just one) in case a problem in your Registry has been hanging around for some time. Many Windows processes, such as installing new software, can run Registry Scanner automatically and in the background. So you might be surprised to find several backup cabinet files in this directory—named RB001.CAB, RB002.CAB, and so on—even though you've never run Registry Scanner yourself manually. When you do run it manually, it can add one more file to this list and give that file a number following the most recent existing file. That way you can still restore your computer to an earlier state following a major software installation, even though you've run Registry Scanner since then.

If you start plowing through your Start menu looking for Registry Scanner, you won't find it. Microsoft apparently didn't want people backing up their own Registries willy-nilly, lest it become some sort of addictive habit requiring treatment and periodic therapy. (Some good habits, such as backing up things, should not be broken—but not everyone realizes that.) So to run the Registry Scanner, here's what you do:

1. Click the Start button, and from the menu, select Run.

2. In the Run dialog box, under Open, type `scanregw`; then press Enter. Registry Scanner will take a moment to look through your System Registry file.

3. If neither you nor any other process has backed up your Registry, the Scanner will do so automatically. Otherwise, it will display a dialog box asking if you want to make another backup. Click Yes.

You might be asking (and if you find yourself asking such things regularly, see your doctor), what happens to all these Registry backups if your hard drive goes down? It would be nice to copy one or all of these backups to a diskette. The trouble is these .CAB files generally are larger in and of themselves than the size of a 3½-inch diskette (1.44MB). So you can't copy one of them to a diskette and you certainly can't compress it any more than it already is to get it to fit. What do you do? This is when having a CD-RW drive, Zip drive, or second hard disk really helps. Periodically (as often as you back up your personal data), you should use your CD-RW drive or other backup media—such as an Iomega Zip drive or second hard disk—to make a copy of the .CAB files in your \SYSBCKUP directory. Chapter 18, "Adding an Optical Drive," discusses the best backup device options currently available to you.

The DOS-mode SCANREG program on your Windows 98/SE/Me emergency diskette will not work right unless your hard disk also is working. If your hard drive goes down, you might have to reformat it and re-install Windows. If you do that, those backup files that Registry Scanner already made for you will be gone...unless of course you were thoughtful enough to copy them onto your backup disc first. Say you've re-installed Windows thoroughly onto your new hard drive; then you've reinstalled all the applications you intend to use. You want these applications to run the way they did before you tried to install that new item. After all your programs are back, reboot your system using your emergency diskette. Your RAMdisk probably is drive E. Type **E:** and press **Enter** to switch to drive E:. Then at the E:\> prompt type this command: **SCANREG/RESTORE** and press **Enter.** The DOS-mode SCANREG program searches all the available drives it can find for the five most recent Registry backups. If your hard disk is available, it will scan that first. In lieu of that, if your backup media is online (which again assumes the DOS-mode drivers for that media loaded properly), SCANREG will scan that media instead.

You'll see a menu showing these five backup files. Their titles reveal absolutely zero about their age or contents, so you're safe to just choose one. SCANREG decompresses the configuration files from the chosen cabinet file, copies them where they belong on your hard drive, and exits. When you re-enter Windows, you should notice the programs you re-installed earlier running the way they used to, with options and settings you had given them before; Windows also should look a little more familiar.

This Is Only a Test ... Be-e-e-e-e-ep

The AUTOEXEC.BAT and CONFIG.SYS configuration files on your emergency diskette may not work entirely right, especially if you relied on Windows 95 to copy those files for you. If you use your diskette in an actual emergency, you may be instructed where to tune in your area for news and official information. In other words, you may be prompted to make use of files located on a device (namely, drive C:) that you can't get to right now—and if you could, you wouldn't need the emergency diskette, would you?

The reason you can't get to these files or the device that contains them (the main hard disk) generally is because the way the commands in the configuration files are phrased presumes that the hard disk is present or that the drivers are located on the same disk as the files themselves. In short, DOS looks for C: but C: ain't around; just A:.

The best way to find out whether your emergency diskette is going to work is to test it out; the best time to do this is *now,* before something truly does go out. When you insert your emergency diskette and reboot your system, at the very least you should be able to access your floppy disk drive (A:), your main hard disk drive (C:), your secondary hard disk if you have one (D:), and your optical disk drive (D: or E:). If you can't, perhaps your hard drive depends on a DOS-mode driver that either hasn't been copied to drive A: or is not being properly addressed from the configuration files on the diskette in A:.

59

Making Your Configuration Files Load the Right Drivers

The most common problem with an emergency diskette is that it does not engage the optical disc drive. If your operating system is older than Windows 98 or if you have an SCSI-based optical drive as opposed to an ATAPI (also known as ATA or IDE), your emergency diskette could fail because no DOS-mode drivers for it have been copied to the diskette. However, even if you copied those drivers yourself, your emergency diskette still could fail because the configuration files are not properly addressing the location of these drivers, even if they're present.

What can you do to make your configuration files work without a doctorate? (In other words, how do you edit the configuration files on your emergency diskette so that they point to the location of your driver files, and when you use the darn diskette, it starts up all the parts of the computer that you need?) Well, if you use Windows 95, you can trick it into making these configuration files (or at least the basis for them) for you. It won't think you're making an emergency diskette—and that's actually the key to the success of this operation. Follow these steps:

1. Go ahead and make the Windows 95 emergency diskette using the procedure outlined in the section "Emergency Diskette for Windows 95" earlier in this chapter.

2. Eject the diskette from drive A:.

3. Exit all open applications.

4. Click the Start button, choose Shut Down, select Restart in MS-DOS Mode, and then click OK. In a minute you'll see the DOS prompt, which is reminiscent of a very old computer.

5. Re-insert your diskette into drive A:.

6. Type the following commands:

   ```
   COPY C:\AUTOEXEC.BAT A:
   COPY C:\CONFIG.SYS A:
   ```

   Remember to press Enter at the end of each command. (You remember DOS, don't you?) If one or both of these files do not exist (you get a File Not Found error), you might not need them to boot your system. In the DOS subsystem of Windows 95, configuration files have become optional. However, you probably will need one of these files to boot your CD-ROM and if neither configuration file actually exists when you exit to DOS, you may need to create one or both of them manually. (Or you could encase your legs in cement and jump off a pier, which might be much more fun.)

7. Now, to get back to Windows, type this command:

   ```
   EXIT
   ```

Windows comes back up in a moment or two, restoring you to the twentieth century. (Even though it's the twenty-first.)

Test the new diskette; if you're still having a problem, begin your investigation of the problem by checking the configuration files on your emergency diskette using Notepad to view the contents of the AUTOEXEC.BAT and CONFIG.SYS files. Edit the files so that all the programs, drivers, and files use a complete path, with a drive letter and directory name. For example, if you have this command in your AUTOEXEC.BAT:

```
MOUSE
```

and you boot your PC from drive A:, DOS assumes that the MOUSE driver is on the same drive that it's currently using. It won't be able to find the driver because it actually is hiding out in either the root directory of the C: drive or one of the directories listed in the PATH statement earlier in the list of commands (if it's there). To fix all this confusion, you have two choices: You could find where the driver is really located, then add its complete path (with the drive letter and the directory) to the MOUSE command, like this:

```
C:\WINDOWS\SYSTEM\MOUSE
```

By adding a complete path to all the programs and drivers in the AUTOEXEC.BAT and CONFIG.SYS files, DOS will be able to find all of them when you boot from drive A:. Of course this assumes your hard disk is in working order. If it isn't, you're in trouble.

Your other option is to copy the necessary driver files to your emergency disk in the first place. These driver files consist of all the files mentioned in both AUTOEXEC.BAT and CONFIG.SYS. This way, if your hard drive goes completely down you may be able to restore some parts of your system. Your mouse—borrowed for the preceding example—may be the least of your worries at such a time.

Here's where that DOS-mode optical disc driver comes in: If you're using Windows 95, or the Windows 98 emergency diskette doesn't boot your CD-ROM, you need to add commands to both AUTOEXEC.BAT and CONFIG.SYS on your emergency diskette (not the files on your hard drive). First use Notepad to add one line to CONFIG.SYS on your emergency diskette. For the sake of demonstration I'll say your driver name is CDROM.SYS. It's probably called something else, so in the following example, substitute CDROM.SYS with the name of your driver. Check whether CONFIG.SYS contains a reference to this driver already. If it does, make sure that reference does *not* contain a drive letter or directory name. (The instruction should look like the following example.) If you don't find a reference to your CD-ROM driver, locate the last instruction that begins with DEVICE= or DEVICEHIGH=, and immediately after that line add the following:

```
DEVICE=CDROM.SYS /d:mscd0001
```

Again, notice there's no drive letter or directory name, as in C:\WINDOWS\SYSTEM \CDROM.SYS. This is because you already copied your driver to the root directory of the boot diskette. Aside from CDROM.SYS, this instruction in CONFIG.SYS should appear exactly as in the previous example. Next use Notepad again to add the following instruction to the very end of AUTOEXEC.BAT (located on the emergency diskette):

```
MSCDEX /d:mscd0001
```

61

The command you added to CONFIG.SYS brings your CD-ROM online but DOS doesn't yet know how to give it the power of displaying its own directories. That's what the MSCDEX utility is for; it was copied to your emergency diskette earlier. The command you added to AUTOEXEC.BAT installs a directory for the device named mscd0001 by the command in CONFIG.SYS.

Isn't this fun? Don't you wish you could do this every day?

The Ins and Outs of Using Your Emergency Diskette

Well, now you can! For your emergency diskette to remain useful, you have to keep updating it. For example, when you install something new such as a new device or program, it probably will make changes to your configuration files. This is what you do:

1. Re-run the **B** creation program using the procedure outlined earlier. Use the same diskette if you need to. Why? Changes you've made to your computer might mandate changes to your startup procedure.

2. Do a dry run to make certain your emergency diskette works, again using the procedures detailed earlier.

3. Before you install a new application or a new device, use Windows Explorer to make a new folder on your emergency diskette (from the **B** menu select **B**). Name this folder **Configs Backup.** Then copy the AUTOEXEC.BAT, CONFIG.SYS, WIN.INI, and SYSTEM.INI files onto this folder. Your emergency diskette won't use these files to start up.

4. If you're using Windows 98, run ScanReg (Registry Scanner) to back up your Windows System Registry files; then copy your RB00*.CAB files to a disk, disc, or disque big enough to hold them.

5. Now that you have your updated emergency diskette and other backups, install your new software or peripheral; then run its setup program. The setup probably will make changes to the configuration files—for example, the setup for a new peripheral may add lines to your AUTOEXEC.BAT or CONFIG.SYS. (Or it might not if it relies on Windows' Plug and Play to recognize it automatically at startup.) Once the setup program is done, you should restart the PC so that any changes that may have been made to the configuration files will be activated.

6. If the changes caused by the setup program end up wrecking your life (and your PC), undo them by copying back onto the hard disk your good, older versions of the configuration files from that **Configs** folder you made on your emergency diskette. If you can't get Windows to start, use these commands from the DOS prompt:

```
COPY A:\AUTOEXEC.BAT C:\
COPY A:\CONFIG.SYS C:\
```

```
COPY A:\WIN.INI C:\WINDOWS
COPY A:\SYSTEM.INI C:\WINDOWS
SCANREG /RESTORE          (Windows 98, 98 SE, Me)
```

7. On the other hand, if the changes made by the setup program seem to work fine (your new toy is happy, you can still run all your programs), repeat these commands to copy your updated CONFIG.SYS, AUTOEXEC.BAT, WIN.INI, and SYSTEM.INI files onto your emergency diskette. Just change the drive letters to copy stuff from your hard disk to drive A:, as in:

```
COPY C:\AUTOEXEC.BAT A:
COPY C:\CONFIG.SYS A:

COPY C:\WINDOWS\WIN.INI A:
COPY C:\WINDOWS\SYSTEM.INI A:
```

8. When you're confident that Windows 98/Me is running just the way you want, run Registry Scanner to make a fresh backup of the System Registry.

If you think one of the commands in your configuration files is messing you up, you can use an old DOS trick to bypass it. Press and hold the **F8** key as Windows 95 is starting up or the left **Ctrl** key as Windows 98, 98 SE, and Me is starting up. Soon you'll see a menu. Press **Shift+F5** to step through each of the configuration commands. Press **Enter** or **Y** to accept a command, or **N** to bypass one.

Now Back Up Your Data

Making a backup of your data is like wearing a seat belt when you drive. It's uncomfortable—and sometimes you can get by without one—but if you ever slam into a wall at 60 mph, you'll be glad you took the time to buckle up. Before you perform any surgery on your system make sure you have backup copies of your important data such as important reports, letters to your lawyer, tax filings, and so on. That way, if the patient dies on the table, you can always restore the important parts after you get the body working again.

Today, the most inexpensive, reliable, useful, and capable backup medium available to the general public is the CD-RW (ReWritable) drive. If you don't have any kind of backup device on your system, Chapter 18 will show you what to look for and how to install one. You'll also be introduced to the software that now comes with CD-Rs and CD-RWs that enable you to back up your data. Earlier editions of this book showed you how to use the tape backup program shipped with Windows. Because tape backups have become historical relics in the wake of CD-RW mass production, the old Microsoft Backup program is no longer shipped with Windows. Instead, Microsoft relies on CD-RW manufacturers to ship their own choice of backup programs—which is a smart move on its part.

The previous edition of this book recommended that you purchase and install an Iomega Zip disk for use as relatively inexpensive and reliable backups. I can no longer make that recommendation in good conscience. A growing number of Iomega customers—myself included—have fallen victim to a chronic problem with their Zip drives that may have been caused by defective construction or design. These customers have dubbed the problem the "Click of Death"; now there is an online support group devoted to these customers at www.geocities.com/iomegano/.

Putting Your Toolkit Together

Before you attempt an upgrade, you'll need to gather some tools so that you can successfully take your PC apart. You'll need a small flat-head screwdriver, and small and medium Phillips-head screwdrivers. You'll also want to make sure every screwdriver you intend to use is nonmagnetic (the kind that's supposed to pick up dropped screws from tight places won't work) so that you don't end up wiping out your BIOS when all you want to do is install an interface card.

If you don't mind looking a little nerdy, get yourself a set of cool computer tools (see Figure 4.1). You can find them at any computer store. They include extra tools for removing chips and retrieving dropped screws—and, at about $20, they won't break your wallet. They generally include those strange, foreign nuthead screwdrivers (yes, that's what they're really called) that look like a combination screwdriver and mini–socket wrench. For some PC tower cases you might need a nuthead screwdriver to take the cover off. Make sure your tools have nonconducting handles (so electricity can't pass through them—you can't zap them; they can't zap you) made of hard plastic, PVC, or ceramic.

A few more handy tips to keep in mind:

➤ Grab a couple of empty pill bottles, 35mm film cans, or even an old egg carton; any of these containers makes a great gathering place for the various screws you'll encounter.

➤ You may also want to grab a flashlight (it gets pretty dark in there), a box (for storing spare computer parts), and a can of compressed air or dust remover. (Hey, while it's open, you might as well do some cleaning.)

➤ One thing you'll find indispensable is paper and a pencil. You can write down the switch and jumper settings of any card you remove in case your fingers fumble at some point and accidentally change one of them. A switch, by the way, is like a tiny light switch, and a jumper is a set of pins connected by a removable gizmo called a shunt. You'll learn how to set switches and jumpers in Chapter 23, "Making Your Computer Boot Up Again." Paper is also handy for writing down part numbers, cable orientation and placement, or any other info you find important.

➤ A Sharpie (or other indelible pen) makes a handy gadget for marking cables and such so you can get them back where they belong after disconnecting them during the installation of some new toy.

➤ Consider getting out your Polaroid snapshot camera, digital camera, or your video camcorder, and taking pictures of how the inside of your computer looks when you open the thing up the first time. This way, you'll at least have a better idea of how to put things back like they were.

➤ If anything on your PC looks dirty, absolutely do not try to clean it with anything liquid that sprays or smells like pine. If a screw gets tight or stuck someplace, absolutely do not use Liquid Wrench or WD-40 to loosen it; these liquids conduct electricity, even from the air itself. Simple contact by any PC component with any of these liquids can short out everything inside of it immediately. Instead, use pure, denatured rubbing alcohol. No, not turpentine (that would be horrible) and not acetone! You can clean the metal pins on the connecting edge of an expansion card with a tiny dab of rubbing alcohol on a cotton swab; the liquid will evaporate naturally as long as you use very little of it.

If the idea of opening up your PC gives you the shivers, invest in a bit of insurance in the form of a *grounding strap*. This neat gizmo straps around your wrist and basically prevents you from accidentally zapping your expensive toy—well worth the money, in my opinion.

Flathead screwdriver DIP chip inserter Flathead and Phillips screwdrivers Tweezers Nuthead screwdriver

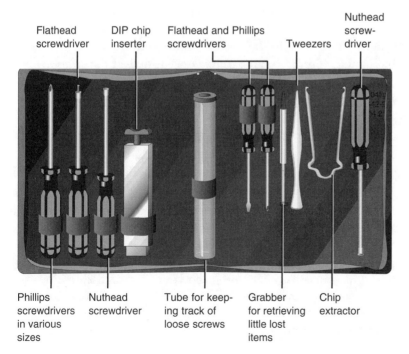

Figure 4.1

Get yourself a set of cool tools.

Phillips screwdrivers in various sizes Nuthead screwdriver Tube for keeping track of loose screws Grabber for retrieving little lost items Chip extractor

Avoiding Frying Yourself on Your PC

Opening your PC's system unit for the first time is a bit like digging up an unopened ballot box in the bottom of a broom closet: There's a lot of anticipation and maybe a little fear, and just when you begin to consider hiring David Boies and heading for the Supreme Court, you discover the fuss was all for naught. You'll soon learn that being a bit scared (therefore, a bit more careful) is better in the long run than tons of confidence (right, Professor Gore?). To open your PC successfully, all you really need is a few screwdrivers and a bit of common sense.

The Twelve Steps to Success

You probably were told you'd need to enter a 12-step program the moment you started taking the job of upgrading or repairing your PC upon yourself; indeed, this book works to meet your every expectation. Step 1: Admit you have a problem. Okay, seriously, here's what you should do to get ready for the big moment:

1. **Prepare for disaster.** Before you do anything—I mean anything—you should back up your data and update your emergency diskette. Remember, anything you don't save you should be prepared to lose. Also make sure you have a copy of your PC's configuration data. See Chapter 2, "Now, Let's Find Out What Kind of Computer You Have," for help.

2. **Read the instructions that came with your new part.** The documentation actually might give you some real information, such as how to get your exact brand of PC to talk to your new part. If it tells you to check out a text file on an enclosed diskette, do it. You may find the documentation online, which is also convenient for the manufacturer to be able to update it to reflect fixed problems or customer concerns.

3. **Turn off your PC and unplug it.** No, it's not enough to just turn the darn thing off. Unplugging the PC from the wall ensures that there's absolutely no possible way that you could plug something into the computer while it's receiving power. And believe me: You really don't want to do that. Also remove any other plugs, such as the one that connects your monitor, modem, or printer to the PC. (You'll probably have to unscrew it first.)

4. **Clear the area.** Remove all potential disasters from your work area such as cups of coffee, cans of soda, any canine, feline, or bovine beings, and any small children who may happen to be juggling water balloons in your vicinity. All those loose computer parts have to go somewhere, so make room on your desk for them before you find yourself struggling to keep your hold on a 20-pound monitor. Use all the magic at your disposal to remove excess electricity from your workplace: stand on a static-free tile or linoleum floor, work over a wooden desktop, touch a doorknob to remove your own static, and so on. Also place

both your PC and yourself on some surface that doesn't conduct static electricity, such as wood, Formica, concrete, plastic, or linoleum. Don't stand (or put the PC) on carpet!

5. **Unscrew the cover.** Check for any plastic panels (*bezels*) that need to be pried off before you find the screws; generally in the back but possibly in the front. Anything to which you have to apply serious force probably wasn't meant to be pried off in the first place. (Ah, the lessons of Watergate!) You might have to use a flathead screwdriver to help you pry but be gentle. However, if you have one of those miracle system cases made by Dell and others, you actually won't have to pry off any panels or even remove any screws at all; you might only have to twist one screw along the side of the case and open the door, which takes all of five seconds. However, for most ordinary system cases you probably need a Philips or nuthead screwdriver and some film cans, an egg carton, or whatever other clever device you plan on using to corral the screws. Once you've found the screws, be sure to undo only the screws holding the cover on. Don't accidentally unscrew the power supply; just stick to the screws along the outer edge of the cover. Figure 4.2 should help you out.

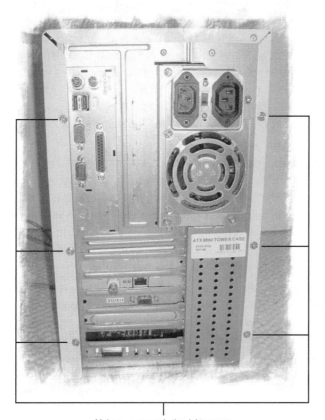

Figure 4.2

Make sure you undo the right screws.

Make sure you undo the right screws.

6. **Remove the cover.** To pull off most tower unit covers, you simply slide the cover backwards; then lift it straight up. With some other PCs you might have to do the exact opposite: Slide the cover forward and then lift it up. You might have to tug a little; be careful to not pull any cords or cables loose. A hatch release secures some covers; you press it to remove the cover. Some systems have more than one release. Keys lock other covers; you have to turn the key to the "unlock" symbol (which looks kind of like an open padlock) to remove the cover. Put the case someplace you won't trip over it.

7. **Ground yourself.** Touch something metal that's resting on the ground, such as your PC's cover, to discharge static electricity. Don't dance (or otherwise move your feet) while you're working. Don't touch anything inside the PC until you're sure you're grounded. After you discharge yourself, no matter how nervous you get, don't scratch your head or shuffle your feet. It takes a minimal amount of static to zap just about any part of your PC so don't move your feet when working on a PC; or, just before touching something inside the PC, discharge any static by touching a file cabinet, a coworker, or whatever.

8. **Get that dust outta there.** Big, flaky, dusty things in your expansion ports literally can short them out if you plug something new in and push them deep into the connector pins. Don't use furniture polish or anything you ordinarily use to dust your candelabra and other valuables. Don't use any detergents, disinfectants, or static removing sprays such as those you'd use in your laundry; don't use a cloth, either. Instead, go to your local computer store and pick up a can of dust-blasting compressed air. It has one of those thin straws but rather than squirting lubricant, it blasts a powerful spray of air that literally eats (blows away) dust without touching it. It's not terribly expensive, but replacing your motherboard is.

9. **Out with the old, in with the new.** The exact procedures for removing and replacing any kind of expansion card you have are in Chapter 12. However, the procedure is generally pretty simple. To remove an expansion card, unplug any cables attaching it to the motherboard or to any of your peripherals. Unscrew the retaining screw and put the little guy where he can't roll away. (Nuthead screwdrivers take off retaining screws in a flash.) Grip the card at the top with both hands and pull straight up. Avoid the metal leads sticking out of the back of the expansion card; they just love to cut fingers.

   To install a new expansion card, find an appropriate open slot. Unscrew the retaining screw holding the slot cover in place. Again, put the screw where you won't lose it. Remove the slot cover and hang it as a decoration in your cubicle. (Don't throw it away; if you ever take the card back out, you'll need it again.) Hold the card at the top with both hands and gently position the edge connectors on the bottom of the card over their slots. Gently rock the card until it slips into place. You may have to apply just the right amount of downward pressure to insert it (see Figure 4.3).

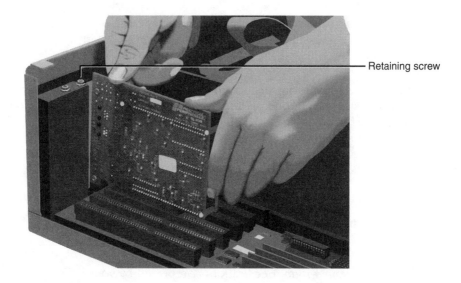

Retaining screw

Figure 4.3

Push the expansion card gently into place.

Removing and installing a memory module is a slightly trickier process and depends on the type of module you're installing (especially whether it's a SIMM or a DIMM). However, it's much, much simpler than removing and plugging in the old, tin-legged DIP chips and bending them up all over the place. Chapter 11, "Memorize This! Upgrading Memory," gives you all the procedures you need to know.

10. **With the cover still off, plug the PC back in, turn it on, and check to see if your new toy works.**   Yes, with the cover off, you should test to see whether you properly connected the new part so you can quickly correct it if it's wrong before you put the cover back on. If something's wrong, you'll usually hear an unusual pattern of beeps. Most PCs beep only once to let you know things are just fine, thank you, but Compaqs for some reason beep twice. If you hear a beep pattern you haven't heard before, something's wrong. The pattern could be telling you exactly what is wrong, so check Chapter 23 to see what it could be.

11. **Close up the box.**   Once you're hearing the number of beeps you're supposed to hear, repeat step 6 in reverse. After Humpty Dumpty's back together again, plug everything back in and start up the PC.

12. **Introduce the computer and your new toy to each other.**   With most new parts, you'll have to run some kind of setup program that comes on some diskette. You also might need your original Windows installation CD-ROM, in case Windows needs to install a few new files of its own to accommodate the

new part. The setup makes changes to the configuration files so that your computer can talk to the new part. See Chapter 24, "Getting Windows to Recognize Your New Toys," for help.

Make sure you mail in your registration now, while you still know where it is. Also keep your manuals in one place. Hang on to any big boxes in case you need to ship something back if it stops working after only a week. Manufacturers won't accept returned parts without their original shipping containers either.

The Least You Need to Know

➤ Create an emergency diskette and update it frequently.

➤ Back up any data you don't want to lose.

➤ Copy your system specifications as reported by your BIOS.

➤ Get a flathead screwdriver and several Phillips screwdrivers together, or purchase a computer toolkit.

➤ You also might want to get something to keep loose screws in, along with a small flashlight, and a pencil and paper.

➤ Make sure you unplug your PC before beginning any work.

➤ Keep yourself grounded as you work, so you don't accidentally discharge any static electricity.

Preventative Maintenance and Other Ways to Avoid Upgrading

Got a klunky keyboard, a malfunctioning mouse, or a pain-in-the-neck printer? Well, in this section, you'll learn some quick fixes for what ails 'em, as well as easy repair solutions for other peripherals such as your monitor, floppy drive, optical drive, sound card, and modem.

In the Second Quarter, you'll see some new moves: how you can extend the life of your software and your operating system (even though at times, you may have felt like not extending it), and how to rev up that old hard disk of yours.

Chapter 5

Fixing the Most Common Problems

In This Chapter

➤ Making the initial diagnosis for what's wrong with your PC

➤ All the little fixes and remedies right in front of your nose

➤ A closer introduction to important parts such as printers and monitors

➤ What to do when nothing seems to work.

This chapter is devoted to all the computer problems that could be solved by doing some quite trivial things—such as jiggling the right cable or knob, or planting your foot in the right location of the system unit with respect to the open window. Up to now, you might not have known which cable or which knob to jiggle; that's okay. Not all computers are made exactly alike, as you probably know by now if you've read all the material up to this chapter.

General Hardware Dilemmas

Your computer's acting strange and you're starting to get that funny feeling deep in the pit of your stomach. Before you panic, it's important to realize this doesn't always mean you'll have to replace something. You can try several simple solutions, including shutting down some programs to free up some badly needed memory or even turning off the darn thing and grabbing a quick cup of coffee. With Windows, restarting the PC solves hundreds of weirdness problems—believe me.

When you return from your java break, turn the PC back on and see whether it's still acting strange. If it is, you'll find some additional solutions in this section. If they don't fix the problem, try the more specific Windows-related solutions in Chapter 6, "Cleaning Windows." They are guaranteed to make Windows behave (well, at least better than it has been). If you decide you need to replace a part, you're in luck: The rest of this book covers that very thing.

When Your PC Won't Start

Although this one is pretty scary, try not to panic—it doesn't necessarily mean you've killed the PC. First thing you do is unplug the PC. Why (perhaps it was unplugged in the first place)? If your power supply is causing the problem, you'll want to disconnect power to it while you check everything else. With that done, check these things:

➤ Start with the data cables. These are the flat, gray cables—also known as *ribbon cables*—that generally have a red stripe along one side. If a data cable is trying to escape, guide it back to its plug. If the plug on the device it's plugged into is marked with a "1" on one side of the plug, the red stripe on the cable should be on the side that has the "1."

➤ If you use a surge protector with your PC, its protective fuse may have blown. If necessary, reset the surge protector by pressing its reset button (it should be marked), or by sliding its fuse switch (generally near its power switch) off and then on again. An inexpensive surge protector might not have a reset button or a way to get to the fuse, which means that if there is a power surge or spike, it just burns itself out to save your PC. Try unplugging all your PC parts (system unit, monitor, printer, scanner, and so on) and plug something trivial into the surge protector, such as a night light. If it goes on, nothing's burned out; if it doesn't, give your surge protector a nice burial and buy a new one. Be thankful it's done its job.

➤ If you've plugged in the computer and the power is on, the next thing to check is the monitor. Is it getting power? If so, are you turning it on? If you have a power saver monitor, it may have switched to low-power mode. Its power light will blink yellow if the monitor is turned on while it's properly connected to a computer. Usually, typing one character or jiggling and clicking the mouse should jog the computer out of low-power mode. If the monitor is on, fiddle with the brightness and contrast knobs for a while. Some newer monitors display TV-station-like color test patterns if they're turned *on* and working properly but not receiving a signal from the computer. Perhaps the data cable is unplugged, or the computer is turned off or not getting power. If you have one of these new monitors, you're not seeing a blinking yellow light near the power button and you're not getting the test pattern, your problem might be in the monitor; not the computer.

➤ If you use your emergency diskette (see Chapter 4, "What You Need to Know *Before* You Open Your PC") can you start the PC? If so, there might be a problem with the hard disk. In Chapter 7, "'Repairing' the Hard Disk Instead of Replacing It," you'll see some of the ordinary hard disk problems you might be able to fix right away.

➤ Are you seeing a message such as "Non-system disk or disk error?" If so, remove the diskette you accidentally left in drive A:, take two steps back, and restart the computer. Does the message say, "CMOS RAM error?" If so, the information in CMOS is wrong, your battery is going out, or something dinked with CMOS. You can easily reset defaults; see Chapter 23, "Making Your Computer Boot Up Again." (See Chapter 10, "Replacing the Motherboard and Its Parts," for help with the battery.) Does the message say, "Bad or missing command interpreter?" If so, you've accidentally deleted an important file called COMMAND.COM. Use your emergency diskette to start your PC; then copy the file back to the root directory from the diskette.

➤ Something might have happened to Windows that's preventing it from starting. (It could be anything.) At the very least, you should be able to start Windows in *safe mode,* which means it loads a minimum of drivers to get you up and running but not working perfectly. When you start your computer, you might see a numbered menu instead of your usual startup screen. Type the number beside the menu entry labeled "Safe Mode" (generally 3 or 5, depending on how your computer is configured). You'll notice during safe mode that your optical disc drive is disabled—this is normal. (Obviously, you can't reinstall Windows while you're in safe mode.) Make sure your hard drive's directories are where you expect them to be, test your mouse, and then exit Windows the normal way and restart. If you don't see that numbered menu a second time but see your normal startup screen, whatever strange thing that might have gone wrong probably has been eradicated by some other strange thing in Safe Mode that you didn't even see.

➤ If you have Windows 95, Win95, OSR2, or the first edition of Windows 98 and you've *exited to DOS* (a way of entering DOS mode by canceling out of the operating system), perhaps you've found that you can't get back to Windows. In this case, the problem with the startup files is that Windows generates

Note

Ever wonder how your PC knows the date and time? There's a chip inside your PC called the CMOS (*complementary metal-oxide semiconductor*) that stores important information such as the current date and time. Once information is entered into the CMOS, it stays there using a battery that helps it remember, even when you cut off the computer's power supply.

for DOS mode. At the DOS prompt, start the DOS-mode text file editor by typing EDIT at the C: prompt. If you've never used this program before, you'll notice it has pretty much the same menus and commands as Notepad in Windows, although you might not have a mouse pointer, depending on how your system is configured. Using this program, open CONFIG.SYS from the root directory of drive C:, and look for a line at or near the top that reads DOS= SINGLE. Delete that entire line. Save that file; then open AUTOEXEC.BAT. Look for a line at the end that refers to win and ends with /wx. Delete that entire line, save that file, and exit the editor. You should be able to start Windows by rebooting your PC. (If you have Windows 98 SE or Windows Me, you can't exit to DOS anymore, so you won't have this problem.)

➤ Do you hear more than one beep when the computer tries to start up (or more than two beeps if you own a Compaq)? If so, there might be a problem with the motherboard or a memory module. Try counting the number of both long and short beeps as if you were listening to Morse Code, and check out Chapter 23 to see what the pattern means. The problem might be your keyboard (make sure nothing is pressing down on it), the monitor (make sure it's plugged in), or a diskette left inadvertently in drive A: (if so, remove the diskette and restart the PC).

When Your PC's Locked Up

If you're working away at the computer and suddenly you realize the PC's no longer paying attention, it might be locked up or stalled. Here are some things you can do to get its attention.

➤ Try pressing Esc. This is the universal get-me-out-of-here key, and it might just awaken your sleeping beauty.

➤ Press Ctrl+Esc to see whether you can reawaken the Windows taskbar. Once the taskbar becomes visible, right-click the problem program and select Close from the pop-up menu. If the program is operating normally, this should terminate the darn thing.

➤ Here is a diagnostic method that works with all versions of Windows: Try pressing Alt+Tab to see if a menu of available icons comes up. These icons represent all your running applications. If it does, release Alt; the program whose icon is highlighted should pop up. Now try pressing Alt+Tab again, and while holding down Alt, keep pressing Tab until the icon for the application you think is locked up is highlighted. If you release Alt and nothing happens, you know it's a crashed application that caused the problem. You then know it's safe for you to press Ctrl+Alt+Delete to bring up the Close Program dialog box, to get rid of the misbehaving program. Choose the program that's giving you the trouble (it might be marked with the words [Not responding]) and click End Task.

If you're shutting down a major application such as Microsoft Word, you might need to repeat this process from the beginning. Why? Because such applications run in two pieces; so if you launch Word again, it will see its other part already running and conclude that some other user is operating it. So any of the files that application was running when you tried to shut it down the first time will be inaccessible until you close that application. Press Ctrl+Alt+Delete again and look for the bad program a second time (in the case of Microsoft Word, don't look for title bar contents; instead just look for "Winword"). If you don't see it, click Cancel; otherwise, choose the application again, click End Task, and then End Task again at the dialog box. Annoyances such as this are the price of progress.

➤ If everything else fails, you might have to reboot your PC to get its attention. Be warned! Rebooting your PC causes you to lose any work you haven't already saved. Sorry—that's the way it goes. Rebooting also might cause its own set of problems: Specifically, Windows doesn't get a chance to delete its temp files. Delete them yourself after you've got everything back in order: You'll find them in the Windows Temp directory. Rebooting in Windows is a matter of pressing Ctrl+Alt+Delete, waiting for whatever dialog box that may come up, and pressing Ctrl+Alt+Delete again.

➤ If the Alt+Tab method doesn't work, your computer might respond to the first or the second press of Ctrl+Alt+Delete with what is popularly known as the *Blue Screen of Death*. There are two possible purposes for this screen, neither of which makes complete sense (but has anything you've read thus far made complete sense?): One such screen might tell you a program has "thrown a hardware *exception*." This is the computer equivalent of your car's engine throwing a rod. An *exception* is a condition that is tripped when a program does something it isn't supposed to do. (You're not at fault; the program is.) Another possible purpose for the Blue Screen of Death is to tell you "System is busy." Well, duh! When is it not? This is Windows saying "Dude, don't bother me! I'm meditating here!" Generally this second screen is a ruse; its only purpose is to try to placate you so that you don't shut Windows off. If you do like the screen asks and press Enter, there's a very small possibility that Windows could come back and everything will be in order. However, most likely you'll see a black screen with a white mouse pointer—a working mouse pointer, mind you, but one with nothing to point to. From there, you could press Ctrl+Alt+Delete again and get the same blue screen. When you can't get past the blue screen to a fully functional Windows, the only recourse is to press Ctrl+Alt+Delete again to reboot your system.

➤ Perhaps nothing happened, no matter how many times you pressed, or hit, or punched Ctrl+Alt+Delete. As a last resort, turn off your PC (or hit the reset button), wait a bit (usually 15–20 seconds), and turn it back on. This certainly gets the PC's attention; however, it also causes the computer to cut the power on every device you have. Keep in mind that if you had been working on something and you haven't saved it yet, it will be lost when you turn off your PC. For newer systems, if the system is completely hosed you might have to hold the power button for at least 4 seconds to activate a hardware override. (Yes, "hosed" is a technical term.)

Here's a curious thing many new computer owners don't find out until a system hang-up happens to them: When you press the reset button on the front or side of the system case nothing happens. Then you press the power switch—and still nothing happens. Your screen stays on and things are still locked up! How freaky can things get? Well, this little feature was not intended to frighten people; however, in today's computers there are a lot of features that can scare the daylights out of me; not just you.

New system cases with the *ATX form factor* (which you'll learn about in Chapter 21, "Classier Chassis: Consider a New System Case") contain power supplies whose buttons often don't do what you expect them to. Sometimes with the reset button, but especially with the main power button, you need to hold it down for four seconds before it does its job.

Keyboard Calamities

Keyboards don't usually die, but they can wear out. When a keyboard is on its last legs, the keys stick, you type G and get GGGGGGGGGGGGG, and the spacebardoesn't workanymore. Even so, there are other things that can go wrong with a keyboard; you don't necessarily have to replace it. In this section, you'll learn the problems that can lead to keyboard calamities and the best ways to fix them.

When the Keyboard Goes Beep! Beep! Beep!

If you hear a beep, a chirp, or a cluck coming from the computer every time you press a key, the problem is not with the keyboard; it's the PC. Your computer has gone into a tizzy over something and locked itself up. Every key you press at this point goes unheard (technically speaking, the *keyboard buffer is full*), which is why you're hearing the beeps. Try shutting down the program you're working on using the methods described previously. (That's right; even though you've pressed every key possible and gotten nothing but cluck, cluck, cluck, you still might be able to press Ctrl+Alt+Delete and get a response. If you're still stuck, only then should you resort to the reset button.)

Little Lost Keyboard

If you start your PC one day and get this message: "Keyboard not found. Press F1 to continue," don't assume your keyboard is still out on an all-nighter with your mouse. This message is telling you that the PC can't communicate with the keyboard; that's probably because the keyboard cable is loose. So return the wayward plug back to its socket (after turning the PC back off again), and restart the PC. By the way, make sure you use the correct socket; a lot of computers have a mouse and a keyboard port right next to each other, and darn if they don't look similar. However, usually they are marked with cute symbols (such as a small rodent) that helps you tell them apart.

Spilled Coffee and Other Common Disasters

If you spill something on your keyboard, don't panic—you still might be able to save the patient. Turn off the PC and use a dry cloth to wipe up what you can. Flip the keyboard over to let it drain for about a day. You can dry the keyboard with a hair dryer if you want (low heat setting, of course), but wait about a day before you try to use the keyboard. After a day or so, plug the keyboard back in, cross your fingers, and turn on the PC.

If that doesn't work, you can do a more thorough job of cleaning by removing the keys with a small flat-head screwdriver. Using the screwdriver as a kind of lever, gently pry up along the bottom edge of each key to remove it. Just make sure you make a note of where each key was located before you actually remove the darn thing. After you get the keys off, use a dry cloth to clean as much as you can. You can spray cleaner on the cloth, but don't spray anything (aside from compressed air) into the keyboard itself. Some keys, such as the Spacebar and Enter key, are real buggers to get back on, so don't bother to remove them. Clean up what you can and try the keyboard again.

If the spill is really bad, you can douse your keyboard in water—it won't ruin anything as long as you unplug the keyboard before you douse it. However, use distilled water because it's free of minerals that can gunk up the keyboard's components. And of course, make sure the entire keyboard is completely dry before you try to plug it back in again.

Perhaps you didn't spill anything on it, but your keyboard has developed a few sticky keys anyway. First, make sure it's not the *repeat rate* that's causing the trouble—the repeat rate controls how hard you must press to get a key to repeat. If the rate's too sensitive, the keys will repeat when you don't want them to. In Windows go to the Control Panel and double-click the Keyboard icon. There you can adjust lots of settings, including the repeat rate.

Note

Absolutely, positively do not use WD-40 on your keyboard or any other part of your computer. Sure, it greases things up fine, but it also conducts electricity! Believe me: WD-40, 4-in-1 Oil, or any other such type of industrial lubrication can do worse damage to your machinery than the strongest cup of coffee.

When You Can't Tell What the Keys Are For

Got some keys that don't work right when you press them? For example, maybe your Backspace key is acting like the letter T? Well, check the logo on your computer. Does it say, "Gateway?" Aha! The problem could be that your Gateway Anykey keyboard (yes, that's what they call it) has remapped the purpose of the Backspace key. Believe it or not, this is a feature. Its purpose is to enable you to create simple macros (a short set of instructions) that can be played back when you hit the key. You also can use this feature to rearrange the keyboard keys (or at least, their purpose) to better suit your exact needs.

With some keyboards, this remapping process can happen quite accidentally (especially if your fingers slip while typing a letter to the manufacturer). To reset the keyboard to its former logical self, you'll need to remove the mapping by pressing Ctrl+Alt+Suspend Macro or some other wacky keyboard combination. Check out the following online document for help: www.gateway.com/support/techdocs/trshoot/portable/32154p.shtml.

The Case of So-Called "Internet Keyboards"

Here's a problem you might be facing with your keyboard that's neither your fault nor your keyboard's: Many retail computer systems sold since 1999 have included *Internet keyboards*—devices that contain a row of buttons along the top designed for one-click access to a number of the manufacturer's chosen Web sites for various categories: games, finance, news, throwing away more of your money, complaining .... These Web sites were chosen because of marketing deals between the system manufacturers and the Web sites themselves or their agents; however, one problem lately is that many of these sites no longer exist because of the Great Dot-Com Crash of 2000.

In any event, these Internet buttons should take you somewhere. Microsoft produces one keyboard model whose buttons take you all over the MSN Web site; eMachines ships a model whose buttons could take you just about anyplace.

The Logitech model of "Internet keyboard" is called iTouch; it comes with software that enables you to program the destination of the keys yourself. Reprogramming is a drag-and-drop operation involving the mouse (you don't have to have a Logitech mouse to do it), so you don't have to hack into any files. By comparison, Microsoft's Internet Keyboard features some keys that you program yourself (called *hot keys*) and others that Microsoft programs for you.

Here's another problem you might face with some Internet keyboards: You install Netscape and suddenly you have all sorts of problems. You check with the manufacturer's Web site (eMachines, Microsoft), and the only solution they'll give you is to uninstall Netscape. Unfortunately, that is the solution unless you prefer for your keyboard to continue to act up. However, if you own the Logitech brand, your programmable Web keys will work fine with whichever Web browser you choose to use—Microsoft's Internet Explorer, Netscape, or even Opera. (Yeah, did you know there's a

Web browser called Opera?) The question you should ask yourself here is this: Do you really want a keyboard that limits the work you do and the way you do it? Replacement keyboards, I'll remind you, are cheap.

When the Mouse Becomes a Rat

There now are two new mouse categories that are quickly becoming commonplace, competing with the industry standard mechanical mouse with the moving ball and the long tail. A cordless mouse uses infrared technology (the same science employed by your TV's remote control) to transmit its location to a receiver unit controlled by your PC. An optical mouse is a revived—and this time, successful—design in which an electronic sensor scans its immediate vicinity to detect changes in its own environment. There are such things as cordless optical mice, enabling computers to have their own relatively solid-state (except the buttons) remote control devices.

Taking Care of Your Mechanical Mouse

In the meantime, those of us in the real world are still using the old rolling rubber balls with the rotary motion detectors. If you've suddenly lost the use of your non-optical, noninfrared, nonturbocharged mouse or if it's acting strange, try some of these tricks:

➤ **Has your mouse gotten loose?** Its tail (the cable) needs to be connected to the back of the PC. Take a good look at your cable. If its plug is round with a series of six pinholes surrounding a rectangular keyhole, there should be a special location for your mouse. Your manual might refer to this as the *PS/2 port—* named for the first IBM computers to include this plug design. It might be marked with a little mouse pictogram (either the rodent kind or electronic kind) or, simpler still, with the word "MOUSE." If the plug is flat with two rows of five and four pins, your mouse is designed to plug into your PC's nine-pin serial (RS-232) port. This plug might not be marked so you'll need to search for a matching connector with nine metal pins poking out. After you plug the mouse back in, you need to restart the PC for the mouse to start working again.

➤ **Is the mouse cable all twisted and torn?** Check the mouse tail for damage; if you see

Check This Out

With your mouse unplugged or disabled, you'll need to use keyboard commands to save your open data files (if any) and exit your running programs; then exit Windows. For example, to open a menu press Alt, then press the menu's underlined letter. You then can use the arrow keys to navigate down the menu until you find Save (for most programs, pressing S works, too).

some, the mouse probably is beyond repair. This damage might be caused by a run-in with a vacuum cleaner or, heaven forbid, a mouse of the other variety. Try borrowing someone else's mouse for a spell; test your system with that to see whether it still works.

➤ **Is the mouse playing hide and seek with you?** It's easy to hide a mouse pointer at the edges of your screen. Move the mouse around and see if its pointer pops out of its hiding place.

➤ **Have you cleaned your mouse lately?** If not, it probably needs it. See the next section for help.

➤ **Is your mouse pointer jumping all around, or moving in only one direction?** First, give it a good cleaning. A dirty mouse roller sometimes results in an otherwise optimal mouse moving the pointer more in one direction than another. If the problem persists, check for device conflicts; see Chapter 24, "Getting Windows to Recognize Your New Toys," for help.

➤ **Have you installed a new device lately, such as a modem?** If so, it might be conflicting with your mouse. Again, see Chapter 24 for help.

➤ **Has your serial mouse been working fine until now, but suddenly it stops working right after you install some kind of serial device such as a modem, joystick, scanner, or serial printer?** The problem is that the new device and your mouse duked it out over a COM port—and the mouse lost. You see, all serial devices communicate with the PC through a *COM* (*communications*) port. Each serial device needs its own COM port; otherwise it gets mucked up and doesn't work. Even a mouse plugged into its own exclusive mouse connector port on the back of your PC is given its own COM port number internally by your computer's BIOS; your PC sees it as just one of the gang, trying to find its own place in line. If your mouse and some other serial device are fighting over the same internal (logical) COM port, you have to switch one of them to a different port. Chapter 23 discusses all the juggling and disposition of your COM ports. If you have infrared input devices such as a cordless mouse or keyboard, there are some extra things you'll need to know to keep them working well in Windows; Chapter 23 also addresses these issues.

➤ **Does the mouse feel funny, or is it too hard to double-click properly?** If so, you can adjust the mouse sensitivity using the Mouse icon in the Control Panel. For example, you can switch to a left-handed mouse, adjust the double-click speed, and make the pointer bigger or slower.

➤ **Does your mouse work only in Windows 95, but not in DOS mode?** If your mouse works only in Windows, but not when you restart in MS-DOS mode, you do not have a DOS driver loading, and you need one. Using Notepad, edit your DOSSTART.BAT (located in the Windows directory) so that it contains a reference to the DOS-mode mouse driver. DOS mode mouse drivers have a delightful tendency to be called MOUSE.COM or MOUSE.EXE, so you should be able to locate one of these on your hard disk drive. Your DOSSTART.BAT command doesn't need any special switches or parameters; just the name of the driver as though you were launching it from the DOS prompt. Here's a delightful surprise: Even if you install the DOS-mode mouse driver MOUSE.EXE for Microsoft brand but your mouse isn't Microsoft, it probably will still work. You might not have access to all the special features your Logitech or Mouse Systems device has on it—but hey, how often do you have to boot in DOS mode? (Windows 98/SE/Me users should not have this problem, as launching a DOS prompt should automatically load up a DOS-mode mouse driver.)

Cleaning a Mechanical Mouse

If you've had your mouse for awhile and suddenly it starts acting weird, chances are all you need to do is clean it. You see, there's a roller ball on the underside of the mouse that just loves to grab dust, dirt, hair, and any other disgusting thing on which it can get its ... uh ... hands. First exit all programs and turn off the PC so it doesn't go nuts with all the screwy signals it'll receive during the cleaning process. Flip your mouse over on its back and open the hatch that holds the ball in place. (You see an arrow telling you which way to twist or push the hatch to get it to open.)

Remove the ball. Now, use a wooden toothpick (not plastic) to gently scrape the gook off of the two or three rollers you find inside the mouse. You can dip the toothpick in rubbing alcohol if you like, but not anything that's oily (like acetone) because this does more harm than good. Someone may have told you before to use a Q-Tip for this, but Q-Tips leave their own fuzz behind; I don't recommend using them.

Use a lint-free cloth or warm soap and water to clean the rolling ball, too. Don't use rubbing alcohol on the rubber—it'll mess it up, and might even dissolve it. When you finish cleaning, put the whole thing back together and try it out.

If you have a mechanical trackball device instead of a mouse (from which the ball sticks up—the industry slang is "dead mouse"), the cleaning process isn't much different. There's a ring-shaped guard that holds the ball in place, and you generally twist it to remove the ring. Once that's off, the ball still might be held down by some strange, weak force; look for a button beneath where the ring would sit, which ejects the ball into your hand. From there you clean the rollers just as you would a live mouse.

A mouse gets all the junk on its rollers from the mouse pad. Obviously the mouse pad has to get dirty first before the mouse gets dirty. Now, you can't avoid the mouse pad getting dirty—it's impossible. As you rest your palm on it, it collects the oils your body naturally emits. In and of themselves, those oils aren't dirty. But they do manage to collect dust from the air, and as they congeal, they form a gray gunk the consistency of Play-Doh. It's that stuff that gets all over your mouse's rollers.

Thus if you want to keep your mouse cleaner longer, try keeping your mouse pad as clean as possible. If it's a fabric pad, avoid the temptation to use upholstery cleaner because it might have chemicals that erode the mouse's roller ball. Avoid any cleansers with powders or grit, and don't use anything with ammonia or chlorine—such as Formula 409, which not only could hurt your rubber ball, it could also bleach your pad. Try a mild antibacterial soap—the kind you wash your own hands with.

Cleaning an Optical Mouse

An optical mouse should never need cleaning, say the advertisements, because its "intelligent" sensor can read clear though dirt, dust, and fingerprints. Yeah, right. You could also decide never to wash your windows again; and in a year or so, you could probably still tell whether a car pulls into your driveway. But if you rubbed your hands over that window every weekday for a year, try telling me that even your own highly evolved intelligence would be able to see who's driving that car.

Cleaning an optical mouse's sensor is a little tricky. You don't want to use cleansers, because a mouse is an electronic device. You'd like to use hand soap, but soap leaves a film. Here again, the best cleaner is distilled rubbing alcohol. The bottom of a newer optical mouse is entirely flat and self contained, so use a paper towel to wipe some alcohol over the surface, then let it dry itself. Don't use a fabric towel, as fabric can leave fibers which will make your optical mouse dirtier—from the sensor's perspective—than it was when you cleaned it. Paper towels leave the least residue.

Infrared Devices: Not Entirely Cordless

Let's make one thing perfectly clear...or, actually, let's make it clear just how *unclear* something is, even though it appears clear on the surface. An infrared input device, although it gives you the freedom to move your input devices pretty much wherever you want—within sight of your monitor—is not really *cordless*. There is a cord; it's just someplace else.

Plugging In Your Cordless Devices

Infrared devices make use of receiver units that receive the infrared pulses of light that your input devices send out. With a TV's remote control system, the infrared receiver is neatly embedded someplace beneath the tube or display screen; your everyday PC monitor doesn't come with this convenience or any place to add such a thing. Thus you have this extra appendage that must be placed somewhere within unobstructed view of your input equipment; this device is plugged into the back of your PC, using a cord pretty much like the old one.

So the old advice, "Check to make sure your mouse or keyboard is securely plugged in," still applies to cordless devices. If you're not getting input, examine your plugs. The receiver device for your infrared mouse may be plugged into your marked mouse port (PS/2 port), and your keyboard receiver may be plugged into your keyboard port.

However, they also might be USB devices, which means their connectors may have small, thin, flat steel plugs that go into USB ports in the back of your computer or onto a USB hub (yet another appendage that sits outside your PC). Infrared keyboard/mouse combinations are more likely to use the USB interface.

Get Accustomed to Resyncing

Periodically, your infrared receiver may lose contact with your input device, even when both are unobstructed and in perfect working order. Unlike your TV remote, infrared mouse devices and keyboards have quite a lot of data to communicate with your computer; in order that they don't say the wrong things to one another, they agree to operate in synch with one another. (If you imagine the space between the letters you're reading accidentally falling in the middle of the letters themselves, you'll get an idea of what it must be like for an infrared receiver to be out of synch with a remote keyboard.)

There's nothing difficult about the *resyncing* process; if your devices are in good working order, you shouldn't have to do it too often. You'll find a "RESYNC" button someplace on the infrared receiver unit. Press it once; the receiver will send out its own infrared signal. Find a similar button on your keyboard or mouse (generally on the side or underneath) and press that once. This will start a "handshaking" process, not unlike what happens when a modem makes contact with a server over a phone line. Wait a minute or so for this process to conclude; then test your input device to make sure it's working. The resyncing process should work right the first time; if it doesn't, check to see what might be blocking the path between the two components. If you're still having trouble, the problem might be your monitor—it might put out too much RF interference (radio noise) and hamper reception.

Note

If your cordless mouse or keyboard acts strange, it may be low on batteries. The batteries go in the device itself, the receiver, or both. Some cordless mouse devices use rechargeable nickel-cadmium (NiCad) battery packs; other brands also are shipped with their own battery rechargers.

When Your Printer Makes You Feel Powerless

With the exception of the mouse and keyboard, the most common troubles you'll have with computers involve solid-state devices. When you start having trouble with your printer, you re-enter the world of do-jiggers, dealy-bobs, and whatzits—in other words, moving parts. In this section you'll find the solutions to the most common printer problems.

Make Sure Your Printer Is Configured Properly

If your new printer is acting goofy, the first step toward finding a solution is to check its configuration. (Steps on how to install a printer under Windows are covered in Chapter 8, "The Easiest Things to Upgrade.")

Since 1998 nearly all the major printer manufacturers have chosen to ship driver software with their systems, each of whose principal operating instructions differ somewhat from the others. So when you bring up the Printer Settings dialog box for, say, an HP DeskJet, you'll see different contents altogether from an Epson Stylus or a Lexmark Z11. However, the categorization of these controls generally is the same—although I can't give you any guarantees here anymore. Here's how to access your printer's main diagnostic features:

1. Click Start, select Settings, and then select Printers.

2. Right-click your printer's icon and select Properties.

3. From the General tab you can print a test page.

4. From the Details tab, you can do the following important things:

    ➤ Change the printer driver. If you've just downloaded a new printer driver from the Internet or you intend to download one from Microsoft's Web site (yes, they do make drivers available there), New Driver is the button for you. If you have Windows 98 or newer, the dialog box actually can launch the process that downloads just the right driver from Microsoft for you.

    ➤ Capture a new printer port. Normally Windows searches for a printer connected to the logical port named LPT1. However, if your PC is on a home network where it and other PCs are sharing a printer, you may need the Capture Printer Port button to help your PC locate the printer being shared.

5. If you have a color printer, the Color Management tab lets you decide whether you allow Windows to manage your colorizing processes for you or you prefer for special software shipped with your printer to do the job instead. This is a decision best left to the manual that came with your printer; if there's some reason for you to use the printer's own color management software, the manual should say so somewhere.

6. From the Setup tab you can set the default paper size and orientation, and adjust the quality of the graphics you print. The higher the quality, the more time it'll take to print them.

There may be other tabs to the right of these, which have been added by your printer driver software and whose functions are defined by your printer's manufacturer, not Microsoft. HP printer drivers tend to add a Features tab, which gives you access to the special features of its printers that couldn't fit in any of the other tabs. You'll probably find other tabs devoted exclusively to the fine art of self promotion.

My Printer Doesn't Print!

If your printer doesn't print at all, make sure it's switched on and online (meaning its communication channel to the computer is open). To put a printer online, press its On Line button or switch. If the printer is on but not responding, check for paper jams. Also make sure it's not out of paper.

Sometimes when your printer won't print, or when the printout looks kinda screwy, the villain is the printer cable. It's sad, but occasionally your cable will just go bad. Before you chuck your printer, consider replacing the cable instead. Better yet, borrow a cable from a friend and see whether your printer works with it.

If everything checks out, you should try printing with another program, just to make certain the problem doesn't reside with your application. If that works, the first program could be set up with the wrong printer or a printer that isn't a printer. Generally to change the designated printer for a program, select Print from the File menu; then in the Print dialog box, under a list marked Name, choose your (real) printer.

Techno Talk

Fax modems often use printer drivers to lay out pages in memory that are being sent out over your fax line, which enables you to print your document to your fax modem as if it were a printer. Your modem's software knows it's not a printer; when it sees your document it asks what phone number it should dial; then goes on from there.

My Printer Keeps Jamming!

A frequent cause of printer jams is that your paper is too thick. If you're trying to use copier paper, don't. *Laser paper* is specially treated so the printer can grip it properly; this is true even if you have an inkjet printer. When buying reams of paper, look for 24-pound bond or higher (written "24# bond"). Thirty-pound bond is best but often is unavailable in recycled form, so generally it's a lot more expensive. Also keep your laser paper in a dry, cool place.

I'm Having Trouble Printing Envelopes and Labels!

If you're trying to print an envelope, generally your printer will provide some special insertion path for it, so it doesn't come out looking like your dog chewed it. On a laser printer, this path might be located above the regular path, or you might have to throw some switch to turn the regular path into a shortened one. An inkjet printer may feature a paper guide not unlike the one you would find on the left part of the platen of an old typewriter, which slides left and right to help guide different widths of paper into their proper place.

If you're trying to print labels with your printer, make sure you purchase labels that are specifically designed for laser or inkjet printing; otherwise the labels will peel off and stick inside your printer. Labels are generally available on 8½"-wide sheets, so avoid using labels on narrow strips.

Which way should an envelope go? Again, look for the little pictogram somewhere on the envelope chute. Then look for the stamp pictured in its upper-right corner; that'll tell you which way your envelope should be pointed as you insert it. Failing that, print the "envelope" on regular paper, and make a note of which way is up, then insert the real envelope and print it.

Nt Bng Abl to Rd Yr Prntot

If your printout looks as illegible as a doctor's prescription, the problem might be the cable. First of all, you want to be sure to place your printer only a short distance from your PC. If your printer uses the parallel port, longer distances—and longer cables—tend to garble up the data. The signal on most parallel cables tends to degenerate after 25 feet. You could boost this signal using a device called a *parallel line extender.*

If your parallel printer cable is loose, remove it. Check all the pins; if one of them is bent gently bend it back using a pair of rubber-handled, needle-nose pliers; then replace the cable and try printing again. If your USB printer cable is loose (the smaller, thinner plug), power down your PC, then remove the cable and reinsert it. By all means, never take pliers to it. A USB connection is tricky enough on the inside as it is.

If you have a PostScript laser printer, disregard anything that states there's only one PostScript version. Actually, there are nearly as many versions as there are people. If your program has both a listing for your particular brand of printer and another listing for "PostScript printer," by all means choose your particular brand for your printer driver. Don't choose the latest and greatest PostScript driver because you think it will improve your PostScript printing. In other words, only choose the HP LaserJet 3200m driver if you own a LaserJet 3200m; if you own an old Apple LaserWriter Plus, don't install the HP drivers.

Check This Out

If you just can't stand having to change the toner in your laser printer all the time, you might just get a bit more out of each one by removing the toner and gently shaking it; then reinstalling it.

When Your Printout Is Only Half There

If your printout is getting light, it might be time to change the printer's *printing medium*—which is the newer, spookier way of saying "toner" or "ink." You can try increasing the print density setting in your program or printer driver before you replace your medium. This makes your printouts darker but if it's really time to change the medium, you won't see much improvement.

On the other hand, if even the lightest subject matter prints too dark, try decreasing the print density setting. With laser printers, this setting generally is a wide-ranging variable from darkest to lightest. Inkjet printers usually provide at least three print densities or *qualities,* which affect the overall speed of printing and the amount of printing medium consumed. You might find your default print density set to something like Normal or Standard in the middle, with your other choices Economy (lighter) and Optimum (darker).

If your print density is set down to almost nothing and things are still dark, the problem might be that your application isn't properly creating gray-scale graphics for your printer. Word processors are especially prone to this problem whenever there is a graphic image on the page. Make sure your program is properly configured to handle gray-scales. (If you're printing with PostScript, you should not have this problem under any circumstance unless something's really, really wrong, such as a toner leak.)

If your PostScript laser printer prints only part of your document, your problem might not be in your computer or your printer but in the document itself. Try ejecting the page manually. If the page is incomplete or the text is in 1,200-point type rather than 12-point, test it by printing out something else—anything other than the same document. If that something else prints just fine, your problem might be with the PostScript instructions your program is sending to your printer for that one document. This is a good time to see whether there are any other types of PostScript drivers that work with your brand of printer.

Cleaning Your Inkjet Print Cartridge

Here's a little-known fact you might not have known about your inkjet printer: Your printing mechanism—the electronic device that is responsible for depositing ink on the page—is embedded in your ink cartridge. (So that's why those things are so darned expensive!) If you have a recent model inkjet printer from any manufacturer, your ink cartridge is an electronic device. The good news here is that, if that device is blatantly malfunctional, you can throw it away and get a new one with your next cartridge replacement.

First you might want to try cleaning the cartridge or cartridges. Color inkjet printers typically have two cartridges: one for black, the other for cyan, yellow, and magenta (the three primary ink colors). As your manual will show you, most cartridges simply lift or snap out of place—there's nothing you have to unscrew. You will want to be careful of dripping ink. Even though many inkjet printing media now are gel based, and therefore don't leak like a pricked water balloon, there still can be junk gumming up the outside of the cartridge or even the print head itself (which again is part of the cartridge).

When you first installed your print cartridge, you probably removed a piece of protective tape from its surface. That tape was covering the print head; if you remember where the tape was, you should be able to easily locate the brass- or copper-colored print mechanism, once you've removed the cartridge from your printer. As a general rule, don't tip or rotate the cartridge if you can, at all, avoid it—keep the cartridge level, now that the tape is off and fluid can still flow from the thing. Using a Q-tip moistened with water only (no alcohol, no solvents, no cleaners), just dab around the print head to remove any dried ink or loose paper fibers; then reinsert the cartridge exactly the way your manual shows you.

Cleaning Your Laser Printer Toner Cartridge

After you change the toner cartridge on your laser printer (by the way, this is best done in the dark to avoid damaging the developer drum unit), use a dry, soft toothbrush or similar instrument to sweep off any loose toner from the components. In any event, your documents will be streaked for a while—this is just spilled toner dust working its way out. (When changing the toner cartridge make sure you don't get any on you or on a carpeted floor—it just won't come out, no matter what superduper cleaner you use on it.) It's always a good idea to run a couple of test pattern pages to get the streaks out of the system.

If your printouts are streaked after you've had the toner in for a long while, there might be a problem with the toner. Check whether your cartridge is the type that you can reseal; if it is, try resealing the cartridge and changing it again. If that doesn't make a dent in the problem, your print drum might be going out, and you'll need to take your printer in to a registered service center for the necessary surgery.

When Your Printout Is Nearly Gone

On your inkjet printer, there are two reasons your printout is faint to the point of invisibility: Your print cartridge is running out of ink or your print cartridge is defective. Your best solution for both conditions is the same: Shell out whatever it costs now to replace the print cartridge.

If your non-PostScript laser printer prints only part of your document, you might be asking it to do too much. You see, for a laser printer to print a page, it first has to cram the image for that entire page into its memory. The imaging system has to have access to the whole page; otherwise nothing works. For most plain text pages, you use only a trickle of the printer's memory when you print these pages because the image is not very complex. If you add a few fancy fonts it gets harder; add a couple of fancy graphics and it gets harder still.

Your only fix here is to either simplify your document by using fewer graphics and only one or two fonts, or by adding more memory to the printer. With some printers, adding memory is about as fun as inserting shrapnel into your stomach, so after checking out the detailed instructions later in this section, you might want to have your registered service representative take care of it for you.

Whether to Add More Memory to Your Laser Printer

I have a laser printer in my office that's 16 years old and counting. Laser printers tend to be the ol' battle-axes of computing, generally surviving far longer than most computers. However, as computing jobs evolve, old laser printers might end up needing new—and more—memory.

Adding more memory to your laser printer keeps it from choking on the big, complex graphics and fancy fonts in your documents. To add more memory to your laser printer, you first have to figure out whether or not it will fit. In other words, do you have an empty memory slot into which you can put more RAM? One-megabyte SIMMs are largely unavailable today. To upgrade memory for a laser printer whose maximum is 4MB, you might have to replace all the memory you have. The good news is that the most commonly used RAM in laser printers today is 4MB 72-pin SIMM modules, which sell for about $25 apiece. They are relatively expensive as RAM goes, but still cheap.

The second thing you need to figure out is how to insert the RAM. Some laser RAM comes in nice, easy-to-insert SIMMs; others come in funky, hard-to-deal-with DRAM chips. Others come on *daughter cards,* which connect to the main memory card. I couldn't upgrade the memory on my 16-year-old Panasonic if I wanted to.

Luckily, I don't want to. Today Windows utilizes the memory of your PC to generate the graphical and textual contents of a page entirely before that image is sent to the laser printer. (The exception is with PostScript printers, which still accept commands from the computer; not image contents.) Because the RAM where the image is made now is in your PC, the only performance gain you would get by adding RAM to a non-PostScript laser printer is in the speed department. Theoretically, your printer could accept image contents from your PC in larger batches at a time, expediting the printing process.

Monitoring Your Monitor Troubles

Today, the market in PC monitors has been thoroughly invaded by flat panel devices, whose prices have descended from the outer stratosphere down to a more reasonable altitude near that of the tip of Everest. The two types of monitor in the modern world—the conventional cathode ray tube (CRT) and the newer flat panel models derived from notebook PC technology (LCD)—are two very, very different orders of beast. Very little about them, technically or even practically, is the same. So I'm going to break this section into two parts, starting with the last vestige of the research of Vladimir Zwyorkin: the old, reliable CRT.

What Could Possibly Go Wrong with a Solid-State Device?

The CRT is the single biggest power consumption device attached to your computer—more than your printer, more than your scanner, more than Quake 3. As long as CRT monitors remain in production, it'll cause troubles whose descriptions and whose solutions seem more analog than digital—because they are.

Before you decide to throw everything out and invest in a new monitor and video card for your PC, here are some items you should check:

➤ If your once-quiet monitor suddenly starts making a loud humming noise, it might be that the old guy is going out, and you'll have to replace it soon. If the monitor only squeaks while you're in a particular program, the program might be trying to make the monitor display stuff that it's not capable of. Perhaps you switched your video card's display mode into a resolution or refresh rate that your monitor doesn't support. Reboot your computer, and then hold down the F8 key (WinMe users, hold down Alt) to bring up your Startup Menu. Type the number for "Safe Mode." Then change your default resolution to a lower number and see if that clears up the problem.

➤ If your monitor starts displaying funny colors or no color at all, check the cable to ensure you plugged it in all the way. Also look at the video plug for any bent pins. If you find some, use needle-nose pliers to bend them back (gently, gently). If the funky colors appear only when you're using a particular program, check its setup to see whether you can change the *palette* (a fancy word for color wardrobe).

➤ If you're having trouble reading what's onscreen, try playing around with the contrast and brightness. Many newer monitors have replaced the old, separate contrast and brightness knobs with a single control or rocker switch, whose mastery would put you on a par with the greatest Nintendo players of all time. If you don't have your monitor's manual handy, go online with the manufacturer's Web site and look for downloadable instructions.

➤ If you still have trouble, try changing the screen resolution. A higher resolution, (such as 1280h × 1024v) allows your monitor to display complex graphics more clearly and forces Windows to display text with crisper edges and smoother curves. You could find text easier to read at higher resolutions, but there are some tradeoffs. Graphics in your Web pages might appear smaller, for instance. Also, your video card could be forced to refresh the display at a lower rate to compensate, possibly causing a flicker that could give you a headache. On the other end of the scale, changing to a lower resolution (such as 640h × 480v) might be more to your liking because objects will appear larger and the screen more steady and solid, without the flicker.

Magnetism and Other Magic Tricks

If the colors in one corner of your CRT monitor appear more vivid or dull than at other corners, the magnetic fields inside your monitor might not be in alignment. This might sound like one of those made up explanations for warp engine accidents in *Star Trek*. However, the truth is that ordinary events—such as moving the monitor, passing something metallic in its vicinity, making adjustments to the display, or exposing it to too many episodes of *Star Trek*—can result in the magnetic fields that guide the electrons in your monitor becoming slightly skewed. The result is that electrons literally bend in directions they're not supposed to, so they strike the wrong color points on the inside of the tube.

There's a simple solution to this problem: *Degauss* ("di-GOWS") your monitor. The degaussing process carefully exposes your monitor to magnetism that neutralizes any internal magnetic imbalances. Many modern monitors come with their own internal degaussing system, activated by a switch on the back or, in the case of monitors with their own menus, by a selection accessible from the front control panel. (Your own TV might have one of these degaussers as well).

Degaussing your monitor while it's turned on will activate a charge within an internal magnetic coil. It will shake your picture around for a moment but it should steady itself, and the strange color shift should go away. If your monitor doesn't have an internal degausser, you can use an external degausser kit, which basically consists of a weak magnet you pass over the surface of your tube as if you were dusting it. (By the way, your monitor could use a good dusting while you're at it.) Do this while the monitor is turned on but remove any magnetic media, such as Zip disks or diskettes, from the area first. As you might have guessed, magnets can zap floppies.

Convening the New Panel

The similarities between flat-panel liquid crystal diode (LCD) monitors and CRT monitors can be summed up by the following: Both hook up to your computer and show you text and graphics. That's about it. What you're paying for when you purchase an LCD monitor is a flicker-free display that might be less of a headache for you (literally), and that consumes far less power and much less space than a CRT.

There are a few tradeoffs: Most notably, LCD monitors have a fixed resolution. In other words, you can't vary the number of scan lines it displays. Most LCD monitors sold today have resolutions of 1024h × 768v, or 1280h × 1024v. Some video cards are shipped with drivers that feature special setup options for LCD monitors, enabling them to simulate lower resolution displays. This means your video card can tell your computer it's generating an 800h × 600v image as it's reformulating that picture to fit the margins of your LCD monitor without shrinking the image. You might notice some chunkiness in the image, which the video card can reduce by means of *anti-aliasing,* or blurring the chunky parts so you don't notice them so much. However, even that's a tradeoff: chunkiness for blurriness. What you gain is the capability for some games or other graphics-intensive programs that require fixed resolution to use the full display area of your monitor.

The manufacturers of LCD monitors advertise that they are not susceptible to the same type of burn-in that affects CRT monitors when you let them display the same image for several hours—or, by accident, several days. Technically, that's correct. LCD monitors are susceptible to a type of burn-in, after they've been showing the same image for a few hours or more. You'll see a faint residual ghost of that image, which might worry you. The good news is with LCD monitors, the ghost image should completely disappear after a few minutes.

That doesn't mean your monitor is completely undamaged. If the image does not disappear, try turning off your monitor's power and leaving it off for about three minutes. Permanent burn-in is physically impossible for an LCD monitor; however, over time it tends to leave ghost images on the screen, even for a few seconds longer than they should remain. You don't want your mouse pointer to look like Tinkerbell's magic wand, so be sure to use a screen-saver program, even with your LCD monitor.

To avoid even temporary burn-in, you use the same tool you would if you had a CRT monitor: a good screen saver or at least something that shuts off the display after five minutes or so. This brings me to my next topic of concern ….

Power Management, or the Lack Thereof

Windows 95 introduced a feature called *power management,* which for a great many users is a euphemism for a monitor that can't seem to turn itself back on until you reboot your computer. In fact, since the advent of power management by way of the operating system, monitors stuck in the "off" position has become the number one monitor problem reported by users. This is ironic, as their monitors generally are not at fault in the slightest.

Windows-driven *Advanced Power Management* (*APM*) enables a computer to set its many parts and peripherals to a low-power mode, or to turn them off entirely, after so many minutes of not being in use. APM has worked relatively well with hard disk drives, which appreciate the occasional break from rotating all the live-long day. Even modern motherboards can sustain low power modes, thus allowing them just to retain the contents of RAM but not feed full power to the CPU during periods of extended disuse. (Sounds like a manual for a nuclear submarine, doesn't it?)

Power management in monitors has led to a system whereby users can effectively leave their monitors turned on, and allow the computer to shut its power off after a while. This way, there's only one power switch the user has to fiddle with—the one on the computer—and the monitor minds the computer's power setting.

This is all very nice, but things start to unravel when we come to the subject of extended disuse: Windows is supposed to be able to set the monitor on *Standby mode,* which means it receives only enough power to keep track of when the computer tells it to come off Standby mode. The tube is powered down during this period. When you press a key or move the mouse, the computer tells the monitor to come off Standby. This should effectively cancel out the need for screen savers.

However, many users like to have their screen savers kick in after five minutes, and perhaps power down the monitor after a half-hour. Because screen saver programs use onscreen animation, Windows tends to kick in a set of internal graphics libraries called *DirectX*, which can change the monitor's scan and resolution modes while the screen saver is running. It's like engaging a second, virtual monitor.

Meanwhile, it's the real, physical monitor that is supposed to receive the signal from Windows that it's supposed to shut down. What's funny is that the physical monitor can receive this signal and go into Standby, but then the screen saver program starts running. So when the computer sends the signal to come off Standby, the screen saver's virtual monitor, thinking it was never on Standby, ignores the signal. Meanwhile, the real monitor, having never received the signal, stays in Standby forever. When the user tries to switch the monitor off and on manually—using the new single-button switch that replaced the old on/off rocker—the monitor actually never comes back on no matter how often the user presses this button.

Here's a variant of this problem: Perhaps your computer is on Standby mode and you turn off the monitor. You can't turn it on again because there is no "on" any more, and you can't launch your monitor directly from "off" into Standby mode. Again, it's APM that causes these problems; not your monitor's power button. In my husband's experience, an APM setting actually confused his Mag Innovision monitor's electronic switch so badly that it short-circuited and had to be replaced.

So what do you do? If powering down your monitor is a feature you think you might need, you should disable your screen saver. From the Control Panel, double-click Display, select the Screen Saver tab, and in the Screen Saver list, choose (None).

Altered States, or the Difference Between "On" and "Really On"

Because Microsoft and BIOS manufacturers utilize their own separate visions of reality in order for them to continue separately developing computer technology, there are now officially five different states your computer can be in at any one time. (You can't just have on and off; no, there have to be several existential states in between!) Get ready to disconnect your brain from the real world as you read the following list of active or altered states your PC and its parts, can attain:

➤ **Ready**—Formerly known as "on."

➤ **Standby**—Power is reduced to the CPU and shut off to the monitor. Meanwhile, memory and the BIOS are fully powered. Whenever the system receives input— say, from the keyboard or the mouse, or from you throwing a brick at something that has a button—your system automatically goes off Standby. Another device in your computer also can take your system off Standby, such as your network card or modem. Why would that ever happen? Suppose you've initiated a long download before you go to bed at night. Your modem actually might keep your PC awake, and prevent your monitor from ever going to sleep, even if you think it's supposed to shut itself off after five minutes. Standby is the setting that confuses most monitors—"Am I on or off? Should I mention that I'm not getting a signal, or should I shut up?"

➤ **Suspended**—This is the low-power state supported by many new motherboards' BIOS. Here, all processing activities within your computer—including its on-board devices—are shut off. You're not on a network, you're not downloading anything, and your devices can't cut in and keep the rest of your system awake. The problem is, Windows doesn't like this state very much. You see, Suspended mode also puts Windows to sleep. Only your BIOS can awaken your PC, usually after you press something on the keyboard. You'll know when Windows fails to appreciate your kicking your computer into Suspended mode, when you notice that not all your running applications wake up after Windows has brought your mouse pointer back. Your pointer might work, but your programs won't.

➤ **Hibernation**—Only Windows Me supports this special state. Here, an image of the contents of memory is stored to your main hard drive (assuming you have enough free space there); then your system is shut off completely. (If you have an ATX power supply in your system, your BIOS can tell your system to power down automatically; if you don't, you'll get the message, "It's now safe to turn off your computer," and you can flick that switch yourself.) Your monitor will be shut off; however, its power light might blink yellow anyway, as if it were on Standby. You can safely turn your monitor off at this point. Whenever you turn on your system again, Windows will read the note it left to itself, telling it to re-load memory with the contents it had at the time you ordered it to enter Hibernation mode. In a minute or two (or 317, or 318 …) you'll see your computer in exactly the state you left it before.

➤ **Off**—As in "off." After several weeks of intense negotiations, both computer and operating system engineers settled upon the name "Off," probably after voting down "Discontinued," "Unengaged," "Disempowered," "Un-reactivated," and "De-planed."

You can entirely disable the capability of Windows to manage power for your monitor. From the Control Panel, double-click Power Management (Windows 95/98) or Power Options (Windows Me). From the Turn off monitor list, choose Never. If you set up your BIOS to manage power for your monitor, you might want to make certain it doesn't conflict with your screen saver. You don't want to try reawakening your monitor, only to find it's stuck showing the screen saver.

Fixing a Drive That's Floppin'

It's now entirely possible for many computer users to go an entire week or even a month without even touching a floppy disk; they're almost extinct. Almost, that is, until Sony came up with a wonderful new use for them: a substitute for film in its new line of digital cameras. I have one and now I find myself breaking into my attic, reusing my AOL sign-up offer diskettes as film.

The PC Won't Read My Diskette!

If you insert a diskette with the hope that your PC can read its data and it can't, check a couple of things before you chuck the diskette (or the drive). First remove the diskette and tap it in your palm a few times. This aligns the magnetic material inside. Reinsert the diskette and see if your PC can read it now. If that doesn't work, remove the diskette and check the metal cover. Slide it back and forth a few times to loosen it up; then try it again.

You might want to try using the diskette in somebody else's computer. If it works there, that can mean your drive is having some problems. Try another diskette in your drive. Same trouble? Well, before you call 911, try using a floppy disk drive cleaning kit to clean the drive. These aren't the easiest items to locate anymore, so try checking online at www.easycart.net/ecarts/AffordablePrinting/. Next check your BIOS settings to see if the drive is set up properly (see Chapter 23 for help). You also can open up the PC and make sure the drive's data and power cables haven't come loose or something equally silly. You also might want to check your system for viruses. Prior to the advent of the Internet, diskettes were the chief transmission method for viruses. If your drive light does not come on at all and you immediately get an error, the diskette drive controller might be bad. Yecch.

If the diskette doesn't work in your friend's drive, something might be wrong with the diskette. Did you format the diskette properly? If you copied data to the diskette, the disk was formatted but it might not have been formatted correctly.

If you're trying to copy something to the diskette and you can't, the problem might be that the diskette is *write-protected,* which somebody did to keep the data on the disk from being overwritten. A 3½-inch diskette's write-protect tab is located in the upper left-hand corner when the diskette is flipped on its back.

If the diskette you're trying came from a co-worker, it might be that his drive or your drive is out of alignment. If the problem keeps cropping up with other diskettes, you should consider replacing the diskette drive. It might be a difficult process (for some smaller systems, it's like solving Rubik's Cube) but it's cheap.

If you get an error message while trying to use your diskette (such as "Sector not found"), you should copy whatever you can off the diskette. If the drive won't let you copy anything but you need to save an important file, you'll have to use a diskette recovery utility. Does anyone still make such a thing? (Check out Do-It-Yourself Data Recovery at www.diydatarecovery.nl/.)

Check This Out

If you borrow a friend's Macintosh diskette, it probably won't work in your PC unless it comes from a Power Mac because most Mac diskettes are formatted funny—at least from a PC's point of view. (Unfortunately, this will sound pretty strange when you discover that your friend's Mac probably can read your PC's diskettes, but I can't help that.) A Power Mac can format diskettes that are readable in both Power Macs and PCs; however, for their contents to be readable in Power Macs, the Mac adds extra directories to the diskette that are meaningless to the Windows user but must not be deleted for the sake of the Mac user. Perhaps this will give you an idea for some good practical jokes you can play on your Mac-using friends.

If, despite all this help you've been given, problems persist with your drive not being able to read diskettes, the drive itself may be going out. Remember first to clean the drive before you make this dire prognosis. Then test to see what types of diskettes the drive is having trouble reading. Can it read diskettes if it formats them, but not others? If so, the drive might be misaligned, and need to be replaced. You might want to open up the PC and check the data and power cables to make sure they didn't accidentally come loose when you drop-kicked the PC after it lost your marketing campaign.

Other Diskette Hassles

Diskettes were the first—and, at one time, the only—storage medium used in DOS- and Windows-based PCs. While they've gotten a little smaller, the things haven't changed to any great extent in the last quarter-century. Here are a few more things that can possibly go wrong with your rapidly antiquating storage device:

➤ If you can't format your diskette because you have two drives, and you're having trouble figuring out which drive is A: and which is B:, from Explorer click the icon for drive A: and look to see which drive light comes on; the drive that lights up is A:. If you get an error message telling you: "Please insert a disk into drive A," click Cancel.

➤ If you still have any of those DOS-based *skew-sector formatting utilities* that were popular back in the Ice Age, get rid of them. They won't work with most modern diskette drives; even if one works on yours, the diskette your machine might read probably will be illegible on 95 percent of the other diskette drives in the world. It's just not worth it for 10 extra kilobytes of storage those programs provide.

➤ If the diskette's stuck in the drive, turn the computer off, and using a small, flat knife or screwdriver, gently pry the diskette out. Be careful to not damage the drive, however.

➤ If you have a 3½-inch diskette that's got a bent metal cover, take the darn thing completely off. The diskette will work fine for now without it. However, copy the contents of the diskette onto a new disk as soon as you can; without the cover, the data on the diskette is not protected.

Optical Drives and Sonic Discrepancies

The optical drive has become the most common way for software to enter your computer (with the Internet rapidly catching up). With writeability one of the key features of the newest drives, opticals are poised to completely replace floppies in the hearts and minds of PC users. Since these drives have a lot of duties to perform, especially with an extraordinary amount of data, it's amazing that things don't go wrong more often than they do.

I Can't Hear My CD!

The best way for you to check for certain whether your entire PC sound system works (CD-ROM or DVD-ROM, sound card, speakers, headphones, CD player program) is to pop an audio CD into your optical drive and see—or rather, hear—what happens. If nothing does happen, don't panic—this doesn't mean you've wrecked your only copy of "Zamfir: Romance of the Panflute." Check the following:

➤ Is the disc loaded properly? Typically, the label side is up, the clear (nonprinted) side is down. (On some drives the exact opposite is true.)

➤ Is this disc a CD-R or CD-RW containing a homemade burn of sound files ripped from another CD or downloaded from the Internet? If so, whoever burned it might have gone too far and actually broiled the thing. Some older CD-RW mechanisms were really sloppy at their jobs, making it difficult if not impossible for other drives—especially ordinary CD-ROM drives—to read them. Try reinserting the disc or cleaning its surface. Some drives might not be able to read CD-R or CD-RW discs at all; yours may be one of them. Try different discs to see whether this is the problem. Is the disc a standard 74-minute disc, or is it one with extra capacity? If so, your drive might not be able to read it.

➤ Try another CD. Does it work? If so, the problem could be the particular CD you were trying to play. Some CDs play well in some drives; not in others. So if the same CD plays perfectly in your stereo, there still could be a defect on your CD that your optical drive can't avoid noticing.

➤ Make sure your speakers are plugged in and turned on. Also check the volume knob on the speakers if they have one.

➤ If your headphones are plugged into your optical drive (CD-ROM) and you play an MP3 or some other sound file from your hard disk drive, you won't hear the sound through your headphones, although you probably will through your speakers. Try plugging your headphones into the jack on one of your speakers or on the back of your sound card.

➤ Do your headphones include a separate volume control? (So that's what that strange-looking sliding bar does!)

➤ Check whether there's a volume knob on the sound card itself. If there is, it would be in the back of your computer where all your cards' plugs are located. Make sure this master volume knob is set to at least medium volume. Sometimes there's so little space on the back of a sound card that there's no way to mark the knob; so medium would be halfway in between as far as the knob can go and as far as the knob can go back. In Windows, this volume knob is augmented by the Volume Control.

➤ Check the volume control on Windows: Double-click the horn icon on the Status bar; then make sure Mute All *is* not checked under Volume Control. If you're using Windows 98, check the separate volume under CD Audio. Make certain Mute is not checked there; then test the volume slider to see whether you can pick the sound up. If you're using Windows 95, to listen to your CD through the speakers make sure Select is checked under Audio CD. If you want to listen only through your headphones and not through the speakers, turn off the Select option.

➤ Windows 98, Win98 SE, and WinMe are shipped with Microsoft's Windows Media Player, which plays the audio tracks from your CD, movies from your DVD, and streaming media from the Internet. You might not have the CD Player program installed on your Windows 95 system, so there's nothing to respond to your CD when you insert it. Since Microsoft no longer makes available a media-playing program for Windows 95, you should download the Internet's favorite audio player, Winamp, from www.winamp.com. (You'll like it better anyway.)

➤ You might want to check the CD-ROM driver to make sure it is properly installed. (If you have a DVD-ROM, that's no excuse; it still should be able to play your CD.) In Windows, right-click My Computer and select Properties. In the System Properties dialog box, select the Device Manager tab. Do you see a yellow circle with a black exclamation point in the list next to "CDROM?" If you do, something is wrong. Click the + next to "CDROM," and then select the name of the drive. Click Properties. In the Properties dialog box, in the Device Status frame, read Windows' assessment of what's wrong with the drive, and its suggestion for what you can do about it. (If you have a DVD-ROM drive, you'll still find its driver listed in Device Manager under "CDROM.")

➤ I know this has nothing to do with hearing sound, but can you access any files through the CD-ROM? In other words, does a directory for the CD-ROM drive show up in Windows Explorer (the file manager program), containing entries like "Track01.cda?" Try it out with more than one disc. If you can't bring up a directory for three or more discs, the problem is with the drive. You should attempt to reinstall the CD-ROM driver; see Chapter 18, "Adding an Optical Drive," for help.

➤ If you can hear some sort of sound but it is unclear or garbled, some other device might be conflicting with your sound card. See Chapter 23 for help.

➤ If you're having trouble hearing sound from just one of the speakers, check to see whether that speaker is the *slave speaker*—the one that gets its power from the other one that has the power cord plugged into it. There should be a thin cable linking the slave speaker to the master speaker.

➤ If you're getting interference through your speakers, try switching to shorter cables. Long cables, especially with amplified speakers, are particularly susceptible to interference. Try moving the speakers and seeing whether that helps. As a last-ditch effort, try an electronics store; they should carry products that will overcome RF interference.

➤ Is the drive itself making noise? If you have a high-speed drive (32x rotation or more), the reason for the noise might be the disc itself. If the paint on the label side of the disc is uneven, it will spin in the drive like an out-of-balance washing machine. You can't do much about this one, but to see whether that's the problem, try out another disc and see whether the noise goes away.

Check This Out

Don't try to use your home console stereo speakers with your PC. For one, they won't work. The signal coming from your PC's sound card is too weak to power most stereo speakers because your sound card does not have an amplifier. (PC speakers either have little amplifiers in them or they employ a pre-amp to give extra boost to the sound.) Even if they did work, or if you were able to rig an amplifier between the PC and your stereo speakers, unless those speakers are shielded, they might interfere with the performance of your monitor.

If you still have problems, there are two major possible causes, which are less easy to detect and fix. First, there could be a conflict somewhere in Windows, perhaps caused by a bad or improper sound card driver. Chapter 24 addresses this issue. The problem also could be inside your PC: Your optical drive needs a teeny little cable to connect it directly to your sound card. Chapter 18 talks about that little part.

How an Optical Drive Head Gets Dirty

If you know something about the way a CD-ROM—excuse me, I mean *optical drive*—reads data from a disc, you know that it beams a laser at it and judges the resonant frequency of the light bouncing off the surface. So optical drives really don't have heads *per se*.

Therefore, what is an optical drive head cleaner really? Some consumer action groups have been asking this question; and a few of them—perhaps hoping to mask the fact that there really *is* an answer to this question—have gone ahead and threatened legal action to save us all from the threat of deceptive advertising. But there's no deception here at all. The inside of your optical disc drive is just as susceptible to invasion from dust and airborne chemicals as any other open part of your computer. (Your hard disk's read head is entombed in a permanent sarcophagus of steel, which is why it never gets dirty.)

As anyone who's ever had to clean windows (lowercase w) will tell you, dust and dirt have a tendency to obscure the entrance of light from sources such as the sun. So when dust and dirt get into your optical drive, the frequency of light emitted by the laser there can be altered by dust and dirt, making the receptor think it's seeing one kind of data when it isn't.

So what does an optical drive head cleaner do about it? Does it get out and wipe the surface with a damp cheese cloth? What exactly reaches out from the surface of this head-cleaning disc to clean your drive? You'd be surprised to note that something does: *light waves themselves*. Sound like science fiction? It isn't fiction but it is science.

A head-cleaning disc cannot clean all the dust from the inside of the drive; however, it can remove from the laser emitter the dust particles of the size that cause the emitter to register false values, by reflecting light waves whose shapes literally budge particles to one side. This isn't something invented in a laboratory; light and sound waves are strong enough to move dust—even suspend particles in mid-air. The moral of the story is: An optical drive head cleaner is *for real*.

Writable Optical Drives

There are now three types of writable optical drives currently for sale in the open market. The most common is the CD-RW drive, which accepts both CD-R (write once only) and CD-RW (write several times over) discs. Newly released is the DVD-RAM drive, which do accept CD-R and CD-RAM discs, but also the newer DVD-RAM discs with four times the storage capacity. CD-R drives are rapidly disappearing as CD-RW drives are mass produced.

Despite their advertising, and how easy their new drivers are to use, writing data to an optical drive is not at all similar—technically speaking—to writing data to a hard disk drive. In the world of hard disks, it's up to Windows to locate the first available slot of open space to start writing a file. If the slot ends up smaller than the file, Windows looks for the next open slot in the sequence—this is why hard disks are said to become *fragmented* over time.

Optical media is a completely different story. Here, you're writing data originally designed to hold audio tracks; so although you're using discs, there's still a sequential aspect to the whole affair that's not unlike the way you used to write data to a tape backup drive. Just think of an optical disc as a flattened spool, and you'll get the picture.

So the process of writing data to your disc has to appear to the optical drive like the process of writing audio to that disc. For this reason, the drive sets up a software driver that streams data to the writing mechanism—the burner—at pretty much the rate of speed it's expecting. Here is where things can go wrong:

➤ Not all CD-RW drives are created equal. Although the data on a disc burned in your CD-RW drive probably will be read by that same drive quite easily, that same data might not be read well—or at all—in someone else's drive. The same is true for a disc burned in someone else's drive. There's no real way to know for sure whether that will happen until it does. The exception to this is audio tracks. Audio that you burn to a CD-R or CD-RW probably will be read pretty well by any CD-ROM drive, CD-RW drive, or stereo CD player.

➤ You'll know whether your disc burner software is buffering your data at too slow or too fast a rate, if the software reports a buffer underrun error (more likely) or buffer overrun error (less likely). The worst possible result if one of these errors occurs is that the last sector of data written to the disc is lost. In the case of a CD-R, where you can write data only once, your entire disc might be shot. For a CD-RW (rewritable), your data-burning software (for instance, Easy CD Creator) should be able to start over again and burn the entire disc image from the very beginning, so long as your CD-RW disc hasn't been overwritten too many times. How do you reduce

Note

If your CD-burning software allows it, you can do a dry run of the burning process to see if it can and will work, before you do the actual burn. The software will go through the motions of burning your disc, except igniting the actual laser. That way, if you're likely to get an underrun error, you'll know it before any damage is done.

the likelihood of a buffer something-run error? Don't overtax your PC while the burn is in progress. Turn off your screen saver before you start; then leave your PC alone for awhile. Otherwise, if you wish to continue using your PC, don't download any streaming media from the Internet at the same time.

➤ If after writing data to your CD-R or CD-RW disc, you can't seem to get anything to eject the disc—not the button on the front of the drive, not right-clicking on the drive in Explorer and selecting Eject—don't panic! Your disc-burning software is still is running in the background and even though it might not be writing data at the moment, it still thinks the write process is in session so you have to find out some way to close the session. Try exiting your CD burner software first. If it doesn't have a window open on your Windows desktop, check the lower-right corner system tray for an icon representing your CD burner software. You might be able to right-click on this icon and select something such as Eject CD.

Deciphering DVD Spaghetti

Playing a DVD movie is the most data-intensive thing a DVD-ROM drive can do. It has to read the track in such a way that it's in sync with the computer's streaming process, which means mathematically decoding both the video and audio tracks separately, and perhaps any other "simul-tracks" that happen to be encoded simultaneously along with the movie. So if your DVD-ROM drive has trouble reading ordinary data, chances are it will loathe playing movies for you, and vice versa.

When you have a DVD-ROM or DVD-RAM drive, the rules of your PC's setup change a little bit. Specifically, there's an extra card called a *DVD decoder* that picks up both your video and audio output and augments them both, before sending them on to the monitor and speakers, respectively. Here are some things you can do if you encounter trouble:

➤ If you're not receiving a picture, check the status of two cables outside your PC (you don't have to open it up). First, check the cable that links your DVD decoder card to your video card—in one card, out the other, like a telephone operator's old patch cord. Then check your monitor cable, which should be plugged into the other slot on the decoder card; not your video card.

➤ If you're not receiving sound, there are two cables outside your PC to examine: First, look for a thin cable that connects your DVD decoder card to your sound card. Specifically, make sure the end in the sound card is plugged into the slot marked CD or AUX. (No such slot? That could be your problem. You might need a new sound card that's ready to play DVD audio.)

➤ Some DVD player software might be incompatible with the drivers for your video card because there are so many of the former, and so many of the latter.

One way to clear up some conflicts is if you manually reset your screen resolution to 800h × 600v, and your screen refresh rate to 60Hz. These settings might be lower than you use for everyday work—but do you really want to be watching *Crouching Tiger, Hidden Dragon* while you're doing everyday work?

Playing and Working at the Same Time: How It's Done

Perhaps you paid extraordinary attention when the sales fellow at the computer store showed you the DVD movie playing on the same screen as a word processor, without the word processor—or Windows, for that matter—appearing to slow down. There's a reason for that: The DVD video image from the decoder card is not being processed by your PC at all. In fact, the CPU won't even know there's a movie playing; it's entirely in the dark. Your decoder card uses a time-proven video trick to overlay one image on top of another by programming a video processor to mask out everything of a specific color in the first image and replace that mask with pieces of the second image.

For this trick to work on your PC, your DVD movie driver software has to turn off your Windows wallpaper—the computer analogy of opening the curtain and letting the silver screen show through. Then it turns your Windows background color to a distinctively ugly shade of magenta—ugly because it's a color you'd probably never choose for your own background. Your decoder card proceeds to mask out the magenta color wherever it appears but leave everything of a different color, such as your word processor document.

This might create an unavoidable problem: If you're using a graphics program while you're watching a movie, there's a chance that the image you're editing in that program has a pixel or two of magenta in it. Your decoder card will dutifully mask out that pixel and replace it with a piece of the movie; the card really doesn't know or care where your graphics program stops and the Great Magenta Sea begins. It's up to you to decide which region of the screen is to be reserved as your movie screen—just one corner of it, or a big stripe through the middle leaving letterbox regions at the top and bottom, of the type a widescreen movie leaves on a standard TV.

Since the DVD image is separate from the Windows image, you can't just drag the window around and drop it in place like you can every other Windows program; instead, you have to use more confusing driver software that communicates with the decoder card directly. To reprint the instructions to that software here would necessitate a "Volume 2" for this book, which I know you don't really want.

In any event, if you've noticed your DVD player software is interfering with your Windows default desktop setup, now you know why. Your alternative may be to use Windows Media Player or some other software that displays streaming images in its own little corner of the screen. The tradeoff there is that the picture may be grainier or choppier.

105

When Your Modem's on the Fritz

If you're having trouble logging on these days, it's statistically more likely that the modem you're calling is the culprit, rather than your own. Why? Because the modems of Internet service providers run practically all the time, 24 hours per day. Sometimes you just have to have patience; however, after 23 seconds or so when you've run out of that, try some of these tricks to see whether your modem is at fault:

➤ First, dumb questions: If you have an external modem, is it turned on, and is it plugged in? Also, is there a phone line running from the modem to a phone jack?

➤ Have you ever used this particular phone jack before? To test a phone jack, plug a regular phone (not one of those digital read-out things) into it and see if it works.

➤ Can you hear a dial tone followed by the modem dialing? If not, first check your modem settings to see if the internal speaker is active, or if it's perhaps turned down so low that you can't hear it. From the Windows Control Panel, double-click Modems to bring up the Properties dialog box for your modem. Under the General tab, in the Speaker Volume frame, check the setting for the slider representing the volume. If that's not the problem, the computer might be having trouble locating the modem. This usually happens when you select the wrong communications (COM) port. Under the Diagnostics tab, the list should show you which COM port your modem is assigned to. If you don't find your modem there—or, for that matter, any modem whatsoever—that's your problem. Go back to your Control Panel and double-click Add New Hardware to locate and install your modem as though it were brand new.

➤ Does the modem you're calling answer your call? If you're not sure that the number you're trying to use is a valid one, dial it using a regular phone. Be sure that the modem is dialing 9 if necessary to get an outside line from your office. In Windows, when you're connecting to the Internet, having your modem dial 9 is not a modem property; it is a feature of Dial-Up Networking. From Windows Explorer, in the left-hand pane, click Dial-Up Networking (scroll to the bottom of the pane to find it; in Windows Me, you'll find it in the Control Panel). Double-click the connection icon you normally use to connect to the Internet. In the Connect To dialog box, click Dial Properties. Then from the Dialing Properties dialog box, in the field marked "For local calls, dial," type **9**.

Check This Out

If your incoming phone line plugs into the same card as your speakers, you might not be able to hear good sound while online. The solution to this problem in the short term is to wait until you've logged off to play any audio files or CDs. However, in the long term replace this combo card with a new sound card and a new modem.

➤ Do you have call waiting installed? If so, you need to disable it before using your modem, or the modem will disconnect you if another call comes in. The best solution is to have separate phone and modem lines. In the meantime, add *70 in front of the phone number you want to call. Bring up the Dialing Properties dialog box as described previously. Check the box marked "To disable call waiting, dial," then type *70 or 1170 in the field just to the right.

➤ Try unplugging your telephone from the extension plug (marked "Phone") of your modem. Sometimes a faulty phone can cause a feedback that affects the modem.

➤ If only a digital phone works in the jack (such as the ones used by most receptionists), don't try to use that particular phone line for your modem, because it carries extra digital gook that can interfere with modem communications. (Normal phone lines are analog, not digital.)

If you use a network interface card (NIC) to connect to the Internet through broadband—as opposed to the old-fashioned modem—there's really nothing about fine-tuning this device that qualifies as easy; thus nothing that belongs in this particular chapter. I do talk about networking and its many hassles in Chapter 13, "The Online Line." (There's a reason I numbered it 13.) In Chapter 24 I throw in a section that talks about some interesting and useful techniques you can use to administer your own home network. You've always wanted to be a middle manager, haven't you?

What to Do When You're Not Sure What the Problem Is

It's hard to define weird. Computers are strange creatures; even when they're well. If your PC is making strange noises, flipping strange little zigzags across the screen, or generally acting uncooperative, try some of these things:

➤ The first thing to check is the cables. Make sure they are not loose. If you find a guilty party, plug it back in and then get a screwdriver to stick it in place permanently. If two cables are supposed to plug in right next to each other but the engineers didn't leave enough room for both cable ends to coexist, consider a trick the pros use: Attach an extension cable to one of the ends, even if you have enough cable anyway. For some reason, the connectors on extension cables are thinner than the connectors on standard cables. Just make sure you don't get a long extension cable—say over 15 feet or so. Long cables cause their own problems with signal degradation.

➤ Try shutting down your PC, waiting 15–20 seconds, and then turning it back on again. This forces the computer to clear all its gook out of memory (RAM). It's amazing how often this can make the Windows weirdos go away; especially if you usually never turn off the computer.

107

➤ If you're guilty of just flicking the main power switch on your PC instead of following the normal Windows exit procedure (selecting Shut Down from the Start menu), Windows was not able to clear out your temporary files from its Temp folder. Delete them yourself (or as many as Windows will allow) and restart your computer.

➤ If the computer is still acting strange, shut down your PC again, remove all your cables, and inspect the little pins sticking out of either the cable or the connector. Are any of them bent over to one side? If so, you can take a pair of needle-nose pliers and carefully bend the pin back in place. But don't yank—it's only wire; thus very cheap and easily broken.

➤ Are you working at home? If so, do you have a fairly big-screen, color TV, big monitor, or a high-wattage stereo set? If so, don't just turn it off but unplug it. Sometimes high-power receiving equipment generates what geeks who love the alphabet like to call RF interference, which cuts right into the electronic signals going on in your computer's bus. (Sound unlikely? Actually, your PC is more likely to catch RF interference than a computer virus.)

➤ Is your surge protector making noise? If it is, its fuse might be about to burn out. No big deal here; toss your surge protector out and get a new one. You see, enabling fuses to be burned out is exactly what surge protectors are designed to do, before something else burns out your computer. (Uh, you do have at least a surge protector, don't you?) If you have an *uninterruptible power system* (*UPS*)—one big step ahead of a surge protector—that is making noise, shut everything off now, disconnect it, and send it away to either be repaired or entombed. Chapter 19, "Powering Up the Power Supply," discusses UPS systems.

➤ Do you keep anything large and magnetic close to your monitor, like, say, a magnet? You're not using your monitor as a catch-all for old sticky notes clamped together with a magnetic clamp, are you? In any case, put anything the least bit magnetic out of the way of your monitor and system unit.

➤ Try defragging (optimizing) your hard disk. Chapter 7 shows you how. Not only is defragging therapeutic for your hard disk, it's a memory-intensive task. You don't even have to finish it; just watch it for the first five minutes. If the defrag process seems to be running smoothly, Windows probably is not at fault, and neither is your hardware. It could be the applications you're running.

➤ Think about installing one of the infinite patches and service pack updates for the operating system you're running. Updates for versions of Windows extending back to Win95 are, surprisingly, still available from Microsoft's Web site. If you use Windows 98, 98 SE, or WinMe, you have Windows Update installed on your system—a feature that contacts Microsoft's Web site and determines just what patches or upgrades your system needs. Select only those you feel comfortable with; don't just pick everything because it's new.

➤ Try using an antivirus utility to check the hard disk for viruses. A virus is a program that can wreak havoc on your PC, destroying files and rendering your computer useless. A mild virus might only display an annoying message. A virus can get onto your computer through an infected file downloaded from the Internet, or from an e-mail message containing a malicious script. There still are some viruses that spread through diskettes. Don't panic; most computer weirdness has nothing to do with a virus—but you should at least eliminate that possibility. If the utility does find a virus, usually it can remove the bugger with no problems.

When All Else Fails ...

If you try all these things and the PC refuses to act normal, it's time to start taking drastic measures. By "drastic," I'm referring to the kind that involves ... get ready for this ... people other than yourself.

➤ **Document the problem.**   Can you duplicate the problem? Does the weirdness happen when you attempt some particular task or is it a one-time thing? Is the weirdness related to a particular program? If so, try backing up your program's data and reinstalling the program—this usually fixes the problem. If you suspect the setup program for your new application or your new part has made changes to the configuration files that are causing your weirdness, use your emergency diskette to copy the original versions of your files back onto the hard disk and restart the PC. Once you get your PC back, try making the changes to your configuration files one at a time so you can isolate the one that caused the weirdness.

➤ **Check the Internet.**   Manufacturers' Web sites often post *white papers* (technical briefings) and *FAQs* (frequently asked questions) about the products they offer; any computer or parts manufacturer that does not have its own Web site now must already have declared bankruptcy. Sometimes you can post a question to the company's own technical support people without having to dial the phone or put up with Lawrence Welk's Tribute to the Rolling Stones while you're on hold. If the manufacturer's own site isn't good enough, check an independent source for advice, such as PC Guide (www.pcguide.com). If you think the problem's source is Microsoft ... heck, what am I saying? Of course you do! Check out support.microsoft.com. You can make queries of Microsoft's extensive knowledge base (George Orwell would just flip over that one, wouldn't he?) to see whether others have reported the same problems you're having. When you've reached the end of your proverbial rope, go to the Google search engine at www.google.com and query its extensive database of freshly indexed Web sites from around the globe. There's also a site that's working on an ongoing, comprehensive index of things that could go wrong (or right): Check out DUX Computer Digest at www.duxcw.com.

➤ **Call for help.** (Sigh!) I know: You're thinking you just spent all this money for a book that tells you to call for help. Actually, it tells you to do that last, doesn't it? That's because it's absolutely a last resort. Before you make the call, make sure you have that documentation of the problem in front of you.

The Least You Need to Know

➤ The most important thing you can do to avert hardware disaster is to keep your system clean.

➤ When the computer stops doing the thing it was doing, it doesn't always mean the computer's dead. There's a series of measures you can take that could at least save the work you were doing.

➤ The only thing you should ever spray directly onto your keyboard is air: literally, compressed air.

➤ The best time for you to clean your printer is while you're changing its ribbon, ink cartridge, or toner cartridge.

➤ Your monitor is an analog output device and as such is subject to RF interference.

➤ If you're using the (old) cathode ray tube, ordinary use can create magnetic fields within the monitor that make colors seem wrong in patches—generally in the corners.

➤ Degaussing is a process that gets rid of those ugly magnetic fields, and leaves your monitor springtime fresh.

➤ Power management...doesn't—so you might want to disable it so you can get some real work done.

➤ If your optical disc drive doesn't seem to be working correctly—especially if you're using it to play musical CDs—the problem could be with your sound card.

➤ If you're having trouble burning a CD-R or CD-RW disc, there could be some simultaneous processes going on that cause the flow of data to come in too slowly. The result is a buffer underrun error, which could cost you your disc.

Cleaning Windows

If you follow Windows instructions to the letter every day and do only what the manuals from Microsoft and others tell you to do, over time you will notice the overall performance of Windows drag, lag, and simply fall behind the peppy, perky system you fell in love with at the store. Like a house guest who overstays his welcome, Windows begins to neglect its responsibilities to your work environment—especially its duty to clean up after itself. This chapter is all about those things you can do to Windows that could benefit your computer at least as much as—if not more than—a memory upgrade or a new CPU.

Crud Windows Leaves on Your Disk

There are many reasons you might want to take the time to periodically go through your hard disk and get rid of unused files. For one, you gain some hard disk space; two, your hard disk runs more efficiently—not a bad bargain. Here's the principal reason: The more hard disk space you have and the more that space is all in one place (*contiguous,* if you want to sound smart), the faster Windows will perform, and the more system resources Windows will think it has available to it.

You see, Windows sees free hard disk space and free memory space all in one pool. The larger that pool is from the vantage point of Windows, the more space it can readily allocate for parts of programs it needs to use, such as Microsoft Office applications. The smaller that pool is, the more often Windows will need to shut down one program part, or *library,* before it launches another. That swapping of resources in memory consumes valuable time and could give your thumbs calluses from all the twiddling.

Cleaning up your hard disk isn't difficult, but it takes some time, because first you have to identify the files you can get rid of. Here are some obvious places to look:

➤ **Your TEMP directory—** Files copied to your TEMP directory are supposed to be just that, *temporary.* However, if you exit a program improperly, or restart your computer while programs are still running or while you're still connected to the Internet, these temporary files are never deleted. (Windows generally places your TEMP directory as a subdirectory of the \Windows directory, although you can place it anywhere by changing the SET TEMP environment variable setting in your AUTOEXEC.BAT file. (See, Windows still relies on DOS for a few things.) As you're deleting entire batches of temp files (and even temporary directories inside the TEMP directory), Windows probably will resist your attempts to delete one or two files it swears are still in use—even if you just rebooted the system. This resistance will cancel any deletion process you'd already started, so you'll just have to start over again; this time excluding whatever file Windows thinks it still needs.

➤ **Your Internet browser's cache—**When you visit a Web page, its contents are downloaded to your system for display: all of its text, graphics, Java apps, and so on. Several separate files make up the average Web page, all of which are stored by your Web browser in its cache, for quick retrieval the next time you visit that same page. With most modern Web browsers, this cache is periodically monitored, and the oldest files in the cache are frequently cleared. But older Web browsers (by older, I mean weeks and weeks older than the newest edition) do not automatically clear their caches. You can clear the cache yourself if you like and re-acquire some hard disk space. To clear the cache for Internet Explorer, bring up the Control Panel and double-click Internet Options. On the General tab, click the Delete Files button.

➤ **The Recycle Bin**—Normally your deleted files are not really deleted but simply moved to the Recycle Bin. This means you can easily recover any file you've deleted by accident (that is, provided your file was deleted from a hard disk. Files deleted from removable media or the network are no deposit, no return). It also means your unwanted files, like some clingy relative, never go away until you push them out the door (by emptying the Recycle Bin.) To empty the Recycle Bin, right-click it and, from the shortcut menu that appears, select Empty Recycle Bin. You can look over the Recycle Bin's own file list before emptying it by double-clicking the Recycle Bin icon. If you see a file or files you'd rather not permanently delete, choose them from the list; then select **Restore** from the **File** menu. Perhaps you've noticed that Windows no longer provides an undelete utility, such as the one that shipped with Windows 3.1.

➤ **Your root directory of each hard drive**—Some installation programs make a backup copy of your AUTOEXEC.BAT and CONFIG.SYS configuration files before making any changes to them. After you install a program and you've determined that your computer is functioning well, you might want to delete these un-needed backups. These files might end in .BAK, .OLD, .001, .002, and so on. Also be sure to delete any files in your root directory (or directories, if you have more than one hard drive) named FILE0001.CHK, FILE0002.CHK, and so on. Believe me, you do not need them. A program called ScanDisk (which I talk about in Chapter 7, "'Repairing' the Hard Disk Instead of Replacing It") is responsible for creating these files; they actually consist of trash dug up from failed deletion operations and improperly completed file move operations (on the computer's part; not yours). ScanDisk converts this rubbish into files, supposedly in case there's anything inside them you want to save for some reason. Unless you really do know how to use the *disk sector editor* (hands up, all of you who do … I don't see any hands), just go ahead and delete these little aftermaths.

➤ **The My Documents directory**—or wherever fine work documents are stored. Many applications, such as the Microsoft Office suite, give you the option of keeping the next-most-recent version of your current documents as backup files; generally ending with .WBK. When your documents are no longer in the editing stage, and are completely finished, use Windows Explorer to delete the .WBK files because your applications won't perform that job for you.

➤ **The Windows directory**—As part of an ongoing operating system bug that has never been properly corrected, Windows generates temp files (with the .TMP extension) apparently whenever an online application makes a request for an uninstalled program component. These components have rather ugly names, which are transposed into the filenames of these .TMP files ... which never seem to go anywhere, and are never deleted even when you shut down Windows. So you could end up with filenames such as fffd4a27_{DD6E3C10-1ED3-4F43-BCAB-088155245243}.tmp. This is a real example; I didn't just pound my fist on my keyboard. (Never mind what it means.) These .TMP files have a total length of 0 bytes and simply clutter up your C:\Windows directory, as well as Windows' capability to locate legitimate files in that directory. So as you're cleaning up your system, just find them (they all begin with lowercase "f") and delete them.

Check This Out

Windows 98, 98 SE, and Windows Me feature a neat utility called **Disk Cleanup,** which removes many unwanted files simply and easily. You'll find it on the **Programs>Accessories>System Tools** menu.

➤ **The Fonts directory**—The more major applications you install on your system, the more fonts Windows tends to collect. As a result, the number of entries in your C:\Windows\Fonts directory can become enormous—does anyone really need that many typefaces? To make matters worse, certain Web pages you might visit actually can install new fonts into this directory, without your ever being notified. Believe it or not, every new TrueType font installed in Windows slows it down. This is because Windows has only so much memory apportioned for remembering all the fonts' filenames each time it needs to typeset a document. If the total number of characters used by all the font files in the Fonts directory exceeds this maximum amount of memory, the act of typesetting a document can slow down tremendously. So you must delete unused fonts whenever you can.

How can you tell which fonts you'll probably never use for anything? If you double-click one of its filenames, Windows will display a sample sheet. You'll probably be able to spot fonts the system uses frequently; however, if you find one or two that look like glued-on macaroni, or fishing gear rearranged to look like letters, generally it's safe for you to delete them. Select the fonts you want to bump off, open the File menu, and select Delete. When the warning appears, click Yes. Windows zaps the files. If you accidentally delete a font you wanted to keep, put on your best "I'm sorry," face and restore the files from the Recycle Bin. Just open the Recycle Bin, select the font you want back, then open the File menu and select Restore.

Before I take Windows to task too much, let me just point out that you may be just as guilty of leaving files hanging around your hard disk as is Windows. Here are some items you might have left behind that you can clear off right away:

➤ **Downloaded files**—Sure, the Internet is cool and full of really neat things such as graphics, sound files, movies, and all sorts of great stuff. It's easy to fall into the trap of downloading and storing everything you see—if for no other reason, to show it off to your friends. Well, months have passed and you probably don't have further need for the preview trailer for *The Mummy Returns*. Hopefully, you're in the habit of storing the files you download in the same directory, which makes it easier to delete them. Remember, when you download entire Web pages with Internet Explorer, all the graphics and other attachments to the page are stored in a subdirectory with the same name as the page itself. So if you delete the Web page, you might as well delete the directory that goes along with it.

➤ **Old data files**—Sure, you completed that sales report last month and you re-ferred to it every day during the annual budget conference. But you haven't looked at it in months, so it's time to back up that file—and its friends and neighbors from the same project—onto a good CD-R; then remove them from your hard disk.

➤ **Old e-mail**—E-mail messages are saved in folders on your hard disk, and they can quickly accumulate. To save hard disk space and make your e-mail program run more efficiently, delete your old e-mail messages periodically, or at least (to coin a new phrase) "archive your archives." In other words, many e-mail client programs such as Eudora and Outlook Express enable you to compress your older messages so they consume less space on your hard drive, although you still can read them.

➤ **Dusty old programs**—Sure, that tax program helped you out of a jam last April. But do you still need it taking up room on the hard disk now that it's October? If not, consider removing it. Double-click the **Add/Remove Programs** icon in the Control Panel; then select the program you want to remove and click **Add/Remove.** If you don't see your program in the list, try looking for an unin-staller called UNINSTAL.EXE or UNWISE.EXE (really, that's what it's often called) in your program's main directory. If you don't find such a beast there, you can look for a SETUP.EXE in your program's main directory and launch that program as if you were installing that unwanted application all over again; this time checking for an uninstall option from one of the dialog boxes that comes up. You can always cancel Setup if you don't find one.

115

Avoiding Crashes

I hate it when a program crashes. Why does it happen? Basically, Windows gets so confused with all the things it's supposed to be doing that it simply loses track of a program, gives up on it, and blanks out. Or, it might be the program's fault; some programs simply do not know how to behave. What can you do to avoid crashes? Well, you can stop running programs—but that's hardly practical. Instead, why not try some of these tips:

➤ **Restart your computer periodically**—Some people like to keep their computers running pretty much all the time, never shutting down at the end of each day. If you're one of these people, you might want to rethink your game plan and shut down every couple of days or so. This enables Windows to completely clear its memory and reallocate its resources.

➤ **Update your applications when you can**—At least in theory, having the latest and greatest versions of your software should eliminate some bugs. (You might just end up trading one set of problems for another, though.)

➤ **Use two hard disk drives**—Huh? You read correctly. Install your main applications on your C: drive; then keep your personal data on your D: drive. This way, if an application failure, an installation glitch, or (worst case scenario) an operating system failure takes out your C: drive, all your personal data on your D: drive is safe even if you have to reformat C:. This measure does not eliminate the need to back up your personal data; however, as long as you keep the installation discs for your applications and your operating system close at hand, even a drive C: failure should not become a complete disaster for you because reinstallation of these things is simple and a waste of a day or so of your time.

Having all your data on a separate hard disk makes it easy for you to always keep it backed up properly (for example, to a CD-ROM disc). Most PCs sold since 1997 support as many as four IDE devices; thus you should be able to install two hard drives plus your IDE (ATAPI) optical drive, and still have one slot left open. If you use the My Documents folder for your data and use lots of Microsoft programs, which tend to look for the My Documents folder on drive C:, you can easily move it to drive D: using Windows Explorer. Just press Shift as you drag and drop the My Documents folder onto drive D:. Any program that provides a My Documents button on the Places bar of the Open and Save As dialog boxes, will know to look on drive D:—not C:—for the My Documents folder. Thus you can keep your most valuable data on D: and let drive C: crash all it wants to, because all it will contain is reinstallable programs. Talk about insurance for the inevitable rainy day!

Attitude Adjustments

When NASA upgraded its manned space rockets from the Titan II to the Saturn V, the number of potential headaches increased along with the benefits. However, they were able to remedy those headaches; mainly because Microsoft Windows didn't exist in 1966. When Microsoft launched Windows 95 in ... well, 1995 ... fortunately it left Windows 3.1 behind. Users certainly were ready and willing, not because Windows 3.1 was by any means a *dog* (techie slang for any less-than-decent program); rather because Windows 95 promised so much—and delivered quite a bit. However, a fresh set of headaches made some long for the old days ... and by that I mean 1966. Windows Me is a product of Microsoft's long journey toward making Windows 95 work. Still, there are quite a few maintenance measures you should take, no matter what version of Windows you use. The following section covers the most critical of these.

Cleaning Up the Registry

The System Registry is an idea that some notable, good programmers (including my husband) wish could be strapped to the third stage of a Saturn V and sent hurtling toward the moon. The Registry acts as a notebook for Microsoft Windows, remembering key details about your computer and its setup. There you find your desktop preferences, device settings, and software and hardware configurations. You also find data pertinent to applications installed in Windows.

A litany of every data file type, its filename extender, and the programs assigned to manage them, is listed here. The single, all-inclusive list of all the different parts of Windows, and how they should make contact with one another, is another part of this file. So important is the System Registry that if something bad were to happen to it, you might not be able to even start Windows! With a faulty Registry, at best you'd be able to boot your computer into command prompt mode.

One problem with the Registry is that, because it holds so much information about Windows, it tends to get pretty cluttered; especially with old data (such as software you've removed or devices you've upgraded). The Registry is so large it holds an amount of data comparable to the size of some metropolitan telephone directories; because it is referenced by Windows and other programs almost constantly, over time it tends to build up entries that become invalid, or perhaps were never valid to begin with.

To streamline your Windows 95 Registry, use a program called RegClean 4.1a, conveniently provided for you by Microsoft, and downloadable online through www.download.com. Although it was never shipped with the Windows 95 package, RegClean is a breeze to use. You basically just tell it to go, wait while it does its thing, and instruct it to commit the corrections to whatever errors it might have found (it will tell you there are errors even when there are none, which is a bit odd). Then

RegClean backs up the Registry for you, makes its changes, and advises you to reboot Windows. There's nothing more to the program than that and it is indeed a lifesaver. If for some reason RegClean causes an error, you can easily undo the changes made to your Registry by simply double-clicking the undo file that RegClean generated automatically during the cleanup process.

For cleaning up the Windows 98, 98 SE, and Windows Me System Registry you use a program called Windows Registry Checker (SCANREGW.EXE), which does ship along with the operating system. Like its predecessor, Registry Checker will back up the Registry for you as well—which is important, because if an application destroys what once was a perfect Windows setup, you'll want to get your PC back to working like it was. You might not find it on the Start Menu, the reason for which probably has something to do with its extreme usefulness. (A corollary to the old adage, "If it ain't broke, don't fix it," goes, "If you don't show 'em how to fix it, they'll never know it's broke.") Chapter 4, "What You Need to Know *Before* You Open Your PC," shows you how to use the Registry Checker. Note this special feature: If Registry Checker finds no errors, it won't try to repair them.

Streamlining Your Startup

One negative aspect of using Windows is that it takes so long to start. Anything you can do to improve the process is a blessing for sure. Here are some ideas:

➤ **Ignore your startup programs.** You may have many programs in your Startup folder (C:\Windows\Start Menu\Programs\Startup). For example, you might have an electronic day planner, your Web browser, and your word processor all loading automatically. Microsoft Outlook Express (the e-mail client that is part of Windows) and Microsoft Outlook (part of Microsoft Office) both take about a year and a half to load. To prevent all programs in the Startup folder from loading, press **Ctrl** while starting Windows. If you need one of your startup programs later on, you can just start it manually. To permanently disable automatic startup of any or all programs, use Explorer to delete their icons from the Startup folder; these are just shortcut icons, not the actual programs.

➤ **Why waste time restarting your computer when all you really want to do is restart Windows?** Click the **Start** button, select **Log Off** [your username here], then answer **Yes**. This is not a smart way to restart the PC if it's been on for several days. If this is the case, power down the PC; then power it back up. However, it is a great way to restart a system that has one running application that seems to have locked up accidentally.

➤ **Speed up startup.** You can speed up the Windows startup process by removing any boot delay and skipping the Windows logo banner. Here's how: From

Windows Explorer, go into your C:\Windows directory. Double-click COMMAND (COMMAND.COM will also work, but COMMAND is better). You'll see an MS-DOS screen in just a moment. Type the following:

`ATTRIB C:\MSDOS.SYS -S -H -R`

and don't forget to press Enter. Nothing earth shattering should happen. Next, type this:

`EDIT C:\MSDOS.SYS`

In a moment, the old Edit program from DOS will bring up the file MSDOS.SYS, which is located in the root directory. Toward the bottom of the [Options] section, but *before* the first line that starts with a colon (:), add the following line: `BootDelay=0`. To refrain from advertising Windows during startup, get rid of the startup banner by adding the line, `Logo=0`. Then from the File menu, select Exit. (These old DOS programs had menu bars!) When you see the MS-DOS screen again, type this:

`ATTRIB C:\MSDOS.SYS +S +H +R`

and finally, this:

`EXIT`

The screen will go away, and your work is done. Next time you boot your computer, you should not see the Microsoft banner, and startup may be a few seconds faster.

➤ **Bypass Windows logon.** If you're tired of logging on to your PC—especially if you're not networked, and no one else has access to it anyway—set Windows up so you can bypass the logon procedure. Double-click the Passwords icon in the Control Panel. On the User Profiles tab select "All users of this computer use the same preferences and desktop settings." Select the Change Passwords tab; then click the Change Windows Password button. Change the password to nothing. From this point forward, Windows will not be able remember the password to log you onto the Internet. However, if it's not a problem for you to remember it yourself and type it in each time you can disable all passwords in this way.

Keeping Your Programs Installed

When you install a new application, it often claims certain file types as its own. As a result, the program with which you intend to open or edit one of these files no longer comes up when you double-click it in Explorer. Instead you get this new application, which you probably don't want claiming your files behind your back. What's worse, some applications are so greedy that they can reclaim those file types every time they start up; thus they always get dibs on your important data files.

The most common examples of applications that claim file types without your permission involve multimedia (sound, graphics, and animation). For example, say you've installed the CorelDraw package to handle .GIF and .JPG image files. When you install Microsoft Office, it changes the System Registry so that, when you double-click one of these files in Explorer, Windows will bring up Microsoft Photo Editor, or Publisher, or something other than the Corel PhotoPaint program you intended. How do you get things back the way they were?

Generally, tech support from one company or the other will tell you to simply re-install the Corel package. However, that will reset all your preferences for each and every one of the Corel programs, including CorelDRAW and PhotoPaint. So what can you do?

You can't stop Microsoft from taking over file types when you install its programs—the case with image files is simply one example. However, you can set things up so that getting things back the way they were is instantaneous. It involves using a program Microsoft doesn't like you to use, but is part of Windows anyway: REGEDIT.EXE, the Registry Editor. Microsoft tells you that using REGEDIT is dangerous: "Do something wrong and you'll blow up your system, and you'll never be able to use Windows again and the country will go into deep depression and California will fall into the ocean!" Baloney. You use Registry Checker (SCANREGW.EXE) to back up your Registry before you begin surgery; then if you do something wrong, you bring back the backup and you're okay. Of course, without a backup of the Registry, there goes California.

The System Registry keeps tabs on all the things that can happen to a file of a specific type whose filename extender is a certain series of letters (generally three, in honor of DOS). When you right-click a file, the menu shows you what can be done to this file (at least Open; but often Edit; sometimes Print; maybe something specific such as Upload.) This list of actions is provided by the Registry, which keeps tabs on which program is responsible for being able to do these things to this file.

In the Registry is a list of known filename extenders. Each extender is assigned a single named entry that contains a list of all the applications that work on that type of file. The first stage of your mission is to rebuild the association between the file type you need and the program you want. This way, to continue the example, when you double-click on a GIF or JPEG image in Explorer, it opens PhotoPaint and not some other program. To do that, follow these steps:

1. In Windows Explorer (the file manager; not the Web browser), from the Tools menu, select Folder Options.

2. Click the File Types tab. In a moment (if you consider eons moments), Windows will bring up a list of every registered file type. In Windows 95 and Windows 98, this will be a list of recognized type names, not extensions, so you may have to look for the name of the application that claimed your file (when in doubt, look under M for Microsoft). In Windows Me this will be a list of filename extensions in alphanumeric order (digits first).

3. Choose your file type from the list. (Note: There might be as many as three such extensions that point to JPEG images: .JPG, .JPEG, and .JPE. You may need to change each of these associations separately in this case.)

4. If you use Windows 95, 95 OSR2, Windows 98, or 98 SE, click Edit. You'll see the Edit File Type dialog box. In the list marked Actions, choose Open (it should be at the top), then click Edit. (Fun so far?) In the next dialog box that pops up, click Browse. Using the file selector that pops up, locate the filename of the application with which you want your file to open (you'll probably find it in the Program Files folder), then click OK. Then click OK. Then click OK. Then click OK. (That's four OKs. Got them all?)

   If you use Windows Me you'll have an easier time of this: Click Change. You'll see a list of titles of installed applications in alphabetical order—not filenames; titles such as "Corel PhotoPaint." Choose the title of the application with which you want your file to open; then click OK. Then click OK just once more. (Just two OKs here.)

At this point Windows should recognize the application you want as being associated with the file you use. However, this state of affairs might not last for very long. What you want is a way to reclaim your file associations when the wrong program claims them. You can't stop new applications from claiming your files, but you can set things up so you can automatically undo the damage they cause. Here's what you do next:

1. Make sure your image files, HTML files, or .TXT (text) files bring up precisely the selections you want when you right-click one of them in Explorer. If not, follow the steps given earlier to fix your file associations.

2. Back up your registry. For Windows 95, run RegEdit 4.1a, let it make the error corrections, and say Yes to the backup. For Windows 98, 98 SE, and Me, using Windows Explorer, bring up your \Windows folder; then double-click SCANREGW.EXE. Say Yes to the backup question.

3. From the same \Windows folder, double-click REGEDIT.EXE. (This program's so useful you might want to add it to your Start menu or make a shortcut to it later.)

4. The Registry Editor runs a bit like Explorer. Click the + sign beside HKEY_CLASSES_ROOT. The list you see drop down contains, right at the very top, all the known filename extensions.

5. Find your filename extension in the list and click it once. In the pane on the right side, at the very top, is an entry marked (Default).

6. Take note of the entry beside (Default), and scroll down the list until you find precisely this entry.

7. Right-click this entry in the left pane; from the pop-up menu, select Rename.

121

8. Type a new name. Make up one. (Perhaps a sensible one, such as renaming a jpg file to MyJPEG, or add your initials as in JPEG_JLF.) Just avoid using spaces because they tend to cause problems. Pick a name you'll remember; then remember the name you picked.

9. Now go back up the list to your filename extension and click it once.

10. Right-click (Default) and select Modify.

11. Type the name you made up and click OK.

12. Now, here's the neatest trick of all: While you're still in the Registry Editor, scroll up the list on the left and choose the filename extension you located in step 5.

13. What you're going to do is create a file in a safe directory that nobody but you can touch. Whenever an application reclaims the association for your file type, you can double-click on the icon for this file, and Windows will automatically restore the association you just built in Registry Editor. So from the Registry menu, select Export Registry File.

14. Find (or create) a directory where this reclaiming file will be stored. Also, under Export range, make sure the option for Selected branch is set.

15. Under File name, type the association name you made up in step 8.

16. Click Save. This file will be saved to your directory with the .REG extension; its icon will appear in Windows Explorer like a pile of blue, stacked blocks.

17. Close the Registry Editor.

Is that it? That's it. But what did you accomplish? You made a Registry entry that no future installation can come in and mess up. It can substitute your setup so that .JPG points to jpgfile again rather than the category that you renamed. However, nothing can delete that new category because it would have to know its name to delete it—and only you know its name, because you made it up yourself. All you have to do is go back to your safe directory and double-click the .REG file you made. This file will change the association for your file from the one your new application created to the one you created for yourself in Registry Editor. There. You're done. A new application you've installed might try to undo your customizations to Windows, and it might think it's succeeded—but now you have a backup plan.

The Least You Need to Know

➤ As often as possible, delete all the unused TEMP files that Windows and its many applications leave parked all over your hard drive.

➤ Whatever Windows version you use, you can speed things up by using your Startup group wisely. In addition, delete any fonts that you never use to add a little extra speed.

➤ You should back up your System Registry just like you back up the rest of your data.

➤ Clean up the Registry periodically to remove any unneeded entries and reduce its size.

➤ Remove duplicate DLL files when possible. Multiple installed programs have a tendency to add the same resource files all over your system, cluttering up your hard drive.

➤ You can create categories of your very own in the Windows System Registry that help prevent newly installed applications from seizing control of common file types, such as .DOC or .TXT or .MP3.

Chapter 7

"Repairing" the Hard Disk Instead of Replacing It

In This Chapter

➤ What to do when your hard disk doesn't respond

➤ Spring cleaning your files

➤ Reorganize your files with DEFRAG

I'm not really much of a mechanic, but given enough time, I can usually take something apart and put it back together with only a few miscellaneous parts left over. In my spare time ... okay, I don't *have* spare time, but while I'm talking on the telephone to someone who thinks he's important (which generally means he's trying to sell me long distance service), I usually take some of those miscellaneous parts and build something new with it. I've got something in the works now that's either a vacuum cleaner or a drink dispenser; I'm just trying to get the *feel* of where it's going. I'm ascertaining its mood. What does it *want* to be? Does it have a place in my life, a role it can fill? And most importantly, which demographic responds best to it—hopefully males, ages 18–35, because if you watch any TV, you'll notice that in the minds of network executives and advertisers, that's all there are now, males 18–35. The women are all gone. Besides myself, of course. What was I talking about?

Oh, yeah, repairing computers. One of the things I've learned by way of tinkering around with Windows for 17 years now (and, in turn, being tinkered with by it) is that, in my spare time, I can avoid *real* repairs to my hard disk, using Windows to make "virtual" repairs to it. In this chapter, you learn how to deal with a malfunctioning hard disk (short of replacing it, that is), and tricks you can perform to keep your hard disk running well.

What to Do When Your Hard Disk Plays Hide and Seek

If your PC won't start normally but it starts when you use your emergency diskette, something is probably wrong with the hard disk. Try investigating these possibilities:

➤ **Did you (or some new program you tried to install) make changes to the configuration files, CONFIG.SYS, or AUTOEXEC.BAT, recently?** You may remember these two pesky little buggers as the configuration files from MS-DOS that are still used by Windows, if only as vestigial remnants. You'll probably know if some program made changes to these files because typically it will tell you so before it starts, although boorish programs make changes without your permission. If you suspect that you (or some installation program) changed the contents of your configuration files, copy them back to drive C: from your emergency diskette and restart the computer.

➤ **Did you or anyone else make changes to your \Windows\System subdirectory?** You see, you might not even have a CONFIG.SYS or AUTOEXEC.BAT file in the root directory of your main hard disk because Windows no longer requires them. However, Windows does use device driver files—for the most part Windows simply tries to select those drivers for itself. In this case, the drivers that Windows expects to see often are kept in the \Windows\System subdirectory; and accidentally deleting one of these files from that directory is as potentially dangerous as deleting a driver file that CONFIG.SYS would have needed in the old system. To see whether you have a missing driver, go into your Control Panel and pull up System. In the dialog box click the **Device Manager** tab and look for any listing whose icon contains a yellow and black exclamation point. If you see one, something has been reported wrong with that device, such as a missing driver. See Chapter 24, "Getting Windows to Recognize Your New Toys," for more info on drivers.

➤ **Your CMOS might be damaged or simply forgetful.** CMOS is a chip inside your PC that stores important information such as how large your hard disk is. If you've recently changed your computer's battery or if you've added some other major part, such as a new floppy disk or more RAM, you might need to update the CMOS info because it might be lost or otherwise incorrect. See Chapter 23, "Making Your Computer Boot Up Again," for help.

➤ **Think back. Has your hard drive given you trouble during the past few months?** Has it had trouble reading files or saving them? If so, you might have a real problem. To figure out what might be wrong, use a diagnostics program. Today, over-the-counter utilities packages don't go far enough in telling you what might be the matter with your hard drive. Your best bet is to find out what brand of hard disk you own (look in Device Manager under System in your Control Panel, if you don't know); then go to the manufacturer's Web site and download the utility program specifically suited to your brand. For example, Maxtor publishes a utility program called POWERMAX that covers all models of Maxtor drives and is available for free download from Maxtor's corporate Web site.

Your best insurance against disaster is a backup of your important data files. See Chapter 4, "What You Need to Know *Before* You Open Your PC," for how-to's.

Checking the Hard Disk for Problems

The format used to store, arrange, and maintain files in Windows is based on the original File Allocation Table (FAT) system designed for MS-DOS. When a file is deleted under the FAT system, the operating system does a mighty sloppy job of it, leaving bits of old, deleted half-files lying around. If you want to know why the FAT system is so sloppy, read the following note. Anyway, these little unused bits of old files that were never actually deleted are called *lost clusters* or *lost chains*. There are several utility programs that come with Windows to help you get rid of these old files and free up otherwise unused disk space.

Check This Out

When you delete a file the File Allocation Table file system doesn't really delete it; instead it erases the reference to that file and marks the spaces it used to occupy as available. The next time you save a file to disk, FAT might place it in one of these available spots, overwriting the deleted file and reclaiming the space for use. Sometimes FAT erases the reference to the file but forgets to mark all the spaces that the file was using as available, resulting in little parts of old file spaces not being reused because FAT goofed. These **lost clusters,** or **lost chains** also can result when the power is turned off while the computer is trying to save something to the hard disk.

If you use Windows 95, Windows 95 OSR2, or the first edition of Windows 98, you actually have two versions of ScanDisk: one that runs in the Windows environment;

one that runs outside of Windows from a DOS prompt. This second version automatically runs itself at startup after your system has crashed or you've exited Windows by turning the system off.

The DOS version of ScanDisk is pretty much the same as the one that shipped with MS-DOS 6.22, with some minor cosmetic differences in the Windows 95 version, a few more in Windows 95 OSR2, and still more in Windows 98. Functionally, they're all alike; although the DOS versions are graphically challenged (not like you need 3D animation with a hard drive utility, do you?), they give you the same choices as the Windows version, with perhaps a different order on screen.

If you don't use Windows Me—which eliminated the DOS version of ScanDisk in an ongoing effort to sweep DOS under the rug—you actually might prefer running the DOS version. For one, it's faster. However, it does have a problem with very long filenames. Because now you can write filenames and directory names with practically any number of letters and symbols, the combined pathname plus filename of any given file can easily extend beyond DOS's old 66-character limit.

The DOS ScanDisk uses the eight-dot-three version of any filename it sees; so the file "My Organizational Files.xls" shows up as MYORGA~1.XLS. That helps matters somewhat. However, even Microsoft Office can install its own files in subdirectory upon subdirectory upon subdirectory, until it gets so buried that the DOS ScanDisk can't make heads or tails of it. It tells you this but treats this as a problem it seeks your permission to correct; tell it No. Have it leave these files alone. The trouble is this seeking of your permission suspends the ScanDisk process; if you were planning to set ScanDisk about its work and come back later, think again. Plant yourself firmly in your chair and begin reading your favorite telephone directory, waiting for problems to crop up.

Note

If your Windows 95 or Windows 98 computer ever does crash or if you hit the reset button before formally shutting down your computer, when your computer powers on again by default it automatically runs the DOS version of ScanDisk in an automated mode. (However, your Windows Me computer runs the Windows-based ScanDisk instead.) If you do absolutely nothing, ScanDisk checks all your hard disks for errors (except for the surface scan part); if you don't respond to any of the prompts, ScanDisk assumes you consent to it fixing any problems it finds, even if those problems are unrelated to the reason your computer crashed in the first place.

The Windows-based version of ScanDisk does not have this problem. Before you run ScanDisk, you should cease any disk-intensive activity you might be running, such as downloading a file or playing a game. You might be able to use your spreadsheet or word processor, as long as you don't save files to disk every minute or so. ScanDisk prefers your hard disk to hold still during its testing. If some process saves data to the disk too frequently, ScanDisk will give up its scan and start over from the beginning.

To run ScanDisk, do the following:

1. Click the Start button, select Programs, select Accessories, select System Tools, and then select ScanDisk.

2. Under Type of test, click Standard. Your other option, Thorough, actually tests the surface media of the hard disk itself, and that's a bit much for today, thank you (you might want to run the test some other time, though).

3. Check the box marked Automatically fix errors, then click Start.

4. ScanDisk does its thing, cleaning up after little lost clusters. When it's done, it proudly displays the results. Click Close.

Reorganizing the Hard Disk

The File Allocation Table in use on every Windows system today is based on the 1984 MS-DOS methodology originally designed for storing files no larger than 100 K on a 5 MB "Winchester" drive. Both FAT16 and FAT32 are pretty sloppy about organizing files on the hard disk. When you (or some program you're running) tell the operating system to save or copy a file to the hard disk, it begins saving the file at the first un-used portion of the disk it finds. Often the OS finds out in mid-save that the unused portion is smaller than the file it's trying to save. So it breaks that file into tiny, bite-size pieces, which it then scatters all over the hard disk in whatever spots seem the most convenient. The more often the OS has to delete one of these multipart files, the more small parcels there are on the drive waiting to break up the next big file that comes around.

As time goes on, although it might appear that you have several megabytes of free space, suddenly you can't save a 150K file because your hard disk space is *noncontiguous*—it's in too many tiny pieces. So if you've been noticing that it seems to take a long time (in PC time, more than a couple of seconds) for your PC to open documents for you, you can speed things up a bit by reorganizing the hard disk. In any case you should probably defragment your hard disk once a month if you use your PC every day. To start the defragmentation process, just click the Start menu and choose Programs. Select **Accessories;** then select **System Tools.** Choose **Disk Defragmenter.**

Select the drive you want to defragment; then click **OK.** The Defragmenter will start immediately, so be ready. It takes a look at your hard disk and gives you a recommen-dation for the best way to reorganize it. If it says that your hard disk is pretty well organized, just click **Exit** to forget the whole thing. If it says you need to organize things, get on with it by clicking **Start.**

Unlike ScanDisk, the Disk Defragmenter program takes a very long time to do its thing, and it is extremely sensitive to being bothered. If you leave your computer unattended and your screen saver comes on after five minutes or so, the Defragmenter will stop its current process and start over from block one. It probably will continue to do so if your screen saver animation happens to be a fairly graphics-intensive process.

Defragmenting used to be a pretty fast process until hard disk drives became gargantuan in size. With the heavy workload the Defragmenter has to perform, it isn't unusual for the program to consume more than an entire day in the process. (My husband reports setting his hard drives to defragment over the weekend; then coming back on Monday morning to find the job only 30 percent completed.) If you want to pause the Disk Defragmenter while it's running, just click the **Pause** button.

It actually might be impossible for your system—the way it's set up now—to complete a defragmentation process in its entirety, uninterrupted. However, you can give it your best shot; first by closing down your e-mail client, Web browser, and any other applications you happen to be running. If you're on the Internet through a modem, log off; then disengage your antivirus program. Normally I'd never advise anyone to do this; however, antivirus programs tend to diligently and dutifully look over any data that has been moved on your hard drive—once they do that, it ticks off Defragmenter and makes it start over. Next, turn off your screen saver and set your Power Management options in the Control Panel to turn off absolutely nothing after any length of time—especially your hard disks, which of course will need to stay powered.

Theoretically, you can keep on working while Disk Defragmenter does its thing. Theoretically, you can also play basketball in an arena that's in the midst of being demolished, as long as you wear a hard hat, as long as the explosives specialists know where you are at all times, and as long as you don't overshoot the basket and hit the little black box with the plunger on it. It just doesn't make sense to work with a hard disk that is in the midst of being defragmented. Do yourself a favor and save this process for overnight or over the weekend. When it's done (hopefully within your lifetime), you see a message telling you basically that defragmentation is complete. If you want to defragment another hard disk, click **No;** otherwise, just click **Yes.** That's it.

Converting from FAT16 to FAT32

If your hard drive is larger than 2GB in capacity and it has only one partition (in other words, it's addressable with just one letter, such as C), it probably uses the FAT32 file management system right now. If not, you can convert any IDE hard disk to FAT32 and save both space and time.

If you installed Windows 95 OSR2 or a newer Windows OS, on a hard disk formatted with a previous edition of Windows or MS-DOS, the hard disk format was not automatically converted. You can convert your hard disk to FAT32 any time you want ... by reformatting it. However, you can convert it from the old FAT (FAT16) to FAT32 when you install Win98 SE or WinMe and still keep your files, as long as your disk isn't full or nearly full. Keep these things in mind if you decide you want to convert to FAT32:

Check This Out

If you're not sure whether your system uses FAT32, right-click the drive within Explorer and choose **Properties.** Look under File System.

➤ FAT32 and disk compression utilities (such as Microsoft's old DriveSpace) do not mix. However, because FAT32 supports such large hard disks, you shouldn't really need disk compression.

➤ Once you convert from Win95 to Win98 or WinMe and convert to FAT32 in the process, you won't be able to uninstall and go back to the way things were. However, this shouldn't affect your ability to run your old programs or to read your old files, because they'll be converted to your new FAT32 format intact, and in their entirety.

➤ Some older disk utilities made for DOS and Windows 95, such as sector editors (Norton Disk Editor), file undeleters, and data removal programs, won't work with FAT32.

With Windows 98 and 98 SE, you can convert your hard disk from FAT16 to FAT32 any time you're ready. Just click the **Start** button, select **Programs**, select **Accessories**, and select **System Tools;** then select **Drive Converter (FAT32)** and follow the steps. If you're using Windows Me, guess what: You have FAT32. WinMe doesn't work with the older format.

Make sure you do a complete backup before you start the conversion process. If you use an image backup program (which replicates your entire hard drive rather than just its files) and your system is converted, you won't be able to use the backup. If you back up to CD-R, tape, Zip disk, or other large media, you will be able to restore any or all of your files if necessary after you've successfully converted your drive's format.

The Least You Need to Know

➤ Clean off old files periodically to make more room on the hard disk for new stuff.

➤ Because your operating system splits files into bits and places them on the hard disk willy-nilly, occasionally you need to get them back in order so your computer can run faster.

➤ Making certain all your files are easily accessible and properly organized, is the job of ScanDisk.

➤ You can reorganize the files on your hard disk with the Disk Defragmenter.

➤ If you run Windows 95 OSR2 or newer, you have the option of reformatting your FAT16 hard drive for the FAT32 file system. However, once you do, you cross an important technological barrier without prospects of return.

Third Quarter

Taking Everything Apart

In the Third Quarter, I'll lead you through the scary process of checking out what lurks below your PC's cover. I'll start out slow, with the easiest upgrades to try (replacing your keyboard, mouse, and printer), then we'll quickly gain momentum. The pain will be worth it, though, because I'll show you how to rev up your PC with a new CPU, a brand new motherboard, a powered-up power supply, a bigger hard disk, more memory, better video, another floppy drive, a new network connection, a new optical disc drive, a removable storage drive, a recordable archive drive, a great sound system, a fast fax modem, and even one of those newfangled cable modems.

You'll appreciate the fact that this quarter begins with the simplest stuff first. You don't have to take your computer apart very much (just a little bit) to replace your keyboard, mouse, printer, or monitor. It's generally no more than a couple of plugs and perhaps one or two Windows headaches. (Aren't you glad I don't sugar-coat anything?) From here—as astronaut Jim Lovell used to warn his crewmates just prior to first-stage separation—the ride gets a little bumpy.

Chapter 8

The Easiest Things to Upgrade

In This Chapter

➤ How to replace a dead keyboard

➤ Replacing or adding a mouse

➤ Installing your new printer

➤ How hard can it be to plug in your monitor?

➤ The different connections between your scanner and your PC

➤ Whether your digital camera is a "device"

There's a common theme in all the components covered in this chapter: USB. Every single category has new models that use the new Universal Serial Bus rather than the ports originally dedicated or assigned to them. This changes the computing picture significantly.

The original goal of USB is to enable every peripheral you own to use the same type of plug. It should be up to the computer, say USB proponents, to determine the identity of the new device you've just plugged in. Often your computer can make that determination; however, because usually it's Windows that decides what happens from there, and Microsoft is not one of the USB proponents (at the time of this writing, it announced its future support for a competing standard from Apple called FireWire), component manufacturers have discovered they need to specialize the setup procedures and routines for their peripherals after all.

Thus for almost everything you own that uses USB, there's a point in the setup procedure that I call the "No, wait—that's not right" part. I promise you'll be able to spot it in each of the following segments.

Replacing Your Keyboard

The truth is PC keyboards today are no big deal. They get sticky keys, have their springs or connections worn out too soon, or have a bad run-in with something as benign as a Pepsi. If your keyboard's showing these symptoms or something even worse, it's probably time to replace it. Lucky for you, replacing a keyboard is a simple and relatively inexpensive thing to do. The classic corded models range in price from $3–$40, with most keyboards averaging $20. Cordless models average about $80.

Before you replace your keyboard you might want to see whether your problem can be solved with a simple cleaning, or some other easy trick. See Chapter 5, "Fixing the Most Common Problems," for how-to's.

Shopping for a New Keyboard

Once you decide to replace your old keyboard, you'll have to make quite a few choices. For the most part, your choice of keyboard is one of personal preference; this section describes your various options.

Make Sure You Buy the Right Connector Type

The conventional keyboard plug on most modern systems is soldered directly to the motherboard—and there's only one. However, it can be one of two types: the larger, "AT" five-pin DIN connector, or the smaller, "PS/2" six-pin DIN connector (see Figure 8.1).

There's not a lot of difference between these two connectors except their size. In fact, you can use an adapter to convert one type of connector to the other; that is, if you can find someone who carries the adapter. Many newer keyboards that use the smaller connector have newer functions that won't translate if you attach the adapter for the larger connector. In most cases you're better off getting a keyboard with the right kind of connector for your PC; many keyboard plugs now come with both in a little chain.

One alternative is the USB keyboard, which is a keyboard with a cord that attaches to the USB port on the back of your computer (if you have one), or to your USB hub. You may be asking, why would you want a USB keyboard? Although USB communication is quite a lot faster than the link between your keyboard and your BIOS (as much as 60 times faster), that probably won't improve your typing speed or even the speed at which Windows processes incoming data from your keyboard. Additionally, major manufacturers of conventional keyboards can charge up to $30 more for their USB models. So why bother?

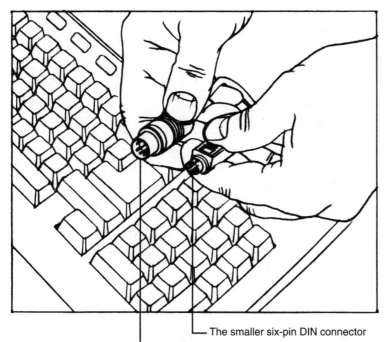

Figure 8.1

The right connections.

└─ The smaller six-pin DIN connector

The larger five-pin DIN connector

USB devices can be daisy-chained, so a good USB keyboard should have one or two extra USB ports right along the side. If you have a digital camera that uses USB, you can plug it into your keyboard rather than the back of the computer whenever you need to transfer photos to your hard disk. Also, if you search carefully you can find USB keyboards that are no more expensive than conventional models. Check out the exclusive online reseller www.ecmore.com for models imported directly from the East that sell for as little as eight bucks.

If you choose to purchase a so-called "wireless keyboard," one thing that comes with it is an infrared receiver unit (see Chapter 5 for the headaches this thing can cause). It can either connect to the same outlet your conventional keyboard would plug into (so it isn't a wireless device entirely), or it might plug into your USB port or USB hub. (See Chapter 12, "Face the Interface," for a description of this little beast.) If it uses USB, something still may have to plug into your keyboard outlet for your computer to boot. You see, if your BIOS doesn't recognize something plugged into your keyboard connector at startup … it might not, um, start up.

Keyboard Layouts

The most common keyboard layout today is the *Enhanced 101-key* keyboard (see Figure 8.2). IBM's original take on this layout was to use a rectangular Enter key, with the backslash key just above. Revisions to this design that became more common restored the backward L shape of the Enter key and shortened Backspace to make room for the backslash key, which scoots in next to +/=.

137

Figure 8.2

The Enhanced 101-key keyboard layout.

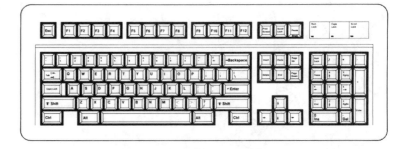

A popular version of the Enhanced keyboard is the *ergonomic* keyboard (see Figure 8.3), whose name is taken from the Latin for "angled Belgian waffle." The premise of ergonomic keyboards is that they are supposed to be gentle on your hands; *ergo,* it reduces the stress normally placed on the hands when they try to twist themselves into position to type on a regular keyboard. The design enables your wrists to stay level with the floor as you type, thereby avoiding repetitive stress injuries such as carpal tunnel syndrome.

Figure 8.3

Microsoft's "Natural Keyboard."

Ergonomic keyboards divide the keys into two sets, pushed apart at the center and angled outward to fit the natural twist of your wrists. Some models enable you to adjust the degree of this space. The better models (including Microsoft's version) position each key at the medically prescribed incline for each finger and at the proper angle for your wrist. In addition, you might find the spacebar hacked in two, giving you one spacebar for each set of keys. Don't fall for a cheap keyboard that calls itself ergonomic but looks like an old IBM XT keyboard hacked in two by a chain saw. Make sure the design fits the way you work by typing on it before you buy it.

Keyboard Features to Look For

Here's a checklist of what to look for when buying a new keyboard:

➤ Many new keyboards have a power button that switches your computer on and off, and a *standby button,* which can switch it into low-power mode. If you've ever used a Mac for any length of time, you might have grown envious of that system's prominent power button on its keyboard—exactly the right spot. For

138

these buttons to work on a PC (specifically, what manufacturers now call "x86" computers), it needs to follow one of the new, so-called ATX form factors and have an ATX power supply—the only kind that can accept an order to switch off or power down from the operating system. Check out Chapter 19, "Powering Up the Power Supply," for details about ATX.

➤ You might like a feature found in many so-called "Windows keyboards": the *Windows key.* This key is marked with the Windows logo; typically you find it hiding next to the Ctrl and Alt keys. When you press the Windows key, the Start menu appears, making it easier for you to start a new program or perform some Start menu task without taking your lovely hands off the keyboard. You might find a second addition called the *menu key,* which mimics the function of your right mouse button. However, because you use the mouse to point at things anyway and all Windows mice have at least two buttons, I don't find myself using the menu key nearly as often as the Windows key.

➤ While we're on the subject of keys ... how many keys would you like? Higher-priced keyboards now come with separate banks of keys, some of which are programmable; others launch your browser and take you to Web sites (see Chapter 5 for all the breathtaking details about that glorious experience). Extra buttons are for those people who don't like mouse pointers but enjoy tinkering with developing their own alternate control schemes for programs. If you're one of those eleven people, you should enjoy a keyboard with 15 or so extra keys.

➤ Test out your keyboard by typing a long passage and making sure you like the way the keys feel, even if you're in a store where the keyboard's not plugged into a display unit. If a keyboard can survive more than two years of my husband's typing style, which resembles a cross between Van Cliburn and a Roto-Tiller, hey, that's good enough for me.

➤ Check out the size of the Enter key, keeping in mind that a larger Enter key causes the backslash key to turn up in odd places. (You'll use the backslash to separate subdirectory names, as in C:\Windows\System.) In addition, look at the position of the Ctrl, Alt, and Esc keys to see whether they are located in the places in which you're used to finding them.

➤ Consider an ergonomic keyboard if you type a lot, or if your wrists hurt. I learned to like Microsoft's Natural (ergonomic) keyboard once I finally got over the feeling of typing on an overinflated balloon. My chronic wrist-ache also went away after I got one—very important for me, the writer, who spends way too much time typing all day.

➤ You might want to see if your keyboard supports *mapping,* which enables the keyboard to mix up the designations for certain keys (for instance, moving the "`" to where the "\" normally is). If it does, make sure the key that maps the other keys is located in a hard-to-bump-when-you-don't-really-want-to-mess-up-your-keyboard kind of place.

139

A wrist rest is a soft pad that sits in front of the keyboard on which you can rest your wrists (say that three times fast). If you're concerned about carpal tunnel syndrome, make sure your new ergonomic keyboard comes with a wrist rest (one model of Microsoft's Natural keyboard does), or buy one to go with the keyboard you choose.

Replacing the Conventional Keyboard

After you've purchased your keyboard, it's easy to connect it (see Figure 8.4). Start by exiting all programs and turning your PC off. You should never plug or unplug anything from your PC while it's on, regardless of what you hear about Plug-and-Play. Disconnect your old keyboard. Put that old thing in a box labeled "Garage Sale." Now connect the new keyboard. Don't worry; the plug fits only one way, with the little dent on the top of the connector facing up. If you accidentally bought a keyboard with the wrong connector, you can either exchange it or buy a converter.

Figure 8.4

Connecting a new keyboard is easy.

Turn the PC back on. The computer should wake up and search for the keyboard. If something's wrong, you'll see an error message; otherwise, you're home free.

If you're installing a USB keyboard or any keyboard that happens to have a USB connection, you may encounter a few problems. Most of the PCs in the world still look for a conventional keyboard before they'll even start up. So if your keyboard is installed in the USB port instead, what happens?

Newer PCs whose motherboards are equipped with chipsets that support the USB 1.1 standard can successfully negotiate the proper location of their keyboards. However, older PCs still might not start. Microsoft's USB keyboard has two plugs on the end of its cord: one is for USB; the other plugs into the conventional PS/2 port. (You'd need an adapter to plug it into the older 5-pin DIN port.)

You would need to connect both plugs into the back of your computer; even then, Microsoft acknowledges, your computer still may refuse to boot. If it does, one enterprising user reported on the Web that she managed to get her computer to boot by simultaneously plugging her old keyboard into the old slot and her new keyboard in the USB port. When Windows started up, its drivers recognized the USB keyboard and disabled the old one automatically. This might be a drastic solution; it certainly is an awkward one. The problem with USB keyboard installation lingers at the time of this writing; even the official USB manufacturers' consortium at www.usb.org hasn't agreed on a single approach to solving it.

Installing a Cordless Keyboard

What truly distinguishes a cordless keyboard from one with a cord is the location of the cordless one's cord. Although it still plugs into your 5-pin or 6-pin port, it leads to an infrared receiving device that needs to be placed in a convenient, open location. It's an infrared device—like the remote control on your TV—so it requires an unobstructed path between itself and your keyboard. Additionally, the receiver and keyboard need to be *synchronized*, which is an easy process but one you may need to perform frequently. Chapter 5 has a section on keyboard problems and their solutions, which deals with the synchronization process.

Mistakes to Avoid

It may surprise you to know that your keyboard is one of the few devices that Windows has almost no direct control over. So while you can change such factors as repeat rate through a Windows Control Panel, if your keyboard appears to be malfunctioning, Windows cannot help you much. So if you get an error message when you try out your new keyboard, try the following:

➤ Turn the PC off and check the cable again. Especially with the larger connector, it's easy to conclude the plug is all the way in the socket when it really has ⅛ inch or so to go. Turn the PC back on; if that doesn't help …

141

➤ You accidentally might have bent one of the pins in the connector when you plugged it in. If so, use a pair of needle-nose pliers to bend it back gently; then try the keyboard again.

➤ Are you using an adapter or an extension cable to lengthen your cord? Keyboard adapters often are screwy and the electrical signals from many keyboards are so faint that they degrade over the distance of an extension cord.

If neither of these tricks coaxes your new keyboard into working, you may want to return it. If the new one has the same problem, take your PC in for a checkup; there may be something wrong with the motherboard's chipset.

Replacing the Mouse

The mouse has become as much a part of our everyday computing experience as program crashes, premature version upgrades, and the Blue Screen of Death. Your hands spend a lot of time operating the mouse. Imagine how worn out someone would be if they had to shake your hand for three hours a day; maybe you'll gain an appreciation for how worn-out your mouse can become after only a few months.

Choosing a Brand and Model

Even though you now know the type of mouse connector you need to shop for, you still face a truckload of choices. Mice (hereafter pluralized as "mouse devices," in order to avoid giving you shivers like some contestant on "Fear Factor") come in all shapes and colors; they even come in lefty and righty varieties. Before you become overwhelmed by all the special mouse features, remember that one of the most important factors is how the mouse feels. If possible, try out your new mouse before you buy it and see if it fits comfortably in your hand. Also check its weight. Some of the cheaper brands are just that—cheaply made, lightweight, and flimsy.

A new mouse costs $7–$60, depending on how picky you are. Once a market as dominated by Microsoft and Logitech as the cola market is by Pepsi and Coke, suddenly there are major brand names getting back into the game—familiar names from the 1980s such as Kensington, 3M, Intel, and Belkin.

A corded mouse may plug into any of the following ports: 9-pin serial, 25-pin serial, PS/2 (6-pin DIN), or USB. (Even a cordless mouse may have a connector. Huh? You'll find out why shortly.) Look at your old mouse and get the same type of connector for your new mouse. If you're adding a mouse to your system, make sure you get one that fits an open connector.

Note

While shopping for a new mouse, you might also want to invest in a new mouse pad if yours is trashed. A mouse pad is a small foam or plastic pad where a mouse hangs out, rather than running around on the surface of your desk and picking up crud from there.

The least expensive mouse pointers come with only the PS/2-style connectors (small and round); however, most devices sold today have two connectors on the end for PS/2 and 9-pin DB (small and flat). Adapters are available to convert 9-pin DB to 25-pin DB (wide and flat) and many mouse packages actually come with one; if they don't, check your computer store for a so-called "DB9/DB25 adapter."

The DB-type connectors are designed to fit into one of your computer's serial ports. This one's easy to identify on your computer: It's the one with pins. If your free serial port has nine pins, fine—your mouse connector will plug right in.

Newer computers—including all models following one of the ATX form factors (shape specifications)—have a PS/2-style mouse port. It's usually marked with a small mouse symbol (either a mouse with buttons and a cord, or a mouse with ears and whiskers) so that it won't be confused with the keyboard port, which might be similar in size.

A USB mouse is designed to plug into one of your computer's available USB ports. Newer computers are equipped with two on the back. However, if you own a USB hub or a USB keyboard, you might have an available USB port right there on your desk.

Cordless Mouse

You could say a cordless mouse is distinguished by its obvious lack of a cord (or a tail), but that wouldn't be exactly right. A cordless mouse may or may not come with its own interface card. In either event, the communication method between it and the port at the back of the computer is either infrared light or, in the case of long-distance cordless devices, high-frequency radio waves.

So how does light bend from the mouse over to the back of the computer? It doesn't. The mouse actually communicates with a small box called the *infrared hub* or *receiver*, which could be located in the vicinity of your monitor or in the middle of your desk. The receiver is connected to the computer by either the usual serial or PS/2 connector, or its own dedicated port on the interface card that comes with it.

As you might imagine, radio waves don't have to be bent or unobstructed. *RF mouse devices* can communicate with the receiver for long distances. You can even make gestures in the air to move the mouse pointer if you happen to be using the device during a seminar in which you're standing beside a projector screen and don't have a mouse pad handy. The radio transmitter uses a very similar principle to that of your garage door opener. Just make certain your RF mouse doesn't accidentally open your garage door.

Buttons, Wheels, and Wild Rides

If Dr. Seuss had written "The Mouse Book," one passage might have read: "Some mice have three buttons; some have four. How about six buttons? You want *more?*" (I like three buttons ... Sam, I am.) Why would you possibly need extra buttons if Windows programs don't make exclusive use of them somehow?

Logitech mouse devices—the most popular of which have at least three or four buttons—come complete with a nifty software driver setup, which enables you to program the middle button for your choice of things, such as Help, automatic click-and-hold, or single-click double-clicking. Top-of-the-line Logitech models have a fourth button for the thumb. I have one in which the thumb button brings up a menu of commonly performed Windows functions; you can program which functions appear in that menu yourself. I have to admit, though, after tinkering with the thumb button for about ten minutes, I've forgotten it's there.

Leave it to Microsoft to invent a wheel for a mouse. Microsoft's newest IntelliMouse incorporates a wheel as its middle button. With it you can quickly scroll and zoom through your Microsoft Office documents, Internet Explorer Web pages, and other applications that support it. If you press it down, you'll also notice the wheel serves double-duty as a button. Logitech now offers wheels on many of its models. At first I thought this wheel thing was a silly gimmick but it's amazing how much I use it; if for nothing other than to slowly scroll through some document or Web page or directory listing I'm reading. For me it's proven quite a bit more useful than button #4.

On the other end of the scale from usefulness comes this interesting concept from Logitech, which incorporates *tactile feedback* into some of its models. The idea is this: When you move the pointer along some of the various screen features, your hand should be able to feel when the pointer crosses the boundary from your word processor window into a dialog box—like your toes feeling the base of your stairs.

The drivers for this device actually instruct the mouse to produce a little "hump" feeling—and can even be instructed to produce a gravel road sensation whenever your pointer crosses over a lot of text, or the grid marks in a spreadsheet. If you don't get enough feedback from your boss, your spouse, your children, your mortgage agent, or your psychoanalyst, now you can get it from your mouse. Once again, society as we know it is saved!

Upside-Down Mice

If you're tired of moving your mouse around or you're limited on space, you might want to consider a stationary mouse, otherwise known to its friends as the *trackball*. A trackball is kind of like an upside-down or dead mouse—the ball is on top and the unit itself does not travel. With a trackball the mouse stays still; you move the mouse pointer by moving the trackball itself. Buttons on the trackball enable you to click, double-click, and drag.

Installing the Thing

First turn off your computer and remove your old mouse. If you're replacing your old mouse with one of the same type, plug your new mouse into the old one's connector (see Figure 8.5). If you're adding a mouse or replacing your old mouse with a new type, plug your new mouse into the appropriate connector. For a serial mouse use the thumbscrews on both sides of the plug to lock it in place.

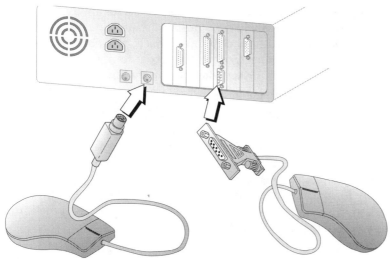

Figure 8.5

Plug your mouse into the appropriate connector.

Under normal circumstances, when you plug a USB device into your computer it should be able to identify itself; the setup procedure should start from there. With the USB mouse, that's a little tricky, because to comfortably operate your computer you need a mouse, which is the very thing you're trying to install. So despite the fact that you have a USB mouse that can be "hot-plugged," you should plug it in while your computer's turned off. Windows will (try to) recognize it the next time it powers up.

Installing a Cordless Mouse

For cordless mouse devices that do not come with their own interface card (which is the case for a majority of them), the installation procedure is pretty much the same as for a PS/2 or serial mouse, except that you connect the receiver to the PC instead of the mouse's cord. Make sure you have a clear path to the receiver so that the mouse signal can get through. Most cordless mice will operate to a maximum of five feet from the receiver, so keep your distance. If you run into any other problems, the mouse might be encountering interference from a radio-like device, such as a cordless telephone.

Announcing the New Guest

Before you can use your new mouse, you might need to teach your PC how to communicate with it. The instructions that came with your new mouse may have you run a Setup program that installs a *mouse driver*. This is a program that tells your PC exactly how to talk with your particular brand of mouse. Think of it as a kind of translator specializing in mouse-speak. Chapter 23, "Making Your Computer Boot Up Again," discusses the topic of running setup software for newly installed devices.

When you reboot your computer, Windows might ask you to insert a driver diskette or CD-ROM disc shipped with your mouse, or the original Windows CD-ROM so

145

Windows can update its mouse drivers. Sometimes the standard serial mouse driver that's already installed as part of Windows will run your mouse just fine, if you purchased an ordinary two-button mouse without any frills, wheels, sixth buttons, biosensory devices, tactile feedback generators, or neuro-precognition waveform detectors. Be sure to update your emergency diskette before you run any Setup program. See Chapter 4, "What You Need to Know *Before* You Open Your PC," for help.

All USB devices are, by design, Plug-and-Play devices. Originally, this term was supposed to mean that you could plug in your new device, your computer would ask it what it is (even if the computer's turned on at the time), the new device would announce itself ("I'm a Logitech three-button USB mouse!"), and you could get on with your life. Despite this, new devices cannot provide the Windows operating systems with the drivers necessary for it to make use of them. So after you've plugged in, you still might be prompted to insert a driver disc. Don't be alarmed and think something is wrong simply because you plugged and it didn't play.

Mistakes to Avoid

Here's a question you probably get asked often: Is your ball not rolling? Open the hatch on the underside of the mouse (the arrows will show you which way to twist); then take out the ball and see whether there's any Styrofoam material left over from when the mouse was shipped.

If your PC uses several serial devices, such as a mouse, scanner, modem, or joystick, and your mouse isn't working after you try to install it, two of your serial devices might be trying to talk over the same COM channel (perhaps they're both fighting over COM1). This is pretty head-grinding stuff; jump to Chapter 24, "Getting Windows to Recognize Your New Toys," for help sorting it all out. If you have a USB or cordless mouse, you won't have to worry about COM ports, channels, or abbreviations.

So your optical mouse isn't tracking properly. Did you take the manufacturer's suggestion about not having to use a mouse pad too literally? If your desk surface happens to be glass, or a solid-color synthetic solid such as Corian, the optical sensor might be having trouble locating how the mouse is moving and where. Consider using a mouse pad anyway—besides, your wrist will be more comfortable.

Acquiring or Replacing a Printer

There have been four prominent categories of computer printers throughout history, in order of their invention: daisy wheel impact, dot matrix, inkjet, and laser. Other types such as thermal transfer have flourished in certain niche markets; however, with the rapid plummet in manufacturing costs, color inkjets and lasers have driven the older dot matrix models into mass market oblivion.

If you still have one of these monsters, it might still be useful as a stopping post in your garage so you can tell when the back of your car has cleared the garage door by listening for the knocking sound made by your front bumper against ancient technology. In this section you'll learn what you should look for in a replacement and how to install your new printer after you bring it home.

Shopping for a New Printer

Your key considerations when choosing a printer are deeper than the brochures let on. Although color inkjet printers have descended beneath any price once thought to be the absolute bottom (some models sell for less than $50), if you tend to print in bulk and purchase paper in crates instead of just reams, you learn quickly about the reality of maintenance expenses. My family has been using computer printers for about a quarter-century now, so we're not only permanently stained with ink from the eons, impervious to all cleansers known to man or beast, we've also learned a few things about making good judgment calls. Consider the following:

➤ The number of pages per minute your printer churns out could become critically important if you use your printer in business and you need to print hundreds of pages or more at a time. One page per minute might be fine for printing out your child's homework—but what about your own? Large batches truly do require a laser printer.

➤ While I'm on the subject of print *quantity,* consider the cost of an inkjet printout. A replacement ink cartridge kit for the average inkjet printer, which contains one black and one color cartridge, sells for about $45. From my experience these cartridges last through about two reams, or 1000 sheets, of paper. So I'm spending about a nickel per sheet for ink. The paper itself sells for around $4.00 per ream, so the cost for paper is a tenth of a cent. So the cost of printing 1,000 sheets could be between 4.5 and 5.3 cents per sheet, depending on my cartridge supplier. Contrast that with laser printer maintenance costs. A toner kit for my laser printer costs $55 and lasts about 5,000 sheets. A developer kit (which contains the print drum) costs $80; for me that lasts up to 18,000 sheets—other users might not be as lucky. Even though I'm printing only in black-and-white, I'm spending about 2.4 cents per sheet. If you make only occasional printouts, that's not a big difference; if you print in bulk, that's real money.

➤ Yet there simply are some tasks that laser printers, because of their bulk, intricate mechanics, and high internal temperature, cannot perform where inkjet printers excel. Even envelopes—which most laser printers are supposed to accept—tend to seal themselves and even scorch, whereas inkjet printers handle them with ease. Also, the best color laser printers produce dynamite color and resolution, yet you can't insert heavyweight bond paper. Meanwhile, many inkjet printers produce crisp output on stockier grades of paper; some will even print on genuine Kodak photo paper.

147

Believe it or not, Panasonic and Lexmark still manufacture dot matrix printers for prices starting at around $350. Why in the world would you want one? Well … do you run a small business? Need something that can print three-part payroll checks? Try that little trick on an inkjet! How about a wide-carriage printer? Take any seismographic surveys lately? Of course you have. You need a 17-inch-wide carriage? You can't fold paper in a laser chute.

Inkjet Printers

An inkjet printer (once known as "bubble-jet") prints by spraying ink through a series of jets, inscribing tiny dots of ink on paper that form characters or graphics. These printers offer printout quality that's only slightly less classy than that of laser printers; however, they do this for an entry cost that has become a pittance. (Notice I said "entry cost.")

Inkjets are by far the least expensive option if you want color printout. They can print on many types and categories of paper, including photographic paper durable enough for a photo album. Inkjet printers also generally are whisper-quiet. On the downside, they are slower and expensive to maintain, mainly because of the high cost of ink. Face it: The manufacturers of printers are realistically in the ink production business. They make little or nothing on the printer itself; once you've purchased it you're locked into someone's brand, format, shape, and size of ink cartridge.

The quality of a printer's output is measured in *dots per inch* (*dpi*). Many general purpose inkjets have print resolutions you can set yourself—300, 600, 720, and 1,200 dpi settings have become common even on entry-level models retailing at $60. The standard color inkjet resolution today is 600 dpi.

Note

Inkjet printer manufacturers no longer advertise the amount of memory their models are shipped with; mainly because their internal RAM is not upgradeable. In earlier models, memory was considered a factor in determining speed; the more memory a printer has, the faster it goes.

Sometimes you'll find print resolution presented like screen resolution, in terms of horizontal versus vertical points (for example, 600 × 600 dpi), even though the two numbers are the same. Don't let the notation fool you; this does not mean 36,000 dpi! This means the printer is capable of producing very square dots, which is important because the formats in which digital images are stored on disk presume that all its pixels are perfectly square.

Inkjet printers' speed has cranked up a notch in the last few years and now is competitive with laser printer speed: 5–17 pages per minute (ppm) for black and white; 1–14 ppm for color. By comparison, laser printers print 6 ppm–24 ppm.

If you have a digital camera, the quality of your color printouts may be more critical. So-called *photo-quality* printers currently average in price around $500 and can exceed $1,000 if you print photos for a living. They feature print resolution of up to 2,880 dpi—albeit at an agonizingly slow 24 minutes per page. Although if you're printing something you intend to frame and hang on your wall, 24 minutes isn't really that slow at all.

The All-in-One Inkjet/Fax/Scanner/Copier

Some manufacturers, including HP and Xerox, produce all-in-one home office devices, which give you the option of having several office peripherals neatly bundled together in one unit. "Why not," says one ad, "have it all together?" That's not a bad rhetorical question if, by putting it all together, you're saving space, money, or time.

An all-in-one device generally starts out with a printer. Grafted onto it might be a fax machine, a scanner, and a telephone; and the box might mention something about an *optical character reader* (*OCR*) for converting your paper documents into electronic files. All these add-ons are marketed as "Everything You Need," which isn't exactly right, because I often find myself needing time, mayonnaise, and sleep. The lessons I've learned from owning two of these monstrosities are these:

➤ The printer part of the combo package generally is not the best printer you can buy. Even today, inkjet and laser printers that come with combo packages are capable of only 300 dpi at 4 ppm.

➤ Before you buy a combo package thinking how much you really need the fax machine, consider this: You may already have a fax machine. Huh? If your computer has a 56K fax modem, decent software that enables it to send and receive faxes on your computer is no more than $50—unless your fax modem came with this software as part of the bundle, in which case, it's free! But suppose you need to scan existing documents rather than stuff you type on your word processor. A flatbed scanner now averages about $100; a combo device starts at about $350 and averages $475. A good fax modem is about $50; and printers, as you've just read, start at $50. If you put all those together for $200–$250, you'll have a much better fax machine and printer than you would have if you went with the $350 all-in-one option.

➤ Some of the copier mechanisms on the bottom-of-the-barrel all-in-one systems borrow the monochromatic page scanner from the fax component. When you make a copy, you literally send yourself a fax. If you like the output of fax, that's alright. (The exception here is Xerox, whose copy quality is quite sharp.)

➤ About that optical character reader: On more than one occasion I've discovered that not only is the OCR based entirely in software; this software is *shareware*. If I intend to use it for 90 days or 100 pages, whichever comes first, I have to shell out more money (in one instance, $120). I can download a demo of something free from the Internet any time I want; if I'm paying money for it, I expect to own it.

Do you get the impression perhaps that I'm not big on the all-in-one hybrid combo Borg drone devices?

Laser Printers

Yes, there really is a laser in a laser printer. First, the printer assembles the page in memory and then uses its laser to burn an image of that page onto a drum. The drum rotates into the toner, picking up ink in the pattern of the image. The drum then brushes against the paper, transferring the inked image onto it. The paper passes near a heated wire on its way out, drying the ink and making the image permanent. Sounds like science fiction, right? Well, expect to pay a bit more for all that technology. Still, noncolor lasers are reasonably affordable ($400–$2,600, with most averaging around $600). Interesting enough, laser printers might be the only category of computer component that has seen substantial price increases over the last two years.

Languages for Printers

Some of the more expensive laser printers come with *PostScript* capability; others that are slightly less expensive are *HP-PCL compatible.* PostScript is a printer language that translates a page into a series of math equations much harder than the ones that stumped you in high school. This enables PostScript printers to print scalable fonts and cool graphics without breaking a sweat. HP-PCL is a printer control language created by Hewlett-Packard, the leader in laser printers. Although not nearly as complex as PostScript, nor as adaptable to heavy-duty graphics, PCL's advantage is its speed. If you get an HP-PCL printer, sometimes you can add PostScript capability (if you need it) through a special expansion card, or through software. Some more expensive laser printers come with the capability to use both PCL and PostScript. If you've followed the various editions of this book through the years and now are wondering, "Hey, Jennifer, where's GhostScript?" both you and your psychiatrist will be pleased to learn that this software-based PostScript interpreter is still going strong. It can still be downloaded free at www.cs.wisc.edu/~ghost/, along with the GSView software, which lets you view PostScript-format document files in your Web browser. GhostScript might substitute for a PostScript interpreter in your printer, giving you much nicer print quality and greater graphics capability. The downside is that it's a separate application—not just a driver—so you have to pretty much lead it by the hand all the way through the print process. However, you can't complain too much because you spent nothing for it.

Common Laser Printer Characteristics

As with inkjet printers, the quality of a laser printout is measured in dots per inch (dpi). To remain competitive with inkjet printers, even the lowest of the low-end laser printers now support 1200 dpi printout. Black-and-white printout speeds range from 9 ppm to 25 ppm, declining to a staggering 4 ppm for 600 dpi color printout.

Why the speed drop for color? Color laser printers are still very complex compared to their monochromatic cousins, because they have to use page sensors to align and re-align the page through four passes of different inks. Prices have stabilized to an average of $2,250 and don't appear to be declining anytime soon, as demand has reduced sharply. By comparison, photo-quality inkjet printers sell for $500, certainly are no slower, and can print directly to photo paper; color laser printers require a premium bond, thin paper that's expensive but not durable.

Many laser printers also come with built-in fonts. You see, when you use a built-in font the PC doesn't have to waste time downloading it from your PC. Also, using built-in fonts allows your printer to handle more fonts and graphics on the same page without running out of memory. Your Windows printer driver will install either identical or similar-looking *screen fonts* on your system that enable the display of your word processor to approximate the built-in fonts in your printer. However, Windows can print almost any document or graphics without the aid of any built-in fonts whatsoever, so they're not a necessity.

Installing Your New Printer Painlessly

Your printer may connect to your computer through either of two ports: the conventional printer port (often marked with some caveman facsimile of something resembling the printing process) or the USB port. If you have a choice you will find a big performance increase with printers with USB capability. With keyboards you don't notice it; with printers USB is a boon.

First, disconnect your old printer. Start by turning it off and removing any paper. Disconnect the cable and the power cord. Next, remove your new printer from its box. Be sure to look inside the printer and remove any shipping materials such as tape and those foam peanuts—sometimes they're placed there to keep delicate parts from moving during shipping. However, if you don't remove them all and you turn on the printer ... well, you get the ugly picture.

Now shut down your computer. I don't care what the USB folks told you about Plug-and-Play. Shut it off. Yes, hypothetically, you can plug your powered-on printer into your powered-on computer through the USB port and your computer will recognize the printer and start doing the cha-cha (see Figure 8.6). Trouble is, your computer will also do some other marginally exciting acts of defiance, one of which has to do with a ploy by Windows to install its own printer driver rather than the one your manufacturer supplied. Of course you want the manufacturer's driver because, well, it's better. You might have spent money for some extra features; you'll want to be able to use them.

If you're using the parallel port instead, you'll still want to shut down your computer (see Figure 8.7). Parallel printer cables can carry enough voltage to shock you (mildly), or to shock your other equipment (terminally).

Figure 8.6

Connecting your printer using the USB port.

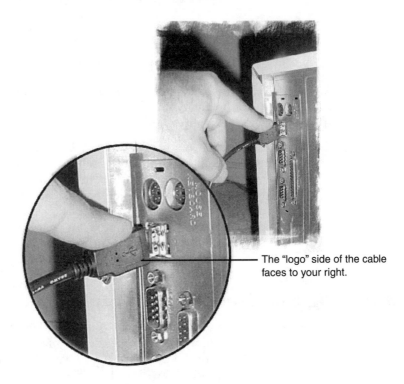

The "logo" side of the cable faces to your right.

Figure 8.7

Connecting your printer using the parallel port.

Parallel port, 25 holes

Printer connector

Follow the steps in Chapter 5 for removing the packing material and tape, and inserting the ink or toner cartridge. Follow the manufacturer's directions for inserting any other miscellaneous parts, such as the developer unit for a laser printer (yecch). Connect the printer cable to the back of the printer. USB cables are not identical on each end so there will be a clearly marked end designated for your printer. If you're using the parallel port, its connector on the printer will have a flat card edge and will be supported by two retaining wires like wings at each end. Connect the other end of the cable to your PC. If you're using the parallel port, you'll want the open plug with

25 holes in it. For the USB cable, either of your two open ports is fine, and your cable will only go in one way.

Plug the printer's power cord in. Add paper and turn your printer on. Wait until the lights on the front of your panel stop blinking—that'll mean the warm-up sequence has concluded.

Now power your computer back up. If you have a Plug-and-Play printer (which is especially true if you used the USB connection), Windows should recognize your new device momentarily, and start the driver installation procedure. Here's the tricky part: Read your printer's manual to find out whether you need to cancel Windows' driver installation procedure now. That's right, you actually might have a Plug-and-Don't-Play-Yet printer (HPs have long suffered from this dilemma). Once you're actually ready to install the driver, then and only then should you put the printer driver CD-ROM disc in your optical drive. If Setup doesn't start automatically for you, look for SETUP.EXE in the disc's root directory and double-click it.

If you don't have a Plug-and-Play printer or it simply didn't play when you plugged, you'll need to formally install the printer drivers using the Add New Printer icon located in the Printers folder. Turn to Chapter 24 for help in this department. After you set up your printer, be sure to open one of your programs and print something as a test.

Check This Out

The single most frequent mistake reported by new printer buyers is the omission of a cable from their purchase. Printer cables almost never come bundled with printers, with the rare exception of certain USB varieties with one end that fits only specific printer models. Don't let yourself get rooked into paying more for a printer cable than you should! Aim for no more than $1.50 per foot.

Mistakes to Avoid

If the printer doesn't print at all, don't forget to turn it on and hit the On Line button. Nowadays this button generally is marked with an icon that, in ancient Egypt, may have been used as a symbol for "place to clean your muddy sandals." In the rare event that your PC has more than one parallel port, you might have connected your printer to the wrong one. One of these ports is known as LPT1; the other is LPT2. Windows generally searches for your printer at logical port LPT1 by default unless you specifically told it LPT2. However, if your printer is connected to the other port, then it's quite likely the print data was sent to a house where no one lives. Try switching your printer cable to the other parallel port.

For your printer driver to be able to produce any kind of graphical printout whatsoever, your hard drive C: needs free space. Try clearing old files from that disk to make room. See Chapter 7, "'Repairing' the Hard Disk Instead of Replacing It," for help in low-space situations.

One last thing to check: Is your printer driver the most current one? I know you just bought the printer, but did they ship the most recent driver? You usually can download the latest driver for your printer from the manufacturer's Web site. With Windows 98, 98 SE, and Windows Me, you can actually have the operating system hunt down the newest driver from the Internet for you.

Improving the View with a New Monitor

Connecting a monitor to a PC is about as difficult as plugging a blender into a wall socket. All SVGA CRT monitors produced since 1995 use a standardized small, thin 15-pin plug; all SVGA video cards' connectors recognize this plug. Some LCD monitors are now being sold with USB connections; the trouble is most video cards don't have interfaces with the USB bus. So until the USB folks get that problem worked out (Britney Spears will be President), you can go on trusting the old reliable SVGA plug.

Talking Monitor-Speak

Before you go out shopping for a new monitor, you should arm yourself with knowledge in the form of "monitor-speak." Here now is a quick summary of all the terms you need to know:

➤ **Resolution**—As you may recall from Chapter 3, "What It Takes to Upgrade Each Part of Your Computer," a monitor's resolution is the number of pixels (dots) that comprise the images it displays. The more dots, the better defined that image can be. At low resolutions, such as 640h (horizontal) × 480v (vertical), there are fewer pixels to fill the screen so they are bigger and fatter, and images are less defined (see Figure 8.8). At higher resolutions, such as 1280h × 1024v, the pixels are smaller, and images are sharper and more finely detailed. Look for the higher resolutions such as 1024h × 768v (good) in Figure 8.8, 1280h × 1024v (better), and even 1600h × 1200v or 1600h × 1280v (best). Expect to pay bigger bucks for monitors that enable higher resolutions. The SVGA monitors sold today support multiple resolutions and are for that reason called *multiscan* monitors. Besides, it's a cool, sci-fi-sounding term.

➤ **Size**—This one's easy: It's the length of the tube measured diagonally. CRT monitors today usually are 15, 17, 19, and 21 inches, measured diagonally.

➤ **Flat screen**—Ordinary CRTs, like ordinary television sets, are ever-so-slightly convex (curved toward the viewer). Sony patented and then licensed the patent for picture tubes with a flat screen; its contents aren't distorted by the shape of the tube. You pay more for flat screen and you might not notice the difference in the store—but just use one for an hour or two and ask your eyes how they feel. (This is not to be confused with *flat panel*, which is a marketing term for LCD monitors.)

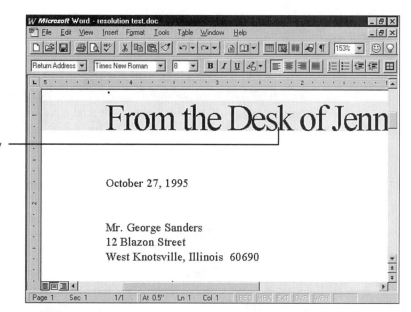

Look here and you'll see some fuzziness in the way the letters are displayed.

Figure 8.8

Here's what text looks like at 640h × 480v resolution.

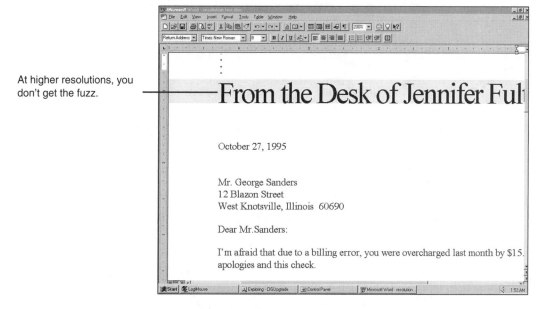

At higher resolutions, you don't get the fuzz.

Figure 8.9

Here's the same text at 1024h × 768v resolution.

155

➤ **Viewing area**—The diagonal length of that portion of the surface of the tube, which is the largest area that can support the actual display. The remainder of the tube around the edges can be considered margins. LCD monitors tout the fact that their viewing area and their screen size are identical.

➤ **Viewing angle(s)**—The angles emerging from the LCD monitor surface, within which your head can reside and you can see the picture. The average LCD monitor offers 120-degree horizontal, and 100-degree vertical ranges of vision. This means your head might be tilted as much as 60 degrees left or right of center and you should still be able to read the display. Top-of-the-line LCDs offer 160-degree ranges of vision. But ordinary CRT monitors, as you know, offer a 180-degree range of vision. Keep in mind that the "corridor of vision," for lack of a formal term, is narrower than this measurement makes it appear. On a 19-inch LCD display, your head could be tilted 0 degrees from the center of the screen but perhaps 8–10 degrees from either edge of the screen.

➤ **Dot pitch**—Basically, this is the onscreen distance between the centers of those little pixels. A good number to look for here is .25mm (millimeters); the lower this number, the sharper the image is onscreen. Each pixel on a low dot-pitch monitor is less fuzzy around its edges so color pictures are crisper. This is because there's less fuzz in between the colors.

➤ **Refresh rate**—Sometimes called the *scanning frequency,* this tells you how often a monitor's electron beams (cathode rays) update the image onscreen. The faster the refresh rate, the less flickering you'll see. For CRT, 75Hz (hertz, not megahertz) is a decent speed for 1024h × 768v, although 66Hz is average for a higher resolution like 1280h × 1024v. (At higher resolutions, it's normal for the refresh rate to go down.) *Multiscan monitors* (monitors that support multiple resolutions) that alter their refresh rates for added clarity at the lower resolutions are called *multisync* monitors (another cool, sci-fi-sounding term). For larger monitors you should opt for higher refresh rates because the flicker in the video signal is more noticeable only when the display is larger.

➤ **Input frequency**—The LCD counterpart to refresh rate. Although an LCD monitor stays in sync with the signal from the video card at a rate of between 50 and 75Hz, the LCD screen doesn't flicker at that rate. So theoretically, a 50Hz LCD display should appear just as rock solid as a 75Hz LCD display.

➤ **Video bandwidth**—This is the maximum frequency at which the monitor is capable of operating. It's the same as the maximum horizontal resolution multiplied by the maximum vertical resolution multiplied by the maximum refresh rate. In short, it's the size of the biggest video signal the monitor supports. The higher the better; 120Hz is a good number to shoot for and is the refresh rate for most new monitors at 640h × 480v resolution. (Compare that to 3.58MHz for the standard North American TV signal.) The video bandwidth of any resolution probably averages out close to this maximum value; as resolution increases, the refresh rate proportionally decreases.

➤ **Luminance**—For LCD monitors, luminance is measured in *nits* (also written cd/m²), or *candlepower* (*candela*) per square meter. (The average candle puts out 1 nit in the 1 square meter vicinity around the flame.) One common complaint is that LCD monitors aren't as *bright* as CRT monitors; however, long-time CRT users have praised LCD monitors for precisely the same reason. The maximum luminance range for modern LCD monitors is 200–235 nits. Here is where technology works against itself: Whereas a CRT produces an image by illuminating pixels, an LCD produces one by *darkening* pixels. Although an LCD array is capable of finer resolution, darker pixels, and finer contrasts (a good thing), the light panel that illuminates this array from behind must have more luminance value to compensate for how much the array can block light. High-performance LCD monitors must put out 235 nits to compensate for their high-contrast, high-resolution, 19-inch displays.

➤ **Contrast ratio**—A measure of how bright a monitor's brightest pixels are (pure white), versus how bright its darkest pixels are (pure black). For a CRT monitor, a low ratio implies a greater amount of ambient light bleeding from the bright areas into the dark areas. For an LCD monitor, a high ratio implies a greater capability for the crystal matrix to darken pixels. In either case, the higher the ratio the better.

Before I go on, I'd like to shoot down a myth for you: Lower-resolution displays are *not* easier to read. High resolution can be good for the eyes as long as your video card and monitor support a high refresh rate. What's high? 60Hz is respectable for 1280h × 1024v. You'll find CRT monitors that are capable of a rock-solid 125Hz—very flicker-free. However, that's only at the lowest resolutions, where text is blocky and choppy.

Check This Out

The refresh rate or input frequency your monitor uses must match at least one of the rates your video card supports. If you buy a multisync monitor that is capable of supporting multiple refresh rates, making a match between it and a video card is easier. If you mismatch the two rates, you can wreck your monitor. On the back of each video card's package is a list of resolutions and corresponding refresh rates that the card supports. Finding the refresh rates for a monitor isn't as easy; you'll need to ask a salesperson or support representative to supply you with literature from the manufacturer. You'll need the monitor's information later when setting up your video card, so it's worth the trouble to get it.

If you use low resolution on a large display (17-inch diagonal or higher), you might end up straining your eyes inadvertently, as they attempt to compensate for text that appears it was typeset by a bricklayer. If you have a big monitor, don't hesitate to try out higher resolutions, until you find one that's a fair compromise between smooth text and steady images.

Connecting a New Monitor (Difficulty Factor –10)

First, there may be pieces of the monitor that you may have to put together. For instance, you may have to attach the base to the monitor. To attach a swivel base, you start by flipping the monitor over onto its top. You may notice some slots into which you can snap the connectors onto the base. Do that and flip the monitor back around. Be careful; these things are heavy. If your monitor came with attachable speakers, don't bother attaching them just yet.

To connect your monitor to the PC, make sure its power switch is off. If you have a DVD-ROM, you probably have a DVD decoder card. In that case only, you'll want to make sure the patch cable, is connected to the port on the back of your video card where your monitor normally would be plugged in.

The other end of this patch cable is plugged into your decoder card; then your monitor plugs into the remaining port on the decoder card. If you don't have a DVD-ROM, there's no patch cable, so it's no big deal. Just plug the monitor's connector into the back of the video card (see Figure 8.10). Now take the power cord for the monitor and plug the female end into the back of the monitor, and the male end into your surge protector.

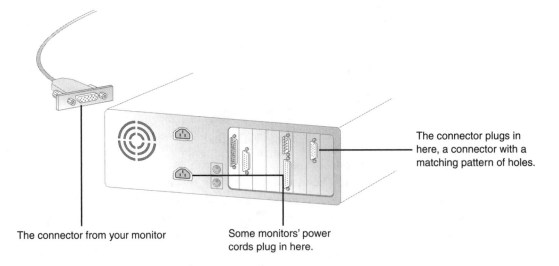

The connector plugs in here, a connector with a matching pattern of holes.

The connector from your monitor

Some monitors' power cords plug in here.

Figure 8.10

Plug the monitor into the back of the video card.

With the advent of Windows 95 came a poorly named piece of software called the *monitor driver*. Unlike the situation with every other type of driver, you do not need to install a driver for your monitor for it to work with your computer. A monitor driver actually is software that helps the video card produce the proper color spectrum and signal for your monitor—in essence, a set of specifications rather than something that actually tells the monitor how to work. It's your video card that requires a driver to help it produce the graphics that you see onscreen; not your monitor. Your monitor will work fairly well without you having to install a monitor driver. However, if you want to improve the quality of your picture, let Chapter 24 show you how to install the so-called driver.

Mistakes to Avoid

Don't power your monitor by running an extension cable through your PC's power supply. It used to be done this way all the time; however, your monitor is a huge power drain. Just plug the power cord that comes with the monitor into your surge protector or UPS.

If you're powering up your LCD monitor for the first time and you notice that Windows comes up as a very small display in the center of the screen, don't panic. Windows might be projecting a 640h × 480v image while your monitor expects 1,024h × 768v or higher. Nothing's wrong; don't go into your Control Panel to adjust display settings just yet. Instead go through the motions while Windows recognizes your devices for the first time. Your computer probably will reboot and your display should come up the right size afterward. If it doesn't, *then* you can go into Control Panel.

Scanners: The Latest Standard Equipment

The color flatbed scanner is now a standard component of many PC systems sold today and a featured item on department store shelves along with the Walkman and the Water Pik. Their scanning resolution ranges from 600 to 2,400 dots per inch (dpi), with 36-bit color ranges that often are richer than those you'll find in a video card with 24-bit color.

The scanning device in principle is the same as you'll find in a digital color copier, so an incredible amount of data needs to be translated to the PC within an interval of 22 seconds for the low-end models, and 4 seconds for the high end. Street prices average about $200, with entry-level models selling for about $80.

Attaching Your Scanner

Nearly all scanners sold today use USB, the new and fast serial bus introduced in Chapter 12. As a result, you can plug a powered scanner into your powered computer and immediately the computer will start by launching the setup process for the scanner. This exercise in Plug-and-Play has proven more successful for scanners than for printers or any other USB device.

For a scanner that isn't recognized automatically, you'll need to run the setup program manually. To start this process from Control Panel, double-click Add New Hardware. Windows searches for the proper driver; make sure you have on hand the CD-ROM that came with your scanner. For Windows 95, the category "Scanner" is not an option in the device type list; if it comes to that point, you'll probably need to choose Other.

Some scanners ask you to power down your computer, plug in your scanner to its appropriate port, and then power up the computer with the driver CD-ROM in the drive. The driver program runs itself and bypasses the Windows Control Panel for you.

Mistakes to Avoid

Windows 98 SE and Windows Me do their darndest to recognize a USB scanner the moment you plug it in. At that time, Windows may try to have you go through one of its "wizard" procedures so you can install scanner drivers from the Windows CD-ROM. Don't fall into the trap! (In fact, your scanner manual might even tell you this up front.)

If you install the Windows version of the generic scanner driver (that word "generic" should tell you something already), you probably will not be able to install the specific driver that came with your brand of scanner—at least not until you uninstall your scanner (because it's a USB scanner, that means unplugging it) and start all over. Double-check your scanner's installation manual just to make sure, but it will probably tell you to cancel the Windows wizard when it comes up. Let your scanner's own driver software do its thing.

When manufacturers go out of their way to point out that the Windows way of doing things doesn't work, they generally have pretty good reason. In my experience with USB (verified against nearly identical experiences shared by others), the two most frequent incorrect guesses Windows makes about what USB device has just been plugged in are: an infrared control device, and a satellite dish.

If you don't follow the instructions from your scanner manufacturer, you could find yourself spending hours convincing Windows that your scanner is not a wireless keyboard, and not a satellite dish. In my satellite dish experience, I'd go into the Device Manager, choose my new satellite dish, and uninstall it. There, gone. Two seconds later, Windows would declare, "New Hardware Found … Satellite Dish!" as if I had just plugged it in again. With my next reboot, there it would be in Device Manager, "Satellite communications receiver." No joke.

Digital Cameras

Once you've transferred a picture you've taken with your digital camera to your PC, you can manipulate it—color-correct it, blend or distort part of it, and get rid of the lettuce hanging out of someone's teeth. You then can print the image out on a color printer or include the image in an e-mail message, a document, or a multimedia presentation. However, the most popular use of digital cameras is to supply photos for inclusion on Web pages. For example, a real estate agent could take pictures of all her clients' homes and put them out on the Web to increase their marketability. If you're into Web page creation, a digital camera is fairly essential nowadays.

A Computer's Eye View of the Digital Camera

A digital camera might only have to plug into your computer on occasion, during those times you're transferring stored images directly from the camera to your PC. Depending on the brand of camera you purchase, you might not have to connect it to your PC at all. Some cameras utilize special memory devices that store several dozen images. There are three types: *memory sticks, SmartMedia cards,* and *CompactFlash cards.*

You might need a USB cable to transfer the images stored from those memory devices to your computer or you can actually install a memory reader into your computer, similar to installing a diskette drive. Sony's Mavica brand of digital camera actually can store images (and even short movies, for the high-end models) on ordinary 3½-inch diskettes, which you can then pop into your floppy drive on your computer when you need to transfer. (At last, a good use for those old AOL giveaway diskettes you never threw away!)

For SmartMedia memory cards, one recent development is the advent of a so-called *FlashPath adapter,* which is an ingenious device shaped like a diskette. You insert the SmartMedia card into the adapter; then slide the entire adapter into your 3½-inch diskette drive. There's special driver software that takes the place of Windows' internal drivers for the diskette drive, but you'll still be able to read ordinary diskettes once it's installed. With the adapter in the diskette drive and the driver software installed, Windows will simply accept the adapter as if it were a 16MB floppy. A similar device for CompactFlash cards enables your memory device to be read by a notebook PC as though it were a PCMCIA hard disk.

Most digital cameras sold today use a specially devised USB cable for transferring files. These cables come with their respective cameras, and feature a very tiny version of the USB connector for the camera end and the conventional USB connector for the computer end. Unlike any other peripheral you'll ever own, you'll "install" and "uninstall" your digital camera quite frequently—for many users, as often as once a week. The very first time you plug in your USB digital camera, you'll need to install its driver software from the CD-ROM disc. Afterwards, you should not have to install the software again; if your computer tells you to insert the CD-ROM each time you plug in the USB, you might have problems.

161

When shopping for a digital camera, you'll need to know some new and very digital-camera-specific terminology:

➤ **Megapixel**—A unit of one million pixels. Suppose a model you're examining can capture images with 1,280h × 1,024v resolution. That's a total of 1,310,720 pixels, which translates to 1.3 megapixels. (You never hear about megapixels when shopping for monitors. Of course, that could change soon.) More megapixels could come at a price. The cameras that offer higher resolutions store fewer images than the lower resolution cameras. Why? Because images with less detail take less memory to save. Look for a camera whose resolution is variable so when you choose, you can take more pictures with lower resolution.

➤ **Optical zoom**—The amount of picture magnification achievable through the lens only. Think of this as "mechanical zoom."

➤ **Digital zoom**—The amount of extra picture magnification accomplished by the electronics of the camera, where the imaging system closes in on a particular frame within the picture being fed to it by the optical lens. (In other words, trick photography.) This uses the same general principle as a zoom option in a graphics application. Advertising often takes the opportunity to multiply a camera's optical zoom capability by its digital zoom capability; so for instance, if it has an 8x zoom lens and 2x digital zoom, the ad will read, "16x zoom!"

Some cameras offer *JPEG compression,* which enables them to store digital images in less space. Making an image smaller for JPEG format requires the computer to use a technique called *lossy compression.* Unlike ZIP compression or the compression technique used for GIF images, you lose some of the image's quality; so this is not necessarily a good thing unless your goal is to capture lots of photos. Most cameras allow you to select the level of compression (if any) that you want, usually through some button or, later, through your computer software.

Don't be fooled into trying to get by with the type of camera that's typically included in a video conferencing kit or Web camera package. Although now some are portable (many Web cameras aren't), the quality of photo they take isn't up to a preservable level. You don't want to give grainy images like theirs to your grandchildren. Web cameras often are made to sit on top of your monitor; generally they take fuzzy, black-and-white images that are suitable for video conferences in which it's okay that the other party can't see that you aren't wearing any pants.

Digital cameras range in price from $400 to $2,500, depending on their resolution, onboard memory, and extras such as sound capture capability, JPEG compression, MPEG movie capturing, and zoom.

Installation, in a Sense

You never really install a video camera into your computer permanently. To underscore this, the very first thing many cameras with cable-driven transfer capabilities have you do is install the camera's driver software, so that Windows thinks your camera is installed permanently.

With most peripheral devices, you plug everything in first, then set up your software. Your digital camera is different because, unlike your other peripherals, you'll be unplugging it often. Sometimes when you unplug a USB device, Windows will go through the motions of uninstalling it, which really isn't what you want to do, because the next time you plug in the camera, Windows won't know what it is. You need to install the setup software first (the old-fashioned way: Insert the CD-ROM in the optical drive, find and double-click SETUP.EXE) before you plug the camera in.

Unlike an ordinary peripheral device, a digital camera is something that isn't designed to be installed *per se*. Still, Win98 or WinMe might treat your digital camera as a category of installed devices, as if it sat next to your PC all the time like your scanner. The actual presence of your camera may or may not be required to install that camera as a device.

For this process select Add New Hardware from the Windows 98 Control Panel, and choose the Digital Cameras category specifically from the list, because the camera won't be a PnP device (especially if it's not really plugged in). However, if your camera doesn't enroll as a formal Windows device, you might be required only to install the image transfer and editing software. That process resembles the installation process for any other application.

Check This Out

The era of digital photography had not yet matured, even when the OSR2 edition of Windows 95 hit the streets. So for digital cameras that hook up to your computer, you'll need at least Windows 98, preferably Win98 SE, if not Windows Me.

If you have a Sony Mavica camera that uses diskettes (folks, that's the one I bought, and I love it), you won't have to worry about this installation business at all. Nothing is needed for your computer to read the images this camera takes. Also, the device has built-in support for FlashPath, so if you purchase the adapter separately, you can store images—and, on the higher-end models, movies—on a 16MB SmartMedia card inserted in a FlashPath adapter disk.

Mistakes to Avoid

If your digital camera transfers images to your computer over cable, don't even think about plugging it in before installing the driver software first; Windows would try to install some kind of generic digital camera driver. Just for the heck of it, I actually tried that once with a Kodak digital model and actually found myself watching Windows invent a new type of camera called "Standard Digital Camera." There's no such thing, let me tell you! And if you have nothing to do on a quiet Thursday night, you won't want to fill your time as I did combing through the System Registry, removing instances of "Standard Digital Camera."

163

Here's a mistake the manuals won't tell you about: Many digital cameras with USB ports put off an extraordinary amount of RF interference—more than you think would be allowed. During beta testing of that same Kodak digital camera over the USB port, I made the silly mistake of stacking some audio cassettes about four feet away. After the transfer was completed, those cassettes were almost completely erased! During the same time, the TV set was going bonkers, and a groovy moiré pattern appeared on my laptop computer's display. Folks, microwave ovens never gave off that many vibes!

The Least You Need to Know

➤ Don't buy a new device simply because it uses USB. Make sure it's the device you need and that you want it enough to put up with the infighting between Windows and USB.

➤ Before purchasing a new keyboard, make sure you test it out to see if you like the feel of the keys.

➤ If you're concerned about carpal tunnel syndrome and you spend a lot of time on your PC, you may want to consider an ergonomic keyboard or a wrist rest.

➤ To replace your keyboard, turn the PC off, unplug your old keyboard, plug your new keyboard in securely, and turn the PC back on.

➤ If your new mouse doesn't use USB, it has either a serial or PS/2 connector, if not both.

➤ To install a mouse, turn your PC off, plug the new mouse in, and then turn the PC back on. Check whether Windows notices your new mouse and requests to install new software for it, and have your driver software ready at that time.

➤ If you run into problems with your new serial mouse, there probably is some kind of COM port/IRQ conflict.

➤ A laser printer is less expensive in the long run than an inkjet printer only if you print hundreds of monochrome pages per week; otherwise, inkjet printers offer low entry cost and easy (if expensive) maintenance.

➤ CRT monitors are more reliable than ever with sharper, clearer images, and reduced cost.

➤ Flatbed color scanners are almost entirely USB driven and provide sharper, more reliable images than the built-in scanner on an all-in-one printer/fax/scanner/copier device.

➤ Some digital still color cameras might connect to your PC for a short time only; generally through a USB port. Others save their images to a floppy disk or flash memory card, which you would take to your PC later.

Accelerating Your PC with a New CPU

The replacement of the central processing unit (CPU) is what most people think of when they consider a PC upgrade. In 1989 Intel began producing CPUs and sockets that were designed to be upgraded (read: replaced, meaning disposable). Intel reasoned that, as long as they were in the business of producing CPUs rather than entire computers, they needed to generate some way for end users to need their products down the road. In this brave new world, the users would be their customers rather than just computer manufacturers. So to that end, Intel perceived a future wherein components such as the motherboard and the system case were more permanent than the CPU. Consumers who lived in this world would consider the purchase of a new replacement CPU as virtually equivalent to purchasing a new computer.

Making the CPU an interchangeable part was the single most catalytic decision in the history of computing, if not of manufacturing as a whole. No other industry in recorded history has witnessed a 12,000 percent increase in product efficiency in less than a 10-year span, except perhaps for political lobbyists.

The Size and Shape of Things

Throughout PC history, the way a processor was packaged wasn't a serious enough factor to warrant consideration by consumers. Now there are many types of processor packages available, such that the technological distinctions between them have become the only factors justifying their differences in price.

Why Packaging Suddenly Matters

The part of a CPU package that actually contains the processor—in other words, the *chip*—is actually just one small part in a complex mechanism. Unlike anything else you can buy—breakfast cereal, camping gear, political candidates—a CPU's packaging is almost as important to the way it does its job, as the processor chip itself. A CPU's packaging is important to you, the buyer, for the following reasons:

➤ **Price**—Less expensive packaging options enable manufacturers to develop multiple product lines—at the very least, creating "standard" and "premium" editions with separate price points. This effectively deposes clock speed as the sole factor determining the relative price of a CPU; now a manufacturer can offer a faster CPU at a lower price than a slower model with premium packaging and more internal features.

➤ **Operating temperature**—Denser components naturally run hotter than looser ones. In order to retain socket compatibility, CPUs must pack greater numbers of transistors and components within the same form factor, or *die*. (No, not "die" as in "death"; "die" as in something cut by a blade from a block—the singular of "dice.") Inventive packaging options enable high-density CPUs to run cooler; by that same token, low-cost packaging could lead CPUs to wear out sooner.

➤ **Performance**—CPU clock speeds have broken clear through the stratosphere and have entered the stratosphere of some other planet. However, CPU performance has not increased proportionately. Simple factors of design, such as the proximity of the L2 cache to the CPU's arithmetic logic unit, can increase the performance of a CPU design by orders of magnitude, without any change in its clock speed.

There are now two main categories of CPU packaging, the differences between which are obvious even at a distance of about 100 feet. Simply put, one's a chip; the other's a cartridge. *Pin Grid Array* (*PGA*) is the common name for the conventional square CPU chip with the little pins sticking out the bottom. (Obviously, the guys who come up with these names don't have hobbies or lives during the weekends.) The different types of cartridges generally are called *Single-edge Contact* (*SEC*) packages, referring to the card edge that connects to a motherboard in a manner very similar to an expansion card.

PGA packaging is represented by both the oldest and newest genre of CPUs (see Figure 9.1). In 1997, Intel made a strategic move to begin production of processor cartridges that enabled the L2 memory cache (an important array of SRAM memory) to be installed on a separate chip from the CPU. The result was more room on the CPU for more transistors and, Intel claimed, better performance, which indeed we saw.

CPGA

PPGA

FC-PGA

Figure 9.1

The different types of PGA processor packages currently available.

In 1999, Intel made the opposite strategic move, reducing and later suspending production of SEC packaging in favor of newer forms of the old PGA packaging. Intel's reasoning, the company claimed, was to enable the L2 cache to be installed along *with* the CPU (which, incidentally, is where it was before). The result, said Intel, was more efficient design and better performance. Since we are indeed seeing better performance, we have no reason to dispute what Intel is saying.

You can easily spot the difference between all types of processor packages just by looking at them; they're not subtle.

➤ **CPGA (Ceramic Pin Grid Array)**—Intel first chose ceramic for its durability and the fact that it doesn't conduct electricity. The first PGA CPUs, beginning with the 80286, used a ceramic mounting, which had both the color and the texture of polished slate. Although Intel moved away from ceramic, AMD has embraced it. The problem with ceramic, though, is that it doesn't dissipate heat as well as other substances. For this reason, AMD's CPGA packages are capped with an aluminum lid that drawhelps draw heat away from the ceramic backing. Although AMD has advanced technology in its silicon, its manufacturing processes are still a few years old and are stuck in the "Ceramic Age." However, AMD does pass on its savings in manufacturing costs to the consumer.

167

➤ **PPGA (Plastic Pin Grid Array)**—This package is identifiable by the tops of its pins, which stick out through the top of the plastic casing. PPGA is the current mounting of choice for Intel Celeron processors. Intel conceived Celeron in 1998 as a low-cost product line, enabling Pentium to become its premium brand. Ironically, plastic is not less expensive packaging than ceramic. The reason Intel switched its manufacturing processes from ceramic to plastic is that plastic dissipates heat more quickly and can more durably support a heat sink or chip fan attachment.

➤ **FC-PGA (Flip Chip-PGA)**—After thousands of hours and millions of dollars in research, someone figured out that you could save valuable real estate in your CPU design simply by flipping the processor mounting over. Up until the advent of FC-PGA in 1999, an expensive manufacturing process was required to spin threads hundreds of times thinner than human hairs, connecting the leads from the embedded silicon to the connector pins on the bottom of the CPU package. By simply flipping the chip backward, a much less expensive process needed only to drop little beads of solder at the points where the chip makes contact with the pins. You can't see it in this book, but you can spot an FC-PGA package a mile away. It's green and uses the same type of plastic substrate material used for the mounting of a motherboard or expansion card. It was the advent of FC-PGA that spelled the end of Intel's experiment with cartridge packaging.

Cartridge design still is widely implemented; however, following Intel's lead, it's being phased out. Here are the three main types of cartridge packages for desktop systems (see Figure 9.2):

➤ **SEPP (Single-Edge Processor Package)**—The simplest form of cartridge mounting, pioneered by Intel's first Celeron processors. Essentially, a conventional-looking CPU is mounted on a card and surrounded by tiny SRAM chips that form the L2 memory cache. SEPPs are often sold with the active heat sink (fan) already clamped on, so you don't get to see this mounting. The technical name for the metal pins along the card edge at the bottom of the cartridge is *goldfingers*. No joke.

➤ **SECC (Single-Edge Contact Card)**—A more complex mounting of processor and surrounding chips, encased permanently in black plastic. The fan is a permanent fixture of this design. In its original form, the goldfingers at the bottom were also shrouded by the plastic case. However, installation required a special *retention mechanism* (a bunch of wires and prongs) that proved flimsy in practice.

➤ **SECC-2**—Intel's second try at this style of mounting, which ended up only slightly more durable. You can distinguish SECC-2 from SECC by looking for the newer version's exposed goldfingers. (If the people naming these things were paying attention, they would have retroactively dubbed SECC "Oddjob.")

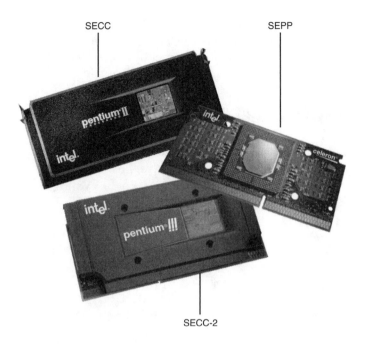

SECC

SEPP

SECC-2

Figure 9.2

The different types of car-tridge packages currently available.

The Wrenching Business of Sockets and Slots

The other determining factor of the size and shape of a CPU is how it connects to the motherboard. PGA packages require sockets; SEC packages require slots (see Figure 9.3).

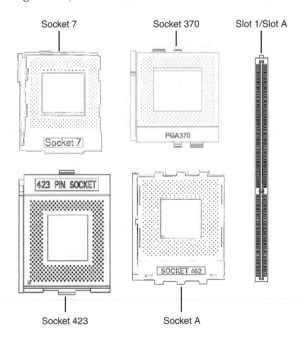

Socket 7

Socket 370

Slot 1/Slot A

Socket 423

Socket A

Figure 9.3

The various sockets and slot connectors currently in production.

169

Table 9.1 lists the types of sockets and slots being manufactured for motherboards (at the time of this writing), and the classes and packages of CPU that fit into these connectors. The "7" in "Socket 7" dates back to a time when Intel numbered its sockets by their generation in its CPU series; not by the number of pins it contains.

Table 9.1 Motherboard Sockets and Slots Currently Manufactured

Socket/ Slot	CPUs Supported	Package	Sys. bus (MHz)	Core Voltage
Socket 7 (296)	Intel Pentium 75–200	CPGA	50–66	3.3
	Intel Pentium MMX 133–233	CPGA	60–66	2.8/3.3
	AMD K6 166–266	CPGA	66	2.2–3.2/3.3
	AMD K6-2 266–366	CPGA	66	2.2/3.3
	VIA Cyrix MII 300–433	CPGA		2.9/3.3
Super 7 (296)	AMD K6 166–300	CPGA	100	2.2
	AMD K6-2 300–550	CPGA	100	2.2
	AMD K6-III 400–450	CPGA	100	2.2–2.4
Slot 1 (242)	Intel Celeron 266–433	SEPP	66	2.0
	Intel Pent. II 233–450	SECC	66	2.8
	Intel Pent. III 450–933	SECC2	100	2.0
Slot A (242)	AMD Athlon 500–1.0G	SECC	200	1.6–1.8
Socket 370	Intel Celeron 366–533	PPGA	66	2.0
	Intel Celeron 566–850	FC-PGA	66–100	1.5–1.65
	Intel Pentium III 450–933	PPGA	100–133	1.5–1.65
	Intel Pentium III 866–1G	FC-PGA	133	1.7
	VIA Cyrix III 333–700	CPGA	66–133	1.9
	VIA C3 733	CPGA	66–133	1.5
Socket A (462)	AMD Athlon 600–1.4G	CPGA	200–266	1.75
	AMD Duron 600–950	CPGA	200	1.6
Socket 423	Intel Pentium 4 1.4–1.7G	FC-PGA	400	1.7
Socket 478	Intel Pentium 4 1.4–1.7G	FC-PGA	100×4	1.4

The Pentium Pro series used Socket 8, which was Intel's largest socket ever, and more rectangular than square. A Pentium II OverDrive processor was developed for Socket 8 and designed to be installed on top of a Pentium Pro; then Intel dropped Socket 8 entirely. Later Intel created a separate category of SEC packaging for workstations and large servers; the connector was called Slot 2; its processors were dubbed "Xeon." Special versions of Pentium II and PIII were designed for Xeon; however, the design just never caught on and Slot 2 is likely to go the way of Socket 8. (However, the Xeon trademark will live on in high-end dual-processor products for workstations.)

The SEC Experiment

The Pentium II was Intel's first CPU series to be mounted on a Slot 1 SEPP package (see Figure 9.4) and is actually the technological equivalent of the Pentium Pro—the sixth generation of the 8086 CPU logic introduced in the first IBM PC. Introduced in 1999, Pentium III actually contains a series of processors that also are based around the Pentium Pro design. In other words, Pentium III actually is an extension—or an upgrade—to Pentium II. Introduced in 2001, Pentium 4 is an upgrade to Pentium III. The trouble is Intel made the upgrade and you didn't. With different upgrades comes different packaging. This is the story of how and why the packages changed even when some of the contents didn't.

Figure 9.4

How Intel envisioned Pentium II would be installed.

(Courtesy Intel Corp.)

All CPUs produced today utilize what is called *cache memory,* which mainly led to the explosion of CPU speed in the last five years. The principle of caching is that a processor tends to seek an address of memory that is very close to the address it sought just a little while ago. During the seek process, the CPU fills this extremely fast SRAM (static RAM) cache with a copy of the memory contents in the vicinity of the requested address.

Even though a CPU might support a handful of cache levels, since the advent of the Pentium it has supported two, dubbed L1 and L2. The L1 cache is smallest, has the fastest SRAM, and gets polled first. If the requested address isn't on L1, the CPU moves to L2, which is larger but perhaps not as fast. If the address isn't there the CPU moves to regular RAM (DRAM); upon finding the address, it reloads both caches. Often the requested address will have been copied to one or the other cache. Because polling SRAM memory is so much faster than polling ordinary DRAM, the effect is

171

like taking out your Chevy 350 engine and replacing it with one from an F-16. Not all CPUs come with their own L2 cache (for instance, VIA Cyrix III has none). By design, L2 cache memory is external to the CPU core; by contrast, the L1 cache is part of the core. On AMD's Athlon and Duron PPGA packages, you can see the SRAM chips as little rectangular bumps surrounding the CPU chip in the center.

When it was introduced in 1995, the Pentium Pro was the first to integrate L2 cache memory directly into the processor package, so that the CPU would not have to apportion cache memory from ordinary RAM. (The L1 cache is on the CPU chip; the L2 is outside.) Pentium Pro also became the first—and the only—CPU to utilize a type of packaging called Dual-cavity PGA. Although L2 cache integration was certainly nice, the narrowing of the distance between components that made room for L2 was blamed for overheating problems that made Pentium Pro the hottest chip since Lay's Chili Cheese & Onion.

The Securities and Exchange Commis...*ahem*, excuse me...The Single-Edge Contact (SEC) cartridge incorporates the CPU and its L2 cache, while enabling SRAM memory chips to be located a respectable distance away from the processor core. That was Intel's first reason for creating SEC.

The second reason was to enable Intel to utilize an interface to the motherboard that it could patent and, at least for awhile, block other chip manufacturers from continuing to follow in Intel's footsteps by producing pin-compatible, less expensive substitutes. For a while this strategy worked. AMD countered by developing an enhancement to the Socket 7 design utilized by Pentium MMX, which it called *Super 7*. It didn't change the size or shape of the socket nor the chip that fit into it, but it did change the allocation of Socket 7's pin assignments. It also enabled AMD's K6-III to support accelerated system bus speeds for motherboards built to support AMD's design. So a so-called "Super 7 motherboard" can only handle an AMD CPU, although a Socket 7 motherboard can support both Intel Socket 7 CPUs and AMD's K6-II and K6-III Super 7 CPUs.

The third reason for SEC was to try to make CPU installation and removal simpler than it had ever been before. This third goal totally backfired, as you'll see when we discuss installation later in this chapter.

In mid-1999 Intel made an unusual design decision, for the first time taking one step backward in history: All new Pentium IIIs and Celeron CPUs are produced for the old Socket 370, and its new Pentium 4 will be produced exclusively for the new Socket 478. So Intel has phased out production of SEPP package (Slot 1 and Slot 2) CPUs; all its competitors will either follow suit or lead the way, depending upon whom you ask. The effect was to make AMD—which had already retooled its factories to produce its exclusive Slot A design—suddenly appear behind the times rather than ahead of the game.

Why did Intel go back? First of all, Intel won its legal disputes with rival AMD, the result of which was that Intel claimed the exclusive right to its pin configuration. AMD would develop its own pin configurations for sockets and slots. This means Intel didn't have to fight the war with AMD by changing the rules of CPU manufacturing and relying upon motherboard producers to follow along; Intel wasn't bound to slots for slots' sake.

Second—and perhaps more important—the distance between the CPU and the SRAM chips forming its L2 cache was creating a huge performance hit on the processor at higher clock speeds. The newer FC-PGA packaging made it possible for Intel to reincorporate the L2 cache into the chip—the way it had intended from the beginning with Pentium Pro. With Intel's move, sockets were in once again. Motherboard manufacturers were designing new arrangements with space set aside for sockets, and AMD had to follow suit.

Slot Upgrade Kits, or Invasion of the Slockets

The coming obsolescence of Slot 1 and Slot A motherboards would be downright unfair if it weren't for the advent of upgrade kits that plug into the old slots and have new sockets attached. Now a growing list of small parts manufacturers, led by a motherboard manufacturer called Iwill, are developing simple devices that plug into Slot 1 and that offer a Socket 370.

With Iwill's delightfully dubbed Slocket II upgrade kit, you can conceivably upgrade a 450MHz Slot 1 Pentium II SECC system into a 533MHz Socket 370 Celeron PPGA system. First you insert the PPGA CPU into the socket just as you would if it were mounted on the motherboard (as you'll see later on, you always install the heat sink first). Then install Slocket II into Slot 1 almost as if it were a SEPP package CPU. The final result actually looks surprisingly similar. Even though Socket 370 has a lower voltage requirement than Slot 1, Slocket II serves as a voltage regulator, forcing the power from the slot to step down a notch or two.

Slocket II is available from IWill for $29 at its Web site, www.iwillusa.com. This is not a paid endorsement; Slocket II just comes highly recommended.

The Manufacturers and Their Products

When you decide to purchase a replacement CPU, your choice will be limited mainly by one of the following: the CPU socket or slot your current motherboard has, or the socket or slot on the motherboard that will replace the motherboard you have (the topic of Chapter 10, "Replacing the Motherboard and Its Parts"). You can't just buy any CPU you want unless you're willing to buy just any motherboard you want. That might not be a bad choice, but even that choice should be an informed one.

So almost like the US automobile industry, the CPU manufacturing industry has a "Big Three." (Although the lesser performer of these three companies isn't owned by Daimler.) Two of these manufacturers now have premium and standard product lines—not unlike the relationship of Mercury to Ford: luxury to economy. Now that we're now considering brand to be a factor in choosing our CPUs, what defines the major brands?

What Defines a Pentium ... Today?

The fifth and sixth generations of Intel CPUs—shown in Figure 9.5—are meshed together under some variant of the Pentium brand name. Today the oldest Pentium still widely available is the Pentium MMX 233. Still a member of the fifth generation, the *MMX* stood for *multimedia extensions*. This CPU was the first to incorporate special instructions for multimedia processing (moving memory around quickly, determining where lines and shapes should go on a display), directly into the microcode of the processor. Today, all sixth-generation Pentiums have ever increasing amounts of embedded microcode for these purposes.

Figure 9.5

Four Intel CPUs that were top-of-the-line in their time.

(Courtesy Intel Corp.)

Pentium MMX Socket 7
CPGA (early 1997-1999)

Pentium II Slot 1
SECC (mid-1997-2000)

Pentium III Socket
370 FC-PGA (1999-)

Pentium 4 Socket
423 FC-PGA (2001-)

MMX microcode was carried on into the Pentium II, which Intel released exclusively as a SECC cartridge. With the need for processors to handle streaming data from the Internet at a more rapid pace and develop faster 3D graphics displays, Intel's Pentium III replaced the MMX microcode with an acronym atop an acronym: Streaming Single-Instruction Multiple-Data Extensions (SSE). It is mainly the replacement of MMX with SSE that differentiates Pentium III from Pentium II in design. Of course Intel stopped producing Pentium II in 1999 at the 450MHz mark, whereas it still produces Pentium III today, having most recently announced, as of the time of this writing, a (corrected) 1,133MHz (1.1GHz) edition.

The PIII was the first Pentium to break away from the cartridge model with the announcement of the 500MHz through 733MHz editions in October of 1999. These new PIIIs were built with the new Flip Chip-PGA (FC-PGA) packaging and reincorporated the L2 cache not just in the package, but back on the chip itself (on-die). Despite these changes, independent testing showed the performance gains were not disproportionate with their speed increases (people expecting a boost didn't get it), and Intel's lower production costs didn't translate into lower street prices.

Intel's most mysterious moves of late have been with regard to the recently released Pentium 4. The first edition of P4 was released with a new form factor and a new socket: 423. Changing socket design is nothing new for Intel. Yet a few months later, Intel announced an "improved" version of P4 that would replace the existing version (already!) and utilize yet another new socket: 478. So anyone who had already purchased a Socket 423 system was cast into the Zone of Obsolescence in a matter of a handful of weeks.

These strange developments, coupled with the recall of high-end PIIIs on account of overheating problems, have placed the high-end Intel product line in the same spotlight as the Ford Explorer, under the category of Chronic Failures. This is sad, especially because both new P4 designs quadruple the data throughput rate of the standard system bus. The Socket 423 model quadruples the system bus clock to 400 MHz; the 478 model relies on new chipset technology, which enables the data bus to fetch four times the data per cycle as a standard 100MHz bus (thus the notation "100MHz × 4").

Celeron Salad

So what, you might ask, is Celeron? A newer brand of Intel processor than Pentium, Celeron (whose name translated into Latin means nothing whatsoever), is essentially "Pentium Lite." Celeron originally (ironically) was designed for Socket 370 motherboards; indeed in 1998 some PCs were released with Socket 370 Celerons on board. Yet the first consumer Celerons featured the new Slot 1 SEPP package (see Figure 9.6).

The first editions of Celeron omitted the L2 memory cache common to Pentium II systems. The result, claimed enthusiasts, was a crippled chip; Intel responded by returning it. Although all Celerons now feature an L2 cache, what has always distinguished Celeron from the corresponding clock speed of Pentium is that Celeron has less L2 cache than Pentium. In fact, some of today's Celerons actually share the same package design as Pentium III (both designs are code-named "Coppermine"), although the Celeron version has either omitted or simply disabled, segments of L2 memory. Today's PIIIs feature 256K of L2 cache, compared to Celeron's 128K.

Pentium has dibs on the highest clock speeds, so at the time of this writing Celeron has yet to break the 1GHz barrier. What has made Celeron so attractive—and successful, especially compared to Pentium—is that its price difference compared to its big sister often compensates more than fairly for its downgraded performance. In fact,

Celeron often is considered a thorn in Intel's ... uh, lower quarters ... because it competes with Pentium for the support of PC manufacturers. Today Celeron is the only Intel CPU still being manufactured that supports a system bus as slow as 66MHz. Newer Celerons support the 100MHz bus but not 133MHz—Pentium has dibs on that too.

Celeron Slot 1 SEPP (1998-1999)   Celeron Socket 370 PPGA (1999-2000)

Figure 9.6

The three Celerons, showing the rapid changes in Intel's bottom of the line.

(Courtesy Intel Corp.)

Celeron Socket 370 FC-PGA (2000-)

Intel Outside: The AMD Story

Today you can easily own a PC where no single part was ever touched by the mighty hands of Intel Corp. Unlike the case with operating systems, you might not always notice any difference at all.

Right now I'm typing on a computer with an Advanced Micro Devices (AMD) processor—a model K6-II. It's clocked at 450 MHz, but its true speed—in other words, its *measured performance*—blows away some Pentium III 650 systems. I know. I did the measuring myself. What do I mean by "blows away?" Some graphical operations were performed by the AMD system thirty times faster than on the PIII system. So "blows away," as in "ground zero," "fallout," and "radiation poisoning."

The K6-II and K6-III were the models that put AMD on the map. AMD still manufactures them, and Super 7 motherboards are still available that support K6. The advanced processing features of K6 are not only comparable to Pentium II, but in some cases hold a slight technological edge. Perhaps even more important, K6-II and K6-III not only fits into AMD's Super 7, but also a standard Socket 7; therefore it is a choice upgrade to a first edition Pentium or Pentium MMX system. Pentium Pro relied upon its own peculiar Socket 8, which demanded its own motherboard and its own specific chipset.

Intel never produced a mechanism for migrating a first edition Pentium system into the Pentium Pro realm. One could argue it would have been pointless, anyway, because such a device would have exceeded the price of a new motherboard. But since Intel chose a design path that led to incompatibility, K6 capitalized by giving Pentium owners a bridge to Pentium Pro–like technology.

AMD now is a major player in the CPU business because of K6's success. Today you can purchase systems from HP, Gateway, Sony, Compaq (soon to be part of HP), and a little blue company called IBM, all of which feature AMD-brand CPUs. AMD's current line of Pentium-competitive processors (see Figure 9.7) is called Athlon (also known as Athlon-K7, in keeping with AMD's own lineage of generations). AMD staked its claim to history by producing the first CPU package clocked at more than 1GHz. At the time of this writing, 1.2GHz models are common and 1.4GHz models are just being released.

Figure 9.7

AMD's newest Athlon processor, with SRAM cache bumps clearly visible.

(Courtesy AMD Corp.)

On the low end, AMD's Celeron-competitive line is called the *Duron series.* The key distinguishing factor between Duron and Athlon—and, for that matter, between Celeron and Pentium—is the amount of on-board cache memory. Duron is limited to 64K of L2; Athlon supports 256K of L2.

What makes AMD so competitive to Intel, besides its fabulous performance numbers, is its pricing schemes. This is where Intel has felt the pinch the hardest. However, if Intel still has an edge, it may be in the compatibility department.

All AMD processors manufactured today require their own sockets and slots, called Socket A and Slot A, respectively. Slot A shared the same physical dimensions as Slot 1, and used the same number of pins; however, the pin configurations were different. (Why? Fewer Intel lawyers in AMD's lobby.) After Intel's move back to socketed CPUs, AMD followed by devising its own socket, with its own shape and pin configurations, which were completely incompatible with Intel's at that time (AMD: 462 pins; Intel: 370).

You'd think AMD would have found itself in the same marketing box as Intel with its unsuccessful Pentium Pro. However, AMD had two advantages: one natural, the other the result of another brilliant marketing move. Naturally, everyone loves the underdog. Motherboard manufacturers want Intel to be a player, just not a dominant force in their industry as Microsoft is in operating systems.

Capitalizing on that sentiment, AMD got into the chipset business and now markets Athlon- and Duron-compatible chipsets for ridiculously low prices, for major motherboard manufacturers itching to have the first models on the market clocked at 1.4 GHz. Today an AMD processor plus a motherboard with an AMD chipset can cost less than an Intel processor alone.

However, although AMD is free to license its "A" specifications to anyone else, including Intel, there's no way we'll ever see Intel manufacturing a Pentium or Celeron CPU that fits in Socket A. So if your motherboard follows one of AMD's "A" specifications, you will not be able to upgrade it with an Intel CPU. Of course you can choose another AMD CPU; when it's time for you to make that decision, AMD will be around.

VIA: Assuming the Cyrix Mantle

The other major competitive brand to Intel is VIA Technologies, which has assumed control of the designs and facilities of the former Cyrix Corporation. Cyrix had a troubled past, especially after having its parent company shift from IBM, to National Semiconductor, to VIA in the course of only two years' time.

However, with each new parent Cyrix acquired some valuable tools. IBM exercised its rights to purchase a majority of Cyrix shares in 1998 as part of a deal that gave Cyrix access to the IBM manufacturing facility that made CPUs for the first IBM PCs, under license from Intel. This plant already knows how to make Intel designs. As part of National, Cyrix was retooled with chip manufacturing technologies patented by National, as part of its first effort to build consumer PC components. That effort failed—but not for technological reasons.

VIA has the marketing savvy that Cyrix never had, that National couldn't build, and that IBM somehow lost. It's a small firm, but it's the world's leading producer of motherboard chipsets—with greater market share than even Intel. (Check your own chipset right now. There's a 40 percent chance it has a VIA logo.) As AMD proved, to be a successful CPU contender, you need to be big in chipsets.

With IBM's old plant and National's patented production techniques, VIA is gambling big. At the time of this writing VIA announced its new top-of-the-line CPU and the next generation of the Cyrix design. What makes the VIA C3 such a big deal is it's walking straight into the Intel minefield, calling its lawyers' bluff. VIA C3 plugs directly into Socket 370 and will be marketed as a low-cost, high-performance upgrade for Celeron-based PCs. No new motherboard required (see Figure 9.8).

Figure 9.8

VIA's C3 makes the CPU market a three-way race again.

(Courtesy VIA Technologies)

What Cyrix gained from National has helped VIA build the C3 into the smallest CPU chip currently available. Why does that matter? Certainly not for motherboard real estate reasons, because all Socket 370 CPGA packages are the same size. First there's the performance factor. When you're dealing with sizes this small, the closer the internal components and transistors can be to one another, the less time it takes for an electron to move from one transistor to another. So higher density can mean greater speed. It also can mean higher temperature, as electrons running so close to one another tend to create friction, resulting in heat. But the chip's diminished real estate compensates for that somewhat. VIA claims its smaller die size more than compensates for any density problem. This is a claim that has yet to be verified...to quote an old movie cliché, this one's gonna be close.

During Cyrix's last corporate transition, VIA continued to market Cyrix's then-top-of-the-line M III. It, too is a Socket 370 CPU, but its fate at that time was undecided. VIA's entry-level upgrade processor is Cyrix's former top-of-the-line M II (read: M2). Cyrix boasted that M II was capable of outperforming an Intel processor with equal clock speed by about 33 percent. That said, Cyrix adopted a nomenclature for M II that refers more to equivalent performance than clock speed (as AMD did in the past with its K5, although not with K6).

For instance, an M II PR433 actually is a 350MHz chip, although VIA claims it has roughly equivalent performance to an Intel Celeron 433. VIA continues to use the "PR" designation for M II but has not carried this little trick on to M III or C3, both of which report correct clock speeds.

Cyrix was largely absent from the CPU wars of 1999 and 2000. Although VIA has gone a long way to bring the Cyrix designs back into the fray, it still has a way to go. The remaining VIA Cyrix III models follow Cyrix's long tradition of omitting the L2 cache altogether to save on costs; the result is a package that is painfully slow for its clock speed. With the new VIA C3, the company dropped the "yrix" in exchange for the first 64K L2 cache in the series' history, vaulting the new CPU's performance back to competitive levels.

Speed: Illusion and Realities

I'm about to make the question, "How fast is your computer?" just a bit more confusing; then I'm going to make the answer to it somewhat clearer than it might have been before. The way I do this is by blowing to bits two of the most proliferated myths about PCs: 1) Your computer is necessarily as fast as its CPU; 2) Your CPU sets the speed of your computer.

Matching CPU Timing with Motherboard Timing

The speed of your computer is regulated by its motherboard—namely by the speed of its system bus. (Some sources call this the *frontside bus* or FSB.) Prior to 1989, the speed of the motherboard's system bus and that of the CPU indeed were the same— that's how we thought it had to be. Then Intel surprised everyone by pulling the 486DX2 processor out of its magic hat—a *clock-doubled chip* whose internal speed could be double that of the system bus. The speed with which a CPU calculated formulas and went about its own business was no longer tied to the speed at which it communicated with the rest of the components on the motherboard.

Today virtually all PCs produced contain CPUs whose clock speeds are some multiple of the system bus speed. It isn't the CPU itself that decides what multiple that is; rather it is a jumper setting on the motherboard somewhere in the vicinity of the CPU.

The system bus is the line of communication between the components on the motherboard—the main highway, if you will. There are little tributaries and dirt roads that divert off this bus. Then there's the expansion bus (or buses in the case of ISA and PCI, which compete for real estate in modern computers), which is an entirely different route that connects to the system bus. Bus controllers, the CPU, and memory all are linked by the system bus. Since the advent of the Pentium CPU, the system bus speed has become slower than the internal operating speed of the CPU.

What is CPU speed, really? Is it some fast pace that has to be worked up to, like some guy exercising on a treadmill? No, actually CPU speed is more like a metronome pedantically counting tick, tock, tick, tock, tick, tock at an amateur piano recital. Four hundred megahertz is four hundred million ticks and tocks per second. (Talk about a minute waltz!) CPU speed is the regulation speed for the processor—the speed at which it expects to perform to perform nominally.

The CPU depends on the motherboard's system bus controller to put out a clock signal—literally to act as the conductor of the orchestra. Because the bus controller doesn't put out a clock signal as fast as the Pentium CPU actually plans to run, it comes up with a way to perform two cycles of work for every beat it hears, or three cycles per beat, or 2.5 cycles per beat. The chosen number—to make things easier on the CPU—is some multiple of 0.5. So if the system bus is clocked at 66MHz (actually 66.66666 … MHz, but the number is rounded off in casual conversation) a 200MHz Pentium MMX achieves its clock speed by means of a 3× multiplier (3 times 66.66666 is roughly 200).

Your motherboard will accept only CPUs whose clock speed is exactly that of the system bus (today that's practically a joke) or whose speed is equal to the system bus speed times a certain supported *multiplier.* The multiplier is chosen either by a jumper setting on the motherboard or through a setting in the motherboard's BIOS. For instance, a Celeron 400 expects a 66MHz system bus speed, which means the motherboard you choose must support a 6x multiplier (very common nowadays).

As a rule, upgradable motherboards built for Intel processors support the following system bus speeds: 25, 33, 50, 60, 66, 75, 100, 133, 166, and 200MHz. (233MHz was forthcoming at the time of this writing.) The 25 and 33 numbers are archaic and no longer used.

Here's a question that might be running through your mind: If the CPU's speed truly is regulated by the motherboard, what happens if you plug a CPU that is designed to run slower than the motherboard setting? For instance, say you plug a 500MHz Celeron processor into a Socket 370 motherboard with a 66MHz system bus and you set the multiplier to 8 instead of 7.5. Will the CPU run at 533MHz? Uh … yeah. It will. Will there be smoke? Probably. What you would have done is something called *overclocking.* It's fast becoming a kind of recreational sport among tech-heads—the computing equivalent of surf-diving (sky diving on a surf board). Super, dude, you did something you weren't s'pose ta'. But is the chance of smoke, sparks, and fire really worth it to save the whopping five bucks difference between the Celeron 500 and Celeron 533?

In light of how cheap hardware is today, overclocking is simply nuts. It's tinkering for the sake of tinkering, to see how far and how long you can bend a rule—in this case, a silly spec. A CPU might be the engine of a PC, but a computer isn't an automobile; you can't just play mechanic and tweak a little bit more horsepower every day out of a system that wasn't built for it just by oiling and polishing it. You either get 33MHz or 50MHz more clock speed, or none at all—unless you like fireworks. Okay, maybe you won't see sparks fly today, and maybe you can tweak a little more speed out of Windows for the time being (a bit like racing with a bunch of lead bricks tied behind you). However, if you're the type who likes to ask for trouble in this way, while you're at it why not try fixing that squeaky power supply fan with a salad fork? If overclocking your CPU really is your idea of excitement, boy, you really need a life.

181

How Do You Really Measure Speed?

Megahertz (millions of processor cycles per second) has been used historically as a marketing tool—a way to emphasize high speed without having to explain to consumers the methodology behind true performance testing. However, after realizing that consumers really do have brains, Intel devised a rating system it calls *iCOMP*, which is a measure of the relative performance of CPUs. Independent sources such as the phenomenally useful CPU Scorecard (www.cpuscorecard.com) also have adapted the iCOMP 3.0 suite of benchmarks for AMD and VIA processors, and report its test results up to the minute on their Web sites.

The iCOMP project arose from an honest attempt by Intel to demonstrate the overall speed gains in its advanced designs when they are put to work doing real-world work—calculating figures, fetching data, projecting graphics images. iCOMP 3.0 is a relative index. For the sake of comparison, iCOMP 3.0 rates a Pentium II 350 at 1000, and an old 16MHz 386SX at 10. If we can agree that a PII 350 is 100 times the computer than the 386SX used to be, we can draw an imaginary performance line in our minds from 10 to 1000 and into the stratosphere. At the point called 4297, we can mark the fastest performing CPU available at the time of this writing: AMD's Athlon 1.4GHz. Following right behind at 4213 is Intel's Pentium 4 1.7GHz. These machines have more than four times the performance of the old PII 350.

Now think about that just for a moment: That Athlon is clocked 300MHz slower than that P4; yet it's still a hair faster. If you equate performance with clock speed, Athlon's 1400MHz certainly is four times that of the PII 350. The Athlon is right in proportion—but the P4 is way off; thus you can no longer trust clock speed to measure performance.

The Issue of Lower Voltage

Voltage has become a critically important issue with regard to CPU packaging. As processors evolve, they require less voltage—Pentium started out requiring 5 volts; now it needs as low as 1.4. The reason for the lower power is processors are so busy these days that, at higher voltage, they would generate way too much heat to live in something as small as a PC case. The motherboard you choose must be capable of providing exactly the voltage requirements of the CPU. This is sometimes difficult to assess, because some manufacturers (even Intel) don't specify all of their voltage requirements.

Power reduction is not an instantaneous thing; you don't simply plug a 2.5 volt chip into a socket built for 3.3 and expect the CPU to know to draw less power. The power is pushed toward the CPU by the power supply; not drawn from the supply like a straw. So the power leading to the socket must be of the voltage expected by the CPU or you get a simulation of the end results of overclocking. Luckily, modern motherboards do feature jumpers that enable you to set the proper voltage levels from the power supply—for most circumstances.

Techno Talk

The Pentium MMX CPU series required two separate lines of power for separate regions of the CPU package: one for the outer I/O area and another, lower voltage line for the processor core. To support the MMX, the motherboard's voltage regulator had to supply *split rail* power levels. Socket 7 motherboards include jumpers that let you set the voltage level; if a motherboard supports split rail it will have two such sets, often marked "INT." and "EXT." If your Socket 7 motherboard doesn't have two sets of voltage jumpers, you absolutely cannot install a Pentium MMX CPU.

The voltage requirements published by CPU manufacturers are recommendations. So you might be able to fudge a tenth of a volt here and there, but you take risks in doing so. Too little power to the CPU and you could get Blue Screens of Death pouring out at you from Windows; too much power and … what's that you smell? Mmmmm! Fried silicon! Breakfast of overclockers! However, depending on how your motherboard's set up, you might be faced with a situation in which you have to risk setting the power to plus or minus a tenth of a volt over the recommended level. Make certain that you have more than adequate cooling and ventilation (the subject of Chapter 20, "Cooling and Ventilating Your System"). Instead of the risks, you might consider replacing your motherboard with one that has a greater variety of voltage settings.

Who do you trust to tell you what your voltage setting should be? In the end, your motherboard manufacturer knows best. CPUs are not built to work with specific motherboards; however, motherboards are built to work with specific CPUs. Board manufacturers have already tested every brand and clock speed of CPU they intend to use, and they know what each voltage setting should be. Your motherboard's manual will tell you explicitly; if it's not available, check the manufacturer's Web site. More about voltage settings coming up in Chapter 10.

Performing Brain Surgery (Replacing the CPU)

Replacing the CPU in your PC is relatively easy; that is, if you try not to think about all the things that can go wrong. Put those ideas of smoke, sparks, electrocution, and massive explosions followed by fire trucks and paramedics, and volcanoes spewing lava in great gushers that blast away whole sides of mountains and terrorize villages, and asteroids colliding with Earth sending shockwaves through the oceans … right

183

out of your head. Be advised at this point that you've already read the most difficult part of this chapter. Deciding what upgrade CPU you need is the most difficult thing I talk about here. Believe me: I've swapped AA batteries in a portable CD with more difficulty than I've swapped CPUs on a motherboard. However, I do take precautionary measures, and I do stay alert and concentrate on the task at hand.

Check This Out

As a precautionary measure, you should make certain the BIOS you have on your motherboard is the most recent version that supports the CPU you are about to install. If it isn't, you should update the BIOS on your PC before you replace the CPU. Why? Because code in the new BIOS might be necessary to support your new processor, and you won't be able to upgrade your BIOS after the installation if the old BIOS code doesn't work and you can't boot your system. Take a look at Chapter 10 for full instructions on how you can update your flash BIOS.

After you have your new CPU ready, follow the steps in Chapter 4, "What You Need to Know *Before* You Open Your PC," for preparing to open your PC. Follow all the steps, such as backing up your data, copying down your BIOS/CMOS information, and updating your emergency diskette. Remove any parts that stand in the way of the CPU. Make a note of what you remove and where the cables go, so you can get everything back together again. A perfectly safe thing to do is mark on the ribbon cables with a magic marker—something simple such as "HD" and an arrow pointing to the hard drive—before you unplug any cables.

Before you touch your old CPU, make sure you discharge any static electricity! Touch your coworker, a metal table, or whatever; then stand still so you don't build up any more static. Or, better yet, invest in a grounding strap that you wear on your wrist—it's worth the money! Keep in mind that, even though your PC might be completely unplugged from the wall, its power supply can still retain enough electricity to send a spike through your body (if you're not properly grounded), which can literally bounce off you and onto another part of your PC, thus frying it. (My husband, who's normally very careful, lost a floppy drive this way.)

Removing the SPGA-Type CPU

All modern PGA-type CPUs utilize the Zero Insertion Force socket, with the little one-armed-bandit lever along the side. Look at the bottom of your CPU for short, stubby pins rather than legs. Then look for the presence of a single lever to one side of the socket. If it's there and the CPU has short pins, you have a ZIF socket—and reason to rejoice (see Figure 9.9).

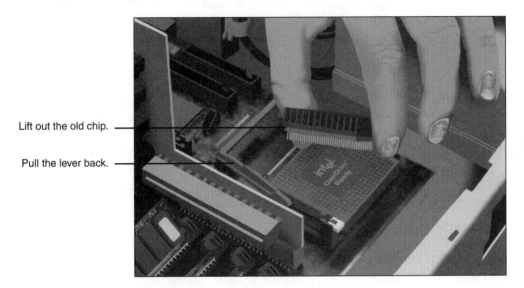

Lift out the old chip.

Pull the lever back.

Figure 9.9

With a ZIF socket, removing a CPU is easy.

Before you go on, notice whether your existing CPU has a fan attached to it. If so, there is a thin pair of spaghetti wires leading to the power supply or to the mother-board. There's a single plug for these two, connected to one corner of the fan. Take note of which color of wire is plugged where, because you might need to plug this wire back into your new fan. If necessary, tear off a piece of masking tape and stick it on the header where this plug goes, unless it's marked well enough ("FAN") that you can't miss it. The plug now should easily slide off of the fan. If your new CPU doesn't have a fan, well, maybe it should because you're about to disconnect one from your old CPU. It's an easy matter to simply clamp the old fan onto the new CPU.

Removing the PGA CPU from the ZIF socket sounds like an emergency room procedure, but it's actually quite a simple matter. The lever on the side is spring-locked down and only swings one direction. Gently pull the lever toward you and it will give way. When that happens, your CPU will be completely loose. Grab two edges of the heat sink mechanism and lift straight up. Done.

Installing Your New PGA-Type CPU

Now's the time to ask this question: Is your heat sink installed? If it isn't, before you clamp the CPU into the socket is the time to put it on. An active heat sink should slide right onto one side. If you have a fan kit that requires a little bit of pre-assembly, be sure you attach the clamp that matches your CPU packaging and socket. Socket 7, Socket 370, and Socket A all are different sizes; so are their heat sinks.

Before you attach a passive heat sink, here's what you do:

➤ If you have a CPGA (ceramic top, completely flat), coat the face of the CPU (not the side with the pins sticking out of it) with a thin layer of heat sink compound. Coat as much as you can all the way up to the edges.

➤ If you have a PPGA (plastic top), there should be a well or moat around the outside where you can lay a bead of compound; just like caulking your baseboards in your house. If your PPGA happens to have a metal cap in the center like the engine block of a Boss Mustang, coat just the metal cap. No need to go out to the edges. Don't worry about touching the compound, either; it feels like moisturizing cream and it isn't poisonous unless you spread it on a sandwich or a cracker.

➤ If you have an FC-PGA (green with a little black hump in the center where the chip is), don't attach a passive heat sink (see Figure 9.10)! It won't fit, so you don't need any compound. Instead use a fan assembly (active heat sink, as in Figure 9.11).

Figure 9.10

A passive heat sink looks like tiny towers attached to the top of a CPGA or PPGA CPU.

Now take a good look at the empty socket. If only one corner of it is notched or beveled in some way, that corner indicates the location of pin 1. Think of pin 1 as polar north from the perspective of the motherboard. Now look at the face of the CPU for a white dot, a black box, a gold box, or a gold arrow in one corner—something. That's the indicator of pin 1 on the CPU. If the logo is facing you, pin 1 should be in the lower-left corner. Can't see the face of the chip because the heat sink's installed? Then scan the sides of the chip beneath the heat sink for a notch in one corner. Can't tell which is a notch and which could be a worn-off part of the corner? Turn the CPU upside-down and look for any type of bright marking around one of the corner pins. That's pin 1. Align that pin with the pin 1 location on the socket (see Figure 9.12).

Figure 9.11

An active heat sink (fan) really cools down a fast CPU.

Figure 9.12

Match the notch on the socket with the one on your CPU.

With the heat sink securely in place, align pin 1 on the chip with pin 1 on the socket. If pin 1 is not marked on your socket look for a corner that is missing a pin hole; that corner is where pin 1 is located. Leave the lever up at this point. Press down on the chip firmly but very carefully; then swing the lever back into its original position. Know that you cannot snugly fit the lever back down with the CPU in the wrong place because of the way the pins are organized. If the lever is stuck, you might not have the chip seated in the proper direction or you might have to wiggle it a bit.

Removing the SEC-Type CPU

To begin, there should be power leading from the power supply to the fan, so disconnect it. There might be support clips supporting the heat sink—not the card with the processor on it—so unhook them. The cartridge now is held in place by two plastic guideposts on either edge. On the top of these guideposts are plastic tabs that hold the cartridge down. With your thumbs, push these tabs out so that the rails on the inside of the posts are unblocked; then firmly but gently lift the cartridge through the rails and out from between the posts.

Installing the SEC-Type CPU

Now's the time to ask this question: Is your heat sink installed? If you have an SEPP (PII or PIII), it actually shouldn't be off. If it's off, now is the time to put it on. Your Pentium II or Pentium III cartridge came with either a passive or active heat sink. You don't need any special creams for this maneuver; just snap the device into place at the marked positions on one side. Use low insertion force here. If you have a fan, plug in its power cord leading from the motherboard. Can't find it? It's a thin pair of spaghetti wires, one red, one yellow; almost all power supplies have at least a few of these in its tangled mess of cables.

The installation process here isn't quite as easy as it was originally supposed to be. The reason isn't technical as much as it is practical: Slot 1 requires guideposts to hold the cartridge in place and to align it with the pins in the slot. The guideposts are two plastic posts that stick straight out of the motherboard itself and are slightly reminiscent of the towers of the Golden Gate Bridge. It's impractical to ship the motherboard with these posts installed because it would increase the size of the overall package and waste airspace. So it's up to you to install these posts yourself. No problem, right? Four plastic screws are all you need; how hard can that be? They're not even electrical parts.

Did you ever have the old A.M.T. plastic model of the Starship *Enterprise* when you were a kid? By any chance do you recall the process of cementing the two long engine pylons in place over the lower secondary hull? And holding onto the engines like Atlas holding up the world for about a week until the cement dried? Of course, at that point, the engines weren't sitting right. So, cursing under your breath with a fake Scottish accent, you had to X-Acto off the pylon connectors and start all over? This is what the process of getting the guideposts exactly right is like. Sure, they're screwed on, they're perpendicular to the motherboard, they stick straight up, no sweat. Right? Try getting the pins on the cartridge to line up over the slot. Just try it. I'll wait. (I'm busy holding onto these engine pylons anyway.)

If you've just removed your old SEC, big deal; you don't have to worry about gluing the guideposts in place. From a technical perspective, there's nothing to this job. Two posts, four screws, four holes. Each post cradles one edge of the slot, which is already on the motherboard. There's a screw on either side of the flange on each post. What you're hoping at this point is that the pilot holes in the motherboard have been drilled at the right spots. If they're slightly off, you're forced to employ a special kind of arm wrestling to maneuver the post into place without breaking it.

Okay, let's say your best estimate is that your posts are securely in place. This should be the easy part: The CPU cartridge can slide through the posts in only one direction; if you have to force it, it's turned the wrong way. Let the guideposts direct it into place. The cartridge's connectors should snap into the slot just like the pins on an expansion card (see Figure 9.13).

At the top of the guideposts may be two plastic tabs that should automatically snap shut, holding the cartridge in place after it's securely fastened into the slot.

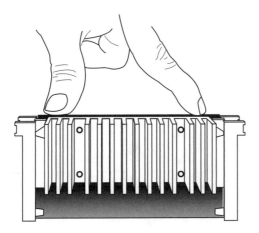

Figure 9.13

Inserting a SEC cartridge.

Your CPU is now in your computer. It probably won't work just yet, so don't turn anything on. Instead, skip over to Chapter 23, to the segment called "Fiddling with Jumpers and Switches and Such," which shows you how to set the system bus speed, set the CPU speed multiplier, and set the CPU voltage. Now that you know what these three things mean, setting the jumpers for them should be incredibly simple. (If only Windows were this simple!)

Mistakes to Avoid

If your new CPU doesn't work, turn the PC off. If you have a ZIF socket, make certain the lever on the side is all the way down so that it feels snapped shut. Also make sure the CPU is aligned properly, with pin 1 in the pin 1 hole on the socket. The chip doesn't fit securely if the pin 1 notches aren't aligned. In addition, check carefully to make sure the CPU is inserted fully into the socket—this might be hard to tell if a fan is in the way.

If the fan is making noise (believe me, it probably will), don't unplug it while your computer is turned on. Don't thump it with your thumb to shut it up. And *do not*, unless you're a pyromaniac, spray WD-40 or any other industrial lubricant on the thing.

If you are dealing with a non-Intel CPU, check with the manufacturer to make sure there are no conflicts with the hardware in your PC, such as the video card. Non-Intel CPUs might come with upgrade software that you must run to make them work with Windows. Your PC should boot fine, but you need to let Windows install some new drivers that are part of that software for it to test the CPU and upgrade Windows to match. Your Intel CPU also might come with software such as a fan monitor program that will warn you if the fan stops working—but you will not need to install this software to get Windows to work with your CPU.

Once you're sure you've got everything right, put your PC back together and get back to your life.

The Least You Need to Know

➤ The clock speed of your new CPU must equal the system bus speed on the motherboard times one of its supported multipliers.

➤ The voltage requirements of your new CPU also must be supported by the motherboard.

➤ The fact that CPU is clocked faster does not mean that it is faster. If you do your research, you'll soon discover some CPUs are faster than faster CPUs. Literally.

➤ The fact that a CPU is clocked faster does not mean it's more expensive. The only reason you could really save money by going with the faster model is because it happens to be more popular.

➤ Overclocking is for people who like to experiment. (Did you ever make your own fireworks when you were a kid?) Something tells me that's not you.

➤ Today's AMD-brand CPUs are built to be compatible only with motherboards that explicitly support AMD. VIA-brand CPUs, on the other hand, are designed for pin compatibility with Intel sockets.

➤ All SEC-type cartridge CPUs come complete with their own heat sink mechanism. Fans are preferable to forests of graphite spikes, although the two together are a powerful combination.

Chapter 10

Replacing the Motherboard and Its Parts

In This Chapter

➤ The important work done by your motherboard's chipset

➤ Finding a motherboard that has a chipset that's right for your CPU

➤ The preparations you'll need to make for installing your motherboard

➤ The "smoke test" method of installing a motherboard

➤ The BIOS error codes you might expect to hear if something's wrong, including the "plaintive wail"

➤ How to re-flash your flash BIOS

➤ How to replace your BIOS chips whether or not you have flash BIOS

➤ Jump-starting a dead battery

Let's get one myth out of the way right up front: Replacing the motherboard of your PC is not that big a deal. In terms of sheer difficulty, although it's probably the most difficult installation job you could do with your PC, it's no more difficult than that outdoor play set or plywood bookshelf you've probably made. When a motherboard installation becomes extremely difficult, the reason most likely is poor system case design. You'll have a few loose screws to contend with and some electrical plugs to coordinate. If your system case is well designed, you should be able to isolate which screw and which plug goes where in a matter of minutes. The all-inclusive answer to poor system case design is to replace the system case. If you look real hard, you can find manufacturers who bundle system cases, motherboards, a CPU, and peripherals like hard drives together in one neat package. (Well, that's one way to replace a motherboard.)

In terms of expense, forget it. The average price of a motherboard in 2001 is about the same as the average price of a modem in 1999: about $75. Remember, a motherboard doesn't usually include a CPU or memory (RAM); those parts usually are sold separately. The CPU is probably your most expensive core component, with RAM coming in a distant second.

Perhaps the most difficult element of the motherboard replacement scenario is determining which one you need or want. There is certainly no monopoly on motherboards in the PC business. Literally hundreds of manufacturers do business in this market, some of whom you've heard (such as Intel, although it isn't the leader in this market), although most probably won't ring a bell within a five-mile radius of you (Asus, Tyan, MSI).

Even these unheard-of companies are strong, well respected, and build reliable products. These products are based on *chipsets,* which are sets of one to four chips (no kidding!) that have taken over the functions of running the system bus, peripheral buses, and the basic interfaces such as FDD, IDE, and PCI. VIA Technologies today is considered the leading chipset manufacturer (you were introduced to VIA back in Chapter 9, "Accelerating Your PC with a New CPU"). Intel also is a chipset manufacturer but now runs second in market share. Companies such as SiS and CPU speed leader AMD follow along behind.

Shopping for a New Motherboard

The one thing you'll notice when going motherboard shopping these days is that political correctness has struck the PC industry. Although engineers years before the days of the PC referred to mother- and daughterboards, apparently even this poetic reference has the potential for offense or insult. The casualty—as is always the case when working to blunt the literary gender dagger—is the English language. Today you'll find numerous replacement names for motherboard floating about: mainboard, systemboard, PC board, circuit board, backplane, mobo, and desktop board.

Motherboard Judgment Criteria

Whether it's truly a board or truly a mother, the one thing a motherboard must do for you is fit, in a number of key ways. Keep these pointers in mind when shopping for a replacement motherboard:

> ➤ Make sure the motherboard will fit your PC's case. When a motherboard is cut to fit within a given *form factor,* the holes drilled into it should align perfectly

with the mounting poles in the system case. If it doesn't, your system case is at fault; not the motherboard. Replace the system case with one made by a company that knows where to put its holes. (Every company should live up to that axiom, shouldn't it?)

➤ Make certain your new motherboard is compatible with your existing power supply and that it supports the same power connector. Your power supply should have plugs that meet the voltage requirements of your chipset and your CPU. Generally these two requirements are the same; however, with newer systems they're different and, as time goes on the required voltage of newer CPUs have decreased; not increased.

➤ Check what type of CPU your motherboard is designed to support.

➤ Make sure the new motherboard will accommodate the memory modules you plan on reusing, if any. If your modules support parity, so should your motherboard. Chapter 11, "Memorize This! Upgrading Memory," will offer some pointers in this department.

➤ Pay attention to the chipset the motherboard uses. You'll want one that supports the widest range of options. Chipsets today support multiple, selectable system bus speeds. The more multipliers you have, the more CPU speed options will be available. Your CPU's clock speed should be equivalent to your system bus speed times your selected multiplier. I'll explain this in further detail coming up.

➤ Find out the types and number of expansion slots the motherboard uses, and whether they match the types of expansion cards you want to reuse. The number and position of expansion slots must match the slots cut into the back of your PC's case. Again, certain form factors prescribe the location of expansion slots; it's up to your system case to match this location. If it doesn't, you'll have an easier time finding a new system case that fits your new motherboard than you will finding a new motherboard that fits your old system case.

Check This Out

Make sure you receive several plastic or brass standoffs with your motherboard; you'll need them for proper installation. They look like oversized tuxedo shirt buttons and act as posts that keep your motherboard fixed in place, providing a space between it and your (metal) PC case.

Fascinating Facts About Form Factors

Breakfast cereal is commonly sold in three form factors: regular size, super size, and economy size. Equally flaky is the nomenclature given to the form factors of today's motherboards. A motherboard's form factor is supposed to describe its general size, and identify the type of system case it fits into and the size of power supply that fits along with it. However, as Table 10.1 shows, the form factor names for a motherboard and its respective system case don't necessarily match. Form factors are listed in order of their relative age, oldest to newest.

Table 10.1   Motherboard Form Factors

Motherboard Form Factor	System Case Form Factors	Motherboard Width	Motherboard Length
Full AT	Full AT, full tower	12"	13"
Baby AT	Baby AT or larger	8.5"	13"
LPX	Slimline	9"	13"
Mini LPX	Slimline	9"	11"
ATX	ATX	12"	9.6"
Mini ATX	ATX	11.2"	8.2"
NLX	Slimline	9"	13.6"
microATX	SFX (power supply)	9.6"	9.6"
FlexATX	SFX (power supply)	9"	7.5"

Here's some more of what you need to know about these form factors:

➤ **Full AT and Baby AT**—You'll find Full AT motherboards in old 386s. A whole foot wide, it simply doesn't fit into today's smaller cases. Baby ATs were used in just about all computers until sometime in 1997. They usually include a single, full-sized keyboard connector built into the motherboard. The CPU and RAM are located at the front of the motherboard. Long expansion cards float over this area; that is, if the heat sink on the CPU doesn't block them. If your system case was built for AT or Baby AT, you really shouldn't keep it when you replace your motherboard.

➤ **ATX and Mini ATX**—The most widely used form factor, especially in Pentium Pro and Pentium II computers. With ATX you'll find your serial and parallel port (and the PS2 mouse port) connectors soldered to the motherboard. You'll find the CPU and RAM located on the right side, in the back, near the power supply. The power supply, by the way, is connected with a single 20-pin connector, instead of the two 6-pin connectors used on an AT/Baby AT motherboard. Also, the power supply on the ATX motherboard is controlled not by the ON/OFF switch but by software. So always treat the power supply in such a system as if it's on.

➤ **LPX and Mini LPX**—Used in older Slimline cases, LPX's most distinguishing feature is the expansion card riser: a tower into which you plug your expansion cards (sideways). Typically, the video graphics, parallel, serial, and PS2 mouse controllers are built in to the motherboard chipset. The word "Slimline," for obvious marketing reasons, was chosen over "minuscule, crammed tight, zero-ventilation brick" to describe the LPX, Mini LPX, and NLX cases. Both Slimline and ATX cases are available as desktops or towers, but Slimlines have proven more popular for desktop units because they leave such a small *footprint*. The truth is a Slimline is the least comfortable case your computer could possibly use. If you're rebuilding your new system from the ground up, avoid a Slimline case unless you intend to use it in a submarine, space capsule, or other tight quarters where air is more precious for your own purposes than it is for your computer.

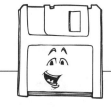

Techno Talk

The **footprint** of a system case is simply its dimensions. Thus, a system case that has a small footprint is small in size.

➤ **NLX**—Used in newer Slimline cases. With NLX you'll find a riser for the expansion cards. As a matter of fact, the floppy disk drive (FDD) controller in the NLX motherboard attaches to this riser. Because an NLX motherboard is slightly fatter than an ATX is tall, the best replacement currently available for an NLX motherboard is another NLX. Because ATX is the form factor in wide distribution, you run into a situation in which you might be stuck with your original brand-name supplier.

➤ **microATX, FlexATX**—What's the least comfortable case ever made? Well, it's a tie between microATX and FlexATX. Intel created these two form factors as a way of appeasing manufacturers who build low-cost PCs for department store retailers that have their own in-house repair outfits. (You know who they are: The ones that charge you the national debt per hour to fix your systems.) These form factors were built exclusively to contain all-in-one components that were exclusively designed to support Intel's new standard power supply (can you believe it?) called SFX. If anything goes wrong with one of these miniscule systems, the idea is you rush to one of these department stores and all their minimally trained technicians have to do is gut the entire case and replace it with a new chassis, expansion parts and all. Leaving, of course, the expensive SFX power supply, for which nothing could possibly go wrong (… go wrong … go wrong …).

In Chapter 18, "Adding an Optical Drive," I tackle the new topic of moving everything out of your cramped system case into a new one, just so you can extend your PC's life for a year or two. For now let's let this topic rest with the following thought: The fact that a motherboard is small and a system case is large doesn't mean that one fits into the other. The system case has to support the motherboard, with the appropriate fixing screws positioned to hold it in place. (With apologies to both Red Green and Tim Allen, here is a case in which duct tape is simply not appropriate.)

Modern Luxuries

What passes for luxury on a modern motherboard are features for which you might pay extra, but don't let that bother you too much because these same features, although a bit more costly, will increase the speed of your computer tremendously. As they say, time is money. In fact, you actually might need some of these features to realize the potential speed benefits of your peripherals.

For example, take the case of Ultra DMA. The newest hard drives from Maxtor and other manufacturers take advantage of a technology that enables the drive controller to assess whether there's a lull in the action inside the computer. It then responds to these lulls (called *latencies*) by pushing the data transfer rate up a notch. With Ultra DMA in place, the ordinary throughput rate is 16.6MB/sec (megabytes per second); when things quiet down, Ultra DMA raises the bar—if only for a split second—to as much as 100MB/sec. However, both the chipset on your motherboard and your CPU need to recognize Ultra DMA or your fancy new hard drive might be stuck in 16.6MB/sec in the slow lane.

Meanwhile, the *Accelerated Graphics Port* (*AGP*) is the newest twist on video technology. The graphics processors in an AGP system are directly linked to the CPU—literally partnered with it—through the AGP port. The AGP processor takes care of much of the initial display work and sets up an independent clock for video processing, whereas the AGP video card provides the system with video RAM and dedicated processing hardware. This clock can be set to a multiple of the PCI peripheral bus clock, so AGP 2x on a 33MHz PCI bus results in 66 MHz of dedicated video processing. Chapter 14, "I Can See Clearly Now: Upgrading Your Video," discusses AGP in greater detail.

The Manufacturers and Their Wares

The world has literally hundreds of motherboard manufacturers; mainly because it's relatively simple for a company to concoct a motherboard out of a brand-name chipset and some spare connectors. However, only about a dozen or so of these names have endeared themselves in the consciousness of PC enthusiasts. Here's a quick list of the names I know, some of which I trust:

➤ ASUS—also known as AsusTek in other countries; easily the technology leader. If anyone tries something bold first—like support for the 266MHz system bus—it's ASUS. One of the most respected motherboard manufacturers among shadetree PC mechanics (assuming those folks ever go outdoors anyway) is ASUS, a premium manufacturer whose models aren't cheap.

➤ **AOpen**—Formerly part of Acer and once known as AcerOpen, AOpen is one of Taiwan's more respected, small consumer electronics companies. AOpen is known for reliable, inexpensive parts. They're not innovators.

➤ **Intel**—They're no fun. You've already heard of Intel.

➤ **Tyan**—A company that tries really hard and sometimes produces some wonderful systems. One of its best is the Trinity 100AT, which supports VIA's Apollo MVP3 chipset. My husband uses a system based on this platform, with a Super 7 socket running an AMD K6-II 450 CPU. This is the system that outperformed the Dell Pentium III 650 laptop.

➤ **Micro-Star (MSI)**—My husband built an MSI system that ran well and performed solidly in a well-cooled case … for 10 months; then quit. Other users have reported similar performance.

➤ **VIA**—Interesting enough, a lot of manufacturers use VIA's brand of chipset but not their motherboards.

➤ **Gigabyte**—As the name suggests, a contender to ASUS in the high-tech engineering department. They produce relatively few models but with premium equipment, such as VIA's best chipsets and frills such as Creative Labs' DSP audio processors. Also not cheap.

Motherboard manufacturers generally are kind enough to etch their own trademark somewhere along the edge of the board or perhaps dead center in the middle of it. But do you really need to open your system to find out what motherboard you have? Perhaps not. Later in this chapter, in a segment titled "Identifying Your Motherboard and Determining Your BIOS," you'll see how the BIOS information you see when you boot your PC can tell you which BIOS you have, whose motherboard you own, and whose chipset is installed on it.

Package Deals: Motherboards + CPUs

Here's maybe the most welcome time- and money-saving news you'll see in this book: If you end up needing to replace everything anyway (CPU, motherboard, and RAM), you should look into online retailers that offer motherboard/CPU combo packages. You can save dozens of dollars this way. Here are some other nonobvious reasons package deals make sense:

➤ Motherboards with CPUs and RAM pre-installed generally have been pre-tested by the dealer before shipping. So you know they work together—or at least, they have worked together. That eliminates a lot of confusing decisions.

➤ Dealers may be generous enough to throw in a warranty on their own workmanship. If something does blow within the first 60 days or so, you get new parts.

199

➤ Many retailers let you choose your own bundles. You see a list of parts that are guaranteed to work together, and you get to choose. They make it for you and do everything but put it in your system case. (If they did that, they'd be PC manufacturers.)

➤ Installation time on your end is reduced. You don't have to reflash your BIOS. You don't have to change out the heat sink. You don't have to locate your fire extinguisher.

➤ You can save on shipping costs. All those loose parts generally come in separate packages with separate Styrofoam. Imagine if they were all in one box!

Here's an example: McGlen Computers (www.mcglen.com) offered a bundle featuring an MSI MS-6337 motherboard with the Intel 815E chipset. (More on chipset types in just a bit.) It supports a Pentium III or Celeron FC-PGA Socket 370. For a hypothetical purchase, I chose the PIII 933MHz. I had them fill it up with 256MB of PC133 SDRAM memory and throw in a top-of-the-line cooler fan. I saved $13 over whatever I would have paid for the components separately, plus several fewer boxes in shipping—so probably close to $50—and I get a system that's already burned in. Another online retailer that specializes in bundles is J&N Computer Services, online at www.jncs.com.

The Importance of the Chipset

The chipset is the reason motherboards have become inexpensive. The key distinction between a chipset and a CPU is this: The CPU performs data processing; the chipset manages data transfer. How any part of data gets from one component to another in your computer is a process driven by the chipset. Among the chipset's data transfer responsibilities are the following:

➤ Control of the system bus, including communication between the CPU and memory.

➤ Control of expansion busses, including ISA, IDE, and PCI.

➤ Management of parallel and serial ports, plus Universal Serial Bus (USB) communication.

➤ Mastery of the main system clock, which is like a metronome that keeps the beat of the system.

➤ Control of all Direct Memory Access (DMA) operations that take place between peripherals and memory, bypassing the CPU.

➤ Monitoring of all basic input and output devices, including the keyboard and mouse, plus any standard infrared devices (sanctioned by the Infrared Device Association, IrDA).

➤ Symmetric Multiprocessing (SMP), which is the capability for a motherboard to support more than one CPU, perhaps as many as four, working in tandem with one another.

➤ Management of the L2 cache for the CPU when that cache is not part of the CPU package (as with Pentium II, Celeron, and Pentium III).

A motherboard's chipset determines what particular models of CPU it can support. Although a CPU might fit into a socket, if the chipset doesn't recognize that model, that socket might as well be empty. Each chipset is designed to support a limited range of one or more CPUs of a particular family or generation. So there might come a point when a particular new CPU is too fast for a given chipset, even if that CPU appears to fit in the designated socket or slot on the same motherboard as that chipset.

Although hundreds of motherboard manufacturers are in the PC market, there are fewer than a handful of chipset manufacturers. These companies are responsible for developing a majority of the logic that goes into every motherboard. Once a manufacturer has chosen and installed a chipset onto one of its models, the design choices it has left are reduced to form factor, number of slots, and variety of jumper settings for such things as system bus speed and multipliers.

So you'll know almost everything you need to know about a motherboard after you've determined which chipset it supports. When you know the chipset, you can soon find out the following:

➤ **The range of system bus speeds the motherboard is likely to support.** For a motherboard to take full advantage of the choice its chipset offers, it should feature a series of jumpers or BIOS settings that enable you to choose the system bus speed you want or need to use. Why would you ever need the system bus speed to be slower than the fastest available setting? Because you might not have the fastest CPU. Keep in mind that many manufacturers will tout their motherboards as capable of supporting certain CPUs at system bus speeds faster than the CPU manufacturers themselves will recommend. Whenever you run a CPU beyond its specs, you're taking a risk.

➤ **The maximum number of IDE channels.** Or storage device interface connections that the motherboard is likely to support. This number now is almost guaranteed to be two, with as many as two devices per channel. A motherboard might support dual IDE or EIDE (ATA-2); the difference from your perspective is negligible. IDE is covered in detail in Chapter 16, "Hands-On Hard Disk Replacement."

➤ **The maximum number of PCI channels the motherboard can contain.** A motherboard might have fewer slots than this number but never more than this number. PCI is covered in Chapter 12, "Face the Interface."

➤ **The fastest PIO mode (Processor Input/Output) the motherboard can support.** The higher this number is, the faster an IDE or other peripheral device may communicate with the CPU.

201

➤ **The highest transfer mode a motherboard containing the chipset can support, for interfacing with storage devices.**   The higher this number is, the faster an IDE or other peripheral device can communicate directly with the memory of the PC, bypassing the CPU. The most commonly supported mode is ATA/33, which enables 33.3MB/sec disk transfers. ATA/66 (66.6MB/sec) and ATA/100 (100MB/sec) are the next higher modes.

➤ **Support for USB, and parallel and serial ports.**   Chapter 8, "The Easiest Things to Upgrade," discusses many of the common peripherals moving to support for the USB interface.

➤ **Support for AGP (Intel's Accelerated Graphics Port), and by what speed multiplier.**   AGP lets special graphics processors (outside of the chipset and CPU) handle some of the more detailed graphics processing. The term "AGP 2x" refers to AGP support at double the speed of the PCI expansion bus and "AGP 4x" quadruple the PCI bus speed.

➤ **The full range of multipliers the motherboard can support.**   When coupled with the full range of system bus speeds, this gives you your maximum supported CPU clock speed. A motherboard that takes full advantage of the choices a chipset offers makes all of these multipliers available through a jumper or BIOS setting. Remember: The system bus speed you choose times the multiplier you choose should equal your CPU speed. It can be less than your CPU speed; CPUs don't mind being run slower than their design specs allow. And yes, it can be faster than your CPU's designated speed, and your CPU might even run faster than it was designed to run (a scenario called overclocking). I like fireworks as much as the next guy, but there's a time and a place for fireworks; the kids need to be kept at a safe distance and you need to wear your fire safety gear. See Chapter 9 for my diatribe about overclocking.

➤ **Dual CPU support.**   This is rare; it permits motherboards to contain two sockets or slots. In the early 1980s, the way you made a PC/XT faster than its turbo speed could muster was by adding a math coprocessor chip. Today the coprocessor (or math extension logic) is built in to every CPU produced. Beginning with the Pentium Pro series, and extending into PII, PIII, and P4 series, you can make some computers faster by adding a second CPU. If the chipset supports such an addition and there's an empty socket for the thing, you know the CPUs will be happy with the arrangement, too so you just plug it right in and set a jumper. Unfortunately, the consumer versions of Windows do not support a second (or third or fourth) CPU even if it were installed; only Windows NT and Windows 2000 have that capability.

➤ **The maximum amount of cache memory.**   This is the sum of the RAM totals for a CPU's L1 and L2 caches. Some CPUs, including the very first Celerons and VIA Cyrix III, have no L2 cache in the package, although they do have L1 (generally 16K, no more than 64K, of extremely fast SRAM). In such cases, if the amount of L1 is less than the chipset's maximum cache support, conceivably the motherboard itself could be set up with external SRAM that makes up for the difference.

➤ **The maximum range of memory that can be cached.** This is important because it can be less than the total amount of memory on the motherboard. Think of this maximum cacheable area as a map and the L2 cache area as a claim made to territory on this map. After you've installed more memory than the maximum cacheable area, any contents stored in this upper area (assuming you have a lot of programs running) will not be cached and access to these contents will be slower.

➤ **The maximum amount of DRAM (main memory) that a motherboard containing the chipset can support.** No matter what strange configurations of modules you may be able to come up with, each motherboard is limited to a maximum amount of system memory. It's literally set to only count so high.

➤ **The different *types* of DRAM the motherboard can support.** This refers to the way the contents of memory are stored on the modules supported by the chipset. As you'll see in Chapter 11, a chipset can use many different "languages," if you will, for addressing the contents of memory. Each of these languages has to do with the math used for storing and verifying the contents of memory, and the timing employed in writing and reading these contents. The CPU doesn't have to know about any of that stuff; it just demands what it wants and expects to find it on its doorstep. The chipset runs the memory bus (or address bus), which is part of the system bus. It's the translator in this little affair.

➤ **The maximum number of memory modules (SIMMs and DIMMs) the motherboard can address.** If the chipset supports RDRAM, the rules change somewhat here, as memory is addressed not by module but by channel. Chapter 11 goes into more detail here.

How Multipliers Change the Picture

When you choose a new motherboard for your CPU, you want to be able to run that motherboard with as fast a system bus speed as it will allow. Therefore, your CPU clock speed should be equal to that system bus speed times one of the multipliers selectable on the motherboard.

That seems fairly simple on the surface. If you divide the CPU clock speed by the fastest system bus speed available you have the multiplier you want to use. For instance, say you have a 400MHz Pentium II. If your motherboard has a 66MHz system bus speed, it should have a 6x multiplier setting for it to support your 400MHz processor. But wait—suppose that same motherboard can be set for a 50MHz system bus and an 8x multiplier. The math still works out right. However, you'll get a slower performing system overall because the system bus is the main flow of data off of your CPU and through your system. So remember, you want as high a system bus speed as you can get for as low a multiplier as you need.

Luckily, you cannot overclock your chipset (thank heavens). Your system bus can go only as fast as it is designed to go and multipliers do not boost the speed of the system bus. They boost the speed of the CPU's internal operations. A high multiplier setting on the motherboard cannot endanger your chipset—otherwise, you would have enough heat sinks all over the place to open a Turkish bath house inside your PC. If your motherboard offers a multiplier, its chipset (perhaps begrudgingly) supports that multiplier.

Who Makes Chipsets?

The design leader in the chipset business—if not always the market share leader—is Intel. Currently, the company markets two generations of its chipsets: the older 400 series and the newer 800. Intel nomenclature uses three-digit numbers to identify chipsets, with the 400s sporting an extra two letters like "BX" or "GX" at the end, and the 800s sporting an extra letter or two to denote variations in a design, such as "E" or "E2."

The last of the 400s still in production is the 440BX, which is simultaneously marketed for low-end consumer PCs and low-end workstations. (Workstations? Why? Because the 440BX was designed at one time to be Intel's high-end workstation chipset. Times have changed—what workstation users demand one month, the Circuit City and Radio Shack customers demand the next month.) Affectionately dubbed "BX" by the motherboard community, the 440BX supports up to eight rows of 66MHz or PC100 memory of type SDRAM up to 1GB. (That support for PC100 also tells you that the chipset supports a 100MHz system bus, or frontside bus.)

That memory can have special reliability and self-policing features such as *Error Correcting Code* (ECC) or *parity*—slightly more expensive but a bit more reliable. (More about these features in Chapter 11.) 440BX can support dual processors; it also supports 2x AGP. You still need an AGP video card; however, a motherboard with 440BX installed likely will enable the 2x mode, which doubles the instruction rate at the speed of the PCI expansion bus. It's like having a dedicated 200MHz bus just for video processing.

At the low end of Intel's 800 series are its 810 chipsets: the 810, 810E (see Figure 10.1), and 810E2. These all have extremely similar features. Built for small consumer computers only, they support up to 512MB of 66MHz or PC100 SDRAM. 810s don't support any type of ECC or parity memory, which is important if you intend to have your system running for long hours. Old RAM gets tired quicker just like any other component (or person); without error correction to back it up, problems can arise.

Figure 10.1

The components of Intel's 810E chipset.

(Courtesy Intel Corp.)

810s also support Intel's all-out implementation of AGP, in which all the video processors are located on the motherboard (you wouldn't need a video card); those processors use ordinary DRAM for their memory. This is a feature geared for consumers who don't intend to get inside their own computers at all, so you won't find it on the higher-end chipsets.

Moving up the product line, Intel's 815 series all support up to 6 rows (up from 4) of PC100 or PC133 SDRAM. That means 815s support a faster 133MHz system bus. All 815s support AGP 4x mode, which quadruples the throughput rate of video processing on the PCI bus but relies on video cards. Only the 815P supports ATA/66 transfer mode; the 815EP, 815, and 815E all support the faster ATA/100.

At the top of the line are Intel's 820, 820E, and 850. The key factor that distinguishes these from their lower-end counterparts is their support for RDRAM (Rambus DRAM), which is a new memory technology jointly developed by Rambus and Intel. As Chapter 11 will show you, RDRAM changes the memory picture entirely by *narrowing* the bus width (a first) while boosting its access speed significantly to compensate. However, because Celeron processors can't address memory as fast as RDRAM, the 820s will work only with Pentium II and PIII processors; the 850 is exclusively reserved for Pentium 4. The 820s can address up to 1GB of memory, the 850 2GB. What separates 820 from 820E is that 820 supports only ATA/66, whereas 820E supports ATA/100—as does 850.

Hey, remember that CPU + motherboard bundle I mentioned earlier? I had a choice between so-called PC150 and PC133. PC150 is great, but I could clearly see that the chipset on board was Intel's 815E. It doesn't support a 150MHz system bus; so although PC150 memory is great, it wouldn't help me. I could stick with PC133 and save 60 bucks.

Check This Out

Motherboards that feature Intel chipsets often borrow the chipset's name for use in their own, as in "BX-455" or "S820." When you peel off the motherboard producer's attachments, you can clearly see which chipset these products support; and as the last few paragraphs reveal, that tells you a lot.

ASUS is pretty choosy about the chipsets it uses for its particular designs; regardless of what chipset manufacturers trumpet, ASUS tends to choose specific chipsets for its performance and specifications alone. Other motherboard manufacturers tend to follow ASUS's lead so sometimes it's a good idea to check out who ASUS is using these days (www.asus.com.tw), even if you don't decide to go with an ASUS motherboard. ASUS's very popular P3B-F, introduced in 1999, uses Intel's venerable 440BX—the chipset that wouldn't die. The "P3" in the name tells you something important about the motherboard right up front; the "B" affirms its support for the BX chipset.

Whereas Intel's own motherboard production has shifted toward supporting its 800 series—hoping others follow suit—the 440BX has proven not only popular among users but also generally less of a hassle. In independent tests, 440BX motherboards outperform 815s and 820s with supposedly similar or even greater features.

ASUS's more recent model P3V133 supports VIA Technologies' Apollo Pro133 chipset (see Figure 10.2) for Socket 370 and Slot 1. VIA has become famous for being among the first to support the higher system bus speeds with relatively stable performance; other manufacturers who release earlier cause more fire hazards. VIA's AMD-supportive counterpart is called Apollo KX133—again, the naming scheme gives it away, as AMD used to name its CPUs with a "K."

The Apollo 133s support 66, 100, and 133MHz system bus speeds, plus AGP 4x. They also have certain proprietary technical features such as burst mode data transfer rates of 533MB/sec (533 percent the rate of the highest storage transfer rate). 133s support up to 8 modules or 1.5GB of SDRAM—which gives VIA an edge over Intel in price and performance.

One of ASUS's other lucky suppliers is Acer Laboratories (ALi), which builds the ALADDiN series for Socket 370 and Slot 1 (Intel) CPUs, and ALiMAGIK series for Socket A and Slot A (AMD). AMD's ALiMAGIK model A7A266 supports ALi's M1647 chipset. To accommodate AMD's higher speeds, the M1647 supports a 266MHz system bus and 4x AGP. Here's something we haven't mentioned yet: *Double Data Rate (DDR)* memory support, which on a 266MHz system bus can be (in a good way) dangerous! Thus when you see "DDR266 SDRAM" out there on a spec sheet by itself, you'll know this refers to two memory fetches per cycle on a 266MHz system bus. Nothing makes an entire system faster sooner than faster memory.

Figure 10.2

VIA's market leading Apollo Pro133 chipset—a set of one.

(Courtesy VIA Technologies)

I've picked three ASUS motherboards with varying features and chipsets from three different manufacturers. What are the differences in price? The popular, time-tested P3B-F sells for about $125 at the time of this writing; the P3V133 hovers at around $100. The reason? BX motherboards are in high demand. The feature-jammed A7A266 is priced around $155.

Here's something you should think about: The difference in price between a standard, decent, time-tested, reliable system and blazing-fast, top-of-the-line speed and performance seems to be roughly the price of dinner for two at an Italian restaurant. But be careful. Don't let this single difference figure fool you. The A7A266 supports other more expensive components, such as a top-of-the-line Athlon processor (which probably will need an amazing cooling system—or an igloo) and DDR SDRAM memory. In the CPU and memory categories alone, the differences between top-of-the-line and reliable middle-of-the-road aren't steep either. However, if you add those differences together we're talking about some real money here. Like dinner for *six* at an Italian restaurant!

Motherboard–ectomy Illustrated

Well, if you're ready, I guess I am. First, back up your data, write down your CMOS, and update your emergency diskette as usual. You must write down the CMOS information because your new motherboard isn't going to know any of it. See Chapter 4, "What You Need to Know *Before* You Open Your PC," for help.

Before you start taking things apart, you may want to use masking tape to mark your cables and other parts of your PC, so you can remember what they're connected to.

207

Discharge your static electricity on something metal but don't use the PC's system case. Again, if you've got a grounding strap, put it on and use it. Attach the other end of the strap to something metallic—not painted (bare metal)—but not to the PC case.

Now is a good time to make sure you have the cables you need. Motherboard kits generally come with at least one IDE cable for your hard disks and optical discs, and one floppy disk controller cable. Cables do burn out over time, so since you're unplugging things anyway, you might consider replacing your old cables while you're replacing your motherboard.

Removing the Old Motherboard

Naturally, if you're building a PC from the ground up, and have a fresh new system case and motherboard, you won't need to worry about this part. However, if you're moving a motherboard from one system case to another, or you're replacing the motherboard in your existing system case, removing the old motherboard is a must.

Start by unplugging everything that connects to your PC from the outside (that's the easy part). Make absolutely certain the power cord is nowhere near your system; then take the cover off. For most metal tower system cases and a fair majority of metal desktop cases, there will be a set of screws along the rim of the back of the case (where all the cables plug in). Don't confuse any of these screws with those holding in the power supply. You do not need to remove the power supply to uninstall your motherboard, even if later you find that it gets in the way.

Just to help you out, so you know which direction is which (in other words, so "to the back of the system case" means something to you), orient your motherboard so that the expansion ports are on the side *away* from you, and the front panel (where the on/off switch generally is) is *toward* you.

With the cover off, unplug the one or two cables leading to your power supply. They're easy to locate, because they're the only cables that come in a rainbow of colors. Chapter 19, "Powering Up the Power Supply," will show you exactly how. Yes, there's a method to it. Why unplug the cables leading from the power supply to the system case if you're not replacing the system case? Because you'll need enough leeway to get your old motherboard out of the case and an attached power cable might as well be a barbed wire fence if it's left in place.

Next, disconnect all of the data cables leading to internal devices, like your diskette, hard disk, and optical drives. You can leave the data cables dangling out the back of these devices if you don't think they'll get in the way, and you can leave the power cables plugged into these devices. Disconnect the cable at the end of each expansion card and unscrew the retaining screw holding it in. Lift each card out and place it on a static-free surface, such as a wooden or plastic desk (not metal). You might want to make a note of the order of your expansion cards—they don't have to be put back in the same order, but why risk it?

Check This Out

If you use a tower case, it may have a removable metal panel on which the motherboard is mounted. If so, after you've taken out the expansion cards, clear the way for this panel and everything on it to come out of the system case; then remove this panel (with the motherboard installed) from the PC. Once you've done that you can remove memory modules and the CPU. Situate the mounting panel so the expansion slots are away from you, toward the back.

Unplug your memory chips or modules and put them on a static-free surface, too. Even if you can't reuse them, you might be able to trade them in for less than the cost of new RAM chips.

At this point you might find your old motherboard is stuck behind the cage that holds your internal peripherals in place. If this happens you may have to unscrew the cage from its mounting rack in the system case. For a tower system, you may find these screws in the front of the case and you might have to pry off the plastic face-plate of the system to get at these screws. Make sure you're supporting the cage with something when you remove that last screw; otherwise you'll have a situation similar to the famous incident during a performance of Tchaikovsky's *1812 Overture* in which the cannons backfired, taking out the cymbals and the gong.

Gently remove the cage from inside the system case; your devices will stay neatly locked in position. You do have one alternative to unscrewing the cage: Get another system case. Why? If your old motherboard is stuck behind the cage, your new one will be, too. Chances are that's not good for its ventilation. Check out Chapter 21, "Classier Chassis: Consider a New System Case," if you need help reviewing this decision further.

Now that all the plugs are off your old motherboard, remove the screws holding it in place. Don't be surprised if there's only two or three. Again, make a note of where they go. Your motherboard's probably loose at this point, but not completely free. You might need to slide the motherboard toward you ¼ inch to release it from the *standoffs* underneath. What's a standoff? Bush v. Gore: The Rematch? No, it's a plastic or steel support whose purpose is to hold the motherboard in place and maintain a safe gap between the motherboard and the (metal!) system case.

With the standoffs slid loose, gently lift the thing out, making sure to hold it by its edges to limit the chance of shorting anything out. Once the motherboard has cleared the system case, with your rubber-handled needle-nose pliers, remove the standoffs from the old motherboard (see Figure 10.3). You might even have to cut the old plastic standoffs off. With what, pray tell? Rubber handled, snub-nose wire cutters, not scissors.

Figure 10.3

Remove the standoffs from your old motherboard.

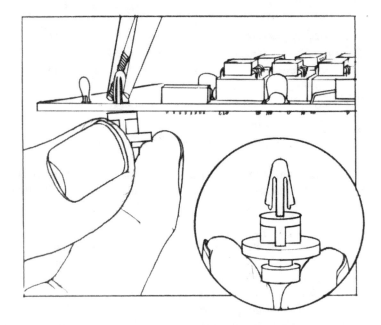

Removing the CPU and Memory Modules

If you plan to reuse the CPU or memory modules from your old motherboard, now's the time to remove them and get them prepared. Chapter 9 gives you the procedure for taking off the old CPU; Chapter 11 shows you how to remove memory.

Is now a good time to prepare your new motherboard for your CPU and memory modules? Perhaps, but the method I'll be demonstrating here is an unorthodox one that some friends of mine developed after some rather significant disasters forced them to rethink their methods. (Smoking silicon—or, more accurately, silicon that is smoking—can make a person rethink his entire approach to life.)

Assessing the New Motherboard

Discharge any static from your body once again and unpack your new motherboard. Look for damage, such as broken wires, little green shavings, and spiky silver or gold things. Take a good look at the mounting holes on your new motherboard. If you chose the right form factor for your system case, some of these holes should align precisely with some of the mounting holes inside your system case, or on the mounting panel you've just removed from your system case.

There may be as many as three horizontal rows of holes (see why I had you put the expansion slots in the back?): three or four at the back, two or three in the middle, and two or three at the front. Not every mounting hole on the motherboard will have a corresponding hole in the system case; big deal. You want at least three holes to line up, otherwise the stability of your motherboard can't be maintained—especially later when you try to plug in a card.

You'll find two types of holes in a system case or mounting panel: one is threaded; the other is not. The nonthreaded holes take the plastic standoffs that come with your new motherboard's mounting kit; the threaded holes take metal *risers* that you twist on, which stand out from the back panel. What's a riser? Marilyn Monroe in a two-piece? No, it's a metal cylinder that has a screw at one end and a threaded opening for a screw at the other.

Consider inserting something into each of your motherboard's holes to ensure stability. For each hole that lines up with a nonthreaded post hole, insert the plastic standoff into the motherboard. Snap the plastic standoff up from the bottom (see Figure 10.4) so that its pointed tip pokes up toward you. When you're ready to insert the motherboard, the lower disc of this plastic standoff will fit neatly into the post hole. For each motherboard hole that lines up with a threaded post hole, screw the lower, pointed half of the metal riser into the post in the system case or mounting panel. Once you've inserted the motherboard, the upper half of this standoff will screw through the threaded hole left open by the lower half, fixing the motherboard in place.

Figure 10.4

Push the standoffs up from below.

If you have enough plastic standoffs to fit through the remaining holes, or even if you have just a few left over, here's a way you can add some extra support: With needle-nose pliers, pry off the bottom disk of a plastic standoff, because it won't be plugging into anything. This leaves a small plastic post. Push the standoff up from the bottom through an open hole on the motherboard, just as before. You've just made an extra spacer that will keep a proper distance between the motherboard and the system case.

Inserting the New Motherboard

With as many of the mounting holes made ready as you can, now's the time to slip the motherboard into place. Align the holes with the standoffs. The plastic standoffs should firmly snap into place. Be sure to use a paper, rubber, or plastic washer when screwing in the metal standoffs, especially if it looks like the screw head is wide enough that it might touch any part of the electric circuitry on the board. Avoid excessive force with your screwdriver or hex-nut driver. Screw in the top half gently until it doesn't give so easily; then slow down and ease up. If you screw it in too tightly, you might bend something—and bending is the absolute wrong thing to do to a motherboard.

How do you know if your motherboard is in precisely the right place? Look for the keyboard connector—a round plug. Your system case should have a cutout location for this plug; each motherboard form factor states explicitly where this plug must be located. If it is anywhere else you have the wrong form factor for your system case. Check this plug to make certain it fits perfectly into its cutout.

Another way you can test for proper fit is to try plugging in an expansion card. You shouldn't have to bend or pry anything on the motherboard to get your card into place; if you find yourself doing that, stop now and remove the card. The card's mounting screw should fit without trouble into the corresponding slot in the back. If you find the fit is just a millimeter or two off, you may need to loosen the steel standoffs and (keeping yourself discharged, mind you) nudge the motherboard in the proper direction.

How do you know whether your motherboard is secure? Hopefully, all four corners are represented by at least one firm attachment. You might get away with three, but certainly no fewer. When you inserted that expansion card, did you jostle something out of place, or did the standoffs hold tight? Did any portion of the motherboard bend or wobble when you inserted or removed the card? There should be zero bending.

If you don't feel confident that your motherboard is secure, take it back out, add some extra plastic standoffs to any open holes (even if you have to buy these standoffs from the hardware store or Radio Shack), and use firm but narrow rubber washers on the top of the motherboard, beneath the metal standoff screw. If it's still not secure, there's a good possibility that your motherboard and system case simply aren't made for each other. Consider replacing one or the other.

Finally, use a ruler to judge the distances between the motherboard's *substrate* (the big green square thing with all the chips on it) and the system case or mounting panel. The distances should be the same all the way around, which means the motherboard is sitting flat and the connectors aren't out of alignment. If your mounting panel is detached, now is the time to reattach it to your system case; don't plug in the data cables just yet.

Plugging In the Motherboard

Whoa. Wait a minute—shouldn't you be inserting your CPU and your RAM modules first? Surprise: No. I know, you've read elsewhere that you should put the RAM in first, then the CPU, and then plug in the cables. There's a good reason you shouldn't: If a motherboard is going to short out, most likely it will do so the first time it receives power. The most common reason for shorting out is a power disruption because of improper mounting or a faulty power supply. When this happens, just about everything that's directly attached to your motherboard fries. That includes your CPU and your memory. Ah-ha! Starting to see my point now? The best way to avoid shorting out your CPU and memory is for it not to be there when you first power on the PC. Same goes for the expansion cards as well; leave them off first time around.

Hold it, hold on, hold the phone, hold the pickles ... if the CPU, memory and video card aren't on board, how do you know whether the motherboard works? Does it cry out, "I'm working now, thank you?" Surprise: Yes. Remember every time you turn on your PC under normal circumstances, you hear a *single beep* (two short beeps for some Compaqs)? That's your motherboard saying, "I'm okay!"

If you hear more than one beep, the motherboard has detected a problem somewhere and cannot continue the startup procedure. Generally that problem is something like not being able to find the CPU or memory. Will you hear more than one beep when you power up the non-processor, non-memory PC? Absolutely. That's what you want to hear. If you hear no beep, something is definitely wrong. You will not hear just one beep; that's for sure. If something is wrong other than missing CPU or memory, your BIOS could beep you a message in its version of Morse Code that indicates what the problem is, before you install your CPU or memory and endanger them in the process. (More on BIOS error codes just a bit later.)

What if you purchased your motherboard with a CPU or RAM already installed? Should you remove them before installing the motherboard? Perhaps. If you purchased your CPU, RAM, and motherboard as a bundle, absolutely not. Forget everything I just said. They've already been tested and burned in by the retailer that sold the bundle to you. However, if for any reason you're in doubt, yes. It could be a shortout waiting to happen.

To begin the power-up process, you'll want to plug in just the necessary power cables. Chapter 19 contains a procedure for reattaching plugs from the power supply to the motherboard. Now reattach your drive controllers, again making sure you align pin 1

213

correctly. Pin 1 on each connector may be marked with a "1," a notch, or a tab. Chapter 12 discusses hard drive data cables and such things.

Birth of a PC

Leave the cover off for now; then plug your power cord into the power supply. You don't need to plug in your printer, your monitor, or anything else just yet—especially if you haven't plugged in your expansion cards. With your main power plugged in and your main data cables left unplugged, it's time for your PC to take the smoke test—the one that determines whether the device that powers all the rest of your devices actually will work, or simulate global thermonuclear war.

If you have a brand-name system ("Compaq": yes; "Joe-Bob's": no), you may need to check the inside frame of your computer for a "safety switch" that prevents your system from powering up while the case is off. This is a silly little rocker switch that can be easily fooled with a small swatch of duct tape.

The type of audible response your lobotomized motherboard will give you when you throw the main switch, depends on the BIOS installed. A bit more than 98 percent of all the installed PC BIOS in the world comes from one of three manufacturers: American Megatrends (AMI), Award Systems, and Phoenix Technologies (which recently bought out Award). There still are some minor manufacturers, and historically there were several more that are no longer in existence. The following section lists the different beep codes and their meanings for the three major brands of BIOS.

AMI BIOS (American Megatrends)

In Table 10.2, for AMI BIOS, each beep after the initial single beep indicates an error condition; the lack of any extra beeps indicates no error.

Table 10.2 AMI BIOS Error Beep Descriptions

Code	Diagnosis
Long, wailing beep	**Can't find the CPU, memory, or video processor.** But hey, the motherboard didn't short out, did it? Consider this the first wail of a newborn motherboard.
1 beep	**DRAM refresh failure.** There's a problem with the system bus. Simple causes: Your memory modules might not be seated properly, or some foreign object might be making contact with the motherboard. Complex cause: You have bad memory.
2 beeps	**Parity circuit failure.** If your memory uses parity (a form of error checking), the component that is used to check for errors is somehow bad. This is more likely a motherboard problem than a memory module problem.

Code	Diagnosis
3 beeps	**Base 64KB RAM failure.** Most likely, your first bank of RAM is bad. Less likely, there's a problem with the chipset or the memory bus.
4 beeps	**System timer failure.** This problem cannot be pinned to any other device than the chipset. To replace your chipset, you replace your motherboard.
5 beeps	**Processor failure.** The CPU has something definitely wrong, if it is *there* (its absence won't cause this problem).
6 beeps	**Keyboard controller failure.** The chipset cannot make contact with your keyboard. It may be absent or defective. If you find the keyboard is not defective, the motherboard may be at fault. Check Chapters 5, "Fixing the Most Common Problems," and 8, "The Easiest Things to Upgrade," for more help.
7 beeps	**Virtual mode exception error.** Most likely, your CPU is having a hard time setting up system services and devices. Less likely, your motherboard's acting up.
8 beeps	**Display memory read/write failure.** The PC is having trouble developing an image for the video card to display. Most likely, the video card may be acting up. If the motherboard is okay, your PC may continue to boot up anyway, albeit more slowly.
9 beeps	**ROM BIOS checksum failure.** A check of the BIOS program currently in ROM reveals that it isn't what it claims to be. You may need to reflash your BIOS or replace your BIOS chips. See the Halftime Report for help.
10 beeps	**CMOS shutdown register read/write error.** This definitely is a motherboard problem. At the very least, your battery may be going out.
11 beeps	**Cache memory error.** The chipset is unable to properly set up the L2 cache for the CPU. If you have a Pentium II, Pentium III, or a Celeron processor with L2 cache on board, you won't get this error from the BIOS because the chipset isn't responsible for the L2 cache for those processors.

AMI reports that 4, 5, 7, and 10 beeps generally mean something's awfully wrong, and you may have to replace your motherboard anyway. Every other beep code can be avoided next time around by reseating your memory, CPU, video card, and cables.

Award BIOS

When something's terribly wrong with a PC that has Award BIOS, see Table 10.3; its diagnostic capabilities will be able to report that problem onscreen, in English.

However, that assumes that there's a display that the BIOS can write to and memory to tell it what to write. So there are some beep codes that take precedence if one of these components seems not to be working.

Table 10.3   Award BIOS Error Beep Descriptions

Code	Diagnosis
Long, wailing beep	**Can't find the CPU, memory, or video processor.** But hey, the motherboard didn't short out, did it? Consider this the first wail of a newborn motherboard.
1 long beep	**Memory failure.** You most likely have at least one bad memory module.
1 long, 2 short	**Video failure.** The chipset can't make heads or tails out of the display. It could be absent.

Phoenix BIOS (4.x and Later Versions)

The Phoenix BIOS, Table 10.4, actually has a few hundred beep code combinations, made up of a group of four beep sets of one, two, three, or four beeps each. Believe me, no more boring reading has ever been produced by the human hand since the Health Security Bill of 1994. Some of the beep codes are reserved for system diagnostic purposes, to tell the listener that something happened during the power-up process that wasn't an error. (Imagine a Saturn V preflight check at NASA; you'll get the idea.)

Phoenix BIOS doesn't have the long, plaintive wail that tells you, "There's no brain in my head, but I'm alright"; however, if you hear what sounds like a Christmas tree made up entirely of sound waves, you know your motherboard is at least working to some degree. There may still be a problem, but it might not be insurmountable. Listed in the following are some of the more important errors that might crop up. Notice Phoenix's names for these conditions are not errors in and of themselves; they are the point at which these errors might occur in the startup process.

Table 10.4   Phoenix BIOS Error Beep Descriptions

Code	Diagnosis
1-1-2-1	**Get CPU type.** If the chipset can't figure out what CPU you have, it's probably plugged in, but something's wrong with the system bus.
1-1-2-3	**Initialize system hardware.** Something is preventing the bus from being a complete circuit. Perhaps something isn't properly plugged in.

Code	Diagnosis
1-1-3-3	**Initialize CPU registers.** The chipset is having trouble placing the CPU in "ready" mode. If the CPU is installed properly, this could be a motherboard problem.
1-2-2-1	**Initialize keyboard controller.** Chances are, your keyboard is unplugged, or your keyboard is defective, or perhaps your mouse isn't plugged in correctly.
1-2-2-3	**BIOS ROM checksum.** A check of the program currently loaded into your ROM BIOS reveals that the program could be erroneous, incomplete, or somewhat fried. You might need to reflash your BIOS or replace your BIOS chips.
1-3-1-1	**Test DRAM refresh.** Your memory modules do not seem to be answering the call of the chipset. You might need to reseat your memory.
1-3-3-1	**Autosize DRAM.** Your BIOS isn't finding all your memory. You may need to reseat your modules.
1-4-2-4	**Reinitialize the chipset.** Something's very wrong with the chipset on your motherboard. Sometimes replacement of the motherboard is your only solution here.
2-1-1-1	**Set initial CPU speed.** If you're lucky, your jumpers may not presently be set to a speed compatible with what your chipset or CPU expect to see.
2-1-3-3	**Initialize all video adapters.** The chipset is having trouble communicating with your video card. This most likely is a video card problem. Maybe it simply needs to be plugged into it a little better.

If nothing whatsoever has fried, you can shut off the system and install your CPU and memory modules. Unplug your power cords again and discharge yourself. Now you're going to be do a lot of book-hopping. Check Chapter 9 for the procedure for inserting your CPU; then hop on over to Chapter 11 for how to insert your memory modules. Finally, scoot over to Chapter 23, "Making Your Computer Boot Up Again," to see how to set your jumpers and CMOS. The most important jumpers you will have to set govern the system bus speed, the processor speed multiplier, and the processor voltage level (extremely critical!). You also probably will need to make some adjustments to your CMOS setup, even if all your devices are Plug-and-Play.

Next put your expansion cards back in the same order in which you had them originally and screw them in. Don't drop any screws! Screws that are accidentally forgotten can ruin your new motherboard when you turn it back on. It isn't the screw that makes the card work; however, if you can get the screw in correctly, you know the card is in correctly. Attach any extra power cords your cards may require, such as the tiny pair of cables that power the fan for the processor on your video card.

Now plug in the data cables leading from your hard drive to the motherboard connectors, or to their host adapter card connectors. Remember to line up the red side of each ribbon cable with pin 1 on the corresponding motherboard or adapter card connector. At this point you can plug the power cable into your CPU's active heat sink (its little bitty fan).

Plug your PC's main power cord back in and turn it on. Now you'll listen for that all-important single beep from the BIOS ("beep-beep" from a Compaq); not the wail of a newborn. If you get something else, check the preceding list to see what you might need to change or alter. Make certain you've disconnected the power and discharged yourself before you proceed. If you hear only that wonderful single beep, congrats on a successful surgery. Turn your system back off and put your PC's case back together; then reattach any fingers, toes, and brain cells you dislodged during the process.

Mistakes to Avoid

First check simple things, such as whether the motherboard is touching any little hanging piece of wire or loose change dropped into the system case. Make sure the motherboard doesn't move around in the case and that it's supported well. You also might want to turn the PC off and recheck all the connections, especially the power connections.

Be sure pin 1 of your drive data cable is lined up correctly on all three ends—it's especially easy to get the hard drive connector on backward. Also make sure all the pins are covered by all the holes in the connector and that you're not one pin off. Check all the critical settings: processor type, bus speed, clock multiplier, and voltage. If your motherboard doesn't have jumpers for them, try plugging in your computer, turning it on, and checking the BIOS settings. (Your CPU doesn't have to even be present for the BIOS Setup program to work.) Make sure you inserted the CPU and the memory chips correctly and that you used the correct type of chips for your motherboard. Also check the video card or video controller connector. If you have a problem with a particular part, check the appropriate chapter for help.

If all else fails, consider stepping up from a smoke test system to a fully installed system part by part to see which part, when installed, causes your motherboard not to give a response code or to give a weird response. Start with an in-between system that includes just the basics: a CPU, keyboard, only one full bank of memory, video card, and a bootable diskette in the floppy disk drive. Disconnect everything else and test the system; then reconnect your other devices (hard drive, optical disc, external backup device) one at a time, until the problem crops up again.

Yes, You, Too, Can Replace Your BIOS!

The way you replace your chipset, or even just the microcoded programming within that chipset, is to replace your motherboard the way you've just seen. However, remarkably, the part of the motherboard whose programming tells the computer that it is a computer—and that teaches it how to receive input every time you turn it on—is very easily replaceable either by hand or, for modern systems, through software. This segment shows you how.

Just What Is a BIOS, Anyway?

In 1981 it was widely discovered that there were no legal impediments to any person or any company producing a program that worked like an IBM PC BIOS, just as long as it wasn't the IBM PC BIOS. This spawned a swarm of new BIOS chip producers, especially in Southeast Asia where entrepreneurs had less fear of the Wrath of Big Blue. The BIOS was the only part of the IBM PC that IBM actually manufactured and to which IBM held exclusive rights. Intel produced the CPU and Microsoft produced the operating system, although neither were under any restrictions for producing the same for anyone else. (Why? Because no one ever thought such a restriction was necessary in 1979. Who knew that anyone else would be manufacturing IBM's computers?)

The abundance of BIOS manufacturers in the mid-1980s led to the explosion of IBM PC clones flooding the market; soon constituting the bulk of all PC sales in the world. After the Great Shakeout, through which only the strongest companies would survive, three major independent BIOS manufacturers remained: American Megatrends (AMI), Award Systems, and Phoenix, Ltd. (AMI and Phoenix merged in 1998.) Throughout the 1990s, only these three companies produced BIOS chips for all the world's PCs—both the brand-name and garage-factory variety—except IBM itself, and even then only for its own systems.

The original objective of the clone BIOS was to make a computer work just like an IBM PC without using IBM's code to do it. Today, because IBM no longer sets the standard, the objective of the modern BIOS is to work with Windows. Believe me: The former objective was far easier to accomplish.

Flash BIOS Versus the Moon Men

For the last several years, the PC's BIOS systems have been provided in the form of single, easy-to-spot, easy-to-remove EPROM (erasable/programmable read-only memory) chips. The equipment for reprogramming these inexpensive chips has become so inexpensive that, in 1996, it became installed on the motherboards themselves. The flash *BIOS* enables you to upgrade your own BIOS without the hassle of installing a new chip; either entirely or almost entirely through the aid of software.

The key reason you would want to re-flash your BIOS is not simply that you need the highest version numbers there are for anything and everything you own. Periodically, and now more frequently than ever, your PC needs to be re-educated on how to communicate with the new hardware you've added or are planning to add.

Also, the BIOS program itself is quite small as programs go: as small as 64K, and rarely larger than 128K. (By the way, a K is 1,024 times smaller than an M.) So the BIOS does not have the luxury of being able to keep a list of all the new hardware components (let's see, infrared scanner, wireless mouse, color laser printer, video capture board …). As a result, the addition of new hardware could force your computer to rethink how it communicates with all the old hardware that's already installed. You might find yourself needing to re-flash your BIOS just to maintain a status quo.

Check This Out

If you don't have a modem or Internet connection yet (perhaps wanting one is why you're upgrading your computer in the first place), you're not left behind. The three—uh, I mean two—major BIOS manufacturers—and, oh yes, IBM too—make their BIOS upgrade programs available to the general public for a nominal fee. Just contact the manufacturer of your BIOS by telephone (you remember the telephone, don't you? It was the thing we used before e-mail.) The distribution method is quite literally the old-fashioned way: a single diskette and a stapled-together booklet in a Zip-lock bag. When you buy one, you're not only keeping up with the times; you get a feel of what the software industry was like in about 1978.

Although both the BIOS programs themselves and the tools you need to flash new BIOS onto your EPROM chips both are downloadable from the Internet, they are no longer downloadable from the Web sites of their own manufacturers. However, generally they are available from the Web sites of your motherboard manufacturer. This actually is a much safer way to go about making BIOS upgrades available, because BIOS versions do have to be tailored, even if slightly, for the particular needs of various motherboards. When you download an upgrade from your motherboard manufacturer, you're assured of at least getting the right BIOS for your system.

Shopping for Your BIOS

Today's BIOS chips are specialized for the motherboards in which they are installed. For this reason, retailers and direct sales outlets are unlikely to carry newer BIOS chips because they cannot order enough of one type in any significant quantity to either create or sustain the relatively low demand for that one type.

Service establishments take advantage of this new reality by performing the rough job of simply finding the right chip set and ordering it, and passing their costs directly on to you. As a result, some BIOS chip sets sold by service or repair shops actually cost you more than a replacement motherboard containing that same chip set. Huh? That's correct: The entire motherboard, including the BIOS chip set, might cost less than just the BIOS parts alone.

Why? A few reasons: First of all, the manufacturer of the motherboard is the only party that can order the BIOS chips in high enough quantity to get them at low enough cost. You, on the other hand, would be ordering one and only one unit. You might be able to order this one unit directly from the BIOS manufacturer—major manufacturers do take orders online. However, if you factor in shipping and handling charges, you may neutralize any savings you would have realized from not ordering from the repair shop.

Second, newer BIOS chip sets are those flash chips I mentioned a few paragraphs ago, whose ROM contents can be entirely rewritten through software. So you can download both the BIOS software-based patch and the program that implements that patch, from the Web site of the computer manufacturer or the motherboard's manufacturer. This capability drives down the demand for replacement chips, which in turn raises their prices.

Identifying Your Motherboard and Determining Your BIOS

The simplest way for you to discover what BIOS brand your PC uses is to simply open it and look. You're looking for one of the old-style *DIP (dual inline package)* chips, hopefully marked with something useful such as AMI BIOS. Recently, BIOS chips have come with prominent brand-name stickers that you can't miss—some of them are even holographic.

But even looking directly at a BIOS chip might not tell you enough. You see, the machine that stamped the front of the chip when it was being manufactured did not know beforehand what type of motherboard the chip would go into. Before it was installed in that motherboard, the chip's own unique flash BIOS program was written into it by the motherboard manufacturer; not the chip manufacturer. This process changes not only the chip's ROM contents; it changes its own serial number. You'll need this serial number—which is no longer on the front of newer BIOS chips—to find out how to replace that chip.

Luckily, this number is not so difficult to obtain. Simply turn on your computer. When the very first screen shows up, telling you what BIOS brand you have (and perhaps displaying the logo of the BIOS manufacturer), press the Pause key on your keyboard. If you look on the screen you should see the serial number of your BIOS, its version, and date. You've paused the Power-On-Self-Test (POST) mode of the computer, so you'll have time to jot this information down. Then press Pause again to continue booting your computer.

Check This Out

There's a highly respected DOS-mode program that can determine your motherboard's manufacturer (assuming you have an Award or AMI BIOS) without you rebooting your system. This program has been dubbed CTBIOS 1.3; it's available for download at ftp://ftp.heise.de/pub/ct/ctsi/ctbios13.zip.

Now, how much can you ascertain from the alphanumeric soup you just jotted down? You might be able to tell what chipset your motherboard uses. More important for your purposes is that there's a good chance you can discover your motherboard's manufacturer.

Within the AwardBIOS serial number is an eight- or nine-character cluster—the third in the series, separated by dashes. The first five characters identify the chipset in use (now that you know what chipsets are, you may just want to know what it is you have). The sixth and seventh characters in this cluster form a code that identifies the brand of motherboard. Check this character pair against the list you'll find on the BIOS Numbers page of Wim's BIOS Web site at www.wimsbios.com. Not only will you find the BIOS manufacturer; if that manufacturer still exists, you might be able to download the newest available BIOS directly from there, or you might at least find a link to the manufacturer's Web site.

Within the AMI BIOS serial number are seven clusters of characters, separated by dashes. The third such cluster is a four-character sequence that identifies the brand of motherboard. Check this character quartet against the list you'll find on the BIOS Numbers page of Wim's BIOS Web site. You won't find links to manufacturers here, although you can check the name you find against the list of links you will find elsewhere on the Wim's BIOS site or www.motherboards.org.

You could say that obtaining this same amount of information from Phoenix Technologies is like pulling teeth, except that when you really are pulling teeth you have a good idea of exactly what it is you're pulling, and you don't get this feeling that something is pulling you. Phoenix Technologies has publicly thrown up its hands (I shouldn't say "thrown up" just after a teeth-pulling analogy, should I?) and admitted that it actually has lost track of its own clients, the motherboard manufacturers. Claiming the identity of the motherboard manufacturer is "impossible to determine" just from looking at the serial number or any other information deposited on the chip itself, Phoenix's Web site tells its patrons, "You've run out of luck." End quote.

One day, Intel decided it didn't like the willy-nilly way Phoenix BIOS were identifying themselves. So it created the following BIOS identifier code out of thin air: 4D4KL0X0. Check your Phoenix BIOS as it boots up. Look for the first cluster of eight characters in the identifier. Does it match these characters? If so, you have a motherboard manufactured by Intel. At least you know that much. Intel is the manufacturer of choice for motherboards featured in Gateway computers.

If you own a brand-name PC with a Phoenix BIOS, such as Gateway, you should be able to locate the appropriate BIOS upgrade through the Web site for that brand. However, if there isn't a major brand on the system case, you might be in trouble. Phoenix's proposed solution to this mess is to purchase one of those newfangled BIOS controller cards from Micro Firmware (www.firmware.com), a licensed distributor of Phoenix products. One wonders, if you don't know which BIOS version you require, how is Micro Firmware supposed to know?

Once you've located the manufacturer of your motherboard, you have found two vital things. The first is the only place you can be guaranteed to download flash BIOS updates because BIOS manufacturers have made agreements with motherboard manufacturers to not provide user support for those motherboards' own unique versions of the BIOS. The second is perhaps the least expensive source for BIOS chip replacements should you ever want or need them.

It actually comes as a surprise to some people that nearly all of the BIOS found on IBM-brand PCs, including PS/2 and Aptiva, are made, manufactured, and distributed by IBM. An article in a major PC industry publication about five years ago condemned IBM for not "getting with the program" and utilizing a "real BIOS" from someone such as Award, AMI, or Phoenix. The author apparently forgot that IBM invented the bloody thing.

Downloading Your BIOS Flasher Package

The flash BIOS chip or chips contain the programs that instruct the computer how to receive and transfer data. (The processing of that data is taken care of by the CPU.) The flash chips were given this program by the manufacturer, which sends electromagnetic signals through the chip of specific polarities at precise locations. This has the effect of flipping arrays of microscopic, washer-like disks one way or the other, so they stay that way. *Re-flashing* the BIOS means sending a new set of charges through the chip, repolarizing these tiny washers so that the memory contents are changed. This memory stays changed even while the power is off; unlike RAM, the BIOS is in ROM (Read-Only Memory). At power-up, the contents of ROM are transferred to an addressable location in the computer's main memory (RAM).

The act of re-flashing your BIOS requires that you download at least two items: One is the program that does the job of re-flashing the BIOS; the other is the binary code for the BIOS itself. The program simply copies the binary code into ROM. It's run in DOS mode; Windows has to be set aside and out of the way. Both items are very, very small as downloads go. The program gets permission from you to proceed, then it might ask to back up your existing BIOS to a binary file. After that, the program goes about its business, and then crashes your computer. This last part can't be avoided; when you override the contents of the BIOS, that's just what happens. You simply reboot, and the work is done.

Precisely what you download from the Internet to re-flash your BIOS depends mostly on what brand of BIOS you will use. If your motherboard does not require the newest

BIOS available, or requires that you not install the newest one available then you may require an older version of the BIOS flash program associated with it. So make certain from your computer or motherboard manufacturer that you're using the right version of the flasher program for the binary BIOS file you downloaded. A general idea of what to look for is in Table 10.5.

Table 10.5   Flasher Programs

BIOS Brand	Program Required
AMI BIOS	AMIFlash—Its filename is generally either *AMIFLASH.COM* or *AMIFLxxx.COM* (the *xxx* stands for the version number). The size of the binary BIOS file will be an even multiple of 128K, and can have any filename at all at the discretion of the motherboard manufacturer, although most likely it has an extender of .ROM. Both files can be distributed together as a compressed .EXE file with instructions.
Award BIOS	Award Flasher—Its filename generally is *AWDFLxxx.EXE* (the *xxx* stands for its version number). Again, the size of the BIOS file will be an even multiple of 128K and can be given any filename, although this time its extender should be .BIN. And again, both files can be distributed together as a compressed .EXE file with instructions.
Phoenix BIOS	*PHLASH.EXE*—The size of the BIOS file will be an even multiple of 128K (generally 256K total). The BIOS binary file can be given any filename; its extender should be .ROM. Both files can be distributed as a compressed .EXE file with instructions.

AMI and Award BIOS flasher programs can be downloaded freely from www.wimsbios.com/HTML1/biosutil.html. Phoenix' BIOS flasher is only available through motherboard manufacturers' Web sites, and not through Phoenix Technologies itself.

Do You Need to Set Your Flash Jumper?

Only in the realm of computing will you ever find yourself doing anything that sounds as profoundly silly as "setting your *flash jumper.*" Sounds like some measure you'd take in preparation for a swimming marathon, doesn't it? You've got your Speedos firmly in place, your swim goggles firmly attached so they don't fall off, your swim cap snapped down, and your flash jumpers set. Now you're ready to dive into the English Channel.

A jumper on a motherboard is a series of tiny, brass poles sticking straight up, pairs of which are covered over by a very tiny, plastic *shunt.* (I'm always finding these little plastic shunts in the junk I dump out of my Dustbuster.) If your motherboard has a flash jumper—a series of three such poles, two of which are covered by a single shunt (not all motherboards have or need this)—it will be located near the BIOS chips themselves. You will need to check the manual that came with your computer or motherboard, or go online with the manufacturer to determine exactly what the flash jumper is called. It will have a simple name such as "J5" or "JP6," and will be clearly labeled on the motherboard in white. The three poles also will be labeled "1," "2," and "3."

Before you begin your shunt-ectomy, you may find out from your motherboard manufacturer that even if the jumper is present, it's entirely useless. You still might be able to re-flash your BIOS even without changing the jumper setting. So if your motherboard has a flash jumper make certain that you actually need to fiddle with it before you take out those tweezers.

Here's the way these flash jumpers generally work (double-check with your manufacturer-supplied information to verify): Poles 1 and 2 will be covered with the shunt, leaving 3 exposed. Using your plastic or rubber-tipped tweezers (as in nonconductive), gently lift the shunt off of jumpers 1 and 2. Just as gently, replace the shunt so that it covers jumpers 2 and 3. You now will be able to re-flash your BIOS. However, you will need to replace your shunt back over 1 and 2 before you can run your computer normally again.

What Do You Mean, Password Required?

Some computer manufacturers simply abhor the idea of enabling everyday users to work on their own computers. As a result, they may have installed a password on your system that prevents anyone from gaining access to the BIOS—including re-flashing it. This really is a lousy trick. Luckily you can undo this intentional damage. Your BIOS password—if there is one—is maintained by CMOS and the battery that keeps that memory running. Sometimes CMOS is set up with the default password used by the BIOS manufacturer, so you may be able to type that default password and gain full access to your CMOS. Here are some known default case-sensitive passwords you can try:

all brands:	bios
	setup
	cmos
Award:	Award
AMI:	AMI
	AMI_SW
	AMI!SW/
	AMI?SW/

To get rid of the password without using a password, you need to get inside your computer and entirely clear the CMOS memory maintained by your BIOS. This clears all the information CMOS has about your system, including what time it is and what types of devices—especially hard drives—you've installed. If you have Plug-and-Play, you won't be in too much trouble. Your BIOS will be able to re-ascertain what devices you've installed, as long as those devices are Plug-and-Play compliant themselves (nearly all hard drives and CD-ROMs produced since 1996 are).

If you don't have Plug-and-Play BIOS or your devices are not Plug-and-Play compliant, it would be nice for you to know the specifications—for instance, drive type number (often just 47 for modern, large hard drives); numbers of heads, tracks, and cylinders; and something called *write pre-comp* (often abbreviated *WPcomp*) and *landing zone* (often abbreviated *LZone*). (Chapter 24 talks all about these settings and how to determine what they are.) The easiest place to find that data is inside your BIOS setup program; however, to get to it you might need that darned password.

So what do you do? Go inside your computer and examine your installed drives. Look for their manufacturer and model number. CD-ROM drives generally do not need any special information to be enrolled as "CD-ROM" within CMOS; you may need to enroll your DVD-ROM as "CD-ROM," if you don't mind the temporary reduction in rank. For hard drives, go to the Web sites of their manufacturers, where you are likely to find in their customer support sections precisely the data you require. In any event, make certain you know what you need to know about your drives and devices (either their operating specifications, or whether they're Plug-and-Play) before you try clearing the CMOS to clear the password.

Here is the easy way to clear your CMOS: Later in this chapter, you'll find the section "Replacing a Dead Battery." Use the procedure outlined there to take your battery out. Wait 15 seconds; then simply replace the battery where it was. You will want to skip from here to Chapter 23 for instructions about how to get your system back up. However, the password will be gone and now you can safely flash your BIOS.

Re-flashing Your BIOS

Need we say it again? Back up everything in sight before you begin this process. Make certain all important files are safe; Chapter 4 shows you how. Also write down all the vital information you can that your BIOS maintains, because it probably will be overwritten. If you don't have Plug-and-Play, you will need to know the specifications of all hard drives on your system (heads, tracks, cylinders, write pre-comp, landing zone).

You will need to have your Windows installation disc on hand once the re-flashing job is done. Why? Ever since Windows 95, the operating system has kept track of certain facts about the computer that's running it on data files contained within the \Windows\System directory. If Windows finds the BIOS has changed, it wonders if perhaps the computer has changed as well. Why should it care? Well, if an unlicensed copy of Windows is being cloned and shipped around from processor to processor, that's a violation of that *end-user licensing agreement* (*EULA,* not to be confused with Beulah, Fibber McGee's housekeeper, portrayed on radio in the 30s and 40s by Ethel Waters) you didn't bother to read because honestly, who has the time to read 450 pages or so of boring text about computers?

Windows maintains as much information as it can gather about the computer on which it is running; when something fundamental about that computer changes, Windows has to reprocess it. In the process it might need to install some files that are found on the CD-ROM. Windows will automatically prompt you to insert the CD-ROM if this is the case.

For safety's sake, you should copy the re-flasher package you downloaded to a diskette. After that's done and you're ready to begin, leave the diskette out of the drive; then reboot your computer. If you're using Windows 95, after you hear the single beep from the motherboard, hold down the F8 key; then at the menu, type the number beside Command prompt only (generally 5 but depending on your computer, perhaps another number), and wait for the DOS prompt. For Windows 98, 98 SE, and Windows Me, after you hear the single beep from the motherboard, hold down the Ctrl key, then at the menu, type whatever number is beside Command prompt only and wait for the DOS prompt.

Next, insert the diskette into your drive, and switch to the A:>\ prompt by typing **A:** [Enter].

The process of actually performing the re-flashing of your BIOS is perhaps more nerve-wracking than it is difficult. Depending on how your PC or motherboard manufacturer set up the file you downloaded, you'll probably execute this process in one of the following three ways:

➤ You'll type the command that launches the flasher and points to the binary BIOS file at the DOS prompt. This is less dangerous than it may seem; if you type something wrong, chances are nothing will happen.

➤ You'll type the command that launches the flasher, which will lead you through a series of menus. At one such menu, you may be asked whether you'd like to back up the BIOS already installed on your computer. This is an option you should take advantage of, especially because if the new BIOS causes problems down the road, you'll have the immediate opportunity to simply bring your old BIOS back.

➤ You'll be asked to copy the entire flasher program onto a blank diskette (to which you may need to copy the DOS system files); then reboot your PC and just let it go.

227

Check This Out

The nonautomated Award BIOS flasher program enables you to back up your existing BIOS to a file so you can re-flash it back to your BIOS chip in case you have problems with the new one. You definitely should take advantage of this opportunity. The AMI and Phoenix flasher programs don't give you this option. So as a precaution, you should download the version of the BIOS that currently exists on your system, in addition to the new version. Let this second download act as your backup.

The grand finale of just about any re-flasher program is a crash or hang of your system. Do not be alarmed; you may even be forewarned by a message that says, "Your system will now hang." This happens. When it's hung, you know it's done. Power down your system completely and count to 10 (or, if you have a Phoenix BIOS, just stop at about 6 just so you can avoid running out of luck and losing count before you reach 10). If you had to set your flash jumper earlier, now is the time to reset the shunt back to its normal position.

Don't be alarmed if after you reboot your computer Windows comes up in the wrong video mode. This is a common occurrence when Windows discovers that the BIOS was changed out from under it. You might find yourself re-installing your video drivers at Windows' request, even if the video drivers already exist on your system (say, in the \Windows\System subdirectory). If, for some reason, Windows cannot locate the drivers it needs on the CD-ROM, the drivers already installed (which Windows for some reason neglected to load the first time around) should work fine.

When Windows asks for driver location, click Have Disk; then when it asks for the disk's drive letter, fool Windows by typing C:\WINDOWS\SYSTEM\. It will respond by finding the drivers it wants and copying them over themselves. (This is the kind of stuff Microsoft gets paid the big bucks to come up with.) Once Windows has you reboot again, everything should be fine.

Physically Replacing the BIOS Chip

If you do not have a flash BIOS, your chipset is simply too old to handle the more modern peripherals your system requires, or if your BIOS is defective, you might have to physically pull the old chip out and put the new one in. Once you have your new chip, take the usual precautions (backing up, copying down your CMOS settings, up-grading your emergency diskette, re-reading Chapter 4, and so on) and open your PC. Locate your old BIOS chip. Make a careful note about which way it faces, because you have to put your replacement chip back in the exact same way. (Look for the location of the notch on the top of each chip. It should line up with the notch location on the socket.)

Once you've written down everything you can about your existing BIOS chip and how it fits, you can remove it. First check your static level by touching something metal. If your upgrade toolkit includes a chip puller (a large set of tweezers), use it to remove the chip. Otherwise, use a small flathead screwdriver to gently pry up one side of the chip a small amount; then pry up the other side a small amount. Repeat until the chip comes loose. Don't play macho chip puller and try to remove the thing in one step—you'll likely break off one of the legs (see Figure 10.5). Just go slow and easy, and you should be fine.

Figure 10.5

When inserting a chip, make sure you don't leave a leg hanging out.

Use your notes to help you place the new chip in the slot, facing the right direction. Line up the notch on one end of the chip with the same kind of notch on the chip's socket. To insert a chip, line up its little legs with the corresponding holes on the socket and apply a gentle downward pressure. You might want to straighten the legs out by pressing one side of the chip against your desktop before you insert the chip. Also flip it over and press the other side against the desktop, which will line up all the legs so they are perpendicular to the chip.

Once you have the chip in, plug in the PC and start it. You see a message during startup displaying the name and date of your new BIOS. If anything funky happens, turn the PC off and check the chip's legs again. One of them probably is sticking out. If so, remove the chip and gently bend the naughty leg back in place. Try inserting the chip again.

Problems You Could Encounter

The fact that a motherboard manufacturer offers the newest edition of a BIOS that has been tested with that model of motherboard does not mean it has been tested with every possible configuration of a PC using that motherboard. Thus it is an unfortunate possibility that a newer BIOS might not work as well in your computer as an older one.

One potential cause of conflict is that, in actuality, there is more than one BIOS in most modern computers. What I generally refer to as "the BIOS" is the historical central Basic Input/Output System of the computer—the part that was "cloned" when the first PC clones were produced in the 1980s. The video BIOS or graphics BIOS is the basic display-handling code embedded in the firmware of your video card (it should just be called "BOS," since not much input takes place from your monitor). Meanwhile, the Plug-and-Play BIOS is a cluster of code that is marketed as separate from "the BIOS," but actually becomes part of "the BIOS" when it is loaded into the computer's RAM at startup.

What have these facts to do with anything? At startup, all of these BIOS elements have to come together to form the key program that defines the computer for the sake of the operating system. New central BIOS programs sometimes dislike older video BIOS. (Which is why some video card manufacturers are installing flash BIOS chips on their cards—but that's a matter for Chapter 14.)

The result can be that suddenly, some video modes become unsupported by the operating system. Which ones practically could be determined by a roll of the dice—it could be the low-res modes; it could be the high-res modes. This is not a problem you should just live with and go on; if legitimate graphics modes become unsupported in Windows, it's the sign of a deeper conflict within your system firmware. You should go back to your earlier BIOS version and report the trouble to your computer or motherboard manufacturer.

One of the most common problems reported after upgrading any BIOS for Windows 98 (actually experienced by my husband) is when, uncertain of just what has happened to the firmware that supported it so wonderfully in the past, Windows freaks out and, in a fit of desperation, insists upon installing that new infrared networking device of yours. You know, that box you spent so much money on so that your six computers could communicate with each other without the need for cables. You must have bought it; Windows says you did and is installing the drivers for it right now. Strange how it doesn't magically blink into existence even after the drivers automatically install themselves.

You can remove the drivers using Device Manager; however, next time you reboot your computer, Windows will insist on you inserting the CD-ROM so it can install the drivers again. What's the solution to this problem? In the short term you could go back to your original BIOS. If you happen to have flash BIOS on your video card, you should upgrade it to the newest BIOS version available from the manufacturer. But most video cards today do not have flash BIOS so you may have to consider re-placing it.

Mistakes to Avoid

The worst possible mistake you could make in re-flashing your BIOS is to turn your system off before you can plainly see that the program has done its job. You should see the completion message perhaps as soon as 10 seconds; no later than 5 minutes after the flash process has begun. If you don't see the message, don't let your worries force you to attempt to reboot and start over. If the flashing process is incomplete, your system will never be able to reboot. Your remedy would be to physically replace the BIOS chip.

Some messages on motherboard manufacturer's Web sites and some instructions packaged with BIOS downloads will tell you that because BIOS performs the same function for the operating system regardless of its brand, you could easily substitute one brand of binary BIOS image with another of the same size—say, swap an Award BIOS for an AMI, or vice versa—and not experience difficulties. This is entirely ridiculous; disregard these messages. Stick with the BIOS brand that's stamped on the chip.

Replacing a Dead Battery

The battery in your PC keeps the CMOS chip charged so that your BIOS can have access to important information, such as what day it is and what kind of hard disk your PC is supposed to be running. This battery is not the same as the power supply, which converts AC current into DC current to feed hungry PC parts. So when the battery starts dying and you turn the power off, the data in CMOS is lost; as a result your PC could get a bad case of amnesia. When this happens, your PC will cry out, "Where am I?" with a message such as "Invalid system settings—Run Setup."

In short, the battery is dead and you're going to have to replace it with a part that'll cost you more than an ordinary AA battery but less than, say, a car battery. After that you have to re-enter the data that was in CMOS. Hopefully, you already copied down that data using the method shown in Chapter 4; without it, there's a good chance your PC's going to be in a coma for a long, long time.

To replace the battery successfully, you've got to find the right kind of replacement. Open up your PC; then locate the battery. It sounds easy; most of the time it's not because PC manufacturers often are ingenious at disguising things. You're looking for one of these things: a set of two batteries the size of AAs, two cylinders sealed in a red plastic sheath, a black and red box, a silver disk like a watch battery, a silver cube, a silver barrel that looks like a miniature oil drum, or a DIP chip that looks like an old-style DRAM memory chip. (This chip probably will be marked with a little alarm clock logo and the word "Dallas.") If you don't find it near the power supply, look close to the keyboard connection.

Some batteries are soldered onto the motherboard and can't be removed. They might be replaceable with a battery pack, which is connected to the external battery connector. A jumper near this connector must be reset to tell the motherboard that an external battery will be used from now on. If there's no way to plug in an external battery connector, the technical term for the replacement for this battery is *new motherboard*. I'm not kidding.

Once you find the battery, take a good look at it. If it's a battery the way you expect a battery to appear (not a chip), jot down a note about the way it's positioned—for example, which way the plus (+) and the minus (–) ends face. If the battery connects to the motherboard with small wires, make a note of their positions, too. You'll have to replace the battery so that it faces the exact same way; otherwise you'll blow up the CMOS chip. And since CMOS is soldered to the motherboard, you'll have to replace the motherboard to fix it—so take a good, long look.

When you're ready to make the replacement and you know for certain that you can, make sure you discharge any static electricity by touching something such as a file cabinet or a coworker. The battery may be removable by lifting a small clip or detaching it from a plug, or by ripping it off of its Velcro. Use this battery as a guide by taking it with you to Radio Shack. If you live in Antarctica, or someplace that might as well be the bottom of the world as far as computers are concerned, find a working computer; then check out www.3klix.com for price and availability of a new battery that matches your old one.

Take the new battery or chip back to your dead PC and replace it in exactly the same location and position as the old one. If the cable connecting the battery to the motherboard comes loose, replace it, too; however, make sure you position it in the exact same way it was before. Put your PC back together and turn it on. Don't expect fireworks—you're not through yet. You still need to re-enter any CMOS data that was lost and that the BIOS cannot re-ascertain when it starts up again. See Chapter 23 for help.

Mistakes to Avoid

I find it hard to get up in the morning if I can't see a clock someplace nearby that absolutely verifies for me that it's time to get up. Your PC might not boot properly if it can't ascertain what time it is. If the PC won't boot after you've changed the battery, pretend to change it again. Take it out and reinsert it using the procedure outlined here.

If you've connected an external battery pack, make certain the jumper setting on your motherboard is correct so your BIOS recognizes you have one of these external packs. Or just be sure that same jumper hasn't been set to enable an external battery connector if you don't have one.

The Least You Need to Know

➤ The capabilities of your motherboard are defined principally by its chipset, including the range of possible system bus speeds, and what type of memory it supports and how much.

➤ You should opt for as fast a system bus as possible for your PC, even if it means setting your CPU's speed multiplier to a lower number.

➤ When you replace the motherboard, you might end up replacing other things so that they are compatible with the new motherboard—such as your RAM chips and video card.

➤ The most important thing to remember during motherboard replacement is keeping yourself discharged. The smallest electrical displacement from your own body or from a metal tool can short out an important part.

➤ Because motherboard shortouts can happen and because such events generally are catastrophic, it's usually a good idea to test your motherboard fully powered, with the CPU and memory modules left out.

➤ Take some extra measures to ensure that your installed motherboard is secured, fixed, and immobilized.

➤ The most critical fix you might ever make to your computer involves replacing the program in your PC's BIOS. This could involve something as simple as reflashing or as difficult as pulling out the old chips and putting in new ones.

➤ Before you replace a dead battery, you must copy the CMOS data about any device specifications and nondefault system settings your BIOS can't recover when it powers up again.

➤ The shape and size of a motherboard battery is about as certain as your next soufflé. However, its size and shape do denote its type.

Memorize This! Upgrading Memory

I changed the title of this chapter. In the Fourth Edition of this book, I called it, "Memorize This: Upgrading Memory *Is Easy*." My editors asked me to update this book to reflect the times … and shorten it if I could. So I did a little trimming, while at the same time changing things to reflect some new realities.

Memory is not easy. When the Single Inline Memory Module (SIMM) was first released in the late 1980s, the acclaim was overwhelming. Suddenly it didn't matter anymore whether you bought gold-lead chips or tin-lead, eight per bank or nine, 150 nanosecond or 120. Suddenly, there was this one little bitty card the size of a pocket lighter. You plugged it in, and there was memory. Memory was supposed to stay that easy.

Then reality happened. You can't release a new idea into the wild without eighteen thousand engineers simultaneously pouncing on it and trying to make something new of it. As a result, there are now so many different types of memory now, I've forgotten them all. I may have to consult my own book after it's printed just so I can pretend to remember them.

Memories Through the Years ... or Rather, Months

Why is memory architecture important? Because certain motherboard chipsets only accept memory modules that are compatible with particular memory architectures. Since 1996, the number of different memory architectures has ballooned into a well-spring of alphabet soup (see Figure 11.1). But you won't be able to make much sense of the differences between them until you understand at least the basics of how memory works in the first place.

Figure 11.1

Six types of PC memory modules.

(Courtesy Kingston Technologies)

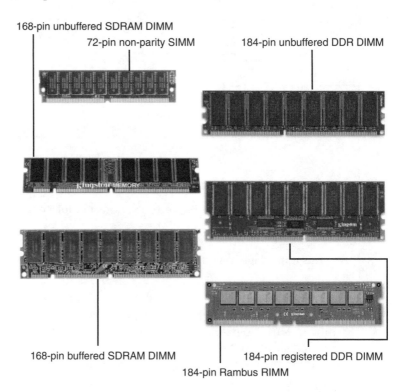

168-pin unbuffered SDRAM DIMM

72-pin non-parity SIMM

184-pin unbuffered DDR DIMM

168-pin buffered SDRAM DIMM

184-pin registered DDR DIMM

184-pin Rambus RIMM

Obviously, SIMM and RIMM designs are somewhat different from DIMMs—radically different from an engineering perspective. But look closely at the differences between the two 168-pin SDRAMs, the 184-pin unbuffered DDR, and the 184-pin registered DDR. Look at the *bottom* of each one, where the pins are located. Notice the notches in the bottom, like someone attacked them with a hole punch. There's an important reason why these holes are where they are: Although SDRAM DIMMs and DDR DIMMs are the same size, they can only plug into their own respective connectors one way, and they cannot plug into each other's connectors. A plastic hump inside the connectors is keyed to the location of these holes. This hump effectively rejects the wrong type of DIMM. So you cannot accidentally plug the wrong DIMM into a connector, or even plug the right DIMM in the wrong way.

How the Address Bus Works

Your CPU has a different comprehension of memory than does your motherboard chipset. The CPU perceives all data as though each element were lined up in a single long, long row, and as if each element were given its own consecutive number, or *address*. What I've been calling the system bus—the link between the CPU and main memory—is what motherboard designers call the *frontside bus,* but what programmers call the *address bus*. Why is that little fact important? Technically, the *address bus* is that part of the system bus used by the CPU to request data, and the *data bus* is that part of the system bus through which this request is fulfilled.

When the CPU needs a memory address, it looks first to its own L1, on-chip cache. Next, it looks to the larger, slightly slower, L2 cache, which generally shares the same package with the CPU but not the same chip—if it doesn't, the L2 could possibly be located in the form of SRAM chips on the motherboard. If the system bus controller part of the chipset gets a request for memory, that must mean the original request could not have been fulfilled by either the L1 or L2 cache. It's up to the chipset to translate the requested address from the CPU into a real address that corresponds to a storage location on one of the installed memory modules.

The way the chipset perceives memory is as one big square full of addresses, like a huge spreadsheet, with exactly as many rows as there are columns. When the address being sought is located in system RAM rather than in a cache, the chipset translates the linear memory address requested by the CPU into a row/column address that can be mapped to a specific location in system memory. How this translation is made, what the translation process resembles, and how the memory module certifies the retrieved data, are the three main distinguishing factors of the various memory technologies.

All the Memory Technologies You Care to Know About

Ordinary DRAM no longer truly exists, but every new technology is an extension of it. In a hypothetical "ordinary" system, the translated address is sent over the address bus in two parts: row first, followed by column. This row/column pairing takes place for each requested address. Now, pay close attention, because I'm going to *try* to be brief.

Fast Page Mode (FPM) DRAM makes it possible for a newly requested address that resides in the same row as the previously requested one, to omit the redundant reference to the row. A redundancy signal is sent instead, followed by the column address. This greatly reduces the overall access time, because a lot of memory requests are *consecutive* ones. For FPM to work in a system, both the memory modules and the chipset must support it.

Extended Data Out (EDO) DRAM skews the internal timing of the memory module a bit so that it can accept a new address request at the same time it's finishing up with the old one. Again, for this technology to be supported in your PC, both your chipset and your memory modules must support it.

Burst Extended Data Out (BEDO) DRAM adds one element to the EDO scheme: If the next four address requests can be guaranteed to be in the same row together, the first address is handled normally, and then the remaining three are processed in "burst mode," consuming just one clock cycle rather than EDO's two. BEDO didn't really have much time in the spotlight before SDRAM took over and crowded the stage.

Error Correcting Code (ECC) is the ingenious name for the type of *error self-correcting* memory that does not use parity. This type of memory must be supported not only by your chipset but by your BIOS as well for it to work in your PC. Almost all BIOS supports parity memory, but not all versions created for all motherboards support ECC. Although ECC does slow down overall memory performance, it does significantly improve its reliability. Like parity memory, ECC also uses one extra bit per byte, but not for parity; so although your PC may support both types, only parity or ECC may be in use at any one time. A chipset either requires ECC or it doesn't. If it does, you need the special DIMMs that utilize ECC; if it doesn't, you need the DIMMs that do not utilize ECC. They are definitely different DIMMs.

Techno Talk

If your memory supports *parity checking*, then it will use one extra bit to store each address (each byte) of memory. You'll recall that a byte of memory is made up of binary digits (1s and 0s). The purpose of this extra bit is to make certain that each address contains an odd or even number of 1 bits (which one depends on your current BIOS parity setting, although one setting is no more preferable than the other). This way, if any one address happens to have degraded so that one or more of its bits have literally flipped, the chipset has a 50/50 chance of detecting this problem because it could result in the number of 1 bits being odd when it should be even, or even when it should be odd.

Synchronous DRAM (SDRAM) changes the entire scene with regard to how memory works. Historically, the bus that links together all installed memory modules or chips on a PC (the *true* memory bus) was timed *asynchronously* with regard to the system bus. In other words, it did its own thing, and kept its own rhythm. Because of that, some memory retrieval operations could theoretically still be in progress at the same time the ever-faster CPU was waiting to receive the results. To eliminate the chances of that happening, *wait states* were added to CPU requests of memory, to ensure that the CPU didn't get ahead of the memory modules. The theory behind synchronous

DRAM is for memory to be able to use the system bus clock to plan when and how retrieval operations take place, so time never has to be added to a retrieval to compensate for the fact that the CPU is so fast. The CPU, in short, never has to *plan* on waiting. SDRAM changed not only the technology of the memory module, but its very shape as well. It was SDRAM technology that helped DIMM architecture quickly overtake SIMMs as the modules of choice.

SDRAM DIMM modules are generally available in 64, 128, 256, and 512MB capacities, although some motherboards will not recognize the 512MB variety. How could DIMM modules keep up with the one-fetch-per-cycle requirements of SDRAM, whereas SIMMs couldn't? A single 168-pin DIMM is made up *internally* of two banks of RAM (surprise!). While one bank is busy wrapping up an address request, the second bank is starting to tackle the next one, because consecutive addresses are skewed among the two internal banks—one in the first bank, the next in the second, the next back at the first, and so on. This is how SDRAM is capable of handling consecutive address requests in just one clock cycle.

For a while, it appeared that SDRAM had matters pretty well in hand. Throughout 1999 and into 2000, PC100 SDRAM comprised a huge chunk of the memory market, supporting the new 100MHz system bus. (PC66 SDRAM was created retroactively to support the next slower speed.) When system bus speeds started exploding (see Chapter 10, "Replacing the Motherboard and Its Parts," to learn why), new SDRAM modules had to be invented to support them, because the "S" in "SDRAM" stands for "synchronous," and a memory module cannot be expected to synchronize itself to whatever clock happens to be out there. In other words, it's pre-synchronized to the right beat before it comes off the factory lines. So suddenly there were PC133, PC150, PC166, PC200, PC233 … all of these being different product lines to account for bus speeds that were coming out of nowhere. Today, these separate categories can't really compete with one another for market share. You either need PC150 or you don't. You can't just decide on an impulse to plunk down the extra twenty-five bucks or so to move up to PC166. If you want the next higher memory speed, you need a new motherboard that supports the next highest system bus speed.

You'd think maybe memory prices would stabilize, seeing as how all the SDRAM categories weren't competing with one another, and competition is the force that usually drives prices down. But instead, with production of all categories at full tilt, there became a bit of a memory *glut* in 2000, and the floor supporting the price of memory started to cave in. Then at last, a new and truly competing technology gave the floor a big shove:

Double Data Rate SDRAM (DDR-SDRAM) uses a trick of technology to be able to retrieve two consecutive addresses in one clock cycle. Try this trick at home and you'll understand how it works: Sing a song in your head, and tap your foot to the beat. Count the number of beats per measure out loud. Now, adjust your method so that you count once when you put your foot *down,* and then again when you pick your foot back *up.* DDR plays with the tick of the system bus clock in exactly this way. This doesn't *exactly* double the retrieval rate (nothing "doubled" in computing is ever really "twice" what it was after marketing gets its hands on the title), but it does give it a significant boost.

DDR uses an entirely new, 184-pin DIMM design. An SDRAM module will not plug into it. To be more accurate, there are actually *two* new DIMM designs: one for un-buffered DDR, and the other for so-called *registered DDR*. This latter type incorporates separate chips (as you can see in Figure 1.1) that serve as an on-module memory buffer. The result is a doubling of memory capacity per module and a potential cost savings, with the tradeoff being that the buffering process makes the registered DDR module slightly slower than its unbuffered counterpart. AMD is a leading proponent of DDR design, and develops chipsets that support DDR along with its Athlon and Duron processors.

Rambus: First Blood, Part II

Here is where the proverbial monkey wrench was cast into the barrel of monkey wrenches: As part of a lucrative business arrangement, a company called Rambus Technologies collaborated with Intel in the production and promotion of an entirely different kind of memory technology—an out-and-out departure from everything we know about the way memory works. New high-end Pentium III and P4 chipsets from Intel will now support this new kind of memory, which doesn't use SDRAM—more to the point, it doesn't use DIMMs at all.

Direct Rambus RIMM—or just RIMM—is an acronym that Rambus's press spokespeople have now gone on record as standing for … nothing whatsoever. The Rambus system actually works by *narrowing* the width of the memory bus from 64 bits to 16, but compensating by implementing a 400 MHz memory clock that is asynchronous to the system bus, and using some of the same tricks DDR uses to double some or all of the data throughput rates.

The Rambus scheme takes everything we've come to know about memory and turns it upside down, stomps on it, beats it with a pick-axe, takes all the little bits, sets them on fire, throws them up in the air, shoots at them with hunting rifles, then sends dogs after them.

Unlike the fully populated square analogy used by traditional memory since the Intel 4004 CPU gave logic to stoplights everywhere, Rambus sees memory as a sort of circular river through which data travels in one continuous direction. The chips on a RIMM form a circuit consisting of mere stopover points for the continual flow of data. A data request from the chipset is merely a passenger on this river, and the response to this request is pushed through the circuit and hits the chipset square in the back.

Like SDRAM (and there are not many instances where I'll use the phrase "like SDRAM" in this segment), RIMMs are available in 64MB, 128MB, 256MB, and 512MB varieties, although the 128 and 256 are the most widely available. Entirely *unlike* SDRAM, you can freely mix and match quantities throughout your connectors without restrictions. You can install a 128 in the first connector and a 256 in the second, or vice versa. Either way, you have 384MB.

240

Now, entirely unlike anything you or I have ever seen before, is this incredible fact: A motherboard that supports Rambus provides a certain number of connectors—say, 4 or 6. All of those connectors *must* be populated with something. If you have a total of four connectors, and you have 256 in the first and 128 in the second, for a total of 384, you still need something in the third and fourth connectors. What do you put there? *Memory modules with no memory*, that's what. They're called C-RIMMs, or *continuity RIMMs*. They're real modules, but they have zero memory. Like the burned out Christmas light in the middle of a chain of 50, the C-RIMM keeps the memory river flowing. So you never leave a RIMM connector open; where there's no memory, you can install a C-RIMM. In fact, you can install a C-RIMM in the first connector, and put your 128 and 256 in the second and third—it doesn't matter as long as no connectors are open, otherwise your chipset will not recognize any memory at all, and your system will fail to boot.

In trying to make a point—and score some points against SDRAM—Rambus calls its categories of RIMM modules "PC600," "PC700," and "PC800." These names will fool you, because it seems like PC800 is going to be eight times faster than PC100. It isn't. Rambus itself claims it's only three times faster, which is still good … but independent tests are confirming it's faster, but not three times as much. These numbers are speed-related, but here's how they work: Rambus uses a 400MHz memory bus clock. If its fetch rate were one 16-bit unit of data per cycle, it would have an effective memory bandwidth of 400MHz. But with PC600 RIMMs installed, the controller chips on the RIMMs themselves regulate the doubling of the data rate for half the requests. PC700 doubles the data rate for 75 percent of the requests, and PC800 doubles for all of them. This way, Rambus has a "good/better/best" marketing scenario.

Now, just because Rambus uses a 16-bit data width, does that mean it makes a Pentium or Athlon system a 16-bit computer? Not at all. Its system bus (it's still there) is 64 bits wide. It just takes four fetch instructions for Rambus to fill an entire data "word." But with a separate clock that's ticking at four times the rate of the average system bus, and with most or all the fetches being doubled, the entire process does end up being somewhat faster.

Battle of the Various Bulges

So, it would appear we have an interesting three-way race going on in the world of memory. On one side, you have the high-performance AMD camp, which is squarely behind DDR technology. On the opposite end of the fork in the road, Intel appears to have taken the road less traveled by, by taking the Rambus, and for all the difference it'll make, it's a helluva lot different. Then there's the established SDRAM, which comprises a majority of memory production and isn't going away anytime soon. That should be enough to keep things brewing quite nicely, shouldn't it?

Synchronous Link DRAM (SLDRAM) is the product of a growing alliance of semiconductor manufacturers, including some major names (Fujitsu, Hitachi, Samsung, TI, Toshiba, and others) that aren't all that thrilled with the idea of paying another company (Rambus) high royalties to use its design. What the SLDRAM Consortium wants to do is further evolve existing DIMM technology by adding a separate clock timed at 200MHz, synchronizing that clock with the system bus clock, then utilizing the double-data rate trick. The Consortium also wants to try Rambus' idea of mixing and matching components (perhaps not with the zero memory module thing, though), so you can have a 128MB DIMM and a 64MB DIMM sitting side by side.

Note

This book will be in print for a little while. During that time, SL–DRAM components, and chipsets that support them, will likely be made available on the open market. There will be one *more* type of DIMM to contend with.

Buying the Right Kind of RAM

Determining what specific module packaging your motherboard requires is more difficult by a long shot than actually installing the modules themselves. You'll need to do some math, so get out your calculator. (You remember calculators, don't you? Those things you find in your Windows Start menu under **Accessories?**)

At the time of this writing, the market price for ordinary DRAM was averaging 22.6¢ per megabyte, based on the price of the "benchmark" 128MB unbuffered SDRAM. There was a time when I used to say RAM prices varied like the price of stocks, and you should wait for the right time to jump in and buy, then buy big. I don't say that anymore. Whatever forces could possibly converge to drive the price of RAM *up*, don't appear to be converging anytime between now and 2003. If you're thinking about waiting for the right time … don't.

Depth, Width, and Speed

Before I go back to talking about Rambus, let me return for a moment to the way things generally work in the world of memory. The Pentium series is a 64-bit processor, which means the width of its data bus is 64 bits. Keep that in mind for a moment. Now, the contents of a DIMM (or SIMM) memory module are arranged in rows and columns, but not exactly the same way as the chipset perceives it (the "perfect square" analogy). Instead, all the chips that make up a DIMM put together have a set number of rows of bits. The number of bits in each row may or may not be 8, even though the old rule still applies that there are 8 bits in 1 byte. A DIMM module is registered by three numbers:

➤ **Depth** refers to the total number of *megabits* that comprise one *column* of storage within the module. A megabit is 1,048,576 bits.

➤ **Width** refers to the number of bits that comprise one row of storage within the module. Multiply depth by width and divide the product by 8, and the result will be the module's memory capacity in megabytes.

➤ **Speed** is reported in either of two ways: 1) as the amount of time it takes a module to fulfill an address request from the CPU, measured in nanoseconds (billionths of a second), or *ns;* 2) as the "PC" trademark for SDRAM that states the system bus speed requirement for the module.

So suppose you're shopping for memory, and you come across the following listing:

```
EDO 4×64-8 ECC DIMM
```

What does it mean? Well, you know what a DIMM is. The "ECC" tells you that the module uses Error Correcting Code, which requires one extra chip for every eight. The "EDO" is the Extended Data Out category, which is older than SDRAM and which some systems still in circulation require. The "4" to the left of the "×" refers to the module's depth in megabits. The "64" to the right of the "×" is the width in bits of one row of storage. Multiply 4 by 64 and divide by the number of bits in a byte (8), and you get 32. This is a 32 *megabyte* (MB) module. The "8" in this listing to the right of the hyphen refers to timing: 8 nanoseconds (ns). It takes 8 nanoseconds for this module to respond to an address request.

Now, here's another possibility:

```
256MB 32×64 PC133
```

The "256MB" is redundant because you already have "32×64." This module has 32 megabits of *depth*—it's a longer DIMM than the previous one. Width is the same: 64 bits. Speed here isn't reported in nanoseconds, but as "PC133"—in sync with a 133 MHz system bus. This is obviously an SDRAM.

Next, let's take a look at a typical RIMM designation:

```
128MB PC800 RIMM
```

The data width of RIMM is already established: 16 bits. The "800" is a kind of made up number. The memory bus speed for Rambus is set at 400MHz— that's not a variable. If Rambus fetched exactly one 16-bit word of data per cycle, it would fetch 400 words per second. But it doesn't, because of buffering chips on each module that enable double data rates for some or all of the cycles. The "800" number is exactly twice the 400MHz bus speed, which means the module doubles every fetch. If it were "PC600," the module would only double half the fetches.

Note

In the days of the Old West when SIMMs ruled the wild frontier, it often took two modules to fill a bank. So you often couldn't buy just one and get away with it. Today, only one DIMM is required to fill a bank of SDRAM. A DIMM is a bank.

Finally, let's examine DDR designations. DDR technology is competing head-on with Rambus at present, and in the marketing department, it simply will not be outdone by Rambus's numbering scheme. So

DDR DIMMs are now all differentiated by their speed, which is recorded like this: PC1600, PC2100, and so on. So suppose you see the following designation:

```
256MB PC2100 DDR
```

What can you discern from this? Data width is not a variable here; all DDR width is 64 bits. So that's assumed. The "2100" is a number derived by multiplying the memory bus speed that the module supports, *times 8,* then rounded to the nearest hundred. (Sheesh!) If you divide 2100 by 8, then round up to the nearest possible bus speed, you get 266MHz. That's the actual bus speed the module requires. (What's the "times 8" all about? DDR manufacturers say, data width is 64 bits, and there are 8 bits in a byte, so 64 divided by 8 is 8. Makes you wish marketing guys didn't know how to use four-function calculators, doesn't it?)

Connector Metal Type

Here's a distinguishing factor of both memory modules and their corresponding connectors that has less to do with vanity than it may appear on the surface: They come in gold and silver. The modules with gold pins fit into connectors that use gold contacts. Likewise, the silver pin modules are designed for use in silver contact connectors. So make sure you get the right metal for your motherboard.

Voltage

Most modern motherboards today use 3.3-volt (v) unbuffered DIMMs. However, both EDO and FPM DIMMs come in 3.3v and 5v models, depending on the voltage requirements of your motherboard. Five-volt memory buses are being used less and less, although they're not entirely extinct; and some motherboards allow you to set a jumper that sets the memory voltage to one or the other. This is one dangerous jumper. No memory module supports both voltages, so there is no reason for you to set this jumper while leaving your current memory installed. This also means you can't mix 3.3v and 5v modules on the same motherboard. Make certain you purchase the voltage you intend to use; and if your motherboard does give you a choice, pick 3.3v.

The voltage requirement for DDR SDRAM is 2.5v. There's no choice about it, so there's no hassle. If your motherboard supports DDR, it cannot support any other type of memory, so its system bus will be set at 2.5 volts.

Rambus bus voltage is also set at 2.5v. However, you can tell overheating can become a problem, because Rambus now recommends you attach an aluminum "heat shield" to the side where the chips are mounted. Now, the heat shield of the Friendship 7 spacecraft kept the heat from getting *to* John Glenn; meanwhile, the heat shield of RIMM modules is supposed to take heat *away* from the chips, not protect them from heat from outside. So when you see Rambus mention the heat shield, know that they got this part backward also.

Mixing and Matching DIMMs: The Limitations

There are fewer and fewer rules regarding the order and capacity of DIMM modules you can install on a motherboard's DIMM connectors. There are strict rules regarding the reduction of those other rules, which may be even more complex than the original rules themselves.

If the DIMMs on your motherboard are of an older type than SDRAM (FPM, EDO, BEDO), then determining the speed you need can be a tough issue. Look for a sticker on one of the DIMMs with the depth/width/speed notation introduced earlier. If you can find the speed, it's always the safest bet to replace or amend these DIMMs with newer ones with exactly the same access speed in nanoseconds. If you exceed this speed with a lower number, the new DIMMs might not work.

How do you know what your motherboard's maximum memory speed is supposed to be? There's only one way for you to find out: *Ask*. Your BIOS will not tell you. Find out what brand and model of motherboard you have, then check on the manufacturer's Web site for special instructions.

Some DIMM connectors on a motherboard are numbered. You'll see little white digits—1, 2, 3, 4 ...—on either end of the connector rows. If they are numbered, then you must install DIMMs in these connectors in sequential order, starting with #1.

All motherboards that do support memory technologies that are older than SDRAM, will have connectors that are numbered. Each connector represents one bank of memory. The speed of all of your banks will be determined by the speed of the module that is installed in the connector marked "1." This speed can be the maximum speed supported by your motherboard (actually, by your chipset), or it can be slower—but not faster. If any of the modules in connectors 2, 3, 4, and so on, happen to be rated *faster* than the module in #1, then those modules will run just fine at the slower speed. If any of those modules are rated *slower* than the module in #1, your system will not boot.

Some BIOS accept any memory capacity that's a multiple of 64MB, and some don't. Those that don't accept any multiple of 64MB, instead expect memory capacities that increase by powers of 2: 64MB, 128MB, 256MB, 512MB, 1GB.

When your BIOS only accepts a memory capacity that's a power of 2, then by virtue of a trick of mathematics, you cannot mix two different capacities of DIMM on the same motherboard. For example, you cannot install a 256MB DIMM and a 64MB DIMM to get 320MB.

How can you tell what your BIOS accepts and what it doesn't? According to Phoenix, the following is now the accepted way for discovering how much memory a system supports: First, install the memory. If your PC doesn't recognize it, your BIOS probably didn't accept it. Now, of course, this assumes you purchased the memory first. You probably don't want to end up having purchased more memory than you can rightfully use. According to AMI, since all motherboards have different specifications, you should go online with the tech support page of your motherboard's manufacturer *before* you make a memory purchase. Now, that makes a bit more sense.

Now, suppose your motherboard allows you to install a 256 and a 64 to get 320MB. But in what order? If your connectors are numbered, then you need to install the *highest* capacity DIMMs *first*. So you'd insert the 256 in connector #1, and the 64 in connector #2.

Suppose you have SDRAM, and your connectors *aren't* numbered. What then? Some literature says you can install your unmatched DIMMs in any connector you want. *Don't*. Instead, choose a connector on either end and call that one in your mind connector #1. It can be either end. *Pretend*. (You can pretend, can't you? The same way you pretend every day that Windows is *so* fast and that you enjoy Windows *so* much.) Then follow the same rules you would if the connectors truly did have numbers: Install the 256 in the connector you've just dubbed #1, then the 64 in the connector just above or below.

Installation: You Must Remember This ...

Get your PC tool kit, do your usual backup, update your emergency diskette, and open your PC (see Chapter 4, "What You Need to Know *Before* You Open Your PC"). Before you do anything, make sure you discharge any static electricity. A grounding wrist strap comes in real handy for this job.

Removing and Replacing DIMMs

Here's something comforting to know: Although an SDRAM DIMM and a DDR DIMM have different shapes, they're installed in their respective connectors with the same technique.

A DIMM is inserted straight down into the socket just like an expansion card. If you are a SIMM veteran, you may have gotten into the habit of installing modules at an angle; you'll need to break that habit with DIMMs. A DIMM can only go into its socket one way, so if its pins aren't aligned with the connections on the socket, don't try to force it (see Figure 11.2).

Here's the trick I use: Holding the DIMM by its left and right edges—*not* by its chips—align the off-center key hole on the connector edge with the hump you can see on its connector. Gently situate the DIMM over the connector. Rock it back and forth a bit; if you feel a fulcrum like the center of a seesaw, you've got it on the wrong way; turn it around. When the connector seems to want to hug the module and it won't rock, then place your thumbs on both corners of the top edge—again, avoid all temptation to grab it by the chips. Using equal force with both hands, gently increase the amount of pressure. The connection will be tight, but don't tap or beat on the module—that could cause the connector to scratch the pins.

As the module enters the connector, the two plastic levers on either side will begin to close, like the bonus "lotus trap" on a Japanese pinball machine. When you can't apply any more force to the DIMMs to make this trap close further, then let go. The DIMM's not installed just yet. Grab both levers, then gently apply force toward the *center* of the DIMM (the way they were headed to start with). You'll feel both levers snap shut. Now, just to make sure, gently pinch the top of the DIMM on one corner and pull up. If it doesn't move, you've plugged it in.

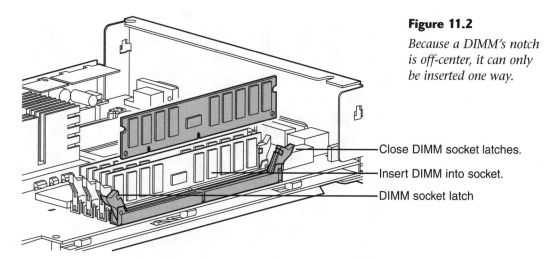

Figure 11.2

Because a DIMM's notch is off-center, it can only be inserted one way.

Close DIMM socket latches.

Insert DIMM into socket.

DIMM socket latch

Leave your system case open, but plug in your power and turn the PC on. Soon it will realize that you added some memory, but it may be confused—you'll know if it is when you check for an error message onscreen or from the audible BIOS "beep codes" (see—or rather, hear—Chapter 10). Don't panic ... at least not yet. You probably just need to ensure the amount of memory recorded in CMOS is correct. Newer BIOSes automatically update this figure, having nothing to do with Plug and Play; the capacity of memory modules should be self-evident to your chipset. But if that capacity figure ends up being wrong, you need to set it yourself. If you need help, see Chapter 23.

To remove a DIMM, unsnap the plastic levers out from the center of the DIMM, and firmly but gently pull them out and down. Not only will they let go of the DIMM, but they'll help shove it out of the socket for you. When the levers are loose, with both hands, pinch the corners at the top edge of the DIMM, again taking care to avoid the chips. With equal force, gently pull up and away from the connector. Try not to rock the DIMM out if at all possible.

Removing and Replacing SIMMs

SIMMs are rarely used in PCs anymore, and the motherboards that use only SIMMs have become too antiquated and too expensive to effectively upgrade. You can still purchase new SIMMs to replace the old SIMMs in your old computer ... but not for long. They're not only out of style, but also out of production. However, there are still some components in the world that do use SIMMs—for instance, *laser printers*. Their manufacturers still make replacement SIMMs available, and probably have enough stored in their backup inventory to last them a few years.

To remove a SIMM, first check to see how it's attached. You'll notice a clip at either end of the SIMM that holds the SIMM in place (see Figure 11.3). To release the SIMM, press down on each clip. The SIMM pops forward a bit. Hold the SIMM at its top edge and lift it out.

Figure 11.3

To remove a SIMM, release the clip holding it in place.

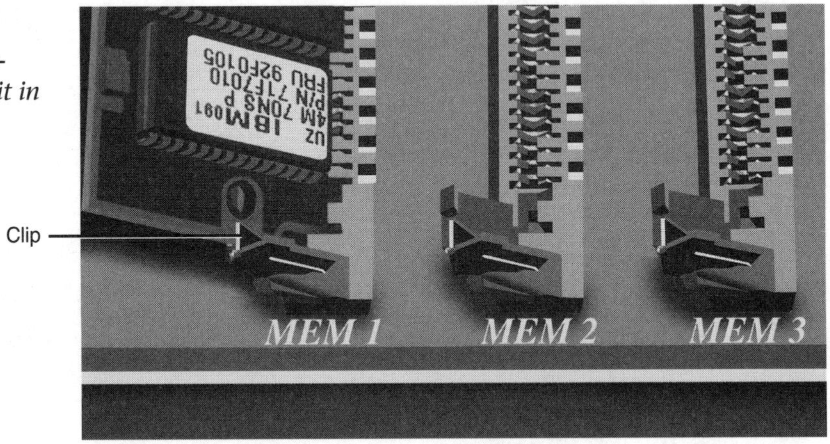

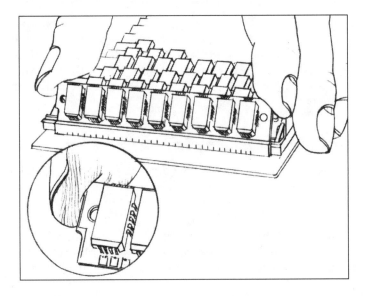

Keep in mind that for SIMMs, modules are added in complete banks and in order. Typically, the first bank of memory is called bank 0, and the second bank is called bank 1 (like how the bottom floor of an office building is the basement, and the next floor up is numbered 1, and so on). Anyway, be sure to fill the banks in order, beginning with the first bank, and proceeding on.

To insert a SIMM, hold it at its top edge (see Figure 11.4). Flip the SIMM so that the notch at one end matches up with the same notch on the SIMM socket. Position the SIMM over the socket and gently insert it at an angle, as shown.

Figure 11.4

Hold the SIMM at the top edge to insert it.

When you insert the SIMM, press it up gently until the tabs pop up to lock it in place. Don't force this; if it doesn't seem to want to work, you may have inserted the SIMM backward, or not completely into the socket itself. Try again. You must insert some SIMMs at a 90-degree angle perpendicular to the socket and rock them backward into a 10 o'clock position to lock them into place.

Removing and Replacing RIMMs

A RIMM is just about the same size as a DIMM, but it won't fit into a DIMM connector. Like DIMMs, RIMMs also have keyed connectors that prevent you from installing them the wrong direction. Each RIMM has a keyhole in the direct center, and a second hole just left of center.

The installation and removal procedure for a RIMM is, thankfully, quite similar to that for a DIMM, except for one very important respect: You will have to remove *something* in order to install your RIMM. If you're adding a RIMM to a motherboard that already has one, that something will be a C-RIMM—a zero memory module. You can easily spot a C-RIMM as a RIMM with quite a bit fewer chips on board (see Figure 11.5).

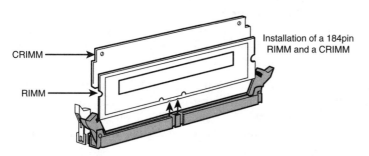

Installation of a 184pin
RIMM and a CRIMM

CRIMM

RIMM

Figure 11.5

You have to get rid of a C-RIMM to make room for a RIMM.

To remove a C-RIMM or a RIMM, you'll find its connector has the two plastic levers on either side, just like a DIMM connector. Pull the levers out and down, away from the center of the RIMM. Then pinch the module by the top and lift up, away from the connector. Which C-RIMM do you remove? Eeny, meeny, miny, mo. Pick any one.

You can use the same trick for installing RIMMs as you do for installing DIMMs. There's one thing you have to pay attention to, though: The chips on a RIMM run very hot, so they need the "heat shield" installed. This part is a cheap little aluminum cap that's very, very thin. If you were to grab the RIMM by the aluminum cap, it could bend or dent the cap, causing it to touch one of the chips. And you don't want that, because that would actually heat up the cap, causing it to be a *provider* of heat for the rest of the chips, as opposed to a remover of it.

Mistakes to Avoid

All of the memory modules in your computer should not only be of the same physical shape, but also of the same *category*. Don't expect to be able to install non-parity memory in a system where parity memory is already installed. If you have ECC now, you'll need more ECC memory to expand it. Same goes for registered memory.

If your PC doesn't recognize your new memory, the easiest thing to do is remove it and start over. Try "rotating" the order of your modules if you're installing more than one, like rotating your tires.

SIMMs are weird. Any Pentium-class motherboard that has a 64-bit memory bus (the part of the data bus that fetches memory from RAM) requires SIMMs to be installed in pairs *if* those SIMMS are 32-bit (72-pin) units. In some unusual (read: "Compaq") circumstances, 32-bit SIMMs have to be installed in *fours*. If a Pentium motherboard uses 64-bit DIMMs, pairing is not required. But many Pentium motherboards that use 64-bit *SIMMs* (not DIMMs) pair up their modules to fill a bank anyway.

Now, as long as you remember to simply fill the entire bank whenever you upgrade, what should this pairing rule matter? If you fill the bank, you follow the pairing rule automatically, right? With some, although the banks do exist, *they're not marked.* You're expected to simply know the pairing rule, either from having read the something-less-than-English manual, from watching smoke rise from your system, or—certainly less hazardous—from having just read it in this book.

If all this fails, then it's time to put your PC back like it was. Take out the new memory modules, reinsert the old ones exactly where they were, and then power on the system with your emergency diskette in the drive. Remember, your emergency diskette has the startup files for your computer backed up before you began the upgrade process. If you get a prompt and everything appears in order, the problem was evidently with something you added (or took away). If the problem persists, however, the problem was caused by the upgrade process itself, and it may be time to take the machine to the shop.

The Least You Need to Know

➤ If your motherboard uses SIMMs, then its BIOS and chipset may be candidates for supporting Fast Page Mode, Extended Data Out, and Burst EDO technologies.

➤ A memory module is identified by its bit depth (the number of megabits per column), bit width (the number of columns), and access speed in nanoseconds. The width of a module determines the number of pins used in its connection.

➤ If your motherboard requires DIMMs, then if it uses technologies such as FPM, EDO, or BEDO, the speed of these modules is determined by their fetch rate in nanoseconds.

➤ If your system uses SDRAM or DDR DIMMs, then their speed is determined by your motherboard's system bus speed: 66, 100, 133, 150, 166, 200, or 233MHz (if not faster by the time this book is printed).

➤ If your system uses RIMMs, then their speed is regulated by a separate 400MHz clock, but their retrieval rate is multiplied by a buffering factor installed on each module.

➤ When a memory module supports error self-correction, such as parity or ECC, it generally adds an extra chip for every four or eight normally installed, to handle an extra bit of memory used in the correction process.

➤ Two other key factors in determining which module you need for your system are voltage requirements and silver/gold connector metal.

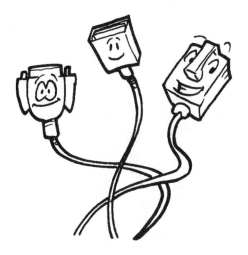

Chapter 12

Face the Interface

In This Chapter

➤ All the expansion interfaces currently manufactured

➤ Making certain your PC has serial and parallel ports

➤ Connecting your motherboard to your I/O connectors

➤ The dual-IDE/EIDE adapter card, and whether you need it

➤ SCSI, SCSI, SCSI, SCSI, SCSI, SCSI, SCSI, and SCSI

➤ USB and World War III

➤ The onset of FireWire

There are two schools of thought with regard to engineering easy ways for you to add things to your computer system. One school believes the best computer is an "open computer," that enables you to replace and augment system components by giving you free and easy access to the system case. The other school believes you're more likely to be afraid of your system case than you are compelled to stick your hands in it, so they would rather you have an easy way to plug new components in from the outside, in universal sockets so you won't have to worry about which plug should go into what socket.

In the true tradition of personal computing, the interplay between these two camps and their conflicting concepts of simplicity, has led to chaos, confusion, and loose connectors. The proponents of the Universal System Bus (USB) are waging their war with the weapons of marketing, spreading their message of goodwill about the joys of plugging in throughout the masses. If you're a person who feels a surge of joy and accomplishment through your veins every time you plug the vacuum cleaner into the wall, your mind should already be open to this message of peace, plugs, and rock-and-roll.

I don't know about you, but I'm just not the sort who can be thrilled by plugging things into other things. I know, I must not be too popular among psychoanalysts. What thrills me most is being able to make something happen *after* the thing gets plugged in.

This chapter is mainly about the act of plugging things in. You might be thinking, this can't possibly be the most exciting chapter in the book. (That would have been the chapter about staging a re-enactment of the Battle of Midway Island with the cast of *Riverdance* on one side, and the cast of *A Bug's Life* on the other, but you know editors and their space restrictions!) You plug cards into your expansion ports so you can add circuitry to your computer. You plug devices into your communications slots so you can add functionality to your computer. You plug storage devices directly into the motherboard. What's exciting about these acts is one principal aspect that they all share: being able to be *done* so your computer works better and you can get on with your life.

An *interface* is a specification for how one thing gets plugged into another thing. Your modem and your printer connect to your computer by way of interfaces. Deeper under the covers, your video card connects to your expansion bus or video bus by way of an interface, and your hard drive connects to your motherboard by way of an interface.

You'll learn about interfaces and the busses to which they connect. Along the way, this chapter will tell you more about SCSI than most anyone truly wants to know. You may not ever have to deal with SCSI in your lifetime; but if, one day, you run across that magnificent backup and archiving device you've always wanted, suddenly SCSI may show up at your door, like eight or nine in-laws that neither you nor your spouse knew you had. You'll also be introduced to the IDE interface, which facilitates hard disks and optical discs (but doesn't manage to resolve the "disk/disc" spelling problem).

Then, if you're still with us, we'll examine USB up close. USB is a separate serial communications bus that can connect to the PCI expansion bus, although newer motherboards support USB directly, bypassing PCI. USB is a valiant attempt to make good on the promise of Plug and Play. Trouble is, Windows still exists.

Everything You Didn't Want to Know About Busses

The width of a bus is like the number of lanes on a highway. Most CPUs produced today have 32-bit, if not 64-bit, system busses. The system bus is the electronic highway over which data travels—from the peripheral controllers or from memory—to the CPU.

The System Bus

If you hear the term *data bus,* or more recently the *frontside bus* (FSB), what's being referred to is the system bus. Consider busses like different *lanes* on the same highway. The speed of the system bus is regulated not by the CPU, but by the chipset on the motherboard. The speed of the CPU to which you attach this motherboard must, of course, not be any slower than the motherboard itself. (Today, that's pretty much impossible.) Meanwhile, your CPU speed should run in sync with your system bus, so that the "beats" they keep aren't off-track. Imagine two songs playing simultaneously, one whose beat is exactly double that of the other. If their melodies are compatible, you just may be able to listen to the resulting noise. This is generally what I mean by "in sync." So the speed of the system bus is just as crucial as the clock speed of the CPU in determining the overall performance of your computer.

For a very long time, the system busses in PCs were limited to a speed of 8MHz—the fixed clock speed of the 80286 CPU. Only with the advent of Intel's 386DX were system busses allowed to be clocked faster; meanwhile, the 386SX was released for motherboards that were still fixed at 8MHz. Also, ever since the '286-based PC AT, the PC's main expansion bus (ISA) has been relegated to a 16-bit data path. What's the problem with that? Data being sent *out*—to your video or modem or printer or speakers— has to stop over at the peripheral bus controller to get chopped into two (from 32 bits to 16), if not four parts, before it can fit onto the narrower bus going to the peripherals. This stopover is the virtual Chicago O'Hare of the computer world; it slows things down, *noticeably*.

Expanding Your PC's Capabilities: Expansion Slots

Located at the back of the system case is a row of slots called *expansion slots* (see Figure 12.1). You can see the tail ends of cards plugged into these slots, as well as cutouts holding places for cards that haven't been plugged in yet.

What can you find already occupying some of your computer's expansion slots? Well, a video card that controls the display to your monitor, for one. If you have a DVD-ROM, chances are that you have a video signal decoder card that connects to your video card from the *outside*. You might also find an I/O (input and output) card that provides a serial and a parallel port on the back of your PC. An internal modem is another common resident of most computer's expansion slots. You may have a modem, a network adapter, or a joystick controller. If you add an external storage device, you might need something called a SCSI (pronounced "scuzzy") host adapter or an ATAPI IDE controller to run it.

Figure 12.1

Expand your PC's capabilities with expansion cards.

Expansion card

Empty expansion slots

The ISA Expansion Bus

The expansion bus in use in all PCs manufactured between 1984 and 1999, and in a declining number of PCs produced since then, is the 16-bit wide Industry Standard Architecture (ISA) bus. The expansion bus (also called "peripheral bus") is the electronic highway that connects the expansion slots and the ports on the back of your PC to the data highway. The connection is made at the peripheral bus controller, which is now integrated into your motherboard's chipset.

If you look closely at an expansion card designed for an ISA expansion slot, you might have noticed the edge that plugs into the slot is often divided into two segments (see Figure 12.2). Each segment handles eight bits of the 16-bit connection. The first segment is designed to be compatible with the original 8-bit plug introduced in the first IBM PC at about the time of Russia's famed October Revolution. The second segment handles the second eight bits of the connection, introduced in the IBM PC AT just prior to the bombing of Pearl Harbor.

Figure 12.2

A 16-bit ISA card and its slot.

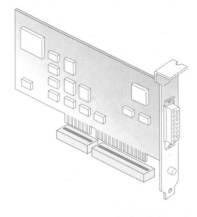

The PCI Bus

The PCI (Peripheral Component Interconnect) bus is the most prevalent expansion bus used in today's PCs, with a 32-bit data path and its own hardware that handles communication with the rest of your PC (see Figure 12.3). This way, data doesn't have to be chopped into sushi bits during the crossover from the data bus.

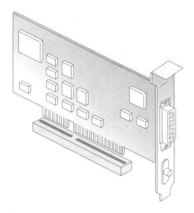

Figure 12.3

A PCI expansion card and its slot.

The AGP Port

Up until 1997, the PCI bus was plenty fast for the graphics requirements of Windows. Then suddenly, as users stopped "exiting to DOS" to run graphically intensive programs, the complexity of PC graphics began growing exponentially, and the strain on both the PCI bus and the system bus made every-day mathematical processing become slower.

Prior to the advent of PCI, the first attempt in 1992 to address the growing problem of ballooning graphics requirements was the advent of something called the "video local bus," or VL-Bus (also called "VESA.") This local bus had its own interface, so it used different types of cards and connectors than ISA. VL-Bus video proved to be popular for its day, until the faster PCI bus destroyed it in the market, on account of its faster speed. (Up until 1998, most users thought PCI was just another, better video local bus.)

Armed with the experience of having produced one successful interface just for video cards, Intel in 1999 devised a new video scheme that would place its top-of-the-line chipsets back in the limelight.

> **Note**
>
> Beginning in September 2000, PC and motherboard manufacturers were treated to Intel's latest technological treat: an interface specification that enables manufacturers to build cards that integrate all the major *analog-to-digital* processing jobs into one unit. So with the advent of the Communication and Networking Riser (CNR) specification, your future audio (sound card), networking, and modem card could be a single card.

Intel's idea was called Accelerated Graphics Port (AGP), as pictured in Figure 12.4. There's some argument among engineers over whether AGP really constitutes a "port" (it's not like the serial *port* or parallel *port*), but they do generally agree that AGP is not a *bus*. In a sense, it's a specialized connection linking video processing hardware to the system bus directly, bypassing expansion busses. Chapter 14, "I Can See Clearly Now: Upgrading Your Video," discusses the video-oriented aspects of the AGP port.

Figure 12.4

An AGP video card and its slot.

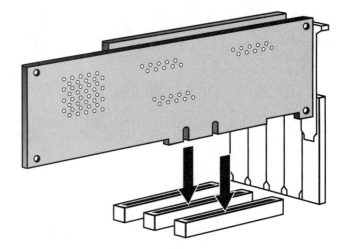

Enabling Your External Parallel and Serial Ports

Since long before an enterprising fellow named Wozniak stuck a TV to the top of a computer constructed inside a wooden crate, designers have been busy developing visions of sleeker, prettier, more ergonomic enclosures for personal computers. But the single factor barring nearly all of their designs from moving from vision to fruition has been the one feature about a PC that simply cannot be designed away by pens, brushes, or CAD programs: all the cables sticking out the back of it.

Personal computers have an awful tendency to have junk sticking out of them. This tendency will probably be inescapable for some time to come. If you've just acquired your computer, new or old, or you're giving your computer a thorough reassessment, just what plugs and connectors truly need to be there? And do you need more connections than you currently have?

The Parallel Universe

Most PCs ever produced contain one *parallel port*—one connection leading from your PC to your printer. On the PC side, it's a 25-pin D-type (DB-25) female plug. You need only one. If you have two or more printers, certainly only one of them will be printing at any one time. The way to connect them all is through a switch box with a single cable connecting to your PC. If you intend to install a parallel-type external data backup system, such as an Iomega Zip or Jaz drive, it will contain its own daisy-chain connector to your printer. You should not try to install two multifunction cards with their own parallel ports in your PC, at least not without disabling one of those ports; and even then, it's not really a good idea. Why? For the same reason a parallel device can assume it's the only such device on a PC, a PC's BIOS (older editions), multifunction card, or operating system can assume your computer has the only parallel port. Given that assumption, a lot of programs that send output to the printer still tend to assume the printer is LPT1, even though, as you might guess, Windows easily recognizes LPT2. This is why it's generally best to have one controlling device that takes care of both parallel ports.

You may be wondering, why is it called "parallel"? Simple reason: All the bits constituting the data signal are flushed through a handful of separate wires in a parallel cable, simultaneously. By contrast, in a parallel signal, all the bits in the signal are sent over a pair of wires in sequence.

Serial Fillers

Very, very few PCs produced anywhere—easily fewer than 1 percent—fail to include at least one external serial connector, and many include two. Such a connection is generally a 9-pin or 25-pin D-type (DB-9 or DB-25) male plug (unlike the female parallel plug), and when there are two serial plugs, you generally find one of both types. These two plugs are nearly interchangeable; with a simple, inexpensive plug converter, a device like a 9-pin serial mouse might plug into a 25-pin connector with no problem.

If you ever run across the license plate-looking designation RS-232, then you should know that it is the technical name for the PC's serial interface. The term *serial port* at one time was used to describe two things: the connectors on the outside of the PC for serial devices, and the processor resources set aside within the computer for exporting data from the CPU to serial devices. Microsoft recently corrected this redundancy, and as a result, logical ports COM1 through COM4 have been re-dubbed *communications ports*.

If you have an internal modem, Windows will assign it to one of these four communications (COM) ports. On top of that, if you have a serial port on the outside of your PC, its connection will be assigned to a different COM port. Here's where the problem comes in: If you have a *second* serial port on the outside of your PC—and many PCs do come with two—Windows should try to assign a third COM port to that serial connector. But some older releases of Windows (most notably Windows 95, prior to release of OSR2) recognize only two logical communications ports (for instance, COM1 and COM2, or COM1 and COM3) at any one time, regardless of the fact that Windows can count to four. This problem was solved for good with Windows 98, so if you look in Device Manager, you'll see under the Ports category that Windows has installed exactly as many "drivers" (really just placeholders for Windows support resources) as there are RS-232 devices and connectors on your PC.

259

Whether or not you plan to use an internal modem, you should keep at least one physical serial connection on your PC. You might need it at some time for a serial mouse or, if your mouse already uses its own dedicated plug, you could use it as a plug for a cheap standby mouse should yours go out. Your internal modem should never use the same COM port as your external serial plug. However, fate might dictate that you acquire a computer where this is already the case. This is a problem you can solve through your operating system, without major surgery; Chapter 24, "Getting Windows to Recognize Your New Toys," will help you out. In any event, even if you never need the one serial plug you find, there is nothing wrong with simply leaving it there, or even turning "off" the unneeded serial port using your BIOS setup program (see Chapter 23, "Making Your Computer Boot Up Again," for details on that). The presence of an unused plug does nothing to slow down your computer or impede its performance. (Believe me, there's a lot of unused junk inside your operating system that you might never use in your lifetime, through no fault of your own.)

Spotting an "I/O Card"

You may remember that I brought up the topic of the motherboard chipset in Chapter 10, "Replacing the Motherboard and Its Parts." One of the reasons for the advent of the chipset in the first place was to "encapsulate," if you will, the functions of the input/output (I/O) system of the computer as standardized hardware. Prior to the advent of the chipset, the parallel and serial ports of a computer were primarily run by an expansion card on the ISA bus called the "multifunction card." But for a little while, even after the first standardized chipsets for the 486 motherboards officially took over the job of I/O, these multifunction cards still presided in brand-name PCs, overriding and nullifying the chipsets' own functions.

If your computer, by virtue of some strange, unseen force, has no parallel port, the way you add one is by way of what is called an *I/O card*. The best among these are PCI expansion cards that have one or two plugs embedded in the metal brace on the end, and headers that may lead to other connectors installed in place of card placeholders elsewhere. The average I/O card features one parallel port and as many as two serial ports. The second serial port, when present, doesn't fit on the same metal brace, so instead a ribbon cable (like a gray, flat lasagna noodle) extends from a plug on the card itself to a second metal brace containing the plug. Some I/O cards may contain provisions for a 15-pin joystick ... uh, *game controller* port.

How can you tell whether your PC uses an I/O card, even if it doesn't need to? When you open your system case, look for the ribbon cable that leads to the parallel (printer) connector. This connector could be installed among your other expansion card slots, or as in newer system cases, it may be in its own dedicated location. Follow that ribbon cable to see what it leads to. If it leads to the motherboard, then your chipset is fully in charge. But if it leads to the side of an expansion card, and you have at least a Pentium-class CPU or newer in your system, then you probably have a redundant or unnecessary component. Chances are, you can get rid of it. But after you do, how will your PC know the chipset is back in charge? Check your BIOS setup program the next time you start up your computer (Chapter 23 shows you how), and look for a setting like "Parallel port enabled" or "I/O enabled." Set it to ON.

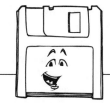

Techno Talk

Many older I/O cards featured jumpers that let you set the logical (COM) port for its two connectors. Newer ones feature headers marked on the card "COM1" and "COM2," that lead directly to connectors that are supposed to be permanently assigned logical ports. Don't be surprised if Windows overrides this assignment, and gives these ports whatever COM port number it darn well wants to. If you installed your mouse in the 9-pin connector you intended to call COM1, then you might be surprised if Windows assigns that connector COM3. Your mouse may still work. If it doesn't, it's best that you go into your Control Panel settings for your mouse, and tell Windows it can locate the mouse on COM3. Believe me, if you get in an arm-wrestling match with Windows about COM ports, Windows could very easily spill elbow grease on the table and switch things back the way it wants, whenever it wants.

Installing Motherboard-Supported Serial and Parallel Ports

If your motherboard uses a Slimline form factor (see Chapter 10 for a discussion of form factors), then its serial and parallel ports are already permanently attached to metal clips sticking out of one side. These clips fit neatly into cutouts on the side of the Slimline system case. You do not have to bother with these ports yourself. (You do, unfortunately, have to bother with all the bad characteristics of a Slimline motherboard.)

If you have one of the ATX form factors, or an LPX form factor, then your motherboard very likely features support for serial and parallel ports. This support relies on the attachment of two or three metal clips that have serial and parallel connectors at the end, and that are designed either to be screwed into cutouts through the back of the system case, or to metal clips that screw into open cutouts in the expansion card area. These connectors are provided by ribbon cables that lead to specially marked headers on the motherboard. If you're swapping out your motherboards from your system case, then you will have to fiddle with these ribbon cables at some point.

261

The connector on the motherboard for the ribbon cable whose other end (on the outside of the system case) is the parallel port, is a row of tiny, paired metal spikes called a *header*. This header will probably be marked with "LPT" or some other relatively meaningful symbol. There may be two similar headers on the motherboard for ribbon cables leading to serial ports on the outside of the system case. These headers will probably be marked "COM1" and "COM2," although whether these headers actually correspond to the operating system's logical serial ports COM1 and COM2 will actually be determined by Windows. These markings *probably* correspond, but don't be surprised if you encounter a situation following installation when they suddenly don't. In other words, the header marked "COM2" may support the port for COM4 if the jumpers or CMOS is set that way.

The plug that inserts into one of these headers on the motherboard is a long, rectangular clip with two rows of square pinholes. Generally, one of the wires along one edge of the ribbon is marked red, to indicate which wire belongs to pin 1. If you don't find such a marking, look on the plastic plug itself for a 1 or a dot, or some telltale sign or hieroglyph along one side that isn't on the other side. On the motherboard header, look for a marking for pin 1 on one corner. Align pin 1, however it's marked, on the ribbon cable with this marking on the motherboard, and then gently but firmly slide the plug in place.

If the external connector for one of these I/O ports does not have a home staked out for it on the system case, the ribbon cable leading from the motherboard (or multifunction card) could be affixed to the same kind of steel clip used to brace an expansion card to the system case. This creates the appearance that the outside plug is attached directly to an expansion card; so just because you see your I/O ports among the expansion card slots does not mean you have a multifunction card. You insert this brace in an open slot and fix it in place with the single screw, in just the same way you would guide the metal brace of a real expansion card in place.

On the other hand, if the external connector has its own home on the system case, then the plug should have metal flanges on both sides with tiny threaded holes. These flanges are designed to fit into pockets on the inside of the case, and then be screwed into place along both sides.

Installing and Replacing Expansion Cards

Generally, the installation of an expansion card into any ISA, PCI, or AGP slot is the easiest part of computing. The act of simply getting any card in any slot is roughly identical to getting any other card in any other slot. For that reason, I can provide you with a general set of directions and techniques you should follow.

Inserting an Expansion Card

As usual, get rid of any static electricity you might be carrying around. Before you install the card, you'll want to make sure you set any jumpers or DIP switches on that card, and plug in any data cables that might be required (your sound card may require one that later connects to the back of your optical disc drive). The simple reason to do this now is because making these adjustments while the card is already in place—especially if you have a small system case—could leave you with a crick in your neck worse than that time you installed the kitchen faucet.

I always begin the surgical part of the procedure by making certain the card is *clean*, especially the bottom "card edge" where the pins are located. If you just removed the card from a sealed anti-static bag, then it's probably very clean right now. One way you can keep it clean is to only handle the card by its silver steel edge—the part that screws into the side of the system case. If you need to clean the card edge, try applying some isopropyl alcohol to a paper towel, then wiping it along the card edge only. If you find some dust hanging around the chips or components, don't wipe them with anything—you could dislodge something. Instead, use your handy can of compressed air to spray it off.

Your first consideration when choosing a slot is, of course, making certain you have the right type. On a Baby AT or ATX motherboard, if you have it facing its own "polar north," the AGP port (if it has one) will be on the top. It's often the putty-colored slot connector. Beneath that (or on top, if there's no AGP port) are the PCI slots. They're often the white connectors. On the bottom will be the ISA slots, if any. They're the black connectors.

Your second consideration, before you start playing "Spin the Slot," is *ventilation*. Now, with this edition of the book, I've devoted the entire Chapter 20 to this topic: "Cooling and Ventilating Your System." One critical aspect of ventilation is making sure nothing disrupts the airflow from your internal fans. A huge, long card installed in the *middle* of your computer can do much more to disrupt airflow than the same card installed at the *top* or *bottom*. You should be able to draw a circle with your hands inside your computer without running into anything.

When you've finally chosen a location (now that I've managed to make that choice such a big deal), then unscrew the retaining screw that holds in the steel placeholder for the slot you've chosen, and remove it. Hold the card by its top or side edges only with both hands, and position the bottom card edge connectors over the slot (see Figure 12.5). Pay attention to where the steel "foot" is falling. As the card edge nears the slot, the foot should fall *outside* the edge of the motherboard. It should not touch the motherboard at all—if it does, you're too far away from the edge of the case.

Stop here for a second. Inspect where the card is lining up with the connector. The slot is designed to *surround* your card edge on all sides, to hold the card in place. If the card's not lining up or, heaven's sake, if it's not the same size, then you've chosen the wrong slot. Take it out, replace the placeholder, and choose another slot.

When you have the card in the right slot the right way, and the foot's not touching the substrate of the motherboard, then gently press the card into place with just the right amount of downward pressure. Don't force the card into its slot.

Figure 12.5

Hold the card by its edges only as you line it up over the slot.

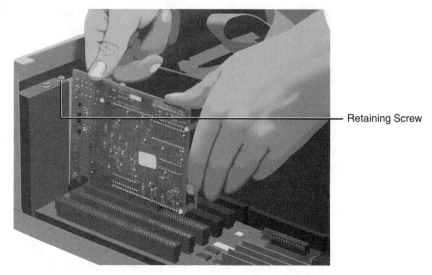

Retaining Screw

Removing an Expansion Card

Getting one of these cards out of your system is a bit more difficult in practice than it is in principle. The instructions are simple: Unscrew the retaining screw, grab the card by its edges, and pull up until the thing pops out.

What's difficult is the *doing* of it (as many new presidents have come to learn). Expansion cards don't have handles. The most stable and safest part of the card is its steel retainer clip, but if you lift up on that part alone, you risk rocking the card too far to one side and damaging the connector.

You don't want to get your metal tools too close to the connector. So what do you do? There's no clear-cut answer for every shape and size of card, but here's what I find myself doing most often: Find the bottom corner of the card *away* from the edge of the system case—cater-corner from the retaining screw. The card often sticks out about a half-inch from the connector. There could be just enough empty space there for you to get a finger or thumb underneath the bottom edge. So with one finger beneath where the retaining screw goes (you *can* use a flathead screwdriver here safely for leverage), and the other hand in this open space you've found, lift *up* (toward you). Eventually the thing will pop out.

Storage Device Controller Interfaces

In Chapter 16, "Hands-On Hard Disk Replacement," you'll see how to connect a hard disk drive to your PC. Chapter 18, "Adding an Optical Drive," covers CD-ROMs and DVD-ROMs, plus their recordable counterparts. The categories of devices covered in these upcoming chapters all depend on the storage device interface your motherboard supports.

Wait a minute ... isn't an interface the thing you see on the screen with the windows, the mouse pointer, and all the little icons and buttons? That's not the same thing. Marketing tends to call the appearance of the operating system or the applications "the interface" because that's a cool-sounding term. They could have called it the "intake manifold" instead, because that's another cool-sounding term. A *real* interface is a way for two computer parts to connect together and communicate with each other. This segment of the book deals with real interfaces—specifically the one that links your PC's motherboard to your main data storage devices.

There are two common types of PC device interfaces in use today: IDE and SCSI. IDE, short for Integrated Drive Electronics because the controller is built into the drive itself. IDE has become the standard storage device supported by today's motherboard chipsets (see Chapter 10). IDE is sometimes referred to as the AT Attachment interface, because that is the technical name for the attachment designed to replace the drive interface of IBM's original AT. Chipsets find one way or another to support four IDE devices, even though a standard IDE channel is limited to two. A revision to the IDE standard, called EIDE (for Extended IDE) or ATA-2, supports four devices per channel, while two simultaneous IDE channels accomplish the same thing. Chapter 16 lists the later revisions and surprisingly ample supply of nicknames for IDE standards.

SCSI, short for Small Computer Systems Interface, a SCSI host adapter can control several types of SCSI devices at once, including a hard disk, a CD-ROM drive, and a tape drive. Although they're pretty fast, SCSI drives are much more expensive than IDE, and are usually considered more reliable. The SCSI interface was designed to facilitate literally any kind of peripheral that might need to exchange data with your computer. In the late 1970s when the first SCSI standard was being hammered out, SCSI printers, SCSI plotters, SCSI tape backups, and SCSI punchcard devices were envisioned. How would a SCSI host adapter determine which kind of device it was talking to? Through an intricately designed system of *conversation* between these devices and the host adapter, using terms and signals that could loosely be associated with, "Hi there, how are you?" "I'm fine, how are you?" and, "Fine, thank you, *what* are you?"

Here's one key difference between the design philosophies of IDE and SCSI: IDE was designed to be a hard disk drive interface, and was later adapted for use in optical and other devices (ATAPI). SCSI was designed for use with any kind of peripheral device that might need to communicate with a PC, but has largely been used for hard drives and other mass storage devices.

Most modern PC motherboard chipsets have been designed to support IDE as its mass storage device interface. If your motherboard only has one IDE channel, you may need to install a dual-IDE or EIDE (ATA-2) adapter card (sometimes incorrectly called a "controller card") to enable your system to run four storage devices. Precisely no chipset is designed to support SCSI. For SCSI to work in your PC, you must install a SCSI host adapter card.

What You Need to Know About SCSI

The single most important thing you will need to know about the Small Computer Systems Interface (SCSI) is that there is more than one. The idea of SCSI is, frankly, rather old, predating even the IBM PC by a few years. So the fact that SCSI has had to change to keep up with the times should come as no surprise. But one of SCSI's most important principles is that of supporting as much downward compatibility as possible. To be truly SCSI compliant, newer SCSI devices theoretically should be workable and compatible with older SCSI host adapters.

As a result of this principle, literally every version of SCSI ever implemented remains supported to this day, even by those SCSI devices that, on paper, support the newer technologies. On paper, there are three official SCSI specifications. In practice, however, there are substantially more than three, all of which go by multiple brand names. The following table lists all the supported SCSI technologies.

Technology	Spec.	Bus Speed (MBps)	Bus Width (Bits)	Cable Pins	Cable Length (Meters)	Max. Devices
SCSI-1	1	5	8	25 50	6/[12]/25	8
Fast SCSI	2	10	8	50 68	3/[12]/25	8
(Fast) Wide SCSI	2	20	16	50+68 68	3/[12]/25	16
Ultra SCSI	3	20	8	50 68	1.5/[12]/25	8
Wide Ultra SCSI	3	40	16	50+68 68	–/[12]/25	16
Ultra2 SCSI	3	40	8	68	–/12/25	8
Wide Ultra2 SCSI	3	80	16	68	–/12/25	16
Ultra3 SCSI (Ultra160)	3	160	16	68	–/12/–	16
Ultra320 SCSI	4	320	16	68	–/12/–	16

The most important characteristics associated with the previous table are as follows:

➤ **Technology** lists the most common brand name for each specification. "Wide SCSI" is also known in some circles as "Fast Wide SCSI."

➤ **Spec.** (specification) shows the number of the official SCSI document in which each technology was introduced. SCSI-3 has actually been rewritten, retroactively, more than once—a sort of Maybe-We-Should-Have-Specified-This-To-Start-With process.

➤ **Bus speed** lists the speed at which communication takes place for each technology, in megabytes per second (MBps). In SCSI terminology, the connection between devices is the *SCSI bus*.

➤ **Bus width** lists the bit width of each data element communicated over the SCSI bus, for each technology.

➤ **Cable pins** lists the number of pins or wires used in both internal and external cables, over the history of each technology. For instance, the listing for SCSI-1 reads "25 50." When SCSI-1 (then just "SCSI") first hit the scene, it used the same 25-wire external cable used today in Centronics parallel printer cables. Later, this cable was replaced in devices and host adapter cards with 50-wire cable, which of course uses a 50-pin connector. When Wide SCSI and Wide Ultra SCSI were first introduced, devices were attached to the bus using *both* 50- and 68-wire cables at the same time. Supposedly, this was done to ensure backward compatibility; and yes, you could certainly say this was backward. Later, the 68-wire cable alone took over.

➤ **Cable length** shows the maximum permissible lengths of the three accepted grades of SCSI cable, for each technology: the so-called "single-ended" cable, Low Voltage Differential Signaling (LVDS, 1.5 or 3.3v), and High Voltage Differential Signaling (HVDS, 5v). LVDS is a relatively recent invention, so the maximum lengths for Wide Ultra SCSI and earlier technologies had to be determined retroactively—thus the [square brackets] around these particular listings. For Ultra SCSI and Wide Ultra SCSI, for every extra 1.5 meters of cable you use beyond the recommended amounts (1.5m and 0, respectively), the maximum number of devices on the bus is cut in half. Your host adapter card supports just one of these cable types, never two or three.

➤ **Max. devices** shows the maximum number of devices that may be simultaneously attached to a SCSI bus, for each technology listed. The devices on a SCSI bus are identified by the host adapter using numbers from 0 to 7 or from 0 to 15. The host adapter itself counts as one of these devices, although its ID number is generally selectable.

Most SCSI devices (all external ones) are designed with two connectors: one that leads back toward the host adapter, and a second that provides a port for the next SCSI device in the chain. So although a SCSI host adapter card may have only one external connector, it begins the "daisy chain" that leads to all the external SCSI devices.

Here's a confusing point you need to keep in mind when installing internal and external SCSI devices to the same host adapter card: The *physical* location of the devices on the connector cable has nothing to do with the ID numbers you assign to them. A bootable internal hard disk, for instance, may be given ID 0. Your external SCSI CD-RW drive may be given ID 1, then your internal SCSI tape backup drive may be given ID 2. You choose the ID numbers for your SCSI devices based on their relative *priority,* not their position in the chain.

Your PC's BIOS will have absolutely no control over your SCSI devices. You may find this, in the end, to be a good thing. The program that controls the software setup of your SCSI devices (and perhaps even sets their ID numbers internally) is a program that comes with your host adapter card, and that you run from Windows. You don't need to reboot your computer to get to it. In fact, for some brands, it can be pulled

267

up through Windows's existing Device Manager. There is one BIOS issue you may need to contend with, however: Suppose you want your SCSI hard disk to be *bootable*—the one that contains your operating system. Because your BIOS doesn't really know what SCSI is, it's going to try to find the first IDE hard disk on the first channel, and not finding it, it may fail to boot your computer. The solution *is* located someplace in your BIOS: Look for a software switch that disables the IDE boot sequence. With that turned off, the next time you reboot the computer, the SCSI host adapter should be able to wrest control of the bus and boot the hard disk given ID 0 after the BIOS gets around to engaging the expansion cards.

If you want to chain several SCSI devices to your new SCSI host adapter, you may run into a situation where one device in the chain renders it impossible for a host adapter to communicate with another, otherwise problem-free device. In such a situation, try swapping their IDs with one another, and then try swapping their physical locations in the connection chain.

Setting Up a SCSI Host Adapter Card

A SCSI host adapter card generally requires a bit of setup on the card itself before you slip it in place. SCSI controllers have switches for all sorts of techie things like IRQ and DMA. See Chapter 23 for help with IRQs, DMAs, and other odd abbreviations.

In addition, you need to set the adapter's own SCSI ID. The SCSI ID determines where in the SCSI food chain your new device will fall. ID 0 is for a bootable device, such as your hard disk. The other IDs are for the rest of your SCSI devices, such as an optical disc, or a Zip/Jaz drive. The adapter card is usually set to the uppermost address, so don't change it unless you have to. If you find an IRQ conflict, for example, then you need to change the IRQ setting in the SCSI card. I can't help you much on this one; you've got to figure out what IRQs other devices are currently using and then select a unique one for this device. Don't let this "IRQ" you too much; see Chapter 23 for more help.

Check This Out

Any adapter card that you buy and that you intend to use for devices that support Direct Memory Access (DMA) needs two things: First, it needs support for *bus mastering*, which is a way for the card to wrest control of the I/O bus from the CPU for a moment to push data directly into RAM, bypassing the CPU. Second, it needs to be a PCI card, because this type of transfer is way too fast for the old ISA expansion bus.

The ID numbers for all your SCSI devices are set either by jumpers or switches on the devices themselves, or by software that came with your host adapter card. You don't need to fool around with all of your SCSI IDs while you're installing your host adapter. For a "Narrow SCSI" adapter that only makes use of IDs 0 through 8, you may find a set of three jumpers or switches, numbered 4, 2, and 1 in that order, generally on the back of the device. To set the ID for that device, set all switches to ON, or shunt all jumpers whose numbers total the ID number you intend. For instance, for ID 5 you would set switches 4 and 1 to ON, but leave 2 OFF.

Setting Up an IDE/EIDE Adapter Card

There's only one reason you'd ever need an IDE/EIDE adapter card: You have more than two IDE/ATA/ATAPI devices (hard drives plus optical drives) and your BIOS supports only two. Older motherboards may support one or two IDE devices with the help of an adapter card that's already plugged in, but most motherboards already have one—generally two—IDE adapter plugs built-in. Each plug is capable of supporting *two* devices, and the IDE cable has a connector in the middle someplace that can plug into the data socket on the back of one device, and then chain to the back of another device. If you have three devices, you'll need to plug two IDE cables into your motherboard. The IDE connectors on the motherboard will be clearly marked "IDE1" and "IDE2." If you only have two devices, you should plug your IDE cable into IDE1 and leave IDE2 open. Chapter 16 will show you exactly how to install your IDE devices.

Most IDE adapter cards are capable of overriding whatever IDE support is already on the motherboard. If you find yourself needing to install one, then there's a bit of configuration you'll need to do beforehand.

If you plan to use both IDE channels, you'll need to set the card's second set of switches to ON to enable the second connector on the card. You could connect two devices to the first controller, and just leave it at that, but you might not want to, because the slowest device on the controller determines its speed. So, whenever possible, connect the hard disk to the first controller (because it's the fastest device), and other IDE devices such as a CD-ROM, Zip/Jaz drive, or your tape drive to the second controller.

In addition, before you can add your EIDE or dual IDE adapter card, you may need to disable the existing IDE connector already on your motherboard. The easiest way to locate the IDE connector is to follow the data cable from your hard disk back to its source. The data cable is the widest one connected to the hard disk. After you locate the controller, look for a set of switches or a jumper nearby that you can set to disable it. You may possibly be able to disable the controller through your BIOS setup program. (You may need some help from your computer manual for this.) Of course, if you can't disable the IDE connector, you're kind of out of luck, and may have to rethink your plan to add another IDE device.

Before you get too confused, you might not have an EIDE or dual-IDE adapter card unless you elected to buy one. If there's only one channel on this card, then its purpose might be to open up a second IDE channel. In that case, you won't need to disable your existing channel. If you did buy a two-channel adapter card, then you have to disable your motherboard's IDE controller. You should be able to disable the IDE controller through the settings in your BIOS setup program (see Chapter 23). You execute this program by rebooting your computer and pressing the setup key it tells you to press before the single beep tells you you're out of time. You will probably also need to look for a setting that enables the "second" IDE controller, even though you've disabled the "first" one and even though your motherboard doesn't have a "second" one.

What You Need to Know About USB

The replacement for your parallel and serial ports, and just about everything else that plugs into your computer, is already well underway. The Universal Serial Bus (USB) is a new expansion interface designed to enable plugging in on the side of your computer, and outside of your computer as well without any differences in functionality. In other words, a USB device could include its own USB socket for plugging something else in. A USB plug is smaller, promises to be less expensive for manufacturers to produce, and is significantly faster than even the parallel interface. Most flatbed scanners, some printers, and at the time of this writing, even keyboards are now rigged for USB. Before too long, manufacturers have already agreed, all devices will be available for USB connection.

Hubs and Other Advantages of USB Design

There are a number of good reasons for you to prefer USB to the serial or parallel port. First of all, a USB connector is small and clasps neatly in place. It's easy to plug in and take out, but it doesn't jostle out of place if you bump it, and you don't need to screw it in. Computers with USB and USB expansion cards both generally contain two plugs, not just one; and if a USB device is equipped with a feature called a *hub*, another USB device can be plugged into the back of it. (New USB keyboards also feature extra USB sockets for plugging in such devices as a digital camera.) The idea here is that plugging something in should not necessarily have to be an *upgrade* every time you do it. Maybe I should think about changing the title of the book.

A USB hub is a simple device that plugs into one of the USB ports on the back of your PC. It leads to a little box that has any number (generally four) of other USB ports where you can plug in things like monitors, printers, scanners, keyboards, and digital cameras. They cost about $30, and you've just seen all the installation procedure you need to see. If you need more USB devices than just four, your computer has two USB ports, so you can get a second hub and have support for 8 devices. (Theoretically, USB can support 127 devices simultaneously.)

Check This Out

Some computer manufacturers simply didn't bother to give you a pair of USB ports for your computer, even though their PCs are supposed to feature USB support. Thankfully, you can rectify this little problem. For no more than $20, you can get a USB connection kit, consisting of a pair of ports screwed into a steel support normally used for an expansion card. You screw this support in place of one of your placeholders for an open expansion card slot. A ribbon cable leads from this pair of connectors to a header on your motherboard that will be clearly marked "USB."

And Then There's That Little Speed Factor You Hear About

USB reflects a gallant, slowly growing movement to develop a very high-speed, low-cost peripheral attachment system. Historically, fast data connections were achieved through parallel connections like the one to your printer, in which all the bits of data were flushed through the cable at one time. Serial connections were theoretically slower because the bits that made up a data element were sent over the wire in sequence, and one had to wait for the other to show up. But serial connections were cheaper because you needed fewer signals in the cable, therefore lower voltage signals, because you didn't have to bother with distinguishing one signal from another.

USB is *fast* because data components in general are, well, let's say, somewhat faster today than when the original RS-232 standard for serial communications was conceived (1977). The serial communications principle for USB is the same—the bits that make up the data are streamed out in sequence rather than all at once. The theoretical maximum speed for USB is 1.5MBps (megabytes per second, or 12Mbps or megabits per second). Fair enough. Meanwhile, the theoretical maximum speed for a serial port is about 115Kbps (*kilobits* per second)—just twice the speed of the fastest phone modem—and the parallel port maxes out at 115KBps (*kilobytes* per second), eight times faster.

If you review the SCSI table earlier in the chapter, you realize that although USB is touted as being "blazingly fast," it's not even up to speed with SCSI-1. That's because SCSI connections are inherently parallel. USB will probably never be used for connections to hard drives or backup systems. But they make excellent and reliable interfaces for higher-speed input devices, such as flatbed color scanners, which sold for over $1,000 as recently as 1997, and sell for under $100 today.

As you saw in Chapter 10, USB support is now being built into many motherboard chipsets. So you'll see more and more off-the-shelf PCs with USB ports attached. When you look for a USB port on the back of your PC, you'll actually find two. These are separate USB ports for two devices, and even all USB attachment cards contain two ports. They are, after all, small enough—smaller than a 9-pin standard serial connection. The average price for a PCI-based USB expansion card right now is $20. Installing this card follows the same process of any other interface card—no switches or jumpers to set, luckily.

Simulated Wargames for Your Computer, Brought to You by USB

If you want to save money on that high-dollar real-world 3D combat simulator for your PC, here's a way you can simulate combat right now: Try getting Windows and USB to play along.

One of the clearly stated goals of the Universal Serial Bus Implementers' Forum—the official body for USB standards development, at www.usb.org—is to enable the operating system to detect whatever you happen to plug into a USB port, recognize that device, and bring up its support drivers and software automatically, even though USB ports all use the same plug. Because the plug is the same, there's nothing *physical* about the plug that would let you or anything in your operating system detect the difference between a printer or a monitor or a scanner or a joystick—no extra pin, no little groove, no little bump poking out from somewhere.

USB works similarly to SCSI. It employs a system whereby the computer asks the device that just got plugged in, "Hello, what are you?" and the device has to respond, "I'm a Hewlett-Packard DeskJet 830 inkjet printer!" (Hopefully that's exactly what it is, too.) The SCSI folks long ago devised a relatively *expensive* piece of hardware in the host adapter to handle the job of arbitrating which device is what. But while the SCSI project is led by interface manufacturers such as Adaptec, USB is supported by *implementers*—companies that make the joysticks and printers and scanners. These companies don't want to invent separate hardware to handle the arbitration process, and feel instead that the *operating system* should assume that role.

In the beginnings of USB, Microsoft Windows 95 tried, but *failed,* to develop a USB support system that actually worked. Windows 95's own idea of Plug and Play, you see, was inconsistent with the USB idea of you-turn-it-on-then-plug-it-in-then-it-works. There is, floating around on the Internet somewhere, a USB support patch for Windows 95. The USB Forum openly suggests that you do not install this patch, and that you instead make the upgrade to a later edition of Windows.

Win98 was the first edition of Windows to get USB support working, for the most part. But it was left to Microsoft to devise a system for supporting USB in a Windows-like way. And Microsoft's second attempt seemed pretty reasonable at first, on paper. You plug in a device. Windows is already running at this point, so it notices something's been plugged in, and puts up a dialog box that reads, "New Hardware Found."

Windows starts the handshaking process with the device, which then introduces itself. Windows then tells you what it believes the device to be, and then if it can't find the support software in its own System directory, it asks you to insert the Windows CD-ROM so it can find it for itself. It installs the driver, does *not* ask you to reboot your system, the device now works, and you can go on with your life.

Uh-huh. The problem with this picture may already be obvious to you. Who knows how many USB devices there are in the world? Are all the drivers for those billions of devices supposed to be located on the Windows installation CD-ROM? Okay, probably not, so suppose you insert the manufacturer's exclusive driver disc instead. Windows should recognize that disc, correlate the new driver to the new device, then install that driver.

Uh-huh. If you've been paying very, very close attention, you already know where this is going: Device manufacturers want to install what *they* want to install: exclusive help files, free software bundles, a few games, perhaps some ads on your desktop. Windows wants to install what *it* wants to install: the driver file that runs the device so Windows can go back to what it was (not) doing. To that end, Microsoft has held steadfast to its USB device installation "Wizard" technology, which does its best to lead you through the process of installing nothing more than a simple, often generic, driver for your new device. But the installation process often fails, and the generic driver often doesn't work. And it isn't always clear who's responsible for that driver not working—this time around, Microsoft might not be to blame.

In any event, as a counterattack, the USB device manufacturers have developed their own unique installation procedures for their components. Especially with printers and scanners, you now are being asked to install the manufacturers' exclusive setup software *first*, before you ever plug your USB device into the port. If you do plug it in first, you're warned, the device may not work and may never work again. No joke.

What does this unique software do? It tries to second-guess Microsoft's USB device installation procedure, by having Windows launch a process when you boot your computer that waits for you to plug in your new device. Hopefully, when you do plug it in, the manufacturers' software runs first, and not the generic Windows Wizard. Sometimes Microsoft gets the upper hand.

So how do the manufacturers respond to that? By having you plug in your USB device with your computer turned off anyway—a return to the ice age from which USB was supposed to deliver us. This way, Windows cannot detect the new device being plugged in.

Here's what you end up doing: First, you install some complicated setup software. Then you power down your computer. You plug in your device, then turn it on. The setup software you've just installed is designed to kick in automatically, before even the Windows desktop is allowed to run. The software leads you through the process of installing your new drivers. When it's done, it will reboot your computer. Afterward, Windows should not notice that this new device was already installed, and will not respond.

273

But sometimes Windows does respond with its generic Wizard, as if you never installed your new device at all. You generally have to cancel out of this Wizard. Believe it or not, manufacturers may be working to thwart this Wizard by including extra software in their setup processes that detects the presence of the Microsoft USB Wizard, and tries to stop it before it comes on. I've managed to detect a few of these safeguard programs myself, doing nothing more than waiting for the USB Wizard to try to come on, so they can shut it down. The result of all this would be hilarious if it weren't so sad: For a machine where one of these safeguards is clandestinely running, if you were to try at some later date to install a different USB device that actually *relied* on the Microsoft USB Wizard (and some do), you couldn't do it. The safeguard from the last setup would cause the current setup to fail.

With all this petty skirmishing going on, you'd think one of the warring sides would try to regain its dignity by throwing in the towel. That is indeed what has happened. In 2001, Microsoft called it quits on USB. Windows XP will not support the new USB 2.0 standard. The skirmishing USB 1.1 standard is yet to be seen.

So it is now up to the USB Forum to devise a way to enroll newly plugged-in devices into the Windows XP operating system. Folks, inventing the stealth bomber was a simpler task. For now, be advised of the following: USB is not the isle of calm and simplicity amid the chaos of computing, that it was intended to be. Choose your new devices for their native capabilities and functions, not for their USB support.

Gearing Up for FireWire

What will Microsoft support natively, if it doesn't support USB? The answer, Microsoft has announced, comes from Apple.

No, don't pinch yourself. Apple submitted its technology for very-high-speed hardware interfacing a few years before USB, and it has since been accepted as a public standard: IEEE 1394, affectionately called "FireWire." (Some device manufacturers call the interface just "1394," and Sony for some reason chooses to call it "i.Link.") FireWire really tries to be the all-encompassing interface standard that USB never was. And by some accounts, it may be much closer to that goal than USB.

Like USB, FireWire generally uses a single, standard, all-purpose plug for connecting any device to the computer, with smaller versions for smaller devices such as digital cameras. And also like USB, FireWire utilizes a very thin, inexpensive cable intended for relatively short-distance connections; if you need longer-distance connections, you should be thinking about *networking* cable.

But the similarities start to end there. The theoretical maximum speed for a FireWire connection is 400Mbps—four times the speed of "Fast Ethernet" networking, and 266⅔ times the speed of USB. (Some FireWire adapters allow this bandwidth to be turned down to 200 or 100Mbps.) This is also four times the speed of the fastest IDE device interface currently in production, so external storage devices would have no need to become slower just because they're outside the box. USB's 1.5Mbps is simply not fast enough to handle external storage devices; and to its credit, that was never USB's intention anyway. But if Microsoft is looking to support a single ubiquitous interface rather than two, then it may be to FireWire's advantage that it can support both slow and fast external devices.

The two categories of products currently in production that utilize the FireWire interface are digital cameras and external optical disc recorders, such as CD-RW and DVD-RAM. No BIOS currently being made supports the FireWire interface, so therefore no motherboard in production for PCs supports FireWire. If you have a FireWire device, you will need a FireWire adapter card. It's a PCI card that sells for about $75 (not cheap), and has as many as three sockets for FireWire plugs. There are no tricks to its installation.

The Least You Need to Know

➤ The most commonly used bus for expansion cards today is PCI, although most modern motherboards do continue the 16-bit derivative of the original ISA expansion bus.

➤ On all modern motherboards, ribbon cables attached to headers lead to parallel and multiple serial ports on the outside of the PC.

➤ Most modern motherboards support two IDE channels for four devices, although some continue to support just one for two devices. An IDE adapter card (sometimes called a "controller card") may add a second channel if your BIOS supports it but your motherboard doesn't.

➤ SCSI has undergone multiple revisions over its long history. However, newer SCSI technologies are charged with the task of staying compatible with older ones, so older SCSI devices can still be connected to newer SCSI host adapter cards.

➤ Today, most inkjet printers and nearly all scanners sold are USB devices. Your BIOS and your operating system will need to support USB for you to attach a USB port connector or USB interface card.

The Online Line

Your computer is a communications tool. And whether the great software companies or media giants continue to bungle the design or mission of the Internet over the next few years, that simple fact is unlikely to change. The Internet, such as we know it, may not be "here to stay" after all. The telephone modem has probably reached the theoretical limit of its technological evolution. Online technology stands upon a precipice from which it can either jump to fly or jump to fall. But the fact that your computer is a communications tool will not change in our lifetime.

Today, there are three choices for ways you may connect to the Internet. The conventional route has you dial up to your Internet service provider (ISP) by way of your telephone line. The second links you permanently (or semi-permanently) to your ISP by way of your cable TV line. The third uses a trick of physics to literally shout an impossible signal through conventional telephone line—either one you already have, or another one installed separately for you. These three technologies are called "phone modem," cable modem, and Digital Subscriber Line (DSL). This chapter discusses all three connection choices rather objectively, standing back and judging the technology of each on its own merits. Then and only then does it kick one of those technologies square in the shins for being substandard and underdeveloped.

The "Telephone" Modem

A telephone modem receives a stream of digital data coming from your PC and converts it into analog beeps and buzzes to be sent over a conventional phone line. At the other end of this line, the receiving modem unscrambles this beeping, buzzing nonsense and converts it back into digital computer data. A communications program or *protocol* at each end controls the whole exchange. In Windows, this protocol is managed by a program called the *Dial-Up Adapter*.

Talking Modem Jive

Now, when you're shopping for a phone modem, you're going to be reading words like "error correction" and "data compression" whether you want to or not. So you may as well read them here first. Here's a brief glossary you can use to decipher modem-speak:

➤ **Downloading**—The process of receiving data. During this process, the modem receives a little bit of data, plus some extra numbers that are used to verify that the data received is the same as the data sent. If it's verified, the data goes into a file, e-mail message, or part of your Web page; if not, the receiving modem asks the server to resend.

➤ **Uploading**—The process of sending data through a communications medium; obviously the complement to downloading.

➤ **Protocol**—A set of standards that governs how two modems communicate with each other. There are many levels of protocols; for instance, a transmission protocol such as V.90 governs how modems maintain higher speeds and detect errors in transmission. "On top of" that protocol rides a content protocol such as FTP or HTTP, which provides the rules for transmitting specific types of content (that is, files or Web pages).

➤ **bps**—Short for *bits per second*, it's the measure of the speed of a modem. Earlier in the history of modems, this was synonymous to *baud rate*, although that's technically incorrect today. Baud rate is the frequency of the wave produced by the modem, and early modems were only capable of transmitting one bit of data per wavelength. Now, thanks to a concept called *quadrature amplitude modulation* (QAM) (I just love saying that), four or more bits can be sent per wavelength by varying the phase of the wave at key points prior to its completion. (In some countries where part of the broadcast spectrum is set aside for "digital radio," QAM is the technology being used instead of AM or FM.)

➤ **Universal Asynchronous Receiver/Translator (UART)**—This is the heart of your modem. Like a CPU, it is one chip, often surface-mounted to the modem card. Rockwell, Lucent Technologies, and AT&T are the leading producers of UART chips for all brands of modems.

➤ **Error correction**—The protocol that a modem may use to discover whether or not an error occurs during transmission. (Duh.) Here's how it works … kinda … The sender of the data stream divides that stream into packets. It performs a mathematical formula on each packet and obtains a result. It then attaches each result to its associated packet before sending it. On the receiving end, the modem extracts the result from each packet and works the formula backwards. If the result could not have come from the data it received, the receiving modem will request that the erroneous packet be resent.

➤ **Parity**—One procedure for determining when an error occurs. (This method was encountered back in Chapter 11, "Memorize This! Upgrading Memory.") A low-grade error-checking protocol uses either even or odd parity, where a ninth bit is added to the eight bits (which make up a character) to make the total number of 1 bits either odd or even. If even parity is being used for example, and a modem receives the nine bits 010010111, then it'll know there's some kind of mistake because there are five 1 bits—an odd number.

➤ **Data bits**—A setting that refers to the number of bits in a single communicated character of data. Although a byte generally contains eight bits, most Internet communication uses only seven. Why? Because this leaves the eighth bit to act as a "fencepost" of sorts, so if the receiving modem gets confused as to where a character starts and stops, it can look for a pattern of zeros (or ones) every eighth bit.

➤ **Stop bit**—A modem setting that determines whether the modem adds a single bit between each character of data to serve as a "fencepost" separating one character from another in the data stream. For proper everyday Internet communication, your modem properties should be set to 8 bits, no parity, 1 stop bit (commonly abbreviated as "8 N 1"). You can access these properties from the Modem Control Panel in Windows 95, or the Modems Control Panel in Windows 98 and Windows Me.

➤ **Data compression**—A protocol or set of protocols the modem uses to shrink its data before transmitting it, so it takes less time. Popular protocols that include both error correction and data compression are V.42 and Microcom Network Protocol, or MNP, (actually, V.42 is an implementation of MNP).

The Different Speeds of 56K

Now for the paragraph you just knew you would be reading: The term "56K" with regard to a phone modem's speed, has become meaningless. Just because a modem advertises itself as 56K, does not guarantee that you'll actually connect at 56,000Kbps. Your modem could actually oscillate faster or slower than 56K, and still get away with the name. Then, of course, the speed of your connection is only as fast as its slowest modem. If you connect to a slow modem, your modem will slow down to meet its speed.

Another nonsurprise: Not all 56k modems transmit at 56K anyway. That's right. Some of the least expensive 56K modems available *receive* at 56Kbps, but *transmit* at 33.6Kbps. (Modems that conform to the so-called *Winmodem* standard, for instance, truly transmit at 33.6Kbps even though they receive at 56K. Perhaps it should have been named "Losemodem.") If a modem claims to follow the international V.90 standard, adopted by the International Telecommunications Union, then it should both transmit and receive at 56K.

On the other side of the scale, even some V.90 modems are capable of generating perceived connection speeds that are *faster* than 56K. Perceived by what, you might ask? The operating system. Some proprietary modulation standards such as HST (developed at USRobotics and acquired by 3Com along with the company) create the possibility of intermittent "burst modes" that mathematically compress the amount of information encoded into the signal, although perhaps not all the time. So some of the higher-priced modems may actually be faster than 56K overall.

The "Fax" Part of a Fax Modem

Most modems sold today are *fax modems*, the chief reason being that fax machines truly are modems in the first place. Of course, you'll need software to handle the faxing details for you, but most fax modems include that, too. With your fax modem and the proper software, you can send a document created with your PC to either another fax modem, or to an actual fax machine. The standard you want to look for here is called CCITT Group 3 Fax; about 98 percent of all the fax modems support Group 3, but at least you can weed out those built on the island of Outer Gamzabia that don't. It's almost impossible these days to locate a new modem that doesn't have fax send and receive capability. But where's the paper scanner? A fax modem doesn't need one. Its image of the page being transmitted exists within your computer's own RAM, and is managed by your computer's operating system.

If you own a flatbed scanner, a decent printer, and a fax modem, then not only do you have a reasonable fax machine, but you own components that are measurably better performing than those that are actually built into devices sold as fax machines.

The "Voice" Part of a Voice Modem

Not all modems sold today are "voice modems." The function of such a device isn't self-evident from its name, but once you realize what it is, you'll wonder why all modems don't function this way.

A voice modem is a digital telephone. It has its own digital signal processor for sending real-world sounds, such as your voice, over the phone line. With the proper software, a voice modem enables you to set up one of those fancy voice mail systems where callers can leave messages for particular people by pressing the right button. Software made for voice modems allows digital messages recorded by you and stored in your computer, to be played through the modem so that the human caller can hear you. This way, your computer becomes a sophisticated answering machine, capable of directing tone-dialed calls through to specific "mailboxes," or to your fax program. A voice modem can also record messages from the caller, so your software can store those messages to your hard disk as .WAV or .MP3 files. Of course, this means you must leave your computer and your modem on all the time, so you can receive messages. (Also, these voice message files can get quite large, so you'd better check your messages often, and delete them.)

Other software such as Blue Starfish's remarkable Veritape (www.veritape.com) can record your business telephone conversations on demand in crisp, clear quality—much better than any tape recorder I've ever owned. You can store these conversations in .MP3 format, and even archive them on CD-R discs. If you're in a business where you conduct phone interviews as part of your job, this can be an invaluable tool. (Again, not a paid endorsement, just me putting in a good word for a good product.)

Now let's put two and two together: If you're to make serious use of the fax part of your fax modem to send and receive data, you'll need to be ready to facilitate fax and data transmission capabilities through the same phone number. Fax transmission has become a polite process for most senders, which now starts the handshaking process with a gentle beep that doesn't blast through your eardrum if you pick up the phone and expect a voice rather than a machine. A fax modem can be set to answer the phone for you. But what if a *person's* trying to call you? What does she hear? This is where the voice modem part comes in. As an answering machine, the voice modem (with the proper software) can kindly tell the person to press a key to talk to you the old-fashioned way. Your phone then rings and you pick it up. So it's entirely possible—albeit tricky—for you to have a fully functional fax machine *plus* telephone answering machine, without installing a second phone line.

Some specialized voice modems let you attach an *electret microphone* that enables you to use your modem as, well, a telephone. Granted, all modems give you a plug for your existing telephone. But with an electret microphone plugged in, your modem becomes functional as a digital telephone. Software on your computer takes the place of the telephone console, so you can use day-planner or office-organizer software not only to store your numbers, but also as a substitute for speed-dial. An electret headset—which looks like a diamondless tiara with a tube pointing to your mouth—leaves your hands free to operate the computer; so the transition of your computer into a fully functional speakerphone with digital answering is complete. You can also use this setup to chat over the Internet with a good telephony program. Although some software lets you use the little microphone that may have come with your PC, you'll be surprised how poorly your voice sounds over a phone line when you use this otherwise decent microphone. You'll find one of these devices at your local office supply store, averaging in price at around $20.

Form Factors

Phone modems are either made to go inside or outside of your computer. (Seems logical enough.) An external modem plugs into a spare serial port, so make sure that you have one. If you've inherited an external modem from a buddy, but you don't have an extra serial port, you should check your motherboard to see whether it supports two serial ports ("COM1," "COM2") but merely lacks the socket for the second plug. If not, you can add a serial port with something called an *I/O card*. (See Chapter 12, "Face the Interface," for the rundown on serial ports.) You can share an external modem with several computers (great idea if you have more than one, such as a laptop PC and your kids' computers), provided they have a spare serial port or a serial I/O PCMCIA card (although not simultaneously, of course).

Check This Out

Most external modems don't include a serial modem cable, which you need to connect your external modem to your PC. Serial ports come in two sizes: 9- and 25-pin, so make sure you get the right cable to fit your needs. Don't accept imitations. Make sure the cable manufacturer rates its cables for use with modems.

Modem Economics

You can only buy a 56K modem today, and you should not have to spend more than $50 for even the most capable modem available; the average price at the time of this writing was $35 for an internal, $50 for an external.

Installing a Telephone Modem

When you're ready to install your modem, go through the usual steps to prepare your system. (If you need hints, see Chapter 4, "What You Need to Know *Before You Open Your PC*," for help.) Take a moment to get rid of that nasty static cling. If you need to remove your old modem, the procedure here is the same as for any other kind of expansion card, as outlined in Chapter 12.

Installing an Internal Modem

You use the same general procedure to install a phone modem card into your system as you would any other type of expansion card. There are few, if any, models that require you to make any on-card settings beforehand. After you have the modem in, connect the phone line to the outside frame of the card (see Figure 13.1), in the socket marked either "LINE," or with an icon that should resemble the RJ11 phone connector end, but may instead resemble a tooth extracted from your eight-year-old. Just leave the PC open if you want; you still need to test the modem, and it's easier to correct problems if you still have access to the problem maker (uh, the modem). Disconnect your telephone from the wall jack. Connect the opposite end of your modem cord into a phone line surge protector. Many surge protectors come with a protected phone jack—use one to avoid damage to your modem from electrical surges.

Now, your phone line surge protector should have come with an extra patch of RJ11 phone cord. Plug one end in the opposite socket of your surge protector, then plug the other end into the wall socket where you disconnected your phone.

Figure 13.1

Plug in the telephone line.

So what do you do with the phone? I said earlier your computer was a communications tool ... but hey, it ain't the *phone!* Luckily, there's a plug for it on the back of your modem. It'll be marked with the word "PHONE," or with an icon that's supposed to look like a telephone but instead looks like a Howard Johnson's (see Figure 13.2).

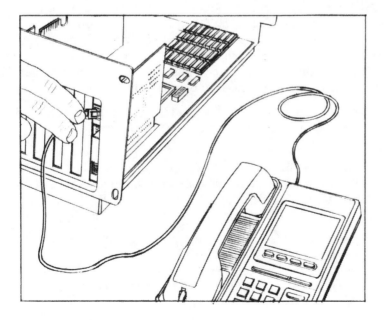

Figure 13.2

You can connect your phone to the modem if you have only one line.

283

Check This Out

When you're using one phone line for both your phone and your modem, you should get rid of extras like "call waiting," which wreak havoc on the modem's capability to send and receive data undisturbed, or disable call waiting by adding the prefix *70 to the front of the number you dial. Doing this requires a trick similar to balancing the federal budget. Windows keeps track of several so-called "Dialing Locations," in case you tend to move your computer from city to city. The default location is called "New Location," no matter how old it gets. Go into your Modem or Modems Control Panel, then click on Dialing Properties. Check the box marked, "To disable call waiting, dial:" Then in the list box just to the right, choose *70. Click OK, then click OK.

Installing an External Modem

There's not a lot to installing an external modem, thank goodness. You need a serial cable that has at least one connector that's type DB25 (flat, 13 pins over 12). The other end depends on which serial port you chose for your modem. If you have a serial mouse plugged into the 9-pin serial port (which Windows generally assigns COM1), then your only open serial port (COM2) might require a 25-pin connection. In this case, the cable you need will have the designation "DB25/DB25 female-to-male." But if your mouse is connected to the PS/2 mouse port, then you may prefer to plug your external modem into the 9-pin serial port that Windows will most likely call COM1. In that case, your cable should be "DB9/DB25 female-to-male." External modems rarely come with their own cables; you'll probably need to purchase one separately.

First, take your serial cable and connect it to the back of the modem (see Figure 13.3). Connect the other end to the serial port you chose on the back of your computer.

Next, plug in the power cable and connect it to a wall outlet, or preferably, a surge protector. Then connect the phone line. You'll see two telephone-type connections; use the one marked "LINE." If you don't see the labels, turn the modem over. Sometimes they're on the bottom. Disconnect the phone cord from the telephone and then plug it into a telephone (RJ11) jack, preferably in a phone line surge protector.

If you only have one telephone line, then to reconnect your telephone, you have two options: You can disconnect your phone from the wall and connect it to the other phone line connector on the modem—the one marked "PHONE." Or, you can purchase a two-way phone line adapter for a few dollars and plug that into your single jack (see Figure 13.4). Then plug your telephone into one socket, and the modem cord into the other.

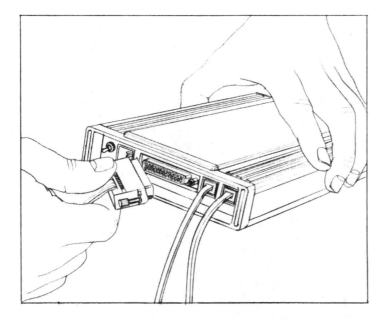

Figure 13.3

Use a serial cable to con-nect your external modem.

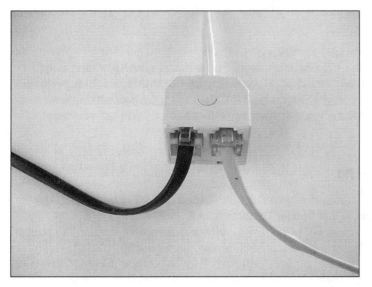

Figure 13.4

Use an adapter if your modem provides only one phone jack.

The Software Part of the Setup

The only place where being a Plug-and-Play (PnP) modem actually counts is here in the setup stage, where it saves you precisely one step. If you have a PnP internal modem, then when you reboot your computer, Windows asks you to insert the

285

CD-ROM that contains your modem's software drivers. If you don't have one, you may need to bring up Add New Hardware from the Windows Control Panel, skip the part where Windows detects your new hardware, and then choose Modem from the Categories list. At that point, Windows asks you for the CD-ROM that contains your modem's software drivers. Wow, that was exhausting. Wish you had gotten the PnP modem and saved those eight seconds?

Surprisingly, something else might save those eight seconds for you, even if you didn't get a PnP modem: Many major modem brands include a CD-ROM that runs itself when you put it in the drive. When you insert this CD-ROM into your drive while Windows is booting up, the program on the CD-ROM starts the process for you of installing the drivers, letting you avoid the Control Panel.

Whether you're using the modem's own setup program or the Control Panel, you should make certain your modem's communications (COM) port is set to the one your operating system needs to use. Generally this is a setting that doesn't conflict with the mouse, or anything else you have that needs a serial port. Windows may attempt to find an open COM port for the new modem automatically, but sometimes even then it's been known to annex a COM port that's in use by something else. How can you tell for sure? Right-click My Computer, and then select Properties. From the dialog box that pops up, click the Device Manager tab. Look for the Modems category in the list, and see if its icon has been marked with a yellow circle and a black exclamation point. If it has, something's wrong. Double-click the listing to see what's wrong, and the dialog box that pops up may tell you that its COM port setting conflicts with an existing setting.

How do you make the change? From Control Panel, double-click Modem (Win95) or Modems (Win98, WinMe). Choose your modem (its brand name may show up, or the listing may simply read "Standard Modem") from the dialog box that pops up, and then click Properties. In the list marked Port, if the COM port setting isn't what you want or if Device Manager said it's wrong, choose the COM port you want to use instead.

Testing Your Modem

Power up the PC. If you have an external modem, turn it on. Then bring up the Modem(s) Control Panel. Click on the Diagnostics tab in the dialog box that pops up, then from the list, choose the COM port you believe is currently assigned to your modem. (There should be a modem icon beside that COM port in the list.) Then click More Info. If you're not already online, Windows conducts some diagnostic tests on the device. In about 15 seconds, you'll see a list of commands that were sent to the modem, and their responses. If something is out of the ordinary in this list of responses, the dialog box tells you there may be an error, so you don't actually have to know what the commands are or what they mean to know something's wrong.

If you're not sure what's going on with these diagnostics, here's another test you can try: Go into your Modem(s) Control Panel and make certain your modem's speaker volume (the only horizontal slider in the panel) is turned up so you can at least hear it. Then bring up your MS-DOS prompt (from the Start menu, select Programs, Accessories, MS-DOS Prompt). Then type **ECHO ATDT>COM1** at the prompt and press Enter (or replace COM1 with the name of the port to which your modem is connected, such as COM3). If you hear something, then everything's fine so far. If something's funky (such as a disconnected modem, or one which is connected to the same COM port as another modem) then DOS responds with the error message, "Write fault error writing device COM1. Abort, Retry, Ignore, Fail?". Press A for abort and check out the next section for help in determining what's wrong.

As a final option, check whether your modem comes with *terminal software* (Windows 95 features an item in the Accessories menu called HyperTerminal; some versions of Win98 and all versions of WinMe omit this program). Use this terminal program to bring up a terminal screen (a blank screen that looks not unlike MS-DOS), where at the upper-left corner, you should see the letters, "OK." This message is coming from your modem, not from DOS and not from your communications software. Type ATDT, then Enter. This time, you should not only hear a dial tone, but you should also see another "OK" message. Finally, type **ATZ**, then Enter. The dial tone should cease, the phone should hang up, and you should see another "OK." If anything's wrong, you'll see the message "ERROR," in which case, you'll need to go back and check your connections once again. But if you see three "OK" messages at this point, your modem has passed the basic tests.

Mistakes to Avoid

When testing your modem from the DOS prompt, if you get the error message: "Write fault error writing device COM1" or "COM2," then either you forgot to turn the modem on, or there's something wrong with the connection. If you're using an internal modem, shut down your computer, try taking it out and then reseating it again.

If you run into problems after you've already got your modem up and running, there could be a COM port conflict with some other device, especially if your mouse (or whatever) begins acting up, too. A conflict might also result in the modem stopping in the middle of transmission.

The Cable Modem: Real, Live Broadband

I can say this now from personal experience: I have seen the future, and the telephone modem plays no part in it. I have a cable modem.

What I'm talking about is a device that borrows the excess bandwidth from my cable TV signal to connect me to the Internet. At this moment, I have no concept of how I survived on a diet of 56k connections. Software downloads that used to take overnight and into the next morning, now take about three minutes. And connections with live, streaming sources of news and music, no longer sound like they're being presented live and direct from the moon by people being periodically pelted with meteoroids. And I can set my e-mail client to check for new mail every 60 seconds. A fast communications device such as a cable modem enables new applications and new functionality that were not possible over the phone.

Despite all that I have come to depend upon so soon with regard to *broadband* technology, I can't make an unqualified recommendation for the technology just yet. I live in a metropolitan area, in a good old-fashioned suburban household. That fact is a key factor in the reason why cable modem works so well for me and my family. People who live in densely populated metropolitan areas, or sparsely populated rural areas, are less likely to even be eligible for cable modem installation. Even small towns where cable TV has already been well established, may be years away from ever having cable modems. The reason is because TV signal distributors (what communications engineers call the *headend*) must install complex and expensive data servers theoretically capable of handling all their cable TV customers, even if only a percentage of those customers choose to subscribe to cable modem service.

Techno Talk

The term **broadband** has come to represent the entire high-speed Internet access industry. The term originated at a time when communications engineers were considering re-allocating the cable TV frequency spectrum into bigger channels, thus leaving a larger open channel, or "band," in which data signals could reside.

What Is a Cable Modem, and How Do I Install One?

There's some argument over whether the cable modem is a modem at all. Technically, a modem modulates and demodulates sound into data, and data into sound. By that loose definition, a cable modem is a modem. But then, so are your ears.

By a stricter definition of communications engineering, a cable modem is not really a modem, but instead a network switching device. It translates data from a signal sent over a channel of cable TV (CATV) not used for television, into a signal interpretable by the everyday Ethernet networks that PCs can connect to with simple expansion cards. (More about networking in Chapter 22, "Installing and Maintaining a Home Network.") Technically, you could make a case that this process is *remodulation*. But it isn't *demodulation,* which is the "-dem" in "modem."

Why was that last bit of technical trivia so important? Because Windows this time around is correct: It does not recognize your cable modem as a modem. More intriguingly, it does not recognize your cable modem *at all*. There's a good architectural reason for this: When you're on the Internet with a cable modem, you're part of a network. Windows' control of the devices you use in that network, has to stop somewhere. Windows cannot and should not "see" the routers, switches, and bridges that make up this big network, even though you're directly connected to it (albeit by billions of miles of optic fiber). It should stick to controlling what it knows, which is your computer. The cable modem, to Windows, is just another Internet switch ... which is as it should be, for once.

The box that is called a cable modem—like the one shown in Figure 13.5—is a specially adapted external network switching device that connects to your cable TV provider's proprietary network. But it doesn't work by itself. For your computer to be part of the network, you need an Ethernet network interface card (NIC), even if you only have one PC in your house. Chapter 22 explains this card in detail; for now, you'll be pleased to learn that it's one of the least expensive expansion cards you can buy—as low as ten bucks—and it can be installed very easily.

Figure 13.5

One of America's most commonly deployed cable modems: the COM21 DOXport 1000.

Cable modem service is offered throughout North America by the cable TV providers for the various regions. You subscribe to this service the way you would subscribe to cable TV. Before televisions became "cable-ready," you used to have to rent the cable channel changer box from your cable company; today, the most practical way for you to obtain cable modem service is for you to rent the cable modem from your cable TV company. For this reason, you do not install your cable modem; that's why there are no physical installation instructions to be found here. For this job, you'll need a service representative from your cable TV company—assuming cable modem service is available in your region.

Just like installing cable TV, a transformer node is placed at a convenient location—say, atop a utility pole—and a high-grade coaxial line is run all the way from the transformer node to your house, sometimes underground. Outside the house, the cable installer sets up the network interface box, which is also known as the "customer point of access." If you already have cable TV, then you already have this box. The installer will split your cable line at this point, and will install a new, dedicated wall socket where your cable modem is to be attached. From that socket, the installer will run a short length of coaxial cable to the cable modem.

At the back of the cable modem is at least one connector, perhaps as many as four, for CAT5 Ethernet cable. It looks like indoor telephone cable, only just a bit thicker.

You or your installer then run a segment of network cable from the back of the cable modem into the NIC card of your PC.

In the initial testing phase of your new cable modem, it will undergo a "handshake" sequence, not unlike the way a phone modem "handshakes" with an ISP when it answers the phone, except 1) your cable modem will take longer (as long as 60 seconds), and 2) you won't hear anything. Instead, the lights on the front of your cable modem will blink, letting you know handshaking is in progress. With a COM21 cable modem, the "RF" light will become a steady green shade when the connection with the downstream ISP is finally made, or it will blink amber if it can't make the connection for some reason.

Now, a cable modem is not a PnP device. It doesn't have to be, because the NIC card *is*. The beauty of the cable modem setup is that your operating system doesn't need to know where the cable modem is or what it does. The cable modem can maintain itself; your PC only needs to be concerned with its Ethernet NIC card. As far as software is concerned, the same Ethernet drivers that run your NIC card for an at-home peer-to-peer network will run that same card for a cable modem. So after Windows has completed setting up your card and it's plugged into a powered cable modem, you're ready to go.

From here on out, your connection to the Internet may be *persistent;* and if it's not persistent in your particular service area, then special software can be set up on your computer so that it at least appears to be. This means you don't have to double-click any dial-up icons or initiate any points of contact. You're online as long as your PC is turned on. (So obviously your cable service provider should not charge you an hourly rate.) You bring up your Web browser, and there's your home page. No waiting, no busy signals, no cursing AOL.

The Cost Factor

You can buy a cable modem. There's just no good reason for you to do so. The portion of your cable modem bill apportioned for renting the modem, is about $5 per month; meanwhile, the retail price of a cable modem averages $200. And as cable modem technology continues to evolve, your CATV provider will (or at least should) replace your cable modem with the newest model, at no charge to you.

On the other hand, you can and should buy your network interface card (NIC), rather than lease or purchase it from your CATV provider. Although you only need a 10Mbps (megabit per second) Ethernet card, ordinary models now feature 100Mbps transfer speed, which could be useful to you if you wish to network two PCs in the future. Even premium brands of NICs sell for about $15, and prices generally average about $10, although you can occasionally find a sale price of $3. By comparison, reports state CATV providers have offered to resell NIC cards to customers for prices in excess of $100, or rent cards to customers for five extra dollars per month.

In most regions of the United States, CATV providers bid for the exclusive rights to provide service within designated regions. As a result, there's no competition within any one region for cable modem service. So your cable modem provider has already been chosen for you, unless you decide to move anytime soon. Today, cable modem subscription prices have settled to about $50 per month, including equipment rental. Installation fees can run as high as $150, but average about $75, except during promotional periods when CATV providers are willing to waive some, if not all, setup fees.

Before you jump to the conclusion that $50/month is excessive, consider the following: If you work at home, or are in a situation where you use the Internet several hours per day, you have probably either considered or implemented the installation of a second telephone line. My husband's and my business paid $30/month for that extra phone line. We then paid our phone-line-based ISP $25/month for access and e-mail. By making the switch to cable modem, where both the line and the access charges are included in the final fee, we actually save five bucks a month.

The Advantages of High-Speed Downloading

Consider also the fact that one reason you may spend so much time online is because it takes so long to get anything accomplished. Suppose, for instance, you need to download the updated version of an installation manual for a computer part you just purchased. The Adobe Acrobat file for this manual could exceed 5 megabytes in size, which with standard 56K modem download speeds could consume 24 minutes. Assuming the manufacturer's server is reasonably fast, you can download the same manual via cable modem in under 5 seconds.

The actual transfer rate of your cable modem will be affected by several factors: One is, believe it or not, the number of other cable modem subscribers in your immediate neighborhood, or "cluster." Everyone whose CATV access is tied to the same transformer, shares the same cable modem channel. So your true bandwidth at any one time could be reduced by your having to share that channel with someone else, though that reduction is not 50 percent as has been reported elsewhere—it's more like 5 to 10 percent.

Another factor, if you live in a metropolitan area, is your distance from downtown, even when your CATV provider is on the outskirts of town. Your perceived downstream speed can be *greatly* reduced in areas where cable signals are more tightly bunched together. Many cable modem users continue to report slow or even non-existent downstream speeds, especially in the largest cities like New York.

I live in a suburban area where I am the only cable modem subscriber on my block. I've done a few things to improve the way my cable modem works (I'll tell you about them shortly). I just had an independent Web site run a test on my service. Right now, it reports that my data download rate (what the cable engineers call *downstream transfer*) is 1.1Mbps—about 1316Kbps (kilobits per second), which is 23 times the theoretical speed of a 56K modem, but is actually 47 times the true download rate I've observed with my top-of-the-line 56K modem on the Internet (28Kbps). Cable companies promise 50 times the speed of phone modem, and that's roughly about right.

Now, to be absolutely fair, I should point out that upload transfer rates, or *upstream* rates, are significantly slower than downstream rates. So it takes a lot more time for me to send an e-mail than it would to receive an e-mail of the same size. How much more? Using the same independent testing service I used to verify the 1316Kbps downstream rate I witnessed, my upstream rate was clocked at 75Kbps. That's almost 18 times slower. However, that's still three times the upload speed of my 56K modem (28Kbps).

Let's put this speed in perspective. Business subscribers to exclusive, fiberoptic ISDN lines experience download speeds of 256Kbps—that's the rate they're guaranteed by their service provider. But that's still more than four times slower than cable modem! So why do businesses continue to spend hundreds, if not thousands, per month for ISDN? Because the upload rate equals the download rate, which enables those businesses to run servers over those lines. You should not expect to be able to run a realistic server with a 75Kbps upstream rate.

Check This Out

By law, in the United States and Canada, you don't have to have cable TV. You can have your home wired for cable modem *only*, and have the split line leading to cable TV terminated. You should not pay any extra for this request. Cable companies can offer CATV/cable modem bundle packages for discounted prices, but they cannot prevent you from saying no to cable TV.

I could simply say you could be downloading files at a faster rate, and be done with it. The truth is, because you'll be downloading data faster, you'll most likely be downloading more of it. You see, the fastest growing segment of the Internet these days isn't even the mighty Web, but the emergence of independent *streaming media* protocols. When you have the fastest persistent connection to the Internet available, chances are you'll take the opportunity to use the Internet as a massive global jukebox and all-around entertainment and informational media center. Downloading MP3 files will be like … *blip* … and you play them. And if you're like my husband, you'll have BBC News 24 running in the corner of the screen all day to complement the CNN or CNBC running on your TV. Through services such as Live365.com, you might be able to find independent "Internet broadcasters," playing popular or unique genres of music through your Dolby AC-3 speakers as though they were radio stations originating from next door. Gone will be the frequent pauses for network interference and rebuffering that you cannot help but encounter with even the most reliable 56K phone modem.

The Disadvantages of Your ISP Being Chosen for You

In the United States, coaxial cable service of any kind offered to residential areas, is considered a public utility. As such, it's regulated by federal and state laws. For most counties in most states, the rights granted a public utility to provide service to certain areas are awarded by exclusive contract. As a result, when you decide to go with cable modem service, the choice of your Internet service provider will have already been made for you.

Just what that choice will be—at least, as of the time of this writing—is more up in the air now than it has ever been. America's #1 broadband ISP, @Home (a division of Excite@Home), probably won't be in business by the time you read this book. America's #2 broadband ISP, Road Runner, is only in slightly better shape. You may find that your cable modem service provider is none other than AT&T. Remember the '70s? Remember *The Phone Company?* History, like a bad sitcom, tends to repeat itself.

Your ISP will not be the same company as your CATV provider. This is important because, if you have a service complaint, your cable TV company isn't the one to talk to. Even if your cable TV support line and cable modem support line have the same telephone number, the answerer might redirect your call to the ISP. But most of the time, for obscure but unavoidable legal reasons, your CATV provider will probably answer your cable modem support call with a recording that tells you to *hang up and dial another number.* (If the CATV provider does anything else, it can be construed as being partly responsible for cable modem service, which is a responsibility it does not want and cannot afford.)

When you finally get your ISP's call center on the phone, its representative can schedule a service appointment with a registered cable modem technician. Surprisingly, though, this technician actually does work for your cable TV company. So it is vitally important that you explain your problem clearly and succinctly to your ISP, because your local serviceperson will receive news of this problem second-hand—generally about as much information as will fit into 80 characters of text on an old-style computer form.

Many online support groups have been established to comfort the many shocked and dismayed newcomers to the realm of cable modems, such as www.cablemodemhelp. com. The horror stories that abounded during cable modem's introduction in 1998— which included one lady's experience in jail for failing to pay for services she didn't receive due to an installation error—have noticeably subsided. But the biggest problem facing most American cable modem customers today is the declining state of the nation's CATV infrastructure. A big chunk of this country's CATV lines are incapable of supporting the high *fidelity* required by digital devices. As a result, some customers are ineligible for cable modem service, even in areas where that service is advertised to be available, and these customers never know for certain until after their CATV provider has attempted the installation.

The most common problem reported by users of online cable modem support sites is not as bad as going to jail, but simply that their cable modems do not work at all *period*, and that the installers know nothing about computers and cannot fix them. Apparently, the truth behind this problem is that the Internet line that piggybacks the cable TV (CATV) spectrum on the circuits owned by CATV companies are not all 100 percent up and running. Because no one in particular owns the Internet, this shouldn't be too surprising. The merger of the multitude of network protocols that makes this entire scheme possible is mind-boggling, and it's a wonder that anything works at all.

There are some other types of problems to consider: When you sign up for a cable modem ISP, your Internet e-mailbox will reside on the ISP's server. At this point, there's appreciable concern that these particular nationwide ISPs may be screening the content being exchanged through these e-mailboxes, under the theory that while the mail isn't their property, the storage space for it is. There is also concern that these ISPs may be keeping tabs on what Web sites you visit, because some of these ISPs do take it upon themselves to screen Web site content on your behalf—whether you want them to or not.

What's That Technician Doing on Your Computer?

The shakiest part of installing your broadband modem comes when your service technician asks you to boot your computer and turn it over to him so he can install some software on it. Try as you might, most technicians will not allow you to install the software yourself. Some may actually make you sign a waiver beforehand, holding them free from any liability for whatever they may happen to do to your PC. Whether you decide to sign this waiver or not is up to you, but if you don't, your technician may walk out the door, phone his office, and say you refused service.

So what can you do? You have the right to watch over this technician's shoulder, ask him what he's up to, and limit him to only installing and setting up the software you need. Here are some things that real service technicians have actually been asked to do, that you have a right to tell your service technician not to do:

➤ **Installing new e-mail software that overwrites your own e-mail software.** Many technicians will try to install Outlook Express on your machine if it doesn't have it already, and will set up Outlook Express as your "default" e-mail program. You have a right to say no to this, especially since Outlook Express is so susceptible to outside attacks.

➤ **Changing your choice of Web browser.** If you use Netscape or Opera, you have a right to continue to use them. They *will* work with your new broadband modem.

➤ **Change the home page of your Web browser.** Ask to see your ISP's home page first, to see if it has any features you might want. But to use broadband ISP, you are under no obligations to visit anybody's home page if you don't want to.

➤ **Install programs that create permanent zones for pop-up ads on your desktop.** You have a right not to make your desktop into a billboard. It's your property. In the US, any agreement you sign with a service provider stating that you agree to witness a certain number of ads per day or week or year, and that you won't tamper with the methods in which these ads are delivered to you, is *legally nonbinding*.

➤ **Install "bonus" software you're not going to use**, such as games or even word processors (!).

➤ **Delete desktop icons that aren't in the technician's manual.** That's your desktop. Nobody has the right to delete anything from your computer but you.

Problems That Could Crop Up

The marriage between the CATV network and the Internet is, by most accounts, not a very cozy one. Problems can erupt, many of which seem to have little to do with you at first, but which you may end up having to account for, or even fight to have fixed for you.

First of all, incremental upgrades of the main downstream loop leading from the CATV provider, from all-coaxial cable to all-fiberoptic cable, have resulted in communities whose signals are carried partly by one type of cable, partly by the other. For cable TV reception, this is generally no problem. But the presence of temporary signal transformers can adversely affect cable modem reception. As CATV lines are upgraded, this problem should be *reduced*.

Also, the quality of the bridge between the CATV network and the ISP network is a variable. Although both @Home and Road Runner made major inroads in improving their networks in the last few years, their capacity to handle multiple simultaneous clients (all of which are very, very fast, by the way) never really measured up to more established national services such as AOL and MSN. When the cable ISP cannot keep up with heavy traffic, the network connection between that ISP and the CATV provider appears to shut down, most often for a few minutes, sometimes for as long as an entire day.

DiSiLlusionment

The Digital Subscriber Line (DSL) is the latest incarnation of an old, old plan conceived by AT&T back in 1968, back when it was known as the Bell System. At that time, Bell's plan was to lay the infrastructure to wire every home in America with a digital fiberoptic line that handles all voice communications, and that might also serve up television while it was at it. The Bell plan was part of its first Integrated Services Digital Network (ISDN) vision. Today, businesses lease fiberoptic ISDN lines as low-cost alternatives to direct T1 or T3 trunks directly into the Internet.

But if you think ISDN never made it to the home, you're wrong. ISDN just made it, and it's called DSL. What's different, besides the newly revised alphabet soup, is the fact that the new system uses new technology to pump new signals over old telephone lines. It's all the things you love about fiberoptics, minus the fiber ... and the reliability, and the fidelity, and the long distance, but we'll get to that part later.

Star Wars Episode II: *The CLECs Invade the RBOCs*

DSL as a technology is a direct result of the US Court of Appeals breakup of AT&T in 1984. Had that event not happened, there would not be such a thing as DSL.

Here's the reason: Prior to the breakup, the Bell System's plan was to systematically rewire all of America with digital, fiberoptic service. At one time, the company believed it could accomplish this goal 100 percent by 1980—and even at the very end of Bell's federally-mandated monopoly of telephone service, it never doubted it could accomplish the goal by the turn of the century.

As part of the breakup settlement agreement, Bell was forced to turn over control and ownership of every one mile of telephone cable extending from every local customers' outlets, to their area's respective "Baby Bell" company. Today, these companies (Verizon, Qwest, SBC Communications, and BellSouth) are known to the telecom and legal communities as the Regional Bell Operating Companies (RBOCs, pronounced "ar-boks," almost rhymes with "Starbucks"). This turnover of The Last Mile, as it has come to be known, rendered any goal of AT&T rewiring America's homes and offices effectively impossible.

But the ISDN dream didn't die. A laboratory jointly owned and funded by the RBOCs, called Bellcore, took over AT&T's old research into ISDN. The RBOCs developed the technology today known as DSL because they wanted to be able to provide high-speed digital service over the phone lines they have in place right now. And all the legal and physical barriers in the world aren't going to stop them.

Their original plan, unveiled in 1987, went like this: The signal carried over conventional copper wires for both the voice and data portions of the telephone network, comprises only a fraction of the range of frequencies that the wire could *possibly* carry—the *theoretical* spectrum. The reason telephone signals are not carried on those higher and lower frequencies today is due to the realities of signal degradation: Certain signals over current grade copper wire die out over so many thousands of feet. But suppose the same data format used to send ISDN were pumped *loudly* over this theoretical part of the spectrum that ordinary telephones don't use. Sure, the signal would degrade over comparatively short distances (say, about 12,000 feet, maybe 30,000 with an amplifier), but if the signal were purely digital, error correction techniques could compensate for that loss. And if every central switching office (CO) in the local phone system served as a "signal pump," then since these offices are situated generally no more than four or five miles apart from each other within most metropolitan areas, these signal pumps could blanket nearly all the territory in every major city.

Thus the concept of the DSL was born: basically a crude but effective attempt to pump ISDN over conventional phone lines. The technical deficiencies of DSL—the principle of shouting a signal over the part of the telephone spectrum that isn't supposed to carry a signal—is at least partly masked by the sheer number of central offices that send the signal throughout a city. If your computer is within shouting range of a CO, there's a good possibility—though not a certain one—that it can receive DSL service.

The AT&T breakup settlement guaranteed the RBOCs ownership of The Last Mile of twisted, paired, copper telephone cable. However, that agreement does not guarantee the RBOCs ownership of whatever could replace that cable. So if Bellcore actually invented a reasonable fiberoptic system, what would prevent a competitive communications company from trying to be the first to deploy that system?

The answer to that question, as affirmed by the landmark Telecommunications Act of 1996, was … nothing. Suddenly, cities and townships had the right to open up local phone access to market competition from a new group of companies called Competitive Local Exchange Carriers (CLECs, pronounced "sea-lecks," almost homonymous with "sea legs"). These are companies who want to be able to provide you with local phone service, or a reasonable substitute.

The CLECs seized upon DSL as a technology that could either break through or bypass The Last Mile, giving them a way to offer new customers an incentive to give up their old phone service. They perceived DSL as a "value-added phone." In regions where CLECs were restricted by law from gaining access to The Last Mile, now they had a way to compel customers to yank that mile out on their own accord. Meanwhile, the CLECs could use the argument that these restrictions burden consumers, as leverage to force the RBOCs to lease bandwidth segments of their mile to them—just enough bandwidth to supply the same type of DSL service that the RBOCs themselves use.

So the reason DSL has suddenly become a major player in the race to bring you broadband Internet, is not because of the wondrous possibilities of the Internet itself, but instead because all the major parties involved in DSL want to be your future phone company.

The DSL Service Categories

There are two categories of DSL service with one very important distinction between them: A *single-line* DSL (SDSL) connection involves a separate copper line of the same grade as telephone wire, linking your home or office to the telephone network, though without its own phone number. CLECs are the ones who offer SDSL service. A *shared* DSL connection may share the telephone line you already have, in which case no second line is installed. RBOCs tend to offer shared DSL, although CLECs that have gained the right to be leased portions of The Last Mile in certain local areas may also offer shared DSL service. It can be a bit slower than SDSL, though it can be cheaper.

The term *Asymmetric DSL* (ADSL) refers to the capability to split the incoming phone signal between a voice and data channel, and then to split the data channel into a larger downstream (downloading) channel and a smaller upstream channel. Shared DSL service is generally of the ADSL variety so that it can make use of your existing phone line rather than make you install a new one. But some companies do offer shared DSL over a separate line anyway. Why? Because, as I've said, CLECs are creating options for themselves to become your next phone company, and ADSL gives them a clear channel to do just that.

The DSL Modem ... Or Not

Nothing more quaintly characterizes the current state of DSL development than the fact that the device used to deploy DSL over phone lines doesn't have a standardized name yet. Bellcore has dubbed the device *termination unit,* and the ADSL variety is called an ADSL Termination Unit-Remote (ATU-R), which I've actually heard pronounced "*aht*-ur." (Evidently Cyrano de Bergerac does not work for Bellcore.) Another term given to this device by network technicians is *bridge.* If you're speaking with a repairman or an equipment supplier, this is the term you may want to use; they may even correct you if you use "DSL modem" instead. But if you're talking your ISP's tech support personnel, and you use the term "bridge," chances are they won't know what you're talking about.

I don't care what anybody says; I'm not calling the thing an "ature." And I know it's not really a modem. But just like the cable modem, the purpose of the *DSL modem* is to capture the incoming signal from the line attached to your telephone wall jack and convert it into an Ethernet signal that your computer will understand. A standard Ethernet-style CAT5 network cable links your computer's NIC to the DSL modem, and either another CAT5 or a standard telephone-style RJ11 links your DSL modem to the telephone wall jack.

Some DSL modems are so well equipped that they enable you, the user, to configure and maintain them through a Web page. Some DSL modems literally act like Web servers, reporting their own status to your Web browser through a page that really does have its own URL. To configure your DSL modem, you fill out a form as it appears on your browser, click on the Submit button, and that's it.

What is it that you'd need to configure? You'll be setting network addresses and protocols because your DSL modem is a true network component—what network architects call a *gateway.* What's important about this fact is that the DSL modem first reports any problems it may have to you, even if you're just renting it. The device can be set up to report its problems to your DSL provider, or to both you and your provider; but oftentimes, you're the one responsible for trying to correct problems first before a service call is placed.

So Close, and Yet So Far

Let's concentrate for a moment on the distance problem. When I talk about the distance between your home or office and your nearest telephone central switching office (CO), I'm not talking about the same kind of distance you could measure if you could stand up on your roof, spot your CO with binoculars, and record the linear distance shown on your radar gun. Instead, imagine if you had to take a walk from your house to the CO, following only the route laid out for you by the telephone cables overhead or underground. The route absolutely will not be a straight line. In some congested metropolitan areas, these two points may be just blocks away on the map, though they are separated from each other by more than four miles of cable. If you're four miles or more from your CO, you do not qualify for SDSL service, and you may not qualify for ADSL. If six miles or more separates you, even the most modern amplified ADSL connection will not reach you. Obviously, if you live in a remote rural area, you may as well live on Mars.

How do you know for sure how much cable there is between you and the CO *without* having to take that little walk? The only way you can know absolutely for certain is to contact the DSL services representative for your local RBOC—whether or not that RBOC is your choice for DSL service. At least until CLECs get a stronger foothold, all DSL service will initiate at the RBOC's switching offices. The reason is because the Internet itself doesn't exist on the telephone network. To be able to relay Internet signals over telephone lines, someone has to provide the bridge between the two. Until further notice, that bridge exists at the CO.

The connection between you and your CO is referred to as the *loop*. The loop contains both upstream (you to the CO) and downstream (the CO to you) connections, and data can be in transit upstream and downstream simultaneously for what is called *full duplex*. Your telephone is also a full duplex communication device because you can talk and listen at the same time; a HAM radio, by comparison, is *half duplex* because it relies upon a single frequency, and only one signal can reside on that frequency at a time.

We know who owns the mile of telephone cable extending from your house. The matter of who actually owns the *remainder* of the cable following the first mile and leading to the central switching office, may easily be anyone's guess. In many metropolitan areas, the only data indicating who owns what span at which point is inscribed by hand on paper kept in a file drawer someplace, perhaps at the bottom of some basement. By law, this is public information; that doesn't exactly mean you can get to it easily.

Why does all of this even matter? Prior to installing your DSL modem, a technician hired by your local RBOC must test the reliability of your phone line. If the technician detects a problem, the next question is going to be, what part of the line may be causing it? It may be up to the owners of a span of phone cable to determine whether a problem even exists in their suspected span; and if those owners have no financial stake in the outcome, how long can you expect to wait for them to act?

How Fast is DSL, Really?

The primary factor affecting the speed of your DSL connection is the *grade* of service to which you subscribe. When you lease a DSL line, you're purchasing chunks of bandwidth. For SDSL service, this chunk is equally divided into a downstream speed and an upstream speed; for ADSL, the dividing line is shifted to favor your downstream speed. In either case, you're leasing between 256 kilobits per second (Kbps) and 8.5 megabits per second (Mbps) of total bandwidth, with the average being 384Mbps.

Easily the best independent source for DSL-related news—as well as a simply well-organized Web site, period—is the impartial DSL news repository DSLReports (www.dslreports.com). According to DSLReports, a reasonable estimate of your maximum real-world data transfer speed for a DSL connection may be obtained by taking the downstream speed in bits per second, dividing by 8 to obtain *bytes* per second, then subtracting 13 percent of the result to account for the data transfer overhead. This overhead is incurred when downstream data is transferred between network loops, and for DSL, this happens twice: once between the ISP and the broadband provider (10 percent), and a second time between The Last Mile of phone cable and your DSL modem (3 percent). Suppose you lease 384K of downstream bandwidth. That's 48 kilobytes per second (K/sec). By the DSLReports standard, that leaves you with a theoretical maximum of 41.76K/sec. Compared with the theoretical 56K modem maximum transfer rate of 3.5K/sec, you have a connection that's about 12 times faster. That's not 100 or 1000, but it's still quite good.

How Much Does DSL Cost, Really?

The average price of consumer DSL service in the United States is right there with cable modem at just under $50/month. Unlike cable modem, though, some DSL providers offer different service *grades* which enable faster download speeds for premium prices. Some services will also offer you faster *upstream* speeds on a premium SDSL plan, so your uploading isn't automatically handicapped as is the case with ADSL. However, under some "fair usage agreements" providers have their customers sign, as a home user, you may be prohibited from using SDSL for the one thing that SDSL service is particularly good for: running your own Web or e-mail server.

But wait … Didn't you read or hear something not too long ago about "free DSL service?" How free is free in this case? Well, kinda free, but not very much. As of the time of this writing, only one company was left offering free DSL service in North America. You'd be given access to a 144Kbps downstream line, which isn't the fastest DSL there is, but it's faster than 56K modems. You'd still pay for the installation fees, which could be phenomenal depending upon what needs to be done to your phone lines. The service was only available in limited portions of major metropolitan areas. And the truth is, it probably won't be available this way for very long. Almost all the companies that were so ready and willing during 1999 to chuck their profits for the possibility of becoming their customers' next phone company, failed to emerge from bankruptcy protection in 2001.

Overcoming DSL's "False Positives"

As with cable modem, you do not install your DSL modem—a service technician does that for you. And you lease that DSL modem from your DSL provider of choice.

But there are still an extraordinary number of things you have to know about, or even do yourself, before you can have DSL installed in your home. The reason has to do with the disturbing number of so-called *false positives*—tests run by DSL providers on customers' lines that resulted in positives (they passed the test), even though those lines ended up being inadequate. According to one estimate submitted to a U.S. Congressional subcommittee in 2000, the number of reported false positives not only exceeded the number of *negatives* (customers whose lines failed the test), but also exceeded the total number of successfully installed DSL customers in the United States. Statistically, your chances of getting a "true positive" line that really does work may be less than 50/50.

The "in" term among technicians for a DSL certification and installation process is a *truck roll*. (In my husband's hometown, a "truck roll" is a big Saturday night event at the Fairgrounds involving pickups with eight-foot wheels.) What is it that a truck roll could turn up, that could render you ineligible for DSL service? Here are the most important hurdles a local loop must clear before you're deemed "positive":

First of all, the total length of the local loop leading from the telephone network interface (TNI) outside your home, to the DSL Access Multiplexer (DSLAM) at the central office, must be within the prescribed range of tolerance. For SDSL, this maximum has never strayed beyond 16,000 feet (3 miles). For ADSL, which may or may not share your existing telephone line, the strange nature of physics has enabled this maximum in some areas to extend to 30,000 feet (5⅔ miles). As a result, some customers too far away from their local CO to qualify for SDSL, are eligible for ADSL.

A phone line may be perforated by hardware designed to enhance its fidelity as a voice signal carrier, but which ironically reduces its fidelity as a DSL carrier—for instance, in-line voice amplifiers, digital added main line multiplexers (DAMLs) which reroute digital voice traffic, and so-called bridged taps which can introduce high-frequency echoes that voice callers never hear. Also, if a line has been excessively repaired, it can create signal degradation at high frequencies—especially if the repairperson leaves her test equipment embedded in the line, which happens all too frequently.

Of all the ironies, newer telephone cables seem to have greater signal degradation at higher frequencies than older cables. Although there is no clear explanation, one extraordinary theory states that modern ore processing has resulted in a different grade of copper that is *too pure* and that, as a result, is free from the impurities that in older cables reduced echoing and reverberation at high and low frequencies.

A clear DSL connection can be subverted by outside forces beyond your control. For example, a conventional ISDN or T1 connection to a nearby business could result in a much stronger signal coming in from elsewhere that could interfere with the weaker DSL signal on the same line. Your technician will refer to one of these stronger signals as a *disturber*. Also, a nearby AM radio station transmitter could drastically interfere with a DSL signal if even part of the cable is not properly shielded. How near is "nearby"? The answer depends on the strength of the AM transmitter. Low-power AM stations intended to be heard within their own close communities, may not cause much problem. A high-power transmitter operating on a "clear channel" (a frequency no other station within a 200-mile radius uses) could render DSL impossible. So if you live close to All-News-Talk-1000, you may automatically be out of luck.

Everyday items *within* your control can render a DSL connection ineffective. Would you believe, the use of halogen light bulbs has also been shown to adversely affect DSL reception. You'll generally find halogen bulbs in overhead track lighting. If a car drives by with its halogen headlights on, you could experience connection troubles for a moment or two. The presence of a rheostat light switch somewhere in your home—also known as a dimmer switch or dimmer dial—has been shown to adversely affect DSL reception. It may take an electrician to solve this problem.

Also, excessive use of older-style AC power adaptors for various electronic devices within your home, will probably cause DSL signal interference. Your telephone answering machines, your battery rechargers, some small kitchen appliances like food processors, your Iomega Zip external drive, and your PC's external speakers all use these fat power adaptor plugs, nicknamed *bricks*. The problem here is the same one caused by rheostat light switches, but this time, there may be a solution. Radio Shack, or your nearest electronics store, sells replacement AC adaptors based on newer *transformer-type* technology. These replacement plugs are advertised to not cause radio frequency interference (RFI). They're smaller and lighter than the older bricks. Make certain you purchase adaptors whose voltage and wattage requirements match those of the adaptors you're replacing.

Broadband Firewalls and Why You Need One

Whether you dial-up your ISP by telephone modem, link to it by cable modem, or establish a "permanent" DSL connection with it, technically speaking, your computer is never truly *connected* to the Internet. There is always a machine somewhere else called an *IP host* that is connected to the Internet on your behalf. This IP host merely echoes the data it receives over the phone line, where your modem or NIC captures it. You send your responses from your computer through your modem, then the IP host captures them and pretends to be you while it forwards those responses through the Internet.

The important distinction between these three types of connections has to do with how the Internet recognizes *you*, the user. With most Internet access schemes including all dial-up schemes, your computer has no permanent *IP address* of its very own for another IP host to be able to contact it directly. Instead, your ISP chooses a temporary IP address from its list of available numbers—not unlike a hotel desk clerk locating the nearest numbered bin with a room key in it—and literally rents that address to you until such time as your modem hangs up the phone.

Separating Your Network from the Internet

When you dial up your ISP with your phone modem, the Internet address it assigns to you is only temporary. You "lease" that address up until the point your modem hangs up the phone. Because of that, you personally cannot be identified by your temporary IP address given to you by your ISP's Point-to-Point Protocol (PPP), and therefore nobody who wants to attack you personally through your computer can make use of that address. (This doesn't render your computer immune from attack through phone modem connections; it merely shields you from the more direct form of computer attacks.)

Some cable modem and DSL services enable a similar system called PPP-over-Ethernet (PPPoE) to lease their customers temporary IP addresses on the fly, in such a way that those customers never have to know their addresses have changed—from their perspective, they're "always on." But PPPoE is becoming less common, as broadband ISPs converge instead on a less expensive system that assigns their customers permanent IP addresses. If your broadband ISP assigns you a permanent IP address, it becomes possible for a knowledgeable malicious user to track you down via your computer.

For this reason primarily, but also for others, you need a *broadband firewall,* like the one shown in Figure 13.6. It is an absolute necessity in broadband communications, and you must not let your cable or DSL provider talk you out of buying one and installing it yourself for any reason.

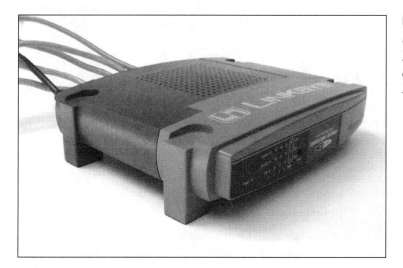

Figure 13.6

One of the most popular broadband firewall/switch combos available: LinkSys' EtherFast Router.

A hardware-based firewall is attached to the line leading *from* your broadband modem. This device's primary function is to serve as a network address translator (NAT). It lets you assign yourself a special redundant IP address that not only applies to your PC within your own network (even if it's just a network of one), but also cannot be routed throughout the larger Internet. In other words, Internet routers cannot accept this redundant address, so it cannot be used to identify your computer to any other computer except a computer in your own network.

A firewall examines ordinary data sent to the IP address that your broadband provider assigned you, and forwards that data to your redundant address. Malicious code addressed to your assigned IP address is intercepted by the firewall before it becomes forwarded to the redundant address. And malicious code that happens to be sent to the redundant address is never received by the firewall anyway.

The best external firewall devices can also serve as switches for your local network, mostly because their technology is exactly the same. Because external firewalls have come into such high demand so soon, firewall/switch combo devices such as those made by LinkSys, have become as affordable at the time of this writing as non-switching network hubs were in 2000, dropping in price below $100. Because of this price plummet, there's no reason for me to recommend you even purchase a stupid network hub any more. So you'll see a cameo appearance of the hardware firewall in Chapter 22.

Malicious attacks have become all too common events on today's Internet. It isn't so much that anyone specifically wants to attack you *in particular;* most often, it's just the fact that your number has come up in some wrongdoer's automatic world havoc-wreaking program. Don't think you can console yourself with the notion that you're as likely to be attacked by some cracker someplace as you're likely to win the lottery—both events depending upon your number turning up. A malicious attack could be waged programmatically on multiple addresses in a given range at one time—not exactly the same odds as six particular ping-pong balls emerging from a hopper in sequence.

Installing a Firewall Device

Your service technician will not install a firewall for you. This is because it belongs to you, not to the cable company, and not to your DSL provider. But don't worry, the procedure is very painless. A firewall works just the same way for a DSL modem as it does for a cable modem—this is why I call it a "broadband modem" in this segment.

You'll need a small patch—preferably only three feet in length—of CAT5 networking cable. Some firewall devices come with this patch, some don't; if you need to buy one, it should not sell for more than $8.

As Figure 13.7 shows you, a CAT5 cable plugs and unplugs into a socket exactly the same way as a modern telephone (RJ11) cable. So start by unplugging your broadband modem from its power source. Then on the back of your modem, find the plastic latch at the top of the network cable socket (on a COM21 cable modem, it will be marked "10BT," which probably means something on a world far, far away from our own). Press down on this latch, then pull the cable out from the modem.

Now, take this cable, and plug it directly into any one of the *numbered* sockets on the back of your firewall—if your firewall doesn't serve as a network switch as well, this socket may just be labeled "PC," but it could also just be labeled "1." *Do not* plug this cable into the socket marked "UPLINK"—leave this one alone.

Take the three-foot patch cable, and plug one end of it into the back of the firewall, in the socket marked "WAN" (Wide Area Network). Plug the other end into the back of the broadband modem, in the socket from which you just removed the other cable. Then plug the power adapter for your modem back into the wall, and connect the power adapter cord for your firewall.

That takes care of the hardware part of the installation. The software comes next, but you'll be happy to learn that your firewall needs no Windows drivers. In fact, firewalls aren't Plug-and-Play devices for a simple reason: For a firewall to truly be doing its job, your computer cannot know it exists. If Windows was aware of your firewall, malicious users could tap into Windows and intercept its translated IP addresses.

So amazingly enough, with many firewall devices including LinkSys' models, you can set up its operating characteristics with your Web browser (see Figure 13.8)! How is this possible? The firewall can pretend to be a Web server, by letting your Web browser contact it with a Web-like address, such as http://192.168.1.1. How come malicious users can't use this same address? Because IP addresses that start with "192" are discarded by Internet routers, so no one can get to this address through the Internet—it's onlyaddressable locally, through your network.

Figure 13.7

Patching your firewall between your broadband modem and your PC.

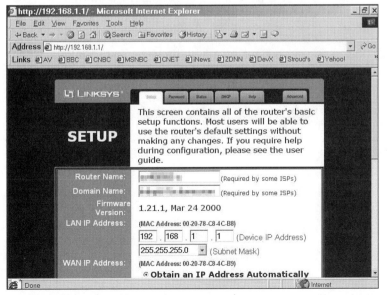

Figure 13.8

LinkSys's firewall/switch setup takes place through your Web browser.

When the service technician sets up your computer, he installed a network address in Windows that identified your computer to your ISP. What you have to do is take this same address and transfer it to your firewall, so that the address will come to represent the firewall *instead* of your computer.

So you start by going into Windows to retrieve this information. From your Network Control Panel, at the top of the dialog box, look toward the bottom of the list for an entry that begins "TCP/IP →", followed by the brand name of your NIC card that you installed (following the instructions in Chapter 22). This entry *will not say* "Dial-Up Adapter." Choose this entry, then click on Properties.

In the TCP/IP Properties dialog box, click on the DNS Configuration tab. Then on a piece of paper, copy down exactly what it says in the boxes marked Host and Domain. Next, click on the WINS Configuration tab, and make sure the option marked "Use DHCP for WINS resolution" is set. If it isn't, set it, then click on OK, click on OK again, and let your computer reboot. Otherwise, click on Cancel, then click on Cancel—you don't need to change anything else here. By the way, DHCP stands for Dynamic Host Configuration Protocol ... which is a better way of saying, "Plug-and-Play for IP hosts."

Bring up your Web browser, and in its Address box, type the Web-like address for your firewall. You'll find it in your manual, although it's generally http://192.168.1.1. You'll be asked for a username and password. Since this is the first time you've used your firewall device, leave Username blank, and under Password, type **admin**, then click on OK. (You'll want to change this username and password later, to prevent possible break-ins from the *inside*.)

Look for a field marked Router Name, then type into that field the name you copied from the Host box in Windows. Next, look for a field marked Domain Name, then type into that field the name you copied from the Domain box in Windows. Toward the bottom of the page should be a button marked Apply or OK. Click on it. Then to be safe, reboot your computer.

When your computer comes back up, try out your Web browser. You should be able to pull up your home page.

The Least You Need to Know

➤ If you opt for an internal phone modem, make sure that you have a free slot, hopefully away from noisy devices like your hard disk or the power supply.

➤ If you buy an external modem instead, make sure you have a serial port available, and be sure to purchase an RS-232 serial cable with which to connect it.

➤ Error correction is the method by which the modem can detect errors in transmission. Data compression is the method the modem uses to compress the data prior to transmitting it.

➤ If you use your home computer for business, or are simply online very frequently, you may be spending extra money for a second phone line. In which case, you could save money by chucking that second line and opting for a broadband connection.

➤ You do not have to be a cable TV subscriber, or even become one, to have cable modem service installed into your home. You should not be charged any extra fee for refusing cable TV service, although cable TV and cable modem are often bundled together for discounted prices.

➤ DSL is currently a marketing tool being used by established phone companies, as well as others that want to be phone companies, by offering you high-speed Internet plus telephone service (perhaps down the road) for bargain prices.

Chapter 14

I Can See Clearly Now: Upgrading Your Video

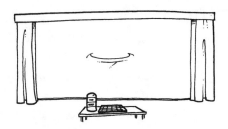

In This Chapter

➤ Pushing down on the graphics accelerator

➤ Sneaking a little *Days of Our Lives* onto your computer screen

➤ What's the deal with video memory these days?

➤ Capturing the moment with a video capture board

➤ Throwing your computer presentation onto the big screen

There are two pieces to your PC's video pie: the monitor itself (which was covered in Chapter 8, "The Easiest Things to Upgrade") and the video card. The monitor is in charge of displaying the best picture it can; it sets the upper limit of what you're going to see. The video card, on the other hand, assembles the image you want to display; it determines the level of detail and the color palette that the monitor can use. To get the best picture, these two parts need to work together.

In other words, if you have a lousy monitor, buying a super great video card isn't going to make you happy. On the other hand, you'll be equally displeased with the combination of a super expensive monitor and a dime-store video card. So match the capabilities of both to get the best results.

Shopping for a Video (Graphics) Card

The main thing to keep in mind when you shop for a new video card is that it must match the capabilities of your monitor. Otherwise, the card may not even work at all. To do that, you should look closely at the resolution capabilities and refresh rates of both the monitor and the video card.

The Funny Terms, and What They Really Mean

When you go shopping for a video card (sometimes called a graphics card, by the way), don't let all the techie terms throw you:

➤ **VGA (Video Graphics Array)**—VGA made its first appearance in 1987, making it possible for the first time for PC users to install a card that overrode the graphics on their motherboard, and projected 256 colors or shades of gray.

➤ **SVGA (Super Video Graphics Array)**—Essentially, the standard governing how graphics data is stored within the memory of every video card produced today. SVGA built onto VGA by adding the capability for the card to display more colors at higher *resolutions*. All new monitors sold today expect SVGA. When any new card you're investigating touts itself as "fully SVGA-compatible," you can say, "Duh." If it didn't fully support SVGA, it wouldn't work.

➤ **Accelerator**—This term has gradually become meaningless. All of today's video cards "accelerate," which means their on-board processors assume the responsibility of handling the video formerly relegated to the CPU (back when Poland was a Soviet satellite state). At one time, there was such a thing as a "graphics accelerator card," whose purpose was to accelerate the graphics coming from a separately installed video card. Such video cards required an on-board connection to the accelerator, facilitated by a ribbon cable installed inside the PC. The existence of such a connection automatically dates your video card. When a modern video card touts itself as an "accelerator" (or even an "accelerater"), just treat that term as a little marketing embellishment (or "embellishmint").

➤ **3D rendering**—A majority of video cards manufactured today contain a processor capable of producing images of shapes, environments, and landscapes. These cards do not automatically create the illusion of depth. But special routines embedded in the processors can create life-like effects such as realistic lighting with shading and shadows, fog, smoke, haze, motion blurs—all of which can give your games, or whatever work you may be doing that requires these routines … ah, the heck with it! We know what these routines are for. They enhance your *games!* There, I said it. Anyway, because 3D rendering has become so commonplace, only the lowest-priced video cards currently available *fail* to have any 3D rendering hardware on-board, and it's no longer considered a "premium" feature.

➤ **pixel**—The smallest visible point on-screen that a video card can render, given its current resolution setting.

➤ **texel**—Short for "textured element." When a video card is rendering a 3D landscape, it perceives its world as though it were projecting a truly three-dimensional display. Of course, monitors are two-dimensional displays (though some video cards do offer 3D glasses that give their output the illusion of three dimensions). In this 3D world, a texel is the smallest point that the card can consider in its own memory. Generally this point lies on the surface of an object it's plotting, such as the side of a wall, or the T-shirt worn by a character in a video game. In terms of visibility, a texel may be smaller than a pixel, and thus you might not be able to see it … if that texel were the only element the card was plotting. But in the context of the larger landscape, each texel plays a role. The performance of a 3D video card is measured either in texels per second, or texels per clock cycle—the video card's clock, not your computer's. Generally, video cards have a 200MHz clock.

Your Choices, in a Nutshell

When a PC manufacturer shows off his computer to you in the store—how fast it is, how resplendent its graphics are, and all the fireworks it's capable of displaying—many times, what he's really showing off is the video card. Today, a video card is a computer unto itself. It has its own BIOS, and its chipset (which it has come to be called) runs its own internal system bus for memory, has its own central processor and co-processor for particular graphics routines. In many low-end computers, the video card is theoretically a more capable computer than the motherboard.

For this reason, among others, a video card costs anywhere from $22 to $600. You can find one with fabulous features for under $100, and $100 is the average price for a video card nowadays. But $600? What does somebody get for that price? The answer is generally: An extremely fast graphics processor, coupled with as much as 2GB of video RAM, resulting in the capability to produce 3D scenes in 1600h × 1200v resolution (which, of course, requires a large and expensive CRT monitor) at about 75 frames per second (fps).

What does one sacrifice when going with the $22 model? Usually, the bottom of the line is limited to a resolution no higher than 800h × 600v, which on a large monitor (17" diagonal or higher) can look pretty blocky. Speed is another factor; the least expensive video cards are *appreciably* slower than the average-price cards. What you save in dollars up front, could be spent down the road in minutes. As fast as your PC is today, why introduce a new bottleneck into your system?

So what can you get for a hundred dollars? Expect 32MB of on-board 128-bit video RAM (most SDRAMs on your motherboard use 32-bit memory), resolution that can exceed most monitors's capabilities (for instance, 2048h × 1536v), AGP 4x (which means, support for clock-quadrupled AGP processing, if your motherboard supports it as well), and a more-than-adequate 3D processor that supports Microsoft's DirectX standard (more on that in a bit). That's quite a lot for $100, and most general users will be quite satisfied.

How AGP Changes the Equation

The Accelerated Graphics Port (AGP) is Intel's new architecture for a direct bus between the CPU and the graphics processor. The purpose of AGP is to allow the graphics controller to access the CPU directly, bypassing the peripheral bus, so graphics can be displayed on your monitor more quickly. That said, you may still need a video card to provide dedicated memory for 3D graphics and other operations, to work hand-in-hand with AGP. For AGP to work, your computer must have a Pentium II motherboard whose chipset and BIOS support AGP, plus AGP processors on the motherboard, Windows 95 OSR2 or later, and either a video card that supports AGP or a motherboard that has AGP processors built-in, and that uses system RAM as its memory.

By Intel's granting AGP direct access to the system bus, it's able to utilize the same main memory bank the CPU uses for other purposes, rather than set aside its own dedicated memory. That said, AGP-compliant video cards set aside dedicated video memory all the time. Why? Because it's just faster. The allocation of resources in main memory is generally managed by Windows, and having video RAM be set aside in a separate pile effectively takes Windows out of the loop.

So why have the AGP port in the first place? It gives the CPU a direct line to the video processor. When the CPU is tackling a tough job—for instance, plotting the placement and color of individual pixels which, when seen from a comfortable distance, represent a sphere with a photograph mapped onto its surface, such as a map of the world—the CPU would normally have to make several types of calculations and decisions, tens of thousands of times in succession. Specialized video hardware takes that load off of the CPU, and performs these redundant tasks using specialized tricks not required for any other form of mathematical processing. The CPU is left free to do other things.

The lowest of the low-end Slimline form factor PCs utilize 100 percent of Intel's original AGP design, in which the system RAM and the video RAM are the same RAM. At one time, this was foreseen as an advancement in the way PCs could work. But in 1998, even the most common graphics cards started rendering graphics using dedicated memory designed with a greater number of bits per word (64, and later 128) than the 32-bit RAM used by the system bus. So even though Intel opened up a direct pipeline to system RAM with AGP, by the time that feature was ready to be shipped, few wanted it.

Recent advances in video processing not only enabled, but *necessitated*, increases in graphics bandwidth. Originally, AGP was designed to use the system bus clock, which in 1999 was maximized at 66MHz. (As Chapter 10 points out, system busses have exploded in speed since them.) This gives "AGP 1x" an effective bandwidth of 254.3MB/s (megabytes per second, assuming the old 8-bits-per-byte definition). If your motherboard supports AGP 2x, its throughput is doubled for every clock tick, effectively doubling its bandwidth to 508.6 MB/s. AGP 4x doubles that yet again to 1,017MB/s.

What do I mean by "bandwidth" in this respect? AGP facilitates a pipeline between the memory and processors in your video card, and your CPU. Your video card needs to be able to take your graphics data as fast as your CPU can pump it out. Broadening the bandwidth fattens the pipe, if you will.

NVIDIA, Oh NVIDIA, Say Have You Met NVIDIA ...?

Intel has always been the dominant force in the production of CPUs, having fended off challenges from IBM twice in its history, and facing its toughest threat yet from AMD today. What Intel has always been for CPUs, a company called NVIDIA (pronounced "en-*VID*-ee-uh") has become for graphics processing.

NVIDIA does not make graphics cards; it doesn't have to. Its trademark ends up stamped on a vast majority of the cards in production today, the same way "Intel Inside" became a feature of computers Intel never saw before. In a realm of business where small fish can very well gobble up bigger ones, NVIDIA has, through creative and selective consumption and digestion of its competition, become the world's dominant graphics semiconductor company in just two short years. In its wake, NVIDIA has left the rubble of some once-towering trademarks. NVIDIA absorbed 3dfx, maker of the pioneering Voodoo rendering standard. S3, once the leading manufacturer of mainstream graphics chips, ended up being scared out of the market altogether, acquiring Diamond Multimedia (a video card manufacturer), changing the combined company's name to SonicBlue, and surrendering its S3 graphics patents.

Today, NVIDIA's closest competition is perceived to come from SiS, which made its name in the motherboard chipset industry; and Trident, the long-time producer of reliable, low-end video cards. ATI, a manufacturer of video cards, produces its own RADEON chipset for its own models, but has been having a hard time keeping up in the performance department this past year. None of these competitors is seen as having much of a chance to topple NVIDIA from its current perch.

NVIDIA's processors are sold to, and resold by, both small and large video card manufacturers. In many cases, the presence of the NVIDIA chipset (again, usually a set of one) determines most of what you need to know about the video card's performance. Intel produces Pentiums and Celerons; AMD produces Athlons and Durons. Here are the graphics processors in NVIDIA's current product line:

➤ **GeForce 3** is, incidentally, the graphics processor chosen by Microsoft to serve at the core of its new Xbox video game. This processor uses 128-bit DDR memory for 256-bit graphics, with total throughput at a rate of 800 billion operations per second. The on-board processors have special routines for providing simulated texture to such objects as slime, fire, ice, and skin. An entry-level card with GeForce 3 generally features 64MB of DDR memory minimum, and AGP 4x support. It sells for about $350.

➤ **GeForce 2** is currently divided into four subcategories: from least to most expensive, MX, GTS, Pro, and Ultra. You'll find the GeForce 2 MX on the standard $100 video card. Since NVIDIA uses different standards of measurement for GeForce 3 and GeForce 2, it's difficult to measure the two series against each other for raw performance. Some say the GeForce 2 Ultra, with its 250MHz clock and one-gigapixel-per-second throughput rate, is faster at some operations than GeForce 3. However, the overall rendering quality of GeForce 3 is very noticeably superior. In some gaming environments, however—where, for instance, you've infiltrated the secret hiding place of World Government Headquarters tunneled 1200 miles below a used car auction house in Sausalito—realism may not be an absolute requirement. GeForce 2 cards also use 128-bit DDR memory and AGP 4x, though entry level cards often start with 32MB and work up from there in powers of 2.

➤ **TNT2** was once a competitor with 3dfx's Voodoo standard, but is now being positioned as a "business" (low-cost) graphics processor. ("Hey, check out the texels on that spreadsheet!" … *Not!*) It's currently being phased out, although you'll find decent video cards featuring TNT2 selling for $40–$60.

Video cards with the same NVIDIA processors and the same amount of on-board memory can have prices that vary wildly from one another. A major brand can cost twice as much as a minor brand. But is the performance of the major brand that much better? Sometimes not. So what is it that you're paying for? Look closely at the boxes and the advertising, and you'll notice that major brands of video cards often include much, much more "free" software—mostly games, most of them not even first-run releases. Quite often, the price difference between the major brand *with* the free software, and the minor brand *without* it, is greater than the cost of the games themselves sold separately.

But couldn't there still be a performance difference in the major brands? Not if you use the right drivers. Some minor brands do take the time to create their own video drivers for their cards … and some fail quite miserably. But if they have NVIDIA processors on board, you have a free option that really is free: NVIDIA produces "generic" drivers under the Detonator brand name that are downloadable for free from its corporate Web site: www.nvidia.com. Since NVIDIA is the first to discover new features in, and correct newly discovered problems with, its own brand of processors, the Detonator drivers are often the best drivers you can use for *any* product that uses NVIDIA processors, including the major brands. So you can opt for a low-cost brand like ASUS (which makes its name in motherboards, not video cards) and get much the same performance as, if not better than, a high-end retail product. Install the Detonator drivers, and you have the fastest video card you can buy for the money, *without* the glitzy software, and having saved as much as a hundred bucks.

Check This Out

If you don't think you need 3D video for the work you do ... then do yourself a favor and get it anyway. Why? Because video cards that don't have 3D video also don't have a lot of other things, such as high-bandwidth video memory. It just so happens that *all* of the video chipsets that can manage 128-bit memory at 200MHz or 250MHz, also have 3D rendering. If you sacrifice the 3D video, even though the work you do isn't 3D (or sometimes even 1D, you might think), you'll have a much slower computer, which is not what you want. A GeForce 2 chipset gives you very fast video memory, and 32MB is an adequate amount, even though you'll notice the speed difference with 64. If you don't need 3D, don't go all out for a GeForce 3 card. GeForce 3 is easy to avoid; just don't buy anything over $300.

Microsoft's DirectX Graphics Standard

If you have the first edition of Windows 98 or any later version of Windows, you have graphics software in your computer that Microsoft, for whatever reason, called "DirectX." (You get the feeling that they don't play Scrabble fairly over there in Redmond, probably attaching "X" to things just to get Triple Word Score.) If you have Windows 95, you can download the DirectX drivers from Microsoft free, at www.microsoft.com/directx.

So what is DirectX? It's software that enables programs to plot graphics in such a way that they don't require windows (small "w"). Normally, everything in the Windows environment is drawn in some kind of window—be it an application window, a dialog box, or a control. Even a push-button is considered a window by Windows. But with DirectX, Windows can "layer" any kind of graphics over, on top of, behind, or in place of all the devices on your Windows desktop.

If you've ever used the shareware music player program Winamp, you've seen a prime example of a DirectX device at work. Winamp is a "skinnable" program whose appearance can be changed to any of hundreds of thousands of designs, most submitted by freelance artists and Winamp users. The point is, Winamp doesn't look like Microsoft Windows, and some say that's one of the program's blessings. Winamp uses DirectX to look any way it wants to look.

Computer games use DirectX in order for you to be able to play them inside the Windows environment. DirectX is why you no longer have to "Exit to DOS" to play

315

games. Any game can display a full screen without the title bar and scroll bar along the sides. The rest of Windows and its applications will ignore your game's existence, or at least try to.

What makes DirectX important in graphics processing is this: A video card that supports DirectX directly can take over the processing of certain graphics from the software running in your CPU, and instead process it much faster, and much richer, using its own internal hardware. DirectX has software that renders graphics on your screen; but unlike any other piece of software ever written, *if DirectX is fully supported by your hardware, that software becomes mostly unnecessary,* except for the fact that it recognizes the superior hardware and passes control of processing over to it directly. A video card that advertises "DirectX acceleration" is one that supports this type of handoff.

MPEG Decoders

Historically, in order for your DVD-ROM player to let your PC play movies, you've needed a piece of hardware called an *MPEG decoder*—and, just as historically, this has been a separate device from your PC's video card. For a separate MPEG decoder card, a patch cord is used to intercept the image emerging from your video card, and then amend it by superimposing your movie on top of it.

Generally, it's up to your DVD-ROM driver software to let you into your full movie screen, in order that you can resize it to one corner of your monitor so you can work in the other corner. This is because your DVD player is not a window—in fact, Windows doesn't even know it's there. But can't you just watch your movie inside an ordinary Windows window? Perhaps. You're not really supposed to be able to, but the only thing *technically* stopping you from doing this are legal restrictions. Companies don't want you to be able to play DVD movies *on* your computer, because if you could do that, you could just as easily *copy* these movies using a DVD-RAM drive.

There's nothing illegal about watching a movie that you own, so the law, in truth, says there's nothing that anyone can do to impose restrictions on how you legally watch a movie you own. For this reason, many video cards on the market today, including ATI's RADEON models and many others with NVIDIA processors, include built-in MPEG-2 decoder hardware. In their software bundles, you'll find included real DVD movie player software, which displays DVD movies in a little window.

Now, the quality of these in-window DVD players may vary, and may not be as smooth or as spectacular as you'll find with the MPEG-2 decoder cards. On the other hand, if you really do want to watch a movie while you work, you want to be able to control where that movie is, and to pause it when you need to. So it could be a worthwhile tradeoff.

Whatever Happened to Adding Memory?

With nearly all video cards produced since 1999, the following fact is true: You can't add memory. Why the heck not? Because of a strange trick of economics. Video cards use 128-bit video RAM manufactured exclusively for them. These days, this memory is *surface mounted* onto the card—it's permanent, and doesn't have a socket. But that's not the economic trick. If video RAM were upgradable, the card would need a socket. Which means, video RAM would need to be produced in a form factor that fits into such a socket—namely, as an old-style DIP chip with the bendy tin legs. For a memory manufacturer to be able to provide video RAM in a DIP form factor, that same manu-facturer would have to pass the cost of that second package on to the buyer of the surface-mount form factor—which, in turn increases the price of the overall card. But that's not all. For video RAM to be cheap, it has to be mass-produced. Which means enough consumers need to demand not just the same form factor, but the same chip.

Despite how many video cards there are in the world, there isn't enough demand for video RAM in DIP packages to keep the price of a *chip* sufficiently below the total price of the entire *card*. In other words, it's cheaper to buy a new card with more total RAM than it is to upgrade that card with just half as much more RAM. For that rea-son, video RAM is no longer widely available.

Performing Video Card Surgery

Removing and inserting your video card is similar to working with any other card in your PC. If you want step-by-step instructions, see Chapter 12, "Face the Interface," for help.

Inserting the Video Card

After you've installed any memory upgrades, reinsert the video card following the steps outlined in Chapter 12, but with one small exception: Your AGP video card will have a little "key" along the bottom corner opposite the metal brace. So you need to insert your AGP card a little on a diagonal, so the key notch fits into the socket side-ways.

Connect the monitor to the card and turn the PC on to test your connection. If every-thing works right, turn the PC back off and put its cover back on. Now you need to install your *driver;* you'll find this on the diskette that came with the video card. The driver is the program that helps your PC talk to the video card so that it can translate its signals properly for the monitor. If you need help installing the driver, see Chap-ter 24.

Removing the Video Card

A PCI video card is removed exactly the same way as any other PCI card, as outlined in Chapter 12. For an AGP card, there's a small difference: Because there's a key-like notch along the bottom card edge, you can't pull the card straight up and expect it to slide right out. Instead, you need to pull slightly more on the metal brace side (after you've removed the screw, of course), and lift up on a slight diagonal until the card rotates out of position.

Mistakes to Avoid

If you are always adjusting the size and position of the onscreen image, there may be something wrong with the timing of your graphics card. You can usually adjust this timing like this: Go into your Display Control Panel, and from the Settings tab, click on the Advanced button. Your specific video driver will dictate what you see next, but look for an Adapter tab. Your timing settings should be located there. Try setting your video for Optimal and see what happens; if the picture's lousy, wait a few seconds, and it will go back like it was. Then try for *lower* refresh rates until your problem clears up. If it doesn't clear up, start suspecting your monitor.

If your screen seems to flicker, the problem could be that the refresh rate is set too low. Sometimes, however, you have to change to a lower resolution (for instance, down to 800 × 600 from 1,024 × 768) to get a higher refresh rate. Check your monitor's manual for details.

While you're looking at your Advanced settings, make sure that Windows has the correct monitor type listed. If not, your video card may think your monitor is more limited in its refresh/resolution settings than it actually is.

If you use Windows and you're having a reoccurring problem with your video, such as the system locking up, or a junky display, you may have an outdated video driver. Check on the Internet with the card's manufacturer for an update, or check with NVIDIA if you have a card with an NVIDIA processor. Oftentimes, the drivers supplied with a card you buy off the shelf, will be older than the newest drivers available.

Your video card will have its own cooling fan. This is because graphics processors can run very, very hot—hotter than even CPUs. If your video card fan does not come on, power down your PC and unplug the card. Check out the fan's little power plug, which is a small, thin double-cord that plugs directly into a header on the card itself. This cord should be plugged in at all times; there's no reason to disconnect it unless you need to change the fan. Chapter 20, "Cooling and Ventilating Your System," goes into more detail about taking care of your fan.

The Long-Awaited Marriage of TV and PC

What can you do with your PC and your TV together? There are some practical applications: With a video capture card, you can acquire moving images with sound and edit them with PC software. Then with TV output on your video card, you can send the edited image back to your VCR. Your PC has become a digital TV mixing studio, giving you the capability to add elegance and music to those movies you took of your family vacation or your wedding. Not a bad mix. But you need both *input* and *output* channels to be enabled. The rest of this chapter explains both.

Adding TV Input to Your PC

TV input is a feature in some video cards that enables them to display TV images on-screen, either full-screen or in a window. If you like to keep tabs on CNN or C-SPAN or even the weekly soaps, you can do it without leaving your precious PC. You can also use one of these cards to capture live video images from the TV input—albeit, as fixed, still images. (To be able to capture full-motion video, see the section on video capture boards coming up.) Some video cards combine the features of a sound card with TV input. In addition, a lot of cards allow you not only to watch TV, but also to listen to FM radio—your choice.

Adding PC Output to Your TV

With the TV *output* feature of some video cards, you can send what's normally displayed on your PC monitor to a television screen, enabling you to present your data to a larger audience. The bundled software includes a PC-to-TV scan converter, allowing you to give dynamic, multimedia presentations anywhere, even in a client's office. Granted, this feature is probably more useful on a notebook PC, but if you use your computer in a classroom setting, suddenly you have a low-cost projection system. Top-of-the-line cards will also include remote control hardware, enabling you to zoom in, pan, and freeze particular parts of your presentation through an infrared input device built into the card.

Adding a Video Capture Device

With a video capture device, you can acquire and edit still images and full-motion video from a video source (such as your video camera, or the TV) or capturing full-motion video, with sound. With the best of these devices, you can edit the video on your PC—clip out the parts you don't need, put all the scenes together in sequence, and even add fancy titles. You can then output the result from your PC, back to video tape! The result no longer looks like it belongs in a "rough cut" music video, but has professional flare and even possibly background music.

Microsoft Windows Me now comes complete with its own video editing program, called Windows Movie Maker. Chances are, you'll never use it. The reason is, Windows can't capture movies without a capture device. And capture devices generally come complete with much, much better video-editing software.

Pinnacle Systems manufactures a video capture device with editing software, which sells for $129. It is not a card, nor does it have one. Its main hardware resides in its own case, and a cable plugs it directly into your parallel (printer) port or one of your USB ports. This is how the video signal gets from the device to the PC with reasonable speed. Another set of cables connects the opposite end of the device to a video source, such as your camcorder. Using the direct control cable of the camcorder, the video editing software can have the camcorder stop, rewind, fast forward, play, and pause. So you can control the entire operation from your desktop, rather than fiddling with your camcorder. Or if your video source is a VCR, which does not have a direct control cable, then (get this!) one end of this same cable has an infrared sending unit. If you point this unit directly at your VCR, it can be programmed to work like your VCR's own remote control. So you can control the VCR from your desktop, borrowing its own infrared control system.

I broke down and bought this unit, and I've had the most fun with it. It's exceptionally well designed, and has failsafes I'd appreciate finding in my word processor! I've edited some family videos with it, and my brother—who is a professional news videographer—has produced a few of his own gems with this thing. Again, this is not a paid endorsement. Just check out www.pinnaclesys.com and see what you think for yourself.

One final note: Many people invest in a high-quality video capture device, and a graphics card that outputs to a TV or VCR, only to forget that the best movies (at least, the best ones produced in the last 70 years) have sound. Video cards have nothing to do with sound. To use your computer to capture, digitally edit, and output to video tape a movie that has sound, you need a more-than-adequate *sound card* to handle the job of processing the sound. An ordinary 8-bit beepity-beep-beep sound card made for such games as "Dueling Fat Worms" will not be appropriate. As long as you're making the investment, you may as well look into a good wavetable sound card (see Chapter 15, "Sensational Stereophonic Sound," for details).

The Least You Need to Know

➤ When choosing a new video card, make sure that it will work well with your monitor. Compare resolutions and refresh rates.

➤ A "3D" video card contains special hardware with programming that renders detailed graphic images of animated, textured *things* at incredible speeds.

➤ Microsoft's DirectX helps establish the software/hardware connection between your applications (or games) and your video hardware.

➤ AGP video cards plug into their own exclusive slots, in order to take advantage of your motherboard's direct graphics support. Your BIOS will determine the clock speed multiplier; AGP 2x will enable throughput at double the rate of the system bus speed, and AGP 4x will quadruple throughput.

➤ The video card is fast becoming its own computer. The acknowledged leader in the production of video card chipsets (processors) is NVIDIA, which produces and resells its GeForce 2 and GeForce 3 series to video card manufacturers.

➤ Memory is no longer an upgradable part of video cards. It's easier and cheaper to replace the card than it is to make video RAM upgradable.

Chapter 15

Sensational Stereophonic Sound

In This Chapter

➤ Shopping for a great sound card

➤ 3D audio and why it's suddenly a hot item

➤ The best speakers money (and more of it) can buy

➤ How to install the darn things

There are two tiers of sound card technology: The more affordable versions provide good quality sound for casual use, such as playing CD-ROM games and audio CDs. The more expensive sound cards appeal to the true sound artist, such as a musician, or to the multimedia maniac. In this chapter, you'll learn how to find the ultimate sound card for your needs.

Sound Card Standards

You need to make sure that your sound card is compatible with the programs you want to run it with. "Sound Blaster" compatibility is no longer the guarantee of conformance and acceptability that it used to be back when the operating system didn't know a sound card from a postcard. Today, compatibility in the sound card arena means, "It works with Windows." This is not to speak ill of Creative (formerly Creative Labs), the company responsible for Sound Blaster. They created a standard for sound card operability back at a time when such a thing didn't appear necessary.

Making Sounds

The capabilities of sound cards are no longer determined by the number of bits in one of its bytes. The older 16-bit sound cards are still available, but are rapidly being phased out. Almost all sound cards produced today have 32-bit sound, which is the equivalent of what the digital signal processor in any CD player uses. It won't go any higher than 32; it doesn't need to.

What distinguishes sound cards today is the number of *voices* it supports—how many distinct sounds it can produce at any one time. While sound cards just a few years ago were limited to 16 voices, today, the bottom-of-the-line sound card supports about 32, the midrange cards support about 100, and the top of the line 512.

Nearly all sound cards today utilize *wave table synthesis* to produce their various voices. Stored in the memory of each of these cards is a large table of exact digitized waveform samples for various sounds. A sample note is taken from an instrument, and then stored in a table as a digitized waveform. These waveforms are exact duplicates of their real-life sounds, so a wave table sound card reproduces sound more accurately than the older sound cards that used only pure FM synthesis. (Some sound cards are wave table upgradeable, which allows you the freedom of upgrading them later on, when you have more cash.)

The best-sounding (thus most expensive) sound cards support several wave tables for different octave ranges, so synthesized instruments sound more true-to-life. In other words, the best wave table sound cards contain multiple tables with several samples from each instrument, instead of just one.

Music in Games and Instruments

If you want to play games and really hear the music, make sure that your sound card is General *MIDI*-compatible. General MIDI is what most games require for the background music. Incompatibility with General MIDI makes a lot of high-end sound cards not suitable choices for game use. You might be surprised to learn that an expensive sound card, when playing the soundtrack of a game programmed just for Sound Blaster compatibility, may sound like an elementary school band practice session. You might also be interested in whether or not your sound card has a game port—a place into which you can plug a game control such as a joystick.

A digital electronic instrument is a MIDI device, such as an electronic keyboard, that supports the MIDI (Musical Instrument Digital Interface) standard. MIDI enables an electronic musical instrument to communicate with your digital computer. You can use your computer to compose a musical score with multiple instruments, and your MIDI instrument set can play it. Not all sound cards support MIDI, but those that do require a weird cabling contraption called a *break out box* that involves commandeering the joystick port. Look for "General MIDI 2" a revision to the old standard that enables 32-note polyphony and 16 channels (thus two simultaneous notes per instrument when all possible instruments are playing). While you're at it, keep your eye open for "DLS extensions," which enable *downloadable sounds*—instrument wave tables or samples that can be downloaded over the Internet and plugged into the MIDI device through software.

Is There Such a Thing As 3D Audio?

Chapter 14, "I Can See Clearly Now: Upgrading Your Video," spent a few paragraphs dealing with the demystification and subsequent re-mystification of 3D video. Even if you're blessed with two ears, you may not fully appreciate the dimensionality of sound as much as of sight.

As is the case with 3D video, the game or music program you use will need to explicitly support 3D audio. Microsoft's DirectX multimedia drivers (part of all versions of Windows since Win98) do provide limited 3D sound, although they're not as crisp as the standards being tossed about these days by the sound card manufacturers. Creative's standard, EAX, is presently proprietary; it isn't sharing this one with its competitors. Meanwhile, the A3D standard, advanced by a company called Aureal, is the one supported by the group unofficially known as "everyone except Creative." I have heard both, enough to know that the factors that distinguish them are only visible to the eyes of the programmer, not the ears of the listener … if you will. A third standard is being introduced by a British company called Sensaura—a division of EMI, which is the inventor of stereo in the first place. The Sensaura standard promises to be crystal-sharp … and, at least for the time being, somewhat more expensive.

One of the most important things you should know about 3D audio is that it cannot create dimensional effects for existing musical tracks, such as MP3 files or CD audio tracks. However, there are audio files—especially DVD video soundtracks—that do utilize 3D sound. That sound is reproduced with Dolby Digital, which is a feature of many digital sound systems (more on that little appliance shortly). But even digital soundtracks do not directly benefit from a sound card's 3D audio capabilities.

What 3D audio standards actually do is make the sound that is generated spontaneously from games and other programs sound as though they belong to the environment depicted by the 3D video. For instance, suppose your game features rustling trees. If the wind kicks up, and you're passing by the right of the tree, you'll want to hear the rustling pass behind you on the left side. Or if you're simulating an aircraft, and one of your right engines gets blown apart, you'll want to hear the explosion on your right side. 3D audio could enhance the effect by making the aircraft creaking noises shudder as though they were being generated by the entire fuselage.

Some Terms You'll See As You Shop

Here are some other terms you'll encounter while shopping for your sound card:

➤ **Digital Signal Processor (DSP)**—The on-board chip that performs the task of rendering sound waves (or any type of waveform, for that matter) in a format most closely approximating analog, or true-to-life, sound. Your sound card has

323

the DSP chip that your CD-ROM drive lacks; without the sound card, you could not hear your audio CD through your speakers.

➤ **Audio line input**—A special input jack for recording sound off of a stereo, TV, VCR, or from your PC. This is not the same as a microphone input, which is usually monophonic and not stereophonic.

➤ **Full duplex**—In the context of sound cards, this implies simultaneous capability to input and play sound.

➤ **Voice**—A nice term for *oscillator*, which is the device that produces the tones used in the composition of parts (instruments) on a sound card. The more the better. Generally, for wave table cards, one voice corresponds to one "part"— such as one instrument or one source of noise. Be careful, though, as some sound cards will combine multiple voices per part, for instruments that sound more realistic, at the expense of timbrality.

➤ **Polyphony**—The number of notes a card can play at the same time. Consider a barbershop quartet "four-tone polyphony."

➤ **Timbrality**—The number of different voices that a sound card can play at the same time. Six-voice timbrality can reproduce orchestral sound. Consider a string quartet "four-voice timbrality," especially because each instrument in that quartet is capable of playing more than one note simultaneously.

➤ **Total harmonic distortion**—The amount of distortion (noise) level that occurs when a sound is amplified. When judging both your sound card and your speakers, look for .1 percent (.001) or less.

Installing Your Sound Card

All sound cards produced today are Plug-and-Play devices. What this is supposed to mean is that they are no longer dependent on you to determine which settings your card should use by finding out which settings all your other cards and devices use. These little wars are now negotiated by computer, every time you turn them on. Which means you should only worry about things when you smell smoke.

I knew it, you smell smoke. That's normal. "Smoke" is the Official Scent of Plug-and-Play Technology. There can be as many as three principal settings which Windows must negotiate and assign for your sound card to work: Its designated interrupt (IRQ), which tells it in which order the CPU recognizes it on the peripheral bus; its Direct Memory Access (DMA) channel number, which gives the card direct access to data stored in system RAM; and the Input/Output (I/O) address ranges, which tell the CPU where the firmware programs installed on your card begin.

You are not supposed to have to know about these three things. However, I just told you about them, first of all, because I've worked with computers for a while and I know better. But secondly, because you don't actually have to fiddle with these settings anymore *before* you install your sound card. Instead, you may have to fiddle with them *afterward*.

When you're ready to install your card, skip back to Chapter 12, "Face the Interface," for details of how to insert a PCI card in its expansion slot. If you're connecting an optical drive (CD-ROM or DVD-ROM) to your sound card, plug its connector cable into the correct slot on the card. Keep in mind that many cards come with several connectors, one for each of the specific types of drives they support. These different connectors are usually well marked so that you can't make much of a mistake, but check with the manual if you're not sure which one to use. You'll also want to connect the optical drive's audio cable to the sound card. See Chapter 18, "Adding an Optical Drive," if you want more help with your CD-ROM drive.

Your sound card typically comes with several outside connectors: a microphone connector, a headphone connector, an external speaker connector, and a joystick or MIDI connector (see Figure 15.1). First, connect your two speakers. If your speakers come with two strands of speaker wire, use one strand to connect one speaker to the other speaker, and another to connect the right speaker to the sound card. If you instead have one strand of speaker wire with a connector in the middle, connect the middle part to the right speaker, one end to the other (left) speaker, and the other end to the sound card. If you want to connect your sound card to your home stereo, it's no trick, but you'll need an adapter that has a ⅛-inch mini stereo connector at one end (to fit your sound card) and regular RCA sound plugs at the other.

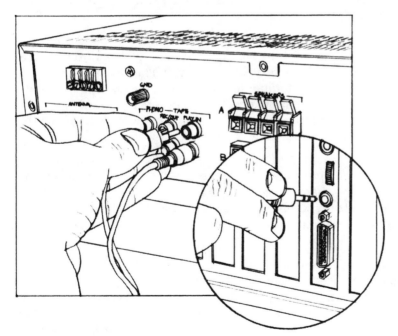

Figure 15.1

You can easily connect your sound card to your stereo system.

Now you can mess with the extras, such as a microphone (for recording all those wise tidbits you come up with every day) and a joystick or MIDI device. By the way, you can connect more than one MIDI device to your sound card by running the output of one device into the input of the previous one in the chain. MIDI devices connect to one another like SCSI devices, in a daisy-chain. So if you have a MIDI multi-timbre module, a MIDI sequencer, and a MIDI drum unit, you can connect them in a chain in any order using 5-pin DIN cable and then connect one end of the chain to the MIDI card.

After you connect your card, close up the PC and turn it on. Next, you need to run the sound card's setup program to install the card's device driver. The device driver, you may recall, is what allows the PC to communicate with the sound card. If you use any DOS games, you'll need to select your sound card from each game's own setup program. You'll have to do some messing around in Windows, too, if you use it. See Chapter 24, "Getting Windows to Recognize Your New Toys," for help in this department.

Mistakes to Avoid

The main problem you'll run into when you add a sound card to your system is IRQ, DMA, and I/O address conflicts. If you don't hear any sound, look in your Device Manager for "Sound, video, and game controllers." (Chapter 24 will show you how.) If you see an exclamation mark icon in a yellow triangle, you know that your computer also knows something's wrong.

So what's the mistake that you should avoid? Don't try to install the sound driver again until you've uninstalled the existing one. Choose the faulty driver from Device Manager, then click on Remove. Then reboot your computer. Plug-and-Play will try to recognize your sound card again. If you run into exactly the same problem a second time, then obviously Plug-and-Play doesn't know how to negotiate its way through a hardware setting discrepancy. Turn to Chapter 24 for help. But before you unplug that sound card, uninstall its driver a second time.

Many 16-bit sound cards prefer using DMA channels 5, 6, or 7. Others prefer DMA 3. For true Sound Blaster compatibility, you may want to use DMA 1. Sound cards with Sound Blaster 16 use two DMA channels, generally 0 and 3. The first is exclusively for the compatibility mode, while the second is for the card's native sound generator. When there's a conflict with the sound card's settings and the settings of other devices, you may get a parity error, or your PC may simply "lock up."

If you still can't hear the sound, make sure that your speakers are on, and that their batteries are working. Check the mixer program and make sure that the master volume is set high enough. In Windows, you can get to the master volume control by double-clicking the speaker icon on the taskbar. You can also test the volume by running the sound card's diagnostic program and playing a test sound file. If you bought cheap speakers, they might not be amplifying the sound enough. Try connecting the sound card to your stereo to see if that solves the problem. You could also try plugging some headphones into your sound card and bypassing the speakers altogether.

Check the cable that connects your speakers to the sound card. Make sure that you use a stereo speaker cable if your sound card is stereo. If you accidentally use a mono cable, you'll either get sound of low volume, or no sound at all.

If you get sound but it's scratchy, make sure that your sound card is not too close to the hard disk or the power supply. The signal that a sound card sends to your speakers is an analog signal, which is susceptible to radio frequency distortions. These are constantly created by things like your power supply, your hard disk drive, and a hyperactive dachshund on a really tight leash. You might also want to move your speakers farther away from your monitor; unless the speakers are shielded heavily against electrical interference, your monitor may be causing a disruption.

Sometimes your PC's BIOS may be the reason your sound card won't work, especially if it handles its DMA channel differently than your card expects. If the BIOS's DMA timing can be changed (slowed), this usually clears up the problem. You can get to this setting through your BIOS setup program. Time to call in the nerds (and Chapter 23, "Making Your Computer Boot Up Again") for help with this one.

Speakers of the House

For some users, the computer has become the central device in their stereo system. In other words, their stereo and their computers are the same cluster of components. This is due to the recent advent of so-called *digital sound systems* that can have as many as seven speakers (four quadraphonic main speakers plus two tweeters and a sub-woofer), and make use of a miniaturized amplifier component that resides outside of the computer. This amplifier receives inputs from multiple channels, including your computer, but also from your CD player (which may or may not be in your computer), your FM or digital radio, and your TV.

Digital sound systems provide such dazzlingly wonderful sonic experiences, that one wonders why a majority of most games produced today feature mainly macho guerilla warriors blowing stuff up with bazookas. Suppose they could use cellos instead, and the enemy could fight back with coronets?

Adequate Sound for Everyday Applications

The depth of sound from speaker to speaker varies a great deal. When shopping for a set of everyday stereo speakers for your computer, look at the frequency response range. This tells the range of high to low sounds the speaker can reproduce. The best speakers can reproduce a range close to that of human hearing (from 20Hz to 20kHz).

You should look at the total power wattage of the speakers, because the sound card produces a fairly weak signal that needs to be amplified before ordinary speakers will be able to reproduce it. Low-cost speakers offer only 4–7 watts, while mainstream PC stereo speaker sets offer as much as 100 watts of power output.

While I'm on the subject of power: The cheap speakers run off two or more lowly C batteries. You might want to seriously consider investing in an AC adapter, which will prevent unnecessary trips to the store when you're in the middle of an intense simulated airplane dogfight. Some speakers come with a built-in AC adapter plug.

Another feature to watch out for is the number and type of control knobs the speakers offer. Most come with a volume control, but the better ones also allow you to adjust the amount of bass, treble, and super bass (dynamic bass boost).

Adequate Sound for Pummeling the Intergalactic Scourge

Quality speakers, on the other hand, are powered by a separate ordinary electrical plug, and possibly a separate power supply. You might be surprised to learn that there are at least *three* speakers in a modern high-quality set. The third is a bass box, and you'll find its best location is *on the floor*, perhaps behind your desk. The bass box is also the home of the speaker set's power plant and amplifier. You'll want it on the floor not only because it gets one more cord out of your line of vision, but also because low frequency sounds resonate best using the floor as a sounding board. You'll be surprised; you won't need as much sound *volume* to appreciate a big, booming bass. The two other speakers in this set are not tweeters to the bass box's woofer, but are instead full-frequency range speakers. You'll be able to appreciate them best if you can place them *above* your head, perhaps in cabinets on either side of you.

Creative manufactures a five-speaker set for use with its EAX 3D sound cards. For this set to be fully appreciated, one pair of speakers should be mounted in front of you, the other behind you, and then the bass box should stay on the floor.

Be careful here: You could pay between $150 and $300 for high-end *speakers*—which is a heck of a lot more than you paid for your sound card.

Keep in mind that many speakers contain magnets to help create their sound. Make sure that your speakers have adequate protection around their magnetic parts, especially if you're going to put the speakers anywhere near your monitor, which is especially sensitive to magnetic fields. This warning applies to your diskettes, as well as other magnetic media.

The Least You Need to Know

➤ "The sound of an orchestra" can actually be several dozen simultaneous sounds, all playing in harmonic polyphony. If your games or other software generate fresh, new sound to go along with the environments they build for you, then you should consider investing in 100-voice polyphony or higher.

➤ There is such a thing as 3D audio, although you should listen for yourself to see if you can appreciate its aesthetic qualities in the game or other program (Who am I kidding? *What* other program?) that makes use of it.

➤ If you're going to invest in superior speakers, make certain the sound card you use can produce a fine, crisp, clear sound worthy of being amplified to a zillion watts per channel.

➤ 3D audio is a real feature that is best put to use with a superb set of at least three speakers.

➤ If you want a high-quality sound card, pay particular attention to voice, polyphony, and timbrality.

Chapter 16

Hands-On Hard Disk Replacement

In This Chapter

➤ IDE, SCSI, ESDI, and all the kids

➤ What to look for in a new hard disk

➤ Performing open PC surgery

The capacity of hard disk drives today is reaching almost mythical proportions—suddenly 60 gigabytes is commonplace! (Don't tell this to Microsoft, please.) Hard to believe what someone might do with that much room—that is, until you load a few programs on your own hard disk and discover you barely have enough room left over for your data.

Issues to Keep in Mind While Shopping

The absolute first bit of information you need to figure out is what kind of hard drive your PC currently has, and whether you plan on replacing it or simply adding another drive to your system. This is not something that either Windows or your BIOS can tell you, believe it or not; they're designed to perceive your hard drive as a generic device, not as a brand name. So they're not really Plug-and-Play devices, and probably shouldn't be, since we don't want to confuse Windows any more than it already is.

What Kind Is It?

So the first place to look for manufacturer information is on the drive itself, on a sticker that has the manufacturer's name, the drive's specifications, and its date of manufacture. This sticker may be located on the top of the drive, or on the rear next to the data connectors. If the sticker on the drive doesn't show its general specifications, at least you should be able to locate the brand name and model name. Go to the manufacturer's Web site and look for a model that has precisely the capacity of the drive on your system. (Windows Explorer will tell you your drive's capacity.) Nearly all reputable hard drive manufacturers keep extensive Web databases with all the important specifications for every drive they currently sell, and every one they've ever manufactured.

Why are these specifications so important? Well, the hard disk connects to a *drive controller*, and it's the controller's job to grab (read) data from the drive when the PC needs it. Likewise, the controller saves (writes) data to the drive when asked nicely. So your new hard disk will have to talk to this controller, because it's the controller's job to act as official interpreter between the PC and the hard disk. An IDE hard drive has its own drive controller, designed to connect to an *interface* on modern PC motherboards. All modern motherboards feature this interface. But a SCSI hard drive—which you may decide is worth the extra investment—needs a drive controller, to be purchased *separately*: namely, a SCSI host adapter card (see Chapter 12, "Face the Interface," for a discussion of that gizmo).

How Big Is It?

Size matters. Get the largest hard drive that you can afford. Studies show that, with the rate at which the sheer size of software is skyrocketing, you're better off with a hard disk that's three times larger than the one you're using now, however large that might be. Sound ridiculous? Not when you consider how much room most applications consume: anywhere from 40MB to 125MB *each*. And of course, if you create any data files at all with these programs, you'll use up even more space.

Another feature you might want to look for in your new hard drive is a cache (pronounced *cash*). This stores the frequently requested data close at hand in a small pocket of on-board memory, so the hard drive can get to it more quickly. SRAM is as useful for hard drive caches as it is for the L2 memory cache of your CPU.

How Cheap Is It?

Nowadays, hard drives are cheap. You can get a 20GB IDE hard drive for $100. New. But not for long, because guess what, it's going out of style; it's too *small*! Larger hard disks will generally cost you even less per megabyte, but watch for those situations where the more popular, higher-capacity model is marked down even less than the not-so-high-capacity model. Today, you should not have to pay more than $150 for a 40GB IDE hard drive. It's no joke.

Of the two competing types of hard drive interfaces, it is the IDE/ATA hard drive that has benefited the most from the price wars. SCSI, although still treading water, has not enjoyed the kind of price plummets in the last two years that IDE has seen, although it has slowly begun to catch up. Today, a 9GB SCSI hard drive costs the same $100 that the 20GB IDE drive costs; and although the SCSI drive's performance might be slightly greater, it might not be worth the reduction in capacity. (If you're wondering what all the alphabet soup in this paragraph means, I promise, I'll sort it all out for you in this very chapter.)

What Does It Come With?

Make certain you also purchase the cables you need to connect your hard drive as well. You may think that the cables come with the drive, but in many cases, they're an extra item. If you're adding a drive to your IDE channel, you may need a new cable that handles two drives if your existing one doesn't. If you're moving up to Ultra ATA/66 or Ultra ATA/100 (more on the alphabet soup in a bit), you'll need special cables that look the same as the old ones, but are specially suited for their lower voltage requirements. In addition, check to see if you need a power cable splitter (Y-adapter) for connecting the new drive to the power supply.

Check in advance to see whether your new drive has the mounting brackets you need to slide it into your chosen empty drive bay in your system case. For example, if the only open area in your system case is a 5¼" bay, you'll need a mounting bracket to make your new 3½-inch hard disk fit. A mounting bracket is another item that not all manufacturers include with their hard drive kits as standard equipment. If you need one, make sure that the kit has one or that you can get a hold of one; don't worry—they're cheap.

If you're adding a hard drive to a small system case such as a Slimline, chances are that you'll need to upgrade the power supply. Which really means you need a new system case with a power supply in it. Don't worry; it's cheaper to get the system case *with* the power supply than to get the power supply by itself (strange, but true). Keep this in mind before you start forking out big cash to upgrade something that's basically an antique. Chapter 21, "Classier Chassis: Consider a New System Case," goes into detail about making a new home for all your existing components.

You could choose to add an external hard drive, which is nice if you don't have any drive bays open, or you don't feel like messing around inside the PC. They cost a bit more, but it may be worth it. Most external hard drives connect through a parallel port, officially listed in the specs as IEEE-1284, in order to avoid having to say printer port. If you have a printer using your parallel port, you may need to add an I/O card that gives you an extra parallel and serial port (the ports, you recall, are the connectors on the back of your PC). Another option, if you're out of drive bays but you do have space in your machine, is an internal mounting bracket attachment. It literally hangs on something in your PC case and supports a 3½-inch drive mechanism. All PCs are fairly different from one another, so this option may not work in your PC, but hey, it's worth investigating.

Deciphering Hard Drive Characteristics

You have to digest a lot of letters and numbers when you take a close look at the specifications sheets for hard disk drives. Sometimes the Marketing Department has a way of fudging the numbers a bit so that slight advantages seem like great advantages, and slight inconveniences seem ... like great advantages. What this segment deals with are just the license-plate-looking terms that you actually need to know; if you ever run across some others, rest assured that you *don't* need to know them.

Interface Types

The two drive interfaces in wide use today have their own respective advantages and disadvantages, which is why neither has been able to knock the other completely out of the market just yet. When you purchase a new PC completely built and off-the-shelf, chances are that its hard disk and optical disc drives are connected to an IDE channel (also known as ATA and/or EIDE, for reasons I'll discuss momentarily). On the other hand, if you go into the offices of any large network administrator, you'll probably find that the drives used on the server system use the SCSI interface, or rather, one of the umpteen million forms of SCSI.

SCSI

The host adapter for the Small Computer Systems Interface (SCSI) can control several types of SCSI devices at once, including a hard disk, an optical drive, and a tape drive. Although they are widely considered to be the fastest, most reliable drives available, SCSI drives are much more expensive than IDE. Also, if you want to chain several SCSI devices (such as a hard disk, optical drive, and a backup cartridge) to your new SCSI host adapter, you may run into problems because a lot of SCSI devices are incompatible with one another—meaning, you might not be able to connect a SCSI optical drive *through* a SCSI hard drive to your computer. SCSI is discussed in greater detail in Chapter 12.

IDE and ATA and ATAPI and Ultra ATA (and Ted and Alice)

The term IDE is short for Integrated Drive Electronics, because the drive's controller is built into the drive itself. This is significant, because prior to the advent of IDE, the processor (specifically, the ST-506 chip) that controlled the connection between the motherboard and the hard drive was located on the motherboard. Some are under the impression that this is where the controller processor is now, because it seems only sensible; but in fact, when you think about it, if you really want to guarantee that a controller works with a drive, why not build them into the same device?

So why did this standard end up having so many names? When its creator, IBM, first proposed it to the American National Standards Institute (ANSI) for adoption as an international computing hardware standard, the name it came up with was the "AT Attachment Standard" or "ATA-4," the "AT" part referring to the IBM AT computer.

Western Digital ended up making the first drives designed to support the attachment standard, although it also actually came up with the idea of putting the controller on the drive rather than the motherboard. So it was Western Digital that came up with the trademark IDE, and thus the term competitors would use to describe their products that work the same way. IBM never specified where the controller went, just how it would work. Some competitors—particularly Seagate and Quantum—went on using the term ATA to describe their drives that use the interface, although other competitors—including Maxtor—used the term IDE to describe their drives that use the same controller technology. Then WD decided to stick with IBM's name for it (ATA) rather than its very own trademark, since WD wanted to promote the fact that it developed a world standard.

This course of events lasted until about 2000, when hard drive vendors began using the different flavors of "ATA" universally to refer to their models' respective bandwidths. You'd think WD would be pleased … or maybe not, since ATA wasn't really their idea; anyway, I'm about to lose track. This universal use of "ATA" caused Seagate and Maxtor (which acquired Quantum's hard drive business) to switch sides and start referring to "ATA" instead of "IDE."

Western Digital—never one to be mistaken for a company that does anything the way anyone else does it—responded by flip-flopping yet again, and now refers to its hard drives as "EIDE" drives—essentially IDE drives that support the four-devices-per-cable standard … that, by the way, no motherboard manufacturer actually uses. The extra "E" is there for show.

So because *you asked for it*, here are all the different names for IDE, and what they mean:

➤ **ATA**   The original name of the standard for the drive interface adopted by ANSI, based on the brand name for the interface suggested by IBM. Today, this term is used mostly with reference to hard disk drives, not optical disc drives.

➤ **IDE**   The first alternative name for the interface as intended by Western Digital, which wanted to promote the fact that it came up with the idea of integrating the controller into the drive assembly. Today, this term is used to describe optical drives—which, only a few years earlier, used the term "ATAPI," though their interface has not changed.

➤ **ATA-2**   The first enhancement to the ATA standard, which increased the maximum number of devices per channel from two to four. ATA-2 was the first to allow for *block mode transfers*—multiple read and write operations grouped together and sent as a collective message to the BIOS. Prior to ATA-2, whenever the BIOS received one of these so-called *interrupts* (literally a request to make a command, as in, "My apologies for bothering you at a time like this, but write this sector, right now, soldier, move, move, *move!*"), it could only respond by reading or writing a single sector of data to the disk. Now it can read or write as many as 32. ATA-2 also introduced *logical block mode addressing*, which freed the controller and the BIOS from always having to register regions of the hard drive in cylinders, heads, and sectors. This way, devices that are *not* hard drives don't have to pretend they *are* hard drives to get noticed. Finally, ATA-2 introduced a type of identity response system—a way for a drive to identify itself when asked by software. This sowed the first seeds for Plug and Play.

➤ **EIDE**   Another name for ATA-2. This is now the term used by Western Digital, which originated IDE but had switched for several years to using "ATA."

➤ **Fast ATA-2**   Yet another name for ATA-2. You think it means "faster ATA-2"? It doesn't.

➤ **Fast ATA**   Okay, fellas, cut it out, already! You think I'm going to say it's another name for ATA. Surprise, you're *almost* right. It's actually *another name for ATA-2*, minus one or two features that some systems that employ Fast ATA-2 don't even use anyway. In other words, Fast ATA is "Slow Fast ATA-2."

➤ **ATA-3**   Uh … folks, this is embarrassing, but … here goes. Remember ATA-2? Sure you do. Who could forget? Take that image in your mind, and add to it one tiny little thing: the capability to self-diagnose using a system called Self-Monitoring Analysis and Reporting Technology (SMART—probably created just to be able to use this acronym before someone else did). Aside from self-diagnosis, ATA-3 is ATA-2.

➤ **Ultra ATA**   Finally! Here's something that's actually different from its predecessor! Ultra ATA broadened the bandwidth (the overall capacity of the data pipeline) of the connection between the on-board controller and the motherboard all the way up to 33.3MB/sec (megabytes per second).

➤ **Ultra DMA**   An alternative name for Ultra ATA, used by the people who don't like using "ATA" in the brand name and thus paying homage to IBM.

➤ **ATA-33**   Yet Another name for Ultra ATA.

➤ **DMA-33**   Another name for Ultra DMA. (Gosh, can't they at least put together a naming committee for these things?)

➤ **ATAPI**   Short for "ATA Packet Interface," this is a form of ATA-2 specifically developed for use by devices that are not hard drives, especially CD-ROMs and DVD-ROMs. The idea is that the ATAPI specification enables the BIOS to map a nonhard drive so that it's addressable as though it *were* a hard drive. A so-called "ATAPI CD-ROM drive" will plug into an IDE channel. Today, the term "ATAPI" has fallen out of favor (apparently too many people confused it with the company that created "Pong"), and modern optical drives are now marketed as "IDE" devices.

➤ **ATA/66**   From dashes to slashes … man, we're moving up in the world, aren't we? Next thing you know, we'll be using tildes! (I can just see ten years from now: "ATA~592! Better than EIDE%364 and Fast DMA#CLXXXIX because it's the same thing!") Anyway, this doubled the bandwidth again to 66.6MB/s.

➤ **Ultra ATA/66**   By now, you get the general theme of this section. Is there a difference between "ATA/66" and "Ultra DMA/66?" No. Some brilliant marketing guy, having perceived that "Ultra" worked before with the original "Ultra ATA," decided in the spirit of "Jurassic Park III" and "Bush II" to create a meaningless sequel. This time around, the "Ultra" means precisely nothing.

➤ **Ultra DMA/66**   Not to be left out, some smaller manufacturers that don't want to pay homage to IBM or WD or anyone else use this variation instead. You thought you'd seen it all! This has to be the ultimate variation on a variation on a facsimile on a theme! Hang on to your foam rubber seat cushion flotation devices, because you haven't seen it all …

➤ **EIDE Ultra-DMA**   When WD went back to using the "EIDE" trademark, the War of Punctuation entered an entirely new phase, and the hyphens were let out of the arsenal. But where's the speed number? Well, since 66.6MB/s is likely to be as fast as hard drive interfaces are going to get, given the fact that signaling voltage over IDE cables is stuck at 5 volts, we can naturally assume this means "66." Right? *Right?*

➤ **Ultra ATA/100**   Wrong. Keeping in tune with the general theme of lower voltage in computer technology, the Ultra ATA/100 standard reduces signaling voltage over the IDE cable from 5v to 3.3v—exactly the same step down that CPUs took when Intel made the move from Socket 5 to Socket 7. In so doing, bandwidth could be expanded to 100MB/s without the signal impedance and line noise encountered by the 5v signal. Now, who do you suppose came up with not only this standard, but this name? Wrong again. *Western Digital* proposed this standard. How does the company reconcile the disparate brands? Today, its models are advertised as "EIDE hard drives" that "offer Ultra ATA/100 interfaces." So you'll find some retailers cataloguing WD hard drives as "EIDE Ultra ATA/100."

➤ **ATA-5**   And then there's this gem. It's short, succinct, and to the point. Is it used to mean Ultra ATA/100? Yes, it is. So that makes Ultra ATA/66, "ATA-4," correct? Nope. Ultra ATA/66 is *also* referred to as ATA-5. Hey, watch your head, that's a hard table you're banging it on! Anyway, as best as I can tell, there is no "ATA-4," nor was there ever an "ATA-4." But if you see "ATA-5" in a hard drive's product literature, look for more clues, because it can mean either 66MB/s or 100MB/s.

Distinguishing Controllers, Connectors, and Adapters

A handful of different parts of IDE/ATA hardware have names that are often confused with one another (imagine that!). But correct terms exist, and I try diligently to stick to them here. The *controller* is the circuit board with the processors that run the hard drive and manage the connection between it and the motherboard. With IDE, the controller is *on the drive,* whether it's a hard disk or an optical disc. Now, suppose your PC needs an interface card in order to plug into an IDE device. That card is an *adapter*. It may say "controller card" on the box, and even on the card! It isn't. Why is that important? Because you might not even need the card to make the connection between the PC and IDE devices. All modern motherboards support IDE directly, building either two IDE adapters, or one EIDE adapter with two connectors, directly onto the board. (Functionally, there's no difference.)

The sockets on the motherboard that connect to IDE devices are simply called *connectors*. Depending on your motherboard, you might have two of these connectors, enabling as many as four devices. You may have either "dual IDE" (two IDE channels with two devices per channel) or EIDE (one EIDE channel with four devices), yet you still have two connectors (dual IDE or EIDE) and they both are configured the same way. So big deal—whatever it is you have in this case.

Recall that for IDE drives, the actual drive controller is located on the drive itself rather than on a separate card (the "I" in "IDE" stands for "Integrated"). There is still a separate IDE adapter, however, which is either a separate card or a part of your motherboard. Each channel in the IDE interface pairs a "master" component with a "slave"; in the enhanced EIDE version of the interface, as many as two masters are paired with as many as two slaves. The first drive in the pairing is the master, and acts as the controller for both itself and the next component in the chain. So if you notice a problem in the future with both your hard drive *and* your CD-ROM, perhaps the source of that problem is on the controller that's built in to your hard drive, assuming it's acting as the master and the CD-ROM as the slave.

If your first drive is IDE, and you buy a new EIDE hard disk, you should make certain that your BIOS is capable of handling the faster throughput rates and often larger capacities of EIDE drives (for instance, 100MB/s). Contrary to what you may have read elsewhere, it is not the EIDE adapter or controller which determines whether your PC can have a larger hard disk. It's actually your BIOS. A new EIDE adapter will be no good for you if your BIOS hasn't been upgraded to handle the higher bandwidth and newer translation modes (explained in a few paragraphs). And if your BIOS is very, very old (months and months), you may need to consider replacing your motherboard to enable you to run your system with the storage capacity you now require.

How SCSI Changes the Picture

Although your motherboard directly supports IDE/ATA, and no motherboard directly supports SCSI (because no BIOS supports SCSI), that should not stop you from investing in a SCSI hard drive, internal or external, if that's what you really want. You will need a SCSI host adapter card, so on top of the SCSI drive's higher price, be prepared to spend at least another $50, if not more, for the card. What do you gain? Better speed and greater reliability.

As Chapter 12 showed you, there are nine types of SCSI, the differences between all of which are nontrivial. In other words, "Ultra SCSI" wasn't just a marketing gimmick. Each SCSI type represents a generation in the standard's development, but today, the most recent *six* generations are still supported. For this reason, you'll find SCSI hard drives that support either 50- or 68-pin cables, and you'll probably want a host adapter card that supports both cables. The 68-pin cable will probably support so-called *LVD mode* (low voltage differential), so you will want to chain your lower-voltage internal and external devices using this cable. The software that comes with your host adapter card will help you assign SCSI IDs to each device, which may be a little tricky if you have your 50-pin cable forming one chain and your 68-pin cable forming another. Tricky, but not impossible.

It makes sense that SCSI should be marketed as a high-performance option for time-intensive computing. If you're going to build a Web server in your home office, you should definitely consider SCSI, not only for its speed but the fact that support for re-dundant storage (RAID) basically requires SCSI. Since Windows utilizes free hard drive space as virtual memory, the general throughput rate of 160MB/s for modern SCSI drives can actually result in a much more manageable system, less susceptible to the frequent memory tangles with multiple running applications, for which Windows has come to be known.

But SCSI is far from a plug-and-play option. Setting up SCSI devices is a science in it-self. And if your goal is simply to speed up your everyday work, SCSI will not make your spreadsheets or word processor documents appreciably faster to process, mainly because the only three roles your hard drive plays in that respect are to store your ap-plications themselves, to store their data files and temporary files, and to serve as re-serve memory. All three of these jobs are not full-time. So when deciding whether to invest in SCSI, you should ask yourself how often you plan for your system to be *seek-ing* data. If you only plan to use Microsoft Office or some other off-the-shelf applica-tion, your answer might end up being not enough to shell out the extra bucks.

Transfer Modes

The two terms *transfer mode* and *translation mode* are the most often confused terms in all of computing hardware. There is a distinct difference: *Transfer mode* deals with how the hard drive gets the data off of its media and onto the bus. *Translation mode* deals with how the BIOS interprets that data after it's grabbed off the bus. The differ-ence will become even clearer over the next few paragraphs.

Each new *real* advance in the IDE/ATA standards brings with it a new series of transfer modes. What this means is that throughput rates and bandwidths are kicked upward, so long as you're ready to replace your controller (which may mean your mother-board) and your BIOS as well. Transfer modes were created so that the CPU, the bus controller, the BIOS, and the drive controller could all agree on timing and transfer rates. Prior to the advent of transfer modes, the transfer speeds were fixed, immutable functions of the interface standards.

PIO Modes

The first set of transfer modes created for IDE was called simply Programmed Input/Output (PIO). There's a lot of complex detail to PIO modes, but the only part that human beings such as yourself need to know is the final transfer rates for each mode, as shown in the following:

PIO Mode	Transfer rate
PIO 0	3.3MB/s
PIO 1	5.2MB/s
PIO 2	8.3MB/s
PIO 3	11.1MB/s
PIO 4	16.6MB/s
PIO 5	22.2MB/s

Up until the latter part of 1997, PIO 4 was the de facto speed limit of IDE data transfers. Because PIO 3's maximum transfer rate is faster than the fixed maximum attainable throughput rate of the ISA bus (approaching 10MB/s), both it and PIO 4 require use of the PCI local bus rather than ISA. If you have an adapter card that supports PIO 3 or PIO 4, it is definitely a PCI-based card. PIO 5, despite reports to the contrary, actually existed for a brief time, and is even supported by some BIOS today, but only as a fallback mode. Faster DMA modes superseded PIO 5 right about the time it had a chance to catch on.

DMA Modes

The use of PIO modes in the disk transfer process involves the CPU in the process of fetching data from the hard drive and storing it in memory, and vice versa. This is important, because the way disk transfers were made faster than 16.6MB/s was by bypassing the CPU altogether. Your PC's BIOS supports a limited number of enumerated Direct Memory Access (DMA) channels that enable a peripheral to address the PC's memory without going through the CPU to do it. To be able to take advantage of these channels, the designers of the IDE/ATA standard developed transfer modes for DMA. The only such modes in use today are the so-called *multiword* modes, because the old single-word, one-tiny-little-data-element-at-a-time modes weren't actually faster than PIO. The order of their development appears in the following:

DMA Mode	Transfer rate
DMA 0	4.2MB/s
DMA 1	13.3MB/s
DMA 2	16.6MB/s
DMA 3 (Ultra ATA/33)	33.3MB/s
DMA 4 (Ultra ATA/66)	66.6MB/s
DMA 5 (Ultra ATA/100)	100MB/s

A DMA transfer mode is not a replacement or a substitute for a PIO transfer mode. In fact, most hard drives support both types simultaneously. DMA transfer modes are designed for periods in which the CPU may be otherwise occupied. DMA itself is nothing new: diskette drives use a type of DMA transfer all the time, and always have. But diskette drive transfers have historically involved the use of a bus controller on the motherboard. Modern hard disk DMA transfers sidestep even the bus controller, and for a short time take over the entire PCI bus, in a process known as *bus mastering*. (One of the Lone Ranger's arch nemeses, I believe.) This way, the IDE controller on the hard drive commandeers the bus. (Sandra Bullock co-stars in this lackluster sequel.) It uses the DMA channel to address RAM directly, and shuttle disk contents to and from RAM, bypassing both the CPU and the motherboard's bus controller.

For DMA transfer modes to work, again, your BIOS is the key. It has the main instructions that tell the computer how to transfer data from one place to any other place. But secondly, your motherboard's chipset needs to support it as well. The chipset contains the bus controller, and bus mastering (who is currently seated at the corner of the saloon, leaning his chair against the wall, with his black hat pulled down over his head and his spurs scarring up the green felt of the card table) requires the chipset to be able to cede control of the bus when requested to do so. ("You got yer'self 10 microseconds to cede yer bus before I take aim at that tin star o' yers.") If the bus controller won't budge, DMA transfer modes never take place, and your investment in Ultra DMA/100 is all for naught. See Chapter 10, "Replacing the Motherboard and Its Parts," for a list of which transfer modes are supported by what chipsets.

Note

A hard drive that claims to support "32-bit transfers" only does so as long as the bus on which its adapter or connector rests is 32-bit as well—for instance, PCI. If your IDE adapter or SCSI host adapter card is on the ISA bus, 32-bit transfers will not happen. However, your BIOS settings may report 32-bit transfers turned *on*, and so may Windows. So you'll never actually know it doesn't work unless you notice the *lack* of a speed difference.

Translation Modes

The *translation mode* of a hard drive concerns how the BIOS addresses particular locations. Your CPU already knows how to address memory. It's up to your BIOS to know how to search for the data that the CPU requests—because most of the time, a CPU request for data is about as technical as, "Next, please!"

CHS Mode

The standard translation mode of a PC—or, more accurately, the way the PC behaves in the absence of a formal translation mode—is called CHS, which stands for "cylinders, heads, sectors." These three categories are the latitude and longitude, if you will, for the geometry of a hard disk. You'll recall that a hard disk is made up of one or more platters that are like a stack of ceramic pancakes that don't touch one another. If you were to take several O-shaped cross-sections of these platters, each one would be analogous to a *cylinder*. Each individual O in a cross-section would be analogous to a *head* (or a *track*, depending upon whom you ask and how many pancakes he's had for breakfast). The head is actually the device that's reading the track, which is itself addressable by number. So there's a one-to-one correlation between a track and the head reading it; the number of heads *is* the number of tracks. Divide that track into equal-length wedges, as though you were cutting pieces of pie, and you have *sectors*. In most hard drives today, a sector contains 512 bytes (characters) of data. I'm not talking about the 32-bit "words" used in DRAM memory, but the old 8-bit bytes.

Extended CHS

Ordinarily, a PC addresses the data contents of a hard drive by what cylinder, track, and sector it's located on. But in much the same way that some PCs can't count past 1999, the PC-compatible BIOS of even the most modern systems cannot count enough cylinders, tracks, or sectors to account for more than 504MB of data. Without getting into too much math, the BIOS and the ATA standard both impose separate limitations as to how many cylinders, heads, and sectors can be addressed in a system. Because the PC is bound by the narrowest of any limitations, the combination of BIOS and IDE/ATA wield their blind magic together to come up with a 504MB barrier. The first technique for fudging a way out of this mess, called *Extended CHS* (ECHS), multiplies the number of addressable heads while dividing the number of addressable cylinders by the same amount. The result, however, is a maximum size all the way up to 7.88GB.

Int 13h Extensions

The first method employed by manufacturers to deploy hard drives larger than 8GB in systems that couldn't count that high was to employ old DOS-style "terminate and stay resident" (TSR) programs, the purpose of which was to trap certain machine language calls made to the BIOS to initiate disk transfers. These calls were identified by the hexadecimal number 13 (which is actually the real-world number 19), thus the calls were called "interrupt 13h," or just *Int 13h*. By trapping these interrupts, the TSR programs were able to reroute the calls away from the BIOS, into special routines that mapped the hard drive beyond the limits of ECHS. The mapping methodology employed here was basically Logical Block Addressing, which is now supported by all BIOS manufactured since 2000.

Computers that included hard drives utilizing Int 13h extensions were shipped to consumers as late as 1999. These PCs have BIOS extension programs that are loaded at startup, by way of a DOS-style driver that's addressed by the CONFIG.SYS file on the root directory of the first hard drive (C:). Many dealers did not offer kits to their customers that enabled them to reinstall these drivers after they reformatted their hard drives. As a result, after a reformat, they for some reason discovered that their hard drive was only 7.88GB rather than the 12 or 16GB they paid all that money for. By itself, an older BIOS that did not support LBA would not format any drive partition for a larger size than 7.88GB. However, if customers knew the right tricks (and few did), using the old DOS-based FDISK program, they could create a second, third, or later partition on the hard drive to make up for the unused size, and then label those partitions D:, E:, and so on. (Chapter 23, "Making Your Computer Boot Up Again," shows you how to use FDISK for yourself, to make multiple partitions, or simply to make just one. You'll have to use both DOS and FDISK if you ever need to reformat your hard drive, because the FORMAT utility isn't enough.)

Logical Block Addressing

The number seven-point-eight-eight gigabytes seemed like a colossal amount for a good while (many months), up until the invasion of the Internet into all of our lives, and the subsequent Need-to-Download-Countless-Reams-of-Stuff. This is where Logical Block Addressing comes in. LBA replaces the old kind of cylindrical geometry with a new kind of linear geometry that is actually *less* complex than the old system. With LBA, each addressable sector is given its own number. *That's it.* Hopefully the PC doesn't run out of numbers before the hard disk runs out of sectors.

The Factors Determining a Drive's True Speed

Obviously, you want the largest and fastest hard disk you can afford. But when you're comparing brands and models, take note of a figure that manufacturers tend to tout, called the *seek time*. This figure tells you how long it takes for the hard disk to locate the first block of data you need. Seek times range from 9.5 to 12 microseconds (ms). Don't let this number fool you: Just because it takes 9.5ms for the drive controller to locate the *first* block of data does not necessarily mean that reading the *rest* of that data will be faster than a drive with a seek time of 11ms.

During that initial seek, what's going on? For a substantial percentage of that time, nothing whatsoever, because it takes some time for the first sector to come around and make its way beneath the drive spindle. This time is chalked up to *latency*. It's not something you add to the seek time; its how much of the seek time is generally spent waiting. Why is this number important? Since the seek time is an *average*, the latency figure gives you a "plus or minus" figure to work from. The luckiest seek operation a hard drive could perform would be one in which the first sector of data being sought were right under the spindle to start with. If the latency for a drive with a 9.5ms seek time is 4.5ms, then theoretically, that lucky shot would result in a seek time for that one operation of 5.0ms.

343

What happens after that initial seek? Arguably, the seek time for the next sector of data after the first sector is 0.0ms. But tracks on a hard disk platter are perfectly round, not spiral like on an LP record album. So when the spindle comes to the end of a track, it must adjust the arm in a quick jump to move to the next track. The time it takes for this jump to occur is recorded as the *track-to-track seek time*. It, too, plays a crucial role in determining overall speed.

When the manufacturer adds together three figures—latency, seek time, and processing time (sometimes the latter figure's an estimate)—the result is an overall number called the *access time*. If you can't find this figure in a manufacturer's specifications, look for seek time and latency, then in your mind add about 0.2ms for processing time. Access time is important, because it indicates not how long it takes for the drive to *find* the data, but how long it takes to respond to a request by *getting* the data. This time is much more analogous to the fetch time of DRAM.

A much more reliable gauge of a hard drive's overall performance is its *sustainable transfer rate,* which is generally a maximum number indicating how much data a drive, when tested, has actually been *observed* to transfer. This number is a bit more difficult to obtain directly from manufacturers, and may only be found in reliable, independent reviews.

Revolutions Per Minute

Any computer industry analyst would tell you that this industry has withstood revolutions at the rate of several per minute. But the revolution that counts when you're evaluating hard disk drives, concerns *rpm*—the same kind of measurement as the revolution of your car's engine, or the revolution of those old vinyl records you used to play with a stylus. You remember those? So-called "LPs"? They revolved on your turntable at a rate of 33.3rpm.

Hard disk drives today generally rotate at either of two speeds: 5,400rpm or 7,200rpm. Of all the components inside your computer, the hard drive platter remains, to me, the most incredible. That anything could rotate that fast continually, for so long continuously, without breaking through its steel sarcophagus and sailing clear through the Earth's molten mantle, staggers the mind.

Rotation is not directly related to seek time or access time, but it does play a secondary role. Theoretically, a 7,200rpm drive could be slower overall than a 5,400rpm drive, but not likely. 7,200rpm drives are generally at the upper end of any manufacturer's product line, though the step up in speed is only partly responsible for a decrease in access time of about half a microsecond.

Performing Hard Drive Surgery

Well, you knew I would get to this point of the chapter sooner or later. Before you scrub up, make sure that you've done the usual: backed up your data, updated your emergency floppy disk, and so on. See Chapter 4, "What You Need to Know *Before*

You Open Your PC," for details. Also, and this is super-important, make sure you copy down your current BIOS settings (see Chapter 23). In addition, make sure that your emergency diskette contains the FDISK and the FORMAT commands. You'll find the originals for them in the \Windows\Command directory of drive C:. You'll learn how to use FDISK and FORMAT in Chapter 23, and this section of the book will tell you explicitly when to skip over to Chapter 23 to continue the hard drive installation process.

Removing an Old Drive

Before you start, you need to know the working parameters of your hard drive: at the very least, its number of *actual* cylinders, *reported* cylinders (which is the lie that your BIOS needs to be told in order for it to work right; generally this false number is 16,383), heads or tracks, and sectors per track. If you don't think you have all the data you need (for instance, what all the jumpers on your adapter card mean), then now would be a good time to go online with the manufacturer's Web site to download those specifications ... that is, before you actually open up your PC and it's too late for you to go online.

Once you have all the data you need, then open up your PC and, as usual, get rid of any excess static. Make any notes as to the position of your devices and locations of your cables right now, while you have a chance. Here's an idea: Do you have your camcorder or digital camera handy? Use it to take a picture of everything in its working position! That way, you have an Instant Manual of The Way Things are Supposed to Fit Together.

With your system case open, check whether your hard drive rests against one of the removable plastic faceplates (5⅞" × 1¾") on the front of your PC. If it does, then once you've disconnected it, you can probably slide your drive out from the front like the drawer of a dresser. This is the safest way to remove a device from your PC. If you're not so lucky to have a removable faceplate in front of your drive, then check whether the entire front panel of your system case snaps off (many, such as cases used by Dell, do). If so, you can remove this panel, then slide your disconnected drive from the front. If you're pretty sure you cannot find a way to remove your drive from the front, then you're stuck with sliding it out the back. It's not the easiest way to do, generally, but it's not impossible.

Even if you are removing just one drive, if there are two IDE cables emerging from your motherboard or adapter card, you should unplug them both anyway, at both ends. Why? Ribbon cables can be like rope nets when you're trying to get both hands into a tight system case. If you buckle a ribbon cable, you could easily snap one of the wires inside. I can't tell you how many times I've done that myself.

Another reason: Ultra ATA/66 and ATA/100 hard drives use different IDE cables. They have 80 wires inside them instead of 40. However, they don't look that much different from their older counterparts. How can you spot the differences? The plugs on both ends of the newer cables are generally blue; older cables use either black or grey.

345

Also, when you hold the two types of cables up beside each other, you'll notice the ridges in the ribbons are tighter in the newer cable. Even with these differences, *you can accidentally connect a newer drive with an older cable.* The result wouldn't be catastrophic—your PC simply wouldn't be able to read your drive. So unplugging the old cables is an obvious prerequisite to plugging in new ones that you know will work.

You should remove the old cables first, before the screws (see Figure 16.1). In addition to the ribbon cables, you'll find a power cable, which has a white plug with separate red, black, and yellow wires. This has affectionately been dubbed the "Molex cable." For both cables, take a firm hold and gently pull away from the drive. The data cable should come out easily; the power cable might take some coaxing. But don't yank, and don't pull by the wires.

Figure 16.1

Remove the cables to free your drive.

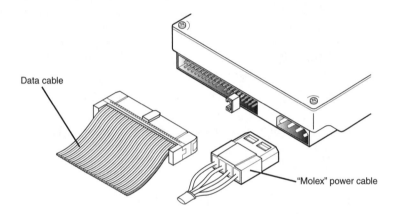

Data cable

"Molex" power cable

Most properly installed hard drives are supported on their left and right sides by something. In a perfect world, that something is a steel bracket or the two sides of a steel inner cage. In this same perfect world, the hard drive is affixed to these two supports by at least two screws on each side. And in this delightful, utopian world of fun and frolic to which Henry David Thoreau once alluded, there's something beneath the hard drive to hold it up, thus counteracting the force of gravity.

Not all hard drives exist in this perfect world. You should thoroughly inspect the area around the hard drive you're removing. Hard drives are safe to handle, but under no circumstances should they be dropped. (Unless they've crashed and no longer work anyway, in which case, who cares?) Up to now, hard drive platters have been constructed of an aluminum/magnesium compound; but recently, companies like Maxtor have taken to using *coated glass,* which is smoother and thus yields increased areal densities (you can store more data in the same area than you could before). I don't need to tell you about what happens to glass when you drop it. One of the worst things that can happen to a working hard drive (after having Windows installed on it) is for someone to remove the screws from both sides of its support, only for it to drop down the tower case and onto bare metal.

Properly installed drives are fastened to their mounting bays by at least two screws on each side. Fastening screws are short, and take very few rotations to loosen. You may drop a few of them. It's better to drop a screw than to drop the drive, so let it happen. They'll probably fall inside the case anyway, so later on, you can rock the case to one side to retrieve them.

If the drive rests in a 5¼" bay, it's probably connected to the mounting cage by way of a pair of 3½" mounting bracket adapters. The best thing about these adapters is that they'll give you something to hang onto as you slide the drive out. Don't fiddle with removing the mounting brackets until after the drive is removed, even if you need to use these brackets for the new drive. The screws attaching the brackets to the drive are simply easier to get to when you can hold the drive up to your face.

If you don't have the luxury of mounting brackets to use as handles, you may have to hold onto the drive with one hand while you're rotating the screwdriver with another to get the screws out, especially if there's nothing supporting the drive from the bottom. This isn't easy, but if the bottom of your drive is exposed, try to find a spot to hold it up with your hand so that the solder beads on the underside of its built-in controller don't prick your fingers.

If you're stuck having to remove your drive through the *inside* of the case rather than sliding it out the front, then this is a job you should do very slowly. Imagine your hard drive is a long, flat, silver, steel automobile (John DeLorean was a visionary after all), backing out of a tight parking garage. Besides the steel support cage, you don't want the drive to touch anything else. Why? Mainly because it's a big hunk of steel, and your motherboard and its expansion cards have lots of tiny parts that can get damaged by it. Use both hands to guide this vehicle, if you will, out of the way of any parts and outside your system case.

Now that the old drive is out, if it has mounting brackets, you should consider whether you want to transfer them to your new drive. Mounting brackets either have plenty of holes, or long, open slits through which screws can be fastened just about anywhere. Hard drives, meanwhile, have at least four, sometimes as many as ten, screw holes on each side. Properly mounted brackets are fastened to the side of the hard drive with at least four screws per side, in any of the pre-threaded locations (see Figure 16.2).

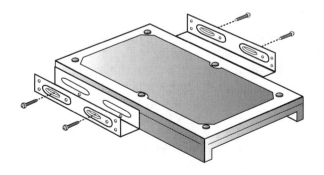

Figure 16.2

How mounting brackets attach to the side of a hard drive.

If the old drive still works, then what do you do with it, now that it's sitting in your hand? If you're replacing it with a new drive, that new drive may be enclosed in an anti-static bag. So cut open the bag, take the new drive out, and put the old drive in. If you're going to install the old drive somewhere else later, then it should be safe resting flat (controller side down) for a little while, on top of a non-conductive surface, such as wood or plastic.

Locating a Spot for the New Drive

If you've just removed an old hard drive ... congratulations, you have a spot for your new drive! All IDE/ATA hard drives and most SCSI drives produced for PCs since 1996 conform to the highly acclaimed 3½" form factor. The larger form factor, 5¼", was originally created for "half-height 5¼" floppy disk drives," but is now used by optical disc drives such as CD-ROMs.

System cases generally provide at least two bays of both form factors. You might want to look through Chapter 21 to see what you might expect from your current system case, and to consider whether you would be better off replacing the case. In any event, it might help you decide the best bay for your new drive ... that is, if your case is large enough to give you a choice.

Regardless of what the marketing brochures tell you, the safest place to install a hard drive in your system is in a designated bay, resting horizontally. The exception, as you'll see in Chapter 21, is when the only open bay sandwiches your hard drive in-between two other insulating devices. Insulation is not what your hard drive needs to stay cool. The steel top of an overheating hard drive can get hot enough to fry eggs on. (Tip: Do not cook food with parts of your computer.) But if there's even a few inches of space between that same hard drive and other devices, it may never have to get any hotter than lukewarm.

Preconfiguring the New Drive

All IDE/ATA hard drives today have a small set of *jumpers* on the back (see Figure 16.3). These are pairs of short metal poles, pairs of which are connected to one another by plastic-coated shunts. You move and reposition these shunts to close particular circuits, thus changing some internal settings in the drive.

The one setting to which these jumpers generally refer is the drive's place in the IDE hierarchy. IDE is like a Cecil B. DeMille epic about ancient Egypt. There are only masters and slaves. The master is the drive whose on-board controller actually runs the IDE channel; the slave is the drive whose controller gets to sit there and do nothing. Some drives have a separate "Solo" setting for when they have the IDE channel all to themselves; others either share the "Solo" setting with "Master," or expect you to realize that "Master" is the same as "Solo." When you set the jumper to "Master" or "Solo," you engage the drive's on-board controller; when you set it to "Slave," you're telling the drive to yield control to the other device on the channel.

348

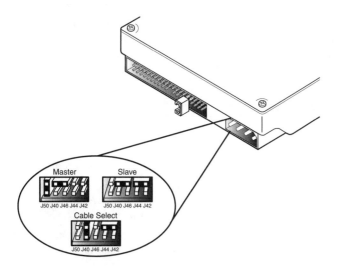

Figure 16.3

An example set of IDE/ATA jumper settings (yours may differ).

Despite all that, most IDE/ATA drives today give you another option: By setting a drive's jumper to "Cable Select," you enable the drive on power-up to determine for itself whether it's a master or a slave, by finding out what end of the IDE cable it's plugged into. Every IDE cable connects to either one or two devices. For the two-device cable (which is the most common), the master connects to the plug at the very end, while the slave connects to a plug toward the middle of the ribbon. (It's not *at* the middle; otherwise, you wouldn't know which end plugs into the motherboard. The slave plug is closer to the master plug than the motherboard plug.) The idea of the "Cable Select" setting is to let the cable decide whether a device is a master or a slave. This may be a convenient setting for you, if you know that the cable you're using is a good one, and you plan to be moving your equipment around your system case relatively often. Be careful, though: If you set the "Cable Select" option on your master drive, be certain you also set the "Cable Select" option on whatever device serves as your slave device.

Changing Out the Adapter, If Necessary

If you purchased an Ultra ATA/66 or ATA/100 drive, and your BIOS only supports Ultra ATA/33, you'll need to take this opportunity to install your new adapter card. Your new drive *will* work with your existing motherboard, but it won't speed up the interface. An Ultra ATA adapter card may solve this problem, although you will need to connect *all* your storage devices to this card, including your optical drive and any other hard drives you have. You will probably also have to disable your motherboard's on-board IDE controllers, generally by way of a BIOS setting (see Chapter 23).

Remember, your old drive cables have not been connected to the back of your new device just yet. Leave them that way while you're installing the adapter card; they'll just get in the way otherwise. Place your thumb, a sticky-note, or a small sleeping furry animal on this page, and then skip back to Chapter 12 for the details on installing your new adapter card. If your old drive controller is part of the motherboard, check the data you found online earlier for the location of the switch or jumper that disables it. There may not be such a switch or jumper; in which case, all may not be lost. The addition of your new adapter card alone may take care of the job, as long as your BIOS is fully up-graded. Getting your new adapter card to work takes more than just plugging it in. You'll have to fiddle with nasty things like IRQs and DMAs, whatever they are. Check out Chapter 23 for help in getting out of this mess.

Inserting the New Drive

If you're replacing your old drive, then you're lucky enough to have paved a route for yourself for installing the new one. If not, then pre-plan your route carefully. Make sure there are no data or power cables obstructing the route. And unless your system case has a very secure mounting cage with guide rails, be prepared to use both hands to guide your drive in place, then to hold it in place with one hand until it's fastened securely.

The larger, 5¼" mounting bays generally have some type of supports at the bottom, en-abling you to slide the drive/mounting bracket assembly through the front without it falling through the bottom. The smaller, 3½" bays are often not so reliable. If your sys-tem case doesn't have a separate cage for the smaller bays, then be very careful to sup-port your drive with at least one hand at all times. If you don't have another pair of hands to help you, then use your hands to thread the first few rotations of each screw before picking up your screwdriver—that's about the only way to reliably screw in your fasteners one-handed.

Connecting the Data Cables

Your main hard drive used to boot your system should be attached to the "IDE1" channel—the first IDE channel—on your motherboard or adapter card. Its jumpers should be set to "Master" or "Cable Select," or to "Solo" if that setting exists, and you know for certain this drive will not be sharing the IDE channel with another device. (Recall that you probably have two channels.) So connect your master/solo drive to the IDE data cable using the plug at the very end, not the one in the middle.

If you're installing a secondary hard drive, you have some more choices. You could set it to be the slave drive on the first channel. Or you could set it to be the master drive on the second "IDE2" channel. A lot depends on your optical disc drive. If it's an IDE/ATAPI device, then it, too, shares your channels with your hard drives. Its on-board controller should perform perfectly well as a master, should you wish to set your second hard drive as a slave. You should not set up any device to be the slave on the second channel, if there's no master on the second channel. That point should be obvious.

Now, attach the data (ribbon) cables to your new drive. Remember that the red wire or stripe along the side of the cable aligns with pin 1 on the drive's connector. Pin 1 is clearly marked with a "1." With a two-device IDE cable, the slave device uses the plug that hangs in the middle.

Motherboards and adapter cards may have either a pair of "dual IDE" connectors, or two EIDE connectors. What's the difference? For the purposes of plugging in your hard drives, *none*. So if the markings say "EIDE1" and "EIDE2," don't panic.

The Highly Anticipated Special Instructions for SCSI Drives

If you're connecting a SCSI drive, there's a bit more to this process, and you just knew there would be. Each SCSI device has to be given its own ID number. Such numbers set the priority of each device on the SCSI chain. Because SCSI devices may be linked together, you may need to use something called a *terminating resistor* to indicate which device is the first and the last in the "chain."

If your SCSI host adapter card supports so-called *Plug and Play SCSI,* then your card is capable of setting the ID numbers and the terminating devices for your SCSI devices automatically, when you boot your PC. Except if your SCSI device does not support Plug and Play SCSI, in which case you'll need to set the ID number for that device manually, and you may need to set the terminating resistors for your chain anyway, wherever they may be. (By the way, Plug and Play SCSI is not to be confused with Plug and Play or PnP, the scheme used by PC devices for identifying themselves to the BIOS.)

Typically, the SCSI host adapter is set to ID 7 (or ID 15 for Wide SCSI), at one end of the chain. The first hard disk is usually set to 0, which means it's at the other end. If the new drive is not the only SCSI device in your PC, and its ID number is set to something between the highest ID number (7 or 15) and the other device's ID number, then you have to remove that other device's terminating resistors or switches. This way, the SCSI host adapter will know that it has to continue on from the hard disk to look for more SCSI devices. Yecch.

Usually all you have to do is identify these terminator critters and pull them off to disable termination of the daisy chain. (Of course, if your hard disk is the one and only SCSI device in your system, leave the termination thingies on.)

While you're rearranging the ID numbers for your other SCSI devices, set your slower devices, such as tape drives and optical disk drives, to the highest priority, so they won't get crowded out of the chain by the fast guys, such as your SCSI hard disk. Some hard drive manufacturers (including Seagate and Western Digital) give you a special SCSI device control program; others make it more difficult by forcing you to set the parameters manually on one line of your CONFIG.SYS file. You may need to set these parameters even though you use Windows.

Connecting the Power Cable

Now that you've inserted your drive and connected the data cable, connect the power cable. This is a cable with four separate wires: red, black, black, yellow. Generally, the white "Molex" plug is shaped to fit only one direction. The male end will have bevels at the top along with a tab, preventing it from being plugged in backward. The female connector on the drive will be notched at the top.

Testing at Full Power

Before you put your system case back together, now might be a good time to reattach all your external cables (power last) and test your PC to see if it boots up with your emergency diskette. If it doesn't—or even if you think it doesn't—you'll have your system case open so that you can make adjustments. Just remember to power back down and unplug the power cord from the power supply before you reach your hands back in there. If you need to format your new hard disk, it's okay to leave the cover off while you're doing this. This way, if you have any severe problems, you can shut down your system, get out your flashlight, and make certain everything's plugged in that needs to be.

Don't expect much when you start up the PC; you have to set up the new hard disk before you can use it. (Chapter 24, "Getting Windows to Recognize Your New Toys," deals with this process.) This is the time when you may want to stop and bake some cookies so that you can bribe some computer guru into helping you.

The Least You Need to Know

➤ Make sure you have an empty drive bay in which you can put a new hard disk. If you're replacing a bad disk, this obviously isn't a problem.

➤ Make sure your system case has enough open space inside of it to enable your new hard drive to breathe once it is installed. In a tight case, a hard drive is as good as a radiator, and can melt things just as easily.

➤ The IDE/ATA family of technologies recognizes six different interface speeds, the four newest of which are still supported by modern motherboards: 16.6, 33.3, 66.6, and 100 megabytes per second (MB/s). Despite whatever the manufacturer chooses to call the standard for these speeds, when it boils down to it, these are the four IDE/ATA interfaces.

➤ The jump from 33.3 to 66.6MB/s came at a cost: Voltage requirements have been stepped down to 3.3v from 5v. So you'll need new IDE cables to support either ATA/66 or ATA/100.

➤ Of all the speed figures you'll read about, the ones that count most with regard to hard drives are seek time, access time (whose formula is seek time + latency + processing time), and average sustained transfer rate.

Chapter 17

Replacing a Diskette Drive

In This Chapter

➤ Adding a new floppy diskette drive to your system

➤ Replacing drives you can't fix

➤ What to look for when shopping for a drive

➤ Installing the darn thing

➤ Some important points of fact about LS–120 SuperDisk floppies

Diskettes (those square things with a disk in them formerly known as "floppy disks") are almost historical remnants of PC technology, and some PCs—including most notebook units made today—don't even include them anymore. Historically, diskettes have two basic sizes, or "form factors": 5¼" and 3½". The 3½" "high-density" (1.44MB) drive is the only standard diskette drive currently being manufactured, and even then, not in very high quantities.

Shopping for a New Drive

Assuming you need to add a new diskette drive after looking at the pros and cons listed in Chapter 2, "Now, Let's Find Out What Kind of Computer You Have," and also assuming that you're not trying to add one to a laptop (which is darn near impossible), then it's time to go looking for your new toy. However, before you go shopping for your drive, take a scout team and assess the situation.

Here's a simple guide to help you shop for diskette drives. Do you have one now? If so, then does it work? If so, you don't need one. If it doesn't work, you might want one if you ever want to use an emergency diskette to boot your PC. Otherwise, your modern PC can actually get by without one. You do not need a second diskette drive. A new high-density 3½" diskette drive can cost as little as $20.

Here are some points you should consider if you find you ever need to replace your old, or worn out, diskette drive:

➤ **How are your drives mounted?**   Do your current drives ride rails, or are they held in place by some screws along the side (see Figure 17.1)? If your drives use rails, then you'll need to make sure that the drive you purchase has its rails included in the box. Otherwise, you'll need to purchase them separately. (If you're replacing a drive, you can reuse its rails to mount your new drive—no need to get new rails.)

Figure 17.1

How are the drives attached to the PC?

Some drives are screwed
directly into the drive bay.

➤ **Will your floppy controller cable accommodate your new drive?**   While you have the PC open (see Figure 17.2), check to see if your existing floppy controller has an additional plug for a second diskette drive (most do). Look at your current diskette drive; there you'll find a fat ribbon cable leading from it to the floppy controller that is located either on the motherboard or on an expansion card. If you see a plug located in the middle of this cable leading nowhere, then you have the connector you need for your new diskette drive. Otherwise you need to replace this cable with what is called a "standard floppy controller cable" or "FDD cable"; if you get this, you'll have the two drive connectors you need. Also, keep in mind that your new diskette drive may have either a pin connector (a connector with two rows of holes into which the drive connector's pins are inserted) or an edge connector (a connector that has a slot instead of holes, into which the flat edged drive connector fits—it's similar to the bottom edge of an adapter card). The cable in your PC needs to support the type of connector on your diskette drive, otherwise you need to get a converter (most drives include such a converter in case you need it, but ask if you're not sure). Some cables contain both pin and edge connectors.

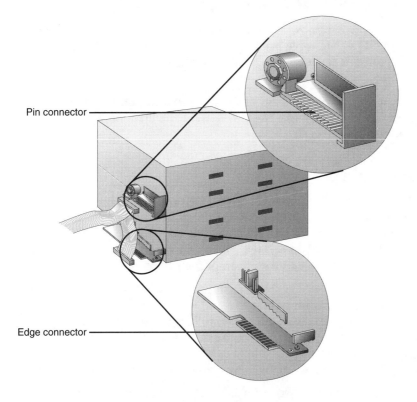

Figure 17.2

Look for an extra connector to attach your new diskette drive.

Pin connector

Edge connector

➤ **Do you have the right power plug?**   All 3½" drives produced today use a specific type of power connector that's smaller than the type used by any other device in your system. All power supplies produced today have one plug that fits into this connector. If you're replacing a 3½" drive, you probably have this plug. If you don't, and you're certain you have a new-enough system, you may need to attach a power adapter to one of your existing, open plugs, in order to convert it to the proper size your diskette drive requires.

Putting Your New Floppy in Drive

After you bring your new diskette drive home, it's time to connect it. To install an external diskette drive, you usually connect its cable to an open parallel port. Then connect the power cable, turn it on, and you're set (except for running the setup software, that is).

To install an internal drive, prepare your system in the usual way, following Chapter 4's instructions: Run a backup, update the emergency diskette, and so on. Then turn the power off, open up the PC, and discharge any static electricity you've built up, or strap on your grounding wrist strap.

Removing the Old Drive (If Needed)

Now, if you're replacing a drive, remove the old drive by disconnecting its data cable and then its power cable. The data cable is a wide, flat ribbon cable, whereas the power cable is made up of four separate wires with a small white connector on the end.

Next, remove the four screws along the sides of the drive that hold it in place. Slide the drive out the front of the PC. Remove the two rails on the drive (if any) and attach them to the replacement drive.

Connecting the Cables

There are several different types of floppy disk drive (FDD) cables you may run into. The first (and, today, the most common) is designed to connect drive A: to the motherboard, and doesn't allow for a drive B:. So there are two connectors at either end of this cable, and none in the middle. You can tell which end goes to the drive by looking for a cut and a twist in the middle of the width of the ribbon itself, just before the connector end.

If you have a cable with one connector at one end and two different types of connectors at the other end, then the cable is still designed to connect one drive to the motherboard. The cable was designed to support the new style of plug that premiered with the 3½" drive, which is a row of paired pins (a *header*) rather than a flat, green card (a *card connector*). You'll only use one of these connectors, never both.

Now, if one end of the FDD cable has two connectors *of the same type*, then the cable was designed to handle drive A: and possibly drive B:. One end of the data cable has a twist in the ribbon just before the connector (see Figure 17.3); this connector identifies drive A:. The other non-twisted connector connects to drive B:. Generally, the drive B: connector is the one near the middle of the cable, while drive A: is at the very end; but check for the characteristic twist to make sure.

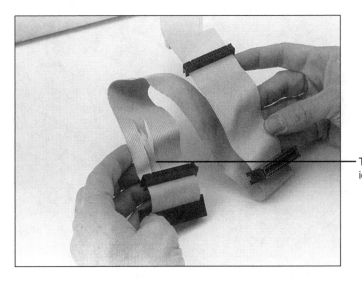

Figure 17.3

A four-connector, dual-drive, "do everything" FDD cable.

The twist that identifies drive A:

Finally, if one end of the FDD cable has *four* connectors, then two will be one connector type (the old card), while the other two will be the other type (the new header). The pair of connectors at the end are (generally) reserved for drive A:, but keep an eye open for the twist that always shows where drive A: should be located. The other pair of connectors is reserved for drive B:, and may be left open (unplugged) if you don't have a second diskette drive.

Once you've decided which cable connector goes where, slide the drive about halfway into its bay and connect the power cable and the data (ribbon) cable. If you're adding a dual drive (combo drive) that has both sizes in one unit, connect it as drive A:. Make sure that you don't connect the ribbon cable backwards—align the striped edge with the number 1 pin on the connector. (If you look at the numbers on the connector, you see that there are lower numbers at one end.)

If you don't have an open power connection, disconnect the power connector from the existing diskette drive and connect a Y-cable to it so that you now have two connectors. Reconnect the power to the existing drive and then use the remaining open connector on the new drive. If needed, attach the converter to the power connector to enable it to be attached to the smaller mini-plug on your 3½" drive. Again, make sure that when you connect any data cable, you align the striped edge of the ribbon with pin number 1 on the connector (see Figure 17.4). In any case, the power connector is *keyed*, which means it can only go on one way (assuming of course that you don't try to force the issue).

Figure 17.4

Connect your new drive.

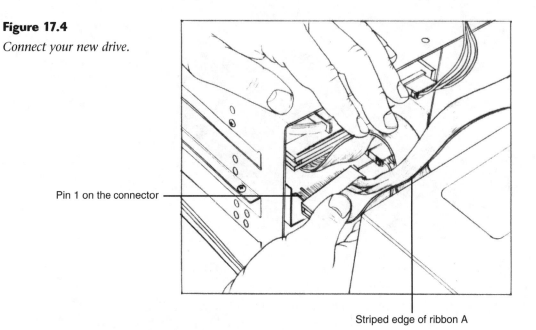

Pin 1 on the connector

Striped edge of ribbon A

Screwing the Drive in Place

After the drive is in place, slide it the rest of the way into the bay and screw it in. Now's a good time to make sure you do not mount the drive upside down. The door on a 5¼" drive closes downward; a 3½" drive doesn't have a door, but instead it has a release button that is located on the lower left.

Most drives have four screws (two on each side). If the drive is not mounted on rails, this can get a bit tricky; just line up the holes on the drive with the holes on the side of the bay and screw each of the four screws just a little (see Figure 17.5). This gives you a little "play" so you can line up everything okay. After you correctly line up the drive, screw everything in the rest of the way.

Mistakes to Avoid

Now that it's connected, leave the cover of your system case off for a moment, power up your PC, and see if it recognizes your new drive. If it doesn't work, don't panic. First, shut down your computer, then check the connections and make sure they're tight. Also, check to make sure you didn't flip the ribbon data cable and connect it upside-down—the striped edge of the ribbon aligns with pin 1 on the connector. In addition, make sure that the pins aren't bent, and that all of them are inserted properly into the connector.

After checking the cabling (Is it backward? Is it inserted correctly?) and the position of the twist in the ribbon cable (the cable with the twist is for drive A:), you should check your BIOS setup information to make sure it recognizes the proper drive type (3½" high-density). Diskette drives are not Plug-and-Play devices; they have to be registered properly in your BIOS.

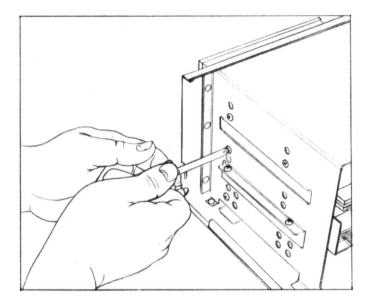

Figure 17.5

Screw your drive into place.

When you work with a PC that is designed to have only one diskette drive, and you add a cable to create a second connection, neither cable has a twist in it. So both drives become drive B. To fix this problem, make sure that drive A has its DS jumper or switch set to the lowest setting, which is usually 0 or 1. Set drive B to the second DS setting, which is usually 1 or 2.

If you notice that the drive keeps showing a directory listing of an old diskette, and not the current one, this could be a sign of an FDD data cable gone bad. Get a replacement FDD cable and try again.

The Least You Need to Know

➤ If your drives ride the rails, be sure to get a pair of rails when adding a new drive.

➤ Check also to see if there's an open plug that's the right type (extra small). If not, again, you should get an adapter.

➤ Keep in mind that some PCs, such as Compaqs or PS/2s, require that you buy their specific drives, and not a generic one such as Teac.

Chapter 18

Adding an Optical Drive

In This Chapter

➤ Narrowing down your choices when shopping for a CD-ROM drive

➤ Is DVD-ROM really a good idea?

➤ The difference between ATAPI and SCSI optical drives

➤ Installing your new optical drive correctly

➤ Installing your recordable optical drive

The optical disc has almost taken its full and rightful place as the successor to the floppy disk. Today, some retail PCs no longer even include a diskette drive, but they all contain some form of optical disc—at least CD-ROM—as standard equipment.

There are two principal reasons why there are now so many different kinds of optical drives. One (which I call "the noble reason") is that PC users have created new and unique purposes for this versatile device, many of which require their own categories of disc to address them. The other (which I call "the *real* reason") is that the optical disc business has become so intertwined with the entertainment media business, that the people involved have become incapable of forming universal standards to their own mutual benefit. The result is that there are now no fewer than *eight* simultaneous types and formats of optical disc—unlike the hard disk drive industry, which really has only one standard, although no one can decide among the 18 different names to call it.

Of CD-ROM, CD-R, DVD-ROM, CD-RW, DVD+RW, and WHAT-NOT

Despite the ongoing argument between the computer media industry and the entertainment industry, when you consider a new optical drive for yourself, you need only ask yourself a handful of sensible questions. First of all, do you need a high-capacity backup device for your important data? If you answer, "No," then you're wrong. There, that was easy.

Seriously, though: The fourth edition of this book featured an exclusive chapter on dedicated backup devices. I removed it for the fifth edition. Why? Because you don't want a magneto-optical cartridge drive, and you don't want a Travan QC-10 tape backup drive. You now have the extraordinarily affordable option of CD-RW (rewritable CD). Whereas in 1999, a 200MB backup cartridge for an Iomega Zip drive would cost you about $10, today, a 650MB CD-R disc costs you about 40¢. The CD-RW device itself can be found for under $100 with reasonable speed, and the older CD-R (write once only) devices can be found for a short time for closeout prices. CD-RWs are faster and, thanks to ingenious software written by Adaptec for its spin-off company, Roxio, you can use no less than Windows Explorer itself to back data up directly to a CD-R or CD-RW disc with a simple drag-and-drop.

What All the "Optical" Business Is About

"Optical" isn't so bad as new computer terms go. Historically, the storage devices for data on the PC have been based in *magnetic* media. The hard drive registers magnetic signals pulsed onto rotating ceramic platters; the floppy diskette drives read the same types of signals from coated film. As the different types of storage systems, new and old, find themselves sharing the same timeframe of history together, they tend to collect into their own little enclaves. Hard drives, diskettes, SuperDisks (LS-120), and Iomega Zip drives are being grouped together as *magnetic media;* while in the red corner, wearing the striped trunks, all the storage systems that involve the use of lasers to read the frequency of reflected light are being grouped together as *optical media.*

What differentiates the CD-R and CD-RW formats from the CD-ROM—and, at the same time, is the reason why you can't just use an ordinary silver CD-ROM disc for writing data—is the fact that the more gold-colored rewritable discs use a trick of optics to magnetically record data (the old fashioned way) onto a film whose optical characteristics change based on the type of charge it carries. So such a disc is writable magnetically, but readable optically. The first type of media to use this technique were the so-called *magneto-optical cartridges* (MO), which went out of style very quickly after the prices of CD-RW drives and media plummeted through the center of the Earth.

Rather than have to say "magneto-optical" all the time, forcing us to sound more like characters from the old "Batman" TV series than sensible, decent, law-abiding human beings, a decision was made that the entire family of disc components should be identified by their shared characteristic. An optical drive, therefore, is a device that uses lasers during the read process. A drive may use something else for the write process (that is, if it has a write process, which CD-ROM and DVD-ROM do not), but it is still considered optical if it has a laser. That's the ticket.

If Cost Is the Deciding Factor

Because CD-RW drives have become so cheap, nonwritable CD-ROMs have become an endangered species. Which sometimes means, you can get a good deal on one. You can find a good CD-ROM drive for $30 to $80, depending on its speed: from 16x to 48x. ("1x" would be the spin rate of the first CD-ROM drive or an ordinary CD audio player; "16x" is 16 times that speed, as will be explained in detail later in this chapter.) But these nonwritable devices are beginning their inevitable process of extinction, and may no longer be widely available after 2002.

Portable CD-ROM drives run from $250 to $350, although CD-ROMs with a form factor thin enough to be installed in a notebook computer may cost below $200. CD-R (recordable) and CD-RW (rewritable) drives average about $225; their write speed currently averages 4x, while their read speed goes as high as 16x.

CD-ROM/sound card combo packages, or so-called "multimedia packages," used to be a reliable way to get a decent CD-ROM drive with an above-average sound card, and save as much as $50 in the process. These packages are already extinct. Margins are already so low that it's difficult for manufacturers to find a way to shave off any more.

If Functionality Is the Deciding Factor

As you may know by now, "DVD" doesn't stand for anything. It used to be "Digital Video Disc," until an industry group decided "Video" was too confusing and changed it to "Digital Versatile Disc." Another industry group complained, so both groups came to a compromise by deciding that it should stand for nothing whatsoever.

The main purpose for having a DVD-ROM drive is so that you can play movies on your PC. Essentially, a "DVD-ROM" drive is a CD-ROM that can play DVD movies. However, they cannot write or "burn" CDs or DVDs, CD-ROMs, or DVD-ROMs. When you purchase a DVD-ROM drive, you sacrifice writability for the capability to watch movies on your PC. However, this will not always be the case, as new generations of writable DVD drives are making their way to retail shelves at the time of this writing.

So here is the rundown of the eight primary types of optical drives, their functions, and their limitations:

CD-ROM

CD-ROM (Compact Disc-Read-Only Memory) drives are capable of reading two types of read-only discs: CD-ROM discs, which include data designed to be read by PCs; and audio CDs, which contain the musical tracks that stereo CD players use. (The word for a CD drive of any kind that does not play audio CDs is "defective.") Because writable CDs were designed to be compatible with older drives, CD-ROM drives (generally) can *read* CD-R and CD-RW discs. Generally. Not all will, and it's difficult to pin down exactly why that's true, but part of the reason may concern the varying frequency and intensity of the lasers used in CD-ROMs.

CD-R

CD-R (CD-Recordable) drives introduce the function of writabilty to the media. Without the "W" at the end, such drives are capable of reading CD-ROM discs, of reading and playing audio CDs, of reading the "gold" CD-R discs, and most importantly, of writing to CD-R discs. CD-Rs are permanent media. Once written to, they cannot be overwritten. So you have to think of them not like removable disks or diskettes (which are "random access" and can thus have files removed and overwritten on demand without the user being concerned about the geometric position of those files on the disk), but like a spool of compressed audio tape, permanently wound together, that you can't write over. The fact that you can't write over them is an exploitable feature—consider, if you will, a backup medium that you can't inadvertently back up over.

CD-RW

CD-RW (CD-ReWritable) drives read CD-ROMs, read audio CDs, read CD-R discs, write to CD-R discs (once only), read the "gold-tinted" CD-RW discs, and can write to and overwrite CD-RW discs. But this doesn't make CD-RW "random access." Even these discs are divided into equal-length tracks, and the process of deleting a file on a CD-RW disc could mean the drive has to rewrite one or even two entire tracks (perhaps more if the software decides to "optimize" the disc) with data that zeroes out the deleted file. So a CD-RW is not at all like a little 650MB hard drive. And although manufacturers claim CD-RW discs can be rewritten thousands of times, independent reports state they can indeed wear out, to the point where even though their data is still readable, they're no longer overwritable. What makes up for CD-RW's deficiencies in the rewritability department is its reliability, and the fact that its price has dropped so low as to push CD-R out of the market.

DVD-ROM

DVD-ROM (DVD-Read-Only Memory) drives are capable of reading CD-ROM discs, audio CDs, CD-R and CD-RW discs, DVD video discs, and DVD-ROM discs. The newest DVD-ROM drives can read DVD-RAM and DVD-R discs also. DVD-ROM drives do not *write* to any of these formats. What is a DVD-ROM disc? It has exactly four times the storage capacity of CD-ROM. However, it isn't a very abundant format. Microsoft publishes its MSDN programmers' libraries on optional DVD-ROM format … but besides Microsoft, that's about it. A vast majority of software sold today is packaged with CD-ROMs. So the key reason to own a DVD-ROM drive is to enable you to view movies on your PC. However, a DVD-ROM drive alone is incapable of doing this; you also need an MPEG decoder card (introduced in Chapter 14, "I Can

See Clearly Now: Upgrading Your Video"). Would you believe that many retail PCs that include DVD-ROMs do *not* include MPEG decoder cards? You need to have both or, as they say, the show's over. DVD-ROM drives currently sell for about $150, with discount models testing the sub-$100 mark.

DVD-R

DVD-R drives are capable of reading CD-ROM discs, audio CDs, CD-R and CD-RW discs, DVD movie discs, and DVD-ROM discs. They can also write *once* and once only to DVD-R discs, which have between four and seven times the storage capacity of CD-R discs: precisely, 3.95GB ("Type 1," or "general use"), or 4.7GB ("Type 2," for whatever reason also called "authoring use"). A DVD-R disc has a fixed capacity and cannot read discs formatted for the other capacities—so if you have a 3.95GB DVD-R drive, it will only read and write to 3.95 DVD-R discs and not 4.7GB. Plus—and this is important—you cannot create a DVD video disc with a DVD-R drive. A DVD-R drive cannot read a DVD-RAM disc, or any of the later "RW" permutations. Some DVD-R drives can write to CD-R discs, and a subset of those can rewrite to CD-RW discs. But unlike CDs, some DVD-R drive mechanisms are *double-sided* like diskettes, capable of writing to both sides of a DVD-R double-sided disc by means of two lasers. So you can have a 9.4GB removable permanent storage mechanism. DVD-R drives barely made it onto the scene, and then faded from view to make way for DVD-RAM; however, DVD-R discs are still widely available. They're sold separately at $25 per single-sided 3.95GB or 4.7GB disc; in bulk, the single-sided high-capacity price drops to about $10. Double-sided CD-R drives were manufactured, but double-sided CD-R discs no longer are.

DVD-RAM

DVD-RAM drives are capable of reading CD-ROM discs, audio CDs, CD-R and CD-RW discs, DVD movie discs, and DVD-ROM discs, but they are also capable of *writing* data to DVD-RAM discs. (The "ROM" in "DVD-ROM" stands for "Read-Only Memory," so shouldn't the "RAM" in DVD-RAM stand for "Random Access Memory?" DVD-RAM is not a random access format. So according to an industry group, the "RAM" doesn't stand for anything either.) A DVD-RAM disc has the same storage capacity as a DVD-R disc. But like CD-RW, the DVD-RAM format is rewritable. A 2.6GB single-sided DVD-RAM disc ("Type 1," although this capacity is lower than for "Type 1" DVD-R) sells for about $23, a 4.7GB ("Type 2") DVD-RAM disc sells for about $25, a 5.2GB disc (*also* "Type 2") sells for about $28, and a 9.4GB double-sided DVD-RAM disc sells for about $52. These prices are still appreciably cheaper than the old MO cartridges, and very appreciably larger. The expense is to be found in the hardware: At the time of this writing, an external SCSI double-sided DVD-RAM drive sells for about $600, while an internal single-sided DVD-RAM drive sells for $350.

DVD-RW

DVD-RW drives are ... confusing, but you're used to that, especially if you read the previous 17 chapters. A DVD-RW disc reads from and writes to everything that a

DVD-RAM drive can, *except* a DVD-RAM disc itself. But here's the catch: Pioneer—the stereo equipment company spearheading the DVD-RW effort—is trying to produce a writable DVD format that enables users to write real movies to their discs ... *without* having to use the same movie format as employed on DVD video discs. The reason for that is to prevent users from using PCs to copy DVD movies onto separate media—a principal concern of the movie industry. Videos written to DVD-RW discs will only be playable in DVD-RW players made by Pioneer, as well as other companies to which Pioneer is licensing its technology (Sharp and Zenith, so far). These DVD-RW players are designed to also work like VCRs, enabling customers to replace their bulky cassette system for a neater, cleaner, and more durable alternative. Which isn't a bad idea; the problem is deciding on a format that both the movie industry and the computing industry will embrace. DVD-RW drives do not write to CD-R or CD-RW discs. They currently sell for just under $1,000, although this is an early price that is expected to plummet well into 2002. A DVD-RW disc is 4.7GB and single-sided, and projections are that its retail price will bottom out at about $25 per disc.

Note

You may be interested in whether the optical drive you purchase supports Kodak Photo CDs. Most CD-ROM drives can display photos placed on a CD in a single session. However, to be truly compatible with the Photo CD format, a drive must be listed as "XA compliant."

DVD+RW

DVD+RW (look closely, the difference is in the punctuation) is the alternative rewritable video format championed by Philips, the creator of the compact disc. Philips and its strong industry consortium believe that consumers should be able to create videos with their PCs using inputs from their camcorders and digital cameras, store those videos on DVD discs, and play those videos on real DVD players that are already in the market. So a consumer-made video on a DVD+RW disc will not require a special player. It may, however, require a new DVD player, because incompatibilities between the new DVD+RW format and older DVD players are foreseen. Like its hyphenated counterpart, DVD+RW discs will be 4.7GB, single-sided. DVD+RW drives are not expected to write to CD-R or CD-RW discs. At the time of this writing, the first batch of DVD+RW discs had yet to be shipped, although retail PCs with built-in DVD+RW drives are expected to be shipped by publication time.

How Fast Is X?

Currently, CD-ROM drives come in 16x, 18x, 24x, 32x, 40x, and 48x speeds; you may even find a few more that claim to be faster (100x). A 16x drive is 16 times as fast as the original CD-ROM drives were. A 32x drive is twice as fast as that ... well, in a sense. Sort of. You know computer marketing by now. Three is one hundred percent faster than two, so because two is one hundred percent of two, and two one hundred percent figures together make three, two times two is three. So three must be twice as fast as two. You get it, don't you?

The "x" in "16x" and "4x" refers to the spin rate of the CD. The first CD-ROMs spun at the same speed as conventional audio CDs. So 4x is four times this speed. Because a 1x drive transfers data at 150KB/s (kilobytes per second), a 4x drive transfers data at 4 times 150KB, or 600KB/s. This is a pretty dependable way to compare drives, at least those 12x and under. You see, CD-ROMs under 12x spin at variable rates, so they can *transfer data at the same rate,* regardless of whether that data is located at the inner- or outer-most edge of the CD-ROM. This is a good thing generally speaking, as long as you can ignore the noise the drives make as they constantly adjust their speed.

CD-ROMs over 12x use a *constant velocity,* which means that they don't speed up when the read/write head is over the outer edge, as opposed to the center of the disc. (Audio CDs, meanwhile, do speed up, unlike their stereo LP predecessors.) Because high-speed drives spin at fixed rates, data transfer rates fluctuate: With a 40x drive, for example, you'll get less transfer speed whenever the drive's reading data at the center of the disc (2.8MB/s, or megabytes per second) than you will if it's reading from the beginning of the disc (6MB/s). Now, a "1x" CD-ROM would transfer data at 150KB/s. This means the outer track speed of a 40x CD-ROM is actually a little over 40x (40 × 150KB/s), while the inner track speed is actually closer to 19x. Unfortunately, data is written to a CD-ROM disc from the center out, so unless the disc is full, you won't *ever* achieve 40x speed. (Yecch!)

Some manufacturers fudge their "x" numbers using formulas they won't reveal to you themselves. For instance, the drives being advertised today as "100x" are definitely not spinning at 100 times normal. They may even be simply 12x drives using a hard disk cache, which is something you could set up for any drive, provided you had enough free hard disk space. If a drive includes its own cache memory, however, you may notice the same type of speed boost you get from the addition of the L2 cache to today's modern CPUs. Dedicated cache memory enables an optical drive to access frequently used data quicker. Most modern CD-ROM drives come with a 128KB or 256KB cache, with higher amounts for writable drives, and as much as 2MB for writable DVD-RAMs.

When you start evaluating the speeds of writable CD drives, you'll find the "x" figures multiply, if you will, to become two or three. A common CD-RW drive, for instance, has this set of speeds: "8x/4x/24x." The trio of speeds is due to the fact that a CD-RW drive slows down during its write processes. The first "x" number in the trio refers to the drive *initial* write speed—when it writes to a clean disc. The second "x" refers to the rewrite

Note

When comparing two drives of similar speed, you should look at all factors: data transfer rate, access time, and seek time. These terms may apply just as well to a singles bar as they do to optical drives. Chapter 16, "Hands-On Hard Disk Replacement," gave a full discussion of what these different terms mean.

speed, which is usually half as fast because the drive must perform two operations: zeroing out the old contents, and refreshing those contents in a separate pass. The third "x" is the drive's reading speed, which can be compared to CD-ROM read speeds.

In my experience with CD-RW drives, I've noticed that even writing to fresh CD-RW discs is a noticeably slower process than writing to CD-R discs. Granted, Windows doesn't make you wait while you're writing data to a disc—you can always run some other program from your hard drive. But if you use a CD-RW disc to perform a periodic backup, as I do, be prepared to wait a bit longer before your CD-RW drive becomes available again, even if you're just breaking out a new disc.

When you're evaluating the speed of a DVD-ROM drive or a rewritable DVD drive, the "x" numbers for rotation will fool you. They're incompatible with the CD numbers, and lead many into the mistaken belief that DVD drives are somehow slower. While "1x" for a CD-ROM is 150KB/s, "1x" for a DVD-ROM is 1,250KB/s. (The average throughput rate you'll find for a DVD-ROM is listed as either 5.2x or 6,500KB/s— the same as a "43x" CD-ROM drive.)

The Interface Factor

Your choice of interface for hard disk drives is not a big deal, as long as you don't mind the fact that the industry came up with nine or ten different names for the same standard. In the end, your hard drive interface choice (as described in Chapter 16) is between two *families* of interfaces: IDE/ATA being the less expensive, simpler to configure option; and SCSI being the premium, faster, more reliable option.

With internal optical drives, this choice is basically the same, only slightly more convoluted: Although SCSI is the premium option for internal optical drives as well, you don't have the same performance gains in read speeds that you have with SCSI hard drives. However, you don't pay much more for SCSI optical drives, if any, than for IDE/ATAPI drives, although you probably will have to shell out some extra cash for the host adapter card.

If you're considering a rewritable drive, portability may become a factor, and for that reason you may want an external model. Suddenly, you find yourself in a veritable supermarket of interfaces. Let's examine this particular choice in greater detail.

IDE/ATAPI: How Safe Is the Safe Route?

Optical disc drives sold today typically follow one of two interface schemes: either SCSI or ATAPI, an offshoot of IDE (some manufacturers have taken to calling it "IDE" anyway). Modern day optical drives have on-board controllers that meet the specifications of Enhanced IDE (EIDE, also known as ATA-2). IDE (also known as ATA) is the most common type of hard disk available, and most BIOS that claim to support IDE actually support EIDE, or even later enhancements.

On the IDE/ATA interface, controllers do not know the difference between hard disk drives and optical disc drives. So a special protocol was created called the ATA Packet Interface (ATAPI), which "re-maps" the contents of an optical disc so it looks like a hard disk to your PC's BIOS. The IDE specifications are upgraded every now and then (and ten or twelve more names are plucked out of the alphabet soup for them) primarily to support faster hard drives. Hard drives have gotten faster, faster than optical drives have gotten faster. So as a result, while your BIOS may have switched on DMA mode 4 or 5 to enable your 66.6MB/s or 100MB/s hard drive, your optical drive will, at best, only require DMA 3 (33.3MB/s). (For an explanation of the key differences between IDE standards and DMA modes, see Chapter 16.)

This can cause some trouble. Regardless of the fact that the EIDE standard was supposed to provide support for four drives per channel, modern motherboards have two connectors designed to support one or two devices each. Generally, you install a hard drive as the master on the first IDE channel; and since this will be your C: drive, you probably want your faster hard drive here. With DMA 4 or DMA 5 going to your master, theoretically a DMA 3 device should work as the slave on that same channel. But in practice, sometimes it doesn't work, and sometimes it does but slower than it should. Luckily, you have two IDE connectors. But if you plan to make a second fast hard drive the master on that second channel, you could face the same problem there, too. And although you can make a device that supports DMA 4 or DMA 5 the slave of your optical drive that only supports DMA 3, you'll be slowing down that fast device by at least half, since the DMA mode of the slave is never greater than the DMA mode of the master.

The SCSI Alternative

The SCSI optical drive has made a comeback as a premium option for writable drives such as CD-RW. New drives with the highest transfer rates and "x" speeds are generally released first with a SCSI interface. (Theoretically, the reliability and wide bandwidth of the SCSI interface actually does very little to improve the throughput of an optical drive.)

If you're considering a DVD option, SCSI becomes even more attractive. For some reason, SCSI-based DVD-ROMs are no more expensive than IDE/ATAPI-based DVD-ROMs. And higher-bandwidth DVD-RAM drives are mainly SCSI-based, especially the external models.

So you may decide to invest in SCSI instead if you plan to reserve your IDE channels for high-bandwidth hard drives, or if you plan to do more with your writable drive than just make hard drive backups, or if portability is something you might desire, or if you want to go all out and invest in DVD.

If you choose SCSI, you'll need a separate SCSI host adapter card to connect your optical drive to your PC. The current flavor of SCSI used by most drives today is Ultra SCSI-3, also known as Ultra160. The host adapter for this card is not a trivial purchase—at the time of this writing, Adaptec's 7-device 50-pin card was selling

369

for about $90. (Chapter 12, "Face the Interface," discusses SCSI flavors and host adapters at length.) A SCSI-based CD-RW sells for about $50 more than an IDE/ATAPI model. So you could be spending more than twice as much for not quite twice the performance. But you could justify the cost if you also were to invest in a SCSI hard drive, which also has measurably greater performance than its IDE/ATA counterpart, and can share the same host adapter as the CD-RW.

The External Bonanza

If you're thinking you need an external optical drive because you've run out of space in your system case, consider the fact that you can save quite a bit of money by investing instead in a new, larger system case, and taking the trouble to transport your existing components there. Chapter 21, "Classier Chassis: Consider a New System Case," tells you how.

There are, however, other reasons you might consider for purchasing an external optical drive, especially a writable model. It uses its own power supply, so it won't be a drain on the power supply inside your PC. It's one less device inside your system case taking up space, and perhaps generating heat. And an external drive is semi-portable, so it opens up the possibility of being able to transport your work between your home and office, and perhaps even telecommute a few days per week.

With an external drive, though, you have the awkward choice of interfaces. It could use SCSI, USB, FireWire (IEEE-1394), the parallel port, or if it's designed to also plug into a notebook PC, a PCMCIA port. So how do you choose?

Virtually all PCs have parallel ports already, so the problem of creating a plug for an external optical drive is already solved. Your printer could daisy-chain to the back of the drive, so you don't lose printing capability, and you don't need a switch box. The price is also fair at about $175. You do, however, sacrifice some performance—the 4x initial write speed of parallel external CD-RWs today is the slowest available.

USB external drives today are slightly more expensive, although some—including models produced by Iomega—have much cooler-looking cases. At about $200, USB-based CD-RWs surprisingly don't provide much better performance than parallel—most are stuck at 4x initial write speed. And since USB devices are more closely monitored by Windows, you could run into the dreaded "uninstallation/reinstallation" problem many users have reported suffering through, when dealing with USB devices designed to be unplugged from and re-plugged into the PC at random.

The FireWire option is worth considering. At about $250, external FireWire CD-RWs offer much higher performance at 12x initial write speed, and 8x to 10x rewrite speed. Three-port FireWire adapter cards are available for about $70; and if you have or are thinking about a digital camera that uses FireWire, both devices could share that card.

With all the new entrants in the external device competition, there's one notable withdrawal: External IDE optical drives are no longer manufactured, and are scarcely available.

Recordable Optical Drives

As incredible as it might seem, you can now "cut" your own compact disc. It isn't exactly the same kind of CD as those that you buy at a music store, but no matter; you can play them in your CD player just as well. How do you get the music on there in the first place, without a studio, a mixer, or even a microphone? You actually copy the data from other CDs. Or (even more interesting ... and controversial) you can download this CD-quality audio from the Internet. You can also create a CD that's full of important data files, and clear up space on your hard disk. Of course, the files should be "finished"—meaning that you don't intend to make changes to them, because you typically won't be able to resave the file back onto the disc.

Although both CD-R (recordable) and CD-RW (rewritable) drives were originally marketed as data backup and archival devices, their newfound popularity has been mainly due to their newfound use as custom audio CD manufacturing stations. Many popular shareware programs enable you to "rip" (to use the technical term so carefully engineered for it) audio tracks from audio CDs and store the tracks as .MP3 (MPEG-3 encoded) files on your hard drive. With programs such as WinAmp, you can actually play these .MP3 files straight from there (with a WinAmp add-on, you can even perform the ripping process). Despite the fact that the term sounds like you're doing something naughty behind your parents' backs, ripping does not damage the original CD. The term merely implies that you're performing a copy process with files that were designed not to be copied—more accurately, not to be *files* in the first place.

A type of program called *premastering* takes these .MP3 files and generates CD audio tracks from them. These tracks contain the full spectrum of audible frequencies that any ordinary CD supports. So you can select as many .MP3 tracks that will fit onto a 74-minute CD-ROM, and then cut your own compact disc that you can take with you to the stereo set or to your Walkman. The write speed of the ordinary recordable optical drive is 4x, but 8x is also available for a little more outlay. (Divide 74 minutes by the "x" write speed to arrive at how long the write process will take.)

Now, these Internet-based .MP3 files come from a multitude of sources, many of them from legitimate bands and musicians all over the world whose work has never been published on CD before. Through their own software and often their own Web servers, these artists manage to publish themselves in the form of .MP3 files, and let individuals provide their own media for the job rather than the big record companies.

There is a third possible source of .MP3 files I should mention: *yourself*. If you have the proper software for mixing your own digital tracks, or converting tracks from your audio tape deck using your PC's audio card, you can produce .MP3 files that, with a CD-R or CD-RW drive, you can then record onto a special recordable ("gold") CD, whose durability is roughly that of an ordinary audio CD.

The Performance DiViDend

DVD-R (Recordable) drives exploded onto the market in 1997. By "exploded" in this previous sentence, I mean in the sense that H. R. Haldeman and John Erlichman "exploded" during their Senate Watergate testimony in 1974. The DVD industry leaders picked up the pieces, decided that $17,000 was not a widely embraced entry-level price point for anything that doesn't bear the trademark "BMW," and decided to shoot for something more in the four-digit range, and then backed up, started over, and exploded onto the market again. I don't recall Haldeman and Erlichman begging Sen. Sam Ervin for more time on the witness stand to bury themselves deeper, but if they had, the results would certainly have resembled the DVD industry's second try at writable devices.

Sensible, affordable writable DVDs are a very recent invention. If you're a sensible person, you probably prefer watching movies on devices originally designed to display movies, such as big-screen TVs ... and big, silver screens with seating for 500. So the real reason you might be considering a DVD is to be able to take advantage of its awesome removable storage capacity: 9.4GB for a double-sided disc! But you might also be considering putting two and two together (which, as the DVD industry will affirm, make three): Since you can edit movies on just about any PC now, properly equipped with a video capture device (see Chapter 14), isn't it possible to write those videos to a real DVD disc and play them on a real DVD player? It's theoretically possible, but today it isn't quite feasible ... not *quite*.

Playing Movies on Your Computer

Much of the infighting between movie studios about which DVD video format to support has subsided but hasn't entirely ended. For now, all the major American studios are releasing movies on VHS and DVD formats concurrently. Notice I said "American." The rest of the world doesn't see DVD the same way North Americans do. At present, the various formats of DVD video have been divided among several global regions: a) Canada, United States, and U.S. territories; b) Japan, Europe, South Africa, and Middle East; c) Southeast Asia and East Asia; d) Australia, New Zealand, Pacific Islands, Central America, South America, and Caribbean Islands; e) former Soviet Union, Indian Subcontinent, Africa, North Korea, and Mongolia; f) China.

You can only play videos with the regional code that matches the regional code of your DVD player. So don't expect to buy a DVD player in Japan and play American movies on it, or vice-versa. The regional codes do not currently affect computer software or DVD-audio, although they might someday.

Check out Chapter 14 also for more details on the *MPEG-2* decoder card your PC may require in order to play movies. With one of these cards, you're not actually playing movies on your PC at all, just on your monitor. If you really want to see DVD pictures in a Windows window, there's a catch to it, and Chapter 14 explains that as well.

In addition to the MPEG-2 decoder card, your PC will also need a sound card capable of handling the three DVD audio formats: MPEG-2 Audio, Dolby Digital AC-3, and Linear PCM (pulse code modulation). (Chapter 15, "Sensational Stereophonic Sound," discusses sound card options.) Plus, your PC's video card will need to support the very high refresh rate of MPEG-2 video. If it cannot, you will not be able to play movies through your monitor. That may be okay if you plan to use the S-video connection on the back of the decoder card to output your movies to a digital TV set. (Most big-screen and high-performance TVs support the S-video connection.) So your system had better be prepared to handle the extreme throughput of high-resolution video and surround-sound.

Techno Talk

The term "MPEG" is actually not a technical one but a political one. It stands for *Motion Picture Experts Group,* and is made up of a group of consultants hired by the major movie studios to come up with better ways to handle the job of storing and transmitting digital video images as well as soundtracks. The standards they all come up with are given the group's name; so **MPEG-2** is a prominent compression scheme used for DVD video and direct satellite broadcasts. Your DVD-ROM might require a separate MPEG-2 decoder card installed in your computer, if you intend to use the drive to watch movies. **MPEG-3** is a replacement standard for compression; if you've ever run across a so-called .MP3 audio file, now you know it's a file compressed using MPEG-3.

However, you should ask yourself, "Do I really need a *computer* to watch my movies on?" Think about it: Your monitor may be big—big enough, in fact, to enjoy a good game of Half-Life—and your sound system may be dynamic and multi-dimensional. But do they compare to the sound and video quality you could get from your own TV and stereo set? Suppose you have friends over to watch a movie. (It could happen.) Do you really want them huddled at your desk around the PC monitor? Unless you really enjoy sampling multiple specimens of breath, the decoder card you purchase should contain a separate *S-video* output. That way, the video signal emanating from the decoder can be output to a real digital television set. The decoder should also have separate outputs for sound, leading not to your PC speakers but to your stereo set. This way, if the movie you're watching supports Dolby Digital Surround sound, you can pipe it into your Dolby Digital Surround speakers.

Of course, this setup basically turns your PC into a dedicated DVD drive. Do you save money this way over a DVD unit for your entertainment unit? After you've spent money for your DVD-ROM drive and your video decoder—and perhaps after you've upgraded some parts of your computer—probably not. But if you compare the price of a DVD-ROM to the total of a writable CD for your PC, plus a separate DVD video player for your entertainment unit, you may end up saving at least $100. Consider whether a hundred bucks is worth all the squinting.

373

DVD Enters the Recording Business

CD-R's and CD-RW's counterparts in the DVD realm are, respectively, DVD-R and the competing trio of DVD-RAM, DVD-RW ("dash-RW"), and DVD+RW ("plus-RW"). Unlike CD-ROM, a DVD-RAM disc can be double-sided, but neither RW standard is expected to support double-sided discs, because DVD video discs have yet to be double-sided. Being double-sided isn't like an LP record, where you can take it out of the spindle and flip it over to read the other side. To support a double-sided DVD, the DVD recorder has to have two lasers reading both sides of the disc.

Recordable DVD drives are generally SCSI-based, and install exactly like a SCSI-based DVD-ROM drive, with one notable exception: They generally interface with a video decoder card (often sold separately) for playback of DVD video.

The less expensive recordable DVD packages do not contain the software necessary for you to actually burn a DVD. Some commercially available software products, including Seagate's Backup Executive for Windows (one of the more expensive packages out there at $150), work just as well for DVD-R and DVD-RAM as they do for CD-R and CD-RW.

How to Install an Optical Drive

Before you remove an optical drive or insert a new one, make sure you prepare your system following the instructions in Chapter 4, "What You Need to Know *Before* You Open Your PC." Then, turn the power off, open up the PC, and discharge that darn static electricity.

Removing an Existing Optical Drive

You can skip this part if there isn't an optical drive in your computer right this moment. To remove the old drive, start by disconnecting its data cable first (that's the wide, flat ribbon cable). Next, remove the audio cable that connects the drive to your sound card. It's a very thin cable with a connector no wider than your pinkie finger. Finally, remove the power cable; it's got four separate wires with a small white connector on the end. It might be kind of hard to remove, but just wiggle it back and forth a little, and it should come out fine. Just don't pull the power cable by its wires; pull it by the white connector instead.

The facts that your optical drive must have access from the front of your PC, and that it must reside in the larger 5¼" drive bay, together mean that you have the added convenience of being able to slide that drive out of the front. First, unscrew the drive from its support cage. It should be supported by at least four screws, two on each side. Once it's loose, give it a little shove from behind, then grab it from the front and slide it out from the front of the PC.

Finally, if the drive you've just removed includes metal drive rails, remove them. You may need to screw them into the same positions on the new drive if your system case requires them, although it may not. Drive rails are a rare feature on modern optical drives.

Installing an Internal Drive

If you've purchased a separate controller card for your drive, and don't plan to use one of your motherboard's IDE channels, now is the time for you to install your interface card. You'll want to put your finger, some other book, or a brick on this page, and then skip back to Chapter 12. There you'll learn everything you need to know about installing whatever adapter or controller card you may have purchased.

Now, you're finally ready to install the drive. Again, before you touch any part of your PC, make sure you've banished the static guy by grounding yourself first. With the cover off, remove the faceplate for the drive bay you've chosen. It's sometimes part of the cover, and other times, it's part of the case itself. You can usually stick a flathead screwdriver just under the rim of the faceplate to pry the thing off.

If You're Installing a SCSI Device

If your new drive's SCSI-based, you need to set its switches so that the adapter can recognize it. These switches control the SCSI address for each device in the SCSI chain (numbers 0, 1, 2, and so on). Just set the drive to the next consecutive number that doesn't match that of any other SCSI devices in your PC. By the way, the adapter has its own ID, too; it's usually set to either ID 7 or 15, so choose something else for your drive. You should be able to set the ID number for the SCSI adapter through its own on-card BIOS setup program; see Chapter 12.

Also, you should remove the terminator on this SCSI drive if you don't plan for it to be the last one in the chain. You see, each SCSI device in your PC connects to the same SCSI adapter card. One end of the SCSI chain is at the adapter, and the other end terminates with the last device. Between the adapter and this last device (whatever it is), there may be up to 6 other devices for standard SCSI, or as many as 14 for "Wide SCSI."

Now, SCSI devices come with something called a *terminating resistor*. Nothing fancy, just a little stopgap that is there to stop (terminate) the SCSI signal at the end of the chain. If your optical drive is one of these middle guys, you should remove the terminating resistor in order for the SCSI signal to continue to other devices further away from the adapter. You're looking for a jumper or a chip called T-RES, or just TR. After you find it, just pull the T-RES plug off of the drive. Of course, if your optical drive is the last device you plugged into the cable leading from the adapter, leave the terminating resistor *on*, and remove the TR resistor from the device in front of it in the chain.

If You're Installing an IDE/ATAPI Device

If your new optical drive uses an IDE/ATAPI interface, you may need to change some settings before you insert it. You will need to set a jumper on the back of the drive to designate whether it is a master or a slave, or to use the "cable select" option (introduced in our discussion of installing hard drives in Chapter 16). The master in this case is the first IDE/ATA device connected to the same cable on the same channel, and the slave is the second device. The master device's on-board controller will be in charge of communications between both IDE/ATA devices and the motherboard. If you plan to install your hard disks on the motherboard's first IDE channel and the optical drive on the second IDE channel, then your optical drive can remain set as "master" even if one hard disk on the other connector is also a "master," because the optical drive is the only device on that cable. If you connect the hard disk and the optical drive to the same cable, then set the optical drive to "slave," and use the connector in the *middle* of the ribbon cable (not the end) to plug into the back of the drive. Check the manual for details, but this usually involves moving one simple jumper.

The idea behind the "Cable Select" option is to attempt to save you some time and energy. With Cable Select engaged, you can avoid having to jumper each drive as master or slave. However, both devices attached to the cable must support this option, and both must have their jumpers set to "Cable Select" rather than "master" or "slave." With this option engaged, your motherboard determines which device is master by what part of the cable it's plugged into; the one at the end, not the middle, is always master. So you have to be certain not to mix up master and slave on the cable.

Connecting the Cables

After your settings have been made, slide your new optical drive into the open bay. Don't bother to screw it in yet; you've got to plug the thing in first (see Figure 18.1).

Figure 18.1

Plug in your optical drive.

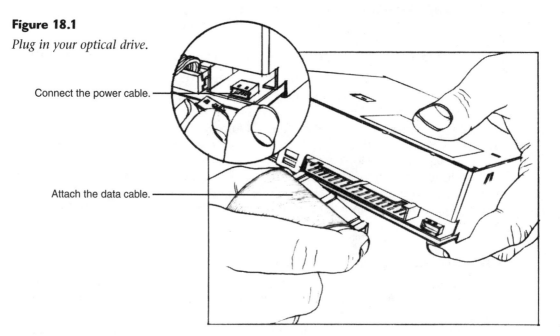

Connect the power cable.

Attach the data cable.

There are at least three, and perhaps six, cables to plug in. Start with the data cable (the big lasagna-noodle-looking one). There should be one connection at the mother-board or adapter card end and two at the device end, with one stuck in the midst of the cable near the device end. The red-striped edge of the cable should match up with the pin marked 1 on the connector. Some thoughtful manufacturers use a triangular arrow to show you which way is "North."

If you have a DVD-ROM, or DVD-*something*, drive and you also have a video decoder card, now is the time to install the decoder card if you haven't already done so. Just like any PCI expansion card, slip it into an open slot and screw on the faceplate in the back. (See Chapter 12 for details about installing cards in general.)

Next, attach the audio cable leading from your sound card or from your video decoder card (in the case of DVD-ROM) to the audio plug on the back of the drive. Although this is officially a "cable," by the standards of other such cables that you've installed thus far, it's really nothing more than a covered wire. It's often in blue or brown spaghetti sheathing, and is about as flimsy as these wires can possibly get. There are tiny plugs on both ends. The plug that has the clip on it goes into the drive, generally in a tucked-away corner. Look at the top of your optical drive for a diagram that tells you where this sound plug is located. If there's no diagram, look for two or four tiny metal prongs in a row, generally on the back end. You might find both two *and* four prongs on some drives. The two-prong set is for digital audio connection; the four-prong set is for analog. You won't mistake one for the other, and your sound card will only support one of these. The clip on the connector going into the drive will face up. A set of two or four metal prongs is located on the sound card. Where the tiny colored wires emerge from the main sheath, look for the red wire, and turn the connector so that the tiny red wire faces to the *left*. Although you can't blow up anything by plugging this cable in wrong, you can still have no sound. So as a word of advice, don't bolt down your PC cover before you've tried out a CD on your speakers.

If you see a *green* wire sticking out of your optical drive and that's permanently attached to it, *that's not the sound cable*. It's a grounding wire that, although not crucial to its operation, may be crucial to its survival in a thunderstorm. At the end of this green wire is a brass antenna lead, which is simply a brass "O." Pick a spot, any spot, on the unused portion of the metal cage inside your system case that houses all of your drives, place a small screw through the O, and screw it into one of the fixing holes of this cage. Next time you forget to ground yourself during an upgrade operation, you may be glad you remembered to screw down this grounding wire.

If you're installing a DVD-based drive, you may need to attach another sound cable leading from the decoder card to the sound card. It's the same type of sound cable as the other one, and it should have been shipped with the decoder card package. If your decoder card doesn't support this cable, you need to attach a patch cable from the "audio out" connector that normally leads to your PC speakers, to an "audio in" connector on the faceplate of the decoder card. However, wait to do this until after you've screwed down the decoder card. Another cable that will have to wait connects your decoder card and your video card.

Next, connect the power cable (the one with the white connector). You probably have a free power cable running from the power supply. If not, you'll need to get a Y-adapter to split one connection into two. Make sure you connect the power cable correctly; if you don't, you can do serious damage to your new drive. Luckily, the power connector is usually notched so that it can only go in one way.

Good job. The patient's alive (at least, I think so). Screw the optical drive in place and close up the PC. But don't attach the final bolts to the back yet until you've heard the sound of music.

If you have an MPEG-2 video decoder card, here's where those external patch cables come in: If you did not connect the sound card to the decoder card *internally*, then you need to do so *externally*. A patch cable that should have been shipped with your decoder card will connect the "audio out" plug on your sound card (where your speakers are plugged in now) to the "audio in" plug on the decoder card. Disconnect the PC speakers from the audio card, and plug them into the "audio out" connector on the decoder card. Then insert one end of the audio patch cable (it doesn't matter which one) into the spot where you unplugged the speakers, and the other into the "audio in" connector on the decoder card.

Another similar connection must then be made between the decoder card and your *video* card, where your monitor is presently plugged in. (Where would we be today if it weren't for about eighteen trillion cables?) Disconnect the monitor from the video card. The video patch cable shipped with your decoder card should look like a monitor plug on one end, though the other end should be small and round, with densely packed pins. Connect this round cable to the connector that's hopefully marked "VGA Card Output Port," or something to that effect, on the decoder card. Plug the other end into the video card where you just disconnected your monitor. Now connect your monitor plug into the open spot on the decoder card.

The Software Part of the Setup

For now, leave the cover off your system case. With everything plugged in, switch your computer on. If you hear the single beep (two beeps for Compaqs), you should be in working order. In a moment, Windows' Plug and Play should detect the presence of your new drive, and lead you through the driver installation process automatically. If this doesn't happen (and it might not, regardless of circumstances), use the Add New Hardware feature of Control Panel to teach Windows the lessons it needs to know. You'll need to know your manufacturer and model number, and have a driver diskette handy. (Having your drivers stored on a CD-ROM or DVD-ROM won't do you much good because, well, you would need your optical drive working to be able to read them, wouldn't you?)

If you're installing a SCSI drive, you'll still need to run some kind of setup program to install the SCSI adapter driver (for the SCSI controller card) and the SCSI CD-ROM driver. Windows' Plug and Play and SCSI are not the best of friends, unless you have a modern SCSI adapter card in your system. So be prepared to install your drivers manually even if you have Windows 98 SE or Windows Me. Chapter 24, "Getting Windows to Recognize Your New Toys," covers the daunting task of waking Windows up to the new realities of the world in which it exists.

Installing an External Optical Drive

Adding an external optical drive is rather simple, because you don't have to get your hands dirty opening up the PC's case. Of course, you might have already had it open to install the controller card for your drive. Oh, well.

In any case, with your PC closed up, attach the cable to your optical drive. Then run the cable to the connector on the appropriate port on the back of your PC, be it SCSI, USB, FireWire, or the printer port. Because a SCSI cable can accommodate multiple devices, you may only have to attach your SCSI drive to any open connector on the existing SCSI chain.

For your SCSI-based optical drive, you'll need to set its SCSI address (devices 0, 1, 2, and so on), either by moving a set of jumpers or a switch on the back of the drive, or by operating the setup software that came with your SCSI host adapter card. Depending on the drive's location along the SCSI chain, you may need to remove the drive's terminating resistor. Basically, if your device is not at the end of the SCSI chain, remove its resistor.

Finally, plug your drive's power cord into a surge protector or UPS and turn it on. (This is especially important if you're installing a SCSI drive, because the PC won't recognize it if you don't turn it on first.) Start your PC and run the setup programs for the card and the drive. You may need to make changes to your BIOS settings, if it doesn't automatically detect the new drive. See Chapter 23, "Making Your Computer Boot Up Again," for help there. You may need to do some manual setup stuff to get Windows to acknowledge your new drive. Your external drive will not be Plug and Play compatible; so you will probably need to run Add New Hardware from Control Panel. See Chapter 24 for how-to's.

Mistakes to Avoid

About a thousand things, as it turns out. Here's a list to help you narrow it down:

➤ If the drive's not working, make sure that you've connected it correctly, and that Windows has chosen the right IRQs and such. See Chapter 23 for help.

➤ If you're using an external optical drive, make sure that it's turned on *before* you turn on the PC.

➤ Got a problem running an audio CD? Well, then, have you installed your sound card, and did you remember to connect your optical drive to the sound card? Did you turn on the external speakers, and play with the volume knob on those speakers?

➤ Some optical drives refuse to work by themselves on their own IDE channel, so you may have to place the drive as the slave on the primary IDE channel with the hard disk as the master. (This is usually due to a conflict with PCI bus mastering and Windows.) You can also try unloading the bus mastering drivers, and your optical drive's manual will show you how to go about that intricate piece of surgery.

➤ Inside your system case, IDE cables should not be any longer than 18 inches, or you'll get intermittent problems with any devices attached to them.

➤ If a game whose CD is in your DVD-ROM drive isn't making any sounds, double-check the connection between the DVD-ROM drive and your sound card. Remember, like a CD-ROM, you must run an audio patch cable between the drive and your sound card's Audio Out connector.

➤ The error message *Mobius hardware not detected* indicates that the external VGA loop cable is not installed properly. Double-check your connections.

The Least You Need to Know

➤ Optical drives come in several speeds. To compare the speed of various drives, check out their data transfer rates, access times, and seek times.

➤ If speed is a factor, make sure that your CD-ROM drive uses a cache of at least 256KB, or that your DVD-ROM drive has as much as 2MB of internal cache.

➤ When comparing CD and DVD speeds, don't forget the "x" factors are different. A "1x" CD-ROM would transfer data at an average of 150KB/s, while a "1x" DVD-ROM transfers at an average of 1,250KB/s.

➤ All optical drive speeds are variable, since the spin rate of the drive is stable for a CD-ROM and DVD-ROM, as opposed to variable for an audio CD or DVD video. So a drive transfers less data per second from the center of the drive than it does from the outside, where the data density is lesser. However, unlike a stereo LP, data is written to an optical disc from the inside out, so actual throughput speeds will almost always be slower than their tested averages.

➤ A recordable CD-R and a CD-RW drive cost about the same, and they both allow you to create your own audio CDs. But a CD-RW drive gives you the ability to have 650MB of removable storage on a very inexpensive disc (a buck or less). So a CD-RW drive is your most affordable, most versatile option for both permanent and temporary backups.

➤ With the new DVD-RW and DVD+RW formats, you should (theoretically) be able to edit and cut real DVD videos on your own computer. However, if the movie studios continue to have their way, you should not have a way to copy commercial DVD movies onto separate discs.

Chapter 19

Powering Up the Power Supply

In This Chapter

➤ When is it time to replace the power supply?

➤ Removing and replacing a power supply, perhaps with more power, perhaps with more cooling

➤ Safer and more uninterruptible power for your system

Believe it or not, your PC does not work on regular household AC current. In fact, the 120 volts that AC current puts out would quickly fry all your wimpy (I'm sorry, I mean delicate) computer parts. So your computer's power supply takes the alternating current (AC) from the wall outlet and transforms it into low voltage (+3.3 volt, +5 volt, and +12 volt) direct current (DC). The stuff in your computer then sucks what it needs from the power supply. Occasionally, the power supply peters out, or, in your upgrading frenzy, you may overtax it.

The power supply also contains a fan that cools down your PC's components, as well as itself. A good word to describe the effectiveness of a single fan in cooling down a tower case system is "joke." Better power supplies, such as those manufactured by Enermax (www.enermax.com.tw), contain two fans: one that faces inside the system case, and a second that faces outside. The interior fan draws air *in*, while the exterior fan acts as exhaust, blowing air *out*. In the best system cases, there's generally an auxiliary fan somewhere. Chapter 20, "Cooling and Ventilating Your System," deals with the subject of proper air circulation and what you can do to help it out.

Going Shopping for a New Power Supply

So why should you concern yourself with the power supply? Simple. If you start adding tons of stuff to your computer, you might need to upgrade the power supply as well. Today, you rarely find replacement power supplies with under 250 watts of power. Such units generally cost about $40, with 300 watt units costing $50, and 350 watt units costing $60.

New system cases come complete with their own power supplies (see Figure 19.1). You never have to buy a system case and power supply separately any more; in fact, the cost of a system case *with* a power supply can be lower than the cost of the same power supply sold separately. Bigger, roomier cases generally have the higher-wattage power supplies. Surprisingly, the price of a power supply alone is often not much less than the price of a system case *with* the power supply.

So when it comes time for you to upgrade your power supply, consider whether it would be worth your while to purchase a new system case, and move all your old components there, saving money in the process.

Note

When your power supply no longer works, you replace it. Don't ever, ever open the power supply box to try to "fix" it. Doing so (even with it un-plugged) is deadly. This is the one part of the computer that could injure you at any time. Leave the power supply closed.

Figure 19.1

An ordinary Baby AT power supply, fully unin-stalled.

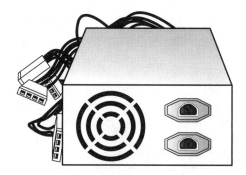

Wattage, Amperage, Voltage, and Other Verbiage

Part of the job of the power supply is to provide power to different types of components that require different voltages. For instance, hard disk drives—which must rotate continuously while the computer's turned on—require +12 volts to sustain constant rotation, although the IDE/ATA interface requires either +5 volts or, more recently, +3.3 volts. With the Socket 7 generation of CPUs, Intel stepped down Pentiums' voltage requirements from +5 volts to +3.3 volts; and although motherboards at first had to employ voltage regulators to step this voltage down a notch, modern ATX motherboards no longer require them.

A power supply's output may be divided into four or five different voltage levels. It then allocates a given measure of the current it generates (measured in amps, or amperes) among those voltage levels. Wattage is generally determined by multiplying the number of volts by the number of amps; but because a power supply's job is to bring down the intensity of the ordinary DC current to a more palatable level for the computer, you actually have to divide the product by 1.4 to get a true estimate of how many watts any device requires.

The range of how many watts of power a component consumes now varies across the board, because almost everything ever made for a computer—RAM, CPUs, expansion cards—has changed its design significantly since 1996. But it's still important to know how much power your new or replaced internal devices consume, especially because these figures determine whether you should replace your power supply or system case. You should double-check the power consumption specifications for any part you intend to purchase.

When Is It Time to Replace Your Power Supply?

If you try to start your PC and nothing happens, it might be a power supply problem, but it's hard to tell. One thing to listen for is the fan—if the power supply is working, its built-in fan should be running. If you're not sure if you hear the fan, hold your hand at the back of the power supply (which can either be the back of the fan, or the exhaust for the internal fan) to see if you feel any flow of air at all. If you feel air coming *in*, there's a chance your power supply can't do enough to cool your system case by itself. If you feel air coming *out,* you're in better shape.

But if you don't feel any air at all, then before you jump to any conclusions, test the wall outlet to see if it works. If it passes the test, unplug your PC from its surge protector and plug it directly into the wall to see if it works, but just until you hear the beep from the BIOS. If it does, the problem's with the surge protector. Reset the surge protector and try it again.

If your power supply peters out, it might be because it got zapped by a lightning strike. If you don't use a surge suppressor, this can happen. After you replace the power supply, make sure you get a good surge suppressor to protect your PC from damage in the future.

If your PC's parts keep burning themselves out, the problem isn't that your power supply is putting out too little power, but rather *too much*. In any case, it's time to replace the power supply.

Selection Criteria for Power Supplies

The first fact you learn about power supplies is that they're designed to fit into the specific form factor of your system case. But this fit runs deeper than just consuming the proper length, width, and depth of space. Newer ATX power supplies have a small degree of integrated circuitry, which enables them to accept their power on/power down/power off signals not from the front panel switch on the system case, but from the motherboard itself. In an ATX form factor system, it is the motherboard—believe it or not—that instructs the PC to go to standby mode, to shut down, shut off, and even come back on again. So if you're replacing an ATX power supply and keeping your system case, you need an ATX power supply to replace it, especially because the switch on the front of your PC … isn't really a switch at all, but just another input device for your motherboard.

The next factor in your selection is getting enough power plugs. Most power supplies come with four, which is adequate although more is better. There are such things as Y-splitters that you can install inline to split one connector into two; but you don't want to have to rely on too many of these splitters for the same reason you shouldn't plug too many extension cords into one another. Most plugs contain four wires in a white plastic casing about an inch wide. Some devices, such as your 3½" diskette drive, use smaller "mini-plugs" to connect to the power supply. They're the same wires but with a smaller plug; so the power supply you choose should have one or two mini-plugs available.

You also need to make sure that the one or two motherboard connectors coming off the power supply will work in your system. The older AT and Baby AT power supplies use a two-part plug to connect to your motherboard, whereas ATX power supplies use only a single, long plug. Your best bet is to simply open up your PC and take a closer look.

Note

You'll still see an abundance of so-called "PS/2 power supplies" still available. They're not just for PS/2s anymore—especially since no one makes PS/2s anymore. IBM wrote the specification for a smaller power supply that connects to an external switch—in other words, it doesn't rely on a "smart switch" supplied by the motherboard like an ATX power supply. PS/2 power supplies are generally smaller than Baby AT or Full AT models. In fact, they're pretty much the same size as ATX, which leads some manufacturers to catalog their models as "PS/2-ATX" or vice versa. But they're actually not interchangeable: PS/2 models use the external switch, whereas ATX models rely on the motherboard for directions.

If the size of your system case conforms to the standards of its form factor (for instance, if it's an ATX case that's roughly the same size as all other ATX cases), then chances are that you have a generic power supply designed to fit that case. If you think your system case is a bit unusual, you may want to take the measurements of your power supply. If you run into problems finding a compatible power supply, you may need to purchase one from your PC's manufacturer. Or you could save a thousand bucks or so and get a new system case. If you feel you have to take the power supply with you to a store, make sure the temperature outside is reasonably moderate, and that you won't be anyplace where you leave the power supply inside your car. (You think Disney World has fireworks.)

If you think the brand name of the power supply is important, or the reputation of the manufacturer ... uh, think again. Will you be able to even recognize the brand name? No. You've never heard of the company that made your power supply. (And neither have I.)

Installing a New System Power Supply

If you opt to replace the power supply by itself, rather than purchase a system case that contains a power supply already installed, you should consider this particular job carefully and soberly. The power supply is the only replaceable computer part that is, by its very nature, deadly and that has indeed killed.

A power supply looks like a set of ordinary screws and a shiny silver box. But in the same way that a cathode ray tube inside a television set or computer monitor retains a jolting, perhaps lethal, amount of power even after it's turned off and unplugged, a computer power supply also retains power at extremely dangerous levels. If you feel that you are any way impaired, mentally or physically, at the time you plan to attempt this procedure, then stop now. Get someone else to do it, or consider getting yourself a new system case with the power supply already installed.

Avoiding Electrocution, or "Who Wants to Be a Million Pieces?"

If you try to open the power supply itself (even if you've unplugged it) the electricity that's built up inside can knock your socks off (and possibly kill you). A modern power supply is turned on and off via the motherboard, and not the main switch. As a consequence, it is officially "ON" as long as it is connected to a motherboard that's receiving power. However, there's no cause for alarm here—power supplies are perfectly safe *as long as you don't try to open them.*

Do not plug your new power supply by itself into the wall to "test" it. A power supply, when it is on, *must be* connected to something it is intended to power, such as the motherboard, the hard disk, the floppy disk drives, and so on. If you simply plug the power supply into the wall while it's not connected to anything else, you may blow it up.

One more suggestion—a minor one, perhaps, but just as important as anything else: When you get your new power supply, you may notice how the unused power cords leading outside have been tied together with either a *rubber* band or a *plastic* belt. If you ever plan to bunch together some power supply cord that has become disused, by virtue of your having removed some unwanted device, then use a rubber band to tie it off, or use a plastic tie-belt. Do not use a *metal* twist-tie like the kind supplied with garden trash bags. Metal twist-ties tend to become unwrapped and exposed. If something bad were to happen to the power supply, it could become a conductor, launching a spike toward some unsuspecting part and perhaps shorting out the entire motherboard.

The Installation Procedure

Start off by taking the usual precautions such as backing up your system (details in Chapter 4, "What You Need to Know *Before* You Open Your PC"). Then, follow these steps carefully to remove the old power supply:

1. Turn off the PC *and unplug everything* (see Figure 19.2). I can't say this one enough: Power supplies retain a bit of power inside, so never, never, never (get the idea you shouldn't do this?) open one up.

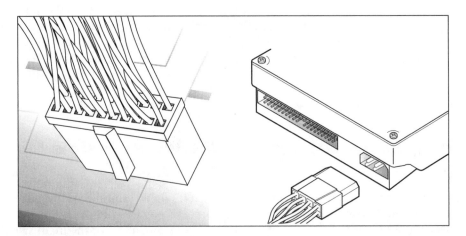

Figure 19.2
Unplug the devices connected to the power supply.

2. Before you start ripping things apart, take a piece of masking tape to mark each plug, and label it so you can remember the device to which the thing connects.

3. Then remove each power plug from the power supply. The one or two big ones connect to the motherboard. Paired power plugs are plastic, white, and have six wires each. Newer power supplies use a single motherboard plug that's roughly

the size of the other two put together. To remove a plug, gently rock it back and forth a bit, tugging ever so slightly upward. Just don't pull on its wires; instead, hold it by the white part, or use needle-nose pliers. Some plugs have "keys" consisting of protruding clips that you must hold onto while rocking the plug. Others cannot be pulled *all* the way straight out; little plastic clips on one side force you to lift the plugs up as far as they will go, then gently bend them 60 degrees to one side, then lift up the rest of the way diagonally. (They go back on the motherboard in exactly the reverse way.)

4. Next, disconnect the main on/off switch (some power supplies have built-in power switches, in which case, skip this step, pass Go, and collect $200).

5. Then unscrew the power supply. Be careful to unscrew the power supply, and not the fan inside—if you keep to the outer edges and stay away from the fan area, you're okay. Also, make sure you put the screws in a safe place so that you can locate them later.

6. Clear a spot on your desk, lift the power supply out, and put it on the space you cleared on your desk. If your PC has a desktop system case, there are probably a couple of retainer tabs at the base of the case holding the power supply in place from the bottom. To release the power supply from these tabs, you need to lift the supply up just a bit and push the supply toward the front of the case. After you free the power supply, use a can of compressed air to clean up the inside of your PC a bit.

Before you insert your new power supply, make sure that it's set for the proper voltage level from the wall (that's 120v for Americans, and 220v for Europeans.) You'll find a switch for this purpose along the back.

Now, look at the side of the power supply that has the two rectangular slots. These two slots need to match up with two retaining clips that you'll find along the side of your system case. Align the clips with the slots, pop the new power supply into place, and then slide it back to engage the retaining tabs. After the power supply is in place, screw it in (see Figure 19.3). Start each of the screws just a little, align the supply, and then screw each one in fully.

Finally, reattach each of the power plugs to its designated location. Here's how you go about doing that:

1. If your motherboard uses two power cables rather than just one (commonly called the P8 and P9 connectors), *make sure that the two black wires on each cable go next to each other, with the colored wires on the outside.* **You absolutely must get this part right—if you don't, you'll blow up your motherboard!** If you're using an ATX form factor power supply, you'll have only one 20-pin power connector, and it can only go in only one way.

Figure 19.3

Screw the new power supply in place.

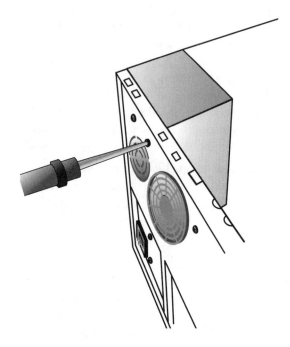

2. Next, plug the following thin power cables into their correspondingly marked connectors on the motherboard, in this order:

   ➤ If you have an ATX form factor, the line going to the power switch (and not the reset switch)

   ➤ The line to the turbo switch (you probably don't even have a turbo switch, but something may need to be plugged in here anyway)

   ➤ Next *and only then*, the line to the reset switch

   ➤ The line to the little LED power light and/or the keylock security switch

   ➤ The line to the other little LED that says the PC's in "turbo mode" (again, you probably don't have a turbo mode, but you may need even a dummy cable plugged in here anyway)

   ➤ The LED that says your hard drive is working

   ➤ Finally, the power to the internal speaker

   Your motherboard transfers power from the main white connectors (P8 and P9 for non-ATX form factors) through to these plugs, which in turn lead to the appropriate locations in the system case. For now, leave the power leading to the CPU active heat sink unplugged since your CPU is unplugged anyway.

   The lights or LEDs and the system lock are typically connected together into a single 5-pin header on the motherboard. You insert the necessary plugs here as follows:

➤ The positive LED plug is placed over the first pin.

➤ The second pin is left open.

➤ The negative or ground LED plug is placed over pin number 3.

➤ The positive and negative system lock plugs take up pins 4 and 5. The colored wire is typically the positive one, and the black or white wire is usually the ground.

➤ The speaker plug may only contain two wires, in that case, connect them to pins 1 and 4 of the motherboard header.

Keep in mind that you need to align the red wire on each cable with pin 1 on the connector, which is marked with a "1" on the motherboard itself, right next to the pin.

3. Next, attach the power plugs to all the peripheral devices, as well as to any cards that may require extra power (very few do). Not all the plugs have a particular device to which they connect. Your 3½" diskette drive will probably use a small mini-plug.

4. Reconnect the power cable, and then turn the PC on to see if anything happens. If everything's okay, turn the power back off and put everything back together.

You should hear the fan when the power supply is on. If nothing happens when you try to restart your PC, double-check all your connections, starting with the connection to the motherboard, and then the main on/off switch. Check the power cable to the power supply, and make sure it is not loose.

If you have the PC connected to a surge protector, make sure that it is on. If one of the drives does not appear to be working, check its connection to the power supply.

Power Security Outside of Your Power Supply

The power supply of the PC is sometimes mistakenly referred to as the "power source;" more accurately, it's more of a reservoir than a source. Like a dam that channels the flow of a river to a narrower level, the power supply's job is to accept power *from* the source and dole it out through separate channels at measured levels. Nothing that the power supply does necessarily makes the flow of electricity any safer; by its very nature, the flow of electricity is dangerous (for further details, see the World Book Encyclopedia under "Chair, Electric"). But if there's anything more dangerous than the natural flow of electricity, it's 1) the *unnatural* flow of electricity, and 2) the *lack* of a flow of electricity. To protect your PC against these two threats, you need to install some form of protection between the power supply and the power source.

The Bare Minimum: A Good Surge Protector

If you don't want to lose another power supply (or the PC itself), you need to invest in a good surge protector. The least a good surge protector should do, in case a huge

389

wave of electricity comes whipping through the line, is blow itself up. Yes, and that is a good thing. Better the surge protector sacrifice itself than allow a surge or a spike to enter your PC. Better surge protectors will serve as shock absorbers, diverting unwanted electricity to useless parts of themselves, and allowing only the necessary voltage to proceed to your valuable parts.

When shopping for a surge protector, remember that you get what you pay for. In other words, if you spend only 10 bucks, you get only $10 worth of protection, which isn't bad, but it's not all that good either. Underwriters' Laboratories (the folks behind the UL symbol, at www.ul.com) regulates which manufacturers are allowed to call their electrical products by certain names. Only qualified products are allowed to be called *surge protectors* and continue to bear the UL logo. A *surge suppressor,* by contrast, could be a legitimate protective device or it could be a cheap extension cord. Cheap surge suppressors offer only marginal protection against surges (if any at all). More expensive surge protectors meet much higher standards and are specifically rated for use with computers.

When comparing surge protectors, look at several factors, including *suppression capacity* (measured in joules or watts/second)—obviously, the higher the capacity for protection, the better. Another feature to look for is *EMI/RFI filtering,* which reduces the impact of nearby electromagnetic fields or radio waves ("line noise") on incoming current. Also, look for telephone line surge suppression for your fax modem. Overall, a UL 1449 rating is an excellent indicator of a good surge protector. Expect to pay between $20 and $80 for one.

Neither a surge suppressor nor a surge protector can protect you against all power problems. For example, if your PC suddenly loses power due to a storm (or little Billy's fascination with wall outlets), then you lose whatever work you haven't yet saved.

Power spikes are real; just because you've never seen one doesn't mean they don't exist. My husband has seen one, and he has a souvenir to prove it: During an electrical storm, lightning struck a nearby lake. From there, it gathered force and leapt to a telephone line. My husband worked a few hundred yards from this lake when a power spike crept up the phone line. Like a loose parasite, this thing came out of the telephone itself (shorting it out, of course), bounced along the top of the desk, shorted out a mouse, crawled through it, and rolled around into a steel-encased Supra brand external modem, where it exploded. The whole thing looked like a Spielberg movie effect; and it lasted about five seconds, so you would have actually had time to follow all this happening. And it left a permanent impression in the modem's case: The stainless steel became "arced," so its surface—which had appeared to be combed in one direction—was now twisted like the surface of a lake stirred by an unseen hand; and if viewed in the right light, you can see a rainbow effect that the spike left in the modem case. For a brief instant, the surface of the metal (not all the way through, just the surface) was literally molten.

What does a surge protector do against a foe like this? It captures it and explodes … internally. It burns out a fuse or two in so doing. It takes its own life, if you will. But it saves your system because the surge or the spike (like the one that hit the modem) stops there.

Uninterruptible Power Supplies

If you can't afford to accidentally lose some work just because nature decides to play a trick on you, then you need to set up your program to automatically save your work for you at timed intervals, such as every 10 minutes. If you still can't relax even with such protection, you may want to think about adding an Uninterruptible Power Supply (UPS). When the power goes off, a UPS (as opposed to a FedEx or an Airborne) kicks in and provides enough juice to your PC so that you can save your work, log off, and go save the ice cream in your freezer while you wait for the power to come back on. As an added bonus, a UPS also acts as a surge protector. The more expensive ones power down your system safely, even when you're not around.

When evaluating UPS systems, the specifications you need to pay greatest attention to are the amount of time required for backup power to kick in when your main power goes out (*switchover time*); the minimum and maximum backup power times (called the *full load time* and the *half load time,* respectively); and, of course, the output wattage.

The least expensive UPS systems available ($90) produce 180 watts, which actually is not the level of wattage that most modern power supplies require (250 watts). A reasonable, though slightly more expensive ($125), UPS system from power supply leader APC produces 330 watts of power, with 4 ms (microseconds) of switchover time for a period of time between 15 and 20 minutes. This should give you plenty of time to power down your system in the event of a power outage or unexpected storm.

The Least You Need to Know

➤ The power supply converts the high voltage electricity coming from the wall outlet into lower voltage electricity that won't burn up your delicate PC parts.

➤ *Never, ever, ever* try to open up the power supply to try to fix it. Even with the PC unplugged, opening up the power supply can kill you.

➤ If you're not sure whether or not the power supply is working, listen (or feel) for the fan. When the power supply is on, the fan is working.

➤ To protect your PC, you need to invest in a good surge protector, which costs as little as $10.

➤ To protect against data loss due to a temporary loss of power, invest in a good uninterruptible power supply (UPS).

➤ If you need to plug in a device and you don't have an open power plug on your power supply, try a Y-splitter to divide one plug into two.

Chapter 20

Cooling and Ventilating Your System

In This Chapter

➤ Why your CPU and other processors can and will overheat

➤ How to install a CPU cooler

➤ Arranging the components in your system case for proper airflow

➤ Adding a new system case fan

When you consider the most vitally important components of your computer, amid your fast processors and fast hard drives, one of them that you might not often consider is *air*. The transistors inside processors have become so small that single electrons could be considered moving parts, almost like ball bearings. And as such, they generate friction, which in turn produces *heat*.

Just a few years ago, computer scientists speculated that one reason we had reached the theoretical speed limit of processor clock speed (which one early 1990s article pinned down at 166MHz) was that the raw material inside consumer PC processors would not be able to withstand the intense heat produced by so many electrons working together inside components that are only 16 ten-millionths of a meter apart (.18 or .25 microns).

The denser the transistors are in a microprocessor, the more wattage that device must dissipate per square centimeter. Even as voltage levels continue to fall, wattage has risen sharply, with the result being that the inexpensive materials used in these devices simply cannot withstand the heat under normal operating temperatures. So cooling systems and ventilation have become a part of our computing lives. If you upgrade a system, chances are it's because you want to make it faster. So when you do, there's an exceedingly good chance that you'll make it hotter. This chapter is about what you will have to do to counteract this trend.

Your Most Valuable Component: The Processor Cooler

Every CPU produced since 1998, and every video processor produced since 1999, requires a powered cooling component. There are no exceptions.

How Hot Can a Processor Get?

CPU manufacturers customarily report what are called *maximum case temperatures*. This title is confusing; this doesn't mean the temperature of the *system* case, but of the packaging of the CPU. A Pentium II processor is designed to operate at maximum case temperatures at or about 70° Celsius (about 160° Fahrenheit). The SECC-based Celerons are more exposed without the plastic case, and with less L2 cache on-board, they could withstand higher case temperatures of up to about 180° Fahrenheit. Newer FC-PGA Celerons can withstand up to 194°F, which is right up there with AMD's CPGA-based Socket A Athlons, which can withstand just over 200°F.

So in just a few short years, we've seen changes in processor design that appear to extend their tolerance level from "Warm" to "Slow Roast." But this development merely speaks to the fact that operating temperature has become a critical concern. None of these processors I've listed are capable of operating by themselves, without cooling apparatus, under room-temperature conditions for longer than one hour—one independent estimate gave the AMD processor under 15 minutes.

Many newer BIOS, especially for ATX form factor systems, include on-board CPU temperature sensors. These devices are capable of sounding alarms through your PC's internal speaker once the CPU reaches a certain temperature—generally 65°C (149°F). Some can actually shut down your system automatically at 69°C or 70°C.

How Cool Should a Processor Be?

With the right apparatus installed, a top-of-the-line, *reasonable* cooling system (one that doesn't use liquid nitrogen or freon gas ... and if you think I'm kidding, I'm not) can bring the case temperature of a properly clocked, socketed, PPGA-based CPU down from 75°C (167°F) to a bearable 32°C (90°F).

That said, some of these reasonably effective cooling systems produced for processors today actually do not fit in the space that system cases make for them. Video processors can become burning hot, but since most video processors are part of a PCI or AGP card, there often isn't enough space between the cards for a proper fan to fit or, when it does, to create proper airflow. Since the AGP connector is generally located above the other expansion slots, you may be lucky enough to purchase an AGP video card whose processor faces up (assuming we're talking about a tower case), but if it faces down, you're in trouble.

Generally, the processor socket on most motherboards situates the CPU in a location where it can come into contact with several cubic inches of air. Generally. But depending on the designs of both your motherboard and system case—which sometimes cannot be engineered with each other in mind—the CPU could end up lodged beneath your power supply, or perhaps behind one of your devices. This is easily the worst possible location, even if your case leaves just enough space to wedge a fan. When your CPU doesn't have room for a fan, or when your CPU with a fan installed cannot draw enough air from inside its tight surroundings to really count, you should consider replacing either your motherboard or your system case. But if there's room for one, your CPU should have a fan.

When choosing a fan for your processor, you'll find that fans fall into two principal categories: So-called *sleeve bearing fans* feature the fan rotor suspended inside a metal sleeve that has been dipped beforehand either in a durable lubricant, or are coated with Teflon. The lubricated fans are inexpensive and quiet, but they're not the most durable; by contrast, the Teflon fans last longer, and are more expensive. Your alternative lies somewhere in-between: *Ball bearing fans* are far more durable, since they reduce the amount of surface contact inside the mechanism. They're not the cheapest fans, but they're not the most expensive either. However, they are the loudest, and you can't do much about that unless your system case is airtight enough to be soundproof. And if it's that tight, then your airflow is going to be so low that fans won't help you much anyway (stick around to the end of this chapter to find out why).

Note

The principal performance measurement unit for *any* fan—including the one you stick in your apartment window—is *cubic feet per minute* (CFM). The average case fan conducts about 40CFM, with power supply fans conducting far less. Ordinary processor fans can conduct as little as 4CFM, but high-grade cooling systems for not much more money, will upgrade that figure to 40CFM or higher.

Cooling Devices That Aren't Fans (and Aren't Cool)

Some CPUs—especially the first SECC and SEPP packages—have a virtual forest of tall aluminum pillars protruding from their tops or from one of their sides. This is called a *heat sink*, not because it looks like a sink, because it doesn't. It radiates the heat outward and drains it into the air, if you will. The pillar contraption has been called a *passive heat sink*, in contrast to the fan being called an *active heat sink*.

To rely solely on a passive heat sink to cool down a modern CPU is a bit like cooling down from a hard summer day's work jackhammering a city street by standing in contact with a turned-off radiator. However, combinations of passive heat sinks and actively powered fans have proven quite powerful working together. For some sockets or slot CPU packages, you can actually purchase a fan that can be attached atop a passive heat sink. But if you don't have room for both, then you should remove your passive heat sink and replace it with a fan. I don't care if your computer works great right now; you should do it.

Sensible, Immediate Precautions to Cool Your System Now

How can you help cool down your CPU today, right now, without purchasing a darn thing? Consider repositioning your internal drives and other devices in such a way that ...

➤ The internal devices don't sit right over the CPU, blocking its airflow.

➤ There's enough space between your internal devices that, between them, they don't create a new source of hot air.

➤ None of your devices block the flow of air from any of the fans to the CPU.

If your system case is so tight that you cannot fit the CPU and its cooling device snugly and safely in place with an adequate degree of air above the fan (or to the side of the fan, in the case of SECC and SEPP packages), then you should not use that motherboard with that system case for your upgrade CPU. You should either replace it for a motherboard whose CPU is positioned in a more adequate location, or get a more spacious system case for your motherboard.

Installing a Cooling Device

The first CPU fans were designed to clip onto or slide over the top of their respective CPUs. You would clip on the fan *before* you inserted the chip package into the socket. The trouble with this design was that not all chip packages were the same. You could clip such a fan to a ceramic package; but today, Intel doesn't make any CPGA packages. Instead, Intel's specifications for CPU sockets (which have carried over into AMD's Socket A specifications as well) call for extended tabs on the sides of the socket, to which a fan can be clipped or strapped on.

Installing a Simple Fan on a Socket CPU

If your fan is designed to slide onto your socket-based CPU, and does not come with a secondary passive heat sink attachment, then the best time to do that is while the CPU is *not* installed. Why? Because you don't want to jostle the grips that hold onto these short, stubby pins while the CPU is in its ZIF socket. But if your fan is designed to clamp onto your CPU (you'll notice a prominent steel belt around it), you'll first want to check to see whether it also slides onto your CPU. Most likely, it will not. Go ahead and insert your CPU into its socket, and clamp it down firmly. Then place your fan carefully, but squarely, over the top of the CPU. There is no "right side up" or "pin 1" for your fan; if it's made to just sit atop the socket, it can sit there in any direction.

Next, with one of the protruding plastic tabs on your socket, thread one of the steel belt loops through that tab. Then stretch the belt over the top of the fan, and to the tab on the opposite edge of the socket, then thread the other loop through that tab.

Installing a Fan/Passive Sink Combo on a Socket CPU

If your cooling device either has or is a passive heat sink, you should have with you a tube of *heat sink compound*, which is a nonconducting gel (known at your hardware store as *silicon grease*). You'll use it to coat the surface of the processor that either comes close to, or comes in contact with, the heat sink. If you just have a fan, then you won't need this goop. By all means don't spread any of this paste on crackers or use as a chip dip. It simply fills the gap between the processor and the passive heat sink, forming a vapor barrier, so that you don't have two metal items in proximity to one another generating a layer of hot air.

First, go ahead and insert your CPU in its socket, then clamp it down firmly (see Figure 20.1). Next, spread a thin layer of heat sink compound over the topmost surface of the CPU. If your processor is a CPGA package (flat ceramic on top), then coat the entire top with a thin layer of the goop. If it's a PPGA or FC-PGA package, you'll only need to coat the aluminum cap on top, and not the surrounding material.

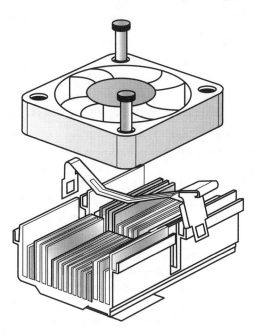

Figure 20.1

The better coolers sandwich a passive heat sink between the socket and fan.

Your heat sink and fan are probably already attached to each other. So with the CPU installed and coated, go ahead and place the cooler gently but squarely onto the CPU surface. There's no "right side up." If there's a metal belt attached to this device, then thread the loop in one side of it through the plastic tab on one side of the socket, stretch the belt over the top of the fan, and thread the loop on the other side through the plastic tab. Instead of a metal belt or strap, you may find a clamping device on one or both sides that's designed to grip the socket tabs tightly. This device works like the metal clasp on the front of an old Thermos lunch box or a portable tool box. You rock it forward and down, and then up to grab the bottom of the tab. Then you push on the upper part of the clasp to lock it down.

Your cooler's manual may show you how to help lock down that clasp by means of a metal flathead screwdriver. *Absolutely, positively, do not do this!* Many screwdrivers have magnetic tips, and even those that don't often become slightly magnetic after heavy use. Besides, if that flathead slips, you could gouge a dent in your motherboard, permanently disabling it. If you need to use a tool, choose something nonconductive, blunt, and expendable, like (I'm not kidding here) the blunt back end of a Bic pen. If it slips from you, you can't hurt much.

Now for the next, weird step: Unclasp your heat sink and take it off. Check the surface of the CPU where you spread the compound. The entire surface should have little stipples in it where it wouldn't let go of the heat sink. Wherever you don't see stipples, you need to apply a very slightly thicker layer of compound. Keep clasping the cooler down and unclasping it until you can plainly see the entire upper surface of the CPU is thoroughly and evenly stippled with goop.

Check This Out

Intel's Pentium 4 CPU effectively ends the era of the Slot 1 CPU by introducing not one but two new sockets. But there's a new catch: The new Pentium 4 sockets are designed with an electrical switch that will prevent the CPU from powering up *unless* there's a cooling device installed. So there's an electrical switch buried in the cooler clip.

Installing a Cooling Device for a Slot CPU

Most slot-based CPUs produced in 1999 and 2000 actually come with their own on-board fans. The key exceptions are SECC-based processors, including the last SECC Celerons before the move back to FC-PGA sockets.

You mount an SECC cooler to the processor package with the CPU disconnected from the slot. (To find out how to remove a Slot 1 CPU, see Chapter 9, "Accelerating Your PC with a New CPU.") While the processor is in your hand, apply a thin layer of heat sink compound to the uppermost portion of the raised aluminum cap in the center of the CPU.

On an SECC package, there are holes near each of the four corners of the central processor. An SECC cooler should have a rear mounting plate with four pre-threaded posts that slip through these holes from the back (see Figure 20.2).

The cooling assembly also has holes for these posts. Unlike socket-based coolers, there *is* a "right-side-up" for SECC coolers, and you may have to check your manual to see just which way is up, because some coolers are not self-evident. Carefully insert the posts through the holes on the cooler, and guide the cooler toward the processor substrate as far as it will go. If it stops before the rear plate of the passive heat sink touches the CPU, then remove the cooler. There may be plastic washers threaded through these posts that need to be removed, or the posts may be cut halfway through, enabling you to remove the upper portions of the posts by bending them off with a pair of needle-nose pliers. This is fine; since SECC CPUs have two form factors, half of the cooler assemblies will not fit until you reduce the size of the mounting posts. Then reinsert the smaller posts through the guide holes in the cooler. This time, the passive heat sink should just make contact with the CPU.

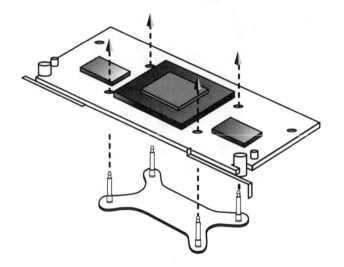

Figure 20.2

Slip the cooler mounting plate through the back of the SECC package.

Finally, there should be some screws or other capping mechanisms that go into the posts and affix the cooler in place.

The Most Important Part: Plugging It In

Most user manuals that come with cooling devices leave out the part where you plug the fan into something to give it power. The power cable from the fan is a thin pair of wires, generally red and black, leading to a single, tiny black plug on the end (see Figure 20.3). This plug is designed to connect to a power header on your motherboard. This header will be marked, generally with "FAN" or "JFAN" ("J" for "jumper").

Some older motherboards (such as this one) have a three-pole header for fan power plugs, although most plugs I've ever seen have just two wires. What's critical is that you line up the red wire over the pole marked "1," which is either at the top or left once you've positioned the motherboard "right side up."

Figure 20.3

The power plug for your fan goes here.

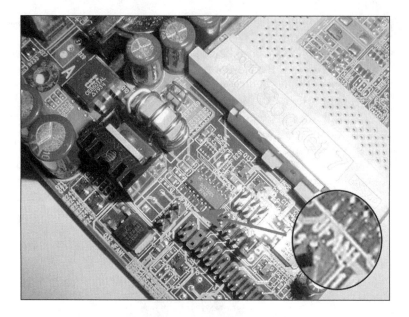

Mistakes to Avoid

Never leave a fan/heat sink combo cooling device attached to your CPU socket if you're not certain it's level, and that the lower heat sink is making flat and even contact with the uppermost part of your CPU.

Don't take the instructions for your cooling device too literally. Most I've read omit the heat sink compound part (a critical element) and would have you fasten the strap down to your socket with a flat-head screwdriver. Whenever you're confused about some specific element of your cooling device, go online with an independent resource such as The Heatsink Guide at heatsink-guide.com.

The Importance of Proper Ventilation

Your heat dissipation apparatus is nothing but cheap ornamentation if your system doesn't have proper ventilation. Your power supply creates some airflow either by drawing hot air out of the system or by blowing cool air into the system (as explained in Chapter 19, "Powering Up the Power Supply"). But that single fan simply isn't enough. Your system case should include a separate, second fan, preferably on the opposite end (if the power supply is on top in the back, then the second fan can be on the bottom in the front), creating a pathway of fresh air that leads into and out of the system.

Just a few cubic inches of airflow on both sides of your hard disk drive make all the difference between a surface temperature of less than 80°F, and a temperature that can actually sear flesh. If you've noticed your hard drive becoming pitfully slow, gradually bringing your entire system down to a crawl, your drive could be overheating.

Now, the platters on a hard drive are made of a substance that resists heat. Trouble is, the resisted heat only dissipates to nearby, more volatile substances. Also, circulating air carries heat away, but only when there's space for it to circulate. By contrast, heat can radiate in all directions through narrow passageways of noncirculating air. Your hard drive could be frying your optical drive at this very moment.

Reducing the Chances of Overheating Through Better Mounting

You may have thought your system case has more than enough space to mount your devices, so you have space in reserve. But with the airspace requirements you just learned about, you may be wondering, what's the safest arrangement for your current devices? All of your critical storage devices should have space between them on both sides. However, in the real world, that's not always possible. So what corners can you cut, and where?

➤ A floppy disk drive generates very little heat, if any. If it's mounted just beneath your hard drive (controller side down), you might not be in any danger. But it can still block airflow to a hard drive mounted directly beneath it. So consider remounting your floppy drive, if you have to, so that it rests on the *bottom* of your 3½" bay cage, and your main hard drive resides on the *top*. In most tower cases, your 5¼" bay cage resides above the 3½" cage, so try, if you can, to leave the bottom 5¼" bay open.

➤ If you only have two 3½" bays, your floppy disk drive is probably parked in one of them. If you have two hard drives, then the best place to install the second one might be in one of the 5¼" bays, with mounting brackets attached to both sides. But in a mini-tower case, you might only have two of these bays available. In that situation—even if you have to remount your optical drive—you should try mounting your second hard drive so that the steel "hood" (the hottest part) is separated from the IDE controller on the underside of the optical drive. You may have to mount the hard drive on top of the optical drive to make this possible.

➤ Many CD-ROM and DVD-ROM drives—which are not the reputed heat generators that hard drives are—can be mounted safely in the uppermost 5¼" bay of a tower case, where there's little space between it and the top cover. But there are exceptions, and I've run into some of them myself.

➤ Some system cases have weird, almost invisible, out-of-the-way mounting rails for second hard drives. They may look like little steel shark teeth with screw holes in them. Look for some in your case.

Why Isn't There Air?

Which way do your fans blow? If you have only one, and it's part of your power supply, you have a serious problem no matter how you answer this question. If it blows *out* from your case, then it's doing very little for your system unless it has proper ventilation in the front. Nowadays, that's about as rare as a celibate intern. If it blows *in*, then it can only generate circulating air *if* there's nothing directly in front of it. Which is entirely unlikely, since directly opposite the power supply in most system cases is the 5¼" bay cage.

Furthermore, a single fan blowing air in, with no proper ventilation for air coming out, can actually become dangerous over time. It's been said that the reason there are system cases in the first place is to keep things like dust, dirt, and dogs out of your system. But if you entirely enclose your system case and attach a single fan blowing in, congratulations, you're the proud owner of a vacuum cleaner. Collected dust, dirt, lint, and hair can, in significant quantities, conduct electricity. (Which is why lint brushes work in the first place.) And since they're drawn toward electricity, eventually lint can situate itself in just the right position to draw power away from your vital components. And in modern systems where voltage is *lower,* and voltage regulation becomes more critical, lint is more dangerous to your computer than ever before.

Now, if you have two or more fans, you have the possibility of real system cooling. In a perfect world, your power supply fan or fans draw air out, while your case fan on the opposite side pushes air in. But just the opposite may be adequate, depending on how much outside ventilation your case fan is exposed to.

Take this simple, nontechnical test: Open your system case, then turn your PC on. (This does not hurt your PC.) Then take a piece of paper, and hold it against one side of each of your fans. This will tell you not only the general direction of airflow, but also the relative strength of your fans.

As Figure 20.4 shows, you'll be able to draw a "weather map" of sorts for your computer, plotting the movement of the jet stream, as it were, over your critical devices.

You may learn the following:

1. Your power supply fan is drawing air in, but a case fan mounted directly over it is pulling this air right back out (or vice versa). Such a situation actually *ensures* stagnate airflow around your other components.

2. Two or more fans mounted on opposite sides of the system are all blowing air in. While this might help you in the temperature department, it's dangerous in the filtering department. System case fans have no air filters, so if they only draw air in, your PC actually *becomes* an air filter; and since tower cases generally rest on the ground, they're located in the optimum spot for picking up lint, dirt, and things the cat left behind.

3. A case fan on the inside of the lower front of your system case is pushing air into your system while your power supply in the upper back draws air out. This

is generally a good arrangement, as long as your storage devices don't protrude so far toward the back that they block the flow of air between the two fans. If both fans reverse directions, the flow of air in might be warmed by the power supply, but the case fan drawing air out can compensate for that.

4. A case fan is mounted above or below the power supply, and is drawing air in the same direction as the power supply. This is good, since it doesn't counteract the force of your power supply (assuming its fan has any force at all). What would be ideal is if you had a third fan at the bottom front moving that air in the same direction.

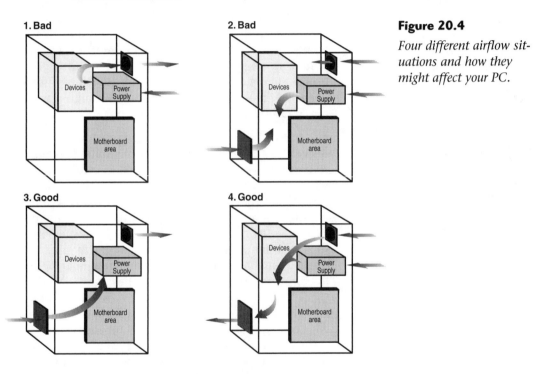

Figure 20.4

Four different airflow situations and how they might affect your PC.

In the past, it was believed that a single fan could provide enough force on one corner of a system case to create air *circulation* in one direction or the other. The engineer of this principle apparently never lived in a high-rise apartment with a single window with a box fan. Sure, the living room stays cool, but the bathroom becomes a toaster. The ideal airflow situation for your system case brings air in and flushes that same air out, as quickly as possible, sending the dust with it.

What can you do to change the direction of airflow for your case fan? If you think the answer is something so simple as, "Turn the thing around" … you're right! Most case fans are reversible.

Adding or Replacing Additional Fans

You need two separate fans. If your power supply has two fans instead of one, that's very nice, but even that's not enough. Those two fans will help draw hot air out of your system. You need a second fan to bring cool air into your system.

A *case fan* is a square, black box that clips onto the side of the system case *somewhere*. Exactly where is uncertain; different system case manufacturers have their own ideas. Some tower cases include steel mounting plates for a case fan, generally at the bottom of the front side, and then close off the entire front side with a nonventilated front panel. But my front panel's ventilated, you may be telling yourself—it has little gills on the side. A Ford Mustang has a little gill on the side of each door—you can't get air to go through it without an acetylene torch to help you out.

The most likely location for a case fan for a tower case is in the front, on the floor, next to whatever sleek shark fin or polka-dot design is used to camouflage the ventilation (which, hopefully, is real ventilation). The installation procedure isn't exactly standard, because although a fan is a computer part, it isn't a *digital* part. However, the power line leading to it from the power supply is standard; it's the same type of tiny plug with one red wire, and one yellow or orange one, designed to connect to the fan (the "active heat sink") on the CPU. If your power supply doesn't have a plug for a case fan, then you should replace your power supply with one that does (see Chapter 19 for instructions). A case fan is that important to your system. You should not have to spend more than $10 for a case fan.

Mistakes to Avoid

If you're going to install two case fans that blow the opposite direction of one another, install them on opposite sides of your system case. This way one fan blows air in, the other blows out.

If your current system case has an overheating problem, never assume that your PC is safer with the case on and the heat locked in, than it would be with the case off and the dust coming in. Heat is a greater enemy to your PC than dust.

Check This Out

You can clean any fan in your system, including the one built into your power supply, by using a can of compressed air to blow the dust away. Of course, the dust you do blow out will probably land right onto the motherboard, so use some more compressed air to blow the excess out of harm's way.

Check This Out

The main fan in your PC's power supply is something you should never try to remove. Although you can replace your power supply safely, you should never under any circumstances try to open one up. If the fan in your power supply makes noise, that's a bad sign. If it draws very little air, that's another bad sign. You should replace it right away.

Speaking of dust, do not use a feather duster to clean any part of the inside of your computer! Would you believe at one time feather dusters were actually sold for cleaning the insides of system cases? Because feathers are organic substances (have you met any plastic birds lately?), they do conduct some electricity, and they also naturally decompose. So imagine what damage little microscopic pieces of feather will do to your system over time.

The Least You Need to Know

➤ Your modern CPU, and even your video processor, *will* overheat without a cooling device installed. Six or seven case fans strapped all over your system case won't beat one good, small fan strapped on top of your CPU socket, or to the side of your CPU slot.

➤ A passive heat sink alone is not enough, but one with a fan on top is the best, and most reasonably priced, cooling device you can buy for the performance it delivers.

➤ Power supply cases can become sources of heat if there's not enough airspace between them and other installed devices, especially your hard drive and optical drive.

➤ A hard disk drive can be an effective radiator for your system if it does not have adequate ventilation on *both* sides.

➤ The fan in your power supply is often not much of a fan. You should supplement it with at least one other fan that blows air into your system.

Chapter 21

Classier Chassis: Consider a New System Case

In This Chapter

➤ Whether your PC needs a new case so its parts can survive

➤ Ordinary replacement system cases versus good ones

➤ Premium features that may be worth the investment

➤ The act of transplanting everything from one case to another

The design of the system case for today's PCs has become a severe problem. We used to think it was safe to entomb our components inside a sarcophagus with little more than a few pinholes and a single, wimpy little power supply fan. The trouble is, with most modern CPUs, today's high-speed hard drives, and especially (surprisingly) today's high-speed video processors, if you cover them all in a 1998 model system case with one fan and no front vent, all of these devices can and will exceed their maximum operating temperature inside of a half-hour.

Now, I spent about all of the previous chapter extolling the virtues of coolness in your system case, and showing you what you can do to add coolness where there isn't any. This chapter is about your other option: Perhaps the most valuable upgrade you can make to your PC is a new system case.

Shopping for a New Case

In Chapter 10, "Replacing the Motherboard and Its Parts," there's a chart showing the standard lengths and widths of motherboards that fit common form factors. Open up your own system case and take a tape measure to your motherboard. If its side measurements match the length and width of one of the form factors on that chart (either vertically or horizontally), you probably can move that motherboard to a new system case purchased separately, either from an exclusive manufacturer of system cases or from a retailer who deals in such cases. Today, they're not difficult to find.

Why Your Existing Case May Be Wrong

How do you know whether your current system case is the wrong one for your components? Ask this important question: Is your case on your desk, and is your monitor sitting on it? Then it's wrong. Replace it with a tower case now. Desktop cases are too small to fit motherboards and devices manufactured since 1999, along with the fans you need to cool them. If transplanting your components into a tower case is physically impossible—or prohibited under the terms of your warranty—then consider replacing your computer now. It's that important. Why go on risking the loss of your valuable data?

Is the tower case you have now wrong for your components? Open it up and consider the following:

➤ Have you used all or nearly all of your 5¼" and 3½" device bays? If they're all full, your devices aren't getting the airflow they require. One reason you might want a system case with more open bays than you'll actually use, is simply for the sake of the airspace. Just a few cubic inches of airflow around a hard disk drive could amount to 50°F of temperature difference. And when your hard drive gets hot, it gets slow, and it could die.

➤ Is there really any source of *true* ventilation besides the airflow through your power supply fan? Secondary fans do little, if any, good inside a sarcophagus. Look for some signs of perforation, preferably in both the front and rear of the case.

➤ Can you even get to the screws in the *back* that are holding your devices in place? With some cases, you have to pry off the front panel to get to the screws in the front that affix the bay cage to the frame, and only when you unscrew those can you get to the back screws that hold your optical drive and hard drive mounting brackets in place. What a waste of valuable time and energy!

➤ How much dust is in there right now? Chapter 20, "Cooling and Ventilating Your System," talked about installing and positioning your fans for proper airflow. If your only fans blow air into the system, dust has no way to get out. (A principle discovered a long time ago by a fellow named Hoover.) But if you have no way to adjust your fans so that it blows air in one side and out the other, your tower case is a vacuum cleaner. This alone is a good enough reason to replace your case.

➤ Can you get to your critical components without risking injury to your hands? Your CPU and your memory modules should not be wedged *under* anything. You may have to change them sometime, and why should you have to remove your device bay cages or your motherboard just to get to them? There should be plenty of room to maneuver a disconnected hard drive through the back and out without banging it or you against something else along the way.

➤ How is your power supply mounted? Even if there's space above and below it, some system cases have them resting against a big metal plate instead of a simple guiderail. These plates can heat up to temperatures beyond what you can comfortably touch, if there's no airflow beneath them to disperse the heat they radiate.

➤ Do your IDE device cables have to make wild twists and turns just to be able to connect to your hard drives and optical drive? Especially with newer IDE cables that use thinner wires for Ultra ATA/66 and Ultra ATA/100 interfaces, they should never have to be contorted to plug in safely and securely.

Why Bigger Just Might Be Better

Tower cases today come in three general sizes, most appropriately described as "small," "medium," and "large." Since only eggs are marketed that way these days, the names generally used instead are "mini-tower," "mid-tower," and "full tower," respectively. There's no real measurement standard governing the *outside* of a system case; when you stack all three types beside each other, you get a general idea of their differences. But when they go so far as to invoke the name "ATX," they do mean something specific: They're designed to hold a 12" × 9" motherboard. Some of the larger system cases go by the designation "AT/ATX," which means they're also adaptable to the older Baby AT motherboard form factor of 8.5" × 13".

In many system cases, only some of the device bays are "exposed"—meaning, you can install hard drives in some of the bays that don't require access from the front, but these bays may be tucked away somewhere, perhaps in a more obscure location. Bigger system cases generally don't include such nooks and crannies, but I've seen exceptions. A mini-tower case can have as few as two 5¼" *exposed* bays, and one 3½" exposed bay, with few or no unexposed. Mid-towers, on average, have three 5¼" exposed bays, one 3½" exposed bay, and one or two 3½" unexposed bays. Full towers have no excuse for economy. They should contain five or six 5¼" exposed bays, two 3½" exposed bays, and as many as three 3½" exposed bays, with room to spare.

If you eliminate mini-towers from consideration, then you'll find that size plays no appreciable role in the price of cases. In other words, you're not saving a cent by going with a smaller case. In fact, you could find a deal on heavily discounted *full* towers that simply look less exciting than some of the cooler mid-towers.

The average price of an *ordinary* system case is about $60, in either mid-tower or full tower. Ordinary may not be want you want, however. In a moment, I'll tell you about certain features to look for, some of which may cost a little extra, but will make the entire transplant operation well worth your effort. For a top-of-the-line system case with premium features, be prepared to spend about $125.

I've mentioned airflow as the principal reason for owning a larger system case. The facts that your power supply should be mounted *above* your motherboard if it's not to obstruct it, and that your power supply should have some airflow above it if it is to stay cool, are enough to disqualify not only desktop cases but "mini-towers" as well from consideration as replacement system cases.

Ease of maintenance is another reason. The smaller a case is, the more difficult it becomes for you to get things in and out of it. You need access to your system case, if only to check things out and make sure they're okay. And how can you do that if you can't even see all your components for all the crazy wires?

Here's a factor that even very few manufacturers consider: A good, solid, steel case is an important electrical component in and of itself. It's a *grounder*. In contact with your floor, it can absorb and disperse electrical discharges, carrying those discharges away from your vital components. One day, a leftover charge from a burned-out power supply in a system my husband was working on, zapped the metal frame of the case. Instead of dispersing the energy, it visibly leapt to the floppy disk drive case, which was instantly fried as though it were struck by lightning. Gratefully, only the floppy drive was toasted, and one reason was because the frame of the system case took the brunt of the discharge, saving the more vital components. If your system case is too small, a static discharge from a bad power supply, or from bad power in general, has a greater chance of damaging your equipment, and even broiling your computer. (This is one advantage to consider when you're investigating the new, "all-urethane" cases.)

Where the Screw Holes Are: The Major Factor

My apologies for invoking memories of Connie Francis. (My heart has a mind of its own.) The location of the screw holes on a system case tell you more than you might think about its usefulness and reliability. On an ordinary tower case (and there are so, so many of those) there are four or six screws in the back that affix the rear flanges on the case cover, to the interior metal frame. Historically, these screws have been more impossible to remove than a husband from his remote.

But what's the alternative? Be careful about cases that grant you "screwless" access from one side, perhaps with a single thumb screw or even a latching door handle.

With some cases where one side opens easily, *the other side doesn't*. Which means you may have to pry the plastic panel ("bezel") off the front to get to the device bay cages, to unscrew them in order to get to the other side of those cages, just to get to the opposite side of the bay cage to remove the screws there. Also, you might have to unscrew the mounting plate where the motherboard rests, just so you can get to the back of it to affix spacers and standoffs. At least with a conventional system case, *both* sides of the case come off easily, giving you rapid access to the entire bay cage and the motherboard backplate.

Here's something else to ask yourself: Does the front "bezel" panel (don't you love that word?) really come off? If so, why? Probably to grant you access to the screws that hold on the device bay cages. This is so you can disconnect those cages from the frame. Now ask yourself this: *Why?* If the system case is designed so you can get to whatever's on the back side of the device bay cages easily, then why would you ever need to disconnect the bay cages? A well-designed system case may very well leave these bay cages permanently welded to the frame, without losing any points in my book.

Design Features to Look For

Retail salespeople don't really know how to show off the features of a system case. It's a box, and it either looks cool or it doesn't. But a system case is the chassis of your PC, and its design is at least as important as that of any other component. Here are some features of the better case designs that, once you realize they exist, you'll wonder how you got along without them:

➤ **Built-in power supply**—There's no reason to settle for less than 300 watts, and you can get as many as 400 watts. Colossal wattage doesn't mean your new system case will be an energy guzzler. It simply means that it can make more wattage available to more devices if you have them. If you have no more than two hard drives and one optical drive, along with your floppy drive and, of course, your motherboard, then 300 watts should be plenty.

➤ **Removable rear I/O port shield**—This is a metal cutout that clips to the back end of a case, and features precut holes perfectly shaped to fit your parallel, serial, and USB input/output connectors. An ATX motherboard has on-board support for I/O, so you can run ribbon cables directly from the motherboard to the back end of this cutout, where your connectors are screwed in. But if a system case supports both ATX and the older AT or Baby AT form factors (many do), those I/O connectors will be provided not by the motherboard, but by an interface card which already has the connectors attached. If you're moving a Baby AT motherboard to an "AT/ATX" system case, you won't need the cutout. So you can take it off and replace it with a flat metal shield that covers over the entire area. In the rare instance that your case also supports the LPX form factor, you'll need an alternate cutout with holes that precisely fit that motherboard's on-board I/O connectors, which stick out from posts on one side.

411

➤ **Front and rear ventilation**—In other words, lots and lots of little drilled holes. In order for your fans to move higher quantities of air around, air has to have other means of entering your case than through the fan itself. Your single power supply fan may draw air in instead of out. Since nature abhors a vacuum (Congress being the exception), if air can get in from perforated holes *around* the fan, it will. Even if the power supply draws air out (which is preferable), peripheral airflow can only help overall circulation. And you need airflow from both sides of your tower case.

➤ **Removable motherboard mounting plate**—You'll have a much, much easier time installing your motherboard if the metal plate it attaches to can be unscrewed from the system case frame. You can lay the plate on your work table, pick it up, adjust the spacers beneath it, without lugging around this 30-pound behemoth or, worse yet, having to clear the power supply or the device bay cages to get to it.

➤ **Redundant mounting holes**—For different motherboards. If a motherboard follows a specific form factor, its mounting holes are supposed to be in particular locations. As I've discovered, this isn't always the case. If your mounting plate has enough extra holes to support variations in the manufacturer's interpretation of the form factor standards, this won't be a problem for you.

➤ **A fan in the front**—Not just the space for a fan—coupled with adequate ventilation in the front plate or bezel. If your rear power supply draws air out, you'll need ventilation in the front to push air in.

➤ **Guide rails for devices inside the bay cages**—Little metal tabs are all that's required to ease the installation of an optical drive or a diskette drive from the front of the case, so you don't have to reach inside and hold it up while you're screwing the thing in.

➤ **Easy access to the on/off and reset switches**—For an AT system case, you'll need to attach the main switches leading from a cable on the power supply, to wherever your switches are located on the front of your case. An ATX system case that does not support AT motherboards will have no mounting units for the AT power supply's main switch. On the other hand, an ATX motherboard has its own "intelligent" switching device, and an ATX system case features its own main power switch, that you shouldn't have to bother with. Leading from that switch on the inside of the case, is a plug that connects to a header on the ATX motherboard. This ATX switch is, of course, incompatible with AT power supplies. If your system case is an "AT/ATX" model, and you intend to install an AT or Baby AT motherboard, you'll need to be able to reach in and unmount the ATX switch and replace it with the switch from the AT power supply. (For that matter, you'll also need to specify you want an AT power supply with your AT/ATX case, because the two power supplies are quite different.)

Premium Features Worth Considering

Not every system case will have the features on this next list, but you might find some of them worth the extra money:

➤ **A mounted side fan**—Since motherboards generally mount on the right side of a tower case (for no particular reason), a fan on the left—particularly one mounted right over the peripheral card area—would be ideal. Peripheral cards are their own barricades to adequate airflow, and your video card is one of the hottest devices in your system. A fan mounted directly over it (in addition to the processor fan mounted on the card itself) could be a savior for your system.

➤ **Color**—Hey. Have you heard? "Putty" is out. Some system case manufacturers have entered the market with all-black product catalogs.

➤ **Mounting drawers**—Now, here's an ingenious concept: Some manufacturers have created drawer systems for the easiest mounting of exposed and unexposed devices you've ever seen. After you pull off the front bezel and flip a locking lever, each of the docking bays can slide forward, giving you easy access to your devices *without* having to pull off the case cover. (Problem: The power and data cables on installed devices would need to be long enough to be pulled forward along with the device, otherwise you'd just have another stuck drawer on your hands.)

Moving Day: Factors to Consider

If you're comfortable with the idea of moving your motherboard and your internal storage devices out of your old system individually, you should be fine with the idea of moving all of them, all at once. Give yourself the whole weekend so you're not under pressure.

What Do You Need That You Don't Have?

Count the number of Molex power plugs your new power supply gives you. Are there enough to power all your devices once you've moved them? If not, you'll need to get a hold of one or more Y-adapters.

Where will your new I/O cables go? One of the problems with your old system case might be that it didn't provide you with a convenient spot for one or more of your I/O cables—this is often the case with older cases that don't have natural locations for USB ports. So the serial, parallel, and USB cables leading from your motherboard may be attached to a clip that takes the place of an expansion card. Or, in the absence of such cables, your current system may be using a serial + parallel and/or USB expansion card so that the I/O ports can be located in your expansion area. If your new system case has cutout holes or an "I/O shield," you'll need ribbon cables that have connectors on one side that screw into these holes from the back, and that connect to your motherboard at the other end. If you don't have these cables, but you do have the cutouts and want to use them, get those cables now. Don't worry; they're cheap. Chapter 4, "What You Need to Know *Before* You Open Your PC," shows you the tools you'll need for this job, and it even shows you the types of toolkits that gather all of them together for you.

Getting Your Stuff Out: What Order?

If you chose your new system case carefully, the hardest part of this job may be getting your equipment out of the old case. Remember, it's the *old* case. You might not need it for anything anymore. So this time around, if the power supply is in the way of a free and clear extraction of your motherboard, then by all means, get that power supply out of there. Chapter 19, "Powering Up the Power Supply," shows you how. Mechanically it's not difficult, but it can be dangerous, because even unplugged power supplies retain reserve electricity. So be extremely careful.

Your new system case will have its own power supply, so you won't need to transplant your old one. If your old power supply was part of the problem with your old case, throw the thing away. It's no good to anyone, and there's no money to be gained from used, worn out power supplies.

Next, you should unplug everything both outside and inside the old case, and get the old cables out of the way. The power cables will still be attached on one end to the old power supply, but the data cables can be disconnected at both ends. So unplug your data cables from both your motherboard and your storage devices. Don't worry; you can't accidentally plug an IDE cable into your diskette drive. Then unplug your power cables from those devices, and unplug all the cables leading from the power supply to the motherboard. Chapter 10 shows you precisely the order in which motherboard cables are most safely removed. To keep the power cables from getting in your way again, tie them all together with a rubber band, then tape the bundle onto the top of the power supply.

Leave the motherboard in place for now, and get your storage devices out. Before you start, consider whether your device bays are in the way of getting your motherboard safely out. If it's a small system case (and I've seen some, believe me) you may want to see if you can unscrew and remove the 5¼" and 3½" bay cages whole and intact, with devices still mounted. You can do this safely, as long as they're all unplugged from both power and data. Bay cages are often screwed in from the front of the case, either from the *outside* of the front (after you remove the old case's plastic bezel, if it has one) or from the *inside* of the front (on the back side of the lip to which the front panel is attached, after you've removed the old case cover). The screws you'll find are just like any others inside a system case—usually short, stubby "hex-head" screws. Once you've removed these screws, the bay cage can probably be removed by sliding it out from under the metal latches holding it in place. Again, you only need to do this if it makes accessing your motherboard simpler, or if the design of your old case makes it otherwise impossible for you to reach both sides of the bay cage to remove your devices. (If you can't get to the other side, how come a repairman can? He has a

414

spot welding torch. One chance in three he knows how to use that thing without spot-welding your CPU to your RAM.)

Chapter 16, "Hands-On Hard Disk Replacement," shows you how to remove your hard drive(s); Chapter 17, "Replacing a Floppy Drive," shows you how to remove that little item; and Chapter 18, "Adding an Optical Drive," shows you how to remove a CD-ROM or DVD-ROM drive. (This is where an author wishes this book were actually on the Internet, because it would make all these chapter references into hyperlinks.)

Now, what should you remove from the motherboard, and what can you safely let alone? Technically, there's no reason why your CPU, your CPU's cooling device, memory modules, expansion cards, and certainly your BIOS chip can't remain right where they are while you're transporting the motherboard. However, if you feel there's any chance that a card could get damaged in transport, then it's certainly safe for you to remove any or all of them. You might want to reposition those cards inside your new case after all. Chapter 12, "Face the Interface," will remind you how to remove expansion cards.

With your devices removed, and your cables and everything else securely out of the way, now you can remove your motherboard using the instructions in Chapter 10. If your old case has a motherboard mounting plate that can be disconnected, do so. After you get the motherboard out, be sure to remove any leftover spacers still attached to the motherboard mounting plate; you may need them for your new system case, unless the manufacturers of that case were nice enough to supply spacers for you.

Check This Out

The one thing you absolutely want to avoid doing when you're gutting your old system, if you will, is bleeding. Water, as you know, conducts electricity. But as a chemist biologist will tell you, blood not only conducts electricity, but can actually retain a small charge. The little spiky beads of solder on the back of an expansion card or motherboard, may be thorny enough to scratch and even cut you. A drop of fresh blood on just the wrong part of an integrated circuit can short it out.

Putting Your Stuff In: What Order?

Here is the order that you want to follow for putting your stuff back into your computer:

1. Since your motherboard goes toward the back of your new system case, it should be installed first. If your new case has a detachable mounting plate (you have been reading this book carefully, haven't you?) then now's the time to unscrew it, and attach your motherboard to it using Chapter 10 to guide you. Then, of course, screw the plate back to the case. Don't connect cables just yet.

2. You should not have to remove any of the bay cages to be able to install all your storage devices. They go in next, using the instructions in Chapters 16, 17, and 18.

3. Now it's time for cables. Your I/O cables should be first. If your system case has an appropriate cutout or "I/O plate," then screw them into the back of the plate as directed by the markings on the plate itself. Then plug the other end into the appropriately marked locations on the motherboard. Chapter 12 contains more details on this procedure.

4. While you're attaching data cables, now's a good time to reattach your IDE and diskette cables.

5. Next, it's time for the power cables, and it's good to get the fiddly bits out of the way first. Your new case will have a few LEDs (little bitty lights) on the front, which tell you whether the thing's turned on and whether the hard drive is accessing data. There are also other cables for auxiliary case fans, and for ATX cases there are the all-important main switch, reset switch, and standby mode cables. Chapter 10 tells you precisely the order in which these tiny cables should be reconnected.

6. With the tiny cables connected, power up your motherboard. There are two types of motherboard power connections, and only some power supplies are equipped with both kinds. All ATX cases will feature the right power plug for ATX motherboards (the new single plug). Chapter 10 shows you how to reconnect your motherboard's main power.

7. Finally, connect the power for your storage devices. Only your diskette drive takes the weird, smaller power plug; your other devices use the big plugs.

With everything reconnected, it's time to try out the PC that you have just built for yourself. There may be a few hitches along the way; don't worry. We have yet another chapter to help you scale these very hurdles: It's Chapter 23, "Making Your Computer Boot Up Again."

Mistakes to Avoid

Before you connect your new system case to a power source, double-check to make absolutely certain that every device is powered, your motherboard is properly plugged in, loose and unused power plugs are out of the way of anything they may happen to shock, and unused fiddly plugs are unused for a reason (your motherboard doesn't need them, for instance).

If you find yourself having to disconnect and reconnect the device bay cages on your new case, absolutely make certain that the reconnected cage is fully screwed down and fully latched and locked. If it isn't, you might not be able to get your front bezel back on. And some system cases contain special switches that prevent your power from coming on if your front bezel is loose or disconnected.

If you turn on your new system, and you don't hear the pleasant, gentle roar of the power supply fan, stop now. You could have a defective power supply.

Never purchase an AT system case thinking that you can refit it to support an ATX power supply. One key difference is in the switching mechanism. There's generally no way to mount an ATX power switch on a case that expects its AT power switch to come from the power supply. Same goes for the reset switch.

The Least You Need to Know

➤ Regardless of what you may have read about how great it is that computers are getting smaller every day, a small system case can be very, very bad for your newer computer components. They need air. Desperately. And newer, larger (tower) cases may have the answer.

➤ Besides the desktop style case you don't want, system cases generally come in mini-, mid-, and full-tower sizes. They're also custom-made to support particular motherboard form factors, especially AT and Baby AT, ATX, and LPX (Slimline).

➤ Your brand-name PC may have a proprietary motherboard that doesn't fit a common form factor, and therefore may not fit in a new system case.

➤ A thumbscrew or latched entry door is a very nice feature, but beware the possibility that such a design leaves the opposite panel bolted and welded shut. In such a case, you may actually have to unscrew and remove your device bay cages to get to both sides of your devices to remove and remount them.

➤ New system cases come with their own power supplies. You can actually purchase some cases for less than you'd spend for the same power supply alone. But be careful and get a case that has the power supply you need; the older AT takes one type, ATX and LPX require another.

Chapter 22

Installing and Maintaining a Home Network

In This Chapter

➤ Do you really need a network if you have two or more computers?

➤ How a home peer-to-peer network works

➤ What the new, inexpensive network switches really do

➤ A formal introduction to the two types of Ethernet network cable

➤ How to "roll your own" coaxial cable segments

This is a chapter about the biggest and most technologically advanced attachment you can add to your computer: another computer. You should consider the potential benefits of linking two (or more) computers together if you're in any of these situations: members of your family are being forced to file computer-time requisition forms four weeks in advance; you cannot upgrade your existing computer to the level you need for the software and hardware you want to use (see Chapter 2, "Now, Let's Find Out What Kind of Computer You Have"); you have your own desktop PC and your work gives you a notebook PC; or you find yourself needing to buy a second computer anyway. To begin, let's focus on whether a two- or three-workstation network makes sense for you right now.

More Than One Computer? How About a Network?

The general notion of a network conjures visions of miles of cable, or hundreds of terminals, or, perhaps more often, of NBC. The Internet is a network, and so are a spider web, the capillaries in your bloodstream, the trail of bank accounts used to launder money flowing into the Nixon re-election campaign in 1972, the neurons in your own brain, and mold. But a network is not usually thought to contain just two computers. However, a two-computer network is not only feasible but also, for some limited purposes, may be quite desirable.

Since the advent of Windows 95, Microsoft has considered each PC a network unto itself—a network of one. Why? Because the one thing a computer does best is move data from place to place. If a computer can act like a network when it moves data from someplace here to someplace ... well, *here,* then it may just be easier to train that same computer later to move that data from here to *there.*

What Do You Gain?

The main benefit of having two networked computers in the home is that two or more people can share some of the same resources. Networked computers can share the same printer, for instance; if the printer is upstairs, the computer from downstairs can send pages to it. You only need one modem for your Internet connections; any computer on the network may access the one modem plugged into your phone line. (Generally, only one computer may access this modem at any one time; but Windows 98 SE and Windows Me have found a way around that problem.)

If you run a small, single-location business, then there may still be significant reasons why you would want to invest in a network, even with only two PCs. If you run a re-tail operation, your business' vital data will be safer if it's stored on a computer in a locked office. However, you'll need at least a second computer up front to be able to access that data—especially your inventory list, and items on order—as well as handle your point-of-sale operations. If your company has more than one officer, chances are that you have more than one PC anyway. Why waste all that time shuttling diskettes back and forth just so you can share your reports and spreadsheets? You'll find it much more efficient for two PCs to be able to get at the same base of company data, or "database" (so *that's* what the term means!).

Why "Peer-to-Peer"?

In networking, the term *peer-to-peer* refers to the way in which the computers in the network perceive one another. In office networks, there is generally one main server and several clients. These clients make requests of the server, and the server responds with data, files, or other shared resources. But in a peer-to-peer system, there is no multi-tier hierarchy. Both (or all) computers in the connection share each other's resources, and neither is perceived as the master (or the server) for the other. A shared peripheral, such as a printer, may be installed on either system.

When you have two computers networked together, the hard drives and other storage devices, such as optical drives, belonging to both computers can be made addressable by both computers. Now, these drives may have to be given different names, because the C: drive on any system is the one from which it boots. So if each of two networked computers has its own hard drive, then the C: drive of computer #1 may be recognized by computer #2 as E:, and the C: drive of #2 may be recognized by #1 as E:. This renaming of one drive to another letter for another system is called *mapping,* and it's not nearly as fun as true cartography.

Mapping also has its downside, and perhaps you've already figured it out: Both the operating system and the applications on one computer are not automatically sharable through the network. In other words, just because Quicken is installed on system #1 does not mean that system #2 can run Quicken right away. You still have to "install" the applications you'll run on #2 through system #2. However, during the installation process, most modern software is capable of examining all the drives in the network for copies of itself. If Quicken or Excel or some other program being installed on #2 runs across an existing installation of itself on drive E: (which is really #1's drive C:), then that installer program will ask if you want to run the already installed program from this computer (or *workstation,* if you want to sound like you earned a degree in this stuff). If you respond with yes, the installer only places a few files on #2—just enough to let it know that the real location of the application is over on #1. It ends up being convenient, because the drive on #2 doesn't have to be cluttered with the installed software on #1. However, you can't say that networking saves you from having to install software on more than one computer; you still have to "install" applications on each system from which they will be run.

Note

Is "peer-to-peer" the same as "P2P"? Not really. They're very, very similar, but the notion of software that makes your PC into an Internet file server, for other similar file servers who want to share files (such as Napster, Gnutella, and their descendants), use the P2P abbreviation to describe their methods of interfacing and communication. Peer-to-peer networking has been around for exactly as long as computer networking, and has always referred to two or more systems (but generally two) that can act as each other's servers or clients dynamically.

Is it worth all that bother just to save some hard drive space? Perhaps so. Suppose you work most of the time from a rather enclosed office, but you have an atrium where you retreat sometimes, or an outdoor patio. If you could wire such a place for a network connection, then you could have either the cheaper desktop computer of the two or, preferably, your notebook computer plugged in when you need it, take that retreat every once in awhile, but take your work with you. Your data files could stay on your main office system, so you wouldn't have to lug a diskette or CD-R disc from place to place.

The Components of a Home Network

The least expensive and most efficient personal network equipment you can buy consists of the following:

➤ Two *network interface cards* (NICs), which are preferably PCI expansion cards that plug into your PC just like an internal modem or sound card. These are among the least expensive expansion cards you can buy, rarely priced above $15.

➤ Two (not one) 25-foot network cables, generally type CAT5 (also known as RJ-45, just slightly thicker than type RJ-11, which is used to connect most telephones to the wall jack). So-called "Ethernet cable" is today generally CAT5.

➤ A self-powered box called the *switch*, which belongs somewhere in between the two systems. The two cables are used to connect the two NICs to this one switch. The switch handles the signaling between both computers, and often contains extra ports in case you ever want to add one or two more systems to the network. In Chapter 13, "The Online Line," I introduced you to a switch that also acts as a broadband firewall, enabling you to not only connect two or more PCs together, but to let them share a single broadband modem (cable modem or DSL) connection safely. An ordinary five-port switch should cost you about $50; with firewall and broadband support added, it should cost just over $100.

➤ A little bit of software, generally in the form of a CD-ROM that contains drivers that should be installed on both systems, so that they can recognize the NICs as legitimate devices.

You may be wondering, where's the network operating system (NOS) in the preceding list of requirements? If you have Windows 95 or any later edition, you already have the NOS. Prior to 1995, the part of the operating system that handled networking was not part of the consumer edition of Windows. It was provided by either Windows NT or Novell NetWare, which is an operating system on top of an operating system that was designed originally to provide networking facilities to MS-DOS. A current version of NetWare is available that enables Windows 95, 98, or Me to act as a network client. Wait a minute—didn't I just get through saying that Windows already was a network operating system? Indeed I did, but NetWare makes it into …

well, a different network operating system, which is arguably better suited for installations and situations having nothing to do with home peer-to-peer circumstances. It's unfortunate, but you don't really need Novell NetWare, just as you don't really need a Corvette. But bigger businesses do need NetWare since it provides all their clients with more sensible access to business resources—in other words, not through Windows Explorer. So NetWare does have its place in a modern society. But unless your office uses a virtual private network (VPN) to enable access to its computers from workers at home, you don't need NetWare.

If you're considering extending your network connection between two or more PCs so that there is 100 feet or more of cable between them (assuming you can station your switch about 50 feet away from each PC), you may need to consider using coaxial cable (10Base2) for your longer connections. It actually costs less per linear foot than CAT5, but it can affect the setup of your network, as you'll see later in this chapter.

The Two Types of Ethernet Cable

There are two basic types of networking cable rated for use with Ethernet NICs:

➤ **10Base2 thin coaxial cable** is pretty much the same grade of cable used for cable TV, only it goes through a few more tests before getting the official networking grade. The odd alphanumeric contraption "10Base2" is shorthand for the meaning of this official grade: a cable that should carry a signal at 10 Mbps (megabits per second) for a distance of 200 meters (about 650 feet). If you go to the hardware store and find multiple grades of networking cable, you now know that "1Base5" doesn't have the right bandwidth; "10Base5" is a little better grade than you may need. The slowest data transfer speed of today's Ethernet NICs is 10 Mbps, which is fine for 10Base2 cable. If you happen to have a 100 Mbps Ethernet card—which is the next step up—then you'll either need a better grade of coaxial (100Base5) or else use CAT5 cable instead. You can find 10Base2 cables at the 50-foot length with connectors preassembled, for about $5.

➤ **CAT5 (Category 5) cable** refers to the grade that telephone engineers have given to twisted-pair cable with little clips on the end, rated for networking. It'll look a bit familiar; in fact, you might mistake it for indoor telephone cable. But telephone cable (CAT3) uses a smaller connector (RJ-11) and a lower internal bandwidth cable than does CAT5 (RJ-45), so they're absolutely not the same. It takes about half a second less time to install a CAT5 cable than it does for a 10Base2 coaxial; you don't have to screw anything in, just push until the clip locks in place. Because CAT5 is thinner, it might not be quite as unsightly as 10Base2, for which you would pay extra if you wanted colors other than basic black or Black-and-Decker orange. But CAT5 doesn't have the range of 10Base2; if the same grades were passed out for CAT5 as for coaxial, it would literally be called "100Base1." CAT5 also averages about three times the cost per linear foot of 10Base2.

423

Today's Ethernet switches are equipped with RJ-45 connectors only; if you were to use coaxial instead, you would have to invest in "10Base-T" converters that convert a coaxial plug to a RJ-45 plug. Although that could make up for the cost savings, you should still consider using coaxial if you're setting up a connection that leads outdoors, or if you have to run a lot of cable, or if you're just now *building* your house and you're running network cable through the walls prior to the workmen putting up the drywall.

How Fast a Connection Do You Need?

The everyday NIC produced today supports two speeds: 10 Mbps (megabits per second) and 100 Mbps. What's a *megabit*? Exactly one million bits (1s or 0s). A single byte constitutes eight of those bits; and depending upon how the network is set up, eight or nine (most often eight) of these bits may be used to send one character. To give you a relative speed factor, 100Mbps (the speed of a so-called *Fast Ethernet* network) is roughly 1,785.71 times the speed of the fastest 56K modems, and 64.77 times the throughput speed of a T-1 digital phone line.

Because you're putting your home network together from scratch, you don't need the 10 Mbps speed; go for the 100. Why? Because there's no price difference; in fact, you could pay *less* for the faster NIC card. The cables may be slightly different; however, they'll be more reliable and no more expensive. The speed of Fast Ethernet throughput is comparable to the average speed of the IDE connection between a hard drive and the CPU (though not in "burst mode" or Ultra DMA). So for most jobs, the remote hard drive will seem like it's right in front of you rather than in the next room, although you won't hear it crunching away.

Techno Talk

In the fourth edition of this book, I recommended that you purchase a hub for your home network. Way, way back then (1999), a two-port connection-sensing switch for networks cost about $500. A hub, meanwhile, while not smart enough to regulate bandwidth and redirect data from point to point, did amplify the signal and simplify the installation process somewhat. Today's switches are cheaper than yesterday's hubs, which have become obsolete. They're not even made anymore for networks with fewer than 16 connections.

If you're purchasing your network cards and hub separately, then if you've chosen the 100Mbps route ("Fast Ethernet"), you should make absolutely certain that the switch you choose is rated for use with 100 Mbps networks, as most are.

You might need to build a network if these situations pertain to you:

➤ You have one printer and two computers and you don't feel like buying a second printer just so your teenagers can print the lyrics to their latest favorite song.

➤ You have one modem/scanner/Zip drive/CD-RW drive, and you want to share it.

➤ You want to set up more than one location in your house where you can access your work—for example, outside on the deck.

➤ You want to connect your notebook PC from work to your home computer with the least amount of fuss.

➤ You've finally gotten good at the latest multi-player game, and you can't wait to beat your kids at it.

Regardless of any advertising you may have read, a network does not make two or more computers act as one. It does not make them share processing power, or run the same application on all systems. It simply opens a channel of communication between them which, although it's quite a bit wider than your channel to that very large network, the Internet, theoretically doesn't involve any different "topics of conversation." Networked computers share files, some raw data, messages meant for each other, e-mail messages meant for each other's users, pathways to each other's peripherals, and access to the same phone modem or broadband modem. That's it.

I admit it. I'm as network-centric as the next person. Who is the next person, you ask? She's the other person on the network who's as network-centric as I am. Anyway, I love the idea that every computer is a virtual network and virtually part of a bigger network … conceptually. In practice, this theory has a few kinks in it, at least for now. As Stephen Wright once put it, "It goes without saying … so I won't."

Are Your Computers Network Ready?

If your computer was made in 1996 or later, the answer is a qualified *yes*. You should have a PCI slot free for your NIC card; although ISA-based cards are still available, they're not the best because they cannot be the fastest. The Ethernet networking scheme actually predates the advent of the IBM PC by some four years; and most PCs manufactured since 1984 have been practically network-ready, save for about two chips and a decent network operating system.

Making Your House Network Ready

The single most expensive feature of a home network is the work you may put in (or have done for you) to install network coaxial cable through the walls in your home.

If you are absolutely dead set against stapling your cable along your baseboard or draping it along the floor, then you should be prepared to spend a lot of money.

Wiring Through the Walls ... While You Can

When my husband and I built our new home in 1995, we had the idea of taking the time to install network coaxial cable and outlets ourselves prior to the homebuilders putting up the drywall. We spent about $200 buying several hundred feet of coaxial cable, plus the blue outlet boxes, the faceplates for those boxes, some doodads with which to create little gold connectors, a drill bit for boring through the studs, and the special tools needed to wield coaxial cable. (Sorry, editors, I know I promised you I wouldn't talk about boring stuff.) We spent about three days on crouched knees and high ladders. But in the end, we saved over $5,000 in installation fees. That's really what it would have cost for a paid team of professional contractors to install cable in the walls *after* the house was built.

If your office is like ours, you could probably drape one more cable along the floor and not really notice it after awhile ... or if it's *really* like ours, you would lose it in about five minutes. Keep in mind that it may cost you at least several hundred dollars to have professionals run coaxial cable through the walls in just one of your rooms. When you couple that with the fact that there are enough junky looking cables hanging out the end of your PCs anyway, you might come to the conclusion that it's not worth it. But don't let the presence of a few more unsightly gadgets deter you from installing a network if you've determined a clear need for one.

There are some "in-between" options for safeguarding your network cable that you can find at your local hardware store or office supply center. A rubber safety strip laid on top of an entire mess of cables can convert a potential source of liability suits into a trip-proof "speed bump." CAT5 cable (with RJ-45 connectors) can tend to draw attention to itself, especially if you buy it in the now-popular fluorescent yellow. 10Base2 coaxial, however, comes in a much more tasteful white; and your hardware store will also have special white tack-on grips that let you tap your white coaxial firmly in place along your baseboards. Later, you can pull your cable right up without much effort. These options will leave you spending less than $100 rather than $5000. Keep in mind, though, that if you choose to go with a "Fast Ethernet" (100 Mbps) network, your choice of cable will probably be made for you: CAT5. There are grades of coaxial cable that allow for greater bandwidth, but you'd have to go to great lengths (are you a government contractor, for instance?) and great expense (how's your mortgage doing?) to get it.

Why Wireless Is Wrong

I'm going to bring up the topic of wireless networking in this section. I'm going to bring it up, and then I'm going to drop it. The reason is, I strongly advocate that you not install a wireless network in your home.

It seems like a wonderful solution to the wires-strung-all-around-your-house problem, and the fact is, wireless networking hardware actually does work very well. It works on the principle that a low-power radio transmitter, broadcasting at frequencies right around that of modern 600MHz and 900MHz wireless telephones, and stationed at the highest possible point you can place it in your house, can transmit a signal *down* toward two or more separate wireless network receiver boxes connected to your NIC cards. The result is that a 10Mbps Ethernet signal can be transmitted between peers without any of them ever knowing there are no wires involved.

Now, this is a more expensive solution than a wired network, but that's not why I'm against it. I'm against wireless networking because of the way Windows works, and because wireless transmitters work too well for their own good.

As you'll probably recall, any user can "log on to" Windows by typing in a personal password. But that password doesn't actually serve as an entry blockade; and perhaps once or twice you've hit Enter or clicked on Cancel without typing anything into the password field—and noticed that Windows came right up without a hitch. You might not see any of your "personalized menus" (hands up, please, of all of you who use Windows' personalized menus ... one ... anyone else?) but you can still get into Windows, start up any application, and load up just about any unprotected or unencrypted data.

Windows Networking for Windows 98 and Windows Me changes this login dialog box only slightly, but the principle is the same: If you click on Cancel, you still get into Windows. Which means anyone can get in.

This fact hasn't raised too many alarms up to now, because a stranger would have to break into your home to gain access to your computer if he really wanted to snoop around your business. And from a psychological standpoint, a person breaking into your home probably doesn't want your PC; he wants your DVD. But when you add a wireless network transmitter to the picture, you change everything. *Any person sitting in his car outside your house with a notebook PC and a wireless receiver on his PC card (available at almost any retail computer store) can log onto your Windows 98 or Windows Me network without you ever knowing it.*

And before you start thinking, "Nah, no one ever *really* does that!"... People really do that. It has become a hobby, especially among tech-savvy adolescents. They cruise the neighborhood, scanning the high frequencies for traffic, such as wireless phone conversations. When they pick up a wireless network carrier wave, they simply power up their notebook and log on.

Why the Other Alternatives Aren't Exactly Right Either

Both engineers and marketers have been busy trying to solve the problem of how you can avoid having to string network cables through your house. They've made some progress, but some of their ideas haven't exactly matured. Here's why.

Electrical wire networking is based on the notion that the wires running to your everyday power outlets have enough spare, unused bandwidth to carry data signals. Which is true—it does. So this type of equipment runs data cables directly into your power plugs without you having to run any new data wires outside or inside the walls of your house. Essentially, your power lines become broadcasters of a data signal, and whoever receives it from whatever socket is responsible for making sense of it. While there's nothing technically wrong with this mode of networking, there is something *practically* wrong with it: It's your *power sockets*. A lot of effort has been spent getting users accustomed to the idea of using some form of surge suppression; and one of the other jobs of a good surge suppressor is *noise suppression*. In this case, "noise" is unused and generally unwanted electrical activity at frequencies outside of the range of ordinary power. Data networking signals would be treated as noise; so to ensure data throughput, we have to eliminate noise suppression, which in turn eliminates surge suppression. So this system uses an unprotected electrical conductor to connect the NIC in your PC directly to your power source! The dangers inherent in this act should be self-apparent. Besides, this mode of networking actually uses less bandwidth than Ethernet, and its equipment is now more expensive than conventional Ethernet—so the only benefit this system offers you is aesthetics, but at the expense of security.

Phone line networking is an intriguing new system that uses CAT3 (RJ-11) telephone cable instead of CAT5 (RJ-45). The bandwidth is lower, so the overall throughput speed is lower, and you'd need NICs that are not Ethernet-compatible. So the system has lower performance and greater expense. Why would you want it? Proponents of phone line networking point to a fully networked future, when appliances such as your refrigerator, your coffee pot, and the leash on your dog are all given IP addresses making them addressable through the Internet from long distances. These proponents are aware that appliance manufacturers are investigating common phone lines as a means of thorough and total home networking. Your PC, attached to all these appliances, might be addressable as a control center that enables you to do such things as set the thermostat, turn on the coffee, and shock your dog by remote control. But these same manufacturers are also investigating Ethernet for the same purposes, and are finding (just as you are) that Ethernet may be less expensive in the long run than a different system that uses phone lines.

Direct Cable Connection is a vestigial feature that is a part of every edition of Windows since 95. The idea here is, you can connect two computers together directly through their serial or parallel ports. You'd need specialized data transfer cables in either case: for serial, something called a "DB-25 null modem cable," and for parallel, something called a "DB-25 pass-through cable." This is perhaps the only alternative to true Ethernet networking that is less expensive, by perhaps a dozen or so dollars. But what you'll end up with is a limited data transfer system, not a true sharing network—that is, if you can get Direct Cable Connection to work in the first place.

Architectural Digest

Simply put, your network should fit your house. Theoretically, you should be able to purchase a switch that resides in the "center" of your network, and connect all your computers to that switch. If you were to draw a sketch of this on a napkin, you'd have what network engineers call a *star topology*—a switch in the center, and a PC at each point. A "topology" is like a map, except that it's actually the study of forms which maps tend to take. So a map of a network that ends up taking the shape of a star uses a star topology.

Unless your house was designed using a similar form of napkin sketching, making a star topology work through several rooms may be cumbersome. Suppose you have three PCs in three rooms, and you plan for your switch to share a room with one of those PCs. You'd need to run two cables out from that switch. Depending on where those rooms are located, you may be running both cables together for several yards—which makes them not too easy to hide.

In such a situation, you do have one alternative: You can purchase NIC cards that are adapted for use with shielded coaxial cable instead of CAT5 cable. Then you can daisy chain your PCs by running coaxial from #1 to #2, then from #2 to #3. There is a performance cost, but you might be able to live with it. I'll discuss this in more detail momentarily.

One principle that applies to any network topology you consider is this: *In any networking scheme that does not employ a switch, the total bandwidth of the network is divided by the number of systems on that network minus one.* For example, if you have three PCs on the home network, then if you monitor the data throughput available to any one of those PCs for any appreciable length of time, you discover that it utilizes one half of the available bandwidth.

This is because, in an Ethernet environment where there are no switches, all messages sent by a PC can be received by any other PC in the network. In a star or bus topology, every PC gets every message. But each message has a designated recipient, so each NIC knows to filter out and discard those messages not directed to it explicitly.

Here are the different types of conventional Ethernet networking architectures, or topologies, available to you as you're designing your home network. (I've left the large-scale business topologies out of this list …. You're welcome.)

Peer-to-Peer Crossover Cable

The least expensive network hardware setup you'd need to connect two ordinary desktop PCs uses one network interface card (NIC) for each PC, and a single *crossover cable* linking those two cards. You would only use crossover cable for this type of setup. Installation could, conceivably, be a breeze; you plug in the two cards, you snap the crossover cable into both connectors, and there it is. Chapter 12, "Face the Interface," deals with some of the specifics for installing an expansion card into a PC—what specifics there are, and there aren't many.

The way a crossover cable works is like this: There are two pairs of wires, one pair that handles data going one direction, and another pair for data going the other direction. You would think that, since there are separate pairs of wires, you could always send and receive data at the same time. This isn't the case for NICs that are only capable of *half-duplex* communication—of only sending or only receiving, but never both. An NIC that supports *full duplex* communication can do both. But why is it so difficult: If the cable seems to support it, why is sending and receiving simultaneously considered an *extra* feature? Because in order for full duplex to work, the data traveling on one pair of wires has to be a different frequency than the data traveling on the other pair; and both NICs in the data exchange process have to keep track of the different frequencies. With only half duplex, the NICs could both be tone deaf and it wouldn't matter.

Techno Talk

One of the distinguishing factors between an ordinary network interface card and a *good* one is whether it offers **full duplex** communication. This sounds more complex than it is. The term merely refers to the capability for the card to receive data while it is sending data, and vice versa. With an ordinary **half-duplex** setup, the card cannot send while it is receiving nor receive while it is sending.

When you study the layout of a CAT5 network cable, it would appear on the surface that there's a full circuit there. But the way Ethernet works, these two pairs of wires have exclusive purposes, with regard to the *type* of data the NICs expect to see on those wires. The pair of wires designated "Transmit" is generally reserved for data being sent from a client to a server; the pair designated "Receive" is reserved for data being received from the server by the client. If you used an ordinary cable to connect two NICs without a hub in between, then because the four pairs of wires (there are two other pairs I didn't mention) are carried straight through without exchanging positions, the arrangement of the wires in the connector at one end would be the reverse of the arrangement of the wires in the connector at the other end. In other words, the pair of wires that form the rightmost two pins of one end, designated "Transmit," would end up being carried through to the *leftmost* two pins on the other end of the cable. And both NICs expect "Transmit" to be the two pins on the right. So "Transmit" on one side would end up in nowhere-ville on the other side; and "Receive" (which is generally expected in the middle) would end up where

"Transmit" is expected to be. Someplace inside a crossover cable, the "Transmit" and "Receive" pairs are flipped, so that one ends up where the other is expected to be, forming a true circuit between the two NICs. (By the way, what are those other two pairs of wires in a CAT5 cable for? Nothing. Literally. They just sit there.)

With 10 or 100 Mbps of throughput and two NICs communicating on half duplex mode through just a crossover cable, the two cards don't always send signals to each other at the same time, so eventually some messages do get through. When they don't, the sending card realizes they don't, and they get resent.

While the performance of a crossed-over network such as this is noticeably lower at half duplex, and somewhat lower at full duplex, than that of a switched network, the improving quality of NICs over the last few years has resulted in fewer complaints and problems about this option than ever before. It is your least expensive Ethernet networking option for two PCs. And there's some weight to the argument that a powered switch between two and only two PCs, with no other data inputs, would be an extremely useless and redundant component.

However, the crossover option does limit your expandability. If you were to install broadband Internet service, for instance, and you wanted the connection to be shared by both PCs, you would need to purchase a second NIC for one of your PCs. The cable modem or DSL connection would need to be run to that second NIC. You would then need to install a Windows software feature called Internet Connection Sharing (ICS) on both PCs, so that Internet data being sent to PC #2 through the second NIC on PC #1 doesn't accidentally end up in the Web browser of PC #1. While this setup might work, it is not the most secure Internet setup you can have; and for reasons of security, you may want to invest in a good switch that handles broadband input and has an Internet firewall, even if you have only two PCs.

There's also no simple way to network three PCs using a crossover topology. You would have to have two NICs in PC #2, one of which connects to PC #1, and the other to PC #3. Even then, any data sharing between #1 and #3 would be spotty at best.

Peer-to-Peer Star Topology with Switch

When you add a third PC or a broadband Internet connection to the mix, a switch becomes a very welcome component. The fact that they're now so inexpensive renders any alternatives, including the use of hubs, obsolete.

A hub doesn't need any programming to be able to do its job, which is essentially to amplify and broadcast the signals from one PC to all the others in the network. But when that happens, the bandwidth available to any one PC is reduced. A switch eliminates this problem (see Figure 22.1). It makes certain that all communications directed from one PC to another in the network take place using 100 percent of the available bandwidth. If necessary, the switch holds up one transmission—like a traffic cop in the middle of a busy intersection—until any other pending transmission is completed.

Figure 22.1

A peer-to-peer network with a switch in between.

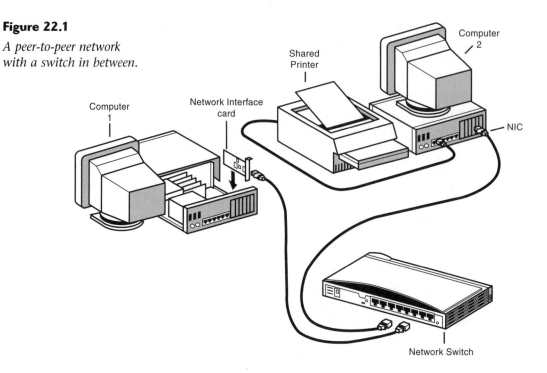

With a switch in your network, its overall shape and scheme—or its *topology,* to use the technical term—becomes what is called in networking circles a *star*. It's easy to see why. The switch is at the center of the star, and all the connected computers form spikes at the end. Okay, so a two-pointed star isn't all that exciting. But it's easy to see where you could add extra points to this star by plugging in extra NICs to the switch.

Peer-to-Peer Bus Topology Without Switch

Suppose you have quite a few computers in your household (a number like three or four is not unheard of nowadays, especially if you throw in a notebook PC). All your kids have their own, there's one in the bedroom, and the main computer's tucked away in the office. This is a situation where a *bus topology* might be workable (see Figure 22.2). Here, the signal from one PC is broadcast to all the others in the network—if the sending PC happens to be in the middle, it broadcasts in both directions.

Yes, I know, the PCs in this diagram are all desktop units, and after all I've been preaching about desktop systems being too small ... You'll just have to forgive me. Anyway, the PCs here have all been endowed with NICs that happen to feature both RJ-45 connectors for CAT5 cable, and BNC connectors for coaxial cable. ("BNC" stands for "British Naval Connector"—what association this has with the British Royal Navy, I haven't a clue.) The device that plugs into the BNC connector is called a *10Base-T converter*. The base of the "T" plugs into the BNC. Coaxial cable can then be screwed into either or both branches of the "T"; and at the beginning and end of the bus, the converter is capped with a *terminator* that effectively designates the "end of the line."

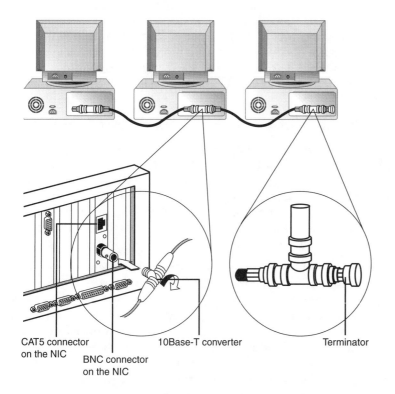

Figure 22.2

A typical bus network, daisy-chained by coaxial cable.

CAT5 connector
on the NIC

BNC connector
on the NIC

10Base-T converter

Terminator

A bus topology gives you the advantage of being able to string just a single cable between any two points in the network, reducing the likelihood that you'll have to trip over anything, or notice some ugly cable defacing your trim moulding. Coaxial 10Base2 cable is less expensive than CAT5, and NICs that have BNC connectors, or both BNC and CAT5, are generally no more expensive than those that support only CAT5.

The price you pay is in the performance department. Although 10Base2 cable is more reliable than CAT5 for 10Mbps connections, it's less reliable than CAT5 for 100Mbps Fast Ethernet connections. Also, since there's no switch involved, and all Ethernet messages are broadcast throughout the entire bus, each PC has to accept its share of the total bandwidth, which is obviously reduced each time you add a new PC to the network.

Installation: You Become the Cable Guy

If you like miles and miles of wires hanging around all over the place, you're going to love installing networks.

Rolling Your Own 10Base2

You can roll your own 10Base2 coaxial cable; I've done it myself. You can buy a few hundred feet of this cable on a long spool, and you can get it from your hardware store for about one-fifth the cost per foot as cable with the connectors already installed. You can then get a package of connectors for no more than a few bucks. You will need, however, three tools that you don't already have in your computing toolkit: a heavy gauge wire cutter, a coaxial cable cutter, and a coaxial connector crimper.

A heavy gauge wire cutter is used to remove a section of coaxial cable from the spool.

A coaxial cable cutter is used by both networking and cable TV technicians to make the proper kinds of splits in the wire. Your heavy gauge wire cutter alone will leave you with this jelly-roll-looking cross-section that you can't get inside to install your connector. To give yourself an easier time with the connector, you need a tool that lets you peel back the outer insulation further than the inner insulation, and that pulls about a half-inch of copper wire out from inside the inner insulation. In short, a well-cut cable looks something like Figure 22.1.

With a real coaxial cable cutter, you score the outer insulation, and then you put it under this little clamp which is like a miniature guillotine. Don't worry; it's not big enough for fingers to get inside, and there's a finger guard on the blade side. When you squeeze the clamp, it automatically peels off the scored outer insulation, pulls out the inner insulation, cuts through that just enough to leave the copper wire, and then pulls back both layers of insulation so that you have just enough exposed wire to make your connector. *A combination crimper/cutter will not do this*; it actually makes more work for you than it saves. A coaxial connector crimper is the device you use to generate a pressure seal so that your connector is firmly entrenched between the two layers of insulation.

If you've ever played with your cable TV's coaxial cable, you're familiar with the twist-on male connector with the sharp-as-all-heck copper wire sticking out the end. That wire is the most important part of your cable connection and, luckily, it's part of your cable, too. Okay, it *is* the cable, or at least a primary part of it. As Figure 22.3 shows, between the two levels of insulation is a copper mesh, which acts as a secondary conductor. The job of the BNC connector is to attach to that mesh to create a contact along its inner rim, while exposing the fully insulated inner copper wire in the center, all the while maintaining a firm connection between the cable and the female connector.

Figure 22.3

The innards of all coaxial cable, including 10Base2.

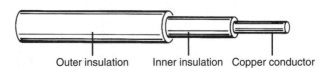

Outer insulation   Inner insulation   Copper conductor

The 10Base-T converter includes the female coaxial connection, called BNC-T. So to plug your 10Base2 coaxial cable into your NIC, you'll need to install a BNC into the end of your 10Base2. This connector is then screwed into the BNC-T end of the 10Base-T. Then you'll attach a terminator to the opposite end of the 10Base-T, and plug the short cable emerging from the base of the "T" into the back of the NIC. This plug may be either another BNC plug that plugs into a BNC-T on the NIC, or a CAT5 plug that plugs into an RJ-45 connector on the NIC. (I can't believe I just wrote that last paragraph. It has more abbreviations than a Defense Appropriations bill.)

A BNC connector straight out of the package is in two parts. One is a tube with an outer rotating rim; the other part is simply a ring of the same diameter as the cable. Using your coaxial cable cutter, prepare one end of your cable so that the copper wire sticks out ¼ inch from the inner insulation, and the inner insulation sticks out ¼ inch from the outer insulation.

Next, insert the ring over the prepared end, and push it back so that it's near the edge of the outer insulation.

Now insert the metal tube into the end of the cable, pushing the tube between the inner and outer layers of insulation as far as it will go. The exposed copper wire sticks up through the center, and you should be able to see white insulating material up against the metal hole.

Here's where your crimper comes in. Cover the foremost area of the outer insulation with the ring, and then with the ring directly under the teeth of the crimper, pinch the ring tightly so that it bends inward, forcing a seal that holds the inner metal tube in place. You'll need all the grip you can muster, otherwise the connector may fall off.

There. Not so bad. On the other hand, unless you truly enjoy waves and waves of disappointment, you should probably not get into the business of installing your own RJ-45 cable connectors. There are eight very, very tiny wires in a CAT5 cable, thin enough that you would think they might blow away in a freak gust of wind. Because you'll probably be using CAT5 for shorter sections than you would for 10Base2 coaxial, it's probably a good idea to just purchase CAT5 cable in preassembled sections.

Cabling the Network Together

For the simplest but most reliable two-computer peer-to-peer network, all you need are two sections of cable (your choice of grades), two Ethernet network interface cards (100Mbps if you can afford it, although 10Mbps is just fine), and a single hub to connect the cable sections together. You can find NICs for as low as $15 apiece, or you can save a little money and purchase a kit that has all the items mentioned previously (if you like short cable, that is) for about $75.

The better hubs you can buy will support more than two PCs—generally as many as four. The better NICs you can buy feature connectors for both grades of cable. If you choose to use coaxial cable and your NICs only have RJ-45 connectors, you'll need four 10Base-T converters with terminators to make each end of cable fit into the appropriate connector. It won't be a pretty sight on the back of the hub; your converters may act as little feet hoisting it an inch or so in the air. If you choose to use CAT5 cable and your NICs only have BNC connectors, you can buy four snap-on converters, however, they are not only expensive but also silly looking. (Why spend as much for a cable converter as you would for the whole card?) So make sure your NIC cards have RJ-45 connectors in any event, and both kinds if you can. In Chapter 24, "Getting Windows to Recognize Your New Toys," you'll see what to do next with regard to installing your networking protocols and drivers.

The Least You Need to Know

➤ A network gives you and other users in your household the ability to share files on the hard drives of the connected computers, as well as peripherals (such as a printer or modem) or other resources connected to any one of them.

➤ A network interface card (NIC) opens up a channel from a PC to the network where data can be shuttled in and out as fast as 100 megabits per second (Mbps), for Fast Ethernet.

➤ The biggest expense you could incur in installing your network is equipping the walls of your house with network cable. If you're building your house, you could save thousands by laying the cables yourself before the drywall goes up.

➤ A peer-to-peer network enables you to connect two, or as many as five, PCs together using inexpensive cards, some cheap cable, and a wonderful device in between called a switch.

➤ A switch allocates bandwidth for messages sent between PCs, as they're sending those messages. As a result, the switch ensures that every connection between PCs uses the maximum available bandwidth.

➤ The least expensive networking connection between two PCs involves two NICs connected directly with one crossover cable. Such a configuration does preclude the option of broadband Internet access or connection of a third PC.

➤ Coaxial cable is graded for use with networks by the maximum length for which it can sustain a normal signal. 10Base2 coaxial is graded to sustain a 10Mbps signal for 200 meters, and a 100Mbps signal for 100 meters.

➤ CAT5 twisted-pair cable (which uses RJ-45 connectors, and thus may be called "RJ-45 cable") is a bit easier to deal with, although it is more expensive and doesn't sustain a signal for nearly as long as coaxial.

Putting Everything Back Together

Unfortunately, it's not enough to sweat off ten pounds in a nerve-wracking contest between you and your PC. You've installed your new device, but chances are pretty good that it's not ready to work just yet. There may be jumper settings you have to make to your motherboard, or switches you need to set within your BIOS so that it can understand what's happening. Finally (and this can be the really tricky part) you have to get Windows to welcome your new friend. Now, Windows has the right idea: It tries to search your computer to see what's changed and what hasn't, every time it starts up. But sometimes it can draw the wrong conclusions, and you may need the setup program that came with your device to help you go back and set things right again ... manually. It's a long road to that happy ending, but eventually you'll be doing a dance in the end zone.

Chapter 23

Making Your Computer Boot Up Again

In This Chapter

➤ Making sense of the CMOS settings

➤ Fiddling with jumpers and switches

➤ Solving annoying COM port conflicts

➤ Dealing with IRQs

➤ The mystery behind DMA

➤ Reformatting and repartitioning a hard drive

When you install some new gadgets in your PC, they bring wine, flowers, and candy, eager to be loved by all the other parts. Other parts bully their way in, steal Dad's favorite chair, and refuse to behave. I'm guessing that you just installed one of these brutes, or you wouldn't be boring yourself with this chapter. Here, you'll learn to tame your beast and get everyone working happily together again.

Before you take the cover off your PC to mess with jumpers, switches, and other junk, take out some insurance in the form of an emergency diskette. See Chapter 4, "What You Need to Know *Before* You Open Your PC," for details.

Configuring Your Reassembled PC

The motherboard is not a Plug and Play device. Everything else in your computer could theoretically be Plug and Play, but only after your motherboard has been made fully functional. After you've installed your new motherboard in your system case (a procedure outlined in Chapter 10, "Replacing the Motherboard and Its Parts"), or whenever you notice your new PC acting strangely from the get-go, you will need to make certain it's properly configured for the CPU you've installed, for the hard drives you've plugged in, and for the memory you've socketed into place.

There are two stages of setup for your motherboard, and you already know at this point how to do the physical part of it. There will most likely be jumpers you will need to set, or at least make sure are set properly. Then, once the motherboard's receiving power and once it has passed the smoke test (another procedure outlined in Chapter 10), you'll need to go into your BIOS setup program to make certain that your PC will recognize the right CPU, the proper IDE devices, and as much memory as you actually have.

Fiddling with Jumpers and Switches and Such

Back in the days of cave men and stegosauruses, PCs got most of their configuration information from tiny pins called *jumpers*, or small switches called *DIPs*. But even with all their fancy-schmancy hardware, some computer parts still prefer this primitive method of communication.

A jumper (demonstrated in Figure 23.1) is made up of two or more parallel pins that are part of a circuit. If the pins are sticking up in the air, then obviously the circuit is open, which is the same as having a switch turned off. To turn on an electric circuit, you need to close, or complete, it; with a jumper, you close the circuit with a little rectangular doodad called a *shunt*, which you slip onto a pair of pins, as shown. The pins are labeled; check the device's manual to find out which pins the jumper is supposed to be put on.

For example, if you're installing an internal modem and the manual tells you to set the J5 jumper to ON to set the modem to COM2, remove the shunt from its current resting spot and place it over the two ON pins on the J5 jumper set. As if this junk isn't hard enough, some jumpers are set in a single row and not in pairs. Here you place the shunt over two numbered pins, such as pins 4 and 5. The number points to the pair of pins that together form the jumper; you have to be careful here, because one pin can be part of two jumper pairs. For instance, you might find three pins (not four) in one row, with markings for J1 and J2. The J1 pair will most likely be the top pair (the first and second pins from the top), and J2 will probably be the bottom pair (the second and third pins).

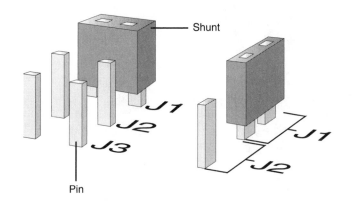

Figure 23.1

Place the jumper over the correct pins to change the setting of the device.

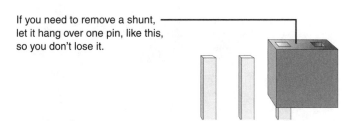

To remove the shunt from the jumper, just pull up. If the shunt's stuck, you may find tweezers or threats helpful. Be careful not to let the metal tweezers touch anything it might short out. So that you don't lose the little guy, consider leaving the shunt hanging over one of the two pins. Since a jumper connection is formed by joining two pins, hanging it over just one pin will have no ill effect. This way, it'll be easier to find it the next time.

DIP switches (sometimes called rocker switches) are like tiny light switches: they can only be set to *on* or *off*. These sets of switches are almost extinct, but from time to time, they crop up on expansion cards that are smart enough not to rely 100 percent on Plug and Play. In case you care, DIP is short for *dual inline package*. Yes, it's the same DIP as in "DIP chip"; the term refers to the way the item is mounted to the circuit board. You'll notice two (thus the "dual") rows of prongs (thus the "inline") sticking out of opposite sides of both a DIP chip and a DIP switch set. They could've called it "two row package" but then the acronym would have been "TRP chip," and you'd have to pronounce it "trip" or "twerp." Although "twerp chip" sounds fitting, it doesn't have that whole double entendre thing going for it.

Before you change a DIP switch's settings, write the old ones down somewhere in case your new ones don't work. To change its settings, use a wooden toothpick—your fingernails will thank you. As Figure 23.2 shows you, flip the switch to the side marked "on" (sometimes marked with just an arrow symbol) if you want to activate it, or to the other side to turn it off.

Figure 23.2

These aren't Grandma's rockers.

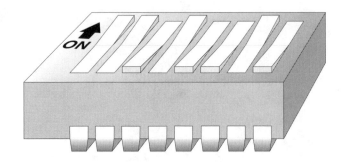

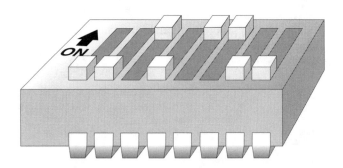

Critical Motherboard Jumper Settings

Most motherboards produced today are configured through their own internal BIOS setup program. However, for some settings, there are often exceptions, and the fact that there are exceptions doesn't necessarily date your motherboard. You're likely to find at least some jumpers for manually setting some critical operating characteristics of your PC. If you do not have jumpers for the following characteristics, check your BIOS setup program for software-based switches for these same characteristics:

> ➤ **CPU voltage level**—The oldest Pentium processors for Socket 3 utilized the old 5-volt level required by the old 486 processors. Later, Intel stepped down the voltage requirements for its newer Socket 7 models to 3.3v. The newest single-edge connector (SEC) packages utilize less voltage still, between 2.1 and 2.9v. The Pentium MMX CPUs utilized so-called *split rail voltage,* which splits the power line into one low-voltage and another super-low-voltage line, the second line reserved exclusively for the processor core. A motherboard that supports split rail voltage will have *two* sets of jumpers for "core" and "external" levels. If you install a nonsplit rail CPU into a motherboard that does support split rail, you'll need to set both jumpers to the same level.

➤ **System bus speed**—For those motherboards that support multiple bus speeds, there may be a jumper that allows you to select this speed. As explained in Chapter 10, set your system bus speed as fast as you can, in accordance with the memory you've installed. Remember, your CPU clock speed should equal the system bus speed times the chosen multiplier; so to reduce the multiplier and to enhance the overall speed of your system, crank up the system bus speed. (When solving this bus speed/multiplier formula, remember that "66MHz" is really 66.66666 … MHz.)

➤ **Bus speed multiplier**—Here's that all-important multiplier setting. This setting tells the chipset exactly how much faster your CPU will be "ticking" than your system bus clock "beats."

➤ **L2 cache size**—Up until the advent of Pentium II, the maximum amount of L2 cache that the BIOS was allowed to annex for the CPU from system RAM was set by way of a jumper. You won't find this jumper if your motherboard supports Intel Pentium II, PIII, or Celeron; AMD K6-2, K6-III, Athlon, or Duron; Cyrix MII or Cyrix III; or Via C3 processors.

➤ **RAM size**—Not many modern motherboards will use a jumper to quantify the total installed RAM any more, but some will. Keep your eyes open.

➤ **Flash BIOS enable**—If you have flash BIOS in your system, you may have a jumper on your motherboard that enables BIOS flashing (programming, as explained in Chapter 13, "The Online Line"). This jumper will have two settings: Enable and Normal. If this jumper is present, you will want to make certain it's set to Normal unless you are about to flash your BIOS.

➤ **CMOS clear**—This jumper, if you have it, is a utility of sorts that "electrocutes," if you will, your BIOS settings retained by CMOS. If you need to reset the CMOS settings maintained by your BIOS, then you set this jumper to Clear, turn on your computer, wait for it to crash (it will), then turn it off again and reset the jumper back to Normal. This jumper should be left set on Normal unless you intend to clear your CMOS.

➤ **Battery source**—Some batteries that maintain the contents of CMOS are permanently installed on the motherboard (one of the most bone-headed design decisions in human history). When the battery burns out, you may be able to install a secondary battery that replaces the old one, even though it doesn't mean the *removal* of the old one. To tell the motherboard you're using a battery from elsewhere, you'd change this jumper setting from Internal to External.

Dealing with BIOS Setup

As you learned in Chapter 2, "Now, Let's Find Out What Kind of Computer You Have," your PC retains certain settings about the operating parameters and characteristics of its devices. Many of these characteristics can be learned through Plug and Play, but those which have to do with the settings on your motherboard are retained in battery-powered memory called CMOS, and are set using your BIOS setup program. This is the program that you can start up the moment after you've turned your computer on. Your CPU doesn't run this program; your BIOS does. So it can run even if your CPU doesn't work, and even if you don't have a CPU installed.

Check This Out

Because much of the information in CMOS is irreplaceable, you should make a copy of it. Follow the steps in this section to start BIOS setup and then print the information out by turning on the printer and pressing the Print Screen key on your keyboard. Then later, when you replace the lithium battery in your system, and whatever was in CMOS has hit the big bit bucket in the sky, you can go into your BIOS setup program, and use this printout to help you restore the settings.

To change the BIOS settings, reboot your computer and watch the screen for a message telling you what key to press for Setup. Then press it. Most likely, it will tell you to press F1, F2, Delete, Ctrl+Alt+Escape, Ctrl+S, Ctrl+Alt+S, Ctrl+Alt+Enter, or Ctrl+Alt+Insert. After you have BIOS setup running, you'll see a screen similar to the one in Figure 23.3. Notice here that you have full access to every operating characteristic of your PC's CPU, motherboard, and storage devices that's of importance to your BIOS.

The program looks like something that would have run in MS-DOS; actually, DOS isn't involved in the slightest. But if you remember DOS programs, you might have a clue about how to use BIOS setup. To move from item to item, you usually press the Tab key or the down-arrow key. You typically use the left- or right-arrow key to change a setting or to move from page to page. Just follow the tips provided at the bottom of the screen. When you're done making changes, be sure to save them. Usually you just press Esc and select Yes to save the changes. You'll end up at the DOS prompt. Restart the computer so your changes take effect.

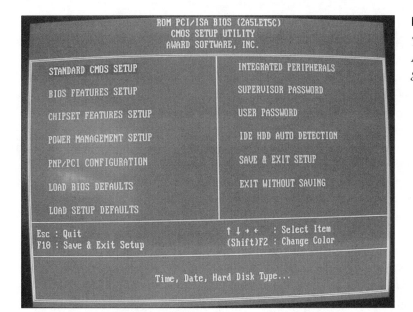

Figure 23.3

The main menu of an Award BIOS setup program.

Critical BIOS Settings

If you have a Plug and Play BIOS in your computer, your IDE, PCI, and some ISA devices should be able to identify themselves to your BIOS on system startup, thereby eliminating the need for CMOS memory to maintain specifications just for these devices. But not everything in your computer is Plug and Play; your CMOS will still need to remember *something* in order for your PC to even work. Here are the most critical settings you may find:

➤ **System bus speed/external clock**—For those motherboards that support multiple bus speeds, there may be a BIOS setting that regulates the current speed.

➤ **Internal multiplier/CPU speed**—If your BIOS lets you choose your processor speed, then this setting actually dictates the speed multiplier for your CPU (this setting is divided by the fixed system bus speed to arrive at the multiplier speed). You may also find, or find instead, a multiplier setting, such as 4x, 4.5x, 5x, and so on.

➤ **CPU power plane**—This most critical setting designates whether your CPU uses a Single voltage or a Dual voltage ("split rail") line. You can make this setting from BIOS setup because, believe it or not, your CPU is turned off at this point. Some BIOS allow you to enter your processor identification code (a five-letter code found on the CPU itself), thereby letting your BIOS determine what voltage(s) your processor requires. When your CPU power plane is set to Single, you then set the *Plane Voltage* attribute to the precise single voltage level that your

CPU requires. When your CPU power plane is set to Dual, you then set the I/O Plane (or External Plane) and Core Plane voltage level attributes to their separately required voltage levels.

If a motherboard is "rated" for use with a specific brand and clock speed or even a specific model of CPU, then chances are that its default settings for processor voltage will be precisely the ones that you require; you may not have to set anything at all. If you want to be absolutely sure, jot down the CPU's five-character processor code located somewhere in the vicinity of its logo (it'll be a mixture of letters and numbers). If you can't find the logo for the heat sink, look in any documentation you might have for your computer, the motherboard, or the CPU—generally at the end of the booklet, under "Specifications." Then check BIOS setup for a special setting for "CPU Label" or "CPU Marking." If its current setting matches what you wrote down, and CMOS maintains settings for voltage levels on behalf of your motherboard, then chances are that the voltage levels are correct. If the setting is wrong, then by all means, type the right one in. Your BIOS may be able to look up the correct voltage for itself.

➤ **Date and time**—Finally, something easy. This is where you enter the system's startup date and time, which you can also do from a DOS prompt or from the Date/Time Windows Control panel later on.

➤ **Hard disk auto-detection**—If you have a Plug and Play BIOS, you'll want to set auto-detect mode to ON right now. BIOS will actually engage auto-detection the moment you do so, and will fill in the gaps for other BIOS settings for any PnP devices it finds.

➤ **IDE primary and secondary channel master and slave parameters**—If you just set auto-detect mode to ON, then there should be numbers for these settings that you don't have to enter for yourself. **Hard drive type** is almost always set to User now, unless you have an ancient hard drive. **Translation mode** is set to LBA (Logical Block Addressing) for hard disks over 504MB in size for which you intend to use a single partition. The alternatives are: CHS (Cylinders/ Heads/Sectors), which is the old-style drive geometry that only counts up to 504MB; ECHS or simply "Large," which still counts in cylinders, heads, and sectors but actually lies about which is what in order to attain larger drive geometries; and Auto, which lets Plug and Play decide what's best at startup. **Block mode** enables the BIOS to transfer up to 16 or 32 sectors in one access rather than the normal 1. **PIO mode** enables certain protocols of data exchange between the IDE device and the CPU, as described in Chapter 16, "Hands-On Hard Disk Replacement." Choose the highest mode your device allows. **DMA mode** enables certain protocols of data exchange between the IDE device and memory, bypassing the CPU, also described in Chapter 16. Choose the highest mode your device allows. **32-bit transfer mode** enables data "words" of 32-bit lengths rather than 16-bit, along the PCI bus. (This does not, as some documentation has suggested, "enable" either 32-bit file transfer mode for Windows, or FAT32 disk formatting.)

How many cylinders does a CD-ROM have? None. (Wow, that was easy.) If you have auto-detect mode set to ON, then your BIOS setup screen should register when a given IDE device is really an optical drive, by leaving blank its drive characteristics, and usually by showing its drive type as CD-ROM rather than User—even if it's a DVD-ROM or a recordable optical drive. If you're not auto-detecting, or you don't have a Plug and Play BIOS, then try setting your optical drive's type to CD-ROM manually. Usually you place the highlight over the drive type parameter, then press the arrow key until it skips over "Type 47," then "User," then the next should be "CD-ROM."

➤ **Floppy drive types** should be set to the proper capacities (generally 1.2MB for 5¼" drives, 1.44Mb for 3½") for drives A and B, or B should be set to Disabled if you only have one diskette drive.

➤ **Boot disk order** should be set to C: first, then A:, unless you really want to be booting off of your emergency diskette for the remainder of existence.

➤ **Plug-and-Play aware OS** setting should be ON unless, for some reason, you decide not to use Windows anymore.

What to Do When Your COM Ports Start a Fight

Various serial devices, such as a modem, mouse, scanner, and serial printer, use COM ports to communicate with your PC. All's well and good, as long as you only use two of these critters, and you set them to use different COM ports. But if you install a new serial device and it grabs somebody else's COM port as its own, you end up with a COM port conflict, which goes by the technical nomenclature, "one heck of a stinking mess."

The easiest way to avoid this problem is to write down the settings your gadgets use. Then, before you install anything new, just choose some settings that aren't being used. You can use this method to avoid not just COM port conflicts, but also IRQ and DMA conflicts as well.

Most PCs can support up to four COM ports, but up until the advent of Service Pack 1 for Windows 95, you could use only two of them at any one time. That's because COM1 and COM3 both use the same *interrupt* to talk to the CPU. (More on interrupts in a minute.) Same goes with COM2 and COM4. (Windows 95 registers this in its Device Manager as an official conflict, although there's no way for you to fix it.) Since Windows 95 SP-1, you can use all four COM ports simultaneously; in some cases, you might not have a choice. But be aware that the operating system is making efforts to distinguish which device is actually invoking the interrupt when two COM ports do share that interrupt. So conflicts can arise, and Murphy's Law has a tendency to play a big role when it comes to conflicts in Windows.

Now, most PCs come with two serial ports on the back, marked COM1 and COM2. It's important to remember that these two ports are active, *even if you have nothing connected to them.* So if you insert a serial device such as a modem, it will conflict with one of these two. To deactivate a COM port, you usually remove some jumper from the I/O card or from the motherboard, or make some change in your BIOS setup.

To change the COM port an external device uses, plug it into a different serial port, or make certain that the serial port it's connected to on the *outside* of your case is plugged into the correct COM port slot on your motherboard *inside* the case. There will be a ribbon cable that leads from the port connector to the motherboard. There, the serial port name should be clearly marked "COM1" or "COM2." Don't disconnect one of these cables unless you've shut down your computer. See Chapter 12 for more instructions about serial port connector cables. These motherboard connectors are designed to lead to serial connectors on the outside of your system case. Through a BIOS setting, you may be able to assign these connectors to point to logical ports COM3 and COM4 (regardless of the markings on the motherboard), especially if you intend to install an internal modem and set it to COM1.

To change the setting for an internal expansion card (generally a modem), you usually have to flip some silly DIP switch or move a stupid jumper. (If you're lucky, you get to use software for this nonsense instead of setting the COM port through switches.) You cannot change the COM port address that any device uses through the Windows Device Manager. After changing COM settings, reset the device by turning it off and then back on, so that the new settings take effect.

Fixing What IRQs You

When a child wants to get someone's attention, he usually yells. When a computer part wants to get the CPU's attention, it uses an *interrupt,* or *IRQ* for short. You see, your computer's CPU is busy all the time. If some device needs immediate attention, it sends an S.O.S. along its private interrupt. For example, if you start pressing keys on the keyboard, the keyboard controller sends an interrupt signal to the CPU so that it knows that someone's pressing keys. If two devices are accidentally assigned the same interrupt, the CPU doesn't know what device actually needs its attention, so either of two catastrophic things can happen:

➤ The CPU just ignores any messages it gets.

➤ The CPU processes one device's message as though it came from the other device.

Imagine what would happen if the CPU were to conclude that someone's typing "DELETE *.*" on your *printer.*

So what you need to do is assign a unique interrupt to each device. Sounds simple, but it's not, because most of the interrupts are already taken by the PC's inner circle of sacrosanct devices. Table 23.1 lists the various IRQs and who normally occupies them.

Table 23.1 Various IRQs

Interrupt	Who Owns It	Problems
IRQ0	System timer	
IRQ1	Keyboard controller	
IRQ2	Controller for IRQs 8–15	IRQs 8–15 don't exist in older PCs. If you own a newer PC, you can sometimes set a gadget to IRQ2 (but it actually ends up using IRQ9).
IRQ3	COM2 and COM4	This is what can get you into trouble using COM2 and COM4 at the same time. Besides modems, your mouse, sound cards, network cards, and tape backup accelerators may use this IRQ.
IRQ4	COM1 and COM3	This is what can get you into trouble using COM1 and COM3 at the same time. Besides modems, your mouse, sound cards, network cards, and tape backup accelerators may use this IRQ.
IRQ5	LPT2	The most common interrupt used by sound cards. Some newer modems allow you to set them to IRQ5. In addition, LPT3 uses this interrupt, along with some network cards, tape accelerators, and the hard disk controller on the very old PC/XT.
IRQ6	Floppy disk drive controller	Tape accelerator cards also try to use this interrupt.
IRQ7	LPT1	Parallel port, generally used by your printer. LPT2 can also use this interrupt, in addition to some modems using COM4, sound cards, network cards, and tape accelerators.
IRQ8	Clock	Clock
IRQ9	Controller for IRQs	Because IRQ2 is used as a controller for IRQ8–15, the computer automatically switches any device set to IRQ2 to IRQ9. A network card often grabs it, or your PCI cards, a sound card, or SCSI host adapter.

continues

Table 23.1   Various IRQs   (continued)

Interrupt	Who Owns It	Problems
IRQ10	Unused	Some gadgets don't support an IRQ this high. What you will typically find here are your PCI devices, AGP video, network cards, sound cards, SCSI host adapters, or the secondary IDE channel.
IRQ11	Unused	Some gadgets don't support an IRQ this high. You will find PCI devices, network cards, sound cards, SCSI host adapters, VGA video cards, and maybe your tertiary IDE channel.
IRQ12	PS/2 mouse	Typically used by the mouse; however, NICs, sound cards, SCSI host adapters, VGA video cards, and even PCI devices might also slug it out for this one.
IRQ13	Math coprocessor	You probably have one and don't know it. Every Pentium CPU, plus every CPU made by Intel, AMD, Cyrix, and Via since then, include their own coprocessors. Today, the processor and coprocessor are the same processor, even though IRQ13 remains allocated.
IRQ14	Primary IDE channel	Hard disk controller, Primary IDE channel, or SCSI host adapter.
IRQ15	Secondary IDE channel	Some gadgets don't support an IRQ this high. But your secondary IDE channel uses this one, in addition to network cards and SCSI host adapter.

As you can see, the only way you're going to make sense of this mess is to know what IRQs your other devices are using. To see how your IRQs are being distributed right this moment, bring up the Windows Device Manager. From Control Panel, bring up System, then click on the Device Manager tab. Now, from the big list in the middle of the dialog box, choose the item at the very top marked Computer. Then click on the Properties button.

In the old world of PCs, no two devices could be assigned the same IRQ, lest all heck break loose. In today's modern world of PCs, in which all heck is already loose without having to break anything to get there, your BIOS can assign two "devices" the same IRQ, but only with certain ones, and only with certain "devices" that know how to share. I say "devices," because some of these items receiving their own IRQs are actually software, not hardware.

Your Plug-and-Play BIOS can assign IRQs to some devices *dynamically*—in other words, on a first-come/first-served basis every time you open the computer. Most of the time, the BIOS will assign the same addresses to the same devices in the same way, but perhaps not 100 percent of the time. In order to make certain everything attached to the PCI bus gets its own IRQ one way or another, IRQs #3, #5, #10, and #11, and possibly #9 and #12 also, are reserved for PCI devices by way of software-based "devices" that hold these places for them—so the ISA devices can't take them first. These software devices show up in Windows as IRQ Holder for PCI Steering.

What am I talking about? When a card on the ISA bus needs to grab the attention of the CPU, it sends a signal along its dedicated IRQ line. There are only so many IRQs to go around in a PC—16, to be exact. So when the PCI bus was first deployed in modern PCs, the very real possibility presented itself that there would be more devices attached to a PC—both real and virtual—than there are IRQs. There are between four and six PCI interrupts mapped to the regular system IRQs depending on the age of your PC. If your PC has more than four PCI slots, then they share IRQs.

In all versions of Windows since Win95 OSR2, PCI interrupts are handled using something Microsoft calls *PCI steering*. The whole idea is to avoid interrupt conflicts by assigning interrupts to devices at startup. Device Manager lists PCI steering as an extra entry just above each PCI device, but don't think it means you have some kind of conflict. The PCI devices still "think" they're receiving a set of interrupts, "numbered" A, B, C, and D, and possibly E and F as well. Under PCI steering, these PCI IRQs are occasionally re-mapped to different system IRQs. The result is that PCI steering allows up to four or up to six PCI devices to still have their IRQs, although using fewer actual IRQ lines to provide them.

So perhaps you can see a pattern here: When two "devices" share the same IRQ, one of them should be a piece of software. *The old fact that no two hardware devices should share the same IRQ still holds true.* When this happens, Windows doesn't always know that this is a bad thing. So when you open Device Manager, it might not show exclamation mark icons beside the two devices that are inappropriately sharing. If you do see them, at least you know exactly what's going wrong. If you don't, scanning Device Manager for two hardware devices—or even a trio of named devices, two of which are hardware-based—can let you know that the hardware hiccups you've been noticing are caused by something relatively simple to fix.

Note

IRQs #14 and #15 can be shared between software devices called *PCI bus masters* (that can wrest temporary control of the PCI bus from the CPU) and IDE controllers that require direct memory access by way of the PCI bus.

If one of your badly behaving devices is an expansion card, then power down your PC, take a look at that card, and search for any jumpers or switches you may be able to reset. Look for a clear "IRQ" marking. If you need help with these monsters, see the first section in this chapter. If you don't find anything there, some civilized devices actually enable you to assign the IRQ through their own setup software, which makes guessing a bit easier. If that doesn't help you, then stay tuned later for a way you can adjust the IRQ assignments using Windows Device Manager.

Messing with DMA Address Junk

First, the good news: Not every device needs a DMA channel or address. Now, the bad news: There aren't that many DMA addresses. Good news again: Although there aren't that many DMA addresses, hardly any of them are taken; this means they're up for grabs by the first device that claims them.

DMA is short for *direct memory access,* and it's the technique that your peripheral devices (mainly your expansion cards) use to address your computer's main RAM while bypassing the CPU to get there. Standard DMA is used by the devices that are attached to the ISA bus—those devices that need DMA, that is. Devices that have their own RAM—for example, your laser printer—don't need DMA. Your video card doesn't need DMA (although it might use DMA through the PCI bus) because it has its own VRAM on board. But your sound card uses DMA because it composes its sound waveforms within main RAM. Your floppy disk (FDD) controller has DMA channel 2 reserved exclusively for it. In addition, most tape drives require a DMA channel, and so does the use of an ECP (Enhanced Capabilities Port) parallel port. Your IDE devices, such as your hard drive (as described in Chapter 16) and your optical drive (Chapter 18, "Adding an Optical Drive,") use DMA for burst mode data transfers; it's the new DMA mode 5 that allows for 100MB/sec speeds.

Peripherals on the PCI bus, along with the best IDE devices, do not use standard DMA. Instead they use a kind of DMA scheme called *first party DMA,* which involves *bus mastering,* where the device itself actually handles—or, more accurately, *marshals*—the transfer of data between itself and main memory. Bus mastering is required here, because the device needs to wrest temporary control of the expansion bus for this transfer to work. First party DMA allows for much higher transfer rates than standard DMA. With standard DMA, the DMA controller in the motherboard chipset handles the transfer operation. Typically, modern hard disks use bus mastering, and so do SCSI cards, some network cards, and even some video cards.

Table 23.2 lists the DMA *numbers* allocated by the BIOS to devices in your computer that request direct memory access. These are not to be confused with DMA *modes,* which are the throughput rates for data along DMA channels, and are listed in Chapter 16.

Table 23.2   DMA Numbers

DMA Address	Who Owns It
DMA 0	Memory refresh
DMA 1	Typically sound cards, but also SCSI host adapters, ECP parallel ports, tape accelerators, NICs, and voice modems
DMA 2	Floppy disk controller
DMA 3	Anything from ECP parallel ports, SCSI host adapters, tape accelerator cards, sound cards, NICs, and voice modems to the hard disk controller for an old PC/XT
DMA 4	DMA controller
DMA 5	Sound cards that can use DMA channels 5–7, also SCSI host adapters, and NICs
DMA 6	Again, only sound cards that can use 5–7, SCSI host adapters, and NICs
DMA 7	Again, only sound cards that can use 5–7, SCSI host adapters, and NICs

Eight-bit expansion cards that use only one slot of the two-slot ISA connector can only access one of the first three DMA channels, and only the first nine IRQs. Sixteen-bit cards can access any of the seven channels that are available, as well as IRQ 10 through 15.

Sound cards, NIC (networking) cards, voice modem cards, and SCSI host adapters are the four most common categories of expansion cards that can inadvertently be assigned the same DMA address. Sometimes these cards have hard switches or jumpers that designate their DMA address; and if two of these cards are set to the same number, the BIOS cannot override these settings. In this situation, to change a device's DMA address, you resort to flipping switches or pulling jumper shunts. (If you're stuck with switches and jumpers, see the first section in this chapter for help.)

How can you detect DMA and IRQ problems in Windows, and how can you take steps to resolve them? For Windows 95 and Windows 98, right-click My Computer, and select Properties. From the dialog box, select the Device Manager tab, right-click Computer at the top of the list, and then select Properties. The Computer Properties dialog box shows IRQs, I/O addresses (the internal "front doors" for devices' control programs in memory), DMA addresses, and reserved RAM blocks. If conflicts do exist, Device Manager points them out on its main list, by flagging the sources of the conflict with a black-on-yellow exclamation point icon. Device Manager is the only real tool Windows gives you to examine and possibly correct these problems. For instance, for modern cards that don't use hardware switches, you can try overriding a DMA designation using Windows Device Manager. Chapter 24, "Getting Windows to Recognize Your New Toys," will help you further.

Partitioning and Formatting a Hard Disk Drive

The single most crucial job you have to perform with respect to getting your PC to start up, to recognize your operating system, and to run programs is to set up the primary hard disk drive. It's a crucial and sometimes grueling job, but it's really not that big of a deal. When you've used computers as long as I have (which reminds me, I have a stack of UNIVAC cards to load into the batch processor tomorrow morning ...), you grow accustomed to the idea of reformatting your hard drive. It begins to be about as familiar to you, and nearly as exciting, as pumping gas. But what's really wonderful is that I get to tell you about this really unexciting job in such an exciting way.

Telling the BIOS About the New Drive

Before you can use your new hard drive, you have to get your PC to realize that it's there. If your hard drive is a Plug and Play drive, this may not be a problem. If you have a Plug and Play BIOS in your computer (which, if it was built since 1998, you do), your hard drive may at least be able to identify itself to your BIOS. If your BIOS knows what that identity means, it can at least enter the drive's specifications into your CMOS settings for you. That's a relief, to be sure. But you'll probably still want to go into your BIOS setup program to make sure this automatic process resulted in settings that make some kind of sense.

If you don't have a Plug and Play BIOS, or the drive you've installed is not Plug and Play-compliant, all is not completely lost. Your hard drive's specifications should be printed up in its manual or, in the case of manufacturers who actually give a rip about their customers (Western Digital, Maxtor, and Seagate qualify in this category), the specifications may be printed on the top of the hard drive itself. These specifications are critical, otherwise you won't be able to even *format* your drive if you need to. So turn on your PC, and as it's booting, do whatever dance you usually do to get the BIOS program to show its face.

Figure 23.4 shows what an Award BIOS setup program looks like as it tries to auto-detect your internal devices. To tell your BIOS about your new drive, you have to know all sorts of creepy things, such as how many *cylinders, heads,* and *sectors* it has, as well as science-fiction sounding things such as write pre-comp and landing zone. Even if you don't understand what these terms mean, the hard drive specs listed on the drive or in the manual are listed the same way as the BIOS setup program lists them, so just type in the numbers from the manual or the drive sticker into the form onscreen. Or, better yet, if you're installing an IDE drive and the BIOS has an auto-detect feature (part of Plug and Play), then use it now. It'll save you tons of headaches.

After you enter the settings manually, the BIOS calculates the size of your hard disk. It may come up with a number that's a little off, such as 2,112MB for a 2.5GB hard disk, but it shouldn't be way off—for instance, 1,064MB.

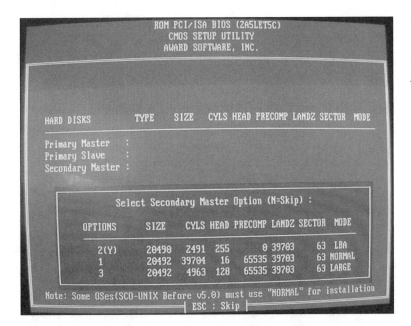

Figure 23.4

The auto-detect feature of the Award BIOS setup program.

Now, if you have to enter the parameters yourself, you may find that you are two parameters short, in terms of what the label on the hard disk told you. For *precompression* or "write precomp" (abbreviated *WPcomp*), use either 0 or 65,535. When in doubt, try 0 first. For *landing zone*, enter the number of cylinders minus one, which will usually be 1,023.

Setting Up a SCSI Drive

If you're setting up a SCSI drive, you have to run its Setup software to add a driver either to Windows or to the CONFIG.SYS file, so that your PC recognizes the drive. Next, you'll have to run the setup program that came with the SCSI host adapter so that it recognizes the drive, and so in turn, you can high-level format the drive using DOS. Before doing that, however, you may have to low-level format the SCSI drive. As a matter of safety, as long as your BIOS isn't controlling your hard drives anyway, you should set the BIOS up for No Hard Drive at all. This way, you won't accidentally use the BIOS to low-level format SCSI drives. Your BIOS thinks you'll always use IDE because nothing else exists except IDE … because it doesn't have a clue about SCSI. To low-level format a SCSI drive, use the special program diskette supplied by the drive's manufacturer, or use utility software that's rated for SCSI drives. *Do not use any low-level format utility that shows up as a selection in your CMOS Setup.*

Partitioning a New Hard Disk (SCSI or IDE)

If your hard disk came with a Setup diskette, you need to run it now. Stick the diskette in drive A:, and if the program doesn't start itself when you reboot your

455

computer, type SETUP at the A:\> prompt. The setup program takes care of the FDISK thing coming up, as well as FORMAT. It also checks your BIOS to see if you need to use a device driver so that your computer will recognize the high capacity drive. Now you can skip gleefully over the next few paragraphs. If your hard disk did not come with a Setup diskette, then reboot with your emergency diskette (which has the FDISK and FORMAT commands on it), and read the next few paragraphs.

Note

Do not, under any circumstances, attempt to low-level format an IDE drive. Unless, of course, you have a sadistic, destructive streak in you, and the only way you can release your inner tiger is by destroying magnetic media. High-level formatting, on the other hand—which you do with the FORMAT command in DOS mode—is not only a good idea, it's required.

After you've gotten the BIOS setup business over with, your next step is to *partition* your drive. A partition is a region of the hard drive's storage space where stuff can be stored. (Thrills.) For most hard disks, a partition should span the entire storage space, for a grand total of 1 partition. The most common reason why anyone puts more than one partition on a drive is because his BIOS only recognizes partition sizes to a certain limit—which generally means his BIOS is too old anyway.

Now, you don't officially have a hard drive yet, so you'll need to boot your system with your emergency diskette in drive A:. Although you can use this opportunity to divide a large disk into several smaller ones, you don't have to do this (unless your BIOS or your operating system forces you). You can, and perhaps should, have just one partition on your hard drive; but having more than one allows you to address one partition as "logical drive" C: and another partition as "logical drive" D:. If you really enjoy this type of confusion, be my guest and sign up for more than one partition.

Sign up for only one partition, that is, *if you can*. As you learned in Chapter 16, if your PC's BIOS is old enough that it did not yet support PIO mode 3, most likely, it can only handle partition sizes up to 504MB. If you have a slightly newer BIOS, it still only may be able to handle partition sizes less than 2.1GB. *Or*, if you're not using Windows 95 OSR2 or newer *and* FAT32, you may still have a 2.1GB limit. If you can't get BIOS upgrades for either of these two conditions, and you don't want to use FAT32, then you'll have to partition your hard disk into two or more smaller partitions that the BIOS can deal with.

To partition your hard drive, first reboot your computer with your emergency diskette in the drive. When you see the A> prompt, type FDISK and press Enter. Be careful when using FDISK, because a simple typo could end up erasing the data of an existing drive. With FDISK, the hard drives your computer recognizes are given *device numbers*, not letters, beginning with 1. So when you tell FDISK to create a "Primary DOS partition" for your main hard disk (the one that will end up being drive C:), make certain that the listing for "Current fixed disk drive" reads 1. If it's not, choose "Change current fixed disk drive," then type **1**.

You may be asked if you want to use FAT32 to partition the drive: What you'll see is a question such as "Enable large disk support?" If you want to use FAT32, then type **Y** for yes. Any partition you create that has over 504MB on it will then use FAT32 automatically. If you replaced your old drive, your new drive is the primary DOS partition. So choose "Create DOS partition or Logical DOS Drive" and then choose "Create Primary DOS Partition." You can only have one primary DOS partition, by the way; that's the whole meaning behind "primary." You'll be asked if you want to use all available disk space for this partition. Type **Y** if you do, and then press Esc, and you're done. Or press **N**, if you want to enter a smaller size amount, to create the first of several partitions for the drive. If you enter a size amount, press Esc to return to the FDISK menu.

Next, you need to make the new partition the active one, so press 2 if needed, to select that option, and then 1 to select partition 1. If you have additional partitions you need to create on drive C:, press Esc to return to the FDISK menu, select 1 (Create DOS partition or logical drive) and then 2 (Create Extended DOS Partition). Press Enter to use what's left as your extended partition (don't worry, you can still divide this up into several logical drives). Press Esc to return to the FDISK menu, where you're prompted to enter the size of the next partition. You can use up what's left, or enter an amount, and repeat these steps to create as many partitions as you like. Press Esc when you're done with FDISK.

If you're adding a second drive instead of a main drive to your computer, you need to partition drive D:. First choose "Change current fixed disk drive" and then select 2 (the second drive). *This is important, because you don't want to do anything to the data on your main drive.* Choose "Create DOS Partition or Logical DOS Drive." Choose "Secondary DOS Partition" and press **Y** to partition it. Follow the steps given earlier if you want to divide the second drive into several partitions.

After you finish with FDISK, insert your emergency diskette, and reboot your PC by pressing Ctrl+Alt+Delete.

Formatting the Drive

After you partition the new drive, you have to high-level format it. Here's some strange-but-true advice: If you're setting up a multi-gigabyte drive, after you've created the main bootable DOS partition for that drive using FDISK, *reboot your computer* with your emergency diskette in your A: drive, before formatting your drive with FORMAT C:. Why? If you don't reboot, FORMAT sets your drive up for no more than 528 MB, no matter how big your drive or main partition really happens to be. After you reboot, your computer will see your drive for how big it really is.

If you replaced your old hard drive, then after you've rebooted, type FORMAT C: at the DOS prompt to format it and press Enter. The "/S" part makes it a "system" disk, so it can run DOS and boot itself without you having to put a DOS diskette in drive A. If you added a second drive or if you partitioned your one hard disk into several logical drives instead, type FORMAT D: and press Enter to format it. You don't need the "/S" part here.

Check This Out

Suppose you replaced your old drive C: with a new hard disk, and then using FDISK, partitioned it into two virtual device partitions. But you left an existing drive D: in your computer. The second partition's letter in this case will be E:, not D:, because D: is already being used by your old hard drive. Get it? Good.

When DOS asks you for a volume label, you can type whatever you want, up to 11 characters—for instance, "BIG_OL_DISK." Anyway, after you've formatted your new drive, remove any diskettes from their drives and restart your PC to test the new format out.

You'll want to repeat the high-level format process for all the partitions you created in FDISK, although you don't need to use the "/S" switch for any other partition except the one that will contain the operating system.

Ah, yes, the operating system. At this point, you'll need to reinstall it. If you use Windows 98 or later, reboot your computer with the emergency diskette in the drive, and then run SETUP from the Windows 98 CD-ROM. And if you use Windows 95 … Remember that emergency diskette that Windows made for you, which didn't have the CD-ROM driver on it? Hopefully you put one there yourself before you started this whole process, didn't you? That way, you can run the SETUP program from the Windows 95 CD-ROM. Chapter 24 will help you with this part.

Mistakes to Avoid

If your new drive won't wake up, open up the PC again and check for obvious things like loose cables and such. Also check to make sure that you didn't put the data (ribbon) cables on backwards. Remember, the red wire or stripe should match up with pin 1 on the data cable connector. Check the controller card as well, and make sure that it is seated properly. Next, you might want to check the BIOS settings for the drive, especially to ensure that Plug and Play is recognizing the proper parameters. Check the master/slave jumpers on the back of the hard disk, to make sure the device you set as the master is connected to the master end of the cable.

Make sure you partitioned and formatted the thing okay. Use your emergency diskette to reboot your computer. Type FDISK at the prompt, and then read the partition table to see if the partitions are really showing up the way you intended. You should have one and only one primary DOS partition. And, one of the partitions must be made the *active* one, or you'll get the message, "No ROM Basic, system halted," or "No boot device found." If needed, just reboot with your emergency diskette and use FDISK again. If you get the error message, "No operating system," you apparently don't have Windows Me, and you forgot the /S parameter when you used the FORMAT command on drive C.

If you're dealing with two IDE drives, they may not want to play together. You can try switching the slave and master drives with each other. If that doesn't work, you may have to take the new drive back and get a drive made by the same people who made the first one.

The Least You Need to Know

➤ To move a shunt from a jumper, pull it off the two pins it currently occupies and slide it back on top of two other pins.

➤ Flipping a DIP switch is similar to flipping a light switch: The switch itself is either on or off.

➤ CMOS keeps track of important info like the number and type of diskette drives, the size of hard disks, and the amount of memory.

➤ COM ports (serial ports) are active, even when nothing is connected to them. You can't set two devices to the same COM port.

➤ An IRQ (hardware interrupt) is a way for a device to get the CPU's attention.

➤ A DMA channel is a high-speed channel for data transfer to the CPU.

➤ Make sure you've copied down your important CMOS information and have verified specifications for your hard disk drive(s), before you begin replacing or reformatting them.

➤ You'll be working from the DOS prompt to create the bootable partition for your hard drive, and to give it a high-level format.

459

Chapter 24

Getting Windows to Recognize Your New Toys

In This Chapter

➤ How to let Windows know that you've installed a new toy

➤ How to get Windows to show you what it thinks is wrong

➤ How adding a printer is different from adding any other device

➤ Installing your network software under Windows

In the previous chapter, you managed to get the computer put back together, switched on, and set up. Your hard disk drives are whirring away, and so are your optical disc drives. Something actually comes up on the monitor, and the BIOS isn't screaming bloody murder like a test of the Emergency Broadcasting System. So you're fine, right? Well, no ... there's one more thing—big thing, actually. It's Windows.

You see, after you switch the computer on, it's the job of the BIOS to tell the computer that it's a computer. But like the Space Center at Cape Canaveral that turns over flight control to Houston after the space shuttle has cleared the tower, the BIOS turns over control of your computer to Windows the moment that the chipset reports to the BIOS that everything is up to speed. This chapter is about getting Windows to want to work with your new or added hardware.

Installing a driver the old-fashioned MS-DOS way through the CONFIG.SYS and AUTOEXEC.BAT configuration files just isn't good enough for Windows. No sir. That's because Windows has its own configuration files: WIN.INI, SYSTEM.INI, and to make matters worse, the gargantuan System Registry. Windows needs a device driver specifically designed for Windows before it can communicate with anything you've just installed. So, for most new devices, you'll need to install a Windows device driver (and sometimes, a DOS driver as well). I know this is like learning you have to fill out your tax forms twice in the same year, but did you really expect your computer to be easy?

If you're joining this chapter from one of the other chapters in the Third Quarter about how to install your hardware, then you've probably just installed your hardware and are on your way to installing the software part—the *driver*. You may recall that a driver is a program the operating system uses to communicate with a specific device. Some devices you add on include both a Windows driver and a DOS driver, but if they don't, you'll find additional Windows drivers on the Windows setup diskettes as well—you know, the diskettes you used to install Windows in the first place. To find those missing DOS drivers, you'll need to check the manufacturer's Web site.

Check This Out

If you restart your PC after using the setup program only to run into a problem (like the PC won't start), use your emergency diskette. Chapter 4, "What You Need to Know *Before* You Open Your PC," showed you how to make one. Just stick it in drive A: and restart the PC. Then edit the configuration files (if you need help, see the next section) to either remove or change what the setup program did, so your PC and the device will work. The new changes will be easy to identify, because they'll be something you won't recognize, but you can always check the manual to be sure. Or you might just copy back to the hard disk the unchanged versions of your configuration files that you put on your emergency diskette just prior to installing the new device.

Introducing Your Shy Operating System to Your New Hardware

"Windows, new device … new device, Windows …" It should be this simple. It never is.

Plug and Play Around

After you install your new toy and restart your PC, the operating system may or may not recognize that something is different. That's because Plug and Play (PnP) doesn't work without a Plug and Play BIOS and a Plug and Play-compliant device that the BIOS can recognize.

In other words, if you've just added a Plug and Play CD-ROM drive, and your PC uses at least a Socket 7 CPU, a modern chipset, and a Plug and Play BIOS, your PC automatically recognizes your new CD-ROM and begins the driver installation process as soon as you turn on the PC and start Windows. This may not be what you want at all … or, at least, not what the manufacturer of the CD-ROM drive may want. Although Windows has become very adept at recognizing new hardware, it isn't always keen on doing precisely what the manufacturer of that hardware wants done with it. So the installation instructions on your new device (CD-ROM drive, printer, scanner, or just about anything else) may instruct you specifically to cancel out of any automatic driver installation procedure that Windows may happen to start, after you first reboot your PC with the new device installed. In the case of USB devices, which you can plug in for the first time while the PC's still turned on, Windows may start up an installation Wizard automatically. For most USB devices manufactured to date, the instructions will probably tell you to cancel out of this Wizard. It will then ask you to insert the installation CD-ROM disc in your optical drive, then either wait for its own installation routine to start itself, or go into Windows Explorer and double-click on SETUP.EXE.

Some USB device manufacturers will ask you to power down your PC before you plug in your new external device, even though theoretically you're supposed to be able to plug them in while the PC is turned on. Chapter 8, "The Easiest Things to Upgrade," dealt with some of the headaches implicit with many of these USB devices.

If you don't have a PnP BIOS in your PC, or if you didn't buy a PnP device, you may actually have an easier time. Windows is pretty good at installing your new device anyway. It just needs a little shove in the right direction.

Adding Just About Anything, Except a Printer

When Windows doesn't automatically welcome your new toy, here's how to tell Windows about it:

First, close down your important applications. Then open the Start menu, select Settings, and then select Control Panel. Double-click the Add New Hardware icon. The Add New Hardware Wizard appears. Not much to do on this first screen, so click Next. You'll see the dialog box shown in Figure 24.1.

The easiest way to handle this is to sit back, relax, and let Windows do all the work. So when it asks you if you want Windows to search for and detect your new hardware, by all means, click Yes. Then click Next.

This whole detection thing takes a few minutes, so feel free to put your feet up while you wait. Meanwhile, Windows starts sniffing around, looking for something new. When Windows finds your new part, it displays the name of that part (or at least what Windows believes that part to be) in a box. If the guess is right, just click Finish, and Windows installs the proper device driver. You may be asked to provide additional information, or to perform additional steps. For example, if you're installing an external modem, Windows asks you to turn it on. Then it asks you to enter your phone number and information about what it normally takes for you to dial out.

Figure 24.1

Getting Windows 95 to search for your new device is easy (later versions appear similar).

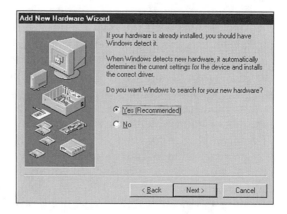

If Windows doesn't find your new toy, or if it guessed wrong, you'll see a message telling you to give it another try. Click Next. You'll see a list of hardware types. Select your hardware type from the list. If you don't see your hardware type listed, choose "Other devices." Click Next. Figure 24.2 shows you what you'll see.

Figure 24.2

The manual method of telling Windows 95 about a new device.

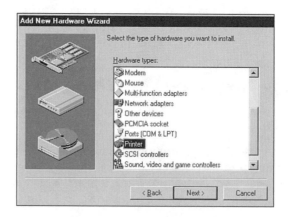

You'll see a list of manufacturers for your particular device. For example, if you select Modem, you'll see a list of common modems. Click the name of the manufacturer that made your modem (such as Supra), and you'll see a list of Supra modems. Pick your model from the list and click Next. You may be asked next which logical port you want to use for your modem (if that feature isn't already preset by a jumper or DIP switch). Don't be alarmed if you don't get asked this question; in fact, *celebrate* if you don't get asked this question. If you do, pick a COM port that you know your mouse isn't using at the time. Windows installs the driver for your new part. In a moment, you'll see its properties dialog box from the Control Panel.

If you still can't find your new part in a listing anywhere, then Windows did not come with a driver for it. Click Have Disk and insert the setup diskette supplied by the maker of your new gadget. Select the driver file from those listed (there will probably only be one file listed) and click OK. Windows installs the driver.

After you've installed your new part under Windows, you might be able to start using it right away. If you do have to reboot Windows, you'll be told so with a dialog box, to which you respond with Yes. If you want to change any of your choices later on (for example, you want to change your modem's phone number) just return to the Control Panel and click the appropriate icon, such as the Modem icon.

Adding a New Printer

Unlike your other devices, the setup for a *printer driver* is somewhat different. Bring up Control Panel, and double-click Printers. In the window that comes up, double-click Add Printer. You'll be greeted by a dialog box that tells you you're about to install a printer. There's not a "Duh!" button, so click Next.

If your PC is attached to a network, you'll see a choice here of whether your printer is directly attached to your PC (Local printer) or attached to a PC on the network, located in some other room (Network printer). If you don't have a network, you won't see this dialog box. Suppose for now that your printer is directly attached. Choose "Local printer," and click Next.

Choose your printer's manufacturer from the Manufacturers list (see Figure 24.3), and its model name from the Printers list. There are about eight zillion printers here. If you can't find yours, click Have Disk, insert your printer's driver diskette or CD-ROM into its drive, and point the dialog box that pops up to the proper device letter. In that case only, you'll see a message asking you if this certain weird-looking .INF file is the right one; click OK.

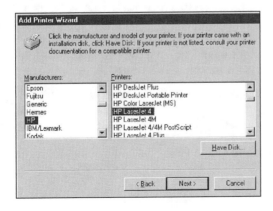

Figure 24.3

Choose your printer's manufacturer from this dialog box.

Next you'll see a list of logical ports that identify the "channel" through which your PC will communicate with your printer. It's a printer. So why you get asked this question, who knows? Choose LPT1:. Then click Next. You get a chance to *name* your printer (haven't you always wanted to give your printer a name?) as well. By default, it's the drab model name, like "Panasonic KX-P4420"; you can replace it with something like "Susan," "Galaxy NGC-7928," or "Something Plug and Play Can't Mess Up." When you're done having fun with this, click Next.

You are given the opportunity at this point to print out a test page. Absolutely do this; it could save you a lot of headaches later. If something's wrong, your botched-up piece of paper (or *pieces* of paper, if something's *really* wrong) will tell you. Leave the option set for Yes, and then click Finish. Your test page, by the way, tells you a few things about your setup and your printer's operating condition.

If your printer's manufacturer intends to offer you some special bonus software, or the incentive to go online and register your printer, it will do this now. In other words, folks, anything can happen from this point on.

Now, if your printer is on a network, in that dialog box you encountered much earlier, you choose "Network printer" and click Next. This takes you to a dialog box that asks for "Network path or queue name." Heck if you know, right? What does Windows think you are, a tax consultant? Click Browse. You'll see the Browse for Printer dialog. The list in this box will be headed with Network Neighborhood if you have Windows 95 or 98, or My Network Places if you have Windows Me. (Contests have already been held as to which sounds the most patronizing, with both ending up tying for first place.) Click the "+" beside Entire Network, then choose the name of the workgroup (not hard, there's only one), followed by the name of the PC to which the printer is actually installed. At last, you'll see the name that the PC has given to this printer. Choose that, and click OK.

Next, if you actually use an MS-DOS program, it's safest to choose Yes under "Do you print from MS-DOS-based programs?" Otherwise, leave the question alone. Click Next.

You're given a chance to create your own name for this printer, although the brand name works just fine. You're also asked whether you want to assign this printer as the "default"—the one that your Windows applications will print to unless you say otherwise. If you already have a different printer attached directly to your PC, No will already be chosen for you. If you don't have one attached, Yes will be chosen for you. Whether you change this choice is up to you. Click Next.

Finally, you're asked if you wish to print a test page. This is worthwhile, especially if you want to spook your family member upstairs on the other PC. Click Next.

What happens next depends on the printer driver installed on the other PC. Generally, your system will automatically copy a set of files that are stored on the system with the other printer. You may then see a wide assortment of unsolicited advertisements.

Using Windows Device Manager to Explore Your System

If you use Windows 95 or 98, you can use My Computer to uncover more secrets about your PC's configuration. Just right-click on the My Computer icon on the desktop, and then select Properties from the menu that appears out of nowhere.

Seeing What's There

On the General tab, you'll see your Windows version, CPU type, and the amount of memory in your computer. Click the Device Manager tab, and you can snoop some more (see Figure 24.4).

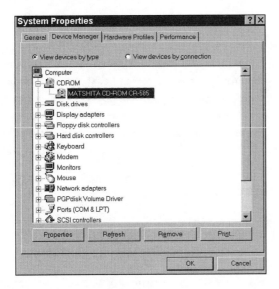

Figure 24.4

Snooping around with the Device Manager.

Click the plus sign next to an item to see more detail. For example, here I've clicked the plus next to "CDROM," and my CD-ROM drive is displayed for all to see.

Device Manager gives you the opportunity to change or update a component's drivers, as well as to alter some of its critical settings. However, rest assured that it's unlikely that you could reset something major—like the COM port where your modem is plugged in—unless you're the sort of person who likes to click on buttons just to "see what this does."

The main list in Device Manager contains items that are categorized by the functions they perform. But it isn't spelled out in this list which items are actually things *per se* (hardware you can hold in your hand), parts of components inside your computer (hardware you should definitely avoid touching unless absolutely necessary), and which are software. It's up to you to keep these distinctions clear in your head. For instance, Monitors is obviously a category of external hardware—a peripheral. The

467

"Ports (COM & LPT)" category, meanwhile, refers to interfaces that reside on your motherboard—the main, big, green square on which your CPU sits. It's hardware, but it's not a peripheral. Under the Network Adapters category, you're likely to find some of the so-called *virtual devices* that help you dial up the Internet—for example, Dial-Up Adapter. This isn't a thing at all, but a piece of software that is installed when Windows is installed that becomes a part of the Windows operating system.

Check This Out

The high-speed burst transfer modes for modern hard drives are provided by way of a ne-gotiated agreement between your hard drive and your BIOS when you switch your PC on. Windows has nothing to do with this. You just have to remember that fact when you check out Windows Me's current "Settings" for your hard disk drives in Device Manager. Windows may show DMA as turned off, even when it's not. But if you check the box and okay the dialog box then, when you restart your system, your hard drive's contents may become, to use Gen. Patton's words, "a bunch of goo." So this word of caution and ad-vice: Leave that DMA check box alone, whatever you do!

Another important point about the Device Manager's list of physical devices and vir-tual devices is that it only shows devices that Windows plays a direct role in control-ling. Notice, for instance, that printers are missing from this list. This does not mean there are no printers installed. It's simply up to a printer to manage itself. Some scan-ners are that way too. So remember, if Windows doesn't manage the device, it's not shown here. In such cases, it's up to you to locate the software on your computer that does manage the device.

If Windows thinks there's something wrong with one of the installed items in the Device Manager list, then next to that item, you'll see a yellow circle with a black ex-clamation point. Click the + next to that item. Click Properties. In the Properties dia-log box, in the Device Status frame, read Windows' assessment of what's wrong with the device, and its suggestion as to what you can do about it.

Changing Critical Settings for Installed Devices

In the previous chapter, you were introduced to IRQs and DMAs —the critical assign-ments given to your computer's various devices before your BIOS gives them their marching orders. Windows ... *pretends* that it is responsible for the act of assigning these numbers to your devices, as part of its policy of making it seem like it's responsible for everything that goes on inside your PC.

You can use Windows Device Manager to change (or at least attempt to change, if your hardware allows it) the interrupt request number (IRQ), direct memory address channel (DMA), and I/O address range of your installed hardware devices, whether Windows thinks there's a problem with those settings or not. Chapter 23, "Making Your Computer Boot Up Again," showed you all the reservations and limitations for IRQ and DMA numbers. If your hardware allows you to make changes yourself in order to resolve an obvious conflict or slowdown in your system, you can use Device Manager to do this.

Now, what do I mean by "obvious conflict or slowdown?" Suppose Device Manager isn't showing you any telltale exclamation point icon signaling a known device conflict. Even in such a situation, I've encountered situations when every sound produced by Windows plays at half speed, staggered, on and off, on and off, like a dinosaur trapped in an empty coliseum. When you hear that kind of sound, generally one of your other devices is fighting your sound card for the same IRQ. The IRQ Steering feature of your BIOS may make it seem to Windows that this IRQ is supposed to be "shared" between these two devices; Windows can't hear what you're hearing.

So here's what you do to attempt a change in your BIOS device assignments using Device Manager: To give yourself something of a safety net—a way to at least get back to the way things were if the setting you make causes things to get worse instead of better—you can have Windows create something for you called a *hardware profile*. In other words, you can make your changes to the computer's setup into a separate list of settings, which you can discard if you find it doesn't work out.

Here's how this works: Right beside Device Manager in the lineup of tabs in the System Control Panel, is Hardware Profiles. To start up a new profile, it's a good idea to start with a copy of the existing one, and just change that. So click Copy, then give your new profile any name you want—for instance, "My Personal Test Configuration." If you think you might try more than one test configuration in the future, it might be a good idea to label this one with the current date beside this name. Click OK. Then shut down the System Control Panel and restart your computer.

During the boot sequence, you'll be given a list of possible hardware configurations. Choose your test configuration (the way you choose this differs depending on which Windows you have). For now, you'll notice nothing different. If there was a problem before, you should still notice it.

Now, bring up Device Manager again. Choose the device whose assignment you need to change, then click Properties. After the Properties dialog box comes up, click on the Resources tab.

The list in the middle of the Resources tab shows you all the critical assignments your BIOS made to this device at startup. The box marked "Use automatic settings" will probably be checked. This is like a safety lock. Uncheck it.

Choose the setting you need to change from the list, then click "Change setting." If it cannot be changed at all, Windows will tell you so now. If it can, Windows will present you with a list of your other options. You can choose one of these options, even if it would definitely cause a conflict with the setting for some other device; Windows will tell you that explicitly beforehand. Don't be surprised if Windows tells you that you can't make the changes you want to make. This may actually be a good sign: When a setting can be changed, that generally means that setting was arbitrary in the first place. A setting that cannot be changed is less likely to be liable for the problem you're experiencing.

Anyway, supposing that you can make this change: Click OK to finalize this change, and OK to exit the System Control Panel. Shut down your computer again and reboot, remembering to choose your test configuration from the menu.

If the problem goes away, don't rush to delete the "Original Configuration" just yet. Work with your computer awhile—perhaps several days—just to make sure. When you're confident you've made the right change, go back into Hardware Profiles. Choose your test configuration, then click on Rename. Give this configuration a name that lets you know you made it, and that it works, such as "My Working Reconfiguration," followed by the date. Click OK, then click OK, and return to your business. Congratulations, by the way! You've just diagnosed and fixed a PC hardware bug!

Now, if you don't notice any change at all, you have two options: Make another change to your test configuration, or go back to the way things were. If you change a setting in Device Manager now, you'll be changing your test configuration, not "Original Configuration." That's still safe. Just remember to reboot to see whether any new changes work.

If your system behaves *worse* than it did before, you'll want to go back to the way things were. Reboot your computer, and choose Original Configuration. Then go into Hardware Profiles, choose your test configuration from the list, and click Delete. Say Yes. At this point, you could start over with a new test configuration, or you could start suspecting hardware troubles that run deeper than just a few BIOS settings. At least you've ruled out the possibility of miscommunication between the BIOS and your malfunctioning device, whatever it is. So when and if you have to purchase a replacement device, whatever that may be, you'll feel more confident that you made that purchase for the right reasons.

Setting Up Your Network

In Chapter 22, "Installing and Maintaining a Home Network," you saw how the hardware for your network works, and how it's installed. Most modern network interface cards (NICs) are Plug and Play devices—even the inexpensive ones. This means that when you install your NIC and reboot your computer, Windows should be able to recognize your new card and install the appropriate drivers.

The Software Parts of the Network

Should. I'm coming close to the end of this book (in fact, I think I hear the Two-Minute Warning coming up) and I'll bet you've read this word quite a lot by now. If Windows installs the right drivers for your peer-to-peer network onto your PC, it will add some components to your Configuration list in the Network Control Panel. If they're not there, it isn't too difficult for you to add them yourself. Here's how to check:

Bring up your Control Panel, and then double-click the Network icon. The Network dialog box pops up (see Figure 24.5).

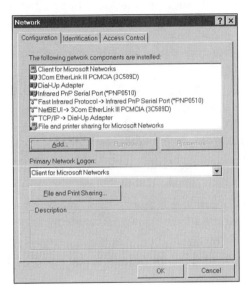

Figure 24.5

Everything Windows thinks your network has shows up here.

There may be several items in your installed components list for both (or all) PCs in your peer-to-peer network, but at the very least, you should have the following items listed:

➤ **Client for Microsoft Networks**—This is the software that actually performs the communication with the server in a standard client/server topology, or with the other PCs in a peer-to-peer topology.

➤ **Your NIC's hardware driver**—This will be represented in the list by the card's brand name.

➤ **Dial-Up Adapter**—You'll still need this for your PC to link to the Internet through your phone modem. (If you have a cable modem or DSL modem, you don't need this.)

➤ **TCP/IP**—Transport Control Protocol/Internet Protocol. Your NIC card might *not* require this, although your PC does need it to connect to the Internet. You'll notice a little arrow beside TCP/IP's listing, showing that it's "bound" to the

471

Dial-Up Adapter, not to the NIC. If your NIC card does need TCP/IP, there will be a separate listing for it, with a binding arrow that points to the NIC's name.

➤ **File and Printer Sharing for Microsoft Networks**—This is the service that makes it possible for Windows on one computer to contact Windows on another computer and send it files to load up or resources to share, like a printer or a network-compatible modem.

If any of these items are missing from your components list, here's how you install them.

First, discharge any hatred or negative emotions that may be hanging around you, by touching your spouse, loved one, or favorite pet. Cancel out of any other programs, applications, games, or doodling you may be working on. Next, place your Windows CD-ROM in the drive. Cancel the song-and-dance dialog box that automatically comes up.

Bring up the Network dialog box (shown in Figure 24.6) by double-clicking the Network icon in the Control Panel. If you notice something missing from the components list, click Add. A dialog box appears asking what you want to add, and giving you four categories for a possible response. Here's what they mean:

➤ A **client** is the software that actually performs the network communications process. Choose this if you need to install "Client for Microsoft Networks."

➤ An **adapter** is either your "NIC hardware," or a "virtual" adapter such as the Dial-Up Adapter used to link to the Internet via your modem.

➤ A **protocol** is the communications method your *workstation* (your PC's been promoted) needs to speak to the other workstations in the network. Choose this if you need to install TCP/IP.

➤ A **service** is something the operating system facilitates for your network, such as File and Print Sharing. If you have Windows Me, you will not see "Service" listed. Don't panic; Windows Me networks still have services, they're just elsewhere.

Figure 24.6

All the stuff that's fit to print on the Windows CD-ROM.

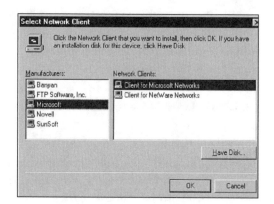

Techno Talk

NetBEUI (pronounced "net-buoy") is an IBM protocol designed to facilitate the exchange of resources over a network. In the previous edition of this book, I suggested that people install NetBEUI, and bind it to their network card so that the network could use it instead of TCP/IP, thus making the network less likely to be tapped into through the Internet. Apparently, enough people took this suggestion from me or somebody else that malicious users found a way to tap into NetBEUI protocol through the Internet. So although NetBEUI is fast and efficient, there are sadly no longer any safety reasons for installing it for exchanging network resources.

Next, you'll see a dialog box that presents you with a list of manufacturers for your chosen category (Microsoft's the manufacturer of the Dial-Up Adapter and all your Services), plus the available items in that category whose driver software is on the Windows CD-ROM. If you're installing your NIC driver, and you don't see your NIC in this list, click Have Disk, and then insert the driver diskette or CD-ROM that came with your NIC card. In the file selector box that comes up, pull up the directory where the .INF file that installs your driver is located (there should only be one .INF file). Otherwise, choose the component you're looking for in the list, and click OK. Your component will be installed forthwith.

Getting Windows to Recognize Your Internet Connection

The way modern Internet connections work in Windows, regardless of whether you have an older version of Windows, you no longer have to set up your computer to pretend that it's actually on the Internet. The least common denominator of all Internet connections, whether dial-up or broadband, is the Domain Name Server (DNS) address used by your Internet Service Provider.

Windows requires these DNS settings so that its TCP/IP protocol *stack* (that's what it's called, a "stack," like pancakes) has a central point of contact with the outside world. A DNS server acts like a "Yellow Pages" of sorts for the Internet, resolving requests like "www.mcp.com" into numeric addresses that routers on the Internet can understand.

So what you'll need to know from your ISP are the following two items: the host name that is being assigned to represent you when you dial up or while your broadband service is turned on (it will be a name, with letters and numbers in it, and with parts separated with dots); and the numeric DNS server address or addresses used by the ISP. Here's how you enter that data into Windows:

Bring up the Network Control Panel. Choose any item from the list beginning with TCP/IP (it actually doesn't matter which one), then click on Properties.

In the TCP/IP Properties dialog box, click on the DNS Configuration tab. Set the option Enable DNS. Then in the field marked Host, type the *first part* of the host address name—everything up to the first dot in the name. Leave that dot out. Then jump over to the field marked Domain, and type the remainder of the host name—everything *after* the first dot all the way to the end, including all dots in between.

The addresses you're given for the DNS servers should be numeric, and in four parts separated by dots. For each address (there's at least one, perhaps as many as three) carefully type the numbers into the field with all the dots in it, just below DNS Server Search Order. Then click Add, and you'll see the number you just typed appearing in the box below. If there are any more addresses, type them into the same field, and click Add after each one.

Click OK. You'll be taken back to the Network dialog box. Click OK to dismiss it. You'll then be told you need to reboot your computer. Click Yes, watch your computer reboot, and wait breathlessly for the magic to begin.

The Least You Need to Know

➤ After you install a new device, you have to get Windows to recognize it. You may be able to let Windows find and install the proper device driver for you using Plug and Play. Otherwise, you'll need to use the Add New Hardware icon in the Control Panel to install your new device.

➤ You might need to download a DOS device driver too, and follow the directions supplied with that driver to install it in the AUTOEXEC.BAT and CONFIG.SYS files of your emergency diskette.

➤ Before making any changes to your Windows setup, update your emergency diskette.

➤ Installing a printer for Windows is a different process than installing any other category of device. Surprisingly, it's actually quite sensible.

➤ Your PnP-compliant NIC card should automatically install all the client, device driver, protocol, and service software your peer-to-peer network may need. If it doesn't, the process isn't too difficult: Just navigate through a few dialog boxes in the Network Control Panel, and reboot your computer.

Index

481

S

493

497

What Are We Talking About?

NIC (Network Interface Card)   An expansion card that contains the processors enabling a PC to connect to a local network or cable modem.

PC100   A grade given to an SDRAM memory module capable of operating in a PC with a 100MHz system bus.

PCI (Peripheral Component Interconnect)   A 32-bit bus used exclusively within a PC for expansion cards and peripherals, and no motherboard components.

PGA (Pin Grid Array)   The packaging for a CPU designed to fit into a socket, as opposed to a slot.

SCSI (Small Computer Systems Interface)   A standard for an interface connecting a CPU to various peripheral devices, including a hard disk drive, printer, scanner, or external storage device, that enables the processors to communicate with one another using a tokenized language.

SEC (Single Edge Connector)   A packaging scheme for Slot 1-based CPUs such as Intel Pentium II, earlier Celeron and Pentium III models, and earlier AMD Athlon models, in which the processor is mounted on a daughterboard and attached to the motherboard via a slot that supports a card edge.

UART (Universal Asynchronous Receiver/Transmitter)   The processor that controls a modem's basic functionality, including its capability to send and receive a signal.

Ultra DMA   1) A brand name for DMA modes 3, 4, and 5, which enable an IDE device to negotiate 33, 66, and 100Mbps data throughput, respectively.

USB (Universal Serial Port)   A new standard for connecting external devices to a PC, utilizing a very fast serial communications scheme that supports Plug and Play.

ZIF (Zero Insertion Force)   A socket design developed by Intel wherein a CPU's pins are not forced into the socket, but are instead gripped by it through the use of an attached lever.

U.S. $19.95
CAN $29.95

ISBN 0-02-864239-2

0 21898 64239 4

Don't buy a new computer just because you need an upgrade!

You're no idiot, of course. You know if your mouse or keyboard goes kaput that you can replace it at your local computer store. However, the complex electronics inside your computer system aren't so easily replaced—or repaired.

You don't have to be a computer technician! *The Complete Idiot's Guide® to Upgrading and Repairing PCs, Fifth Edition,* will show you exactly how to improve the performance of your computer without calling tech support. In this updated and revised *Complete Idiot's Guide®,* you get:

- Information on the latest PC-related technology, including the latest Windows OSs, CD-RW, DVD-RAM, DSL, cable modems, PDAs, firewalls, and more.

- An analysis of the inner components of your computer—and whether or not it's feasible to upgrade them.

- Instructions on replacing and upgrading the components your PC needs to help you become a multimedia maven.

- Advice on how to choose the best replacement components, how to install them, and mistakes to avoid.

 JENNIFER FULTON is the co-owner of Ingenus Communications, a consulting firm started with her husband in Indianapolis, IN. She has authored more than 75 books covering many areas of computing including DOS, Windows Me/98/95/3.11, and Office XP/2000/97/95. Her most recent titles include *How to Use Office XP, Easy Microsoft Outlook 2000, How to Use Publisher 2000,* and *Teach Yourself Excel 2000 in Ten Minutes.*

Cover image © Brandtner & Staedeli/SuperStock

Visit us online at: www.idiotsguides.com

A ALPHA

Get tech savvy without getting technical!

- ◆ Discover how your PC operates—in easy-to-follow language.

- ◆ Organize your desktop so that your PC runs more smoothly.

- ◆ Learn the advantages and disadvantages of telephone, cable, and DSL lines for faster Web surfing.

- ◆ Configure new components so your operating system recognizes them.

- ◆ Increase RAM to improve memory capability.

- ◆ Repair your hard disk without replacing it.

ISBN 0-02-864239-2

51995

9 780028 642390